DATE DUE

Video-Mediated Communication

Computers, Cognition, and Work
A series edited by
Gary M. Olson, Judith S. Olson, and Bill Curtis

Finn/Sellen/Wilbur (Eds.) • Video-Mediated Communication

Fox • The Human Tutorial Dialogue Project: Issues in the Design of Instructional Systems

Hoschka (Ed.) • Computers as Assistants: A New Generation of Support Systems

Koschmann (Ed.) • CSCL: Theory and Practice of an Emerging Paradigm

Moran/Carroll (Eds.) • Design Rationale: Concepts, Techniques, and Use

Oppermann (Ed.) • Adaptive User Support: Ergonomic Design of Manually and Automatically Adaptable Software

Smith • Collective Intelligence in Computer-Based Collaboration

Video-Mediated Communication

Edited by

Kathleen E. Finn
Consultant

Abigail J. Sellen
Rank Xerox Research Centre, Cambridge

Sylvia B. Wilbur
Queen Mary & Westfield College, University of London

LAWRENCE ERLBAUM ASSOCIATES, PUBLISHERS
1997   MAHWAH, NEW JERSEY

Lawrence Erlbaum Associates, Inc., Publishers
10 Industrial Avenue
Mahwah, NJ 07430

Cover design by Kathryn Houghtaling

Library of Congress Cataloging-in-Publication Data

Video-mediated communication / edited by Kathleen E. Finn, Abigail J.
Sellen, Sylvia B. Wilbur.
    p.   cm.
Includes bibliographical references and index.
ISBN 0-8058-2288-7 (alk : paper).
1. Videoconferencing—Congresses. 2. Work groups—Audio-visual
aids—Congresses. I. Finn, Kathleen, E. II. Sellen, Abigail J.
III. Wilbur, Sylvia B., 1938–
HF5734.7.V527   1997
658.4′5—dc20   96-33431
                                                                     CIP

Books published by Lawrence Erlbaum Associates are printed on acid-free paper,
and their bindings are chosen for strength and durability.

Printed in the United States of America
10 9 8 7 6 5 4 3 2 1

Contents

Preface

In autumn 1994, we organized and conducted a workshop on video-mediated communication (VMC). The workshop, which was held at ACM CSCW'94 (Computer-Supported Collaborative Work) at Chapel Hill, NC, was attended by about 25 researchers. The aim of the workshop was to bring together the principal researchers in the field of VMC to compare their results and methodologies, and to propose a strategy for advancing understanding of the field. Participants were asked to submit position papers addressing their research, and how they interpreted the differences between their results and the results of others.

Out of that workshop grew a consensus that, although the workshop attendees might not be able to agree on a number of finer points, the fact that there was no single volume that adequately pulled together the now substantial body of work on VMC was an omission that we could address. In the 1970s and 1980s, some comprehensive and much cited volumes did impact the field, focusing on the social psychology of telecommunications (Short, Williams, & Christie, 1976), the role of gaze in communication (Argyle & Cook, 1976), models of groups and group processes (McGrath, 1984), and models of communication centering on the telephone (Rutter, 1987). But the most current work, to a large extent represented by the authors of chapters in this book, is mainly found only in journals, conference proceedings, and corporate technical papers, and has never been published in one comprehensive volume.

To the end of producing such a publication, another meeting of the CSCW workshop participants took place, this time prior to ACM CHI'95 in Denver, CO, in May 1995. During this second meeting, we refined the goals of our book, agreed on its overall organization, and committed ourselves to writing specific chapters. We also identified a set of researchers whom we considered to have carried out significant research in the field, but who had not attended the original workshop, and agreed to solicit their contributions. Surprisingly (in view of their heavy schedules and commitments), almost everyone we approached committed to contributing a chapter, allowing us to present the full breadth and scope of work we had hoped to achieve.

There are four major sections to the book. The Foundations section sets the stage for the rest of the book by providing related background information: an introductory chapter that presents some of the difficulties in comparing related research; a discussion of the major research on vision and its significance in communication; an overview of the video technology underlying representative systems used in VMC research; and a framework presenting how group characteristics, tasks, and technologies interact with one another.

The Findings section constitutes the bulk of the book, and presents chapters by researchers mainly working from psychological or sociological perspectives and adopting a range of analytic techniques. One result of this methodological and, to some extent, philosophical diversity is that the role of video in communication and collaborative work is explicated at a number of different levels. It is therefore both interesting and challenging to compare and contrast the findings across chapters, and to consider the use of video in a range of contexts: from the detailed study of tasks in controlled laboratory settings, to observations of its broader organizational impact in the "real world." Such studies also vary in the degree to which they consider the use of video systems over time, which raises a number of important issues to do with adapting and habituating to video technology by living and working with it.

The chapters in the third section, Design, present a variety of different approaches to the application of video in the workplace. A major goal of this area of research is the creation of a "virtual space" for collaboration based on audio, video, and data connections. Each approach focuses on particular aspects of the design of a virtual space, aiming to provide a context for communication that is as rich in opportunities for visual and verbal interaction as face-to-face environments. The roles of video and associated design issues are discussed from the point of view of the authors' varying technical and theoretical backgrounds.

The final section, The Future, comments on new and innovative applications of VMC technology and points out how its role may be tied to other emerging technological trends. This section also offers discussions of how the role of video may be changing insofar as it is moving away from the concept of "talking head" video systems for conversation. Rather, these chapters present evidence that suggests that video systems of the future might be most useful in supporting informal communications and awareness, and for focusing on work-related objects and artifacts.

The book is intended for use by researchers, engineers, user interface designers, and anyone with an interest in the results of current VMC research. It should prove useful to college students and professors studying human–computer interaction, computer-supported cooperative work (CSCW), human factors, interface design, multimedia systems, communication theory, psychology, and sociology. It should likewise be of value to university and corporate researchers in related fields. It will have something to offer those looking for background material, a historical perspective, work by specific researchers, work in specific applications areas, work on particular systems, or a view to what the future holds. Because of its organization, it is intended for use either as a cohesive whole, by section, or by individual chapter.

As editors of this comprehensive volume, we feel privileged to have been able to bring together the work of so many leading researchers in the area. We hope the publication of the book will be seen as timely, as after a long and difficult period of inception, video is at last establishing itself as a medium for organizational communication. With its broad coverage of the past, present, and future role and impact of video, the book represents a unique source of reference on the subject. As our readers browse in the following chapters, we hope they will experience some of the enthusiasm we feel for the research reported here, and the potential of video communication.

ACKNOWLEDGMENTS

The editors thank their respective employers for support during the preparation of this book and the workshop that engendered it: SRI International, Menlo Park, CA; Rank Xerox Research Centre, Cambridge, UK; and Queen Mary & Westfield College, London. We would also like to thank our authors and reviewers, too numerous to list, for their patience and diligence in producing such high-quality material under adverse conditions, including the vagaries of electronic communications, incompatible platforms, and tight deadlines. And finally, we express our appreciation of our long-suffering families: During the course of the workshop preparation, conducting the workshop, planning the book, and the ensuing deluge of time-consuming book-related activities, no fewer than four children and one grandchild were born to the three editors. For putting up with all those missing evenings and weekends, our enduring thanks.

—*Kathleen E. Finn*
—*Abigail J. Sellen*
—*Sylvia B. Wilbur*

REFERENCES

Argyle, M., & Cook, M. (1976). *Gaze and mutual gaze*. London: Cambridge University Press.
McGrath, J. E. (1984). *Groups: Interaction and performance*. Englewood Cliffs, NJ: Prentice-Hall.
Rutter, D. R. (1987). *Communicating by telephone*. New York: Pergamon Press.
Short, J., Williams, E., & Christie, B. (1976). *The social psychology of telecommunications*. London: Wiley.

Contributors

Anne H. Anderson
Human Communication Research
 Centre
Department of Psychology
University of Glasgow
62 Hillhead Street
Glasgow G12 8QB
Scotland, UK
anne@psy.gla.ac.uk

Susan Anderson
Xerox Corporation
1350 Jefferson Road, MS 801-27C
Rochester, NY 14623 USA
anderson@eso.mc.xerox.com
http://www.mcg.gla.ac.uk/

Joel S. Angiolillo
Lucent Technologies
Room 1M-514
101 Crawfords Corner Road
Holmdel, NJ 07733 USA
joel@hocpa.att.com

Kazuho Arita
Nippon Telegraph and Telephone
 Corporation
Multimedia Service Promotion
 Headquarters
Multimedia Business Department
UrbanNet Otemachi Bldg. 16F
2-2-2 Otemachi, Chiyoda-Ku,
 Tokyo 100 Japan
kazuho@mbd.ntt.jp

Victoria Bellotti
Apple Computer
1 Infinite Loop, MS: 301-4A
Cupertino, CA 95014 USA
victoria@atg.apple.com

Harry E. Blanchard
AT&T Bell Laboratories
Room 1J-325
101 Crawfords Corner Road
POB 3030
Holmdel, NJ 07733 USA
harry.blanchard@att.com

Sara Bly, Consultant
24511 NW Moreland Road
Hillsboro, OR 97124 USA
sara_bly@acm.org

William A. S. Buxton
Computer Systems Research Institute
University of Toronto
 &
Alias I Wavefront Inc.
110 Richmond St. East
Toronto, Ontario
Canada M5C 1P1
buxton@alias.com
http://www.dgp.toronto.edu/
    people/BillBuxton/billbuxton.html

Jon Crowcroft
Department of Computer Science
University College London
Gower Street
London WC1E 6BT UK
jon@cs.ucl.ac.uk
http://www.cs.ucl.ac.uk/staff/jon

Gwyneth Doherty-Sneddon
Department of Psychology
University of Stirling
Stirling FK9 4LA
Scotland, UK
gds1@stir.ac.uk

Paul Dourish
Rank Xerox Research Centre
Cambridge Laboratory (EuroPARC)
61 Regent Street
Cambridge CB2 1AB UK
dourish@europarc.xerox.com
http://www.xerox.com/RXRC/
    Cambridge/people/dourish

Elizabeth Dykstra-Erickson
Apple Computer
2 Infinite Loop, MS 302-1HI
Cupertino, CA 95014 USA
elizabeth_dykstra-erickson@
    quickmail.apple.com

J. Robert Ensor
Multimedia Communication Research
    Department
Bell Laboratories, Lucent
    Technologies
Room 4F607
Holmdel, NJ 07733 USA
jre@big.att.com

Kathleen E. Finn, Consultant
21361 Milford Dr.
Cupertino, CA 95014 USA
kfinn@best.com

Robert S. Fish
Bellcore
445 South Street
Morristown, NJ 07962 USA
robf@thumper.bellcore.com

Anne Marie Fleming
Human Communication Research
    Centre
Department of Psychology
University of Glasgow
5 Hillhead Street
Glasgow G12 9YR
Scotland, UK
annemari@mcg.gla.ac.uk
http://www.mcg.gla.ac.uk/

David Frohlich
Hewlett Packard Laboratories
Filton Road, Stoke Gifford
Bristol BS12 6QZ UK
dmf@hplb.hpl.hp.com
http://www-uk.hpl.hp.com

Richard Harper
Rank Xerox Research Centre
Cambridge Laboratory
61 Regent St.
Cambridge CB2 1AB UK
harper@cambridge.rxrc.xerox.com

Steve Harrison
Xerox PARC
3333 Coyote Hill Rd.
Palo Alto, CA 94304 USA
harrison@parc.xerox.com

Christian Heath
School of Social Studies
The University of Nottingham
Nottingham NG7 2RD UK
christian.heath@nottingham.ac.uk

Richard Hertz
Suite 340
US West Advanced Technologies
4001 Discovery Dr.
Boulder, CO 80303 USA
rhertz@advtech.uswest.com

Ellen A. Isaacs
Electric Communities
10101 De Anza Blvd.
Cupertino, CA 95014 USA
ellen@communities.com
http://www.communities.com

Hiroshi Ishii
MIT Media Laboratory
E15-485, 20 Ames St.
Cambridge, MA 02139-4307 USA
ishii@media.mit.edu

Edmond W. Israelski
AT & T Bell Laboratories
200 Laurel Ave. S.
Middletown, NJ 07748-4801 USA
e.w.israelski@att.com

Minoru Kobayashi
Nippon Telegraph and Telephone
  Corporation
Human Interface Laboratories
1-2356 Take, Yokosuka-Shi
Kanagawa, 238-03 Japan
minoru@aether.hil.ntt.jp

Robert E. Kraut
Carnegie Mellon University
5000 Forbes Ave.
Pittsburgh, PA 15213 USA
robert.kraut@cmu.edu

Allan Kuchinsky
Hewlett-Packard Laboratories
1501 Page Mill Road
Palo Alto, CA 94304 USA
kuchinsk@hpl.hp.com

Steve Langton
Department of Psychology
University of Stirling
Stirling FK9 4LA
Scotland, UK
srhl1@stirling.ac.uk

Robert Leichner
Hewlett-Packard Laboratories
1501 Page Mill Road
Palo Alto, CA 94304 USA
leichner@hpl.hp.com

Paul Luff
School of Social Studies
The University of Nottingham
Nottingham NG7 2RD UK
paul.luff@nottingham.ac.uk

Amir Mané
AT & T Bell Laboratories
Room 1F-306
101 Crawfords Corner Road
Holmdel, NJ 07733 USA
amir.mane@att.com

Catherine Marshall
Collaborative Technologies
2600 Garden Rd., Ste. 201
Monterey, CA 93940 USA
crm@collabtech.com

David Meader
Department of Management
  Information Systems
Karl Eller Graduate School
  of Management
430 McLelland Hall
University of Arizona
Tucson, AZ 85721 USA
dmeader@bpa.arizona.edu

Scott Minneman
Xerox PARC
3333 Coyote Hill Rd.
Palo Alto, CA 94304 USA
minneman@parc.xerox.com

Gale Moore
Ontario Telepresence Project
c/o University of Toronto Library
130 St. George Street
Toronto M5S 1A5 Canada
gmoore@dgp.utoronto.ca

Jim Mullin
Human Communication Research
   Centre
Department of Psychology
University of Glasgow
5 Hillhead Street
Glasgow G12 9YR
Scotland, UK
jim@mcg.gla.ac.uk
http://www.mcg.gla.ac.uk/

Bonnie A. Nardi
Apple Computer
1 Infinite Loop
Cupertino, CA 95014 USA
nardi@apple.com
http://www.atg.apple.com/
   personal/Bonnie_Nardi/

Alison Newlands
Department of Psychology
University of Glasgow
5 Hillhead Street
Glasgow G12 9YR
Scotland, UK
alison@psy.gla.ac.uk

Brid O'Conaill
Hewlett Packard Laboratories
Filton Road, Stoke Gifford
Bristol BS12 6QZ UK
boc@hplb.hpl.hp.com
http://www.uk.hpl.com

Claire O'Malley
ESRC Centre for Research in
   Development, Instruction
   & Training
Department of Psychology
University of Nottingham
Nottingham NG7 2RD UK
com@psyc.nott.ac.uk
http://www.psyc.nott.ac.uk/credit/
   people/com.html

Gary M. Olson
Collaboratory for Research on
   Electronic Work (CREW)
The University of Michigan
701 Tappan Street
Ann Arbor, MI 48109-1234 USA
gmo@umich.edu

Judith S. Olson
Collaboratory for Research on
   Electronic Work (CREW)
The University of Michigan
701 Tappan Street
Ann Arbor, MI 48109-1234 USA
jso@umich.edu

Carrie Rudman
Suite 340
US West Advanced Technologies
4001 Discovery Dr.
Boulder, CO 80303 USA
crudman@advtech.uswest.com

Heinrich Schwarz
Program in Science, Technology,
   Society
MIT
E51-070
Cambridge, MA 02139 USA
schwarz@mit.edu

Abigail J. Sellen
Rank Xerox Research Centre
Cambridge Laboratory
61 Regent St.
Cambridge CB2 1AB UK
sellen@cambridge.rxrc.xerox.com
http://www.xerox.com/RXRC/
   Cambridge/home.html

Michael C. Sheasby
SOFTIMAGE/Microsoft
3510 Boul.St-Laurent, Bureau 400
Montreal, Quebec
Canada
H2X 2V2
msheasby@microsoft.com

John C. Tang
SunSoft, Inc.
2550 Garcia Ave.
Mountain View, CA 94043 USA
john.tang@sun.com

Jeroen Van der Velden
Technical University of Delft
De Vries van Heystplantsoen 2
2628 RZ Delft
Netherlands
email: c/o andriessen@wtm.tudelft.nl

Steve Whittaker
Room 2C-404
AT & T Research
600 Mountain Ave
Murray Hill, NJ 07974 USA
stevew@research.att.com

Sylvia B. Wilbur
Department of Computer Science
Queen Mary & Westfield College
Mile End Rd.
London EC1 4NS UK
sylvia.wilbur@dcs.qmw.ac.uk
http://www.dcs.qmw.ac.uk/
export23/users/sylvia/

Takashi Yagi
Nippon Telegraph and Telephone
Corporation
Business Communications
Headquarters
System Services Department
Kouwa Kawasaki Nishiguti Bldg. 14F
66-2 Horikawa-Cho, Saiwai-Ku,
Kawasaki-Shi
Kanagawa 210 Japan
yagi.takashi@ss.bch.ntt.jp

Part I

FOUNDATIONS

Chapter 1

Introduction: An Overview of Video-Mediated Communication Literature

Kathleen E. Finn
Consultant

The field of video-mediated communication (VMC) is well represented in the literature, but trying to integrate the various results reported in the literature is problematic. This is because of the heterogeneity of the research studies, with respect to methodology used, experimental design, variables looked at, and a number of other issues. This chapter presents a brief sampling of the diversity students of VMC are likely to encounter in conducting their own examinations of the related literature.

INTRODUCTION

Video-mediated communication (VMC) has been touted as an invaluable tool for such applications as remote collaboration, conferencing, and distance learning. In many cases its desirability is taken for granted, much as was the case of color for computer monitors. But on closer scrutiny, we find that numerous studies have yielded conflicting results. A cursory examination of the related research reveals that the individual studies themselves are widely disparate in a number of areas, making side-by-side comparison of studies—and their results—difficult.

This chapter illustrates some of the dimensions along which the studies differ, and cites some of the primary examples of published works in each category. By examining each dimension, or aspect, in turn, we can evaluate how it might have factored in the research, and assess its impact on the conclusions drawn by the researchers. This will leave us in a better position to perform comparative interpretations of the seemingly disparate results.

The chapter begins at the end, so to speak, in the sense that the first topic reported on is the results of related studies, because that is where the apparent differences are most striking. The results of several major studies are given, along with brief descriptions about the conditions under which the results were obtained, and the researchers' conclusions or interpretations of the results. Following the summary of results are two sections that address, with relatively coarse granularity, the different experimental conditions, namely, the architecture of the technology and the equipment used. Next, the finer aspects of the analytic approach are dealt with, including the analytic methods used, the questions asked by the researchers, the characteristics of the participants, the tasks being performed, and data collection and analysis methods. Finally, a related background material section details resources available in subsequent chapters in this volume.

RESULTS OF STUDIES REPORTED IN RELATED LITERATURE

Unless one were familiar with the intrinsic and fundamental differences across studies, as briefly touched on in the following sections, one might be quite startled to compare the related studies based on their results alone. Although in some cases the results cannot be compared because they really address different aspects of the VMC issue (e.g., some studies compared VMC with face-to-face, whereas others compared VMC with a condition in which there was no video channel or other visual component), in other instances the results do not seem to have much in common with one another. It is not so much the case that some studies concluded, "VMC is equivalent to face-to-face communication," whereas others concluded it is not, or that some research proved the value of adding a video channel, whereas other research claimed video has no effect on anything. There are as many areas of discontinuity across studies as there are of overlap, making direct comparisons of studies an inexact science.

Several studies concluded that the use of a video channel or video-mediated technology has no effect on the variable of interest, whether that was task performance, user satisfaction, or some other measurement. For example, Chapanis, Ochsman, Parrish, and Weeks (1972) found that the voice mode makes the single most important contribution to task completion, and the availability of a video channel has no significant effects on communication times or behavior. Gale (1989) found no significant differences in the quality of the output or in the time taken to complete tasks.

Other work has determined that availability of a visual channel benefits the process, outcome, or user experience of communication, such as in Olson, Olson, and Meader (1995), and Rutter, Stephenson, and Dewey (1981). Rutter studied a variety of conditions, including face-to-face, audio-only, same room but separated by curtains, and separate rooms connected by a CCTV link. He found that visual cues and physical presence both make critical contributions to the quality of communication, as measured by task orientation, depersonalization, or communicative style.

Still another body of research yields more finely grained results, in which specific variables are found to differ between VMC and face-to-face (FTF) interactions, between different VMC conditions, or between VMC and some other communication modality. In this section, several examples of differing results are presented, just to give the reader some sense of the range of results obtained.

FTF Versus PicturePhone Meeting Service (PMS)

Cohen (1982) compared a VMC system called PicturePhone Meeting Service (PMS) with FTF interactions. In the PMS condition, six to eight participants sit around a conference table in a room equipped with two monitors, one for the incoming display and one for the outgoing display, and two speakers. Each of three cameras is focused on two adjacent positions around the table; the cameras are voice-switched to display either the current or the last participant to speak. The participant and observer data show more speaker turns in FTF than in PMS in general, and fewer interruptions and simultaneous speech events within the same room with PMS than with FTF. Cohen suggested that PMS produces "more orderly turn-taking and fewer speaker exchanges that are viewed as interruptions." Although the social dynamics and degree of participant satisfaction are similar, participants rate FTF as slightly more enjoyable to use, and considerably more effective in handling discussion tasks. Observer data show more interruptions, and almost twice as many speaker exchanges, in FTF as in PMS. Cohen interpreted this data as evidence that FTF meetings are more interactive, less orderly, and less polite than video teleconferences.

FTF Versus ISDN Versus LiveNet (LN)

O'Conaill, Whittaker, and Wilbur (1993) compared FTF with ISDN and with a system called LiveNet (LN). The ISDN condition is characterized by half-duplex audio, transmission lags, and poor-quality images. LiveNet (LN), a high-quality analog system used for lectures, seminars, and meetings, operates over optical fiber; a central video switch links studios in eight sites across London.

Informal observations of the videoconferencing conditions include difficulties in identifying the remote speaker in ISDN, detecting small movements, attaining mutual gaze, and gaining floor control; and tendencies toward exaggerated user movements, staring at the screen displaying remote participants, and having to conduct more advance preparation. Even so, participants express a preference for videoconferencing over audioconferencing, citing several advantages: knowing who is at the remote site, being able to identify the speaker, and not feeling as if they were "talking into a void."

Compared with FTF, the researchers found that in ISDN speaker turns are longer, turn-taking is more formal, and there are fewer interruptions, backchannels, and projections, producing a more lecture-like effect. In the LiveNet condition, there are fewer backchannels and more formal handovers using questions, and speakers are less likely to hold the floor than in FTF.

O'Conaill et al. attributed these findings to channel properties (the high visual quality and full-duplex, nearly instantaneous audio transmission of FTF), as predicted in their model. However, they stated that those properties alone do not account for all the behaviors seen. They went on to suggest use of directional audio and video, participant control of remote audio and video, and the use of multiple monitors with one reserved for a high-quality image of the current speaker or still. They recommended studies on the effects of task outcome, and on the use of video images of something other than participants' head and shoulders.

FTF Versus Picture-in-a-Picture (PIP) Versus Hydra Versus Audio-Only

Sellen (1995) compared conversations occurring in three videoconferencing conditions, with same-room (FTF) and audio-only conversations. The three videoconferencing systems studied are a picture-in-a-picture (PIP) setup, Hydra, and LiveWire.

In the PIP system, a color monitor displays images of each of four remote participants simultaneously, and a single speaker broadcasts the voices of all the participants. A video camera transmits the video of each participant; each person wears a headset microphone. In the generic Hydra setup, a four-party meeting is simulated by having each remote participant face three separate color monitors (8-cm diagonal), a camera mounted below each monitor, and a speaker mounted below each camera. The positioning of the equipment mimics the relative locations of the participants with respect to one another. In LiveWire, voice switching activates a video image of the current speaker; this video is displayed to all participants except the current speaker, who is shown an image of the last speaker.

All three systems use full-duplex audio and high-quality video; there is no perceptible audio or video lag in any of the systems.

In the first experiment, Sellen predicted that, compared to VMC, FTF conversations would produce more and shorter turns per session, more equal distribution of turns among speakers, and more simultaneous speech. However, her statistical analysis of session transcriptions showed fewer differences between same-room (FTF) and video-mediated multiparty conversations than predicted, and no differences between PIP and Hydra were detected in the statistical analysis. However, participants' responses in their questionnaires and discussions showed that about two thirds prefer the Hydra system because it supports selective listening and gaze, and simultaneous conversations. One third prefer PIP, listing such reasons as not having to turn their heads, and seeing images of themselves onscreen. Contrary to Sellen's predictions, there were more interruptions in the FTF condition than there were in the video conditions. She concluded that interruptions serve as indicators of interactivity, rather than problems in turn-taking.

In a second experiment, the same design was used but the conditions were audio-only, PIP, and LiveWire. Again, statistical analysis showed few differences across conditions, whereas participants' own responses showed their preference for PIP as having fewer inappropriate interruptions, being more natural, being more interactive, offering the best support for selective listening and attending to others, and being best for knowing when others are listening to or attending to them.

Citing the general lack of differences across video-mediated conditions, Sellen concluded that perhaps the technology interferes more with a conversation's formality and interactivity than with its synchronization (turn-taking, for example). Furthermore, the similarity of the audio-only and video-mediated conversations points to the impact of any technology mediation, not just video mediation, and Sellen suggested that the gating factor is whether or not participants share the same physical space.

Shared Whiteboard With and Without Audio and Video

Gale (1989) studied three conditions: a "data share," data share with audio, and data share with both audio and video. The data share is similar to a shared whiteboard; multiple users can draw and type in the same workspace simultaneously, with updates occurring within 10 msec. His users judged video as being effective in assessing the attention of other people; it helped them know when to start and stop. Only 14% of them indicated that the video was seen as effective for "discussions" or a "more personal medium."

Although 14% felt use of video is effective for discussions and more personal communication, 61% felt it is poor while working, because they have to read material both on and off screen, requiring them to divert their eyes away from video monitors and toward what they are working on. Thirteen percent found the use of video to be weak during discussions, particularly because of poor eye contact; other responses indicated it is difficult to talk to someone directly.

Interestingly, users rated themselves as never using the video channel beyond 4 on a scale of 1–7, with 1 indicating no usage and 7 indicating extensive usage. However, examination of the video data showed that they used it constantly. The author suggested that use of the video channel may be so intuitive and transparent to the communication process that users are unaware of it.

FTF Versus Phone Versus Desktop Video Conferencing (DVC)

Using a desktop videoconferencing prototype (DVC) that supports digital audio-video conferencing, Isaacs and Tang (1993) found that videoconferencing provides team members with several benefits over phone conversations. It allows them to indicate their understanding, or lack thereof, to the speaker; they can augment their verbal communication with gestures; they can respond purely visually (gesturally), as in smiling or nodding; they can convey attitudes by their expressions and posture; and they can better interpret the significance of conversational pauses.

In comparison with face-to-face interaction, DVC does not measure up in terms of users' ability to manage turn-taking, acquire or retain floor control, notice expressions or gestures, or have side conversations. However, the researchers noted that DVC has some advantages over face-to-face: Besides the obvious benefit of being able to stay in their own offices, users feel distanced from one another and therefore less obligated to engage in social pleasantries, making their meetings more efficient.

The researchers cautioned against voice-activated videoconferencing, which might show only the current speaker instead of all participants. They noted that small delays in audio can seriously disrupt participants' ability to reach mutual understanding and reduce their satisfaction with conversation.

Existing Tools Versus Desktop Conferencing Prototype, With and Without Video

Tang and Isaacs (1993) studied a team under three conditions: using existing tools, that is, phone, e-mail, and videoconference rooms, using the desktop conferencing prototype (DCP), and using the DCP without the video channel. The DCP supported real-time audiovideo conferencing and ShowMe, a shared markup and drawing tool. They found that the DCP does not increase overall interactive communication, reduces the number of e-mail messages, is used more in full-DCP mode than in DCP-minus-video mode, and increases gaze awareness. Users feel that they are using the phone less, and are using DCP instead of some face-to-face and video conference room meetings. Perhaps most significantly, however, the DCP is not used at all when there is no video channel available.

Different rules of etiquette seem to apply to other visual meetings than in DCP interactions, in which team members read e-mail and take phone calls or are otherwise distracted, to the annoyance of some other members. DCP interactions resemble FTF interactions more closely than videoconference-room meetings, in terms of interruptions, turn-taking, and joking.

Tang and Isaacs concluded that users' desire for video (as derived from the drop in DCP usage without video, and from interviews) results from its impact on the *process* of their interpersonal interaction, rather than from its perceived effect on any *product* of their interaction. The researchers also concluded that audio is critical, and that high-quality audio is more important than high-quality video.

"ARCHITECTURE" OF THE TECHNOLOGY

As can be derived from the thumbnail descriptions in the preceding summaries of results, the architectures used in studies of VMC technology differ quite extensively. To a certain extent, the setup of the various equipment follows a chronological trend. For example, the earliest work cited used closed-caption TV (CCTV), in which dedicated lines transmitted video directly to other participants, often just in adjoining rooms, in real time. Instances of research using this model include Chapanis et al. (1972), Hoecker, Brown, Wish, and Geller (1978), Ochsman and Chapanis (1974), and Rutter et al. (1981).

Then we see a videoconferencing era, in which a group in one room is connected to a group in another room, with each group looking at the other via a common monitor. Work of this nature is reported in the ISDN and LN conditions of O'Conaill et al. (1993) and in Tang and Isaacs (1993).

From here we move on to desktop videoconferencing, with many variations of a common theme, commonly referred to as a "talking heads" or PIP (picture-in-a-picture) setup. Individual users sit at their respective computer workstations and communicate with other users via an audiovideo connection, manifested as a picture of each participant on each workstation monitor. This would include, for example, Isaacs and Tang (1993), Sellen (1992, 1995), and Tang and Isaacs (1993).

Initially the focus of these systems was merely the support of an audiovideo link between participants. This expanded to the point where the audiovideo connection (or the communication it enabled) was but one dimension of a more fully defined collaborative environment, in which users also collaborated on their tasks via shared applications (drawing, editing, simulation, etc.) on their workstations. Here we begin to see more of a focus on what types of communication the technology will support (e.g., informal vs. application-centered), perhaps in recognition of the many earlier findings that suggest that video technology might be more supportive of informal communication (Fish, Kraut, Root, & Rice, 1992, 1993; Fish, Kraut, & Chalfonte, 1990; Root, 1988). Different designs or architectures were developed to support specialized tasks (Gale, 1989; Isaacs & Tang, 1993; Tang & Isaacs, 1993).

In a further development along this path, the PIP model and its variations gave rise to the concept of *media spaces*. In a media space, the area around the user (such as an office or lab), as well as collaborative tools or other artifacts, was included in the space to be shared across the network. Much of the literature in this area is less related to the formal quantification of the effects of the technology on communication, and more concerned with the users' perception and awareness of others' presence (teleproximity, privacy issues, etc.). Such is the case with the direct office share in Adler and Henderson (1994); the Xerox PARC Media Space of Bly, Harrison, and Irwin (1993); Xerox PARC and EuroPARC's Portholes in Dourish and Bly (1992); Gaver (1992); Gaver et al. (1992); the Multiple Target Video (MTV) study of Gaver, Sellen, Heath, and Luff (1993); the ubiquitous office environment in Heath and Luff (1991, 1992); CAVECAT in Mantei et al. (1991); and the DCP in Tang and Isaacs (1993).

Extrapolating from this, we find the human-to-human audiovideo connection undergoing some mutations, resulting in images of something other than pure talking heads being presented. One example of a rather asymmetrical configuration is Forum, a system for conducting distributed presentations developed at SunSoft (Isaacs, Morris, & Rodriguez, 1994; Isaacs, Morris, Rodriguez, & Tang, 1995), in which a distributed audience could see the speaker and the speaker's slides but the speaker did not have similar access to the audience. More unusual examples include Xerox PARC's VideoWhiteboard (Tang & Minneman, 1991), which displayed shadows of collaborators working at a whiteboard space; NTT's ClearBoard system (Ishii & Kobayashi, 1992), in which images of the participant's entire head and torso are superimposed on a whiteboard (and inverted to maintain perspective); and MAJIC, developed at Keio University (Okada, Maeda, Ichikawaa, & Matsushita, 1994), which projected life-size images of remote participants onto a large screen, positioning them as if they were all seated around a conference table.

The talking heads, or video images of the remote collaborators, are supplemented or replaced by actual data in research that explores how video of the workspace and artifacts can be used as a means of facilitating collaboration. This is a more recent development with relatively little literature associated with it, the most notable exception being the work performed by Nardi et al. (Nardi, Kuchinsky, Whittaker, Leichner, & Schwarz, 1996; Nardi, Schwarz, Kuchinsky, Leichner, & Whittaker, 1996; chapter 23, this volume). In that work, video images of remote surgery were transmitted to remote consultants, as well as being viewable in the operating room on a large monitor and through a microscope. Tani, Yamaashi, Tanikoshi, Futakawa, and Tanifuji (1992) developed a system for manipulating real-world objects via "object-oriented video," although in that case the video was not being used for collaborative or communicative purposes. In Gaver et al. (1993), participants could choose to view either video images of other participants or of shared objects.

EQUIPMENT

Another factor that cannot be overlooked in comparing the results of studies is the differences in conditions of the experimental setup, especially the quality of the equipment used. A fuller treatment is provided in the Olsons' chapter, "Making Sense of the Findings" (chapter 4, this volume). However, the examples[1] cited next should suffice to give the reader a sense of the range in quality in the equipment used, and an appreciation for the role this might play in the outcome of the studies. Keep in mind, too, that published results do not always include technical specifications, making it more difficult to conduct direct comparisons across studies.

Consider audio as one of the major variables in VMC. Audio can be either full duplex (Fish et al., 1992; Sellen, 1992, 1995) or half duplex (Cohen, 1982). The audio and video signals can be synchronized (Cohen, 1982) or not (Isaacs & Tang, 1993; Tang & Isaacs, 1993). There can be a delay in transmission of the audiovideo signal from when it is actually produced. Cohen (1982) introduced synchronized transmission delay of 0.705 sec; Isaacs and Tang (1993) and Tang and Isaacs (1993) introduced audio delays of 0.32–0.44 sec. Systems can use noise-cancelling microphones or not; they can use directional sound, or multidirectional microphones (Heath & Luff, 1992).

Looking at the visual signal used, there are differences in frame rates ranging from very low (5 fps used in Isaacs & Tang, 1993; Tang & Isaacs, 1993) to broadcast quality. There is a similar range in resolution of the images, although this is often not mentioned in this body of research. Most of the experimental work has been based on analog technology, providing high-quality images (because analog video is transmitted on separate wires, thus offering more or less unlimited bandwidth). More recent systems have moved to digital video, in which available frame rate becomes more of an issue (such as Montage; Tang & Rua, 1994).

Some systems offer support for directional gaze, which can increase the sense of telepresence and may help in reducing miscommunications. This is the case with the Hydra system (Sellen, 1992, 1995), which uses a separate camera and monitor for each participant. Okada et al. (1994) used a unique projection mechanism to support directional gaze. Acker and Levitt (1987) used multiple cameras capturing different angles of the participants to provide a display that offered a sense of improved eye contact. Multiple cameras can be used to focus on different objects or areas, as in much of the media space work (e.g., Gaver et al., 1993). In Gaver, Smets, and Overbeeke (1995), the remote camera's field of view is controlled by tracking a participant's head movements in front of a local monitor, which causes parallel movements in a remote camera. SharedView (Kuzuoka, 1992) attempted to achieve a three-dimensional collaborative environment with the use of a head-mounted camera and a head-mounted display. This has been refined in GestureCam (Kuzuoka, Kosuge, & Tanaka, 1994), which supports both shared and independent fields of view.

For a more in-depth discussion of these and many other technical aspects of the experimental setup (including audio and video, as well as quality of service, etc.), and the implications of selecting from a spectrum of options, refer to Angiolillo et al., "Technology Constraints of Video-Mediated Communication" (chapter 3, this volume).

It is not so easy to divide studies into those that looked at "high-quality" video-mediated technology and those that looked at "low-quality" technology, because many studies involve a mixture of high and low quality. In general, the earliest work, which tended to use CCTV, might be considered high quality, because there were direct television links involving high-quality images and sound, and no delay, asynchrony, and so on (e.g., Chapanis et al., 1972; Gale, 1989; Ochsman & Chapanis, 1974; Rutter et al., 1981). Even these, however, sometimes entailed voice switching for floor control, which introduced artificial constraints on conversation. More recent work on media spaces also tended to be of higher quality than some of the intervening work.

The effects of the varying quality of conditions were specifically studied in O'Conaill et al. (1993), in which the researchers examined how properties of the communication channels (full- or half-duplex audio; audio delay; video quality) influence specific features of the communication process. Whittaker (1995) gave a table comparing experimental VMC systems in terms of quality of technology, method used, outcome (product) of experiment, and process coordination. He reviewed three subhypotheses about the role of video in nonverbal communication: cognitive cuing, turn-taking, and social cuing, distinguishing between the effects of high- and low-quality systems. He concluded not only that the benefit of video in providing nonverbal information has been exaggerated, but that the emphasis on video has a detrimental effect in lower quality systems, where video quality is provided at the expense of audio quality.

ANALYTIC APPROACH

Analytic Methods

Different research studies were designed based on differing experimental methodologies, reflecting the backgrounds of the researchers or their purposes in conducting the studies. Such methodologies include psychological, ethnographic, conversational analysis, and other approaches, which are discussed in further detail by Sellen in "Assessing Video-Mediated Conduct" (chapter 5, this volume).

Questions Asked

Each piece of research seeks to answer one or more questions, which may be explicitly stated up front, or merely implied. For instance, some studies have been conducted to evaluate a specific system. In others, researchers may be examining how to optimize user satisfaction with a system by modifying specific conditions, such as the quality or arrangement of the video views seen by participants. For example, Acker and Levitt (1982) studied the effect of providing improved eye contact (images presented without parallax angle) between participants. Still other researchers may be looking at how to measure user satisfaction or some other parameter to capture the efficacy of a system; an underlying assumption of some work has been that the closer VMC approximates face-to-face communication, the better it is. The nature of the questions can influence the slant or scope of the reported research.

A recurring focus of much of the research has been communication: How well is human–human communication supported by a system, or how is that communication altered by use of the system, or how can that communication be characterized?

- Chapanis et al. (1972) felt that the richer the communication modality, the better the problem-solving performance, and studied the effects of different communication modalities on problem-solving and linguistic behavior.
- Short, Williams, and Christie (1976) and Williams (1977) asked how telecommunications, in general and in different modes, affects task performance and human behavior.

- Hoecker et al. (1978) explored how the nature of the particular view of participants (voice-switched vs. continuous) transmitted to other participants affects the communicative aspects of videoconferences.
- Cohen (1982) sought to add objective data to previously reported subjective results of market research on the extent to which speaker interactions differ as a function of the communications medium by comparing speaker interactions in face-to-face (FTF) versus PICTURE-PHONE Meeting Service (PMS) environments.
- Gale (1989) wanted to determine the value added to an office system by incorporating audio and video performance, and in doing so studied three conditions: data share, data share plus audio, and data share plus audio plus video.
- O'Conaill et al. (1993) investigated the claim that properties of the communication channels (full- or half-duplex audio; audio delay; video quality) influenced specific features of the communication process, in ISDN versus LIVE-NET (LN) conditions.
- Fish et al. (1993) studied the extent to which VMC and face-to-face informal communications were similar, in terms of frequency, expressiveness, and interactivity.
- Sellen (1995) compared the properties of spoken communication used in three videoconferencing systems with respect to their support for selective gaze and listening, and how their differing visual access to other participants affected the communication.

Some of the literature presents mostly anecdotal—as opposed to quantitative—reports of the experience of using video-mediated technology (e.g., Abel, 1990; Adler & Henderson, 1994; Mantei, 1988; Nardi et al., 1993) or, in some cases, the experience of developing such technology (Harrison, Mantei, Beirne, & Narine, 1994; Mantei, 1988). And Root (1988) presented a conceptual design of the system that would become Cruiser.

The purpose of some papers has been to evaluate or summarize existing reports of research (Short et al., 1976; Whittaker, 1995; Williams, 1977). Other papers offered the authors' assessments of whether VMC is a worthwhile undertaking and, if so, suggested ways in which it can be advanced. Examples of such work include Egido (1988, 1990), Fish et al. (1992), Gale (1992), Gaver (1992), and Whittaker (1995).

Group Characteristics

At least partly related to the choice of analytic methodology is the composition of the group of subjects participating in each study. Because few of the studies were longitudinal (but cf. Dykstra-Erickson et al., 1995; Tang

& Isaacs, 1993), one would expect some effect from whether or not subjects knew each other prior to the study. Particularly in earlier lab study work (e.g., Hoecker et al., 1978; Chapanis et al., 1972; Cohen, 1982; Ochsman & Chapanis, 1974), the subjects were recruited solely for purposes of brief studies, and usually were not familiar with each other, the equipment, or the assigned tasks.

On the other hand, more current, naturalistic work involving workplace studies tends to use participants who know each other, have a previously existing working relationship, and are familiar with the technology used. This is true in Fish et al. (1992, 1993), Gaver et al. (1992), Isaacs and Tang (1993), O'Conaill et al. (1993), Tang and Rua (1994), and Tang and Isaacs (1993). A group of this composition is likely to exhibit different communication patterns among themselves, because they are already familiar with nuances of each other's communication styles and have a shared social and historical context.

Besides the variables of familiarity and previous experience with the equipment, another factor that contributes to differences in communication styles across studies is the actual number of participants in any given interaction. Most of the earlier work studied dyads, groups of only 2 (e.g., Chapanis et al., 1972; Ochsman & Chapanis, 1974), whereas later work, tending more toward naturalistic studies, needed to accommodate real working groups. Thus, the Tang and Isaacs studies (1993) were based on interactions ranging from 2 to 5 people; in O'Conaill et al. (1993), the FTF and ISDN meetings involved 4 to 7 people, and the LN meetings 7 to 9. The significance of the number of participants is that with more than two participants, the possibilities exist for richer, more complex, and more realistic conversational styles. For example, in a group of 3 or more, 1 person can make an aside to another; in groups of 4 or more, parallel conversations can be conducted simultaneously. Although these are more representative of "real" (i.e., face-to-face) conversations, they also introduce more room for miscommunication, as it becomes less clear whom is being addressed, who has the floor, and so forth. Sometimes the technology can be seen to provide inadequate support for such sophisticated communication.

There are many other dimensions of group characteristics, discussed by Olson and Olson in "Making Sense of the Findings" (chapter 4, this volume).

Tasks Being Performed by the Users

Also somewhat dependent on research methodology is the task that participants perform during the study. Earlier and lab-based studies tend to use artificial or contrived tasks, whereas later, workplace-based ethnographic studies use more naturalistic tasks. Thus, Chapanis et al. used a problem-solving task; Hoecker et al. (1978) had subjects solving a consensus problem; Cohen (1982) used role-playing and consensus tasks; and Gaver et al. (1993) developed two tasks, both contrived, for subjects to perform during the course of the research session.

In contrast, participants tend to perform their normal everyday work-related tasks in media space and other environments used for workplace collaboration and communication. See, for example, Heath and Luff (1992), Isaacs and Tang (1993), Nardi et al. (1993), O'Conaill et al. (1993), and Tang and Isaacs (1993).

The Olsons, in "Making Sense of the Findings" (chapter 4, this volume), discuss other aspects of the tasks used in VMC research. The issue of naturalistic tasks and how they fit into the analytic methodology is also dealt with further by Sellen in "Assessing Video-Mediated Conduct" (chapter 5, this volume).

Data Collection and Analysis

The studies also differ widely in the data they examined, both in the nature of data collected and in the variables they measured. The ways in which data has been collected include participant questionnaires, quantitative measurement of individual actions, independent evaluation of results of sessions, experimenter observation, and quantitative analysis of transcripts of videotaped sessions. Many studies are based on some combination of data from these resources.

Participants are sometimes questioned about their experiences using video-mediated technology to determine their level of satisfaction, how closely they felt the VMC interactions approximated face-to-face interactions, what sorts of tasks/interactions they found VMC particularly useful for, and so on, as in Hoecker et al. (1978), Cohen (1982), Gale (1989), Nardi et al. (1993, 1996), Sellen (1992, 1995), and Tang and Isaacs (1993). Participants fill out questionnaires, are interviewed by the experimenter, or take part in focus groups.

In some cases, experimenters sit in the same room as the participants, categorizing the participants' utterances or actions. In the work by Chapanis et al. (1972) and Ochsman and Chapanis (1974), individual behaviors were classified as sending, receiving, searching, taking notes, handling parts, waiting, or combinations thereof. In ethnographic studies, experimenters may even "shadow" individual participants, following them around for long periods of time and recording their daily procedures and tasks, as in Nardi et al. (1993, 1996). Sometimes participants are asked to perform self-reports, as in Fish et al. (1993), whose participants reported on the content (e.g., report work status, discuss nonworkplace topics) and outcomes (e.g., did productive work, maintained relationship) of their conversations via different media.

Session videotapes were analyzed in many desktop videoconferencing studies. For example, Isaacs and Tang (1993) examined transaction logs of the events in all conditions, and the ability of the different modes to support communicative behaviors, such as expressing understanding, forecasting responses, enhancing verbal descriptions with gestures, conveying nonverbal information, expressing attitudes through posture and facial expressions, managing pauses, managing turn-taking, controlling the floor, using peripheral cues, having side conversations, pointing, and manipulating real-world objects.

Tang and Isaacs (1993) applied interaction analysis and determined at what points in the collaborative design process team members were using each of the media available. They studied the pattern of interactions chosen by team members, measuring frequency, duration, and distribution of the different interaction modes available. In that study, participants had a choice of using e-mail, phone conferencing, video room conferencing, desktop videoconferencing, or face-to-face meetings.

Transcribing the entire contents of videotapes is less common, and there are differences among the transcription systems used. Even here, however, there are difficulties in making direct comparisons, as the transcription systems used either were not specified or differed in focus, scope, and methodology. Tang and Isaacs (1993) used transaction logs rather than verbatim transcriptions. Heath and Luff (1992) mapped visual gestures onto transcriptions of sessions. O'Conaill et al. (1993) provided details on which segments of the sessions were transcribed, and explain the conversational analysis transcription system used. Sellen (1992, 1995) removed backchannels, laughter, and cross-talk from the measurements obtained by a special-purpose speech tracking system.

The variables measured differ widely from study to study, reflecting differences in both the theoretical and methodological inclinations of the researchers. Studies that examined variables of particular interest include:

- Chapanis et al. (1972) measured the time it took to solve the problem and the number of "button pushes" on an electronic switching system, which roughly equated to turns taken, or messages exchanged.
- In Cohen (1982), the data collected included participants' ratings of the two environments with respect to such features as ease of communication, social dynamics, and the effectiveness of the communications media, compared to regular telephony, for performing different types of tasks.
- O'Conaill et al. (1993) measured variables based on channel properties: backchannels, interruptions, overlaps (projections/completions, floorholding, simultaneous starts), explicit handovers, turn number, turn length, and turn distribution.

- Sellen (1992, 1995) defined each of the speech events being measured, such as turns, switch time, or categories of simultaneous speech and handovers. Video and audio recordings of sessions were made. After the sessions, participants completed questionnaires and a group discussion was held.
- The participants in Tang and Isaacs (1993) and Tang and Rua (1994) kept logs of the frequency and duration of their interactions with one another; videotapes in each of the three conditions were analyzed for interactions, and each team member was interviewed at juncture points throughout the life of the study.

FURTHER BACKGROUND MATERIAL

The three remaining chapters in this section provide the reader with a broad-based foundation for approaching the works in the rest of this volume, addressing the role of vision, relevant aspects of video technology, and a vocabulary for pulling together discussions of related works.

Whittaker and O'Conaill, in "The Role of Vision in Face-to-Face and Mediated Communication" (chapter 2, this volume), present a general framework within which they describe communicative features and characterize the types of visible information that factor into communication. They evaluate several predictions regarding the benefit of video in mediated communication, and discuss related technology and design implications.

The next chapter, "Technology Constraints of Video-Mediated Communication" (chapter 3, this volume), by Angiolillo, Blanchard, Israelski, and Mane, provides a comprehensive introduction to many of the technologies that are factors in the viability of VMC. The authors present both a historical and a lifecycle view of the technology, as well as making predictions about how the technologies might evolve in the future.

In "Making Sense of the Findings" (chapter 4, this volume), the Olsons examine the many variables that comprise a suggested framework. The hope is to engender a common ground on which researchers can meet to design their studies, compare results, and evaluate theories.

NOTE

1. The example citations are merely representative, not all-inclusive.

REFERENCES

Abel, M. J. (1990). Experiences in an exploratory distributed organization. In J. Galegher, R. E. Kraut, & C. Egido (Eds.), *Intellectual teamwork* (pp. 489–510). Hillsdale, NJ: Lawrence Erlbaum Associates.

Acker, S. R., & Levitt, S. R. (1987). Designing videoconference facilities for improved eye contact. *Journal of Broadcasting & Electronic Media, 31*(2), 181–191.

Adler, A. & Henderson, A. (1994). A room of our own: Experiences from a direct office-share. *CHI'94 Conference Proceedings* (pp. 138–144). New York: ACM Press.

Bly, S., Harrison, S., & Irwin, S. (1993). Media spaces: Bringing people together in a video, audio, and computing environment. *Communications of the Association of Computing Machinery, 36*(1), 28–47.

Chapanis, A., Ochsman, R. N., Parrish, R. B., & Weeks, G. D. (1972). Studies in interactive communication: II. The effects of four communication modes on the behavior of teams during cooperative problem-solving. *Human Factors, 14*(6), 487–509.

Cohen, K. M. (1982). Speaker interaction: Video Teleconferences versus face-to-face meetings. In L. A. Parker & C. H. Olgren (Eds.), *Teleconferencing and electronic communications: Applications, technologies and human factors* (pp. 189–199). Madison, WI: University of Wisconsin Extension, Center for Interactive Programs.

Dourish, P., & Bly, S. (1992). Portholes: Supporting awareness in a distributed work group. *CHI'92 Conference Proceedings* (pp. 541–547). New York: ACM Press.

Dykstra-Erickson, E. A., Rudman, C., Hertz, R., Mithal, K., Schmidt, J., & Marshall, C. (1995, March). Supporting adaptation to multimedia desktop conferencing. *Proceedings of the 15th International Symposium on Human Factors in Telecommunications* (pp. 31–38). Melbourne, Australia.

Egido, C. (1988). Video conferencing as a technology to support group work: A review of its failures. *CSCW'88 Conference Proceedings* (pp. 13–24). New York: ACM Press.

Egido, C. (1990). Teleconferencing as a technology to support cooperative work: Its possibilities and limitations. In J. Galegher, R. E. Kraut, & C. Egido (Eds.), *Intellectual teamwork* (pp. 351–371). Hillsdale, NJ: Lawrence Erlbaum Associates.

Fish, R. S., Kraut, R. E., & Chalfonte, B. L. (1990). The VideoWindow system in informal communications. *CSCW'90 Conference Proceedings* (pp. 1–11). New York: ACM Press.

Fish, R. S., Kraut, R. E., Root, R. W., & Rice, R. E. (1992). Evaluating video as a technology for informal communication. *CHI'92 Conference Proceedings* (pp. 37–48). New York: ACM Press.

Fish, R., Kraut, R., Root, R., & Rice, R. (1993). Video as a technology for informal communication. *Communications of the Association of Computing Machinery, 36*(1), 48–61.

Gale, S. (1989, September). Adding audio and video to an office environment. *Proceedings of the 1st European Conference on CSCW*, London.

Gale, S. (1992). Desktop video conferencing: Technical advances and evaluation issues. *Computer Communications, 15*(8), 517–526.

Gaver, W. W. (1992). The affordances of media spaces for collaboration. *CSCW'92 Proceedings* (pp. 17–24). New York: ACM Press.

Gaver, W., Moran, T., MacLean, A., Lövstrand, L., Dourish, P., Carter, K., & Buxton, W. (1992). Realizing a video environment: EuroParc's RAVE system. *CHI'92 Conference Proceedings* (pp. 27–35). New York: ACM Press.

Gaver, W., Sellen, A., Heath, C., & Luff, P. (1993). One is not enough: Multiple views in a media space. *INTERCHI'93 Conference Proceedings* (pp. 335–341). New York: ACM Press.

Gaver, W. W., Smets, G., & Overbeeke, K. (1995). A virtual window on media space. *CHI'95 Conference Proceedings* (pp. 257–264). New York: ACM Press.

Harrison, B., Mantei, M., Beirne, G., & Narine, T. (1994). Communicating about communicating: Cross-disciplinary design of a media space interface. *CHI'94 Conference Proceedings* (pp. 124–130). New York: ACM Press.

Heath, C., & Luff, P. (1991). Disembodied conduct: Communication through video in a multi-media office environment. *CHI'91 Conference Proceedings* (pp. 99–103). New York: ACM Press.

Heath, C., & Luff, P. (1992). Media space and communicative asymmetries: Preliminary observations of video-mediated interaction. *Human-Computer Interaction, 7*(3), 315–346.

Hoecker, D. G., Brown, E. F., Wish, M., and Geller, V. J. (1978, December). A behavioural comparison of communication using voice-switched and "continuous presence" videoconferencing arrangements. *NTC 78, Proceedings of the National Telecommunications Conference* (pp. 34.2.1–34.2.3). Birmingham, AL.

Isaacs, E. A., & Tang, J. C. (1993). What video can and can't do for collaboration: A case study. *Proceedings of ACM Multimedia 93* (pp. 199–206). New York: ACM Press.

Isaacs, E. A., Morris, T., & Rodriguez, T. K. (1994). A Forum for supporting interactive presentations to distributed audiences. *CSCW'94 Conference Proceedings* (pp. 405–416). New York: ACM Press.

Isaacs, E. A., Morris, T., Rodriguez, T. K., & Tang, J. C. (1995). A comparison of face-to-face and distributed presentations. *CHI'95 Conference Proceedings* (pp. 354–361). New York: ACM Press.

Ishii, H., & Kobayashi, M. (1992). ClearBoard: A seamless medium for shared drawing and conversation with eye contact. *CHI'92 Conference Proceedings* (pp. 525–532). New York: ACM Press.

Kuzuoka, H. (1992). Spatial workspace collaboration: A Share View video support system for remote collaboration capability. *CHI'92 Conference Proceedings* (pp. 533–540). New York: ACM Press.

Kuzuoka, H., Kosuge, T., & Tanaka, M. (1994). GestureCam: A video communication system for sympathetic remote collaboration. *CSCW'94 Conference Proceedings* (pp. 35–43). New York: ACM Press.

Mantei, M. (1988). Capturing the Capture Lab concepts: A case study in the design of computer supported meeting environments. *CSCW'88 Conference Proceedings* (pp. 257–270). New York: ACM Press.

Mantei, M., Baecker, R., Sellen, A., Buxton, W., Milligan, T., & Wellman, B. (1991). Experiences in the use of a media space. *CHI'91 Conference Proceedings* (pp. 203–208). New York: ACM Press.

Nardi, B., Kuchinsky, A., Whittaker, S., Leichner, R., & Schwarz, H. (1996). Video-as-data: Technical and social aspects of a collaborative multimedia application. *Computer Supported Co-operative Work, 4,* 73–100.

Nardi, B. A., Schwarz, H., Kuchinsky, A., Leichner, R., & Whittaker, S. (1993). Turning away from talking heads: The use of video-as-data in neurosurgery. *INTERCHI '93 Conference Proceedings* (pp. 327–334). New York: ACM Press.

Ochsman, R. B., & Chapanis, A. (1974). The effects of 10 communication modes on the behavior of teams during co-operative problem-solving. *International Journal of Man–Machine Studies, 6,* 579–619.

O'Conaill, B., Whittaker, S., & Wilbur, S. (1993). Conversations over video conferences: An evaluation of the spoken aspects of video-mediated communication, *Human–Computer Interaction, 8,* 389–428.

Okada, K., Maeda, F., Ichikawaa, Y., & Matsushita, Y. (1994). Multiparty videoconferencing at virtual social distance: MAJIC design. *CSCW'94 Conference Proceedings* (pp. 385–393). New York: ACM Press.

Olson, J. S., Olson, G. M., & Meader, D. K. (1995). What mix of video and audio is useful for small groups doing remote real-time design work? *CHI'95 Conference Proceedings* (pp. 362–368). New York: ACM Press.

Root, R. W. (1988). Design of a multi-media vehicle for social browsing. *CSCW'88 Conference Proceedings* (pp. 25–38). New York: ACM Press.

Rutter, R. R., Stephenson, G. M., & Dewey, M. E. (1981). Visual communication and the content and style of conversation. *British Journal of Social Psychology, 20,* 41–52.

Sellen, A. (1992). Speech patterns in video-mediated conversations. *CHI'92 Conference Proceedings* (pp. 49–59). New York: ACM Press.

Sellen, A. J. (1995). Remote conversations: The effects of mediating talk with technology. *Human–Computer Interaction, 10*(4), 401–444.

Short, J., Williams, E., & Christie, B. (1976). *The social psychology of telecommunications.* Chichester: Wiley.

Tang, J. C., & Isaacs, E. (1993). Why do users like video? Studies of multimedia-supported collaboration. *Computer-Supported Collaborative Work: An International Journal, 1*(9), 163–196.

Tang, J. C., & Minneman, S. L. (1991). VideoWhiteboard: Video shadows to support remote collaboration. *CHI'91 Conference Proceedings* (pp. 315–322). New York: ACM Press.

Tang, J. C., & Rua, M. (1994). Montage: Providing teleproximity for distributed groups. *CHI'94 Conference Proceedings* (pp. 37–43). New York: ACM Press.

Tani, M., Yamaashi, K., Tanikoshi, K., Futakawa, M., & Tanifuji, S. (1992). Object-oriented video: Interaction with real-world objects through live video. *CHI'92 Conference Proceedings* (pp. 593–598). New York: ACM Press.

Whittaker, S. (1995). Rethinking video as a technology for interpersonal communication: Theory and design implications. *International Journal of Human–Computer Studies, 42,* 501–529.

Williams, E. (1977). Experimental comparisons of face-to-face and mediated communication: A review. *Psychological Bulletin, 84*(5), 963–976.

Chapter 2

The Role of Vision in Face-to-Face and Mediated Communication

Steve Whittaker
AT & T Laboratories

Brid O'Conaill
Hewlett Packard Laboratories

This chapter uses a general communication framework to predict where visible information supplied by video might be critical in mediated communication. We first identify fundamental features of communication that have to be supported in any conversation, regardless of the available communication modalities. We characterize the different types of visible information that play a role in face-to-face interaction and the communication features they support. We then use the framework to evaluate three predictions about the benefits of video in mediated communication: (a) Video supports visible behaviors and hence supplies nonverbal information that is missing from the speech channel; (b) video provides visible information about the availability of other people, and hence supports connection for unplanned communications; (c) video provides dynamic visual information about objects and events that is important for certain collaborative tasks, an application that we refer to as "video-as-data." We evaluate existing work on VMC in terms of these three hypotheses. Current evidence suggests weak support for video as communicating one type of nonverbal information, that is, affective information. We conclude that there is insufficient data to evaluate the connection and video-as-data hypotheses. We discuss what refinements are needed in our theories about how visible information operates in mediated communication, and briefly examine the technology and design implications of these results.

INTRODUCTION

Face-to-face communication is a multimodal process. It involves complex interactions between verbal and visual behaviors. As people speak, they gesture for emphasis and illustration, they gaze at listeners and visually monitor their environment, their facial expressions change, and their body posture and orientation shift as they talk. Likewise, listeners look at speakers, as the speakers talk. Listeners monitor speaker's facial expressions and gestures, they nod their heads to show assent, and their facial expressions and physical posture change depending on their interest in and attitude to the speaker's utterance. Furthermore as people interact, they orient to, gesture at, and manipulate physical objects in the environment they share.

Despite the multimodal nature of face-to-face communication, the most pervasive and successful technology for communicating at distance is the telephone, which relies solely on the voice modality. Early attempts to supplement the voice modality by adding visible information about other conversational participants have not led to the expected improvements in remote communication. Laboratory studies to demonstrate the benefits of adding a visual communication modality to voice have in general shown few objective improvements (Chapanis, 1975; Chapanis, Ochsman, Parrish, & Weeks, 1972; Reid, 1977; Rutter & Robinson, 1981; Sellen, 1995, this volume; Short, Williams, & Christie, 1976; Williams, 1977). Furthermore, technologies premised on the advantages of supplementing voice with visible information, such as the videophone and the videoconference, have not yet proved greatly successful in the marketplace (Egido, 1990; Noll, 1992).

This prior work shows that the role of visible information in communication is both complex and subtle. From a theoretical viewpoint, it indicates that we need more detailed understanding of the precise functions that visible information plays in communication. From a practical viewpoint, we need to understand when and how visible information is vital for communication. This understanding is important in the design of technologies that exploit visible information to provide more effective remote communication than is currently supported by the telephone. Much of the prior technology-oriented work on video-mediated communication (VMC) has been based on the intuition that visible information will necessarily benefit interaction, without having specific hypotheses about how those benefits will come about.

The aim of this chapter is to use a general communication framework to predict and evaluate where visible information might be critical in mediated communication. The structure of this chapter is as follows. We begin by presenting a communication framework, specifying fundamental features of communication that have to be supported in any conversation, regardless of the communication modalities available. We then describe the different types of visible information that play a role in face-to-face interaction and the conversational features they support. We distinguish between two main classes of visible information: visible behaviors produced by the participants, and information about the visible environment. Visible behaviors include the gaze, gesture, facial expressions, and posture of the participants. The visible environment includes information about objects and events that have been observed by the conversational participants, as well as information about the availability of other participants. On the basis of this analysis of the communicative function of visible information, we evaluate three predictions about how video might improve communication. The three hypotheses are:

1. Video supports visible behaviors and hence supplies important nonverbal information.
2. Video provides visible information about the environment, specifically the availability of other people; this in turn facilitates connection for unplanned communications.
3. Video provides dynamic visual information about objects and events in a shared visual environment. This is important for certain collaborative tasks, an application that we refer to as *video-as-data*.

We evaluate existing work on VMC in terms of these three hypotheses. We conclude by discussing the impact of these results for theories about how visible information operates in mediated communication, and exploring the implications for technology designers.

COMMUNICATION FRAMEWORK

There are a number of key aspects of communication that have to be supported regardless of what communication modes are available (see Table 2.1). Communication is a joint activity that requires coordination of both process and content between speakers and listeners (Clark & Brennan, 1991; Whittaker, Brennan, & Clark, 1991). Content is the subject matter of conversation, and concerns what participants talk about. Content coordination addresses how participants build up common beliefs and understanding about that subject matter. Process is concerned with the mechanisms and management of conversation. The key issues for process coordination are (a) the set of procedures by which participants agree to begin and end entire conversations and (b) the rules that allow participants to switch roles between speaking and listening.

Coordination of Process

We address two aspects of process coordination: turn-taking and availability. Turn-taking is concerned with how participants jointly determine who will speak, who will listen, and how transitions are made between these roles

TABLE 2.1
A Taxonomy of Conversational Mechanisms
and Their Communication Functions

	Conversational Mechanism	Communication Function
Process coordination	Turn-taking cues	Determine who will speak, who will listen, and how transitions are made between these roles
	Availability cues	Determine when to initiate or end a communication episode
Content coordination	Reference	Allow participants to identify the objects and events they jointly want to talk about
	Feedback cues	Inform speaker of listener's understanding; contribute to maintenance of mutual beliefs and common knowledge between speaker and listeners
	Interpersonal cues	Allow participants to infer the emotional stance, affect, and motivations of other people to what is being discussed, and to other conversational participants

(Sacks, Schegloff, & Jefferson, 1974; Walker & Whittaker, 1990; Whittaker & Stenton, 1988). A striking feature of conversations is that in general only one person speaks at any point. Less than 5% of speech is delivered in overlap (two people speaking at the same time), and yet gaps between one speaker finishing and the next starting are frequently measurable in milliseconds (Levinson, 1983). Turn-taking addresses how these transitions are successfully achieved (Sacks et al., 1974). Process coordination also addresses how entire conversations are initiated and concluded (Schegloff & Sacks, 1973). Many communications are unplanned. They therefore require participants to establish precisely when other people are available for communication and when it is opportune to initiate such spontaneous interactions, based on awareness of others' movements and activities (Heath & Luff, 1991; Kendon & Ferber, 1973; Kraut, Fish, Root, & Chalfonte, 1993; Whittaker, Frohlich, & Daly-Jones, 1994).

Coordination of Content

Coordination of content is concerned with how participants arrive at, and maintain, common understanding in conversation (Clark & Brennan, 1991; Clark & Marshall, 1981; Grosz & Sidner, 1986). Coordinating content presents problems for both speakers and listeners. From the listener's perspective, one of the fundamental problems with human communication is that the literal meaning of an individual utterance underspecifies the speaker's intended meaning (Clark & Marshall, 1981; Grice, 1975). Listeners have to infer the speaker's intended meaning by supplementing what was said with contextual information external to the utterance. In general, listeners are able to generate such external inferences quickly and accurately, and hence determine the speaker's intentions (Levinson, 1983). How are listeners able to do this and how do they know which information not directly stated in the utterance should be used in deriving inferences? Clark and Marshall (1981) argued that this external information is a restricted set, common knowledge, which is shared between participants.

Common knowledge is crucial for achieving an important aspect of communication, namely, reference. Reference enables conversational participants to jointly identify the objects and events that they want to talk about. Speakers have multiple communication choices when they wish to refer to an object or event (Clark & Marshall, 1981). A speaker may therefore verbally refer to a dog as "the dog." Alternatively, there may be more precise or specific ways to describe the animal, such as "Marvin," "the dachshund," or "whoever chewed my slipper." If the animal is present they may point at it, or gesture and say "that animal" or even "that." Speakers make these choices based on the common knowledge they share with listeners: It would be of little use to describe the dog as "Marvin" to a complete stranger. Likewise, the term *dachshund* is almost certain to fail with a very young child. When speakers make these reference choices they must therefore balance the additional precision these terms provide, against the likelihood their audience may not understand (Clark & Marshall, 1981).

A second problem for speakers in coordinating content is to determine whether their utterance had the intended effect, that is, whether the listener drew the correct set of inferences from what they said. Listeners' knowledge and beliefs are usually not directly accessible to the speaker (Walker, 1993), so feedback mechanisms are crucial for the maintenance of common knowledge. Speakers provide listeners with frequent opportunities to offer feedback about what was just said (Kraut, Lewis, & Swezey, 1982; O'Conaill, Whittaker, & Wilbur, 1993; Yngve, 1970)—to show acceptance (Clark & Schaefer, 1989) or to clarify their level of understanding (Walker & Whittaker, 1990; Whittaker & Stenton, 1988). These feedback processes take place on a moment-by-moment basis in conversation, so that misunderstandings can be quickly identified and rectified (Clark & Brennan, 1991; Kraut et al., 1982; O'Conaill et al., 1993).

Communication is not restricted to the exchange of propositional information, however, and a final aspect of content coordination concerns the affective state or interpersonal attitude of the participants. This is social information about participants' feelings, emotions, and attitudes to the other conversants and to what is being discussed. As with conversational intentions, participants generally do not make this information verbally explicit, so it usually has to be inferred. Access to affective information is important: It can change the outcome of conversations in situations where emotion plays a critical role, such as negotiation (Short et al., 1976).

THE ROLE AND FUNCTION OF VISIBLE
INFORMATION IN COMMUNICATION

We now turn to an analysis of the types of visible information that are used to support some of these features of face-to-face communication. In face-to-face conversation, there are two different types of visible information. The first is information about the behaviors of other conversational participants, that is, the set of communicative actions that they perform with their eyes (gaze), faces (facial expressions), hands and arms (gestures), and the movements and orientation of their bodies (posture). The second type of visible information is about the visible environment that conversational participants share, with its set of shared objects, access to shared events, and information about the movements and activities of other people.

It is important to note that the correspondence between visible information and communication function is not direct: The same type of visible information can support multiple communication functions, and likewise one communication function may be supported by different types of visible information. For example, one type of visible behavior, gaze, supports multiple functions. It can coordinate reference, give feedback of understanding the utterance, and aid turn-taking. Similarly, one communication function may be mediated by multiple different types of visible behavior. Thus turn-taking can be supported by gaze, gesture, and posture (Beattie, 1978, 1981; Duncan, 1972; Kendon, 1967).

Visible Behaviors

Gaze. Gaze is the way people extract visible information from their environment. The direction in which a person looks, the amount of time looking in that direction, and the patterns of gaze are all important aspects of this visible behavior. The communicative functions of gaze are shown in Table 2.2.

Gaze is a general indicator of attention and can be directed at other conversational participants, as well as at features of the physical environment. By gazing at the speaker, listeners derive important information from the speaker's facial expressions, posture, and gesture. In this way, the speaker's visible behaviors help clarify the content of what is being said. Speakers interpret listeners' attentional behavior as feedback for determining how well their message is being understood and coordinate their content accordingly (Beattie, 1978, 1981; Clark & Brennan, 1991; Goodwin, 1981). On some occasions speakers also try and elicit this type of feedback: They may pause in their speech until they detect visible attention from listeners (Goodwin, 1981).

TABLE 2.2
Communicative Functions of Gaze

Conversational Mechanism	Gaze Behaviors	
	Speaker	Listener
Process coordination Turn-taking cues	Speaker predominantly looks away from listener while talking—negotiated mutual gaze used as "turn-yielding" signal	Listener predominantly looks at speaker while speaker is talking; negotiated mutual gaze used as "turn-accepting" cue
Availability cues		
Content coordination Reference	Gaze at an object indicates person's interest and attention to that object; joint attention allows pointing	Gaze at an object indicates person's interest and attention to that object; joint attention allows pointing
Feedback cues	Gaze at listener can be an attention-eliciting device	Gaze at the speaker indicates interest in what the speaker is saying
Interpersonal information cues	Patterns of gaze interpreted as indicating sincerity, trustworthiness, friendliness; indicate speakers' affective attitude to utterance	Patterns of gaze interpreted as indicating sincerity, trustworthiness, friendliness; indicate listeners' response to utterance

Gaze may also be coordinated between conversational participants to achieve mutual gaze or joint attention. Mutual gaze occurs when two participants are concurrently looking at each other. Joint attention is when participants are mutually oriented to a common part of their shared visible environment and are aware that their conversational partners are also looking at it. People are very good at determining where others are looking. This facilitates joint attention, which allows greater flexibility in referring to objects, because the speaker can infer which objects are highly salient to listeners (Clark & Marshall, 1981).

Gaze is also an indicator of interpersonal attitude or affect. Speakers tend to gaze at a listener's face more when they are being more persuasive, deceptive, ingratiating, or assertive (Kleinke, 1986), and are more likely to look at conversants whom they like (Exline & Winters, 1965). In addition, people tend to evaluate others by their patterns of gaze: People who look at their interlocutor only a small part of the time are judged as "defensive" or "evasive," whereas those who look a lot of the time are "friendly," "mature," and "sincere" (Kleck & Nuessle, 1968).

Gaze is also a key mechanism in the co-ordination of the conversational process of turn-taking (Kendon, 1967). As speakers draw to the end of a natural phase in their utterance, they are likely to gaze directly at their listener. By looking at the listener, speakers signal that they are ready to finish speaking. They then wait for a gaze from the listener confirming that the listener is ready to continue. When the listener and speaker achieve mutual gaze this serves as a confirmation of the transition, and the listener then takes over as next speaker.

Finally, it is important to note that participants spend relatively small amounts of time gazing at others while conversing. The amounts of gaze directed at others can be as low as 3% to 7% of conversational time, in the presence of relevant visible objects (Argyle, 1990; Argyle & Graham, 1977). Mutual gaze is even lower with recent studies reporting levels of below 5% (Anderson, Bard, Sotillo, Newland, & Doherty-Sneddon, in press). Given these low frequencies, it appears that conversational participants have restricted opportunities for eliciting visual information about others and neither speakers nor listeners have access to all the visible behaviors of others. This work also shows that conversationalists are often more visually focused on their environment than on other people (Argyle, 1990; Argyle & Graham, 1977).

Gesture. Gesture is the set of dynamic movements and shapes formed by a person's hands and arms during communication. Like gaze, it also supports multiple communication functions, shown in Table 2.3. It is used to coordinate conversational content, achieve reference, and assist in turn-taking. Some gestures, known as emblems, have conventionalized meanings, such as the "thumbs up," and "V for victory" (Efron, 1982). These can substitute for spoken words or phrases. Other iconic gestures can express propositions with a spatial or dynamic aspect: "It was this big," or "it moved like this," where the word "this" is illustrated by an appropriate gesture. A final class of gesture (known variously as "beats," "batons," or "speech primacy movements"), allows speakers to emphasize, evaluate, or "comment on" the information they are conveying verbally. In some cases "beats" serve the function of coordinating talk with the listener (Cassell, McNeill, & McCullough, in press; McNeill, 1992).

Given joint attention, pointing gestures can be used to achieve reference. Pointing gestures can also be used to manipulate or direct the attention of others, either by pointing and using speech, such as "look at that" or by pointing alone (Goodwin, 1981). Gesture can also be used to communicate more abstract characteristics of the space the speaker is talking about, such as the relative positions of the objects it contains, and their relative orientations (Cassell et al., in press; McNeill, 1992). Finally, gesture can serve to coordinate turn-taking transitions, and hence serve to coor-

TABLE 2.3
Communicative Functions of Gesture

Conversational Mechanism	Gestural Behaviors	
	Speaker	Listener
Process coordination Turn-taking	Termination of speaker gesture interpreted as "turn-yielding" cue	Listener gestures signal desire to speak
Availability		
Content coordination Reference	Pointing facilitated by joint attention	Pointing facilitated by joint attention
Feedback		
Interpersonal information		

dinate process. The continuation of any speaker hand movement—of whatever gestural type—acts as a cue that the current speaker wishes to hold the conversational floor. Similarly, the termination of gesture—again regardless of gestural type—acts as a signal that the speaker is ready to hand over the conversational floor, and is therefore referred to as a "turn-yielding" cue. Hand gestures can also be used by listeners to signal that they want to say something (Goodwin, 1981).

Facial Expression. Facial expressions are conveyed by the eyes, eyebrows, nose, mouth, and forehead. Information from the eyebrows and mouth is of prime importance in facial expressions (Ekman & Friesen, 1975). Facial expressions play a role in coordinating content: They provide listener feedback and serve as general indicators of emotional state. Information from the speakers' lips can also serve to disambiguate spoken content. These functions are shown in Table 2.4.

Facial expression offers speakers information about listeners' level of understanding. There are two methods by which the face provides feedback. The first, head nods, provides the speaker with concurrent feedback about what has just been said, and modification of the normal frequency and duration of head nods disrupts speakers' ability to communicate (Birdwhistell, 1970). Listener's facial expressions also reveal interest, puzzlement, or disbelief about what they are being told (Ekman & Friesen, 1975).

The face is also a rich source of information about the affective state of the conversational participants. The eyes, mouth, and eyebrows are highly expressive. Ekman and Friesen (1975) have shown that people across a number of cultures are able to recognize seven distinct facial expressions from posed photographs (happiness, sadness, surprise, anger, disgust, fear, and interest). Affective expressions allow listeners to infer speakers' current

TABLE 2.4
Communicative Functions of Facial Expressions

Conversational Mechanism	Facial Expressions	
	Speaker	Listener
Process coordination — Turn-taking		
Availability		
Content coordination — Reference	Visual information from reading the speaker's lips decreases the ambiguity of speech	
Feedback		Head nods indicate assent or dissent; expressions indicate interest, understanding, puzzlement, or disbelief
Interpersonal information	Expressions indicate happiness, fear, interest, surprise, sadness	Expressions indicate happiness, fear, interest, surprise, sadness

emotional state, and expressions allow their audience's emotional reaction to what is being said.

Finally, facial expressions, especially lip and teeth movements, can help decipher speech. The lip shape, teeth, and to a lesser extent tongue position give listeners visual information about the phonemes that the speaker is producing. Unintelligible speech can be rendered interpretable by visual information about lip shape. When lip shape information is available, listeners can interpret an additional 4–6 dB of noise and achieve the same level of intelligibility (Summerfield, 1992). The effect of visual information on speech perception is also demonstrated by the "McGurk effect," in which conflicting information from face and voice is "heard" in a way that combines both modalities. If the lips say "ga" and the voice "ba," then people hear it as "da" (McGurk & MacDonald, 1976).

Posture. This is the information supplied by the inclination and orientation of a conversational participant's body, in particular their trunk and upper body. The positions of both the arms and legs are also important here. Posture is less dynamic than other visible behaviors, with variations occurring less frequently. The communicative functions of posture are shown in Table 2.5. Posture is another cue as to the degree of interest or

TABLE 2.5
Communicative Functions of Posture

Conversational Mechanism	Postural Behaviors	
	Speaker	Listener
Process coordination Turn-taking		Listener activity can signal a desire to interrupt
Availability		
Content coordination Reference		
Feedback		Attention, interest in what speaker is saying
Interpersonal information	Reveals speaker's attitude to utterance	Reveals listener's affective reaction to utterance

engagement of a conversational participant. It therefore provides feedback to the speaker about how the message is being received. Interest is signaled in listeners by leaning forward, and by speakers in leaning forward and drawing back their legs. In contrast, boredom is signaled by head lowering, or turning the head to one side, supporting the head on one hand, leaning back and stretching out one's legs (Bull, 1978). Body position and orientation can also be used by the speaker to include or exclude people from the conversation (Goodwin, 1981).

Sharing a Visible Environment:
Information About Shared Events, Objects, and People

We have so far focused on the role of visible behavior, namely, the gaze, gestures, facial expressions, and posture of other conversational participants. In face-to-face conversation, however, the fact that participants have access to a shared physical environment means that other types of visible information are available, such as information about physical objects, events, and people. For the purpose of coordinating content, sharing the same physical environment enables people to make inferences about the set of objects and events that others in the same environment are likely to know about and want to talk about (Clark & Marshall, 1981; Whittaker et al., 1991, Whittaker, Geelhoed, & Robinson, 1993). Listeners can reduce the ambiguity of an incoming message, by using this physical information to infer what the message is likely to be about. Similarly, speakers can make inferences about what their audience might expect them to converse or know about, based on this shared physical information. Finally, people can make inferences about the availability of others for communication, based on visible information about those people. This availability information helps the process of initiating and terminating conversations.

Using Visible Information About Objects and Events in Collaboration. The visible environment includes information about the objects and events in the participants' shared environment, as well as their spatial configuration and interrelations. Information about the visible environment often interacts in important ways with verbal and visible behaviors, such as when participants gesture at, orient toward, and manipulate aspects of their environment. As we have seen, the visible environment provides crucial contextual information that can help participants determine what things are likely to be communicated about, and what entities are likely to be salient to others (Argyle & Graham, 1977; Cooper, 1973; Whittaker et al., 1993; Whittaker et al., 1994).

For tasks that require participants to jointly manipulate or modify complex objects, it is crucial to have access to a shared environment containing these objects to help coordinate content (Nardi, Schwarz, Kuchinsky, Leichner, Whittaker & Sclabassi, 1993; Nardi, Kuchinsky, Whittaker, Leichner, & Schwarz, 1996; see chapter 23, this volume; Gaver, Sellen, Heath, & Luff, 1993; Whittaker et al., 1993). Having access to a shared environment can be beneficial in multiple ways: Not only can participants mutually directly observe changes to that environment, but the shared environment also provides straightforward methods for people to exchange and simultaneously look at objects. Thus many workplace interactions involve documents, and a shared environment enables people to easily hand over a document, or for both participants to mutually orient to the document (Whittaker et al., 1994; Whittaker, Swanson, Kucan, & Sidner, in press). Furthermore, objects such as documents can be used as "context-holders" for intermittent workplace communications between colleagues. There are often long delays between different fragments of workplace conversations about ongoing shared tasks. Workers sometimes leave documents relating to current ongoing communications on their desktops as reminders of tasks in progress (Whittaker et al., in press). Similar "context-holding" functions were observed in intermittent interactions around different types of shared objects (Nardi, Kuchinsky, Whittaker, Leichner, & Schwartz, 1996; chapter 3, this volume).

Using Visible Information About People for Availability. Most simply, one can infer the presence of another person if the person is visible.[1] Furthermore, information about the proximity, current activities, and movements of other people has been shown to influence certain aspects of communication, such as its initiation and termination, as well as how interruptions are handled (Heath & Luff, 1991; Kendon & Ferber, 1973; Kraut et al., 1993; Tang, Isaacs, & Rua, 1994; Whittaker et al., 1994; Isaacs & Tang, chapter 9, this volume; Isaacs, Whittaker, Frohlich, & O'Conaill, chapter 22, this volume). This information is easily derived from the visible mode. In addition, other information about physical appearance is conveyed visibly and can support inferences about other participants' gender, age, and possibly dispositions.

Workplace interactions are generally unplanned (Isaacs et al., chapter 22, this volume; Kraut et al., 1993; Whittaker et al., 1994), and visible information provides mechanisms for initiating those types of communication. First, sightings of others can lead one to fall into spontaneous conversation, such as in public areas like coffee areas (Kendon & Ferber, 1973). In addition, seeing a colleague may remind one of an issue that needs to be discussed, so that the sighting serves as a reminder that a conversation needs to take place (Kraut et al., 1993; Whittaker et al., 1994). Visible information is also helpful in determining whether a colleague is receptive to an unplanned conversation, offering vital clues as to how available or interruptible they are. For example, passing by a colleague's office, it is possible to determine whether they are present and, if so, infer whether they can be interrupted and in some cases, how long such an interruption should last (Frohlich, 1995; Isaacs et al., chapter 22, this volume; Whittaker et al., 1994). Finally, this class of availability information can influence the termination and character of conversation. A substantial number of dyadic workplace communications are ended or changed by the arrival of a third party. Often this person indicates a desire to interrupt or join the conversation by "hovering," waiting for the current conversation to reach a point where the person can break in (Whittaker et al., 1994). Again, the information indicating to the conversationalists that another person wishes to interrupt or join them, is available in the visual channel.

EVALUATING THE EFFECTS OF ADDING VISIBLE INFORMATION TO AUDIO-ONLY COMMUNICATION

Given the analysis of critical communication features and the different functions of visible information, where might we expect to find benefits to supplementing audio with visible information? The preceding analysis suggests three distinct hypotheses about how visible information provided by video might improve audio-only communication. Extensive reviews of these hypotheses are also provided in Whittaker (1995, 1996).

Nonverbal Communication Hypothesis

The nonverbal communication hypothesis is that visible behaviors such as gaze, gesture, facial expressions, and posture provide information that is absent from audio-only communication. One evaluation of the hypothesis has been to conduct short-term laboratory studies comparing video-mediated with (a) audio or (b) face-to-face interaction, in the context of a particular communication task. The comparison with audio reveals how and when video information enhances speech-only communication, and the comparison with face-to-face communication about how effectively video/ audio mimics face-to-face conversation. Another technique has involved longer term field studies, installing video systems to evaluate their use (Abel, 1990; Bly, Harrison, & Irwin, 1993; Fish, Kraut, & Chalfonte, 1990; Fish, Kraut, Root, & Rice, 1993; Gaver et al., 1992; Mantei et al., 1991; Tang et al., 1994). There are methodological difficulties with the two types of data from field evaluations, however. The first type of data is from workgroups at the same physical location using high-quality video systems. Here, the ready availability of face-to-face communication may reduce the incidence and use of video technology. There is also data from geographically distributed workgroups that have higher incentives to use the system but are using inferior video technology because of the constraints imposed by wide-area networking bandwidths.

There are three distinct versions of the nonverbal communication hypothesis, each of which addresses different features of communication (Whittaker, 1995, 1996): (a) video provides cognitive cues that facilitate shared understanding; (b) video offers process cues to support turn-taking; (c) video provides social cues and access to emotional information. Cognitive and social cues address the issue of coordinating conversational content, whereas turn-taking addresses process coordination. The prototypical systems here are the videoconferencing suite or videophone. We review evaluations of each of the three subhypotheses about the role of nonverbal communication, first for high-quality and then for low-quality systems.

Chapanis and colleagues (Chapanis, 1975; Chapanis et al., 1972) conducted a series of laboratory experiments testing the cognitive cuing hypothesis, namely, that visual cues such as head nods and gaze help speakers to evaluate listener's understanding and attention. They compared the effectiveness of a variety of different media combinations for different cognitive problem-solving tasks, by looking at task outcome measures such as time to solution and quality of solution. The tasks involved complex instruction giving and route planning. In one task, subjects had to jointly construct a mechanical object where one person had the physical components and the other had the instructions. In another task, one person was given a map and the other given a copy of the *Yellow Pages*. They were asked to identify a map location satisfying a number of criteria, such as the nearest dentist to a given street address. The research compared two media conditions: audio-only communication, and high-quality video/audio, where the video showed the head and shoulders of the remote participant. However, the studies showed that adding visual information in tasks where it is important to track the understanding of remote participants did not increase the efficiency of problem solving, or produce higher quality problem solving.

Furthermore, other experiments comparing different combinations of media indicated that speech was the critical medium for interpersonal communication in collaborative problem solving: Removing the speech channel had huge effects on the outcome of communication. If participants could use the speech channel, then the addition or removal of video, text, or writing media had little effect on task outcome or quality of solution.

These results showing little impact of visual information on cognitive problem solving have been replicated by several other laboratory studies (Reid, 1977; Short et al., 1976; Williams, 1977). Most importantly, this is not an issue of video quality: Even face-to-face interaction is no better than speech only communication for this class of task (Williams, 1977). Similar negative results are suggested by field study research. A study of high quality local area videophone conducted over several months in a research laboratory showed few objective usage differences compared with the telephone (Fish et al., 1993).[2] Phone and videophone calls have similar durations, and are used for the same set of communication tasks. The researchers also administered a questionnaire asking people to state the tasks for which they felt that different communication techniques (e.g., videophone, telephone, face-to-face) were appropriate. Multidimensional scaling techniques applied to people's answers indicated that videophone is viewed by users as more similar to the telephone than face-to-face communication.

There is some counterevidence to these negative results, however. For a design task, Olson, Olson, and Meader (1995) showed that groups communicating face-to-face generated higher quality designs than audio-only groups, when those groups had access to a shared workspace. There were also differences in mutual understanding. Audio-only groups spent more time in stating and clarifying issues than groups that also had a high-quality video link.

The results are more mixed for the turn-taking hypothesis. Sellen (1995) investigated this in a series of laboratory studies of negotiation tasks, in which groups discussed contentious issues and tried to reach consensus. There was little evidence to support the claim that high-quality video information improves conversation management and turn-taking, when compared with audio-only conversations. For objective conversation process measures such as pausing, overlapping speech, and interruption management, there were no process differences between the video/audio systems and speech-only communication. Furthermore, none of the video/audio systems replicated face-to-face conversational processes. The video/audio systems reduced the ability of listeners to spontaneously take the conversational floor, as measured by number of interruptions.[3] Video/audio systems led speakers to use more formal techniques for handing over conversational initiative, such as naming a possible next speaker or using "tag" questions,[4] when compared with face-to-face interaction. Similar data are reported by O'Conaill et al. (1993), who also found speakers holding real meetings using high-quality videoconferencing used more formal turn-taking techniques than were observed in face-to-face interaction. One explanation of the failure of even high-quality videoconferencing to replicate face-to-face communication processes is that most videoconferencing systems do not support directional sound or visual cues. They tend to present sound and picture from a single monitor and speaker, which may compromise sound direction, head turning, and gaze cues in group interactions. Testing his hypothesis remains an outstanding research issue.

However, there are some differences in subjective data about turn-taking gathered from questionnaires. These differences concerned subject's impressions of the impact of video on conversational processes (Sellen, 1995). Video/audio is perceived to be better than speech in a number of ways. It is perceived to support interruptions; lead to more natural conversations that are more interactive; increase the ability to listen selectively to particular speakers; allow one to determine whether one is being attended to; and to generally keep track of the conversation. People also believe that they are better able to track the attention of others when they have video. Similar qualitative data are reported by Isaacs and Tang (1993), who found that video seemed to allow participants to manage pauses better than in speech-only communication. Despite this, Tang and Isaacs (1993) also found that high-quality video was not perceived as equivalent to face-to-face interaction: Subjective data showed that video was seen as less effective in supporting interactivity, selective attention, and the ability to take initiative in the conversation.

There is stronger evidence for the claim that video supports the transmission of social cues and affective information. Adding video information to the speech channel changes the outcome and character of communication tasks that require access to affect or emotional factors. Example tasks here include negotiation, bargaining, and conflict resolution. Participants focus more on the motives of others when they have access to visual information, and video/audio conversations are more personalized, less argumentative, more polite, and broader in focus. They are also less likely to end in deadlock than speech-only communications (Reid, 1977; Short et al., 1976; Williams, 1977). These results can be explained in terms of affective cues: Providing visual access to facial expressions, posture, and gesture allows people to make inferences about other participants' affective or emotional state. There are also subjective benefits to providing visual information: Participants believe that video/audio and face-to-face interaction are better than audio only for tasks requiring affect, such as getting to know other people, or person perception tasks. In addition, groups conversing using audio and video tend to like each other more (Reid, 1977; Short et al., 1976; Williams, 1977).

The preceding evaluations all used high-quality audio and video. Current technology limitations and restricted networking bandwidth mean, however, that high-quality systems will not be available for some years. It is therefore crucial for design and implementation that we understand the utility of low-quality video. One key finding from studies of low-quality video systems is that in certain circumstances adding visual information can detract from the interaction processes, if the video is implemented in a way that interferes with audio. There are two ways that audio can be affected in low bandwidth systems. First, certain commercial systems delay audio transmission, to allow time for video compression and decompression over wide-area networks, in order to present synchronized audio and video.[5] Second, some videoconferencing systems enforce half-duplex[6] audio to preserve bandwidth for video.

There is evidence that reducing audio quality to incorporate video is highly disruptive of turn-taking processes. In a naturalistic study, O'Conaill et al. (1993, chapter 6, this volume) compared face-to-face and video-mediated interaction in a low-quality wide-area system. The system had one-way half-duplex audio with one-way lags of between 410 and 780 msec and poor picture quality. The study measured a number of characteristics of conversation processes. Interactive aspects of conversation that required precise timing such as giving feedback, switching speakers, and asking clarifying questions were much reduced in the low-quality system compared with face-to-face interaction. Given the half-duplex audio and lags, speakers were unable to time their conversational contributions, with the result that backchannels or interruptions arrived too late, or at inappropriate points in the conversation. As a consequence, people had to explicitly manage speaker switches and there was increased formality in handing over the conversational floor, using devices such as selecting the next speaker by name. The result of both decreased interactivity and increased formality was a "lecture-like" style of interaction, with conversational turns in the videoconference being three times as long as face-to-face ones, making the system only suitable for certain types of conversational tasks, such as information exchange, that do not require quickfire exchanges.

Similar results showing the impact of audio lags on conversational processes are reported elsewhere. Cohen (1982) compared communication processes in face-to-face communication with low-quality videoconferencing for a series of laboratory tasks. The system she investigated had a 705-msec lag in both video and audio to simulate the performance of the AT & T PicturePhone. Participants found it hard to switch speakers and hard to ask clarifying questions in videoconferences. There were twice as many speaker switches in face-to-face communication compared with the videoconferencing system, and many more interruptions. Tang and Isaacs also evaluated low-quality videophone and videoconferencing systems (Tang & Isaacs,

1993; Isaacs & Tang, 1993). They found that lagged audio is highly disruptive of turn-taking, producing many fewer, longer turns. Their study also provides strong subjective support for the importance of low-lag audio. Participants preferred to use a separate half-duplex speakerphone to reduce delays in audio, even though it meant that synchronization between audio and video information was lost.

Connection Hypothesis: Using Video to Provide Availability Information

The second hypothesis is that video provides availability information about the movements and interruptibility of coworkers. This visible environment information can facilitate connection for unplanned interaction. Two separate classes of video application have systematically tested this hypothesis: (a) glance, which enables a user to briefly "look into" the office of a coworker to assess their communication availability, and (b) open links, in which persistent video/audio channels are maintained between two separate physical locations. There are again methodological problems in drawing conclusions about the video for connection hypothesis. In wide-area connection applications, video quality is poor. There may therefore be less motivation for using video for achieving wide-area connection, when the ensuing conversation will be over low-quality video. In local-area applications, visual connection information about coworkers' availability may already be accessible, as people move around their workplace. These confounding factors may lead to reduced use of video for connection. Nevertheless, when people do choose to use the technology for assessing availability, we can still ask how successful the technology is in achieving connection, and we now turn to this data.

For a local-area system, Fish et al. (1993) tested the use of different types of glance and their differential success in promoting opportunistic interactions. A brief glance at a user-selected recipient was the most frequently chosen type of glance: 81% of user initiated interactions were of this type, with 54% of these leading to an extended conversation. All other modes of glances were much less frequent and had much reduced likelihood of resulting in conversations. One type of glance was intended to simulate chance meetings such as "bumping into" another person in a hallway. In face-to-face settings neither participant normally intends such encounters, but they can promote extended work-related conversations. These types of chance encounters were implemented as a system-initiated connection between two arbitrary participants. These system-initiated connections showed very high failure rates, with 97% being terminated immediately without conversation. Overall, the glance options that callers chose indicate that they want direct control over who they connect to, and when they connect, rather than having the system do this. Furthermore, people wanted to use the "glance" as a preparation for communication, not merely to know "who is around." Glances that allowed "looking into" another office without the option of communicating were an infrequent user choice, accounting for only 12% of user selected glances.

The relationship between glances and opportunistic communication was also explored by Tang et al. (1994) for a system operating across multiple sites in a local area. Participants could first "look into" the office of a remote coworker, with the option of converting this into an extended conversation. Altogether, only 25% of glances were converted into conversations. This is no better than connection rates using only the phone (Whittaker et al., in press). Why was successful connection so infrequent? A significant proportion of failures (38%) occurred when recipients were out of their offices, but the reasons for the remainder are unclear; only 4% were when the recipients explicitly signaled that they were unavailable for communication. Many of the other failed connection attempts may occur when the recipient is in the office but busy with another activity, or another person. Tang et al. did not report this data, however.

Video and audio can also be used to support continuously "open links" between the offices of remote collaborators (Fish et al., 1993; Heath & Luff, 1991; Mantei et al., 1991). This is intended to approximate sharing the same physical office, so opportunistic communications can be started with minimal effort between connected participants, and visual and auditory information about communication availability is persistently available. However, Fish et al. (1993) reported that only 5% of connections lasted more than 30 min, and Tang et al. (1994) reported that only five interactions (out of a possible 233) lasted more than 30 min. Thus, both sets of usage data suggest brief interactions, rather than open links, are the main uses of the system. Open links can also be constructed between public areas of geographically separated sites (Abel, 1990; Bly et al., 1993; Fish et al., 1990). Cameras can be installed in common areas, transmitting images of people at remote sites, so that people can see, for example, who happens to be in the coffee area of a remote site. This is intended to promote opportunistic conversations of the type that can occur when people meet in public areas of the same site. Field trials report frequent use of open links for social greetings or "drop-ins" between remote sites, with 70% of open link usage being of this type (Abel, 1990; Bly et al., 1993). Clearly, these brief interactions would have been unlikely to occur in the absence of the system. The use of the open link was mainly limited to these brief social exchanges, however, and the link was seen by the users as being ineffective in supporting work (Fish et al., 1993). Fish et al. (1990) also examined how often extended verbal communications resulted from sighting someone over the videolink. They compared this with the likelihood of interaction following face-to-face sightings, and found that sightings over a videolink were less likely to convert to extended conversation than face-to-face sightings.

Taken together, these preliminary results on glance and open links indicate a lack of evidence for the utility of video for connection: (a) Failure rates with glancing are as high as with phone alone; (b) open links are an infrequently chosen user option; (c) open links are less likely to promote conversation than face-to-face sightings; and (d) open links between common areas are not adequate to support work. These failures may, however, be due to confounding factors in the evaluations, or to implementation problems, such as lack of support for overriding or interrupting an existing open link (Whittaker, 1996).

Video-as-Data: Video Provides Information About the Visible Environment

An alternative hypothesis is that a major benefit of video lies in its ability to depict complex information about dynamic 3D shared work objects, rather than images of the participants themselves. This approach is partially motivated by finding that participants spend more time looking at relevant work objects than other people (Argyle & Graham, 1977). Thus, the video image can be used to transmit real-time information about work objects, and this can then be used to coordinate conversational content among distributed teams, by creating a shared physical context. The example discussed here is remote surgery, but other tasks such as concurrent engineering, or training also have similar requirements (Egido, 1990; Nardi et al., 1993; Nardi et al., 1996; chapter 23, this volume).

This work is discussed in detail in chapter 23, but to summarize, four different types of communicative use of the image were found. First, the dynamic image of the surgeon's actions allowed detailed coordination of interleaved physical action between the assisting nurse and the surgeon in the operating theater. By monitoring the surgeon's actions, via a shared video image viewed through the microscope, the nurse could anticipate the surgeon's requirements and provide the correct surgical instrument, often without it being directly requested. A second communicative function of the video image was that it served to disambiguate other types of surgical data that were supplied to remote consultants, such as neurophysiological monitoring data. The interpretation of these neurophysiological data depends critically on precise information about the physical actions that the surgeon is currently executing, such as the exact placement of a surgical clamp or the angle and direction of entry of a surgical instrument. Without the video image depicting these actions, the remote consultant had to rely on verbal reports from those who were present in the operating theater, and the inadequacy of the descriptions meant that the consultant often had to resort to physically visiting the operating theater to observe the actions directly. Third the video image served as a physical embodiment of progress through the operation. Members of the team who were involved in multiple operations at different locations and also those within the operating theater could see the current stage of each operation by inspecting the physical image, and observing what stage of the procedure the surgeon was at. The remote consultants could thus coordinate their visits to each operating theater accordingly, so as to arrive at times when their physical presence was critical.[7] Finally, the image was used for learning and education. The application was installed in a teaching hospital that undertook innovative surgical procedures. Academic visitors and trainees would often come to the operating theater to observe the novel procedures on the large monitor in the operating theater as they occurred. Some surgeons also recorded these procedures, to use them as aids in teaching classes.

Similar arguments for this use of "video-as-data" were made by Gaver et al. (1993). They looked at the use of images of 3D objects in design tasks. Users could choose between a number of different images, including between an image of the other participant, and various views of the object under study. Participants rarely chose facial views of their coparticipant (11% of the time), and "mutual gaze" (where both participants were simultaneously viewing each other) occurred only 2% of the time. Instead, people were much more likely to choose an image of the object, spending 49% of their time with the object views. This shows that for this class of design application, information about gaze and gesture of the other conversational participant seems to be less important than information about the shared physical context. An extensive research program has also been executed by Ishii, who has built a series of prototypes that use video to combine a semireflective writing surfaces with images of the participant's upper bodies. This enables the fusing of an image of another participant onto the work surface itself, making it possible to see both participant and object simultaneously and hence accurately track visual attention, while writing or manipulating the object (Ishii & Kobayashi, 1992). Again, a major focus of the work is that crucial collaborative information is embodied in the work object, although systematic evaluation of the benefits of adding this attentional information has not yet been conducted.

CONCLUSIONS

We have provided a framework for identifying potential functions of visible information in communication, reviewed evidence for three different hypotheses about the role of video in interpersonal communications, and identified outstanding research and design issues. With the exception of tasks that require access to affective information, we found that evidence for the nonverbal communication hypothesis is not strong, with few task outcome and process differences being found between audio and video-enhanced communications.[8] Furthermore, despite the absence of compelling evidence for the nonverbal communication hypothesis, certain current implementations may have compromised overall system utility by focusing on video at the expense of providing full duplex, low-lag audio. Failing to provide this type of audio information disrupts conversational processes that require precise timing and bidirectionality (O'Conaill et al., 1993).

Nevertheless, methodological and theoretical questions remain about the nonverbal communication hypothesis. We need to refine the hypothesis, so that more specific predictions can be tested and better systems designed. Visible information changes the outcome of tasks depending on affect or emotion, supporting the social cuing hypothesis. Neither process nor cognitive cuing accounts are well supported, however. For cognitive cuing, even face-to-face communication is no better than speech only, and even high-quality video cannot replicate the conversational processes of face-to-face communication (O'Conaill et al., 1993; chapter 6, this volume; Sellen, 1995). We therefore need to understand why even high- quality audio and video do not replicate face-to-face processes. One possibility is that current systems do not accurately simulate the presentational aspects of face-to-face interaction; spatial audio and video may therefore be needed to replicate conversational processes (O'Conaill et al., 1993; Sellen, 1995). However, there are other possible explanations that also need to be tested.

Another possible explanation of the results on the nonverbal communication hypothesis is that certain types of information are substitutable across different conversational media, whereas others are not. Thus in face-to-face communication, cognitive and process information is partially transmitted by head nods, eye gaze, and head turning. However, data on the efficacy of speech-only communication indicate that cognitive and process information can also be communicated effectively by other nonvisual cues (Walker, 1993; Walker & Whittaker, 1990). In contrast, the removal of the visual channel changes the outcome of tasks that require access to affect suggesting affective information is not substitutable. Part of the reason might be that affective cues are often not generated intentionally, so that although speech can signal affect, speakers omit the full range of affective cues when using audio-only communication. Future theoretical work should address this issue of the substitutability of different media and information types, and the role of intentional cuing. Another unresolved problem concerns inconsistencies between subjective and objective measures: Although outcome and process show few differences between audio and video conversations, people reliably prefer video-mediated communications (Fish et al., 1993; Isaacs & Tang, 1993; Tang & Isaacs, 1993). One possibility is that subjective preferences are an aspect of social cuing, but the social cuing account must be clarified for this argument to be sustained.

The connection hypothesis has yet to be systematically tested. The putative connection function of providing availability information for the process of conversation initiation is therefore undemonstrated. Although workplace studies show the importance of opportunistic communications, it is currently unclear how well video can support their initiation. One problem is the methodological limitations of current studies. Evaluation work needs to focus more on situations in which there is a critical mass of users who are geographically remote: Early evaluations have suffered from only investigating small user populations who often share the same physical space. Other design factors such as long delays in initiating communication, style of initiation, and, most importantly, privacy issues also have to be addressed before we know about the effectiveness of video for connection (Tang et al., 1994; Whittaker, 1996; Whittaker et al., 1994). Work should also be done to investigate whether alternative technologies, such as active badges (Pier, 1991), could also supply availability information and hence substitute for visual information. There is also the question of the extent to which other asynchronous technologies can partially substitute for opportunistic meetings. Can a brief e-mail or voicemail message replace a short synchronous discussion and hence reduce the need for remote opportunistic meetings (Whittaker et al., in press)?

Finally, video-as-data is a promising area, where more applications should be built and evaluations conducted. Much early work on video has neglected the importance of shared objects as part of a shared context. Given the lack of clear support for nonverbal communication, video-as-data may be a more successful use of video if we can identify tasks that are focused on complex dynamic 3D objects. Recent work on the nonverbal communication hypothesis also indirectly offers support for shared objects and a shared environment. For desktop videoconferencing applications, the presence of a shared workspace improves cognitive problem solving (Olson et al., 1995). However, as with opportunistic connection, there are also outstanding social issues about privacy and access that have yet to be addressed for "video-as-data."

Overall, this chapter suggests that the role of visible information and the successful application of video technology for interpersonal communications still require extensive research. Rather than the single function of broadening communication bandwidth implied by the nonverbal communication hypothesis, we need to extend the set of hypotheses we entertain about video, to think about video for initiating opportunistic communication and representing shared objects. The work reviewed here also suggests that the benefits of video are task and situation specific. Future research must explain when and why this technology brings benefits to interpersonal communication.

NOTES

1. Of course there are other indicators of presence. One can often infer presence from hearing another person, or from hearing others talking to them.
2. Many other recent field trials have investigated videophones, open links, and media spaces (Abel, 1990; Bly et al., 1993; Gaver et al., 1992; Mantei et al., 1991; Tang et al., 1994), but few of these studies have explicitly addressed the enhanced audio hypothesis. Instead, their focus has either been on the technical feasibility of building distributed video systems or alternatively on discovering novel uses of video applications such as video for connection. We review these novel applications in the next section.
3. The ability to interrupt the speaker at any point of the conversation, such as to ask a clarifying question, is regarded as a positive aspect of conversation, indicating spontaneous speaker switching (O'Conaill et al., 1994; Rutter & Robinson, 1981; Sellen, in press; Walker & Whittaker, 1990; Whittaker & Stenton, 1988).
4. Examples are "isn't it?," "aren't they?," "couldn't you?," and involve an auxiliary verb and question syntax, at the end of a sentence.
5. Exact lags depend on the system and network, but typical figures for one-way lags are 705 msec for the PicturePhone system (Cohen, 1982), between 410 and 780 msec for an ISDN system operating between the United States and the United Kingdom (O'Conaill et al., 1993; Whittaker & O'Conaill, 1993), and 570 msec for an ISDN system operating from coast to coast in the United States (Tang & Isaacs, 1993; Isaacs & Tang, 1994).
6. Half-duplex audio only allows unidirectional transmission of audio. This prevents certain key conversational processes that depend on multiple participants at different ends of an audio link being able to speak simultaneously, for example, backchannels to provide feedback to the speaker, or interruptive clarifying questions.
7. This function is similar to using video for connection, in that video information is used to coordinate a communication episode between people at remote locations.
8. Although more recent work with very-high-quality directional video may show small differences (Olson et al., 1995).

REFERENCES

Abel, M. (1990). Experiences in an exploratory distributed organization. In J. Galegher, R. Kraut, & C. Egido (Eds.), *Intellectual teamwork* (pp. 489–510). Hillsdale, NJ: Lawrence Erlbaum Associates.

Anderson, A., Bard, E., Sotillo, C., Newland, A., & Doherty-Sneddon, C. T. (in press). Limited visual control of the intelligibility of speech in face-to-face interaction. *Perception and Psychophysics.*

Argyle, M. (1990). *Bodily communication* London: Routledge.

Argyle, M., & Graham, J. (1977). The Central European experiment: Looking at persons and looking at things. *Journal of Environmental Psychology and Nonverbal Behaviour, 1,* 6–16

Beattie, G. (1978). Sequential patterns of speech and gaze in dialogue. *Semiotica, 23,* 29–52.

Beattie, G. (1981). A further investigation of the cognitive interference hypothesis of gaze patterns in conversation. *British Journal of Social Psychology, 20,* 243–248.

Birdwhistell, R. (1970). *Kinesics and context: Essays in body motion communication.* Harmondsworth: Penguin.

Bly, S., Harrison, S., & Irwin, S. (1993). Media spaces: Bringing people together in a video, audio and computing environment. *Communications of the ACM, 36,* 28–45.

Bull, P. (1978). The interpretation of posture through an alternative method to role play. *British Journal of Social and Clinical Psychology, 17,* 1–6.

Cassell, J., McNeill, D. & McCullough, K. E. (in press). Speech gesture mismatches: Evidence for one underlying representation of linguistic and non-linguistic information. *Cognition.*

Chapanis, A. (1975). Interactive human communication. *Scientific American, 232,* 34–42.

Chapanis, A., Ochsman, R., Parrish, R., & Weeks, G. (1972). Studies in interactive communication: The effects of four communication modes on the behavior of teams during cooperative problem solving. *Human Factors, 14,* 487–509.

Clark, H., & Brennan, S. (1991). Grounding in communication. In L. B. Resnick, J. Levine, & S. Teasley (Eds.), *Perspectives on socially shared cognition* (pp. 127–149). Washington, DC: APA.

Clark, H., & Marshall, C. (1981). Definite reference and mutual knowledge. In A. Joshi, B. Webber, & I. Sag (Eds.), *Elements of discourse understanding* (pp. 10–63). Cambridge: Cambridge University Press.

Clark, H., & Schaefer, E. (1989). Contributing to discourse. *Cognitive Science, 13,* 259–292.

Cohen, K. (1982). Speaker interaction: Video teleconferences versus face-to-face meetings. *Proceedings of teleconferencing and electronic communications* (pp. 189–199). Madison: University of Wisconsin Press.

Cooper, R. (1974). The control of eye fixation by the meaning of spoken language. *Cognitive Psychology, 6,* 84–107.

Duncan, S. (1972). Some signals and rules for taking speaker turns in conversation. *Journal of Personal and Social Psychology, 23,* 283–292.

Efron, D. (1972). *Gesture, race and culture.* The Hague: Mouton.

Egido, C. (1990). Teleconferencing as a technology to support co-operative work: A review of its failures. In J. Galegher, R. Kraut, & C. Egido (Eds.), *Intellectual teamwork* (pp. 351–372). Hillsdale, NJ: Lawrence Erlbaum Associates.

Ekman, P., & Friesen, W. (1975). *Unmasking the face.* Englewood Cliffs, NJ: Prentice Hall.

Exline, R., & Winters, L. (1965, April). Effects of cognitive difficulty and cognitive style on eye contact in interviews. *Proceedings of the Eastern Psychological Association.* Atlantic City, NJ.

Fish, R., Kraut, R., & Chalfonte, B. (1990). The Videowindow system in informal communications. *Proceedings of Conference on Computer Supported Cooperative Work* (pp. 1–12). New York: ACM.

Fish, R., Kraut, R., Root, R., & Rice, R. (1993). Video as a technology for informal communication. *Communications of the ACM, 36,* 48–61.

Frohlich, D. Requirements for interpersonal information management. In P. Thomas (Ed.), *Mobile personal communication and co-operative working* (pp. 35–65). London: Alfred Waller.

Gaver, W., Moran, T., Maclean, A., Lövstrand, L., Dourish, P., Carter, K., & Buxton, W. (1992). Realizing a video environment: Europarc's Rave system. *Proceedings of CHI '92 Human Factors in Computing Systems* (pp. 27–35). New York: ACM.

Gaver, W., Sellen, A., Heath, C., & Luff, P. (1993). One is not enough: Multiple views in a media space. *Proceedings of CHI '93 Human Factors in Computing Systems* (pp. 335–341). New York: ACM.

Goodwin, C. (1981). *Conversational organization: Interaction between speakers and hearers.* New York: Academic Press.

Grice, H. P. (1975). Logic and conversation. In P. Cole & J. Morgan (Eds.), *Syntax and semantics 3: Speech acts* (pp. 225–242). New York: Academic Press.

Grosz, B., & Sidner, C. (1986). Attentions, intentions and the structure of discourse. *Computational Linguistics, 12,* 175–204.

Heath, C., & Luff, P. (1991). Disembodied conduct: Communication through video in a multimedia environment. *Proceedings of CHI '91 Human Factors in Computing Systems* (pp. 99–103). New York: ACM.

Isaacs, E., & Tang, J. (1993). What video can and can't do for collaboration: A case study. In *Proceedings of the ACM Multimedia 93 Conference* (pp. 199–206). Anaheim, CA.

Ishii, H., & Kobayashi, M. (1992). Clearboard: A seamless medium for shared drawing and conversation with eye contact. In *Proceedings of CHI '92 Human Factors in Computing Systems* (pp. 525–532). New York: ACM.

Kendon, A. (1967). Some functions of gaze direction in social interaction. *Acta Psychologica, 26,* 1–47.

Kendon, A., & Ferber, A. (1973). A description of some human greetings. In R. Michael & J. Crook (Eds.)., *Comparative ecology and behaviour of primates* (pp. 591–668). London: Academic Press.

Kleck, R., & Nuessle, W. (1968). Congruence between the indicative and communicative functions of eye-contact in interpersonal relations. *British Journal of Social and Clinical Psychology, 7,* 241–246.

Kleinke, C. (1986). Gaze and eye contact: A research review. *Psychological Bulletin, 100,* 78–100.

Kraut, R., Fish, R., Root, B., & Chalfonte, B. (1993). Informal communication in organizations. In R. Baecker (Ed.), *Groupware and computer supported co-operative work* (pp. 287–314). San Mateo, CA: Morgan Kaufman.

Kraut, R., Lewis, S., & Swezey, L. (1982). Listener responsiveness and the co-ordination of conversation. *Journal of Personality and Social Psychology, 43,* 718–731

Levinson, S. (1983). *Pragmatics.* Cambridge: Cambridge University Press.

McGurk, H., & MacDonald, J. (1976). Hearing lips and seeing voices. *Nature, 264,* 126–130.

McNeill, D. (1992). *Hand and mind: What gestures reveal about thought.* Chicago: University of Chicago Press.

Mantei, M., Baecker, R., Sellen, A., Buxton, W., Milligan, T., & Wellman, B. (1991). Experiences in the use of a media space. *Proceedings of CHI '91 Human Factors in Computing Systems* (pp. 203–209). New York: ACM.

Nardi, B., Schwarz, H., Kuchinsky, A., Leichner, R., Whittaker, S., & Sclabassi, R. (1993). Turning away from talking heads: An analysis of "video-as-data." *Proceedings of CHI '93 Human Factors in Computing Systems* (pp. 327–334). New York: ACM.

Nardi, B., Kuchinsky, A., Whittaker, S., Leichner, R., & Schwarz, H. (1996). "Video-as-data": Technical and social aspects of a collaborative multimedia application. *Computer Supported Co-operative Work, 4,* 73–100.

Noll, M. (1992). Anatomy of a failure: PicturePhone revisited. *Telecommunications Policy,* May/June, 307–316.

O'Conaill, B., Whittaker, S., & Wilbur, S. (1993). Conversations over video conferences: An evaluation of the spoken aspects of video-mediated communication. *Human–Computer Interaction, 8,* 389–428.

Olson, J., Olson, G., & Meader, D. (1995). What mix of video and audio is useful for small groups doing remote design work? *Proceedings of CHI '95 Human Factors in Computing Systems* (pp. 362–368). New York: ACM.

Pier, K. (1991). Active badge panel. In *Proceedings of Conference on Organisational Systems,* Atlanta, GA.

Reid, A. (1977). Comparing the telephone with face-to-face interaction. In I. Pool (Ed.), *The social impact of the telephone* (pp. 386–414). Cambridge, MA: MIT Press.

Rutter, R., & Robinson, R. (1981). An experimental analysis of teaching by telephone. In G. Stephenson & J. Davies (Eds.), *Progress in applied social psychology* (pp. 143–178). London: Wiley.

Sacks, H., Schegloff, E., & Jefferson, G. (1974). A simplest systematics for the organization of turn-taking in conversation. *Language, 50,* 696–753.

Schegloff, E., & Sacks, H. (1973). Opening up closings. *Semiotica, 7,* 289–327.

Sellen, A. J. (1995). Remote conversations: The effects of mediating talk with technology. *Human–Computer Interaction, 10*(4), 401–444.

Short, J., Williams, E., & Christie, B. (1976). *The social psychology of telecommunications.* London: Wiley.

Summerfield, Q. (1992). Lipreading and audiovisual speech perception. *Philosophical Transactions of the Royal Society of London, B335,* 71–78.

Tang, J., & Isaacs, E. (1993). Why do users like video: Studies of multimedia-supported collaboration. *Computer Supported Cooperative Work, 1,* 163–196.

Tang, J., Isaacs, E., & Rua, M. (1994). Supporting distributed groups with a montage of lightweight interactions. *Proceedings of Conference on Computer Supported Cooperative Work* (pp. 23–34). New York: ACM.

Walker, M. (1993). *Information redundancy in dialogue.* Unpublished doctoral dissertation, University of Pennsylvania, Philadelphia.

Walker, M., & Whittaker, S. (1990). Mixed initiative in dialogue. In *Proceedings of 28th Annual Meeting of the Conference on Computational Linguisitics* (pp. 70–78). Morristown, NJ: ACM.

Whittaker, S. (1995). Video as a technology for interpersonal communication: A new perspective. *IS&T SPIE Symposium on electronic imaging science and technology, 2417,* 294–304.

Whittaker, S. (1996). Rethinking video as a technology for interpersonal communication. *International Journal of Human–Computer Studies, 42,* 501–529.

Whittaker, S., Brennan, S., & Clark, H. (1991). Co-ordinating activity: An analysis of computer supported co-operative work. In *Proceedings of CHI '91 Human Factors in Computing Systems* (pp. 361–367). New York: ACM.

Whittaker, S., Frohlich, D., & Daly-Jones, O. (1994). Informal workplace communication: What is it like and how might we support it? In *Proceedings of CHI '94 Human Factors in Computing Systems* (pp. 130–137). New York: ACM.

Whittaker, S., Geelhoed, E., & Robinson, E. (1993). Shared workspaces: How do they work and when are they useful? *International Journal of Man-Machine Studies, 39,* 813–842.

Whittaker, S., & Stenton, P. (1988). Cues and control in expert client dialogues. In *Proceedings of the Conference for the Association for Computational Linguisitics* (pp. 123–130). Cambridge, MA: MIT Press.

Whittaker, S., Swanson, J., Kucan, J., & Sidner, C. (in press). Telenotes: Managing lightweight interactions in the desktop. *Transactions on Computer–Human Interaction.*

Williams, E. (1977). Experimental comparisons of face-to-face and mediated communication. *Psychological Bulletin, 84,* 963–976.

Yngve, V. (1970). Getting a word in edgewise. In *Proceedings of the Sixth Meeting of the Chicago Linguistics Society* (pp. 567–577). Chicago, IL: Chicago Linguistics Society.

Chapter 3

Technology Constraints of Video-Mediated Communication

Joel S. Angiolillo
Harry E. Blanchard
Edmond W. Israelski
Amir Mané
AT & T Bell Laboratories

This chapter provides an overview of the technology underlying video-mediated communication (VMC) that directly impacts the users' experience. After a brief discussion of types of VMC systems, technologies are introduced in the framework of the life cycle of a video call. First, call setup involves establishing a communications connection. Capture involves camera technology and control. Image processing includes compressing and coding for transmission over the allowable bandwidth of communications system. Next, the different types of transmission systems are discussed: POTS (plain old telephone service), ISDN (Integrated Service Digital Network), LANs (local area networks), private lines, CATV (community antenna television), the Internet, and so on. Finally, there is discussion of the technology characteristics of the output display devices and their impact on the user experience.

INTRODUCTION

When one asks what video adds to an auditory channel, such as that provided by the common telephone, the answer, as it emerges from the body of work presented in this book, cannot be understood, interpreted, or integrated without basic understanding of the underlying technology of VMC. As illustrated in the studies presented by O'Conaill, Whittaker, and Wilbur (1993), to understand and interpret the different findings obtained by using different systems one has to understand the technology in use: What is ISDN?[1] What is broadband transmission? What is audio delay and why is it introduced? What is the implication of using a satellite for transmission?

The purpose of this chapter is to focus on those aspects of the technology that directly impact the user's experience in VMC. Thus, although topics such as communication protocols and network topology are important parts of the infrastructure, they are only briefly mentioned. Instead the focus is on topics such as the image and its implications to VMC, for example, the impact of the time delay associated with image processing on sound quality and the synchronization between sound and sight.

TYPES OF VMC SYSTEMS

Before describing the technologies, it is important to distinguish among the various types of VMC systems, to illustrate how various combinations of user groups and tasks led to the creation of distinct market segments.

Video Telephones

The longest sought-after system is one that simply adds a video image to the audio connection provided by the familiar telephone. Envisioned as the next generation of telephones, these devices are variations on the theme of a telephone with a small screen and a camera lens. Grandparents will use it to talk to their grandchildren and teenagers will chat with their classmates. Price dictates the level of technological sophistication that will be built into personal videotelephones. Another design constraint is that the existing public switched voice telephone networks must be used for transmission, at least if the service is to become ubiquitous.

Desktop Video Conferencing

When the user is in the business environment, and the purpose is collaboration among individuals who are physically distant, one solution is the integration of video capability into the personal computer (PC). The user may add a camera near the computer monitor and use a telephone line or a local area network (LAN) to connect to other users. The use of the PC is conducive for adding data exchange: In addition to seeing each other and talking, the users can share data, either by transferring files or images, or by sharing an application and working on it jointly. These systems can be used as a point-to-point connection between two employees, or in a multipoint connection, in which a conference is held among multiple participants.

Group Systems

Designed to support business meetings between groups in different locations, group systems have already established VMC as a viable business. Initially, group systems required that users travel to a specially designed videoconference facility. The specialized rooms are typically equipped with several cameras and monitors. However, the field has grown to include a new category of "roll-about" systems. These systems have an integrated camera and monitor mounted on a cart that can be moved from one office to another. The group systems often use dedicated transmission facilities that support the presentation of a better quality image at a cost that is significantly higher than that of a regular telephone call.

Media Spaces and Special-Purpose Systems

Media Spaces are unique VMC systems designed to create for distant locations a virtual meeting room that gives the people who visit the room a sense of copresence with the people in the other location(s) (e.g., Abel, 1990; Buxton, 1992; Fish, Kraut, Root, & Rice, 1993; Olson & Bly, 1991). They were developed mainly to allow researchers to experience and study the mechanisms and dynamics of remote collaboration. On the commercial side, one can find a variety of special-purpose systems, most of them designed to address specific business needs, for specific user populations. One such example is the banking "kiosk" that allows a distant banking expert to provide personalized advice to customers in a remote branch.

THE LIFE CYCLE OF A VIDEO CALL

The primary technology challenge in VMC is how to transport the video image from a camera and the audio signal from a microphone in one location, to a monitor and a speaker in another.

Regardless of the media in use, the participants in a VMC must *set up a call*, establishing a physical connection between the two or more locations. Once a connection is established, the camera and microphone can begin to *capture* the sights and sounds of the participants. Because of limited transmission capabilities, it is necessary to *process the image*, that is, move it from its analog form to a digital one, and compress it. The compressed digital signal can be sent to its destination through the *transmission* facilities. Once at its destination, the signal has to go through additional processing, this time decompressing the data and transforming it back to analog signal that can be *displayed* to the participants in the other location. Of course this process is most often bidirectional and symmetrical, and can take place among multiple locations.

The sections of this chapter follow the life cycle of the audiovideo call, and describe the technology that is required to accomplish the communication, with a focus on the relevance of this technology to the user experience.

Call Setup

The basic function in VMC is to set up a video call. Yet the ease with which the user can initiate a video connection, or lack thereof, could be the most serious barrier to the use and acceptance of this new technology. Spontaneity has not been a characteristic of traditional teleconferencing: rooms, communications channels, and/or equipment have to be reserved beforehand. Yet the full promise of video cannot be met unless users have the same spontaneity they enjoy with voice communications. Indeed, experiments with continuously available video links (Fish et al., 1993; Olson & Bly, 1991; Tang & Rua, 1994) demonstrate the interesting possibilities when video can support informal and spontaneous communication across distances.

Unfortunately, the complexity of the telecommunications systems is not always hidden. Frequently, videoconference setups require the dialing of two telephone numbers (which may be different) to acquire the appropriate bandwidth (this is common for ISDN-based communications in the United States). And the situation gets more complex when multipoint conferences must be made, and when communication must be established between different equipment (using different protocols and/or networks). At the very least, a third number must be dialed to a teleconferencing center and/or interworking center in the network. Users often do not know what type of equipment they or their callers have, and it is difficult for the network to identify what equipment the users have. Call setup problems can be eased by having expert technicians set up all the proper equipment beforehand, but then that destroys spontaneity of communication.

Capture

The video call begins in a specific room, in a unique physical environment in which a particular camera and microphone are placed, capturing the words, gestures, and displays of the speakers.

Physical Environment. The size and shape of the room add constraints to many other important physical variables such as room acoustics and lighting, and placement and size of video monitors, cameras, and audio equipment. The physical layout of the room will determine the critical placement of monitors, cameras, microphones, and speakers. Rooms with poorly planned wall space may not allow all participants to have good viewing angles to maintain good eye contact.

Video communication experiences can be successful if and only if audio communication quality is excellent. Besides the sophistication of the electronics, audio quality depends on the quality of room acoustics and microphone placement. Reverberation must be minimized to reduce unwanted echoes and boomy, unpleasant sound. Full-duplex sound, in which a two-way voice path allows both parties to speak at once, is desirable but can only be achieved with superior room acoustical treatment, such as sound-absorbing wall coverings and furniture.

Another important variable is room lighting. Professional direct and indirect lighting must be designed to allow video cameras to work effectively so as to produce acceptable video images with minimal shadows and with even lighting of people and objects. Often, when VMC is integrated into the office environment, the room lighting is inadequate and results in a dark and blurred image of the speaker.

Camera. The camera can transmit its image in analog or digital form. It could be a simple fixed-focus, fixed-iris, and fixed-position camera, or an expensive video camera with a motorized mount. Most videotelephones today use inexpensive digital cameras called CDDs (charge-coupled devices), which are optically sensitive semiconductors. CDD cameras capture images as a matrix of picture elements or pixels. (The word *pixel* comes from picture element, a single dot on a display monitor.) The resolving capacities of CDDs vary considerably and are often designed to match the computer screen or TV resolution. Common resolutions are 320×240 and 640×480 pixels. Higher resolutions are also now available.

Camera Control. Camera control is the electronic equivalent to a person's eye gaze and where the person might choose to sit in a face-to-face meeting. A user may want to control his or her own camera, the remote camera, or both. In any case, the participant may want to control zoom (focal length or width of view), focus, exposure (usually automatic), pan (left and right movement), and tilt (up and down movement). Local camera control also includes the important abilities of switching among other video sources such as document, slide, or overhead projection cameras.

A special case of the need to control the local camera is self-view, the state in which the user's own camera output is displayed on the local screen. Self-view mode can either be full screen or a small picture within a larger picture. Conforming to human control movement stereotypes will allow error-free camera control. For self-view, the human stereotype is based on years of viewing ourselves in a mirror. Moving one's body to the left would produce a leftward movement on the screen as in a mirror. Moving a camera pan control to the left would produce a scene shift to the left as the participant views the screen. A left movement should not have the camera move to its left as this would cause an opposite, nonstereotypic direction of movement.

In systems that allow the remote control of the cameras in other locations, the stereotype is such that the viewer is taking the same perspective of the camera in the remote location—that is, a left movement would cause the camera to move to its left. Interesting control protocol problems arise as multiple local and remote parties try to control the same cameras.

Hands-Free Communications.   Hands-free communication is the most natural and allows VMC to be most like a face-to-face meeting. Thus, most VMC systems offer it. There are times, however, when users will prefer a telephone handset for a personal video station, such as in a noisy work environment or when privacy is desired. Even in these situations, a telephone headset might be a more desirable choice for audio communications. Two important variables for hands-free communication are use of full versus half-duplex audio, and microphone characteristics and placement.

Full-duplex audio allows complete and simultaneous transmission of all audio communications from all endpoints. This is the most natural, and is overwhelmingly preferred over switched-loss, half-duplex audio transmission. In half-duplex audio, only one side of the audio conversation can be heard at any time. This results in clipped audio transmission, which can only be avoided if users are very disciplined and which allows only one talker at a time, adhering to strict turn-taking rules of conversation.

Microphone placement is a critical variable. Placement interacts with room size and room dimensions. Good audio pickup can be obtained with microphones placed in the ceiling, in the conference table, or by the use of special microphone arrays that can be centered on a conference table or on a wall. The directionality of microphones is also very important to ensure that as much of a speaker's voice energy is picked up as possible, while minimizing unwanted acoustical energy or noise. Multiple microphones have been used to allow stereo transmission of sound that allows stereo imaging for localizing multiple people speaking around a conference table. In multipoint video conferences in which video is switched on the basis of voice energy, the quality of microphone audio pickup is especially important to avoid delayed video switching and false switches due to noise.

Image Processing

As described in this section, to simply transmit the captured sound and image would require transmission facilities that are far too rare and too expensive. The raw image from the camera must be processed by special-purpose hardware and software before sending it to the remote site.

Transmission media come in different sizes, as measured by the number of bits they can carry reliably in a second. A standard copper telephone line is commonly used to transmit 9600 bits per second (bps) or, more recently, 14.4 and 28.8 kbps (kilobits per second, or a thousand bits a second). This is the work-a-day service you get from your local telephone company for your home costing between $10 to $20 a month. Modern digital service costing two to three times that much can deliver 128 kbps. A private line broadband service could deliver 30 Mbps (megabits, million bits per second) at thousands of dollars per month. How many bits per second do you need?

The Burden of Video. Suppose you want to send TV-quality full-motion color pictures from one site to another. The TV screen is composed of approximately 525 rows by 525 columns of pixels, or 250,000 in a single frame. To get smooth motion, you will want to send at least 30 frames per second (the NTSC standard in the United States; the PAL standard in Europe is only 25 frames per second, but it has more pixels per frame). The color and the luminance of each pixel needs to be described, as does the sound, of course. The result is that a single TV channel requires approximately 90,000,000 bps, equivalent to more than 1,300 voice channels. A good analog connection, like that which carries telephone calls to your home, will give you at most 28,800 bps. A common digital connection (ISDN-BRI) in offices today might provide 128,000 bps. In either case, you are trying to fill the pool with a squirt gun.

Compression. What are your choices? You can wait until we all have optic fibers able to carry billions of bits per second to our homes and offices, or you can reduce the data required to display images. There are a number of ways to do this. First, you can *reduce* the size of the signal by eliminating some of the information, for example, by making the screen smaller or by sending, say, 5 frames a second instead of the 30 required to produce the perception of smooth motion. Second, you can *compress* the signal. Compression is simply taking out the bits that are not needed, by finding the statistical redundancy in the data stream. For example, if there is a blue bar in the frame, you can send a few bytes to say "the next 5,000 pixels are blue" instead of sending 5,000 individual pixel descriptions. Extracting the redundancy in a frame is called *intraframe coding.*

You can also predict what will happen at a particular pixel, based on what was at the same location (or a nearby location) for the last several frames, or even the *next* several frames. Extracting this temporal redundancy in the signal is called *interframe* or *predictive coding.* Interframe coding schemes send only the bits that have changed from the previous frame, or, more precisely, the bits that were not predicted correctly. Some compression/decompression algorithms will return exactly the same information as one started with so-called *lossless compression* with a typical savings of 2:1 or 3:1. *Lossy compression* loses some of the information so that the displayed image is not exactly the same as the encoded ones. Because the best of these algorithms achieve a 600:1 savings or more, and because the human eye is very forgiving when viewing moving pictures, lossy compression schemes are used on most videoconferencing systems. A number of compression algorithms are in use today. For more detailed descriptions see Netravali and Haskell (1991).

Codecs.   Analyzing the frames to extract redundant and unneeded information requires both standards and devices that can perform billions of computations per second. The device that processes the frame on the sending side and, likewise, processes the same frame at the receiving side is called a *codec* (for coding/decoding). There are two types of codecs: *software-only* and *hardware-assisted.* Software-only codecs are fine if you are encoding a video clip for later viewing using an *asymmetrical* algorithm like *MPEG,* motion coding, or *JPEG,* still-image coding (Motion Picture Experts Group and Joint Photographic Experts Group, respectively). These algorithms decompress quickly for normal viewing, but require a relatively longer time for compression. However, if you want the compression and decompression to be *symmetrical* (to take the same amount of time to compress as to decompress) and to happen in *real time,* as you do in a videotelephony service, you need extremely fast, special-purpose integrated circuits.

Much of the technologist's excitement in visual communications centers on these small, thumbnail-sized chips, specially designed to code and decode images hundreds of times a minute. Although the 10-foot-tall refrigerator-sized codecs of 10 years ago are now a handful of chips, they are still one of the most costly components in a visual communications system.[2] The world of ISDN video has adopted the ITU-T[3] H.261 standard for coding moving images. This standard is also called the P × 64 standard because it provides for video at a number of different data rates, all at multiples of 64 kbps, the most popular being 64, 128, and 384 kbps.

All codecs are not equal, even those using the same compression/decompression algorithms. Each codec performs differently for different types of visual material, at different bandwidths, with different types of impairments. In the world of digitized video, there is no single agreed-on standard to measure video quality and therefore codec quality. (For a discussion of the complexity in measuring compressed video quality see Hearty, 1993.)

Video Standards and Interoperability.   Both processes, encoding and decoding, must speak the same language. These languages can either be *proprietary* (owned by one company) or *nonproprietary* (developed by international standards bodies). It should be noted that there are many protocols governing VMC, from how the video is compressed (ITU-T H.261), to framing synchronization (ITU-T H.230), to the algorithm for 7-kHz audio in 64 kbps (ITU-T G.722), to the numerous communication protocols that determine how calls are set up and maintained (e.g., the ISDN protocols). Viable markets can not be developed until there are widely held standards to build to, but at the same time, the technology is changing so quickly that as soon as a standard is agreed upon, there are better ways of doing things. Table 3.1 gives a list of relevant audio and video standards.

However, it is not exactly true that both devices must speak the same language. *Interoperability services* are available that will connect two video devices that operate with different protocols or at different data rates. These services often provide multipoint bridging as well. Unfortunately, these conversion services add cost and delay to the transmission.

Audio Delay and Lip Synchronization. Bandwidth limitations cause the second major technical issue behind VMC: audio delay. Delay caused by terrestrial transmission and by switching equipment is negligible. In the public analog voice telephone network in the United States, transmission delay is typically 20 msec to 30 msec. Delay in ISDN is around 10 msec. T1 service (large bandwidth private trunk lines) is down in the single digits. In contrast, a single-hop satellite adds 260 msec delay one way. Thus, satellite links are not appropriate for two-way video communication.

The significant delay in a video call is caused by video image compression. All video compression techniques share one thing in common—they require processing time to perform their function. Although the digitization and compression of the audio channel require only a few thousandths of a second, the compression of the video image introduces a typical delay of 200 msec to 400 msec. The exact length of delay varies from one algorithm to the other. It also varies within an algorithm from moment to moment, because the length of the computation depends on indeterminate elements, such as the amount of change in the image from one frame to the next.

A misalignment in which audio precedes the video by 200 msec to 400 msec will be perceived by the user and will adversely impact the user's experience. Most vendors of codecs assess the average delay incurred by the processing of the video and introduce a similar delay to the audio channel in order to maintain the synchronization between the image and the sound—to maintain lip synchronization.

The value of lip synchronization has been established in tasks that required "speechreading," tasks where it takes a real effort to make sense of the speech, typically because of some background noise (Östberg, Lindström, & Renäll, 1989; Smeele & Sittig, 1991). We have less information on

TABLE 3.1
Audio and Video Standards

CCITT	International Telegraph and Telephone Consultative Committee (old name for the ITU-T)
CIF	ITU-T common intermediate format; H.261 standard for displays of video: 288 lines × 352 pixels
CELP	Code-excited linear prediction; used for low bit rate (4–16 kbps coders)
G.711	64 kbps, 3kHz audio
G.722	64 kbps, 7kHz audio
G.728	16 kbps, 3kHz audio
H.221	Frame structure for audiovisual services
H.242	Establishing communications between audiovisual terminals
H.261	Video codecs for audiovisual services at P × 64 kbps
HDTV	High-definition television
ISDN	Integrated services digital network: a set of standards for digital communications on the local loop and for long haul; provides for two B-channels of 64 kbps each, and one data (signaling) channel of 16 kbps in the local or BRI (basic rate interface); provides for 23 B channels and 1 64-kbps data channel on the long haul or PRI (primary rate interface)
ITU-T	International Telecommunications Union Technical standards committee, formerly known as the CCITT; a committee of the ITU, which has some international treaty powers, it sets telecommunications worldwide
MPEG	Motion Picture Experts Group
NTSC	National Television Systems Committee: collection of standards for broadcast TV
P × 64	Another name for the H-series standards where P is an integer value and 64 stands for 64 kbps
PAL	Phase-alternating line: broadcast TV standards used in Europe and other parts of the world
QCIF	ITU-T quarter common intermediate format: H.261 standard for display of video, 144 lines × 176 pixels
X.25	Packet switching protocol

how much of a gap would adversely affect users' performance in a normal conversation, or their perception of the quality of the connection. We do know that given our expectation from the video connection, a complete disregard for lip synchronization has a negative impact. However, some researchers have argued that lip synchronization should be abandoned altogether, because users are more frustrated with the audio delay than with the absence of lip synchronization (Tang & Isaacs, 1992).

Audio transmission delay is known to have an adverse effect on performance as well (Brady, 1971; Kitawaki, Kurita, & Itoh, 1991; Krauss & Bricker, 1967; Wolf, 1982). People who experience the delay often are not aware of it. They experience it generally as "confusion." In some cases they may attribute the problem to the other party in the conversation (Brady, 1971; Kitawaki et al., 1991). Each speaker may experience himself or herself as quick to respond, whereas the other party seems to take a long time to respond.

Coordination of conversation relies on very refined timing by the participants. Speakers effectively regulate the flow of the conversation by timing their contribution to fall within a fraction of a second after the current speaker's contribution is over, sometimes even creating a slight overlap.

The presence of delay is detrimental to this process. It can be illustrated with an assumed delay of 300 msec in each direction. Let us say that John approaches the end of his contribution, and expects a quick response. Jane hears John with a delay of 300 msec, and times the beginning of her contribution to overlap with what she expects to be the end of John's utterance. However, Jane's contribution is heard by John 300 msec later—that is, a full 600 msec after John terminated his utterance. This is long enough for John to notice that Jane is not responding as expected, and to start another sentence. Of course, the new sentence will be quickly overlapped by Jane's response. Now it is no longer clear who "has the floor" and the result is a breakdown in the communication.

When enough breakdowns take place, people adjust to the situation by resorting to a more formal way of communication with fewer interruptions. Indeed, when observing the style of interaction of participants in videoconferences, a more formal pattern of interaction emerged when an audio delay was present (Isaacs & Tang, 1993, 1994; O'Conaill et al., 1993). This pattern was not as evident when the audio was not delayed (O'Conaill et al., 1993).

Video Messaging. There is another way around the limited-bandwidth problem. We have only talked about real-time, two-way video in which both parties are seeing and being seen at the same time. Often it is more convenient, or more economical, to provide *asynchronous* communication in the form of video mail. Like voice mail, one party records a presentation and sends it to another, for later viewing. With video mail, one can transmit the video more slowly than it will be seen, reducing the need for high-bandwidth transmission lines. At the same time, there is an additional need for large amounts of storage. A convenient rule of thumb is that one frame of an uncompressed VGA-quality image will require about one megabyte of storage. Or the same megabyte can be used for about 1 min of compressed ISDN-quality images and video. Either way, hard disks can fill up quickly with video data.

Transmission

There are a number of choices when it comes to transmitting the image. It can be sent on *analog lines* or *digital lines,* over a *wired* or *wireless* connection, over *private line* or *public switched facilities.* Regardless of the transport chosen, the major technical issue is the bandwidth of the transmission line, that is, how much information can be economically sent down the channel per

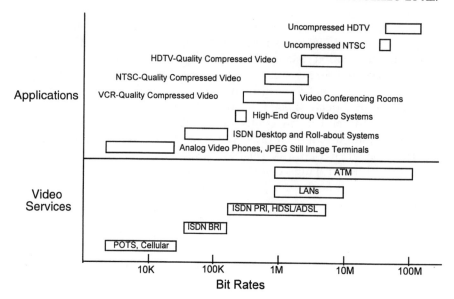

FIG. 3.1. Relationships between bandwidth, transmission medium, and types of VMC.

second. Figure 3.1 provides an overview of the transmission rates needed to support various video applications and the communication services that offer these transmission rates.

Analog transmission is cheap and ubiquitous. However, sending the images in digital form is much more efficient, allows for error free transmission, and it is easier to store and manipulate the images. The Picture-Phone of the 1970s used a 1-MHz analog signal. In the network the signal was digitized and transmitted as a T2 signal at about 6.3 Mbps, equivalent to 96 voice calls.[4] In contrast, today's videotelephones use the same room on the network as one or two voice calls.

What about going wireless? Broadcast TV is video and it is wireless. However, TV requires a large amount of bandwidth. One TV station takes up 6 MHz of the FCC-regulated, fiercely contested airwaves, the equivalent of approximately 90 Mbps of digital traffic or 1,300 voice calls. It is also not two-way. Other important wireless technologies are satellites and cellular. Using satellites for person-to-person transmission is not recommended for two reasons. First, the 50,000-mile round trip adds unacceptable delay to video communications. Second, although the down-link receivers are cheap, the up-link transmitters are not. Finally, cellular frequencies are too much in demand (and too expensive) for video. Nevertheless, the transmission of color still images over wireless links is now being perfected in the lab. Our conclusion: Multimedia communications will remain wired for the near future.

POTS. POTS is the analog public telephone service provided to nearly all homes in the United States. A personal computer or videotelephone hooked up to a common modem[5] on a POTS line can currently transmit somewhere between 2400 and 28,800 bps. This data rate is going up every few years. The advantage of a POTS connection is that telephone lines are literally everywhere and they are cheap to use. The disadvantage of POTS is that, because it was designed 100 years ago to carry voice, it has difficulty supporting the high data rates needed for video.

ISDN, HDSL, and ADSL. To go beyond the bit rates that modems provide there are special types of commercially available digital telephone lines, called ISDN, a local access service that comes in multiples of 64 kbps channels. The most common variety for the home and office is called *basic rate ISDN* (BRI). BRI provides two channels of 64 kbps each, for a total throughput of 128 kbps.

An advantage of ISDN is that it works on (most of) the local telephone lines out there today, although it requires special equipment at both ends of the line. It also an international standard. The number of ISDN lines being installed by businesses is growing rapidly, although the home market is lagging far behind.

In ISDN, all traffic remains digital from one end to the other. Because of this, more of the bandwidth on the telephone line can be used. Experimental digital services called *asymmetrical* and *half-duplex subscriber loops* (ADSL and HDSL) can push the humble copper telephone line to 1.5 Mbps (million bits per second) if one-way or 384 kbps if two-way.

LANs, WAN (Wide Area Network), and Private Line Service. If all you need to do is get video calls from one employee to another within a building, a LAN carrying 10 Mbps or more may be sufficient. Unfortunately, video conferencing requires a dedicated virtual circuit between the two parties on the LAN. LANs were not designed for time-critical electronic traffic. When you are sending an e-mail message, it is acceptable if things are a little slow because of heavy LAN traffic. However, a phone conversation is different. You want your words to reach the other end as soon as you say them, not a second or two later.

New technologies, such as *isochronous Ethernet, FDDI* (*fiber-distributed data interface,* a standard for high-speed LAN traffic), and *ATM* (*asynchronous transport mode,* a standard for high-speed packet networks) are more promising, although they are fairly expensive. The network interface cards and hub ports on these "video-enabled" LANs are pricey—between $500 and $2,500 per user. An ATM connection at 600 Mbps, servicing an entire building, costs upward of $30,000 per month.

In order to get from the LAN to a remote location, a service like basic rate ISDN (128 kbps) or primary rate ISDN (1.5 Mbps) must be used. With a significant amount of video traffic, leased lines can be purchased (for example, T1 circuits at 1.544 Mbps, or fractional T1 service for private point-to-point connections). These private line facilities are offered by large telecommunications companies, but are expensive. This is the solution for companies that wish to link only a few sites with high-quality video. Because of the higher cost of private line service (a T1 line is approximately $15,000 a month), there has been a dramatic growth of *switched digital services*. These are purchased only when needed at a per minute charge, much like a long-distance voice call.

Internet. The Internet represents a new technology for carrying video transmissions. It has not taken the vanguard long to exploit it. An interesting software solution, developed at Cornell University, is CU-SeeMe, which provides a one-to-many connection, delivering audio and video from one "speaking" participant to a multitude of listeners. Although it does not deliver truly two-way communication, it may be the harbinger of things to come. Another approach was taken by Apple Computer company. Special Quicktime software and a $100 camera and microphone combination makes the desktop computer an endpoint on an Internet video conference. Software for other PCs and workstations also exists. The picture and voice are not what we are used to on a typical circuit-switched connection, but we can perhaps expect dramatic improvements in the coming years.

CATV. Cable television is referred to as CATV, short for "community antenna television." It delivers television programming to 60% of the households in America and is yet another architecture for supporting video communications. CATV today is in some ways more like a LAN than POTS service, in that each subscriber does not have a dedicated line. In another way it is more like POTS service than ISDN: It is (in most places) analog. And it is like neither in that it is one-way, or radically asymmetrical, with all or almost all of the bandwidth dedicated to the downstream (into the home) traffic.

To support video calling, the infrastructure would need to be upgraded with digital facilities that can handle more channels and two-way traffic. Proponents of a CATV infrastructure to support video calling generally agree on a basic architecture that includes three components:

- A *set-top box* in the home to connect TVs, computers, and telephones to the cable.
- A *fiber-coax access network* consisting of coaxial cables to neighborhood hubs, and then fiber to the cable head end.

- SONET (synchronous optical network) optical fiber multiplexors and RF modems to connect the access network to the *SONET ATM backbone network* operating at gigabits speeds.

For interoperability, the cable head end would also need to be connected with the public switched network via high-bandwidth facilities. Contention schemes need to be worked out so that thousands of people could use the same cable lines. Fortunately, this development is happening today as cable companies upgrade their facilities with fiber optical cables.

Display

When the information, in the form of bits, arrives at the destination, it must be converted back into images and sound. Once again, but in reverse order, you need the proper network interface, a device for decoding the bits, and a device for displaying the image and playing the sound. If the network interface and the decoder do not follow the same standards as did the sender's equipment (an all too common problem), the video call fails.

Display Size. In videotelephones, small displays are necessary due to cost and/or portability factors; they also may enhance the perceived video quality. Computer-based video displays are also small, limited by what can be presented inside a computer monitor, and often shared with other windows in a graphical user interface. Videoconferencing systems often have larger displays, usually larger television screen sizes. Yet it is possible to provide a life-size display of a whole person or a whole conference table, using, for example, projection screen technology (e.g., Okada, Maeda, Ichikawaa, & Matsushita, 1994).

There are certainly advantages to a small display. Small displays allow a device to be portable. The video picture may have to share real estate on a computer screen. Small displays also make lower resolution images look better. However, users show a preference for large displays up to the point where the image is life-size (Inoue, Yoroizawa, & Okubo, 1984).

Why might this be so? A large or life-size display may provide a feeling of *virtual presence*, an "instinctive" feeling that the remote participants are physically present in the room. Prussog, Mühlbach, and Böcker (1994) used a display that provided a life-size full-body image, with surrounding, and reported that users' subjective impressions of actually being in the same room were remarkable. Is there anything to be gained from increasing the display size even further? There may be. Cinematic and virtual reality techniques have shown that displays that cover a viewer's peripheral vision provide a qualitatively more intense, "virtually real" experience (users will have less opportunity to notice the borders of the display; Pausch, 1993).

Despite possible advantage of size, video display sophistication must have limits due to cost and bandwidth. A trade-off is required to be practical but also to preserve what may be the advantages of having video in the first place, increasing the sense of personal participation (Blanchard & Angiollilo, 1994; Pye & Williams, 1977; Williams, 1977).

Video Image Attributes.   Compression is the foremost method for reducing the amount of video data that needs to be transmitted. Reduction of the data size is achieved by setting the resolution of each picture (or frame) and the frame rate of the display to values that, although less than optimal, are acceptable for the user and the task.

One can achieve a reduction in the amount of data that needs to be transmitted by reducing the number of pixels per square inch, or the *resolution* of the image. The ITU-T H-series standards specify a few acceptable resolutions, including *CIF* (common intermediate format, 288×352 pixels, and *QCIF* (quarter common intermediate format, 144×176 pixels). For comparison, the SVGA standard for computers is approximately 800×600 pixels, and the NTSC standard for TVs is 480×440 pixels. Reducing the number of pixels can give the image a grainy quality, like a cheap newspaper photo.

One can also reduce the number of *frames per second* (fps; the *frame rate*). The movie industry standard is 24 unique fps, with each frame showing twice for an equivalent frame rate of 48 fps. The existing practice in ISDN-based systems is to maintain about 10 fps, which provides the viewer a jerky picture, but this is sufficient if there is little motion in the picture. In the extreme, VMC could use still images that are transmitted whenever the user presses a button. Operating at 9.6 kbps, still-image videophones send a high-resolution image in 10 sec to 120 sec, depending on the complexity of the image. Frame rate, image size, and resolution can all be traded off, and most of the standards allow for this.

Local Views.   Many systems will have more than one local image source, only some of which may be transmitted, and any of which may be viewed on the output screen. Control of these various views quickly becomes a usability problem: It must be obvious to users that, for any image on their screen, they know what image they are looking at, where that image is coming from, and what other conferees on the video link are viewing. The latter is more significant than may appear at first pass. Potential privacy concerns appear when users do not know when they are transmitting their picture. Usability studies at AT & T Bell Laboratories indicated that when users can see themselves on their screens, many have the intuitive impression that no one else can see them, even when on-screen messages are provided.

An additional caution is required with local views: Views of people must be mirrored, whereas views of texts must not. Mirroring of an image may be simple or may pose some challenges depending on system architecture, but users will have great difficulty with a nonmirror image of themselves, as they must relearn firmly established eye-body coordination habits.

Eye Contact and Gaze Awareness. Gaze direction plays a number of roles in conversation. Eye contact is necessary for starting conversations, greeting, and reinforcing during conversation. But people spend most of the time looking at their environment, at the gestures and positions of others, and sending signals by mutual gazes and facial expressions (Argyle, 1972). Gaze awareness communicates liking, status, emotions, attitude, and truthfulness (Cook & Lalljee, 1972).

To truly preserve eye contact in a video system, the participant must look directly into the camera, but because the person must also be looking at the video image of the other person, or at a computer screen, eye contact must be compromised. The most typical compromise, both in computers and videotelephone and conferencing devices, is to place the users' camera above the screen. This causes people to appear to be casting eyes their eyes downward—but this is better than other positions, as people appear suppliant when they gaze upward and deceitful when they gaze sideways (Kenyon, White, & Ried, 1985). There have been several novel solutions to preserving eye contact: The ClearBoard project (Ishii & Kobayashi, 1992; Ishii, Kobayashi, & Grudin, 1992) superimposed video of the other participant on a common whiteboard, while a camera preserved eye contact using half-silvered mirrors, and the MAJIC system (Okada et al., 1994) solved the problem using full-size video images.

Technical constraints that limit users' gaze awareness and eye contact contribute to the inability of video to fully convey nonverbal signals, and, again, are one of the causes for a surprising weakness of video to provide value to teleconferencing (Williams, 1977; Pye & Williams, 1977; Blanchard & Angiolillo, 1994).

Sound Quality. The issues for sound are the same as those for video. Sound sampled at 44.1 kHz with 16-bit resolution (so-called "CD quality") requires over 700 kbps. The quality of voice on the long-distance network, so-called *toll-quality speech*, does not require the same fidelity. It is sampled at 8 kHz with 8-bit resolution, which is then transmitted at 64 kbps. By reducing either the sampling rate or the resolution and then compressing the data (taking out the redundancy), we can reduce the required bandwidth to 16 kbps, or even less for POTS video calls. The AT & T Videophone 2500 uses a CELP (code-excited linear predictions) algorithm for compressing sound to 6.8 kbps. ISDN personal video systems generally follow the ITU (International Telecommunications Union) G.711 (64 kbps, 3 kHz audio) or the G.728 (16 kbps, 3 kHz audio) standard. However, you should not trade off sound quality for a better picture. Ample research has shown that users are not willing to sacrifice good sound quality in order to get a picture.

The lower limit of acceptable audio was long ago determined in the initial design of the telephone network, and was standardized as 200 Hz to 3,200 Hz. This range may not be good enough for music, but enough of the voice information is passed to be quite intelligible. At the very least, telephone quality bandwidth is something with which users are intimately familiar. If quality is reduced from the public telephone network standard by limiting bandwidth and applying compression techniques, not only is the intelligibility of speech at risk, but users may lose the ability to identify the speaker: Friends, relatives, and associates just don't "sound like themselves."

There may be an advantage to moving in the other direction: increasing the bandwidth and quality beyond public telephone network level. High-fidelity or *7-kHz audio* passes frequencies from 50 to 7,000 Hz. Another direction is to provide *multichannel audio,* such as stereo.

Multipoint VMC. In the work environment most meetings involve more than two people. Some systems are explicitly designed for a meeting in which there are several people in the room, but are still restricted to *point-to-point* connection (i.e., only two locations). However, a large proportion of the meetings require the presence of participants from more than two locations—hence the need for technological support for a multipoint connection. Network topology that requires each node to have a full connection to every other node on the connection is impractical, and thus the connection is done through a multipoint control unit (MCU).

The solution for multipoint connection over the audio channel has evolved over the years. An audio bridge receives input from every endpoint and uses a sophisticated algorithm to detect which of the endpoints are talking and which ones are listening. A subset of the points is selected, the audio level for these points is adjusted, and a summation of all audio signals is sent to all the points on the conference.

The video channel presents a challenge—summation of audio is far easier than summation of video. Two basic solutions were developed. In the *split-screen* solution, multiple "windows" present the visual images that come from the various points. In the *switching* solution, a single image is selected at any given moment and transmitted to each participating endpoint.

In principle the MCU could transmit the images from each point to every other point and let the end-user device determine what images to present. In practice, the current cost of bandwidth dictates that the bridge must transmit a single image, be it a composite image that the bridge created or a single selected channel. Thus, for most systems, the choice of split-screen or switching is implemented in the video bridge.

Switching can be done manually. Typically this is done by one party to the conversation that is designated as the "chair." Among the drawbacks of a *chair control* is that one party has to dedicate quite a lot of attention to the switching of the signals, and often has to choose between participation and performance of this duty. The other is that other participants may not be content with the decisions made by the chair.

An alternative approach to switching is to do it automatically. Usually this is done through *voice-activated switching.* An algorithm makes use of the changes in audio signals from the various points to determine who is the current speaker. All endpoints are then presented with the video signal that this point is transmitting, and the speaker typically sees the image of the speaker that preceded him or her. An interesting side effect of this algorithm is that sometimes the last speaker is entirely unaware that his or her image is still being seen by one other party, that is, the current speaker.

Other variations of switching may combine the broadcasting of a single source, designated as the "broadcaster," to all other endpoints. Meanwhile, the broadcaster receives the video image of other endpoints either based on voice-activated switching or based on some random scanning algorithm. This is appropriate for a *lecture* style presentation where all locations see the main speaker, and the speaker can view the points that have questions or comments to make, or simply scan to see the reaction of the audience.

In the split-screen alternative, the video bridge composes a single image from the multiple images, and sends this image to all participants. The most common example is the *quadrature* screen, which integrates images from up to four other endpoints. When the number of parties is not greater than five, this technique allows each point to view each other point.

An advantage of the split screen is that it provides a sense of social presence. Participants do not appear and disappear from view: They are presented at all times, whether they are speaking or listening. One obvious drawback of such a solution is in the reduction of "screen real estate" that is dedicated for each one of the images, further reducing the ability to discern body gestures or subtle changes in facial expressions. And if one of these views is local and the rest are remote, a challenging control situation is created if mirror imaging is used for local view and not for remote views.

CONCLUSION

In order to understand the future one must know the past. We open our conclusion with a brief history of commercial video telecommunication and follow with future directions.

A Brief History of Commercial Video Telecommunication

The origins of video telecommunications can be traced back over 65 years to a most historic, one-way full-motion video call in 1927 from then Secretary of Commerce Herbert Hoover in Washington, DC, to AT & T executives in New York City (Dorros, 1969; Mainzer, 1984). The frame rate was 18 fps. This technology became the foundation of commercial television that was first introduced in Britain in 1936. Some of the notable events along this evolutionary path include the failed commercial introduction of PicturePhone video telephone service in 1970 by the former Bell System in the United States. In 1985 ISDN was introduced and codecs were developed that produced acceptable video quality at 128 kbps. In 1991 the former CCITT (now ITU-T) approved the P × 64 standards for video coding, which opened the market for video telecommunications significantly. Also in 1992, AT & T introduced the VideoPhone 2500, which worked with regular analog telephone lines, had a 3-inch screen, and transmitted at 1 to 10 frames per second. Many video telecommunications vendors have entered the markets and some are making significant profits. Among the more successful equipment providers are PictureTel and CLI, especially in the area of group video systems including "roll-abouts."

Future Directions

One can distinguish among three periods in the progress of VMC technology. The early period, from the 1920s to the 1960s, saw both success and failures. Two-way video communication, which was the original direction pursued by inventors, failed. One-way video communication, which gave birth to broadcast television, was a great commercial success that shaped the world as we see it. The 1980s were characterized by the successful, although limited, emergence of group videoconferencing, along with a renewed research interest in the topic as part of the growing field of computer-supported collaborative work (CSCW). This chapter is written in the midst of the third period, dominated by the promise of integration of the near-ubiquitous personal computer, the telephone, and video components in a powerful multimedia connection that allows a far richer form of interaction and collaboration. Is this third period going to be a success story? Ultimately the question regarding the value of VMC will be answered by the marketplace.

As we witness the exponential growth of traffic and innovation in the Internet, we have to pay close attention to the emerging use of the net for real-time audio and video communications. The MBone, short for multicast backbone, is a virtual network that supports multicast of real-time audio and video across the Internet. Multicast provides one-to-many and many-to-many network delivery services. Although frame rate is limited, the MBone supports VMC over a network connection that is typically rather inexpensive to the end user. Although audio quality at the time of writing may be reminiscent of a bygone era, and speakers may have to resort to taking turns speaking, this is a key technology to watch because it may deliver on the promise of a truly inexpensive transmission infrastructure. VMC may initially appear close to periodical transmission of still images, but the next few years may present some innovations that are beyond what we can envision at the present.

Usually "incremental" innovation in technology can be adopted by a single user. One can make a decision to purchase a cordless phone, and find it useful even when the rest of the world does not. This is not the case for VMC; having a single VMC device has no value if you have nobody to communicate with. In order to be useful, it is essential that a critical mass of users use this technology and that the devices manufactured by all vendors can communicate with each other. Will there be a critical mass of users to make VMC a common technology? There are some reasons to believe the time for this technology may be near:

1. Some penetration has already been established, mostly in support of group videoconferencing. In 1995 there are tens of thousands of video endpoints worldwide that can communicate with each other.
2. International video coding standards (P × 64) now allow different types of vendor equipment to work together.
3. The price/performance ratio for the underlying technologies keeps improving, with great improvements in the cameras, processors, codecs, and flat-panel displays.
4. Broad bandwidth is more readily available and cheaper. It is getting easier to obtain ISDN service, as well as switched 56 kbps and 384 kbps, from a local carrier. The introduction over the next few years of broadband networks, such as ATM, will bring about far greater bandwidth at prices that are more affordable for many businesses.
5. Video compression technology is more advanced and significantly improved, offering a significantly better image and sound quality.
6. People are getting more comfortable with being on camera as a result of the extensive use of camcorder and VCR machines.
7. Saving the cost, the time, and the inconvenience of undesirable travel is more important as today's businesses operate in a global economy.

NOTES

1. Integrated Services Digital Network.
2. Costly, yes, but we should all appreciate the dramatic drop in price of these devices. The first codecs cost $150,000. By the mid-1980s the price had dropped to $75,000. Today

they are a few hundred dollars. If there were a single reason why visual communications is feasible today, it would be the affordability of these coding/decoding drones.
3. International Telecommunications Union Technical Standards, formerly known as CCITT, an international body for developing engineering standards for communications networks.
4. The bandwidth requirements were eventually reduced to 1.544 Mbps, or 24 voice calls.
5. A modem modulates the digital picture information, encoded as a string of 0s and 1s, onto an analog signal and then sends it down the wire. A modem on the other end of the line must turn the analog signal back into the original 0s and 1s to reconstruct the picture as best as it can.

REFERENCES

Abel, M. J. (1990). Experiences in an exploratory distributed organization. In J. Galegher, R. E. Kraut, and C. Egido (Eds.), *Intellectual teamwork; Social and technological foundations of cooperative work* (pp. 489–510). Hillsdale, NJ: Lawrence Erlbaum Associates.

Argyle, M. (1972). Non-verbal communication in human social interaction. In R. A. Hinde (Ed.), *Non-verbal communication* (pp. 243–269). Cambridge: Cambridge University Press.

Blanchard, H. E., & Angiolillo, J. S. (1994). Visual displays in communications: A review of effects on human performance and preference. In *SID '94 Digest of Technical Papers* (pp. 375–378). Santa Ana, CA: Society for Information Display.

Brady P. T. (1971). Effects of transmission delay on conversational behavior on echo free telephone circuits. *Bell System Technical Journal, 49,* 115–134.

Buxton, W. A. S. (1992). Telepresence: Integrating shared task and person spaces. In *Proceedings of Graphic Interface 92,* 816–821.

Cook, M., & Lalljee, M. G. (1972). Verbal substitutes for visual signals in interaction. *Semiotica, 6,* 212–221.

Dorros I. (1969). The evolution of PICTUREPHONE service. *Bell Laboratories Record, 47,* 137–141.

Fish, R. S., Kraut, R. E., Root, R. W., & Rice, R. E. (1993). Video as a technology for informal communication. *Communications of the ACM, 36,* 48–61.

Hearty, P. J. (1993). Achieving and confirming optimum image quality. In A. B. Watson (Ed.), *Digital images and human vision* (pp. 149–162). Cambridge, MA: MIT Press.

Inoue, M., Yoroizawa, I., & Okubo, S. (1984). In *Proceedings International Teleconference Symposium* (pp. 66–73). International Telecommunications Satellite Organization. Reprinted in D. Bodson & R. Schaphorst (1989). *Teleconferencing* (pp. 211–218). New York: IEEE.

Isaacs, E. A., & Tang, J. C. (1993) What video can and can't do for collaboration: A case study. In *Proceedings of ACM Multimedia 93* (pp. 99–206). Anaheim, CA.

Isaacs, E. A., & Tang, J. C. (1994). What video can and cannot do for collaboration: A case study. *Multimedia Systems, 2,* 63–73.

Ishii, H., & Kobayashi, M. (1992). ClearBoard: A seamless medium for shared drawing and conversation with eye contact. In *Proceedings of ACM CHI '92 Conference on Human Factors in Computing Systems* (pp. 525–532). New York: ACM Press.

Ishii, H., Kobayashi, M., & Grudin, J. (1992). Integration of interpersonal space and shared workspace: ClearBoard design and experiments. *Proceedings of the Conference on Computer-Supported Cooperative Work 92* (pp. 33–42). New York: ACM Press.

Kenyon, N. D., White, T. A., & Ried, G. M. (1985). Behavioral and user needs for teleconferencing. *Proceedings of the IEEE, 73* (pp. 689–699). Reprinted in D. Bodson, & R. Schaphorst (1989). *Teleconferencing* (pp. 219–229). New York: IEEE.

Kitawaki, N. Kurita, T. & Itoh, K. (1991). Effects of delay on speech quality. *NTT Review, 3,* 88–94.

Krauss, R. M., & Bricker, P. D. (1967). Effects of transmission delay and access delay on the efficiency of verbal communication. *Journal of the Acoustical Society of America, 41,* 286–292.

Mainzer, E. A. (1984). *AT&T Picturephone: The dysfunctionality of a functional structure.* New York: New York University.

Netravali, A., & Haskell, B. (1991). *Digital pictures.* New York: Plenum Press.

O'Conaill, B., Whittaker, S., & Wilbur, S. (1993). Conversations over video conferences: An evaluation of the spoken aspects of video-mediated communication. *Human Computer Interaction, 8,* 389–428.

Okada, K., Maeda, F., Ichikawaa, Y., & Matsushita, Y. (1994). Multiparty videoconferencing at virtual social distance: MAJIC design. *Proceedings of the Conference on Computer Supported Cooperative Work* (pp. 385–393). New York: ACM Press.

Olson, M. H., & Bly, S. A. (1991). The Portland experience: A report on a distributed research group. *International Journal of Man-Machine Studies, 34,* 211–228.

Östberg, O., Lindström, B., & Renäll, P. O. (1989). Contribution of display size to speech intelligibility in videophone systems. *International Journal of Human–Computer Interaction, 1,* 149–159.

Pausch, R. (1993). Three views of virtual reality. *IEEE Computer,* February, 79–80.

Prussog, A., Mühlbach, L., & Böcker, M. (1994). Telepresence in videocommunications. *Proceedings of the Human Factors and Ergonomics Society 38th Annual Meeting, 1,* 180–184. Santa Monica, CA: Human Factors and Ergonomics Society.

Pye, R., & Williams, E. (1977, June). Teleconferencing: Is video valuable or is audio adequate? *Telecommunications Policy, 1,* 230–241.

Smeele, P. M. T., & Sittig, A. C. (1991). *Effects of desynchronization of vision and speech on the perception of speech: Preliminary results.* Contribution to CCITT, Study group XII, Brasilia, September, 6–13.

Tang, J. C., & Isaacs, E. A. (1992). *Why do users like video? Studies of multimedia-supported collaboration* (SMLI Tech. Rep. No. 92–5). Mountain View, CA: SUN Microsystem Laboratories.

Tang, J. C., & Rua, M. (1994). Montage: Providing teleproximity for distributed groups. *CHI '94 Conference Proceedings: Human Factors in Computer Systems* (pp. 37–43).

Williams, E. (1977, June). Experimental comparisons of face-to-face and mediated communication: A review. *Psychological Bulletin, 84,* 963–976.

Wolf, C. G. (1982). Video conferencing: Delay and transmission considerations. In L. A. Parker & C. H. Olgern (Eds.), *Teleconferencing and electronic communications* (pp. 184–188). Madison: University of Wisconsin.

Chapter 4

Making Sense of the Findings: Common Vocabulary Leads to the Synthesis Necessary for Theory Building

Gary M. Olson
Judith S. Olson
The University of Michigan

We present a framework for variables that are thought to influence the behavior of groups working with various types of technologies, either face-to-face or remote, real-time or asynchronously. The framework urges researchers to describe in full the features of the group members and their relations, the particulars of the situation, the technology support, and the task, as well as the dependent variables having to do with the group process measured and the outcome. Only when we have all variables described can we sort out the factors that indeed influence group work. Only when we have clear pictures of these influences will we be able to build a theory of computer supported cooperative work. In this chapter we present the framework, then illustrate its usefulness by reviewing the other chapters in this book. This review illustrates four benefits: It points to clear clusters of chapters, shows where effects are undertested, helps sort out apparent contradictions, and points out consistent results ready for theory building.

The chapters in this book represent various answers to the question: Does the addition of video to a communication path improve people's remote work? The answer, understandably, is that it depends. Each chapter examines a situation in which people who do or do not know each other are asked to do a task in a controlled laboratory setting or their own work in their workplace, using various modes of communicating with each other. In some cases the communication channel is delayed; in others it is not; the video is large or small; audio is monaural or stereo; and so on. Furthermore, some groups have other technologies available to them, such as a shared work object.

It is no surprise that the results are complex and occasionally appear to conflict. Review and synthesis of all these results is difficult. Some of the difficulty stems from the fact that we have no common vocabulary, no way of describing in detail all the potentially important aspects of the situation. Without the common vocabulary we cannot build a theory that links cause and effect. What kind of group doing what kind of task in which situation will benefit from what sorts of video connections? The purpose of this chapter is to offer such a vocabulary and to organize the individual factors into a simplifying framework.

The framework we present here includes specific features of the group members and their relationships, the particulars of the situation, technology support, and the task. Furthermore, in doing empirical studies, we measure different things. Various studies measure the process of working, task outcome (like quality of the product), group outcome (like satisfaction), and organizational outcomes (like employee retention).

We borrow many of the group and situation factors from the framework presented by Kraemer and Pinsonneault (1990). Because their focus was on group decision support system (GDSS) and we wish to cover that plus video-mediated communication (VMC), we extend their technology descriptors in a major way. We include, as they do, group, task, and situation factors, as well as process and outcome measures.

It would be foolish to claim that the framework we present here is complete, covering all there is to know about the behavior of small groups. Tomes have been written on this topic (e.g., Forsyth, 1990; McGrath, 1984; Shaw, 1981; Steiner, 1972, 1976). Rather, we focus on those factors that are likely to be important in the assessment of real-time video communication channels, primarily for real-time distance work and asynchronous work whether at a distance or collocated.

The body of the chapter presents the framework, listing the key variables that researchers should describe in their reports so that comparisons and syntheses are possible. To show the usefulness of this framework, we end this chapter by using it to describe some of the other chapters in this book. There are four points that emerge in this analysis:

1. Chapters in this book *cluster* into sets of covariables—particular niches. The framework helps identify these niches.
2. Of the large set of situations in which groups work, most of our collective research has explored only a small fraction. We use the framework to *point to new situations* in which technology in general, and video in particular, could help.
3. There are some apparent *contradictions* in the empirical literature. Close examination of these results shows that the situations in which

the tests were made could have differed in important ways. The framework's vocabulary points to those aspects in the situations that may explain these apparent contradictions.

4. As findings stabilize and relationships are drawn, we can build a *theory* about the ways in which various types of technology affect group work.

THE FRAMEWORK

Our framework is similar in style to that of Kraemer and Pinsonneault (1990), in that it divides the context variables into classes having to do with the group members and their relationships, the situation, the technology, and the task. We modify the contents of the first two categories, groups and situations, and greatly expand the latter two categories, technology and task.

Some variables one might expect, like size of the group, are missing. This is intentional. We are looking for those key constructs that shed light on why certain things happen. When the size of the group increases, a number of other variables change concurrently: the homogeneity of abilities, the mix of status or power, and the probability that someone will assume leadership. By describing these process-oriented variables, which can vary independently in other situations, one can account for effects that are attributed to the single variable, size of group.

Characteristics of the Group

Characteristics of the group include individual characteristics, group composition, organizational factors, and particulars of the moment. Our list of important group characteristics is a synthesis of a number of frameworks generated in the field of social psychology. Books by Shaw (1981) and McGrath (1984) and papers by Hackman (1987) and Morgan and Lassiter (1992) provide a lot of detail about what factors in both the individual group members and the interactive effects of group compositions affect group process and outcome.

Individual Characteristics. Skill, ability, and *knowledge* are resources the individual brings to bear in a group task. Some enduring aspects of people's *personality* determine, among other things, the amount of effort the person will expend in a setting. This in turn can determine how much tolerance they have for communication tools that are not as easy as talking face-to-face. We add the characteristic of *enduring motivations and agendas* to reflect the goals the person may bring to the situation that are not related to the stated task at hand. For example, we have seen people show up at meetings only to have "face time," to be visible to their peers and manager, thinking this would lead to more favorable future performance reviews. Also, we have seen people whose agenda was to avoid taking on any new tasks, commonly called "lying low." Biographical characteristics, such as age, gender, and experience, are captured by these constructs.

Group Composition. Important characteristics include homogeneity of abilities, knowledge of others' abilities, knowledge, motivation, fit of personalities, cohesiveness and trust, communication structure (connections, availability), and homogeneity of status, roles, and power. Most of these variables are self-explanatory. However, one of the key constructs in this list that has clear importance for the assessment of VMC is the knowledge of the others' abilities, knowledge, and motivation. Gabarro (1990) reported, for example, that mature, stable groups can use alternate modes of communication to convey the same message because they have a shared repertoire of meaning and ways of expressing those meanings. Thus, a group that knows each other well may not benefit from video as much as less well-established groups. For them, e-mail may do as well as video. Similarly, Gabarro noted that this familiarity may support the group's ability to be spontaneous and informal in their exchange, because they have shared meanings that can be quickly, efficiently picked up.

Aspects of the group's normal communication structure can also affect the nature of work and the ease with which it can be conducted remotely or asynchronously. Some heterogeneous groups communicate via a "line of reporting" structure (to the manager of a group before being disseminated to the members of that manager's group). Others communicate directly, person to person regardless of organizational lines, sometimes keeping the manager informed of major issues. Various technologies fit these various communication structures or not. Also, the effectiveness of all these communication modes can be severely affected, either positively or negatively, if the various parties are often unavailable. For example, e-mail, Lotus Notes, and calendars would serve a nomadic group member, whereas desktop video may not.

Organizational Factors. These include reward structure, work norms (participation, individual responsibility), and organizational routines. Note that the effectiveness of various technologies has been shown to be dependent not only on the individuals or group composition, but also on the organization's reward structure (Orlikowski, 1992). For example, an organization that rewards individuals on their personal accomplishments, in competition with others, will not easily take to Lotus Notes where the expectation is that one will share what one knows.

Particulars of the Moment. Here we consider differences in contextual time, and momentary attitudes or motivations. Interestingly, the one variable about distance work that technology cannot overcome is time. Here, time refers to contextual time, such as when in the day the interaction occurs (early morning for those in Hong Kong is early evening for those in Ann Arbor, both participating in a video-based distance learning experience). Furthermore, holidays, celebrations, moods, and weather affect the local participant in ways that may be opaque to the distant group member. We participated in a videoconference between London and Chicago on a day when Chicago had a major snowstorm, which was of course invisible to the London participants. On another occasion we were in an audioconference between Ann Arbor and Rotterdam on the day that the Netherlands celebrated the 50th anniversary of its liberation from Nazi Germany. The loss of such local context among group members can be quite jarring to the participants, and of course often exacerbates cultural differences that characterize global work (O'Hara-Devereaux & Johansen, 1994).

Characteristics of the Technology

We can see that as technologies to support the conversation, and technologies to support the work object. Technology to support group work today is increasingly varied. Kraemer and Pinsonneault reviewed the effectiveness of group decision support systems, but our goal is to cover a much wider range of technologies. Furthermore, we wish to describe the technologies in enough detail to understand the differences in their effectiveness with different groups and different tasks.

We separate here technologies that support interpersonal communication from those that support the shared work object. This is an important distinction. People codevelop work products, like proposals, white papers, budgets, and so on. In today's world of distributed group members, these products are often faxed, sent by FTP (file transfer protocol) or e-mail attachments, or stored on a shared file server so others can retrieve them. In addition, the group will converse about those objects, using face-to-face meetings, e-mail, voice mail, and discussion databases. The features that groups need in these technologies differ, and thus are separated in our framework.

Technologies to Support the Conversation. Factors considered here are what is visible (video clarity, field of view), what is audible (audio clarity, e.g., feedback and echo; spatial sense, e.g., stereo vs. mono), delay (between the audio and video channels; of the message, by milliseconds; of the message, by minutes to days), and control over what is sent and received, in terms of passive or active initiation of conversation, ability to signal whether you wish to be contacted, and control over the channel characteristics. Other factors are support for linking the conversation to the work objects, reciprocity (homogeneity of channels), the ability to review and revise messages, correspondence of the sent and received sequencing of messages, anonymity of message, access (how hard it is to schedule the channel), cost of the channel relative to other channels, and support for coordination. The list of factors blends those from Fussell and Benimoff (1995) and Clark and Brennan (1991) and is augmented by a review of the various types of communication channels explored in this book.

Most of the items in this list are self-explanatory, with variants explored in the papers in this book. Clearly, *what is visible*, and in particular the *field of view*, is important both to the conduct of the discussion, but also for helping the participants understand the context of the remote participant. We know from the field of proxemics (Hall, 1966) that angle of regard, eye contact, and physical distance all impact the conduct of a discussion. These important factors are often overlooked in the display of people on videoconferencing—we see talking heads, full frontal, and sometimes with camera angles that hide the eye position, all of which disrupt the turn-taking and possibly the participants' attitudes and motivations.

Delay manifests itself in these situations in a variety of important ways. Any delay (longer than 200 msec) to the audio channel disrupts conversation (Fussell & Benimoff, 1995). This suggests that when technology dictates a delay for video, it is better to decouple the audio and video channels and keep the audio delay very short.

There is a separate effect of delays longer than a second or two. Natural conversation builds on the fact that the participants share common ground (Clark & Brennan, 1991). We commonly use *deixis* to refer to things presumed to be in all participants' recent memory, and understand where we are in the flow of a conversation. When we move to asynchronous communication, we lose the thread of the conversational sequence and, because of memory loss, lose the ability to refer to things efficiently.

In addition, remote communication often disrupts the conversants' abilities to use a shared physical referent (Bekker, 1995). That is, if one's hand gesture points to a place, that place may not have the same meaning to the remote participant. What one sees is usually not what the other sees. Some systems have "telepointers" to transmit pointing gestures on a shared object, allowing the recipient to disambiguate referents. But telepointers are very impoverished media for all of what is available in shared physical space.

Lotus Notes allows shared documents and conversation databases, but does not support the linking of the two to enable comments to appear near the point of reference. PrepEditor (Neuwirth, Kaufer, Chandhok, &

Morris, 1990), a prototype shared editor, puts comments on text next to the areas they refer to, making it easier both to produce the comments and to understand them later.

Reciprocity and homogeneity of channels are related, referring to the ability of the group members to interact on equal footing. Reciprocity refers to similarity of the channels among all participants: If I can see you, you can see me; if I can hear you, you can hear me. Physical space offers these characteristics; artificial communication technologies can alter the symmetry, leading to "bugging" and "Big Brother" spying. Similarly, if the specific characteristics of the communication channels are different (you can hear me loud and clear, but you sound distorted and soft to my ears), it may alter the apparent personality or status of the participants.

The next two features, *sequence* and *ability to be reviewed and revised,* refer to asynchronous interactions. E-mail and chat windows are the prime examples where the "utterance" can be reviewed and revised before being sent. There are occasions, however, where the messages arrive out of order to the time in which they were issued, disrupting the comprehensibility of referents and grammatical links. And, in both e-mail and chat windows, it is hard to pull together the "thread" of the conversation.

Frequency of use and satisfaction are affected by the ease of *access* to the communication channel. It matters whether the video connectivity is on the desktop or down the hall, whether one has to rent a room far in advance of the meeting, and how many people are required to support the endeavor. Cost figures in the decision to use various channels—not necessarily absolute costs but those relative to other available alternatives.

Support for coordination among the participants is a general category that includes people's abilities to be aware of the work of others. This can happen through seeing them work, seeing notes about their progress in a revision control system, or a shared view of a constantly updated project plan. There are systems that alert the user when certain activities have occurred, or when someone has changed a document in an area in which another has responsibility. One could present indicators of who is currently logged on to a distributed session, or even indirectly by showing work being carried out by others in the same document (Dourish & Bellotti, 1992).

This coordination can also involve live video displays of a remote area, either a continuous view of a hall or room, or glances into individuals' offices. Some systems combine this with access to others' calendars and an easy ability to leave e-mail messages or sticky notes on the screen to notify people when they return to their offices (Tang, Isaacs, & Rau, 1994).

The clear description of all of these features is critical if we are to synthesize the effects of VMC. The rich variety of features available in face-to-face communication is subtle and easily taken for granted. Only when they are not reproduced in VMC do we discover how significant their effects are on the progress and product of the work.

Technology to Support the Work Object.   Group work involves not only conversation, but the objects to support the work (e.g., meeting minutes, project plan, draft proposal, item to be repaired, CAD drawing). Tools that have been built for creating shared objects and editing them vary widely on important features that interact with group members' style and the task they are engaged in. Here are features of technology modified from a list first presented in Olson, McGuffin, Kuwana, and Olson (1993): whether others have access to the object, control over participant read/write permissions, extent of functionality for editing and navigating the shared object, correspondence between participants' views, the ability to locate the position of others in the work, the ability to capture the others' attention, control over turn-taking, support for specific types of work, and ease with which tools can be accessed from one another.

Access refers to the permissions the various group members have to read/write, as well as to their homogeneity. If there is access, it is important to describe the basic *functionality,* the editing capability of the underlying application. The notebooks in many of today's shared work systems, like ProShare, are simple sketching tools that do no global formatting or "smoothing" the way text editors do (e.g., they do not rewrap when one wishes to insert something in a previously drawn list).

Correspondence of the participants' views, ability to locate the position of others in the work, and *ability to capture the others' attention* refer to the group members' interface to this object. They refer to whether they all see the same view or not (WYSIWIS; Stefik et al., 1987), and whether if the group members have different views the members can be aligned so the members can discuss a common referent. Interestingly, in some systems views are aligned by a participant grabbing control over another's view, and in others it is initiated by the one wanting to align. These different schemes have very different fits to the group members' personalities and power and status relations.

We also need to know how *turn-taking* is implemented. Most shared-object groupware allows access to editing only one at a time (various kinds of selection or file locking), with control either being grabbed by the one who wants it, or requested from and released by the current holder of the pen.

Group work changes its task moment by moment. At one time or another, people are generating ideas, evaluating them, organizing and presenting them. Similarly, people are working together for a while, then breaking into phases of parallel, individual work. Technologies are variously suited to different work modes, with or without support for smooth transitions. That is, many systems are built solely for asynchronous parallel work; Lotus Notes is an example, as is use of a shared file server with and without file locking. But it is not easy to bring a file of this sort into a meeting room to use it in a shared-editing mode. And the LiveBoard drawings, created in a synchronous distributed meeting, are not amenable to editing in any other piece of software, such as a graphics editor, for use in meeting minutes or a report.

Characteristics of the Task

There are a number of everyday English ways of describing tasks, such as brainstorming, design, teaching, or decision making. But these are at the wrong level of granularity for determining exactly how various kinds of technology can help or hinder. For example, the task of design has many phases to it, and these phases might be mixed together in complex ways. These include gathering of requisite constraints and solution components, critiquing these, deciding, carrying out the documentation, and so on.

We have created a smaller granularity descriptor set, adapted from the synthesis of tasks in Teasley, Olson, and Meader (1994): the nature of the material, major information-processing activity, dependencies among the work of the participants, mental resources necessary to do the task, and duration and scope. This descriptor set builds on those of McGrath (1984), Hackman (1987), and Hackman and Morris (1975), Morgan and Lassiter (1992), and Shaw (1981). We aligned and synthesized these other schemes to create a level of description that appears to be important in discerning the effect of various technologies on group work.

The Nature of the Material. The easiest part to describe is the nature of the *material* of the work, whether it be abstract ideas or concrete objects. The chapter by Nardi et al. in this book (chapter 23) best illustrates the use of video to show the object of work, in this case the microscopic view of neurosurgery. Because the material of the work is concrete (or in this case flesh), video can be used well to share the object. In other cases, when the content of the work is abstract, video typically supports the conversation rather than the object, although perhaps capture of the ideas in shared visual form (in a shared editor) could help the memory loads incurred in this task.

The Major Information-Processing Activity. We consider exchanging information about other team members' capabilities, planning and orchestrating the team, gathering or generating information, explaining or sharing information, discussing to come to agreement, and planning and producing a product. These items are described at a particular level of granularity, intended to join to form recognizable composites of work. For example, the task of design includes gathering information, explaining and sharing, discussing various ideas to come to agreement, and planning and producing a product. Tutoring involves explaining and sharing information. Decision making is gathering information and discussing to come to agreement.

Dependencies Among Team Members. Different tasks are variously decomposable, allowing the groups to work easily in parallel (divide and conquer) or tightly integrated. The dimension of "dependencies" is intended to reflect this aspect (see Malone & Crowston, 1994, for a more extensive discussion of the dependencies that are managed in coordinated activities). When groups have to merely collect resources on a topic, the task is *loosely coupled.* The group can work in parallel finding material, and only at the end coordinate it so that duplicate finds are eliminated. On the other hand, people who are designing the components under the hood of a car have to be *tightly coupled.* They have to be concerned with designing something that will impact something else, such as changing the size of the engine block so that the path of the air conditioning hose has to change. Groups performing a jazz piece are *tightly coupled,* as their actions have to be integrated actions moment by moment to produce a whole.

Mental Resources Necessary to Do the Task. These can be viewed in terms of number of constraints and familiarity. Work varies in difficulty, both with the inherent resources necessary and with how familiar this problem is. Building software in a team for the 5ESS switch at AT&T has many more constraints and interactions among components and individuals than jointly building, with a coauthor, a graphic to illustrate a point in a paper. Similarly, developing the nth spreadsheet model for calculating household taxes is more familiar to a tax analyst than the first was. These variables, contributing in some sense to overcomplexity of the task, interact with the processes in the next category, the duration, scope, and time pressure. For example, a task may be short but repetitive, engendering an eventual degree of familiarity.

Duration and Scope. The duration of the task has implications for many of the other variables here. Short-term tasks are often much less complicated than longer term, and often involve a fixed set of players. Longer term projects often are more mixed and difficult, involve people with varying amounts of knowledge about each other (but the potential of knowing others very well), and produce management and motivational challenges that short-term tasks do not. Time pressure puts additional burden on the ability of the group to coordinate their work, to be aware of each other and of their progress, and to be able to plan the next steps. Personalities often are exaggerated in this situation, making some of the personal and interpersonal dynamics different than in other, less stressful situations.

Measures of Group Process

To make sense of the effects of the many factors we have described so far it is necessary to be clear about what aspect of group performance is affected. Our descriptive measures, dependent variables, are divided into those dealing with the process in which the group engages, and those dealing with the outcome. We consider task process, communication process, and interpersonal process and roles.

Task Process. The factors here are depth and breadth of analysis, time spent in various activities, structure of the conduct of the work (serial, parallel), and efficiency. A number of the papers in this book use measures of the group's process. Some are time based (Olson, Olson, & Meader, chapter 8, this volume) and track the time spent in various kinds of activities, also showing the transitions among those activities over time. Other measures are content based (e.g., Olson, Olson, Storrøsten, & Carter, 1993), where the ideas generated are diagrammed along with the argumentation surrounding the ideas' adoption. In longer term projects, it is perfectly reasonable to track the global aspects of how the work was done, whether in meetings or in individual work modes. The Anderson et al. chapter, this volume (chapter 7), calculates efficiency as the time to reach a particular state or the number of ideas or utterances per unit time.

Communication Process. This process entails clarification, pattern of the management of discussion (turn-taking), nonverbal communication, and digressions and socializing. Closely related are details of the communication patterns in group work. Anderson et al. and Olson, Olson, and Meader (chapters 7 and 8 in this book), for example, code activity surrounding people's clarification of their ideas, responses to questions, etc. Clearly, this is an important potential measure of the clarity of the video/audio channel. Similarly, several people (Sellen, 1995; Boyle, Anderson, & Newlands, 1994; Anderson et al., chapter 7, this volume) claim that a good measure of the efficacy of the video channel is how the conversation is managed, how easily people take their turns in conversation, and how many interruptions happen. Bekker (1995) catalogued the various kinds of gestures people use to communicate complicated ideas, which are likely to vary as people either lose the video channel or find they cannot convey things effectively that way because of a too small video window. Others report the use of posture and larger bodily gestures in service of conveying attitude, attention, and intent to speak.

Interpersonal Process, Roles. Relevant features are conflict and cooperation, affect, and participation. Early coding schemes such as Interaction Process Analysis (Bales, 1950) emphasize the mood or *affect* of the interaction, whether the interactions reflect *conflict* or *cooperation,* and whether comments are pleasant or hostile. People will also vary their participation with their perceived value or difficulty in the communication modes. One more specific form of participation is the role that a person will play in an encounter, such as meeting manager, devil's advocate, or idea generator. These are likely to be important measures of how video technologies impact remote group work. One can imagine, in particular, that if the communication channels are heterogeneous (e.g., one person is on a speakerphone and all others have high-bandwidth video), participation will vary and may change the affect of the meeting.

Measures of Outcome

Task Outcomes. Often the easiest measure of the group's success is to score the product *quality* against some criteria. This could include percent of a target goal the team finished, or how many defects reside in the product, e.g., in software production. Some lab tests include tasks that have right answers; others have to be judged by a panel of experts or evaluators. Some tasks lend themselves to easy counts (e.g., brainstorming number of ideas), and others are more difficult (e.g., quality or creativity of a design solution). But one can also look at more global features such as the total amount of *time* the group took to finish and the *cost.* These last two are the features commonly included in assessment of productivity.

Group Outcomes. Sometimes it is as important to know how well participants know and buy into the final decision or product as it is to assess the product's inherent quality. The work that individuals engage in after a meeting can either succeed or fail, depending on this *buy-in* and *understanding.* One can also assess the *satisfactions* people have with the process and product. A simple measure of satisfaction with the process is the frequency with which a particular communication channel is used. This choice is driven in part by a group member's satisfaction and in part by the support the channel and tools offer to the important aspects of the task.

Organizational Outcomes. We especially want to stress the organizational outcomes, including learning (individual knowledge and skill acquisition), willingness to work with members of the group again, group member loyalty and retention, changes or reinforcement of work norms, and individual status changes. Organizational outcomes are long term and can be more difficult to assess, but are nonetheless very important. Changing the organization's knowledge base or skill set or decreasing employee turnover may be much more important to the organization than affecting the quality of a particular task outcome. Members of the group may either refuse to work with a group member again or seek that member out, given the experience in this group. Some technologies may change the work norms. For example, in some technologies it is easy for managers to monitor the work of group members, engendering changes in trust and willingness to share. On the other hand, some people may end up being rewarded for their participation, where they were reluctant or unable to make their ideas known in other kinds of communication situations. In order to fully understand the role of VMC, these kinds of longer term, more difficult to measure outcomes need to be examined as well.

We would also like to encourage multimeasure studies of VMC, particularly with a focus on both process and outcome. Process analysis is usually more difficult than just measuring outcomes, but it is only through process analysis that we can learn why outcomes were affected in the way they were. This is especially critical in field studies where experimental manipulations are usually not possible.

MAKING USE OF THIS FRAMEWORK

The value of this framework can be illustrated by applying it to the set of papers in this book. There are four major benefits to using the framework in terms of the ability to:

1. Cluster findings into similar sets, having to do either with the type of group, their task, or the details of the technology employed.
2. Point to situations (group types, tasks, technologies) that have been undertested in empirical work. By filling in the table of empirical research relevant to feature or combination of features, one finds holes. These holes indicate areas of needed research, and in some cases even potentially fruitful applications to be built.
3. Focus on areas where researchers have found apparently contradictory results. By looking at the full set of variables in the framework, it is possible to find explanations.
4. Where findings are stable and clearly comparable, begin to build a theory.

Clustering the Findings

The empirical work on this book clusters into three major categories. A number of papers explore the value of video in communicating during focused, real-time, cooperative work. Anderson et al., Olson et al., Rudman et al., Sellen and Harper, and the review by Whittaker and O'Conaill (chapters 7, 8, 10, 11, and 2, respectively) focus on this situation, comparing work with various communication technologies to face-to-face work. The collection of papers reports not only process and outcome measures, but also interviews of people about the higher level organizational factors that impact the frequency with which these technologies are chosen.

A second cluster explores the value of "media spaces" where video is used both to converse and to support general awareness of the activities and whereabouts of people. Isaacs and Tang, Harrison et al., Heath et al., Isaacs et al., and the review by Kraut and Fish (chapters 9, 13, 15, 22, and 25, respectively) emphasize this aspect of cooperative work. Interestingly, these studies derive their conclusions from field studies, looking both at people's perceptions of the value of these technologies and at the frequency with which they choose these over other methods of communicating.

A third cluster has only a single exemplar in this book. This is the use of video for showing the *object* of work, not the participants. This is the work by Nardi et al. (chapter 23), in the neurosurgery application. Here, video supports coordination of team work by showing all the group participants (and some remote people, both experts and novices) the flow of work, work that would normally, without technology, be visible only to the surgeon. Although this is the only paper of its kind in this book, others have illustrated the use of video in real-time work for showing the object of the work, for example, for remote tutoring about a mechanical process (e.g., Ishii & Miyake, 1991).

Undertested Situations in Need of Future Work

Most of the empirical work focuses on groups that know each other and are cooperating while performing shared tasks. There is need for research about groups who are contentious, who have to negotiate as opposed to create a communal object, or whose memebers differ in status or power. Many people experiencing videoconferencing ask about the effect of working with people who do not know or trust each other. They also ask about the common situation in which some participants in a multipoint conference have less bandwidth than the others. And, although we have collected both process and outcome measures of group work under a variety of technologies, we have not yet measured some of the anticipated longer term effects, like willingness to work with others again or organizational learning.

Unraveling Apparently Contradictory Results

One important benefit of having a list of important situational descriptors is to help disambiguate apparently contradictory results. Potential for this benefit is revealed in two papers in this book. The review by Whittaker and O'Conaill (chapter 2) and the paper by Anderson et al. (chapter 7) report mixed results of the value of video on the conduct of turn-taking. In some cases, face-to-face work is characterized by more interruptions than video or audio remote work, in some cases less. By examining the list of features in the framework with respect to these studies, two potential explanatory sources arise.

The video technology used in the studies does not match exactly. In some cases, the video is large-screen videoconferencing with delays, and in other cases the video consists of video tunnels that preserve eye contact but are "in a box" and not large. These two technologies differ in the strength and timing of peripheral cues offered to the participants, known to affect turn-taking.

The second source of conflict centers on the dependent variables: the ways in which these studies measure the concepts *turn-taking* and *interruptions*. Interruptions can arise from several sources. Interruptions can occur when participants are "in sync." They finish each other's sentences or indicate through interruption that they understand and that the other person need not continue. The other kind of interruption comes from the awkward pauses that arise from communication channel delays. The original speaker pauses but, hearing no uptake of the turn from the other, begins to speak again. Perhaps the results from these studies could be disambiguated by sorting out their use of the term *interruptions*.

Building a Theory

The good news is that some of the empirical studies are finding common results. For example, there is a growing body of research confirming that when people who know each other are cooperating in a complex task, video does not seem to add much over audio to the quality of the end product. If there are any delays to the audio, quality suffers. All remote work, no matter how high the bandwidth and how small the delay, still makes people behave differently. They often either explain more or need to clarify their ideas to their remote group members. But clearly, throughout these studies, people prefer video connectivity over audio only.

These results form some of the basic links between important factors in this framework, building essential facts for theory. Although we are nowhere near understanding all the interactions among these variables, for all the kinds of groups, technologies, tasks, and situations, we are at least beginning to find consistency. Theories are on the horizon.

ACKNOWLEDGMENTS

This work was supported in part by grant IRI 9320543 from the National Science Foundation, and by grants from the Intel Corporation's Natural Data Types Research Council and the AT & T Foundation.

REFERENCES

Bales, R. F. (1950). *Interaction Process Analysis: A method for the study of small groups.* Cambridge, MA: Addison-Wesley.

Bekker, M. M. (1995). *An analysis of user interface design practice: Towards support for team communication.* Doctoral dissertation, Delft Technical University. Delft: The Netherlands.

Boyle, E. A., Anderson, A. H., & Newlands, A. (1994). The effects of eye contact on dialogue and performance in a co-operative problem solving task. *Language and Speech, 37*(1), 1–20.

Clark, H. H., & Brennan, S. E. (1991). Grounding in communication. In L. Resnick, J. M. Levine, & S. D. Teasley (Eds.), *Perspectives on socially shared cognition* (pp. 127–149). Washington, DC: APA.

Dourish, P., & Bellotti, V. (1992). Awareness and coordination in shared workspaces. *Proceedings of the Conference on Computer Supported Cooperative Work* (pp. 107–114). New York: ACM.

Forsyth, D. R. (1990). *Group dynamics* (2nd ed.). Pacific Grove, CA: Brooks/Cole.

Fussel, S. R., & Benimoff, N. I. (1995). Social and cognitive processes in interpersonal communication: Implications for advanced telecommunications technologies. *Human Factors, 37*(2), 228–250.

Gabarro, J. J. (1990). The development of working relationships. In J. Galegher, R. E. Kraut, & C. Egido (Eds.), *Intellectual teamwork* (pp. 79–110). Hillsdale, NJ: Lawrence Erlbaum Associates.

Hackman, J. R. (1987). The design of work teams. In J. W. Lorsch (Ed.), *Handbook of organizational behavior* (pp. 315–342). Englewood Cliffs, NJ: Prentice Hall.

Hackman, J. R., & Morris, C. G. (1975). Group tasks, group interaction process, and group performance effectiveness: A review and proposed integration. In L. Berkowitz (Ed.), *Advances in experimental social psychology.* (Vol. 8, pp. 47–99). New York: Academic Press.

Hall, E. T. (1966). *The hidden dimension.* New York: Anchor Books.

Ishii, H., & Miyake, N. (1991). Toward an open shared workspace: Computer and video fusion approach to TeamWorkStation. *Communications of the ACM, 34*(12), 37–50.

Kraemer, K. L., & Pinsonneault, A. (1990). Technology and groups: Assessments of empirical research. In J. Galegher, R., Kraut, & C. Egido (Eds.), *Intellectual teamwork.: Social and technological foundations of cooperative work* (pp. 375–405). Hillsdale, NJ: Lawrence Erlbaum Associates.

Malone, T. W., & Crowston, K. (1994). The interdisciplinary study of coordination. *Computing Surveys, 26*, 87–119.

McGrath, J. E. (1984). *Groups: Interaction and performance.* Englewood Cliffs, NJ: Prentice Hall.

Morgan, B. B., Jr., & Lassiter, D. L. (1992). Team composition and staffing. In R. W. Swezey & E. Salas (Eds.), *Teams, their training and performance* (pp. 75–100). Norwood, NJ: Ablex.

Neuwirth, C. M., Kaufer, D. S., Chandhok, R., & Morris, J. H. (1990). Issues in the design of computer support for co-authoring and commenting. *Proceedings of CSCW'90 Conference on Collaborative Work* (pp. 183–195). New York: ACM.

O'Hara-Devereaux, M., & Johansen, R. (1994). *Global work: Bridging distance, culture and time.* San Francisco: Jossey-Bass.

Olson, G.M., McGuffin, L.S., Kuwana, E., & Olson, J. S. (1993). Designing software for a group's needs: A functional analysis of synchronous groupware. In L. Bass & P. Dewan (Eds.), *User interface software* (pp. 129–148). New York: Wiley.

Olson, J. S., Olson, G. M., Storrøsten, M., & Carter, M. (1993). Group work close up: A comparison of the group design process with and without a simple group editor. *ACM: Transactions on Information Systems, 11*, 321–348.

Orlikowski, W. J. (1992). Learning from Notes: Organizational issues in groupware implementation. *Proceedings of the Conference on Computer Supported Cooperative Work* (pp. 362–369). New York: ACM.

Sellen, A. J. (1995). Remote conversations: The effects of mediating talk with technology. *Human Computer Interaction, 10,* 401–444.

Shaw, M. E. (1981). *Group dynamics, The psychology of small group behavior.* New York: McGraw-Hill.

Stefik, M., Foster, G., Bobrow, D., Kahn, K., Lanning, S., & Suchman, L. (1987). Beyond the chalkboard: Computer support for collaboration and problem solving in meetings. *Communications of the ACM, 30,* 32–47.

Steiner, I. D. (1972). *Group process and productivity.* New York: Academic Press.

Steiner, I. D. (1976). Task performing groups. In J. W., Thibaut, J. T. Spence, & R. C. Carson (Eds.), *Contemporary topics in social psychology* (pp. 393–422). Morristown, NJ: General Learning Press.

Tang, J., Isaacs, E., & Rua, M. (1994). Supporting distributed groups with a Montage of lightweight interactions. *Proceedings of Conference in Computer Supported Cooperative Work* (pp. 23–34). New York: ACM.

Teasley, S., Olson, J. S., & Meader, D. (1994). *Toward the task/technology fit for group work: An analysis of task characteristics.* Unpublished manuscript, CREW, University of Michigan.

FINDINGS

Chapter 5

Assessing Video-Mediated Conduct: A Discussion of Different Analytic Approaches

Abigail Sellen
Rank Xerox Research Centre (EuroPARC)

In this introduction to the 10 chapters in Part II, a practical categorization of their various analytic approaches is offered. The different disciplines, analytic orientations, and methodologies that arise within this framework are discussed. One goal is to discuss the strengths and weaknesses of each approach; another is to point out the underlying assumptions behind a range of approaches in order to help in interpreting the findings.

INTRODUCTION

Even those of us who are well acquainted with the literature on video-mediated communication (VMC) can sometimes feel overwhelmed by it. As the chapters in Part I attest, one reason for this is that the research has tended not to follow a well-defined path. Although researchers themselves may be systematic about their own work, there seems to be little systematicity or cohesion across VMC studies, resulting in a body of work that is unusually diverse. One consequence of this is that each set of findings needs to be carefully considered within the context of the specific methods used and measures taken, as well as the particulars of the tasks, systems, and people being studied. For this reason, the chapters in Part I are important in that they try to impose some structure on to the now substantial body of research, attempt to make sense of the findings by introducing common vocabulary, and help to explain the technical aspects and terms that permeate the literature.

By way of introduction to the 10 chapters in Part II, which concentrate on findings, I offer another framework within which to categorize and interpret the results, this time based on what I call *analytic approach*. Here I use the term as a general way of referring to the range of disciplines, methods, and analytic orientations used in the research. Analytic approach is tied to, and to some extent determines, all of those other research dimensions discussed in Part I: the kinds of questions being asked, the kinds of measures selected, and the kinds of systems, work settings, and people that are the focus of study. But as analytic approach often reflects a deep-seated commitment to an orientation within a particular discipline, it can go much further than this. It can show itself in what the researchers consider to be the true object of inquiry, from the mechanics of behavior to the social world. It can show itself in methodology—for example, some researchers construct the situations in which the data are to be collected, whereas others immerse themselves in naturally constructed situations. It can show itself in how the data are interpreted: as a set of cause-and-effect relationships among variables, as events that unfold and have meaning over time, or as events that find their place within the social order of behavior.

Before expanding on these issues with reference to specific chapters, it is perhaps useful to start with a practical categorization. I say practical categorization because it is difficult to impose any clear-cut taxonomy on what follows: Many of the chapters are interdisciplinary, most employ a variety of methods, and several describe extensive programs of research. However, it is possible to cluster the chapters together by considering some of their underlying commonalities and differences, and then to use this as a framework for discussion.

Chapters 6, 7, and 8 might be called *experimental studies* in that they rely on the application of what is often called the "scientific method" to the study of VMC. Although not limited to the laboratory, they aim for the kind of control usually found only under laboratory conditions, and adopt a reductionist, psychological orientation in doing so. Chapters 9, 10, and 11, which I call *field studies*, put the emphasis on use of technology in real-world contexts. Having said that, one might still call these studies experimental, and indeed the main disciplinary influence in these chapters is psychological; however, they tend to be concerned with the impact of technology over time, rather than across controlled conditions. One other characteristic of chapters 9–11 is that they assess the impact of video on users who have no vested interest in developing or testing the technology. This is quite unlike the next three chapters, 12 through 14, which represent what I call the *living with technology* approach. These chapters represent three different laboratories known for their research on media space technologies: Rank Xerox's Cambridge laboratory and its RAVE system, Xerox PARC's media space, and the Ontario Telepresence Project at the University of Toronto. Although each laboratory has conducted a range of empirical studies, each has also studied those technologies to a large extent through their own long term experiences of use. Finally, chapter 15 represents an amalgam of all of these, combining and reporting on the results of psychological and ethnographic studies in both laboratory and sociologically informed field settings.

In outlining these different classes of studies, one is, I believe, justified in generalizing these observations to the VMC literature at large. The collection in Part II is very much representative of the techniques and approaches that exist more broadly. I next comment further on the disciplinary background, analytic orientations, and methodologies that arise within each of the categories just outlined.

CHAPTERS 6, 7, AND 8: EXPERIMENTAL STUDIES

The experimental approach to the study of VMC seems to follow naturally from the kinds of questions often asked about video systems: What is the advantage of a videophone over a telephone? Can a video system replace face-to-face meetings? Implicit in these sorts of questions is an assumption that adding a visual information channel to an audio channel somehow brings remote participants closer to a face-to-face, copresent conversational context. In other words, video systems are conceptualized as lying somewhere in between audio and face-to-face meetings along an information bandwidth continuum. In order to build on this underlying model, one natural course of action is to perform direct comparisons of audio, video, and face-to-face conditions in order to map out the differences in conversational conduct between them. As such, audio-only and face-to-face meeting situations often form the baselines against which various video systems are compared.

The experimental approach offers a systematic way in which one might make such comparisons. It is a psychologically based, reductionist approach that tries to map out a set of cause-and-effect relationships between experimentally isolated aspects of communicational contexts and the behavior these contexts engender. One of the goals of this approach is to define the function of visual information in terms of a mechanistic model of communication, as is well illustrated by Whittaker and O'Conaill in chapter 2. From a practical perspective, one might then hope to be able to specify which aspects of video system design might be important for supporting particular kinds of behavior.

Central to this approach is an inevitable trade-off between experimental control and realism. If too many factors differ across conditions, one may be at a loss as to what to attribute any observed differences in behavior.

Too many systematic variations across conditions confound interpretation of cause–effect relationships and muddy the waters of analysis. On the other hand, tasks and systems that are too contrived may yield results with no relevance to real-world systems and real work; people who are brought together only for the purpose of a short-term experiment may fail to exhibit characteristic behaviors of real working groups.

The three experimental chapters in this section attain this balance in different ways. The chapter by Anderson et al. maintains the firmest grasp on experimental control, using subjects, tasks, and systems (with one exception) all carefully designed with the aims of the experiment in mind. However, the authors are well aware of the importance of choosing tasks with realistic properties. Similarly, Olson et al. choose their experimental procedures with an eye to realism within the confines of a laboratory setting, using well-established tasks and tools. O'Conaill and Whittaker venture out of the laboratory, observing real systems in use in meetings by real working groups. They maintain control not so much by imposing it, but rather by carefully selecting which groups and systems to observe. They are the first to admit, however, that because of this it is sometimes difficult to draw conclusions about which variables may be held responsible for which observed effects.

Another characteristic of these experimental studies is their emphasis on operational definitions of behavior. Broadly, the measures of interest in VMC research of this kind can be divided into two kinds of "objective" measures of behavior: measures of task outcome and measures of communicative process. Typically such studies often also gather what they call "subjective" data, or, people's perceptions and opinions collected through questionnaires, rating scales, and interviews.

Anderson et al. (chapter 7) and Olson et al. (chapter 8) make use of all three kinds of measures, whereas O'Conaill and Whittaker (chapter 6) concentrate on the structural properties of conversational process for their objective measures, supplemented by interview data for their subjective assessment. Measuring aspects of communicative process, in particular, can be extremely labor-intensive. But as Anderson and colleagues observe, it is sometimes important to collect both outcome and process measures, as they can illuminate different aspects of the same phenomena.

Objective and subjective measures can also tell very different stories in the same situation. The three experimental chapters in this section (as well as chapter 9 by Isaacs and Tang) indicate that subjects' comments, as revealed through interviews and questionnaires, often paint a more complex picture of the benefits and drawbacks of visual access than objective speech measures would suggest. Sometimes these measures serve to strengthen and confirm the objective findings, but at other times they reveal differences across conditions where objective measures do not. In all three of the experimental chapters in this section, subjects express strong preferences for video systems over audio systems, and for good-quality video systems over poor-quality systems. Further, they often articulate reasons that receive no support in the objective data. This suggests either that the objective measures are not adequately capturing the relevant phenomena, or that subjects' perceptions are not manifested in, or derived from, any outward measurable behavior. Whatever the case, it tends to cast doubt on the efficacy with which these kinds of operationally defined, objective measures offer a comprehensive assessment of the impact of video within an experimental context.

In addition to difficulties in choosing appropriate measures of behavior, there are also problems in knowing how to interpret differences in these kinds of objective measures across conditions. The measurement of interruptions serves as a good example. Although frequent interruptions in conversation might be taken a priori to be an indication of difficulties in turn-taking or speaker coordination, as the chapters by O'Conaill and Whittaker and Anderson et al. help to illustrate, frequent interruptions can also be interpreted as an indication of a highly interactive and informal conversation. In other words, frequent interruptions can be seen as a feature of a good conversation rather than as a bad one.

Despite these various problems with the experimental approach, operationalization does offer a basis on which we can compare results across studies. The fact that this kind of comparison is difficult is largely a function of the multivariate nature of the research and the apparent sensitivity of such measures to small differences in experimental context. As we struggle to resolve inconsistencies and arrive at models that fit the data, we can be somewhat assured that if the experimental approach does reveal some consistent findings across studies, then those findings are very likely both robust and generalizable. Simple bandwidth models of communication (or models that attempt to "count up" the number of variables available for communication) do not yet provide the interpretive or predictive framework we need. I am, however, optimistic that such models are on the horizon and that the experimental approach will be largely responsible for their development.

CHAPTERS 9, 10, AND 11: FIELD STUDIES

Laboratory-based experimental studies aim to produce theoretically based predictions for the impact of video on conversation and collaborative work. Another approach is to study the impact of video in situ. Because each organizational context is unique, one could argue that findings from in situ studies are difficult to generalize: Any set of findings from one organization may not hold true in another. On the other hand, many would

argue that it is just these unique properties of real organizations that matter
when assessing the impact of video on work—that the group dynamics,
political hierarchies, work practices, and social order of work settings are
what really matter when considering whether technological systems will
find their place in the real world. Likewise, short-term laboratory studies
ignore issues of adaptation to and adoption of technology. Thus long-term
studies of use are needed, and these are always difficult to carry out in
laboratory environments.

The chapters by Isaacs and Tang (chapter 9) and by Rudman and
colleagues (chapter 10) describe studies that reach a compromise between
experimental and field research in that they are sympathetic to the point
of view just presented, without wishing to sacrifice some of the benefits of
experimental control. To this extent these two sets of field studies rely
heavily on psychological methods. This holds true both for the design of
the studies and for the ways in which the data are collected and analyzed.

This view of a workplace as a "living laboratory" is typified by Isaacs and
Tang. In chapter 9 they report on a series of studies in which patterns of
behavior are measured and analyzed both with and without the technology
of interest. This technique of observing the same group of "subjects" over
time and under different conditions is very similar to what one might choose
to do in the laboratory. Likewise, Rudman et al., in their studies of graduate
student teams, impose a series of different technological "conditions" on the
same groups to examine how they impact behavior across time.

Psychological methods also show themselves by the kinds of measures
that are employed in these two sets of studies. Isaacs and Tang make use
of quantitative measures of system use as well as measures of other aspects
of collaborative activity such as frequency of phone calls, face-to-face meetings, and so on. Other attempts at gathering quantitative data in this
chapter and in that of Rudman et al. include the use of rating scales and
questionnaires. Such methods, theoretically, are replicable because they
are operationalized.

Chapter 11, by Sellen and Harper, exhibits some methodological simi-
larities with the other two chapters in placing the emphasis on observing
system use over time in a nonexperimental work context, and in using a
mix of quantitative and qualitative analytic techniques. However, the orientation of this chapter is more clearly ethnographic rather than psychological. Such ethnographic undertones can also be found in both the Isaacs
and Tang and the Rudman et al. chapters in the degree to which the
investigators rely on interviews and observations, and more generally in
the way in which they attempt to gain an understanding of the people
they are studying. Rudman et al. cast out a particularly wide net in doing
this, observing and interviewing people from 20 different organizations.
Sellen and Harper focus only on one group in one organization, but

observation of this group takes place over a long period of time in order to discover the salient properties of the social world, which tend to reveal themselves only by long-term observation of a work setting.

As one might expect, the result of studying the impact of video systems in the field reveals new insights. Isaacs and Tang discuss ways in which their systems find their place within the context of other work activities. They also make observations such as the extent to which people are concerned with privacy issues a priori, but then fail to take advantage of features to protect their privacy in the course of actual system use. Rudman et al. describe how organizational goals, economic factors, and logistical constraints impact on system use. For example, they describe the ways in which people appropriate and adapt the technology at hand to suit their needs, often changing their tasks in order to exploit the resources they have available. Sellen and Harper discuss how video systems are important in showing presence in the face of fluctuating group membership, how they allow working groups to break off into fractionated discussions, and how groups choose technological systems depending on the kind of work they wish to accomplish. All of these observations would not emerge in the natural course of laboratory work.

As these three chapters show, the creativity and flexibility that working groups exhibit in using the technology they are given offer some fascinating insights into technology and work practice. However, the very fact that people are so adaptable may work against developing design innovations, because they may often be willing to "make do" with what they have. If the people using the technology have no vested interest in developing it, unless pressed, they may have little to say about what else they need, what changes they would like to see, and what form future systems should take. Thus although one can make a good argument for evaluating new systems in use with relatively disinterested parties, one can also make an argument for developers and designers having a closer working relationship with their own systems, which brings us to the next three chapters.

CHAPTERS 12, 13, AND 14:
LIVING WITH TECHNOLOGY

Chapters 12, 13, and 14 are characterized by very-long-term experiences of use where the designers and developers of media space technologies attempt to live and work with their own technology. These sorts of "living experiments," to quote Bellotti and Dourish, can lay claim to many of the benefits already outlined in relation to field studies in general: in providing a real context in which to study the use of systems for diverse purposes over a long period of time. Indeed all three of the chapters here represent extensive media space projects lasting anywhere from 3 to 10 years.

One of the main contributions of such studies is in offering an analysis of the ways in which system design changes over time as its users adapt the technology to suit their needs. Similarly, the behavior of the users themselves changes through the course of living with the technology. Thus, users and technology can be seen to co-evolve, and this process is one in which its users can have direct influence, as the designers and developers of the system. This is one theme that chapter 12 by Bellotti and Dourish is helpful in elucidating.

Another feature of this kind of work is an emphasis on the flexibility of the design of media space technology, and how it differs from the conception of video systems as face-to-face videophones. Media spaces are different from the videophone model in that they provide a range of functionality, are ubiquitous, and have a persistent presence. As all three chapters illustrate, media spaces can be used for much more than point-to-point connections. The utility of services that support background awareness, for example, extends our notions of what video can be used for and offers good evidence for the range of ways in which video, audio, and computing systems can be creatively configured. Further, chapter 13 by Harrison et al. points out the importance of media spaces as malleable, flexible systems that can be appropriated and modified by the communities they support.

So one of the benefits of living with the technology one is also developing is that this allows the opportunity for a system to naturally evolve. Engagement between users and designers is ensured. As such, its users are more likely to be on the lookout for design opportunities, and are more likely to be tolerant of bugs and breakdowns. One can contrast this with putting technology into field settings outside one's own domain where, as Moore points out in chapter 14, one walks a fine line between providing a robust prototype and a prototype that is not yet fixed in its design. In researching field settings outside one's own research laboratory, as any field worker knows, it is of utmost importance not to get in the way of the work. Systems that fail or that represent too much of an imposition on the natural course of work may upset the delicate relationship between field worker and field site. There are many other kinds of practical obstacles that one must overcome when attempting to deploy technology outside the realm of one's own research environment, as Moore's chapter well illustrates.

Another benefit of this approach is the richness of the data that one has available. Partly this has to do with the length of time at one's disposal, but partly it is because of the depth of one's own understanding of the work context. The impact of technology can be assessed and confronted within one's own experience and thus within the extensive grounding one already has of the setting in which the technology is embedded. Another advantage over field studies outside of one's own workplace is that there is no need to be preselective about which group, which set of activities, and which aspect of system use one chooses to study. Observations within one's own workplace can be largely serendipitous; design modifications can be opportunistic and involve very little overhead and investment.

But it is also instructive to ask whether this kind of approach has any inherent drawbacks. One issue characteristic of many papers of this sort is that the chapters tend not to reflect or rely on any one particular analytic orientation. In itself this need not be problematic, yet many of the studies that rely on anecdotal evidence tend not to be accompanied by the ethnographic analysis one might hope to see, and thus seem stripped of the organizational context within which to interpret the anecdotes. One has the sense that the authors sometimes withhold comment on the social world within which the technology is placed. There may be good reasons for doing this. Research laboratories often consist of communities within communities, each supporting different technologies. For this reason, as a member of the development team for a given technology, one may be under some (implicit) pressure to show support for one's "own" technology. Further, it may often be more politic not to comment in detail on the social factors that impact on the use of technology in one's own place of work. Thus, just as a psychological orientation rules out introspective analysis because of the potential for distortion and bias, there may be significant sociological difficulties for a research community in attempting to be self-reflective and self-analytic.

A final point is that there may be problems in trying to generalize from research environments to other places of work. As Harper (1992) noted, research environments are, organizationally speaking, quite unlike most other places of work in that there is a disproportionately large amount of professional staff, with all the rights, autonomy, and aloofness from organizational constraint that goes with that status. This high concentration of knowledge workers likely has significant impact on the ways in which such communities use collaborative tools, media space systems included.

Unsurprisingly, this approach has its own set of advantages and disadvantages, but as the three chapters in this section illustrate, these long-term analyses of experiences of use provide important converging evidence for understanding the ways in which video can support a diverse range of interaction.

CHAPTER 15: A HYBRID APPROACH

Chapter 15 by Heath et al. cannot easily be classified into any of the preceding three categories. It reports on sociological and psychological studies, in both field and laboratory settings. Unlike the other studies in this section relying on ethnographic methods, the analytic orientation behind the field work draws on conversation analytic techniques, meaning that the emphasis is not on the impact of technology on the social world, but is rather focused on behavior at a more local level. This approach is concerned with such things as the sequential organization of behavior, how behavior draws meaning from its temporal context, and how people working together construct shared meaning within the developing course of interaction. Thus the essence of this approach is that it considers actions in their local context through very detailed analysis of videotaped interaction.

This technique is very different from any of the techniques used in the other chapters in Part II, and Heath and colleagues show how it can be broadly applied in analyzing video-mediated conduct. For example, they report on an analysis of Rank Xerox's media space system as well as the use of a Xerox Television link. They also show how this technique can be applied to a variety of collaborative work settings in places where no video systems per se are involved. The purpose of this is to shed more light on the interactive processes underlying collaborative work in general. An integrating theme, and one that leads into the experimental Multiple Target Video (MTV) studies, is that collaborative work requires much more than a face-to-face view. In addition to this view, collaborative work requires flexible access to the local environment of the other, to work-related artifacts, and to the relation of one's coparticipant to those activities and artifacts. The MTV experiments are designed to test out ways in which that flexible access might be provided.

This chapter provides one example of how interdisciplinary research can speak to the same issues in different ways. It also shows how very different analytic orientations and their accompanying methodologies can work toward informing the design of new kinds of video systems.

CONCLUSIONS

I have offered a practical categorization of the 10 chapters in Part II in order to provide a framework for discussion of the various analytic approaches that exist in the VMC literature. These approaches stem mainly from the disciplines of psychology, sociology, and anthropology, and as such most chapters adopt an experimental or ethnographic orientation, or a combination of both. Within this broader classification, one can see many different kinds of methodological techniques: experimental laboratory techniques, experimental measurement applied to field settings, ethnographic observation and interviews, and video analysis with conversation analytic leanings.

Approaches over such a range are often fundamentally philosophically different from one another. At one extreme, the research may aim to reduce phenomena to its behavioral elements and from there synthesize a model; at the other extreme it is essential that behavior is not stripped from its context as context confers meaning on action. Approaches also fundamentally differ according to the level of the phenomena of interest. On the one hand the research may focus on local behavioral phenomena, whether they be measurable behaviors across conditions or within a spatiotemporal context. On the other, the research may focus on the more global aspects of working life and the social world—on the organizational, work practice, and even moral aspects of behavior.

A final dimension along which these approaches differ, and one that is worth emphasizing, is in the sorts of assumptions made about what aspects of human interaction video is intended to support. Much of the experimental psychology work on VMC concentrates on video in support of conversation during focused group work (e.g., O'Conaill & Whittaker). The model for much of this experimental work is a face-to-face model, which is like the model underlying most commercial video systems. The support primarily of face-to-face talk may also incorporate work-related objects such as computer-based tools, paper and pencil, and whiteboards, especially for support of focused problem-solving activities (e.g., Olson et al., Anderson et al., Rudman et al.) and also decision-making activities (Sellen & Harper). The experimental work reported in the Heath et al. chapter attempts to extend beyond this face-to-face model for collaborative work by providing more than a face-to-face view, and emphasizes the importance of viewing data and artifacts, as does chapter 23 in Part IV by Nardi et al. However, these chapters still concentrate on the support of groups deliberately brought together for the purpose of focused work. In contrast, in testing their Montage and Forum prototypes, Isaacs and Tang begin to experimentally explore other kinds of interaction one might wish to support with video, including the mechanisms involved in making contact with others in an organizational environment, and ways in which one might support presentations to large audiences. The three "media space" chapters go furthest in exploring a whole range of ways in which video might be used for various types of interaction from the support of informal, background awareness of others, moving into more engaged, focused collaborations.

So what are the practical implications of all of this? What does the research have to say about how we can best configure technology to support different kinds of work at a distance? As this chapter has outlined, different analytic orientations have their own strengths and weaknesses, and can provide help in guiding and evaluating the design of video systems in complementary ways. But as we can also see, assumptions about what kinds of interaction video is intended to support are often made before the research is begun, and this also needs to be taken into account in interpreting the findings. As researchers, we can help by making these assumptions explicit. Perhaps this will be helpful not only for practitioners, but also for other researchers seeking to make links across studies and seeking to facilitate more systematic, cohesive research.

REFERENCE

Harper, R. H. R. (1992). Looking at ourselves: An examination of the social organisation of two research laboratories. *Proceedings of CSCW '92* (pp. 330–337). New York: ACM Press.

Chapter 6

Characterizing, Predicting, and Measuring Video-Mediated Communication: A Conversational Approach

Brid O'Conaill
Hewlett Packard Laboratories Bristol, UK

Steve Whittaker
ATT Labs Research

We present a method for comparing the spoken aspects of communication for meetings held in three different communication settings: (a) low-quality video-mediated communication (VMC); (b) high-quality VMC; and (c) face-to-face meetings. Based on an analysis of the media characteristics of face-to-face communication, we derive a set of predictions about how the spoken characteristics of communication will differ in these two systems, as compared with face-to-face communication. As predicted, we found that adding video can detract from spoken conversation when networking bandwidths are limited. Contrary to our expectations, however, we found that even high-quality video does not replicate all properties of face-to-face communication, and we attempt to explain why.

INTRODUCTION

Many video communication technologies are premised on the hypothesis that adding a visual channel to audio-only technologies, such as the telephone, will improve communication and simulate many of the important properties of face-to-face communication. Thus, the added benefits of having the visual information afforded by gaze, gesture, and facial expressions will enrich the quality of the communication (Whittaker & O'Conaill, chapter 2, this volume). For organizations, the promise of increased remote collaboration through improved mediated communication is very attractive. It means they can increase the number of potential coworkers while

107

decreasing travel costs: Fewer employees need to journey to meet their distant colleagues because they can interact effectively with their colleagues using videoconference or videophone (Johansen, 1984). It is clear, however, that these promises have not been fulfilled (Egido, 1988, 1990; Noll, 1992). Why then have video technologies failed to be the commercial success that was forecast as far back as their first introduction in 1927? Two answers have been put forward: inadequate analysis of user needs (Johansen, 1984; Johansen & Bullen, 1984; Panko, 1992) and a failure to identify a strong task outcome benefit from the addition of a video channel (Chapanis, 1975; Reid, 1977; Short, Williams, & Christie, 1976; Williams, 1977). Here, we explore another possibility—that adding video can compromise basic communication processes. A number of key processes in face-to-face communication are heavily dependent on two-way interaction and involve very precise timing. Our hypothesis is that, in commercial systems where audio is buffered to synchronize with the video channel, concurrency and timing are disrupted. As a result, such systems may not support basic communication processes.

Unlike many laboratory prototype video systems, commercial systems are subject to bandwidth constraints in transmitting video data. Video data has to be compressed to travel over these commercial networks, and this introduces delays in communication. The time taken to compress, transmit, and decompress video data is greater than that for audio data alone. To provide synchronized video and audio, it is common practice to buffer the audio until the video image is processed, and this introduces delays. Additionally, in the case of conferencing systems, there is a need to prevent feedback from the audio stream being retransmitted from the destination side. To alleviate this problem, many systems are half-duplex—that is, the audio is transmitted from only one location at a given time. These channel properties are very different from the properties of face-to-face communication where the audio channel is both immediate and full duplex. In this chapter, we predict and test how these channel constraints in video-mediated systems make the spoken aspects of communication in such systems different from face-to-face communication.

Previous theoretical work has addressed the question of how mediated communication differs from face-to-face interaction. Prior attempts to characterize the differences have relied on notions such as *social presence* (Short et al., 1976), *cuelessness* (Rutter & Robinson, 1981), and *media richness* (Daft & Lengel, 1984). However, such terms are difficult to measure objectively and are open to interpretation. We wished to quantify differences in terms of measurable characteristics of speech processes that have independently been shown to be important in face-to-face interaction (see also Sellen, 1992, 1995). In understanding how these speech processes are affected in VMC, it should be possible to explain why video technologies have not succeeded and to suggest more limited applications for which they might be appropriate.

We compared the interaction in real meetings that took place in two wide-area videoconferencing systems with that in a face-to-face (FTF) setting. The first system (ISDN) is representative of currently available commercial video conferencing systems. It has half-duplex audio, transmission lags, and poor picture quality. The second (LiveNet) is a higher quality prototype system that is representative of future systems. It uses an analogue infrastructure with the properties of duplex audio, no transmission lags and full bandwidth video. All the meetings took place for work-related reasons and had been scheduled to take place regardless of the study. We describe the three conditions briefly, concentrating on the channel properties that may influence conversations over those systems. Further details of the systems can be found in O'Conaill, Whittaker, and Wilbur (1993). We then present some conversational features that are important to communication. For each of these features, we derive predictions about how they will differ in the two videoconferencing systems as a result of their different channel properties.

ISDN System (ISDN)

This system is located at Hewlett Packard Laboratories, Bristol, and the majority of the transmissions are to the United States. The available bandwidth after rate adaptation to the United States is 112 kbps (kilobits per second) of which 16 kbps is used for audio, 90 kbps for video transmission, and the remainder for communication between codecs. Due to compression and propagation delays, the lag between a person on one site speaking and the signal arriving at the other site can vary between 410 and 780 msec, depending on the propagation route. The audio channel is half-duplex, so the voice of only one person can be transmitted at any time. This is necessary to eliminate problems caused by echo or feedback when the sound from the loudspeaker is picked up by the microphone and retransmitted across the line. The conference room contains a table at which three people can sit comfortably. A 26-inch monitor displays the live picture of the remote location. If the user is looking at the monitor it appears at the remote location almost as though the user is looking into the camera. However, the distance and the video quality make eye gaze and head movements unclear.

LiveNet (LN)

LiveNet is the London Interactive Video Education Network, which is used for intercollegiate lectures, seminars, and meetings over distances of up to 42 km. LiveNet is an analog system with the sites connected by a pair of optical fibers each carrying four full-bandwidth video channels. The result is a full motion picture with none of the frozen picture motion that is associated with some digital video systems. As there is no video or audio processing, the time lag is simply the propagation time at the speed of light. Delays can therefore be measured in microseconds. The audio sub-system is full-duplex. The rooms used are typically lecture theaters or seminar rooms in which the participants sit at a table and face a set of four 20-inch monitors and a CCD camera. Where four or fewer sites are being connected, the sites are shown in full on the four monitors in front of the participants. If more sites wish to take part, a system called *chairman's control* is used. The sites are shown in a "picture in picture" format in quadrants on the monitors. The chairman of the session chooses and displays the active speaking site on a full monitor. The broadcast-quality video means that head movements are easily discernible.

Face-to-Face Meetings

The face-to-face meetings took place in the conference rooms available on site at Hewlett Packard Laboratories, Bristol. The room layouts were very similar to the one containing the ISDN system. Participants sat around tables approximately 6 feet long and 4 feet wide. Documents were shared by passing them around the table. An overhead projector was available but was not used in the meetings we observed.

PREDICTIONS

Our focus is on aspects of conversation concerned with speaker transitions, an issue that has been addressed extensively in the conversation analysis literature (Jefferson, 1987; Sacks, Schegloff, & Jefferson, 1974). However, our definitions of the techniques speakers and listeners use to transfer the floor are different from this literature. Our aim was to study both codable and replicable aspects of such transitions. The data were transcribed using a simplified version of the system developed by Jefferson (Atkinson & Heritage, 1984; Jefferson, 1987). We did not code the phonetic information such as prosodic turn-switching cues. Examples are shown using the transcription notation. The following extract shows some of the conventions in use and is followed by a glossary of the symbols.

```
A:    So it's it's moving to Italy ahm and ah we're not ah we I got a thing
B:    (bet they) get lost on the way (.) [(    )
A:                                       [we've got some market stuff which
      eh
```

B: Oh [yes
A: [Tim I [ga I gave to Timmy oh it's circulating is
      it yeah [it seemed it was=
B: [it's circulating
B: [(   )
A: =quite interesting ah

[A single left square bracket indicates the point of overlap

=   Equal signs at the end of one line and the beginning of the
           next indicate no gap between the two lines

(.)   A dot in parentheses indicates a tiny gap within or between
           utterances

( )   Empty parentheses indicate the transcriber's inability to hear
           what was said

(word)   Parenthesized words are especially dubious hearings

(( ))   Doubled parentheses contain transcribers' descriptions

From the descriptions of the two videoconferencing systems we can see
that their channel properties differ from the face-to-face condition. The
ISDN system introduces a transmission lag of between 410 and 780 msec.
for both audio and video, and a half-duplex (one-way) line for audio. In
addition, both the LN and ISDN systems allow only limited visual cues,
reducing the multimodal quality of the conversation. Both have relatively
fixed camera angles, and in ISDN the picture quality is poor and subject
to jitter and occasional frame loss. How might we expect these differences
to impact the nature of communication over the two systems? Table 6.1
summarizes our expected findings for a number of spoken conversational
characteristics. We now discuss how we arrived at these predictions.

Backchannels

Communication is a joint activity that requires coordination of both process
and content (Clark & Brennan, 1990; Clark & Wilkes-Gibbs, 1986; Whittaker, 1992). To allow this coordination to take place, conversation is both
incremental and interactive. The speaker delivers utterances incrementally,
and the listeners provide concurrent feedback that the conversation is on
track, by giving both short feedback utterances and visual feedback in the
form of head nods and eye gaze. This positive concurrent feedback is
called backchanneling and serves several functions including attention,
support, or acceptance of the speaker's message. For the purpose of this
study only auditory backchannels were measured and not head nods or
gaze behavior.

TABLE 6.1
Expected Characteristics Relative to Face-to-Face Interaction
for the Two Videoconferencing Technologies

	ISDN	*LN*
Backchannels	Fewer	Same
Interruptions	Fewer	Same
Overlaps	(?)	Same
Handovers	More	Same
Turn size	Larger	Same
Dominance	More	Same

In face-to-face interaction, backchannels are produced by the listeners concurrently with, or directly after, speaker input. However, in ISDN the audio channel is half-duplex, and there is a substantial transmission lag. This means that at the remote location the backchannel will not be concurrent with or directly follow the material it is intended to reinforce. This serves to reduce its communicative impact. More significantly, it may disrupt the speaker at the remote location by its late arrival. In addition, the half-duplex line means either (a) the backchannel is suppressed altogether, or (b) it takes the audio channel from the remote speaker, so that information generated at the remote location is not received locally. All these factors should lead to fewer backchannels in ISDN. In contrast, in the LN system the audio channel is full-duplex and transmission nearly instantaneous. This allows both concurrent and timely backchannels to be delivered. In LN, therefore, we expect backchannels to occur as frequently as in face-to-face interaction.

Interruptions

Interruptions are often associated with simultaneous speech. However, simultaneous speech can arise for a number of different reasons (Levinson, 1983). We distinguish between two different classes of simultaneous speech: (a) overlaps—those instances where there was a clearly identifiable reason why the next speaker should have broken into the current speaker's utterance, for example, where two speakers attempt to gain the floor simultaneously; and (b) interruptions—those instances of where there was no such reason for the next speaker to have broken into the current utterance. We begin by discussing interruptions. We defined interruptions as those instances of simultaneous speech where there is no indication by the first speaker that they are about to relinquish the conversational floor. As such, they are deliberate attempts to gain the conversational floor without the prior consent of the current speaker. Here is an FTF example of an interruption:

A: my worry would [be my worry would be that
B: [No I don't I don't I'm not saying this person has to
      have

The same predictions hold here as for backchannels. In ISDN, with half-duplex and transmission lags in audio, we should witness reduced attempts to interrupt the speaker. The half-duplex line means that either interruptions are highly disruptive, in that they take the channel and mask whatever the speaker is saying, or they are suppressed and never transmitted to the remote location. In addition, the transmission lag may mean that by the time the interruption arrives at the remote location, the speaker has already gone beyond the relevant material. This can lead to further disruptions, for example, if the interruption deletes material that then has to be repeated, and turn-taking reestablished. In contrast, we expect that in LN, with full-duplex audio and almost zero lag, the interruptions will be much easier to achieve successfully. They can be delivered in overlap with the speaker, and the absence of lag means that the conversation has not moved on by the time they are transmitted. We therefore predict an equivalent number of interruptions in LN as in FTF.

Overlaps

Overlaps are instances of simultaneous speech that follow a signal the speaker gives indicating that the speaker intends to relinquish the conversational floor (Levinson, 1983). We made predictions for three different types of overlaps: projection/completions, floorholding, and simultaneous starts.

Projection/Completion. This type of overlap occurs when the next speaker anticipates that the current speaker is about to finish, or tries to help the "forward movement" of an ongoing utterance (Clark & Wilkes-Gibbs, 1986, Clark & Schaefer, 1989). In predicting the possible finish by the current speaker, the next speaker may recognize that the message of the current speaker is semantically complete, although the speaker may continue. The next speaker may then begin to speak over the redundant part of the original speaker's message. Overlaps may also occur when the next speaker attempts to complete an utterance, for example, when the current speaker is having some difficulty in completing a turn.

A: ahm how the work [ho how how it works=
B: [pans out
A: =with [how the work pans out between the people
B: [pans out

We expected fewer projections overall in ISDN, because deliberate attempts to complete or overlap the end of the current speaker's turn may either delete the relevant material, or arrive at the remote location after the speaker has already finished their turn. In LN we expected equivalent numbers of projections as in face-to-face interaction, because low-lag full-duplex audio should support this type of intervention.

Floorholding. This occurs when the next speaker tries to take the floor while the current speaker attempts to hold the floor while producing utterances that do not contain any information (Jefferson, 1984). Examples of floorholding can range from self-repetitions to function word repetition ("so . . . so"):

> A: that's not true you is it you could have an annotation which can either
>   be a structured annotation or a free text annotation
>   [so   [so
> B: [some but [somebody has got to own the interface the top level inter-
>   face=

We expected less floorholding in ISDN, because of adjustments by both speakers and listeners. Speakers should be less likely to hold the floor because they want to avoid the disruptive effects of the half-duplex line on simultaneous speech, in deleting one speaker. Listeners should avoid trying to seize the floor for the same reason. There should be no such constraints with LN, where floorholding should be possible without such disruptive effects.

Simultaneous Starts. These occur when two or more speakers compete for the floor when the previous speaker has just finished. In some instances this may include an attempt by the original speaker to resume. This can happen when the original speaker yields the floor and after some time has elapsed believes there to be no contenders and so begins a new turn (Sacks et al., 1974).

In ISDN, we should expect more simultaneous starts because of the problems that participants have in timing speaker switches. Because of the lag, and the desire not to overlap the end of the previous speaker's turn, listeners may deliberately wait to respond to ensure that the speaker has finished. Given the slow response, the original speaker may assume that no other person wants to speak and may then begin to speak again. Meanwhile at the remote location another participant may have already begun to speak. This situation conspires to produce simultaneous starts in ISDN. The situation is different in LN where low lag times and full duplex should allow equivalent numbers of simultaneous starts as in face-to-face interaction.

Overall we expect LN to result in the same number of overlapping speech acts given the similarity of the audio properties to FTF. For ISDN, we have different predictions for each of the subtypes of overlapping speech.

Explicit Handovers

Turn-taking is central to the process of conversation. There are a number of intonational, syntactic, pragmatic, and nonverbal devices that speakers use to indicate that they are about to finish their conversational turn. We identified three verbal devices used by speakers to indicate that they intend to relinquish the floor: (a) the use of questions; (b) tagging, using stereotyped questions such as "isn't it?," "arent they?," or statements such as "you know," or by the addition of redundant information on the end of a turn, for example,

> A: . . . ahm now I don't have I don't have a problem with that at all but
> it but it wouldn't it would not mean that we have at any one point one
> interface you know it would just be [you know

and finally (c) naming the next speaker (Levinson, 1983; Sacks et al., 1974).

We expected that given the timing and concurrency problems in ISDN, speakers would be much more likely to explicitly signal that they had finished their turn. We therefore expected more instances of questions, tagging, and naming of the next speaker. This should not be true in LN, where speaker switching should be unproblematic, and explicit handovers unnecessary.

Total Number of Turns and Turn Length

Turns are defined as attempts by speakers to gain the conversation floor. We expected a number of factors to conspire to increase turn length in ISDN. Where feedback, such as backchanneling, is absent or even delayed, the speaker's ability to formulate efficient messages is reduced (Krauss & Bricker, 1967; Krauss & Fussell, 1990; Kraut, Lewis & Swezey, 1982). Without feedback, speakers are unable to assume the message has been understood; they may therefore attempt to clarify or reiterate points, sometimes unnecessarily, to ensure that the listener has not misunderstood (Kraut et al., 1982). Absence or delay of feedback can therefore encourage the speaker to take long turns (Krauss & Bricker, 1967; Oviatt & Cohen, 1991). In addition, the difficulty in interrupting the speaker in ISDN would reduce the number of "quickfire" interchanges. We therefore expected the ISDN meetings to have more of the characteristics of formal presentations or lectures where speakers deliver large amounts of material as an uninterrupted monologue. In LN there should be no problems with rapid speaker switching or quickfire exchanges, and turn number and length should be comparable with face-to-face interaction.

Turn Distribution

Finally, we expected that turns would be unequally distributed in the different technologies. In face-to-face interaction, all participants, in principle, have equal access to the conversational floor, although there are external factors such as knowledge and power that influence participation levels (McGrath, 1984, 1990). In each videoconference, it is possible for people to communicate with people at the local site (via standard face-to-face interaction), as well as with the remote site using the system. Given the difficulty of interacting over ISDN, our informal observations suggested that groups attempt to manage this problem by channeling their responses to the remote location through one specific individual at each location. We therefore expected that these local coordinators would dominate their group's contributions: The overall distribution of turns would be unequal with these individuals having more turns than the average group member. In contrast, we expected turns to be more evenly distributed in the LN meetings.

To summarize the preceding analysis and predictions, it can be seen that certain critical features of face-to-face conversation depend on three properties of the communication channels: (a) low-transmission lags—that is, messages are received almost instantaneously by listeners; (b) two-way transmission—for example, feedback can be produced at the same time as the speaker's utterances; and (c) multiple modalities—that is, both verbal and visual channels are used in synergy (Whittaker, 1992). We have predicted how the channel limitations of the two systems will impact some conversational features.

METHODOLOGY

Recording Method

The ISDN videoconferences were recorded by placing a video camera next to the monitor and camera stack in the conference room. An additional monitor displaying the remote participants was placed beneath the table at which the participants sat. The video camera thus captured the local participants, with the remote participants visible on the monitor under the table. The stills screen was not monitored. The LiveNet meetings were recorded at the central video switch site. The picture on each of the two quadrant monitors was recorded on to videotape. The face-to-face (FTF) meetings were audiotaped. An observer was present at each meeting and noted any events not picked up on tape.

The Meetings

Five ISDN videoconferences, four LiveNet (LN) meetings, and five face-to-face meetings were recorded and analyzed. All meetings were scheduled for work-related reasons and were not arranged for the study. We attempted to identify analogous groups and meetings for the three conditions. The meetings were cooperative in nature, with their main function being to exchange information. Secondary functions and activities such as problem solving and idea generation also took place. The FTF and ISDN meetings were to report progress where participants described the work that they had recently been doing. In some cases this involved the demonstration of software. These meetings centered around project teams with one or two project managers being present. The LN meetings were technical discussions between representatives from different colleges. Participants from the various colleges gave updates on the developments and progress made at their site.

In the majority of cases, the participants knew each other before the meetings, although in a few of the videoconferences the people at either end of the link had not all previously met face-to-face. We could not control for certain parameters of familiarity: for example, participants at either end of a videoconference link are likely to know each other better and have a greater understanding of local work. Where possible, however, we tried to reduce this problem by our choice of face-to-face meetings: Two of the face-to-face meetings were between collaborators from the United States who were visiting the United Kingdom, and therefore had little day-to-day contact. All participants were familiar with using videoconferences. As they already had experience with the systems, we did not expect participants' conversational strategies to alter significantly during the meeting. We therefore did not analyze whether conversational behaviors changed in the course of each meeting.

In the FTF and ISDN conditions there was a mixture of agenda- and non-agenda-based meetings. All the LN meetings were agenda-based. Both the FTF and ISDN meetings had an average of six participants. For FTF and ISDN, the smallest meeting had four participants, and the largest had seven. The LN meetings were slightly larger. The largest had nine participants, one had eight, and the remainder seven. With the exception of one meeting in which three sites took part, all the LN meetings took place using four sites. The ISDN meetings took place between two sites. Typically all meetings lasted between 1 and 2 hrs.

Analyzing the Data

A 20-min segment from the middle of each meeting was transcribed in
detail. Each segment was taken 20 min from the start of the meeting so
that differences in the opening sequences would not bias the results. For
the same reason the closing sequences were not analyzed. The data were
transcribed using the simplified version of the system developed by
Jefferson (Jefferson, 1987), described earlier. Sentences were transcribed
as they were spoken, including any syntactical errors. From these transcripts
measures were taken of the number of utterances, the number of words
per utterance, backchannels, interruptions, overlapping speech, and
handovers according to the definitions given earlier.

The transcripts did not replace the tapes for scoring purposes, but were
used in conjunction with the tapes. We also conducted a reliability analysis
with two judges independently scoring two meetings in each condition.
Both tried to identify every instance of backchannels, interruptions, overlaps, and formal handovers. Reliability scores were measured using Cohen's
coefficient of agreement for nominal scales (J. Cohen, 1960). These were
as follows: backchannels (.91), overlaps (.74), interruptions (.62), and handovers (.92). We also compared reliability of coding across the three conditions and found coding was most reliable for ISDN (.89) and LN (.88),
but slightly less reliable for face-to-face interaction (.79).

RESULTS

Overview

The following section summarizes the findings from the study. Where
differences are discussed, these differences are statistically significant.
Unless otherwise stated the differences were analyzed in a one-way analysis
of variance (ANOVA), and post-hoc ANOVA tests were subsequently
administered to make pairwise comparisons between the conditions
following the recommendations of Kirk (1982). All analyses apply to the
20-min segment we analyzed for each meeting and not to the whole
meeting. Table 6.2 summarizes our findings for the different spoken
characteristics across the three conditions.

Backchannels and Interruptions

Mean levels of backchanneling were low in ISDN compared with FTF (7.00
vs. 60.80), confirming our prediction that people in ISDN would avoid
backchannels. The following example shows why backchannels were
reduced in ISDN: Where backchannels do occur, their arrival at the remote
location is delayed, which can lead to a disruption of the flow of the

TABLE 6.2
Predicted and Actual Outcomes for the Spoken Characteristics in the
Two Videoconferencing Technologies Relative to Face-to-Face Interaction

	ISDN		LN			
	Prediction	Actual	Prediction	Actual	FTF	p
Backchannels (mean number)	Fewer	Fewer 7.00[a,b]	Same	Fewer 30.50[b]	60.80	< .001
Interruptions (mean number)	Fewer	Fewer 1.40[a,b]	Same	Same 13.00	18.60	< .01
Interruptions excluding channel breaks		0.20[a,b]		11.75	18.60	< .01
Overlaps (mean percentage)	?	Same 9.6%	Same	Same 12.3%	10.1%	n.s.
Projection/completion	Fewer	Fewer 2.9%[a,b]	Same	Same 9.2%	7.3%	< .01
Floor holding	Fewer	Fewer 0.0%[b]	Same	Fewer 0.6%[b]	1.8%	< .01
Simultaneous start	More	More 6.7%[a,b]	Same	More 2.5%	1.0%	< .01
Handovers (mean percentage)	More	More 30.8%[b]	Same	More 21.2%[b]	8.8%	< .01
Question	?	More 23.8%[b]	Same	More 18.2%[b]	7.7%	< .01
Tagging	?	Same 4.3%	Same	Same 1.9%	0.8%	n.s.
Naming	?	Same 2.7%[b]	Same	Same 1.1%	0.4%	< .05

[a]Significantly different from LN in post-hoc ANOVA test.
[b]Significantly different from FTF in post-hoc ANOVA test.

speaker. In this instance B responded with a backchannel to A's comment, "it would be interesting to see if ah we could marry that." Locally the backchannel was placed after the suggestion overlapping A's "because." However, because of the lag, A does not receive the backchannel until some words later leading him to hesitate ("ahh").

A: portion of the interface that's been put there it would be interesting to see if ah we could marry that [because that was the intent of the ahh an original interrogation=

B: [mm

We did not predict, however, that backchannels would also be reduced in LN compared with FTF (30.50 vs. 60.80). We discuss this finding in the following section. Again as predicted, interruptions were also significantly less frequent in ISDN. In the face-to-face meetings, almost 10% of turns were interruptions, compared with less than 2% in ISDN. This occurred despite technical reasons for interruptions in ISDN, producing line breaks with consequent loss of audio and video for several hundred milliseconds. Many of the interruptions in ISDN followed line breaks and represented requests for a repetition of information lost during a break of the channel. There were fewer of these problems in LN and none in face-to-face, where the majority of interruptions are to clarify what the speaker has said and not requests for repetition. A second analysis, which removed interruptions following line breaks, showed that there were large differences between the media, with both face-to-face and LN having more interruptions than ISDN.

Overlapping Speech

Overlaps were analyzed in terms of their frequency per turn. This was to allow for the fact that there were many fewer turns and speaker switches in ISDN, and the chance of generating an overlap is clearly dependent on the number of speaker transitions. The overall number of overlaps per turn did not differ substantially. However, the different types of overlaps showed different distributions in the three conditions.

For projections we found, as we predicted, that there were differences between the conditions with more overlaps following projections in the face-to-face and LN media (7.3% FTF and 9.2% LN vs. 2.9% ISDN). The combination of half duplex and lags seem to combine to reduce projections in ISDN, with listeners avoiding overlapping speech even when this could assist the speaker in composing their message.

We found that floorholding was much more frequent in face-to-face than in either LN or ISDN (1.8% vs. .6% and 0%). The difference between ISDN and FTF is explicable as a combination of speaker and listener adaptations to lag and half-duplex: Listeners try not to break in on current speakers, and speakers immediately stop talking when they have nothing further to say. The extent of this adaptation was that, strikingly, there were no examples of floorholding in the ISDN meetings. Contrary to our expectations, however, was the finding that floorholding was reduced in LN compared with face-to-face. We provide possible explanations for this in the Discussion section.

The picture was different for simultaneous starts. These can be regarded as breakdowns in the process of speaker switching brought about by ISDN lags. As predicted, they were much more likely in the ISDN medium than in both LN and face-to-face (6.7% vs. 2.5% and 1.0%). Additionally, when turn-taking has been disrupted in this way it can be difficult for it to be reestablished. Unlike the face-to-face situation where one speaker drops out, it is usual in ISDN for both speakers to stop and then for one to be granted the floor either verbally by being told "go ahead" or visually by using hand gestures. Where this does not occur, a second or third clash can happen. In the following ISDN example both speakers stop, then start again. This is finally resolved by a third party telling the remote speaker to go ahead.

```
A:                              the visual [appearance
B:                                         [uh just out of curiosity wh
A:     the appearance of [that
B                         [just out of curiosity what difference (    )
C:     go ahead
```

Explicit Handovers

We predicted that speakers would try to remedy the problem of speaker transition in ISDN by explicitly handing over the floor. Again this was measured in terms of frequency per turn because of the different numbers of turns across conditions. As we predicted, there was a greater number of each of these formal handovers in ISDN compared with FTF, (30.8% vs. 8.8%), because of the need to explicitly manage speaker transitions. Contrary to our expectations, however, we found the same overall pattern of formal handovers in LN (21.2%) as in ISDN. Again we suggest possible explanations in the Discussion section.

Further analysis of the different classes of handover indicated that handovers using direct questions were more frequent in both videoconferences (23.8% ISDN, 18.2% LN, and 7.7% FTF). In the ISDN condition participants used questions at the end of long turns to encourage speaker transition, for example:

```
A:     there are only two possible choices either there is an inpu an input
       file or there is none or rather either it is empty or not If it is if there
       is data in it then the job runs correctly otherwise all the subsequent
       steps test the condition code and if it is different from zero then they
       don't run as simple as that any ah ((pause)) any counter indication
       on your end?
```

Handovers by naming the next speaker were more frequent in ISDN than in face-to-face (2.7% vs .4%). LN (1.1%) was more like FTF. In some instances names were used to address a question to a particular individual. Tagging with questions such as "is that okay?" or "you know" or redundant information was equally frequent in all media (4.3% ISDN, 1.9% LN, .8% FTF).

Turn Size

We predicted that the problems encountered in speaker transition, coupled with listeners' reluctance to interrupt or provide backchannels, would result in longer turns in ISDN meetings. Table 6.3 shows the number of turns taken

TABLE 6.3
Mean Number and Size of Turns Showing Levels
of Statistical Difference for the Three Conditions

	ISDN	LN	FTF	p
No. of turns per meeting	74.2[a,b]	180.0	199.2	<.01
No. of words per meeting	3,212.0	3,529.5	3,386.8	n.s.
No. of turns by participant	12.37[a,b]	23.77	34.82	<.01
No. of words by participant	535.3	455.5	603.2	n.s.
No. of words per turn	43.61[a,b]	19.23	17.08	<.001
No. of words per turn not including turns of less than five words	62.19[a,b]	30	31.3	<.001

[a]Significantly different from LN in post-hoc ANOVA test.
[b]Significantly different from FTF in post-hoc ANOVA test.

and their average word length. Typically, the meetings held over ISDN were characterized by fewer turns of greater length. There were significantly fewer turns per participant in ISDN compared with LN and face-to-face. The complementary result was that the number of words per turn was significantly greater in ISDN than in the other two media. It is possible that these effects are due to the reduction of brief turns (such as backchannels) in ISDN. To investigate this we repeated the analysis excluding all turns of less than five words, but both effects were still present.

These differences in turn size were observed despite the fact that there were no overall differences in the total number of words per meeting in each condition. Although the total number of words remained constant across conditions, the differences between the conditions lay in how the words were distributed across turns. These results strongly support our prediction that ISDN would produce a "lecture-like" interaction with speakers holding the floor for lengthy uninterrupted monologues. In contrast, in both LN and face-to-face we see many more short turns with higher frequency of interruptions and backchannels.

The following examples show typical interactions for ISDN and LN. The first clearly shows the "lecture-like" style in ISDN. Here speakers supply large amounts of uninterrupted information, with transitions often being accompanied by pauses.

A: and ah essentially what they are doing is they're ah comparing preoperative waves with with the actual interoperative ones they're looking at what the guy was like before they did anything to him to what he's like now ahm and its kind of you know they sort of look at this thing and they sort of say its its a bit different isn't it type of thing and your thinking yeah it is I suppose and and then they sort of say well actually I think I'll tell him but I I don't quite I don't I haven't quite got a grip on what the algorithm was they were sort of saying well it looks similar and look its sort of kind of moved that that way a bit ahm and that's how they were doing delays it was it was very approximate. ((pause))

B: Yeah I mean the two things that they seem to be looking at predominantly are latency over the preoperative signal and also some characteristics which we couldn't fathom which were like the shape of the waves you know something to do with peaks and you know like when they hit or you know how their characteristics changed and you know in some way that related to ahm you know the particular nerve that was being tested but . . .

In contrast, LN, like FTF, has many more short turns with conversational exchanges being incremental and interactive.

A: Is there any significant difference?
B: ahm there was a problem there was a mouse problem on two point one which occurred intermittently
A: It's a bug fix
B: yes yes
A: Not a new functionality
B: I don't think so no There's also a new version of of meta software (Etches) available
A: yes I know

Turn Distribution

Finally, we expected that the different conditions would lead to unequal distribution of turns between participants. We expected that in ISDN, given the problems of managing the channel, participants would rely on two people ("chairpeople"), one at either end of the link, to manage interactions across the connecting link, and they would direct their responses through these people. However, when we examined the data for dominance by two speakers this was not the case (see Table 6.4). We measured the number of turns that were produced by the two most frequent speakers in the three conditions. However, there was no overall difference either in the percentage of turns taken by these people or in the number of words that they spoke. We also investigated whether ISDN served to exclude certain speakers: the fact that they were less able to interrupt might prevent participants who are not chairpeople from having the opportunity to speak. Again this hypothesis was not born out by our results. There were no differences in the number of words and the number of turns for the two people who spoke least. This result is interesting because it runs contrary to the perceptions of the people using ISDN and LN. They report feeling both that certain participants are able to dominate the meeting and that others are less able to contribute to it.

TABLE 6.4
Normalized Mean Percentage of Turns and Words Spoken
by Most and Least Frequent Speakers, Showing Levels
of Statistical Difference for the Three Conditions

	ISDN	LN	FTF	p
Turns taken by the two most frequent speakers/total turns	66.84%	58.48%	73.45%	n.s.
Turns taken by two least frequent speakers/total turns	8.28%	2.29%	10.56%	n.s.
Words spoken by two most frequent speakers/total words	78.10%	70.76%	76.58%	n.s
Words spoken by two least dominant speakers/total words	5.24%	1.38%	11.6%	n.s.

DISCUSSION

Consistent with our predictions, our results showed that compared with FTF, spoken conversation patterns are disrupted over ISDN with its half-duplex line, transmission lags, and poor quality image:

- Listeners produce fewer backchannels and interrupt less.
- Listeners are also less likely to anticipate turn endings, and hence complete speaker utterances.
- Speakers also alter their behavior, being more likely to hand over turns formally using a question or naming the next speaker. They are also less likely to hold the floor with redundant phrases.
- The result of listeners reducing interruptions and speaker feedback, combined with the general difficulty of switching speakers, is a formal "lecture" style of interaction, with long turns, handed over by a very deliberate process.

Our theoretical claim is that these findings result from the properties of the communication channels disrupting basic communication processes. Face-to-face interaction has full-duplex, almost instantaneous transmission of audio as well as high-quality visual information. When these channel properties are changed to those of the ISDN system, we produce a style of interaction that is lecture-like and lacks spontaneity. These findings are supported by other studies of systems with lagged audio (K. Cohen, 1982; Isaacs & Tang, 1993). Listeners in ISDN seem to be more polite, waiting for a pause or for a speaker to finish before making their conversational contribution.

However, a comparison of LN and FTF, contrary to our expectations, also demonstrated differences. Despite having a full-duplex line, immediate transmission, and broadcast-quality image, the properties of the spoken communication still differed from face-to-face interaction in the following ways:

- Although listeners interrupt as frequently as in FTF, they are less likely to give backchannels.
- Speakers use questions to formally hand over the floor more frequently, and they are also less likely to hold the conversation floor with redundant information.

Thus, although LN was similar to FTF it was still characterized by highly formal conversational behaviors. How can we explain these findings? The argument that lagged half-duplex audio and poor-quality video are solely responsible for communication disruption can no longer hold true. If these channel properties underlie all the communication disruptions we observed, then we should have seen no difference between LN and face-to-face. In fact we did observe differences between LN and face-to-face. This suggests that other channel properties are also critical here, and the account should be extended to include these properties and the conversation features they impact.

What are these other channel properties and how could they affect conversation? ISDN and LN both have nondirectional audio and video: In both, sound and vision originate from a restricted number of sources, that is, one or two monitors and loudspeakers. This contrasts with FTF where sound and visual behavior are directional, because they emanate from the different participants. In FTF, head turning, eye gaze, and localized sound may be used to support the speaker switching process (Duncan, 1972; Kendon, 1967). The absence of such cues in ISDN and LN may explain the reduced floorholding and more explicit handovers. Speakers are forced to be more verbally explicit in managing intended speaker switches, possibly because they cannot use cues such as eye gaze to indicate the next speaker. Recent research on directional audio and video attempts to test this hypothesis (Mantei et al., 1991; Sellen, 1992, 1995). Sellen (1992) directly addressed the impact of directionality on conversations in video conferencing systems. Few objective benefits were found, though this may have been due to the small size of the screens. Further exploration of this area is required.

We also need to refine our explanations of ISDN in the light of the unexpected differences between LN and FTF. Which disruptions of communication were exclusively due to ISDN channel properties? Comparison of ISDN and LN enables us to determine this. ISDN differed from LN for backchannels, interruptions, projections, simultaneous starts, and turn size. One explanation here is that the channel properties of ISDN reduced listener participation. It prevented listeners from indicating assent or dissent and caused them to wait for the original speaker to finish before taking the floor. The effect of reduced listener participation is to decrease the total number of speaker switches and hence the overall number of turns. We did not, however, isolate whether audio lag, half-duplex audio, or visual quality was mainly responsible for these disruptions in ISDN. This was because we attempted to gather data for real systems for which these properties were not independent. Other laboratory work should be done to confirm which of the channel properties of the ISDN system was most disruptive of these conversation features. Currently we cannot rule out any of these channel properties, and other research has independently shown that removing visual cues, lags, and half-duplex audio can all independently produce these types of effects (K. Cohen, 1982; Krauss & Bricker, 1967; Rutter & Stephenson, 1977; Tang & Isaacs, 1993; Whittaker, 1995b; Wolf, 1982).

Turning to more subjective results, are participants aware of differences between the different media? Our interviews with users and informal observations suggest they are. When interviewed, people stated that video-conferences involved more "effort." For example, participants complained about the difficulty of assuming control of the conversation in both video-conferencing media. One participant reported for ISDN: "I have the feeling that I want to say something, but there's no opportunity to speak. Then when the opportunity does arise, I don't take it because my comment often isn't relevant anymore." Other people exploited the problems of speaker switching to their advantage: One LN user acknowledged the greater formality of LN meetings compared with face-to-face but said that she sometimes exploited this to hold the channel for longer periods. On the other hand, despite the problems with the videoconferencing systems, people preferred these to audioconferencing. The main stated advantages of videoconferencing were knowing who was at the remote location and knowing who was speaking, notwithstanding the poor image quality in ISDN. Another stated advantage was the feeling of "not talking into a void." Finally our users had clear ideas about the limitations of ISDN for certain tasks: They commented that they found it appropriate for only certain types of meeting such as information exchange or project updates.

CONCLUSIONS

This method aimed to show how the nature of communication was affected by the channel properties in VMC systems. Previous research has explained the characteristics of videoconferencing in terms of concepts that are difficult to operationalize such as "social presence" (Short et al., 1976), "media richness" (Daft & Lengel, 1984), or "cuelessness" (Rutter & Robinson, 1981). We aimed to quantify these characteristics to allow replication and comparison of results with other similar studies. We argue that high-level phenomena such as "cuelessness" and lack of "social presence" are explicable in terms of disruptions in basic conversational processes, such as lack of support for backchannels or interruptions. These disruptions result from definable characteristics of communication channels, such as lags and half-duplex audio. In turn, we argue that "media richness" can be defined in terms of the set of conversational processes supported by a given medium and derived from the channel properties of that medium.

Other work has shown that the structure and conduct of mediated communication is critically dependent on the properties of the communication channels (Whittaker, Brennan, & Clark, 1991; Whittaker, 1992). Using a framework based on face-to-face communication and examining how the channel properties in mediated communication differ from it, we have been able to generate and test predictions about how lags, half-duplex audio, and poor-quality video information would disrupt specific aspects of communication. In doing so, the study contributes to a developing theory of mediated communication.

The results from this study also add to our practical knowledge about the nature of VMC. Many potential explanations have been suggested for the failure of videoconferencing to gain widespread acceptance, including cost, incorrect marketing, and the questionable value of a video channel. However, there have been few detailed empirical studies of the actual communication. Our results generate practical implications for the improvement of video technology.

First, we can draw implications about the kinds of tasks for which the current ISDN quality videoconferencing is appropriate. The "lecture-like" character and the inability to support quickfire exchanges may mean that ISDN is unsuitable for tasks such as conflict resolution, planning, or negotiation, where the ambiguity of the information and the requirement for rapid clarification and feedback are critical for the success of the interaction (Daft & Lengel, 1984; Whittaker, 1992). If ISDN cannot effectively support these tasks, this may contribute to the lack of success of this quality of videoconferencing. It may be that future remote collaborators have to choose media appropriate to the task at hand and ensure that certain types of task, such as conflict resolution and negotiation, are resolved in face-to-face situations.

From a technology perspective it would seem that introducing low-lag, full-duplex channels will lead to improvements in communication, as evidenced by the superiority of LN over ISDN. This suggests that we should continue to work on high-speed wide-area networks and compression technology to reduce the disruptions to communication described earlier. However, the LN results also suggest that improving these properties alone will not exactly reproduce face-to-face interaction. Perhaps the implementation of directional audio and video might address the outstanding differences between LN and FTF (Sellen, 1992). Other technical improvements might follow from the comments and suggestions of the users of such systems. In interviews the users of ISDN and LN suggested providing remote audio and video controls, so that remote participants are able to choose what they want to see and hear rather than have these choices made for them. They also suggested the use of several monitors to enable one monitor to be used to provide a high-quality image of the speaker or object of interest, and other monitors could then present lower quality panoramic images of other remote participants for visual context.

However, there are some limitations to the method we describe here. An inherent problem is that it does not compare the effectiveness of the different communication modes as laboratory studies have done (Chapanis, 1975; Morley & Stephenson, 1969, 1970, 1977; Wichman, 1970). With real-life meetings, it is not clear what is an appropriate objective measure of successful communication, nor how we can easily compare the success of the different meetings. Other work suggests, however, that the types of communication characteristics measured here have implications for task outcomes. Laboratory studies have shown that lack of support for interactive processes such as backchannels and interruptions has effects on outcome measures such as time to solution and participants' understanding (Kraut et al., 1982; Oviatt & Cohen, 1991). We have also suggested that in the future collaborators may choose appropriate media for different tasks. Naturalistic studies of remote collaborators who are using multiple media would be more appropriate than our current method in determining how people currently allocate media to communication tasks, and more theoretical work might help to specify the relationship between communication task requirements and the basic communication processes that are needed to support them.

Another hypothesis that is not addressed by this method is whether media differences result in changes in the content of conversation across different media. It has been suggested that video-mediated meetings are more task focused and as a consequence save time for participants (Johansen, 1984; Short et al. 1976; Rutter & Robinson, 1981). This work cannot support or refute such a hypothesis.

It is also important to note that users' subjective reactions to the technology and the conversations it supported did not match the objective aspects of communication we measured here. For example, although our users had strong perceptions that the meetings were dominated by a few speakers, our measures of conversational characteristics did not support this. Similar discrepancies between subjective and objective measures have been found elsewhere (Sellen, 1992, 1995; Tang & Isaacs, 1993; Isaacs & Tang, chapter 9, this volume), and future work needs to explain these differences. Another area that we have not explored is the alternative uses of video technology. Elsewhere an alternative application of video in the form of "video as data" is presented (Nardi et al., chapter 23, this volume; Nardi et al., in press; Whittaker, 1995a, 1995b). This work suggests that in some environments, it may be better to transmit pictures of the work itself rather than of the participants who are carrying out the work. Further applications can be seen in the area of "open distributed offices" where video is used to provide background awareness rather than as a direct communication channel (Fish, Kraut, Root, & Rice, 1992; Harrison et al., chapter 13, this volume). Methods that support these type of investigations are presented elsewhere in this book.

Finally, some practical difficulties in applying this method should be noted. Because of the detailed nature of the analysis, the method is a time-consuming one. Analysis must be carried out on each verbal utterance, determining its origin, function, and timing. There have been some attempts to automate this process using recording systems that can time utterances and determine if they were uttered in overlap and so forth (K. Cohen, 1982; Sellen, 1992). However, as we have seen, a single measured feature of speech may arise for multiple conversational reasons: For example, speech delivered in overlap may arise for one of several reasons and gross measures will not capture these differences. It is likely even where automated analysis is used that additional manual measures will need to be undertaken.

Nevertheless, the method has useful practical and theoretical implications. By quantifying the different conversational characteristics of different mediated communication systems, we have been able to identify critical interaction processes that are compromised by system properties. We have therefore been able to suggest how system redesign might improve these processes. In addition, we have been able to refine theoretical terminology such as "cuelessness" and "media richness" to identify and predict measurable characteristics of conversation that are affected when conversation is mediated. This allows replicability and comparison of results with other similar studies (e.g., K. Cohen, 1982; Isaacs & Tang, 1993, and chapter 9, this volume; Sellen, 1992, 1995).

REFERENCES

Atkinson, J. M., & Heritage, J. C. (1984). *Structures of social interactions: Studies in conversation analysis.* Cambridge: Cambridge University Press.
Chapanis, A. (1975). Interactive human communication. *Scientific American, 232,* 36–42.
Clark, H., & Brennan, S. (1990). Grounding in communication. In L. B. Resnick, J. Levine, & S. D. Bahrend (Eds.), *Perspectives on socially shared cognition* (pp. 127–149). Washington, DC: American Psychological Association.

Clark, H., & Schaefer, E. (1989). Contributing to discourse. *Cognitive Science, 13*, 259–294.

Clark, H., & Wilkes-Gibbs, D. (1986). Referring as a collaborative process. *Cognition, 22*, 1–39.

Cohen, J. (1960). A co-efficient of agreement for nominal scales. *Educational and Psychological Measurement, 20*, 37–46.

Cohen, K. M. (1982). Speaker interaction: Video teleconferences versus face-to-face meetings. *Proceedings of Teleconferencing and Electronic Communications* (pp. 189–199). Madison: University of Wisconsin.

Daft, R., & Lengel, R. (1984). Information richness: A new approach to managerial behavior and organizational design. In B. Straw & L. Cummings (Eds.), *Research in organizational behavior* (pp. 191–223). Greenwich, CT: JAI Press.

Duncan, S. (1972). Some signals and rules for taking speaker turns in conversation. *Journal of Personal and Social Psychology, 23*, 283–292.

Egido, C. (1988). Videoconferencing as a technology to support group work: A review of its failures. *Proceedings of the Conference on Computer Supported Co-Operative Work* (pp. 13–24). New York: ACM.

Egido, C. (1990). Teleconferencing as a technology to support cooperative work: Its possibilities and limitations. In J. Galegher, R. Kraut, & C. Egido (Eds.), *Intellectual teamwork* (pp. 351–372). Hillsdale, NJ: Lawrence Erlbaum Associates.

Fish, R., Kraut, R., Root, R., & Rice, R. (1992). Evaluating video as a technology for informal communication. *Proceedings of the Conference on Human Computer Interaction* (pp. 37–48). New York: ACM.

Isaacs, E., & Tang, J. (1993). What video can and can't do for collaboration: A case study. *Proceedings of the ACM Multimedia 93 Conference.* Anaheim, CA.

Jefferson, G. (1984). On stepwise transition from talk about a trouble to inappropriately next-positioned matters. In J. Atkinson & J. Heritage (Eds.), *Structures of social interaction* (pp. 191–222). Cambridge, England: Cambridge University Press.

Jefferson, G. (1987). *On a failed hypothesis: "Conjunctionals" as overlap-vulnerable.* Unpublished manuscript, Tilburg University.

Johansen, R. (1984). *Teleconferencing and beyond: Communications in the office of the future.* New York: McGraw-Hill.

Johansen, R., & Bullen, C. (1984). Thinking ahead: What to expect from teleconferencing. *Harvard Business Review, 62*, 164–174.

Kendon, A. (1967). Some functions of gaze direction in social interaction. *Acta Psychologica, 26*, 1–47.

Kirk, R. (1982). *Experimental design: Procedures for the experimental sciences.* Belmont, CA: Brooks/Cole.

Krauss, R., & Bricker, P. (1967). Effects of transmission delay and access delay on the efficiency of verbal communication. *Journal of the Acoustical Society of America, 41*, 286–292.

Krauss, R., & Fussell, S. (1990). Mutual knowledge and communication effectiveness. In J. Galegher, R. Kraut, & C. Egido (Eds.), *Intellectual teamwork* (pp. 111–146). Hillsdale, NJ: Lawrence Erlbaum Associates.

Kraut, R., Lewis, S., & Swezey, L. (1982). Listener responsiveness and the co-ordination of conversation. *Journal of Personality and Social Psychology, 43*, 718–731.

Levinson, S. (1983). *Pragmatics.* Cambridge: Cambridge University Press.

Mantei, M., Baecker, R., Sellen, A., Buxton, W., Milligan, T., & Wellman, B. (1991). Experiences in the use of a media space. *Proceedings of the Conference on Computer Human Interaction* (pp. 203–208). New York: ACM.

McGrath, J. (1984). *Groups: Interaction and performance.* Englewood Cliffs, NJ: Prentice Hall.

McGrath, J. (1990). Time matters in groups. In J. Galegher, R. Kraut, & C. Egido (Eds.), *Intellectual teamwork* (pp. 23–62). Hillsdale, NJ: Lawrence Erlbaum Associates.

Morley, I., & Stephenson, G. (1969). Interpersonal and interparty exchange: A laboratory simulation of an industrial negotiation at plant level. *British Journal of Psychology, 60*, 543–545.

Morley, I., & Stephenson, G. (1970). Formality in experimental negotiations: A validation study. *British Journal of Psychology, 61*, 383–384.

Morley, I., & Stephenson, G. (1977). *The social psychology of bargaining.* London: Allen & Unwin.

Nardi, B., Kuchinsky, A., Whittaker, S., Leichner, R., & Schwarz, H. (1995). Video-as-data: Technical and social aspects. *Computer-Supported Cooperative Work, 4*(1), 73–100.

Noll, M. (1992). Anatomy of a failure: Picturephone revisited. *Telecommunications Policy,* May/June, 307–316.

O'Conaill, B., Whittaker, S., & Wilbur, S. (1993). Conversations over video conferences: An evaluation of the spoken aspects of video-mediated communication. *Human Computer Interaction, 8*, 389–428.

Oviatt, S., & Cohen, P. (1991). Discourse structure and performance efficiency in interactive and non-interactive speech modalities. *Computer Speech and Language, 5*, 297–326.

Panko, R. (1992). Managerial communication patterns. *Journal of Organizational Computing, 2*, 95–122.

Reid, A. (1977). Comparing the telephone with face-to-face interaction. In I. Pool (Ed.), *The social impact of the telephone* (pp. 386–419). Cambridge, MA: MIT Press.

Rutter, D., & Stephenson, G. (1977). The role of visual information in synchronizing conversation. *European Journal of Social Psychology, 2*, 29–37.

Rutter, R., & Robinson, R. (1981). An experimental analysis of teaching by telephone. In G. Stephenson & J. Davies (Eds.), *Progress in applied social psychology* (pp. 143–178). London: Wiley.

Sacks, H., Schegloff, E., & Jefferson, G. (1974). A simplest systematics for the organisation of turn-taking in conversation. *Language, 50*, 696–753.

Sellen, A. J. (1992). Speech patterns in video-mediated conversations. *Proceedings of the Conference on Computer Human Interaction* (pp. 49–59). New York: ACM.

Sellen, A. J. (1995). Remote conversations: The effects of mediating talk with technology. *Human Computer Interaction, 10*(4), 401–444.

Short, J., Williams, E., & Christie, B. (1976). *The social psychology of telecommunications.* London: Wiley.

Tang, J., & Isaacs, E. (1993). Why do users like video: Studies of multimedia-supported collaboration. *Computer-Supported Cooperative Work, 1*, 163–196.

Whittaker, S. (1992). *Towards a theory of mediated communication.* Unpublished manuscript.

Whittaker, S. (1995a). Video as a technology for interpersonal communication: A new perspective. *IS&T/SPIE Symposium on Electronic Imaging Science and Technology: Multimedia Computing and Networks, 2417*, 294–304. San Jose, CA.

Whittaker, S. (1995b). Rethinking video as a technology for interpersonal communication: Theory and design implications. *International Journal of Human–Computer Studies, 42*, 501–529.

Whittaker, S., Brennan, S., & Clark, H. (1991). Co-ordinating activity: An analysis of computer supported co-operative work. *Proceedings of the Conference on Computer Human Interaction* (pp. 361–367). New York: ACM.

Wichman, H. (1970). Effects of isolation and communication on cooperation in a two-person game. *Journal of Personality and Social Psychology, 16*, 114–120.

Williams, E. (1977). Experimental comparisons of face-to-face and mediated communication. *Psychological Bulletin, 84*, 963–976.

Wolf, C. (1982). Videoconferencing: Delay and transmission considerations. In L. Parker & C. Olgren (Eds.), *Teleconferencing and electronic communications* (pp. 184–188). Hillsdale, NJ: Lawrence Erlbaum Associates.

Chapter 7

The Impact of VMC on Collaborative Problem Solving: An Analysis of Task Performance, Communicative Process, and User Satisfaction

Anne H. Anderson
University of Glasgow

Claire O'Malley
University of Nottingham

Gwyneth Doherty-Sneddon
University of Stirling

Steve Langton
University of Nottingham

Alison Newlands
Jim Mullin
Anne Marie Fleming
University of Glasgow

Jeroen Van der Velden
Technical University of Delft

In this chapter we report the results of four studies of collaborative problem solving supported by various forms of video-mediated communication (VMC). We analyze task outcome, the process of communication, and the user's reactions to the technologies with similar data obtained from face-to-face interactions. VMC was not found to deliver all the advantages observed for face-to-face interactions. The possible reasons for this are explored, as well as the implications of the data for evaluation techniques.

INTRODUCTION

Previous research on the impact of VMC on collaborative tasks has produced mixed findings. Whether or not seeing one's partner has an effect on performance seems to be highly dependent on the type of task. Reviews of the literature report little benefit in seeing one's partner in collaborative problem-solving tasks, whereas other studies suggest that the visual channel is of benefit for more "social" tasks, such as negotiation or bargaining (Williams, 1977). Other reviews report equally mixed findings with respect to the impact of VMC on communicative processes (Sellen, 1995). One of the problems with much of the research is that studies comparing video-mediated or face-to-face interactions with audio-only conditions have tended to focus on one or two measures in isolation—for example, task outcome (Chapanis, 1975; Short, Williams, & Christie, 1976; Williams, 1977), or structural aspects of the communicative process such as turn-taking (O'Connaill, Whittaker, & Wilbur, 1993; Sellen, 1992), or user satisfaction (Tang & Isaacs, 1993). However, as writers such as Monk et al. (1996) have argued, a multidimensional approach to the evaluation of VMC is likely to be more informative about the relative benefits of this technology. Such an approach has also been adopted by researchers such as Olson et al. (Olson, Olson, Carter, & Storrosten, 1992; Olson, Olson, Storrøsten, & Carter, 1993) and Strauss and McGrath (1994). We need to understand the relationship between these variables in order to get a clearer picture of how technology mediates communication and collaboration. In this chapter we describe a number of studies we have conducted on the impact of VMC on collaborative problem solving where we adopt such an approach, exploring the effect of such technologies on task outcome, on the process of communication, and, in later studies, on user satisfaction.

GENERAL APPROACH

We explore the performance of users on two collaborative problem-solving tasks: the Map Task (Brown, Anderson, Yule, & Shillcock, 1984) and the Travel Game (Anderson, Mullin, Newlands, Doherty-Sneddon, & Fleming, 1994). In the Map Task participants collaborate to complete a map route as accurately as possible. In the Travel Game the participants are engaged in planning an itinerary around the United States. Their goal is to visit as many destinations as possible given the restrictions imposed by available connecting flights. Both tasks produce objective measures of task success against which the corresponding task dialogues can be compared. We use an experimental approach when conducting evaluation studies: We systematically compare the performance of users who attempt such tasks when the system incorporates video technology or provides only an audio link. In addition, we compare the performance of subjects who tackle the tasks when communicating face-to-face or with only an audio link. As well as calculating task success we also perform detailed analyses of the structure and content of the task dialogues. This involves examining the lengths of the dialogues, in turns and words, and examining how the process of turn-taking is managed. For the Map Task, the content of the dialogue is analyzed in terms of the pragmatic functions that the speakers are attempting to convey as the dialogue progresses. This involves coding of all the communicative behaviors or "conversational games" (Kowtko, Isard, & Doherty, 1991) that are attempted and how these are distributed across dialogues when speakers communicate face-to-face, in VMC, or in audio-only conditions. We also explore aspects of the nonverbal communication (gaze) on task.

For the Travel Game we examine the decision-making process and how frequently "clients" change their plans and decisions. We examine the lengths of the dialogues in the different conditions and the turn-taking behavior of speakers. In the Travel Game we also conduct a detailed posttask questionnaire on aspects of user satisfaction with the task, communication, and technology. We briefly report on four studies of the impact of VMC on two different forms of collaborative problem solving. We compare face-to-face and audio-only interactions with collaborations supported by high- and low-bandwidth VMC and explore the effect of long-distance VMC across the European Internet. These evaluation studies involved over 200 participants. An overview of the comparisons made and the results obtained is shown in Table 7.1

BACKGROUND: THE BENEFITS
OF FACE-TO-FACE INTERACTION

In earlier research on collaborative problem solving we had found that in face-to-face interaction, participants needed to say significantly less to achieve the same level of performance than in audio only conditions (Boyle, Anderson, & Newlands, 1994). This study is unusual in showing subtle but significant benefits of the availability of visual signals for collaborative problem solving. Most earlier studies that focused only on task outcome showed no advantage for face-to-face problem solving (Davis, 1971; Chapanis, Ochsman, Parrish, & Weeks, 1972; Williams, 1977). Only in tasks involving conflict or negotiation was there some evidence of a benefit for communication with visual contact (Morley & Stephenson, 1969; Short, 1974). The task we used in the study by Boyle et al. and in subsequent explorations of video-mediated communication is a form of collaborative problem solving known as the Map Task (Brown et al., 1984). Two participants each have a copy of a schematic map. One subject (the instruction giver) has a route shown on her copy of the map and her task is to describe this route so that the instruction follower can draw this on his copy of the

TABLE 7.1
Overview of Studies

Study	Measures			
	Task Performance	Dialogue Length	Number of Interruptions	Dialogue Structure
Boyle et al. (1994), face-to-face vs. audio only	No difference	Face-to-face significantly shorter	Face-to-face significantly fewer	Face-to-face less verbal feedback
Study 1, VMC +/− eye contact, audio only	No difference	VMC + eye contact significantly longer	VMC + eye contact significantly more	VMC + eye contact less verbal feedback
Study 2, video +/− delay, audio only +/− delay	Video and audio + delay significantly poorer	No difference	Video and audio + delay significantly more	[Not analyzed]
Study 3: Travel Game (local) Face-to-face vs. audio only	No difference	Face-to-face significantly shorter	No difference	Face-to-face more optional changes of plans
VMC vs. audio only	No difference	No difference	No difference	No difference
Study 4: Travel Game (remote collaboration) VMC vs. audio only	No difference	No difference	No difference	No difference

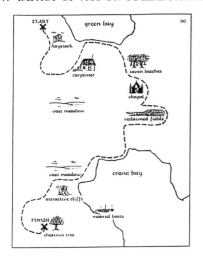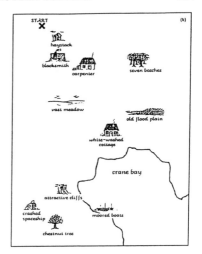

FIG. 7.1.   Illustration of a Map Task used in Study 1.

map. Some landmarks differ between the maps, providing problem points that the participants have to overcome (Fig. 7.1). The task produces an objective measure of task success (how well the route has been completed) and provides clear and comparable communicative goals for users who participate in evaluation studies.

In the Boyle et al. study, 32 pairs of undergraduate subjects tackled versions of the Map Task sitting at opposite sides of a table, either communicating face-to-face or with a screen between them. In face-to-face dialogues speakers used 28% fewer turns and 20% fewer words than in the audio only condition. Yet face-to-face participants achieved equally good levels of task performance with this reduced verbal input. The interaction was also managed more smoothly in face-to-face collaboration, with 8.7% of turns containing interruptions compared to 12% of turns in the audio only condition. These face-to-face advantages suggest that speakers can use visual signals to supplement the information presented verbally and to assist in managing the process of turn-taking.

DIALOGUE ANALYSIS

All 128 dialogues from the Boyle et al. study were coded using conversational games analysis (Kowtko et al., 1991). Our aim was to discover what kinds of communicative functions caused the greater length of audio-only dialogues, and thus what kinds of functions may be substituted by the visual signals in face-to-face communication. conversational games analysis charts the way speakers achieve their communicative goals. The analysis is derived from the work of Power (1979) and Houghton and Isard (1987), which proposed that a conversation proceeds through the accomplishment of speakers' goals and subgoals—with these dialogue units being called conversational games. (For example, an instruction is accomplished via an INSTRUCT game.) Conversational games analysis was developed to detail patterns of pragmatic functions in Map Task dialogues. Utterances are categorized according to the perceived conversational function that the speaker intends to accomplish. This involves taking several sources of information into account: the semantic content of the utterance, the prosody and intonational contour accompanying the utterance, and the utterance location within the dialogue. So, for example, "Go right" could function to instruct, to elicit feedback or to provide feedback depending upon its dialogue context and intonation. Table 7.2 shows the full set of conversational games and their definitions. Two trained coders independently coded the dialogues, and the interjudge agreement on a test sample produced a kappa value of .7, $p < .001$.

DIALOGUE ANALYSIS RESULTS

Which communicative functions differ between face-to-face and audio-only dialogues and underlie the efficiency benefits of face-to-face communication? This kind of analysis should be valuable for understanding the potential impact of VMC. The analyses of face-to-face dialogues showed that speakers check less often that their listener understands them (ALIGN) or that they have understood their partner (CHECK) than in audio-only interactions. There were significant increases in the frequency with which

TABLE 7.2
Six Types of Games Found Necessary and Sufficient to Capture the
Speaker's Communicative Intentions in Coding Map Task Dialogues

INSTRUCT: Communicates a direct or indirect request for action or instruction.
CHECK: Listener checks their own understanding of a previous message or instruction from their conversational partner, by requesting confirmation that the interpretation is correct.
QUERY-YN: Yes–no question. A request for affirmation or negation regarding new or unmentioned information about some part of the task (not checking an interpretation of a previous message).
QUERY-W: An open-answer Wh-question. Requests more than affirmation or negation regarding new information about some part of the task (not checking an interpretation of a previous message).
EXPLAIN: Freely offered information regarding the task, not elicited by coparticipant.
ALIGN: Speaker confirms the listener's understanding of a message or accomplishment of some task; also checks attention, agreement, or readiness.

speakers used ALIGN and CHECK games in audio-only conditions, with these games occurring 50% and 28% more often, respectively. Where visual signals are not available speakers do more verbal checking, whereas in face-to-face conversations nonverbal signals may be substituted (for a full account of these data see Doherty-Sneddon et al., 1996).

Support for this idea comes from pilot analysis of gaze behavior. Two judges coded 32 videotaped Map Task dialogues and noted each time a speaker looked up at their partner. Interjudge agreement on a sample dialogue was 97%. From detailed analysis of a sample of 8 face-to-face dialogues, it seems that gaze often seems to occur in face-to-face interactions at the same points in dialogue structure as additional verbal checking occurs in audio-only dialogues. We are extending these initial observations to elucidate the role of gaze in face-to-face interactions.

STUDY 1: VMC WITH THE MAP TASK

We investigated whether high-bandwidth VMC "videotunnels" (see Smith, O'Shea, O'Malley, Scanlon, & Taylor, 1991), could replicate the advantages of face-to-face interaction. The face-to-face condition was replaced by a high-resolution video link, which could be set to allow direct eye contact between speakers and which included a full-duplex audio link. We compared the impact of three conditions: VMC where participants could make eye contact with their partner, VMC where eye contact was not possible, and an audio-only condition. In all conditions the participants sat in separate but adjacent rooms. The videotunnel apparatus is illustrated in Fig. 7.2. By altering the position of the camera, subjects are able to make direct eye contact with each other in the eye contact condition. The condition in which subjects could see each other via video but without making eye contact was achieved by displacing the camera's position so that each subject was now looking slightly down on his or her partner. Microphones and speakers were arranged such that the direction of the sound was roughly the same as the viewing angle.

Thirty-six pairs of undergraduates took part in this study. Participants who knew one another were recruited, and each pair tackled three versions of the Map Task, one in each of the conditions: VMC with eye contact, VMC without eye contact, and audio-only communication. All orders of presentation were counterbalanced. If VMC is to confer the benefits we have observed for face-to-face interactions, then our high-quality VMC condition where users can engage in eye contact should elicit similar communication benefits over audio-only conditions as found in the study by Boyle et al. We would expect task performance to be comparable across conditions but task dialogues to be significantly shorter in the VMC plus

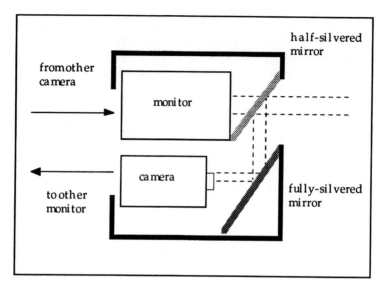

FIG. 7.2. Illustration of the Videotunnel apparatus used in Study 1.

eye contact condition. These efficiency gains should be derived from similar changes in dialogue structure described earlier. As this study used a different subject pool, design, and locations, direct statistical comparisons with the Boyle et al. study are not possible, but broad comparisons of the patterns are made where appropriate.

Results

As we would predict, we found no difference in levels of task performance obtained across conditions. We found, however, that dialogues from the VMC with eye contact condition were significantly longer than dialogues from the other two conditions, containing 11% more turns and 10% more words than the other two conditions, which did not differ. A full account of the results of performance and conversational analyses from this study is given in Doherty-Sneddon et al. (1996). As the level of task performance was the same, not only did VMC with eye contact not replicate the length advantage of face-to-face communication, but it was significantly less efficient. More speech was used to achieve the same level of performance as in audio-only communication.

We used our system of dialogue analysis to explore these differences—in particular, to compare the different ways that dialogues are structured in face-to-face, video-mediated, and audio-only conditions. We analyzed sample dialogues from VMC to examine the distribution of conversational games when visual signals are technologically mediated and compared these with the observed patterns from our analyses of face-to-face and audio-only dialogues described earlier. Are there differences in dialogue structure that explain the failure of VMC to deliver its expected benefits? How are dialogues structured when the visual signals are technologically mediated? Do speakers make the same adjustments to their dialogues in VMC?

To answer these questions, 34 dialogues, 11 from each VMC and 12 from the audio-only conditions, were coded and compared. These formed a representative sample of this corpus, as they were the first dialogues from each pair of participants in the three conditions. The sample did not differ from the complete corpus in performance or dialogue length. Conversational game analysis showed only one significant difference between VMC and audio only dialogues: There were significantly more ALIGN games in audio-only than in either VMC conditions. So, as we would have predicted from our analysis of face-to-face and audio-dialogues, speakers check that their listener has understood what they are saying (ALIGN games) more frequently when they only have an audio link than when visual signals are available. In this respect VMC seems to deliver the same type of dialogue benefit as face-to-face communication. VMC failed to deliver the other advantage of face-to-face interaction: the significant reduction in the number of CHECK games, where listeners check on their understanding of what the speaker has just said. Even if the visual advantage is restricted in VMC, why do speakers produce significantly longer dialogues? The conversational games analysis showed no significant increase of any particular communicative behavior; rather, there was a general increase in the amount of interaction in VMC conditions that allowed eye contact between participants.

What was happening to cause these longer VMC interactions? Was there something about large high-quality video images with eye contact that encouraged greater interaction and hence more dialogue? To tackle this question in a different way we explored the gaze behavior of speakers in the sample of 22 game-coded VMC dialogues. Judges again assessed the videotaped interactions and noted each occasion when a speaker looked up at their partner. On a sample dialogue coded by both judges, interjudge agreement on gaze was 92%. When we compared the amount of gazing in VMC conditions, we found that there was significantly more gazing in the eye contact possible condition, with on average 239 gazes per dialogue compared to 144 where no eye contact was possible. As this rate of gazing was more than double that recorded in face-to-face interactions on the Map Task, we conclude that VMC with eye contact may encourage participants to "overuse" the visual channel.

This level of gaze behavior is unusual for a collaborative task, and may be counterproductive. In several previous studies, such as Goldman-Eisler (1967) and Beattie (1981), it has been suggested that gaze may interfere with cognitive processing and speech planning. So with the high levels of gaze that we observed in these VMC plus eye contact dialogues, the benefits of having access to visual signals may be counterbalanced by users becoming distracted by their partner's face and so using significantly more speech to achieve a comparable level of task success. It is possible that a novel communicative environment encourages users to explore and exploit its capabilities and so elicits more gaze and hence more interaction. It would be interesting to observe users over a period as they gained experience of VMC to see if such effects are a transient novelty factor or a more stable consequence of video-mediated interaction.

We also examined how turn-taking was managed in the different conditions of the study. The total number of interruptions and the rate of interruptions by turn was calculated for each dialogue. Video-mediated dialogues contained more interruptions than those in the remote audio-only condition. The same significant effects resulted even when the length of the dialogues was controlled. This is somewhat surprising given the finding reported in Boyle et al. (1994) that there are significantly fewer interruptions in face-to-face dialogues. When the relative interruption rates are considered the pattern becomes less confusing. In VMC dialogues, on average, 5.6% of turns contained interruptions compared to only 3.6% of turns in the audio-only condition, whereas Boyle et al. reported interruption rates of 8.7% for face-to-face compared to 12% for audio-only interactions. Remote interactions even between separate rooms seem to produce a more formal and less interactive communicative style in general, which VMC goes some way to ameliorate. When speakers are physically copresent as in the Boyle et al. study, the dialogues are more interactive, with a higher incidence of interruptions in general, but visual signals may allow speakers to time their contributions somewhat more precisely and reduce the incidence of overlapping speech. However, the interpretation of interruption data is difficult given the variability reported here and across other studies in the literature.

One possible explanation might be that interruptions may reflect rather different interactive dimensions in different communicative tasks. The presence of visual signals may encourage a more interactive style of conversation so that in social interactions this more relaxed communication will be reflected in an increase in overlapping speech. In problem solving it may be more important to synchronize contributions so that important information is not obscured by frequent interruptions, in which case speakers may use visual signals to help them avoid this sort of communicative problem. Comparisons of the rates of interruptions across different types of dialogues in contexts with and without visual clues might help to clarify such issues. It must be remembered that interruption and overlap in dialogue are very delicate phenomena, and it may be that different transcribing and coding practices may cause some of the differences reported between studies in the literature. It may be best to interpret interruption data with caution, and more advisable to relate it to other observable dimensions of the communicative process and task outcome.

In this study, the only added value of VMC seemed to be that speakers felt able to engage in interaction more freely than in audio-only conditions. High-quality VMC did not replicate all the benefits of face-to-face communication. As the effects on communication seemed to depend on the nature of the VMC, such as whether eye contact was or was not possible, we next explored the impact on users of attempting the same collaborative problem-solving task with a different type of VMC. We investigated whether lower bandwidth video technology, as found in "off-the shelf" videophones, offers advantages in collaborative interactions. One of the limitations of such relatively inexpensive and accessible VMC is that the limited available bandwidth results in delays in transmitting the video signal using current compression technology. Do these technical limitations impact on users? Does VMC offer benefits to task outcome or communication in such conditions?

STUDY 2: EFFECTS OF DELAY

Twenty-four pairs of volunteers attempted our collaborative problem-solving task using different forms of communication technology. We compared the effects on task performance and communication of collaboration supported by high- or low-bandwidth VMC, with and without delay in the video and audio signals. High-bandwidth VMC was provided by videotunnels, as described in Study 1, with direct eye contact possible between speakers. Participants in this condition used a telephone audio link. This represented the video/no delay condition. In the audio-only/no delay condition subjects only had access to the telephone link. In the video/delay condition, participants used off-the-shelf videophones with an analog signal that has a delay of approximately 500 msec, due to the limited bandwidth and compression of the video signal. (The video and audio signals are synchronized, which results in approximately a half-second delay for the whole message.) In the audio-only/delay condition the same system videophone system was used but the video monitor was covered. As the video signal was still being sent even though subjects could not see the monitor, the audio signal was still delayed. Pairs of subjects, who were familiar with each other, tackled two versions of the Map Task: one with the video link and one in the audio-only condition. Pairs of participants were randomly assigned to the delay or no delay conditions. The orders of presentation of conditions were counterbalanced.

Results

When the lengths of dialogues were examined in the various conditions we found no significant differences. The length advantage reported for face-to-face communication in Boyle et al. (1994) again failed to emerge in VMC. An analysis of task outcomes showed no difference in the success of pairs attempting the task with or without visual signals. This is what we would have predicted from our earlier studies. The surprising effect that emerged was the impact of delay, which produced significantly poorer performances. When the audio signal was delayed, performances were on average 36% poorer than those in the no delay conditions. This decrement in performance was also present when subjects could see and hear each other but where there was a delay in both signals: The effect of delay did not interact with visibility. Speakers using videophones performed no better than telephone users where the same audio delay was involved and were 40% worse than normal telephone users. Signal delay also affected turn-taking behavior, causing a significant rise in the total number and the rate of interruptions in dialogues, particularly in the videophone condition. When using videophones over 50% of a speaker's turns were interrupted by the listener. When telephones had a delayed audio signal, over 40% of turns contained interruptions, whereas only 15% of turns had interruptions in the other conditions. In other words, nearly three times as many interruptions occurred in conversations where the audio signal was delayed. In comparison, Boyle et al. report less than 9% of turns containing interruptions in face-to-face dialogues. Visibility was also found to affect turn-taking, with significantly more interruptions in total and a trend toward a higher rate of interruptions where speakers are visible. Visibility did not interact significantly with delay in its effects on turn-taking. Speakers using videophones interrupted on average 69 times per conversation, compared to 21 times in normal telephone conversations, 56 times in telephone conversations with audio delay, and 23 times in VMC with no delay.

We conclude that low-bandwidth VMC with a noticeable delay between audio and video signals (even though they are synchronized) can have adverse effects on collaboration and communication. This delay effect is striking because of the impact on task performance. Most previous studies show no effects on task outcome, but only in the subtler aspects of the communication process. Delay seems to be a salient detrimental factor that should be avoided in the design of communication systems.

In our studies to date we used an experimental procedure to evaluate the effects of different communication modes. This involves a carefully controlled laboratory task, where task difficulty is held constant across all the conditions and different versions of the task can be presented to the same subjects to track the effects of communicative context on the same individuals. Although this has obvious advantages for detailed analysis of performance and communication, the tasks employed are necessarily contrived. In our next two studies we attempted to increase the similarity of our experiments to real-world tasks where VMC might be used. To this end we produced a new and more realistic task, the Travel Game, and used a system incorporating video windows on large computer screens with various shared tools, which is more like those in use or development in nonlaboratory settings.

STUDY 3: VMC WITH THE TRAVEL GAME

In this task, participants plan an itinerary around the United States. They compete for a cash prize for the best itinerary, which includes visits to the most states and cities in the United States. Each "tourist" has a map of the United States, showing states and main airports, but has to communicate with a "travel agent" to obtain details of available flights and connections. There is an objective measure of task success in terms of the number of destinations involved, and the accompanying dialogue and user satisfaction questionnaire provides a rich view of the impact of VMC on such a collaboration.

The Travel Game was designed to elicit collaborative problem solving that involved a more social dimension than the simple exchange of information involved in the Map Task. This aim is reflected in the analysis of the communication process. If visual signals are useful in establishing social presence and have a greater impact on tasks involving negotiation, we might expect that the extent to which "clients" felt at ease with the communicative situation would depend on the availability of visual contact with their conversational partner. As well as including questions about such aspects in our task questionnaire, we also attempted to identify features of the task dialogues that might reflect such a difference. Travel Game clients have to make a series of decisions about their travel plans based on the information they have obtained from the travel agent. To optimize their itineraries they might request a considerable amount of information from the travel agent, who has to consult files to check on the details of available flight connections for each request. We considered that the extent to which the client felt comfortable in involving the travel agent in additional information searches would depend in part on the degree of social presence in the communicative setting. In face-to-face interaction we predicted the client would feel more relaxed about making additional requests for input from the travel agent. Where no visual contact was available to provide emotional/expressive cues we predicted that such requests would be less common.

Undergraduate volunteers were assigned the role of client. They had to communicate with the travel agent to access flight information required to plan their itinerary across the United States. Their goal was to visit as many cities and states as possible on an Airline Travel pass that has restrictions on lengths of stay in a single state and financial penalties for changing airline or backtracking to an earlier destination. Twenty volunteers took part in a comparison of face-to-face interaction and audio-only conditions, where the information was presented on paper. Ten were randomly assigned to each condition. In the second part of the study there were a further 20 participants, and again each was randomly assigned to one condition, attempting the task in either video-mediated or audio-only conditions.

In the computer conditions, users had an audio link, two shared screen facilities, one a map of the United States, one a whiteboard where the travel decisions were logged. Half the users also had a video link showing the face of their partner in a 3.5 × 4.5-inch window. In the paper-and-pencil conditions participants tackled the task while communicating face-to-face, or via an audio link between adjacent rooms. In paper-and-pencil conditions both participants had a copy of a map of the United States showing the major airports. The travel agent had the timetable of flight connections, and the shared travel log, which was visible to both. For the VMC conditions, the Travel Game was presented on two 20-inch color computer monitors on a dedicated local area network (Fig. 7.3). The video image refreshes at 4–5 frames per second. There was an audio link through microphones and headphones, providing full-duplex sound.

The travel agent was a member of the research team familiar with the multimedia communication tools, and had been instructed to work to a loose script in her interactions with clients to ensure she was equally helpful to all clients. She was naive about the details of the experimental hypotheses. Her task was to provide information from standard files about the availability of flight connections and timings and to log the clients' itinerary on the shared screen or notebook. Task performances were assessed by the number of cities and states visited in the time limit for the session. Minor changes were made to the rules of the Travel Game to ensure that it could be completed within 15 min between the two parts of this study. This means that the dialogues were shorter for transcription and analysis, and that in subsequent studies participants could attempt more than one version of the Travel Game task in a single session. We standardize for length in the cross-condition comparisons described later.

When we compared the task performance data, no significant differences emerged. Participants managed to visit just as many destinations in face-to-face and audio-only conditions. In the computer-presented Travel Game the itineraries did not differ when participants did or did not have a video link to the travel agent. Good levels of task outcome were achieved in all conditions. As in previous studies in the literature, problem-solving perform-

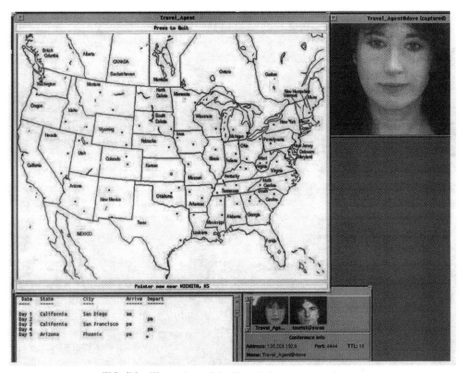

FIG. 7.3. Illustration of the Travel Game screen display.

ance was generally unaffected by communicative context. (See Anderson et al., 1994, for more details of this study.) We next examined the lengths of the dialogues in the different conditions. In the paper-and-pencil conditions, we found that when the client and travel agent communicated face-to-face, the travel agent used 22% fewer words than when they were using an audio link between rooms. So the length advantage found in face-to-face interaction on the Map Task has been replicated in another problem-solving task. When the dialogues from the computer conditions were compared (with and without videolink), no differences were observed. VMC again failed to deliver the efficiency gains of face-to-face interaction.

To explore the structure and the content of the task dialogues, two types of analyses were conducted. Turn-taking was examined by calculating the number and rates of interruptions in each dialogue. An analysis of rates of interruptions across the four conditions showed a significant effect of mediated communication. On average, speakers interrupted one another less often in the second part of the study, where the task and communication were computer mediated. There was no significant effect of visual signals, but across the conditions the rate of interruptions rose from

10.9% of turns containing an interruption in the video window condition, 12% in the computer condition without video link, 13.8% in the face-to-face condition, to 14.5% in the audio-only condition. There was a significant difference ($p < .05$) between the ends of this distribution. The combination of access to visual signals and the greater formality of mediated communication seemed to combine to reduce the incidence of overlapping speech.

We next wanted to explore the content of the clients' contributions in the Travel Game in all the conditions of the study. Our dialogue analysis in the Travel Game aimed at exploring the impact of visual signals on the decision-making process. We assumed that in face-to-face communication the greater sense of shared social presence would lead clients to be more willing to engage the travel agent in extra searches and thus there would be more optional changes of travel plans as clients sought to optimize their itineraries. To test this hypothesis we looked at decision making in each dialogue. We coded as optional or forced all the changes to the planned itineraries made by clients. Forced changes were those that resulted from the information provided by the travel agent, such as there being no available flight connection between two cities. Optional changes were those where the client decided on a new destination from choice, for example, by revising an earlier part of their itinerary, asking for alternative possible destinations, or using the surcharge option in the rules of the game to backtrack to a previous destination. All such optional changes involve more work from the travel agent in terms of additional information searches or alterations to the logged itinerary.

When the number of such forced and optional decision changes were calculated, there were significantly more optional changes in face-to-face than in audio-only interactions. On average there were 6.6 optional changes per dialogue in face-to-face interactions compared to 2.7 in the audio-only condition. No such difference emerged in dialogues from video-window and audio-only conditions. VMC again failed to deliver the same benefits as face-to-face interaction.

Was this because users were dissatisfied with the technology or felt uncomfortable with task presentation or communication? We explored such issues in a posttask questionnaire given to all participants. We asked participants how easy it was to communicate with the travel agent, asking for a choice from very easy to very difficult. The questionnaire showed that in face-to-face interactions 90% of subjects felt that it was very easy to communicate with the travel agent, compared with 50% of audio-only participants. In the video-window condition again only 50% of participants felt it was very easy to communicate, but surprisingly this rose to 80% in the audio-only (computer-based) condition.

How easy was it to make changes to the planned itinerary? In face-to-face communication 70% felt it was very easy compared to 20% in the audio-only condition. In the video-window condition 30% felt it was very easy to make changes compared to 20% in the corresponding audio-only condition. We asked participants to rate their satisfaction with the final outcome of the consultation with the travel agent. In face-to-face interactions 100% reported that they were satisfied or very satisfied with the outcome, as did 90% in the audio-only condition. In the mediated conditions, user ratings were again high with 80% in both conditions satisfied or very satisfied with the outcome.

The questionnaire data provide some useful confirmation that the impressions of users are largely in accord with the objective measures of performance and communication. Although VMC users were satisfied with their performance, and often commented on the appeal of the new technology, they felt slightly less at ease in the communication process than those engaged in face-to-face interaction. VMC did not seem to generate the same sense of social presence as face-to-face communication and indeed showed no benefits over the same technology without video signals.

In our most recent study we explore a context where the possibly subtle benefits of VMC may prove of value: distance collaboration. We investigate the impact of VMC on task outcome, communication, and user satisfaction, where users are aware that their conversational partner is several hundreds of miles away, in a different country.

STUDY 4: EFFECTS OF REMOTENESS

Here we assess the impact of VMC on long-distance collaboration over the European Internet. The quality of video and audio links provided by the Internet is rather variable. The United Kingdom–Netherlands link is generally one of the best connections. In pilot tests and in the main study described here we found that the video signal rarely suffered breakup of the image and the audio signal was clearly audible on almost all occasions. Twelve undergraduates at the University of Glasgow participated as tourists in this Travel Game study. Each tackled two versions of the Travel Game, one with and one without a video link. The order of presentation was counterbalanced. The Travel Agent was at the Technical University of Delft in the Netherlands but operated to the same script as had been used in earlier studies. The students were informed that this was a long-distance link between Glasgow and Delft, and the travel agent, although a fluent English speaker, spoke with a noticeable Dutch accent. In pretask chat while setting up the task, the conversation clearly indicated that this was a genuine long-distance experiment. The communication link over the Internet used public-domain network video and audio tools. The same computers and monitors were used as in Study 3.

Results

The first finding was that the Internet connection between the United Kingdom and the Netherlands was able to support this kind of collaboration. Of 24 experimental sessions, only one had to be abandoned and rerun due to technical difficulties with the network link. Reasonably good audio and video reception was obtained in the remaining sessions, with clear sound and little noticeable lag or breakup of video images.

The results of the Travel Game showed no difference in the task outcome for video or audio link conditions. Although this again shows no advantage for VMC on outcome measures, it is encouraging in other respects. The level of task success was very similar to that obtained in earlier studies. The differences imposed by using network communication tools, such as the need to click a pointer in a designated area of the screen before speaking, and the performance of the Internet compared to a dedicated local area network did not impair performance on the task.

When we assessed the communication process, we found no difference between VMC and audio-only conditions in terms of the lengths of the dialogues in words or speaker turns. The number of interruptions was low and did not differ between conditions.

The questionnaire data again showed some subjective benefits for VMC. Although 83% of users found it very easy to communicate in both conditions, in VMC 83% of responses were very satisfied with the task outcome compared to 67% in audio-only. When users were asked about social presence (i.e., how aware they were of the travel agent), 92% of responses in VMC were fairly or very aware, compared to only 50% in the audio-only condition. When asked how often they were worried that they had lost contact with the travel agent, 75% of audio-only users were worried on some occasions about losing contact, compared to 50% of VMC users. These data suggest that in truly remote collaboration there may be some benefits for VMC in establishing and maintaining social presence.

DISCUSSION

Video-mediated communication potentially offers us the benefits of face-to-face interaction while collaborating with a distant partner. We have tried to illustrate what benefits accrue in face-to-face interaction that VMC systems might be designed to emulate. We found that the visual signals in face-to-face conversation seem to be used in several ways. First, speakers use visual cues to judge that communication is proceeding smoothly and hence need to elicit verbal feedback less often. Second, listeners are more confident and check their understanding of messages less often. Third, visual cues may be used to establish a sense of social copresence that makes us feel at ease with our conversational partner and so feel able to ask for additional information or help in a shared task.

Video-mediated technology has been designed to facilitate collaborative communication at a distance. To simulate such conditions we compared task performance and dialogue between participants in different rooms. The visual signals transmitted in high-bandwidth VMC elicited dialogues structured in certain respects like face-to-face communication. Compared with speakers in the remote audio-only condition, speakers using VMC requested verbal feedback less often, presumably because the available visual signals provided feedback information. Video mediation encouraged speakers to interact more freely, interrupting one another more often. But even high-bandwidth VMC that allowed eye contact between speakers failed to deliver the same efficiency benefits as face-to-face communication. Speakers said significantly more in VMC to achieve the same level of task success as in audio-only conversations. The increased length of the dialogues may have arisen because of the high level of speaker gazing that was elicited in VMC with eye contact. This may have encouraged more interaction, either because of the heightened sense of social presence that frequent gazing produces or because the frequent gazing at the listener distracts the speakers from planning and producing utterances, so longer dialogues are needed to complete the task. This effect seemed to "swamp" the length advantage of reduced verbal feedback.

In contrast, low-bandwidth VMC, where audio and video signals are delayed, had pronounced detrimental effects, impairing task outcome and smooth communication. With limited bandwidth and the demands of video compression there is a trade-off between delay and synchronicity. One might choose to have no delay in the audio signal, but that would result in lack of synchronicity with the video signal. One also might suppose that having visual information would help in managing conversations where the audio signal is delayed (e.g., because listeners can see when their interlocutors are ready to "hand over" a turn). However, our study shows that having both signals delayed, even though synchronized, still disrupts the timing in normal conversation. Seeing your partner does not help to overcome this disadvantage. Teasing apart the relative detrimental effects of lack of synchronicity or delay will require further research.

Our small study of long-distance collaboration suggests that VMC may offer some advantages in this area by making the conversational partners more aware of one another and reassuring them that they remain in contact even across a remote Internet connection. Further analyses of these remote dialogues continue to explore whether there are any differences in dialogue structure that reflect these subjective impressions.

It remains to be seen whether the effects of VMC that we observed are transient and would diminish with increased experience of VMC. This factor may be important, because reports in the literature that claim added value for VMC (e.g., Tang & Isaacs, 1993; Olson, Olson, & Meader, 1994; Isaacs & Tang, 1994) use either fairly lengthy exposure or repeated exposure over time.

What we have shown has implications for the development and use of video-mediating technologies. The visual channel is useful for task efficiency even for a task where social factors are not a central component (compared to, for example, negotiation and bargaining tasks). The impact of the visual channel depends on the medium through which it is transmitted. Video-mediated communication does not necessarily bring the same efficiency benefits to communication as face-to-face interaction, even when it elicits some similar dialogue characteristics.

We have been concerned with the impact on collaboration of video-mediated images of the conversational partner. The conclusions that we might draw from these studies are that the benefits of face-to-face communication are rather subtle and the forms of VMC that we have investigated to date do not seem able to replicate these advantages. This is, of course, only one possible use of video data in collaborative tasks. The possibility of sharing other forms of video data would almost certainly have a large impact on task performance and communication. In the Map Task, for example, the collaborators only have access to their own copies of the maps, but the instruction giving and following tasks would have been greatly altered by having shared access to both individuals' maps. We would expect that the task would have been performed more accurately with less discussion required between participants in such a communicative context. In the Travel Game task we provided shared access to relevant video data in the form of the shared map of the United States, and the whiteboard where travel decisions were recorded. If such information had not been accessible to both participants we assume the task would have been considerably more difficult and would have required longer dialogues between tourist and travel agent. In future studies we intend to go further in making systematic comparisons of the impact on users of video data compared to video images of the conversational partner.

A final point that we wish to make is methodological. Monk et al. (1996) proposed that a full evaluation of communication technology requires measures of both task outcome and communicative process. This is the approach we have adopted. Only by looking at both of these aspects in conjunction can we adequately evaluate the impact of VMC. By looking at task performance alone (as in many earlier studies) we would have concluded that there is no difference between video-mediated, face-to-face, and audio-only communication. By looking only at measures of process, such as the number of turns per dialogue, we may have concluded that VMC is either equivalent to or worse than audio-only communication. By looking at process and outcome together we see that communicative structure, verbal and nonverbal, differs across the contexts in ways that offer advantages and disadvantages to the efficiency of the interactions. The visual channel provided by VMC is useful to speakers, but the remoteness of the interaction invokes a change in communication style that offsets the benefits.

The studies reported in this chapter show that here is no simple answer to whether VMC "works" or offers advantages. Different technological configurations of VMC will have different impacts on users, and some systems such as low-tech videophones may actually disadvantage users. In general, however, the pattern is a complex one. Successful collaboration depends on a number of complementary processes: how the process of communication is managed, the level of task success achieved, and the users' satisfaction with all the aspects of these processes. VMC has been shown to influence each of these aspects of collaboration within our laboratory studies of joint problem solving. Although designers will naturally be concerned with the impact of VMC on users in the workplace using systems for more extended time periods than those we employed, the data we have presented suggest that such studies must also deploy evaluation methods that consider the multidimensional aspects of collaboration. In any of our studies we would obtain a different answer to the question of whether VMC "works" if we considered task performance, communication process, or user satisfaction, in isolation. The same dangers apply to field studies in the workplace.

ACKNOWLEDGMENTS

The research reported in this chapter was supported by the Centre for Research in Development, Instruction & Training (University of Nottingham) and the Human Communication Research Centre (University of Glasgow), both funded by the UK Economic and Social Research Council; and a grant from the Economic and Social Research Council to Claire O'Malley, Anne Anderson, and Vicki Bruce. Support from the EC COST 14 Project PAMWAC facilitated the Internet study between Glasgow and Delft.

REFERENCES

Anderson, A. H., Mullin, J., Newlands, A., Doherty-Sneddon, G., & Fleming, A. M. (1994). Video-Mediated Communication in CSCW: Effects on Communication and Collaboration. In *Proceedings of Workshop on VMC, at CSCW 94*, Chapel Hill, NC.

Beattie, G. (1981). A further investigation of the cognitive interference hypothesis of gaze patterns during conversation. *British Journal of Social Psychology, 20,* 243–248.

Boyle, E. A., Anderson, A. H., & Newlands, A. (1994). The effects of eye contact on dialogue and performance in a co-operative problem solving task. *Language and Speech, 37*(1), 1–20.

Brown, G., Anderson, A. H., Yule, G., & Shillcock, R. (1984). *Teaching talk.* Cambridge: Cambridge University Press.

Chapanis, A. (1975). Interactive human communication. *Scientific American, 232,* 36–42.

Chapanis, A., Ochsman, R. B., Parrish, R. N., & Weeks, G. D. (1972). Studies in interactive communication: The effects of four communication modes on the behavior of teams during co-operative problem-solving. *Human Factors, 14,* 487–509.

Davies, M. F. (1971). *Co-operative problem-solving: A follow-up study* (Rep. No. E/71252/DVS). Cambridge: Post Office, Long Range Intelligence Division.

Doherty-Sneddon, G., Anderson, A. H., O'Malley, C., Langton, S., Garrod, S., & Bruce, V. (1996). Face-to-face communication and VMC: A comparison of dialogue structure and task performance. *Journal of Experimental Psychology: Applied.* Manuscript submitted for review.

Goldman-Eisler, F. (1968). *Psycholinguistics: Experiments in spontaneous speech.* London: Academic Press.

Houghton, G., & Isard, S. (1987). Why to speak, what to say, and how to say it. In P. Morris (Ed.), *Modelling cognition* (pp. 249–267). London: Wiley.

Isaacs, E. A., & Tang, J. C. (1994). What video can and cannot do for collaboration: A case study. *Multimedia Systems, 2,* 63–73.

Kowtko, J. C., Isard, S., & Doherty-Sneddon, G. (1991). *Conversational games in dialogue,* A. Lascarides (Ed.) (Tech. Rep. No. HCRC/RP-26 Publications). University of Edinburgh.

Monk, A., McCarthy, J., Watts, L., & Daly-Jones, O. (1996). Measures of process. In M. MacLeod and D. Murray (Eds.), *Evaluation for CSCW* (pp. 125–139). Berlin: Springer Verlag.

Morley, I. E., & Stephenson, G. M. (1969). Interpersonal and interparty exchange: A laboratory simulation of an industrial negotiation at plant level. *British Journal of Psychology, 60,* 543–545.

O'Connaill, B., Whittaker, S., & Wilbur, S. (1993). Conversations over videoconferences: An evaluation of videomediated interaction. *Human–Computer Interaction, 8,* 389–428.

Olson, G. M., Olson, J. S., Carter, M., & Storrøsten, M. (1992). Small group design meetings: An analysis of collaboration. *Human–Computer Interaction, 7,* 347–374.

Olson, J. S., Olson, G. M., & Meader, D. K. (1994). What mix of video and audio is useful for remote real-time work. *Proceedings of Workshop on VMC, CSCW 1994* (pp. 33–42). New York. ACM.

Olson, J. S., Olson, G. M., Storrøsten, M., & Carter, M. (1993). Groupwork close up: A comparison of the group design process with and without a simple group editor. *ACM Transactions on Information Systems, 11,* 321–348.

Power, R. (1979). The organisation of purposeful dialogues. *Linguistics, 17,* 107–152.

Sellen, A. J. (1992). Speech patterns in video mediated conversations. *Proceedings of CHI 1992* (pp. 49–59). New York: ACM.

Sellen, A. J (1995). Remote conversations: The effects of mediating talk with technology. *Human–Computer Interaction, 10,* 401–444.

Short, J. (1974). Effects of medium of communication on experimental negotiation. *Human Relations, 27,* 225–243.

Short, J., Williams, E., & Christie, B. (1976). *The social psychology of telecommunications.* London: Wiley.

Smith, R., O'Shea, T., O'Malley, C., Scanlon, E., & Taylor, J. (1991). Preliminary experiments with a distributed, multi-media, problem-solving environment. In J. Bowers & S. Benford

(Eds.), *Studies in computer-supported co-operative work: Theory, practice and design* (pp. 31–48). Amsterdam: Elsevier.

Strauss, S., & McGrath, J. (1994). Does the medium matter: The interaction of task and technology on group performance and member reactions. *Journal of Applied Psychology, 79*, 87–97.

Tang, J. C., & Isaacs, E. A. (1993). Why do users like video? Studies of multimedia collaboration. *Computer-Supported Cooperative Work, 1*, 163–196.

Williams, E. (1977). Experimental comparisons of face-to-face and video mediated communication. *Psychological Bulletin, 84*, 963–976.

Chapter 8

Face-to-Face Group Work Compared to Remote Group Work With and Without Video

Judith S. Olson
Gary M. Olson
University of Michigan

David Meader
University of Arizona

We report results from two studies that compare the quality of the work, the process, and the perceptions of participants when working in four conditions: Face-to-face with whiteboard, paper, and pencil; face-to-face with a shared editor; remotely with the editor plus high-quality spatial audio; and remotely with the editor plus audio and high-quality video. Results showed that the quality of the work with remote high-quality video is as good as face-to-face. Remote work without video is not as good as face-to-face. Face-to-face work is better when supported by a shared editor than when the group uses traditional tools such as a whiteboard and paper and pencil. However, the process of remote work differs from that of face-to-face. There is more clarification, regardless of the presence of video. Contrary to expectations, video does not encourage the participants to be more engaged nor to discuss things more critically. But video in remote work is preferred by the participants over audio-only, and equally to face-to-face work.

INTRODUCTION

Meetings are a central component of collaborative work in organizations. They can range from formal meetings that are scheduled in advance with a predefined agenda to informal, ad hoc meetings where the members of a work group get together to work interactively on some problem on the spur of the moment. Traditionally, all forms of what we think of as meetings took place face-to-face, in meeting rooms, commons areas, and lunchrooms. But as we all know, groups no longer need to meet in the same location; new technologies are allowing us to relax the constraint of colocation. Alternatives to face-to-face interactions have distinctive properties, and have not, in any real sense, replaced what it is possible to do in face-to-face interactions. We need to understand better what the opportunities and constraints are that are offered by each mode of synchronous interaction.

This chapter integrates the results from a line of research whose aim is to understand these issues. We have focused on synchronous interactions among small teams working on design problems. In this line of research, we began with field studies of groups in real organizations doing software system design (Olson, Olson, Carter, & Storrøsten, 1992). Our goal was to understand better what small group behavior was like for design tasks, and what opportunities existed for supporting this activity with technology. We learned much about both, leading to our developing a simple shared editor called ShrEdit (McGuffin & Olson, 1992) that we felt had properties that would be useful for groups doing these kinds of tasks. It provided the members of a group with an electronic workspace into which they could all enter and edit their ideas as they worked.

We created a design task that elicited design behavior similar to what we had seen in the field, and compared real groups of three people using ShrEdit with groups working with the more traditional meeting-room media of whiteboard and paper and pencil. The groups using ShrEdit produced higher quality designs, as judged by a rater who was blind to which design came from which group. To our surprise, the groups with ShrEdit did this by exploring fewer ideas rather than more. They were also somewhat less satisfied with their work process than the groups working in a traditional fashion. Details of this are reported later, as appropriate to understanding how groups working in remote situations differ from those working face-to-face.

Modern networking has brought about the possibility for these small groups to be located in different places while working. A fundamental consideration in ShrEdit's design is that we assumed that the members of a group would always have other communication channels available to them. In a face-to-face setting, of course, the groups can talk and gesture in their usual interactive ways. Indeed, the groups in our studies engaged in extensive discussion while using ShrEdit as a workspace to capture and revise their emerging ideas. So our next step was to investigate the use of ShrEdit by distributed groups.

We decided to provide communication for our groups that was as ideal as we could make it given their distributed setup. We wanted a baseline for later studies that looked at other kinds of communication, and in particular digital desktop video.

A number of sources indicate that high-quality audio is important to synchronous work (Fish, Kraut, & Chaltonte, 1990; Pagani & Mackay, 1993; Tang & Isaacs, 1992). So we had half our groups work with high-quality audio in addition to the shared workspace. Our audio was full duplex, directional for both input and output, and of far better quality than found in teleconferencing or most commercial video conferencing systems.

More controversial is whether video adds significant value for groups doing distributed problem solving. Although the research record is quite mixed, many theories, and most people's intuitions, are that video should add substantial value to such work. Thus, the other half of our groups had our good-quality audio plus high-quality analog video connections to each of their colleagues. The video was arranged in an optimal fashion to create the feeling of sitting around the a table with one's colleagues, with the shared workspace in the center (see Fig. 8.1). We took more care than usual to create what we felt would be the best possible videoconferencing setup.

We were interested in how these video/audio groups using ShrEdit would compare to face-to-face groups using ShrEdit from our earlier study (Olson, Olson, Storrøsten, & Carter, 1993) on a range of measures: quality of the work product, satisfaction, and characteristics of the group process. We also compared these audio/video groups to the audio-only groups to assess the added effect of the video. What distinguishes our study from previous investigations is the use of a task that has been established to be representative of design in the real world, the use of an established workspace tool of known value for sharing the work, and the care we took to ensure that the audio and video were of the highest quality we could get with present communication technology. We used a variety of measures to assess the process and product of the work.

FIG. 8.1. A diagram of the audio and video configuration in our remotely connected offices.

METHOD

Although we report two different studies here, the conditions were constructed and run to be comparable. Therefore, we report the combined method, indicating where the two studies differed and in what ways the analyses we report draw on different samples of data.

Subjects

Seventy-four existing groups of three professionals participated in the study—a total of 222 individuals. All of the groups consisted of three MBAs,[1] each enrolled in the Michigan Business School. In all groups, the members had worked together before in class or work projects and all knew at least one Macintosh or Windows application.

Settings and Their Communication Support

Thirty-eight groups worked face-to-face in the Collaboration Technology Suite (CTS) (see Fig. 8.2). They were seated at workstations that were slightly recessed in the table so that they did not interfere with eye contact and gestures. The 19 groups that used ShrEdit, two people sat on one side of the table, one on the other. The 19 groups that used traditional technologies, whiteboards, paper, and pencil typically sat on one side of the meeting table, facing the whiteboard. All freely talked and gestured throughout the session.

Thirty-six groups worked in a distributed mode. They were seated in three separate rooms made to look like offices. In these rooms, a workstation with a large screen was centered on a desk, with two 13-inch video monitors on each side of the screen, as shown in Fig. 8.1. A camera and microphone were mounted on each video monitor, with the camera placed at the center of the top of the monitor so that when the participants faced each other, they appeared to each other to be making near eye contact.[2] Furthermore, when the other two remote participants were facing each other, their images projected to the receiving participant made them look as if they were looking at each other. All of the remote groups used ShrEdit.

The microphones and speakers were similarly situated to either side of the central screen, corresponding to the person shown on the video screen. They were open full-duplex channels that offered a sense of spatial location. Indeed, in the audio-only condition, group participants often moved their heads to face the speakers of the people they were addressing. The audio condition used the identical microphones and speakers of the video condition; the only difference was that the video monitors were turned off.

FIG. 8.2. Groups meeting in the CTS, the groups on the left using ShrEdit and the group on the right using the whiteboard, paper, and pencil.

Document-Sharing Technology

The technology used here was one we designed and built called ShrEdit, which stands for Shared Editor (McGuffin & Olson, 1992). ShrEdit is a simple text editor that allows all participants to view and change the same simple text document, with all participants being able to type simultaneously within one character position of each other. Although the individuals' views of the document are normally independent (each can scroll to a different part of the document or arrange the windows on the screen in a unique way), the views can also be locked together if the discussion calls for it. Although the task, described next, may appear to require sketches, the problem statement clearly indicated that lists and descriptions in text would suffice, making ShrEdit an appropriate tool for this task.

Task

We chose to study the task of group design, that of early requirements definition, because it is both important and interesting. In terms of McGrath's (1984) task taxonomy, this activity is a blend of Planning, Creativity, Decision Making, and Cognitive Conflict.

In this study, all groups were instructed to draft the initial requirements for an automatic post office (APO), a collection of postal services offered through a stand-alone device similar to an ATM (automatic teller machine) for which a prototype could be built by their fictitious company of 30 people in a year. They were instructed to determine the core services they would offer, some of the required equipment, the rough cost/benefit analysis, and a list of things they would like to investigate before the next time they would (hypothetically) meet. They were given 1½ hr to complete the assignment, producing meeting notes that could be read by a (fictitious) additional group member who could not attend that day's meeting.

Procedure

The subjects came to the CTS for a single 3-hr period, broken into two 1½-hr portions with a 15-min break in between. In the first half, the subjects filled out background questionnaires and permission forms. Those groups that used ShrEdit were then trained in a 20-min session. The instructions demonstrated the system's capabilities and how to control them, but did not prescribe how to use these features to support work. After the training session, the groups working face-to-face remained in the CTS. Those groups in the two remote conditions were then taken to their individual remote offices. They first took a few minutes to acclimate to the setting, to set camera angles and audio levels.

All groups were asked to solve two small problems of 20 min each. These tasks served both to allow the subjects to warm up to the task situation and, as appropriate, to learn the software and adjust to the software's capability for simultaneous editing. Following a 15-min break, the groups did the APO task in a single 1½-hr sitting. All groups filled out a questionnaire after the session assessing their satisfaction with the work they did and the functioning of the group. For the remote groups, we also asked their rating of their ability to understand others in the group and to be understood by them.

Study Design

Groups were recruited en masse through various MBA classes and fliers and encouraged to sign up at convenient times, either morning, afternoon, or evening sessions for 3 hr. The groups in the face-to-face conditions were run in entirety before the groups in the remote conditions, with these being two experiments. Because the subjects were drawn from the same population and two of the three experimenters were the same, we did not worry about infusing differences in the conditions other than those we intended. In each study, the groups were assigned to the two conditions at random as they came in, with the proviso that at the end of each week the conditions were balanced for time of day, and each of the experimenters served in an equal number of the different conditions.

Measures

Our goal was to assess three things: the quality of the product, the participants' satisfaction with the process, and the process of design and coordination.

Outcome. We assessed how the technology affected the outcomes of the meetings and the quality of the design as reflected in the final document of each group. We used the same quality measure as was used in Olson et al. (1993). This measure was developed after extensive discussion with both designers and researchers of design. Three major aspects of the groups' output were scored: how completely the output covered all the aspects of the assigned task, the ease of understanding of the ideas reported in the document, and the judged quality of the post office design, including the feasibility of producing a prototype of the suggested post office within the stated time and manpower constraints, the coherence of the ideas, and the judged success of the ideas if marketed. The average pairwise correlation between raters was .85. Because this was well above acceptable range for reliability of measures, one researcher then coded the quality of the remaining meetings' outputs using the same instrument. Out of a possible score of 80 points, the quality of the meetings' output ranged from 25 to 74.

Satisfaction. To assess satisfaction, we constructed a post-session questionnaire that asked the participants to

1. Rate their satisfaction with the process that they used (adapted from Gouran, Brown, & Henry, 1978; Green & Taber, 1980) as well as with the design result (Green & Taber, 1980)
2. Assess the evenness of the participants' contributions (Gouran et al., 1978) and identify a leader if one emerged
3. Rate how easy it was to understand the other participants and be understood

The first two sets of questions were asked of all groups; the remaining 23, which focused on various details of the communication media, were asked only of the groups working remotely.

Process. All sessions were video- and audiotaped. From audio, we transcribed the conversations. In addition, we captured timed keystrokes from ShrEdit; we integrated this typing activity into the verbal transcript as appropriate. These transcripts were then coded for what kinds of activity were taking place at each moment, using the categories devised and tested in our study of field design meetings and the earlier related lab study (Olson et al., 1992, 1993). We identified times when the participants stated the issue on the table, when they generated alternatives, and when they critiqued the ideas. These categories have origins in the design rationale literature (Olson et al., 1992, 1993). We also catalogued the time it took the participants to organize themselves (an activity we call *meeting manage-*

ment), to clarify their ideas, talk through difficulties with the technology, or engage in side digressions. The division of activity into task and process management was inspired by work in the literature (Putnam, 1983; Zigurs, Poole, & DeSanctis, 1988).

Several new categories were required to account for the work surrounding producing the output: times when they would plan the organization and wording or dictate the words, called *plan* and *write*. In the supported groups, we required yet another two categories: times when they were confused about something having to do with the technology, and other comments about the placing of their work into the windows on the screen. We called these *technology confusion* and *technology management*, respectively.

Interrater reliability of the core 22 categories was measured in two ways. A strict measure shows the correspondence of categorization, second by second; our interrater reliability is 68%, with a Cohen's $\kappa = .64$. If we look at the summary measures used, the correlation between the two raters' summary statistics on time in category was .97.

For a subset of the audio and video conditions, we assessed two additional processes: engagement and critical discussion. *Engagement* was defined as the degree to which individuals invest themselves in and contribute to task-oriented group discussion. Sproull and Kiesler (1986) found that without social context cues (in e-mail conversations) people were more self-absorbed and less engaged. We expected that the groups working remotely would have a tendency to be more engaged if they could see each other, with the video providing the social context cues.

Engagement was operationalized in several ways:

1. The time spent in sequences of act–response interactions whether the participants agreed with each other or not, including time discussing things written in the shared document
2. Speaker turn change density, rapid interchange of statements and their responses
3. Length of time the groups met

To be sure, people can be engaged in other ways than arguing, and meeting long, such as by attending to a discussion without speaking, or by entering thoughts into the shared document. However, because both these other types are harder to measure, we took the verbal repartee and meeting length to be reasonable measures of the groups' engagement. Reliability of coding this category was .94 for segmenting the speech stream, and .80 for agreeing on the category label for relevant segments. Reliability of the count of turn density was .98. (See Meader, 1995, for details of both the operationalization and reliability calculations of both engagement and critical discussion.)

Critical discussion refers to the aspects of design discussions in which both positive and negative evaluations are offered. Critical discussion is the antithesis of group think (Janis, 1982), in which only positive support is offered for ideas generated. The presence of critical discussion has been positively related to group effectiveness in solving problems that have some ambiguity (Sambamurthy & Poole, 1992; Eisenhardt & Bourgeois, 1992). We expected that the remote groups with video would engage in more critical discussion, because the interaction was natural and easy, not requiring additional attention to maintaining the conversation. It was thought that the effort needed in the audio-only condition to maintain the conversation would take away from the energy required to engage in critical discussion, resulting in poorer quality output.

The concept was operationalized as the amount of time in which discussion on the design included both positive and negative criteria. Reliability of coding this category was .94 for segmenting the speech stream, and .68 for agreeing on the category label for that segment.

Analyses of engagement and critical discussion were performed on 30 groups, 15 of the groups who were remote with video and 15 of the groups who were remote with audio only. This subset has the same overall characteristics of time use and quality of outcome as the whole 38 remote groups.

RESULTS

The results are organized by the major classes of measures as described above: outcome, satisfaction, and process.

Outcome Differences

Figure 8.3 arrays the quality scores for all four conditions. This shows that the average judged quality of the groups supported by audio plus video was not significantly higher than that for groups supported by audio only, $t(36) = 1.41$, $p < .16$.

Although these quality differences were not significant, they showed a pattern of differences with the face-to-face conditions that is interesting. All four quality ratings were not significantly different from their adjacent values (FTF Unsupported = Remote Audio; Remote Video = FTF with ShrEdit). However, FTF with ShrEdit was significantly higher than the Remote Audio, $t(35) = 2.67$, $p < .01$, and FTF Unsupported, $t(36) = 2.71$, $p < .01$. Remote Video was not significantly higher than FTF Unsupported, $p < .09$.

In sum, the quality differences when one takes away video connections are small and do not always overcome the large between-group variances in performance. But more interesting, work with remote high-quality video

FTF	Remote	Remote	FTF
Unsup.	Audio	Video	Supported

54.7 = 56.7 = 61.5 = 64.4

```
            |--------------p<.01------------|
|-----------------------p<.01---------------|
|---------(p<.09)-----------|
```

FIG. 8.3. Analysis of quality of the output.

to support conversation is as good as face-to-face. Remote work without video is not as good as face-to-face.

Satisfaction

Analysis of the questionnaires revealed that when there is no video connection, the participants reported in the questionnaire that the quality of the discussion was significantly poorer, $t(106) = 2.32$, $p < .02$ (Fig. 8.4). Furthermore, remote work with video was as satisfactory as face to face (with ShrEdit support). The normal way of working, however, face-to-face with whiteboard and paper and pencil, was the highest of all. This is not surprising because all of the mode of working with ShrEdit was new and may have temporarily unsettled people.

In other questions, the remote group with audio only reported being less able to tell how their other group members were reacting to things said, $t(106) = 2.28$, $p < .025$. They also reported that the communication system got in the way of their being able to persuade others about their ideas, $t(106) = 3.52$, $p < .001$, or to resolve disagreements, $t(106) = 2.15$, $p < .03$.

Process Differences

We now look at how the groups conducted their work, in particular how they spent their time and how they moved among activities in the course of design.

We coded the transcripts of the spoken parts of the meetings, noting the kinds of activities they engaged in, and then summarized how much total time was spent in each activity as well as the flow between activities. Figure 8.5 shows a view of the flow of activities, with the two face-to-face conditions at the top and the two remote conditions at the bottom. In these diagrams, each category of activity is represented by a circle, the area

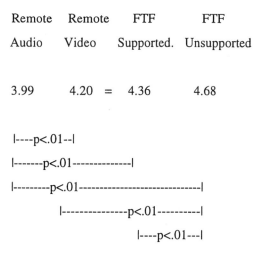

FIG. 8.4. Mean ratings of the rated quality of the discussion.

of which represents the total time the group spent in that activity, aggre-
gated over the whole meeting. White portions of the circle represent the
direct introduction of the idea; the black wedges represent the time spent
clarifying that topic. The arrows denote the transitions between them, the
width of which reflects the likelihood of going from one category to the
next.[3]

The groups in both conditions spent their time in almost identical ways.
Furthermore, they are almost identical to the way in which face-to-face
groups worked with the same shared editor tool these groups used. The
differences that were significantly different included: Video groups spent
less time than audio groups stating and clarifying the Issues, $t(34) = 2.54$,
$p < .02$; $t(34) = 2.25$, $p < .03$. Remote groups (both Video and Audio)
spent significantly more time managing their meeting than the FTF group
using ShrEdit (Video: $t(35) = 2.92$, $p < .006$; Audio: $t(35) = 3.18$, $p < .003$).
Remote groups (certainly Audio and marginally Video) spent significantly
more time clarifying what they meant to each other (all categories combined) than the FTF group using ShrEdit (Video: $t(35) = 1.81$, $p < .08$;
Audio: $t(35) = 2.31$, $p < .003$).

Engagement

Engagement has three measures: time in interaction, speaker turn density,
and length of time the groups met. Recall that these analyses were done
on 30 of the 38 remote groups, but that this subset represents the whole
on the other measures.

None of the anticipated differences emerged (Table 8.1). Time in interaction and speaker turn changes per unit time were equal in the remote

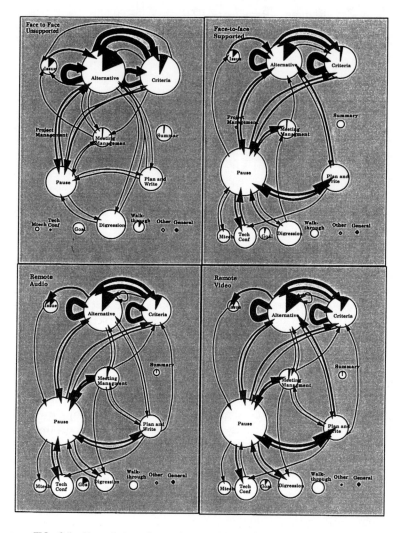

FIG. 8.5. Use of time for various activities along with the pattern of
transitions between the activities for the face-to-face (top) and remote
(bottom) groups.

four conditions. Overall, the mean time spent in the meetings was 87 min,
which was not significantly different over the four conditions. Furthermore,
the groups talked a great deal during this 87 min; they were not just silently
typing. On average the groups spent 64 min talking. The three groups
that had ShrEdit talked significantly less than the group using whiteboard
paper and pencil, by 13 min, $F(3,70) = 6.06$, $p < .001$. There was no

TABLE 8.1
Measures of Engagement in the Remote With
Audio Only and Remote With Video Conditions

	Remote Audio	Remote Video
Time spent in task-based interaction	46.2 min	47.2 min
Number of keystrokes	6,380	7,210
Speaker turn change density	7.8/min	7.8/min
Meeting length	83.8 min	89.6 min

difference among the groups supported by ShrEdit, whether they were FTF or remote, or supported by video or only audio.

Critical Discussion

We thought that video groups, having an easier time understanding each other and being understood, would engage in more critical discussion. The groups with video spent 10.6 min in critical discussion and the groups with audio only 10.7. There was no difference, $p < .17$.

Correlations With Quality

Although there were no overall differences between the audio and video conditions except in perceptions of ease of communication, there were some other variables that correlated with quality of outcome. Combining both remote conditions, the more the group typed (total keystrokes), the higher the quality output, $r = .58$, $p < .01$. Furthermore, the more highly the group rated the communication ease, the longer the meetings, $r = .62$, $p < .01$, and the more turn changes, $r = .49$, $p < .05$. Putting these two results together, using engagement as measurable by either turn change, meeting length, or keystrokes, we find that the easier the perceived communication, the more the engagement and the higher the quality of output. We found earlier that remote video groups rated the communication as easier; we might then be led to think that video could lead to better quality output.

CONCLUSIONS

With high-quality communication (both audio and video) and a shared workspace tool, distributed groups can produce work that is indistinguishable in quality from face-to-face groups using the same workspace tool. Taking away the video from remote groups leads to poorer quality designs when compared to face-to-face groups. The audio-only groups were marginally different from the video groups. Thus, high-quality group intellectual work is possible under distributed conditions, and video appears to add some value.

The perceptions of the users, however, is that video clearly adds value. The groups working at a distance without video do not like it as much as those that have the video. They reported being less able to tell how their other group members were reacting to things said. They also reported that the communication system got in the way of their being able to persuade others about their ideas or to resolve disagreements. Groups without video report having a harder time communicating, and that perception is loosely correlated with engagement in the task and outcome quality. Tang and Isaacs (1993) found that groups in a field setting that were offered video in addition to shared workspace and audio used the system more heavily than those that had audio and workspace tools, suggesting that the preference we saw in our study could be a harbinger of usage patterns when these capabilities were discretionary.

However, judged by how people used their time, distributed work does require greater process overhead. The remote groups spent more time managing their work and clarifying what they meant than the face-to-face groups. Working under distributed circumstances is not equivalent to working face-to-face. Perhaps there is more sense of what others are doing and what they mean when we are face-to-face than can be presented via even very good video channels.

These results are important. We confirm the results of others (Chapanis & Ochsman, 1972; Minneman & Bly, 1991; Smith, O'Shea, O'Malley, Scanlon, & Taylor, 1989) in that remote work can be done without loss of quality. This work has added to this body of findings, however, in that it uses intact groups doing a more realistic task, and uses measures of process as well as quality and satisfaction. In addition, we found that remote work takes extra effort to manage the group and clarify things meant. Adding video to remote work has some value in terms of the work accomplished by the groups, and has a clearer effect on the satisfaction of the group members. People like to see each other. Video makes them feel more able to communicate with each other, to persuade and resolve issues. This in turn makes them more engaged, resulting in higher quality work. For work that extends over long periods of time, these preferences and indications of engagement are very likely to be important, as shown in the Tang and Isaacs (1993) field study.

ACKNOWLEDGMENTS

This work was supported by the National Science Foundation (grant no. IRI-8902930) and by grants from Ameritech, Anderson Consulting, Apple, the Ameritech Foundation, Steelcase, and AT & T. Many people participated in the collection and analysis of the data reported here, including Mark Carter, Stacey Donahue, Sue Schuon, Barb Gamm, Patsy Gore, Arona Pearson, Sidney Levy, Shawn Salata, Michael Walker, Rodney Walker, David Sisson, and Isabelle Byrnes.

NOTES

1. Ninety percent of the MBAs at Michigan have significant work experience before coming back to school. These are professionals with practical group experience.
2. Eye contact was not perfect. Participants reported that the other person appeared to be looking at their throat when they looked into their eyes.
3. To make this diagram less "busy," we include here only those transitions that occurred 1% of the time or more.

REFERENCES

Chapanis, A., & Ochsman, R. N. (1972). Studies in interactive communication: I. The effects of four communication modes on the behavior of teams during cooperative problem solving. *Human Factors, 14,* 487–509.

Eisenhardt, K. M., & Bourgeois, L. J., III. (1992). *Conflict and strategic decision making: How top management teams disagree.* Unpublished manuscript, Department of Industrial Engineering, Stanford University.

Fish, R. S., Kraut, R. E., & Chalfonte, B. L. (1990). The VideoWindow system in informal communication. *Proceedings of the Computer Supported Cooperative Work—'90* (pp. 1–11). New York: ACM.

Gouran, D. S., Brown, C., & Henry, D. R. (1978). Behavioral correlates of perceptions of quality in decision-making discussions. *Communication Monographs, 45*(1), 51–63.

Green, S. G., & Taber, T. D. (1980). The effects of three social decision schemes on decision group process. *Organizational Behavior and Human Performance, 25,* 97–106.

Janis, I. L. (1982). *Groupthink: Psychological studies of policy decisions and fiascoes.* (2nd ed.). Boston: Houghton Mifflin.

McGrath, J. E. (1984). *Groups: Interaction and performance.* Englewood Cliffs, NJ: Prentice Hall.

McGuffin, L., & Olson, G. M. (1992). *ShrEdit: A shared electronic workspace* (CSMIL Tech. Rep. No. 45). University of Michigan.

Meader, D. K. (1995). *Supporting distributed, design discussions: A study of video effects on engagement and critical discussion in desktop, multimedia conferencing.* Unpublished doctoral dissertation, University of Michigan.

Minneman, S., & Bly, S. (1991). Managing a trois: A study of a multi-user drawing tools in distributed design work. *Proceedings of the Conference on Computer Human Interaction, CHI-91* (pp. 217–224). New York: ACM.

Olson, G. M., Olson, J. S., Carter, M., & Storrøsten, M. (1992). Small group design meetings: An analysis of collaboration. *Human–Computer Interaction, 7,* 347–374.

Olson, J. S., Olson, G. M., Storrøsten, M., & Carter, M. (1993). Groupwork close up: A comparison of the group design process with and without a simple group editor. *ACM Transactions on Information Systems, 11,* 321–348.

Pagani, D. S., & Mackay, W. E. (1993). Bringing media spaces into the real world. In G. DeMichelis, C. Simone, & K. Schmidt (Eds.), *Proceedings of ECSCW'93* (pp. 341–356). Milan: Kluwer.

Putnam, L. L. (1983). Small group work climates: A lag-sequential analysis of group interaction. *Small Group Behavior, 14*(4), 465–494.

Sambamurthy, V., & Poole, M. S. (1992). The effects of variations in capabilities of GDSS designs on management of cognitive conflict in groups. *Information Systems Research, 3*(3), 224–249.

Smith, R. G., O'Shea, T., O'Malley, C., Scanlon, E., & Taylor, J. (1989). Preliminary experiments with a distributed multi-media problem solving environment. *Proceedings of ECSCW'89* (pp. 19–34), London.

Sproull, L., & Kiesler, S. (1986). Reducing social context cues: Electronic mail in organizational communication. *Management Science, 32*(11), 1492–1512.

Tang, J. C., & Isaacs, E. (1992). Why do users like video? Studies of multi-media supported collaboration (Rep. No. TR-92-5). Mountainview, CA: Sun Microsystems Laboratories.

Zigurs, I., Poole, M. S., & DeSanctis, G. L. (1988). A study of influence in computer-mediated group decision making. *MISQ, 12*, 645–665.

Chapter 9

Studying Video-Based Collaboration in Context: From Small Workgroups to Large Organizations

Ellen A. Isaacs*
John C. Tang
Sun Microsystems, Inc.

Over the past few years, our group has developed and studied a variety of video-based prototypes to support remote collaboration. We started with a basic desktop videoconferencing system with a shared whiteboard and found that it was effective in supporting a distributed group's conversations, but that many of the users' attempts to contact each other were unsuccessful. We went on to build another desktop videoconferencing prototype called Montage, which focuses on awareness and helps people find good times to interact by integrating other coordination and collaboration tools. We also built Forum, which allows people to give live, interactive video-based presentations to distributed audiences. We describe the methods we used to study the long-term use of these prototypes among existing distributed groups and the lessons we learned by doing so. Finally, we discuss the roles that video plays in supporting distributed collaboration and we provide a list of design principles for those who wish to use video to support such activity.

INTRODUCTION

Lydia is developing some marketing materials for an upcoming customer presentation and she decides to show her latest idea to her colleague Sonia for feedback. From her computer workstation, she initiates a "glance" into Sonia's office, 500 miles away. As the image fades in, she sees that Sonia is away from her desk. She checks Sonia's online calendar and sees that she is in a meeting for another

---

*Currently at Electric Communities.

hour, so she leaves a Stickup "electronic note" asking Sonia to glance her back when she gets in. A few minutes later, a notice pops up on her screen indicating that the CEO's quarterly talk is about to begin. She "attends" the talk by opening an application, and she is presented with a video window of the CEO, who will be broadcasting from the corporate headquarters, along with the presentation slides and a list of others starting to join. After 5 minutes, over 600 people have joined the talk. Lydia looks through the slides to preview the CEO's remarks. She sees that the CEO will not address certain issues that are important to her. She decides she will ask about it if no one else does, although she will probably keep the question anonymous. Perusing the list of names and faces, Lydia notices that her colleague Bjorn is attending and she sends him a note asking if he wants to have lunch after the talk. He replies quickly saying he's free and they make arrangements.

This scenario illustrates the range of tasks and group sizes our Collaborative Computing group has been trying to support through the use of video. For example, the "glance" tool (which we call Montage) supports one-on-one interactions and attempts to help people find opportune times to interact. It is integrated with other online communication and coordination tools (e.g., calendar and Stickup electronic notes) to support the "pre-interaction coordination" that is often needed to set up an interaction. The video presentation tool (Forum) supports one-to-many presentations among potentially hundreds of people. It also supports questions from the audience and passing notes among the audience to retain some of the interactive richness that makes presentations collaborative events.

STUDYING COLLABORATION

Since 1991, our group has developed a variety of video-based prototypes to support remote collaboration. Our approach begins by studying collaborative work activity to identify how the existing technology does and does not meet the collaborators' needs. These studies guide the design of prototypes that help address those needs and in particular enable more natural collaboration across distance. Once we have developed a functioning prototype, we deploy it into real use over a long period of time and study how people react to it. We take a combination of quantitative and qualitative measures of users' activities, and we compare the group's behavior using the prototype to their behavior without it so that we can learn how the prototype affects their ability to work together.

Although our work shares much in common with other chapters in this book, we have made some choices that have enabled us to explore new issues. For example, nearly all the other experimental video systems aim to support small groups of people with relatively informal interactions, yet Forum supports large communities by broadcasting formal presentations. Most projects, including Cruiser at Bellcore (Fish, Kraut, Root, & Rice, 1993), CAVECAT and Hydra at Toronto (Mantei et al., 1991; Sellen, 1992), the Media Spaces at PARC (Bly, Harrison, & Irwin, 1993) and at EuroPARC (Gaver et al., 1992), the research at University of Michigan (Olson, Olson, & Meader, 1995), and others have focused on analog video, whereas we have used digital video. The latter is currently of lower quality (e.g., 4–10 frames per second, grainy resolution), but it allows us to better integrate our prototypes with other applications and to use digital video effects when appropriate. So far our work has used a "connection-based" model of communication, in that contact is explicitly initiated by one person, rather than leaving audio–video links on all the time. Other projects, such as the Media Spaces, have explored using continuous audio–video connections to enable extremely short, spontaneous interactions. Finally, although many other use studies[1] involved the developers of the system or other early adopters, we have tested our prototypes with people who were not affiliated with the prototype development to better approximate the response of nontechnical users.

This chapter reviews the three video-based prototypes we have developed to support remote collaboration. We started with a basic desktop video-conferencing (DVC) prototype, which gave small groups of about 5–10 people the means to see each other and share documents. Studies of the DVC prototype in use indicated that people often had problems finding opportune times to make contact. This finding prompted us to design Montage, which made it easier to start interactions or coordinate future times to interact. In parallel, we worked on Forum, which enabled people to give interactive presentations to hundreds of people watching from their workstations. The following sections describe these projects and summarize lessons learned. In each case, we describe our techniques for studying the use of the prototype, in part to demonstrate how we reached our conclusions and in part to illustrate techniques we believe are effective for studying the social implications of introducing new technology. We conclude with some lessons learned about the use of video, the design of video-based applications, and our methodology for studying collaborative activity.

DESKTOP VIDEOCONFERENCING PROTOTYPE

Goals

We began our research on the support of remote collaboration by studying how people used existing technologies to collaborate over long distances (Tang & Isaacs, 1993). We surveyed users of our company's video telecon-ference rooms to learn how that system was or was not meeting the needs of remote collaborators. The biggest problem identified was availability; the teleconference rooms were often booked weeks in advance. Respondents also complained about audio quality and delay in hearing the remote collaborators. When asked which additional videoconferencing capabilities they desired, users most often requested a shared drawing space.

We also studied the work of a four-person team that was split between East and West Coast sites of the United States, about 3,000 miles apart. We studied their work activity in three settings: face-to-face meetings, video teleconference room meetings, and phone conferences. By studying videotape records of the team's activity, we found that the main problem in using the video teleconference rooms was the delay in transmitting the audio from one site to the other. This delay disrupted many mechanisms of natural conversation (e.g., interrupting a speaker, completing sentences, timing jokes). Eventually, the team elected to turn off the audio of the video teleconference system (which was delayed to preserve synchrony with the video) and use speakerphone audio through the phone system. They strongly preferred this arrangement because of the negligible latency in phone audio, even though it disrupted the synchrony between the audio and video (the audio arrived before the accompanying video).

Observations from the survey and the preliminary use study suggested that users would benefit from a system that provided videoconferences on demand, with minimal audio latency, and a shared drawing space. Thus, we designed a desktop videoconferencing (DVC) prototype (Tang & Isaacs, 1993) that provided real-time audio and video links and a shared drawing program. The DVC prototype used digital video and audio transmitted over standard computer networks. This DVC prototype enabled us to explore the technical issues of using digital audio and video and introduced us to the interface and usability issues of desktop videoconferencing.

Design

The user interface for establishing and managing desktop videoconferences was modeled after the process of placing a phone call. The interface, shown in Fig. 9.1, allowed users to specify the recipient of a conference request. When a request was made, a copy of the interface appeared on the screens of all the specified users, accompanied by an audio alert. A shared message area allowed users to type text messages to negotiate their entry into the conference. Users could also select which collaborative tools would be used in the conference. The tool supported multipoint (up to three-way) conferences, but once a conference was established no one else could join.

Figure 9.2 shows a screen image of a typical desktop videoconference. For a two-way conference, each user's screen displayed:

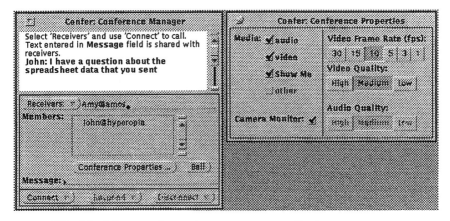

FIG. 9.1. John uses the conference manager application to request a conference with Amy.

- A video window of a remote collaborator
- A preview window of the video being sent to the remote collaborator
- A shared markup and drawing program (called Show Me) for drawing, typing, pointing, and erasing over shared bitmap images

Show Me allowed users to create shared freehand graphics and to grab bitmap images from their screens and share them with the other conference members.

When designing the DVC prototype, we made sure to minimize the audio transmission delay. We did so by designing the infrastructure for making connections to handle the video and audio data streams separately, which enabled us to give priority to the audio transmission during periods of heavy network usage. At these times, the quality and/or latency of the video was degraded to preserve minimal audio latency.

Study

To understand how people would use the DVC prototype, we conducted a study of distributed collaboration. We studied a five-person team that was distributed among three locations: two buildings on a campus site on the West Coast, and another building on the East Coast. We observed their collaborative work under three conditions:

- *Pre-DVC*—using conventional tools (phone, e-mail, videoconference rooms, etc.)
- *Full-DVC*—adding the DVC prototype (audio, video, Show Me)

FIG. 9.2. The desktop videoconferencing prototype consists of the Show Me shared drawing tool, receive video window of remote user, and preview video window of outgoing video signal.

- *DVC-minus-video*—subtracting video from the DVC prototype (audio and Show Me only)

We studied the team for 3 weeks in the pre-DVC condition, 6 weeks in the full-DVC condition, and 4 weeks in the DVC-minus-video condition. This team had previously been located together in neighboring cubicles at one site, so they were particularly aware of things that became difficult in their distributed locations.

We used a variety of observational methods to get different perspectives on their work activity. We monitored the team's observable collaborative activity, including the number and duration of phone calls, their usage of electronic mail, the frequency of their face-to-face contact, and their usage of the DVC prototype. Additionally, selected samples of collaborative activity in the three conditions were recorded on videotape. These tapes were analyzed by a multidisciplinary group in the tradition of interaction analysis (Brun-Cottan & Wall, 1995). Furthermore, at various stages during the study, we interviewed each team member to gather their perceptions about their work activity. Details of the study are described in Tang and Isaacs (1993).

Lessons Learned

Although this study was not specifically intended to measure the value of video, one finding that clearly emerged is that video was very important to the users. The group used the prototype when video was provided, but their use declined dramatically when the video was removed. They commented that the main reason they stopped using the prototype without video is that its audio was worse in quality than the phone and exhibited an annoying echo and a noticeable transmission delay. This pattern indicates that the main benefit the prototype offered was through the video. In fact, the users were willing to endure the poor audio to gain the advantages of the video.

Qualitative analyses of the videotapes of their use of the prototype helped identify why video was valuable. The visual access provided cues that facilitated the mechanics of turn-taking and the interpretation of gestures, facial expressions, and pauses. We observed that nonverbal cues were especially important for signaling disagreement and handling sensitive issues. (See Isaacs and Tang, 1994, for a further discussion.) Furthermore, the users commented that the video capability made their interactions generally more satisfying (see also Rudman et al., chapter 10, this volume). This support for interactional mechanisms makes VMC more efficient, effortless, and effective. A richer communication channel affords greater mutual understanding among the participants, and we would expect it to help improve the quality of their collaborative work in the long term.

One related issue is the role of eye contact in VMC. Although direct eye contact is expected in face-to-face meetings, conventional desktop videoconferencing configurations can provide only near eye contact by positioning the lens of the camera as close as possible to the video window of the remote collaborator. In our DVC setup, this arrangement gave each collaborator a clear sense of their partners' direction of gaze, known as gaze awareness (Ishii & Kobayashi, 1992). All the team members initially remarked that their inability to establish direct eye contact felt strange. However, we found considerable evidence in the videotapes that the collaborators were able to make use of gaze awareness in their interactions. For example, if someone paused and looked upward, their partner could infer that they were searching for the right thing to say. In another example, one collaborator expressed disagreement by avoiding looking at his partner until they moved on to another topic.

Only 43% of the call attempts turned into desktop videoconferences. Most of the call requests were not answered because the person being called was not in the office. This statistic suggested that an application supporting audio–video interactions should also help users find a good time to interact. The usage logs also showed that desktop conferences tended to be relatively long, with a median duration of 8 min and 55 sec. In the interviews, users commented that the interface for requesting a conference felt heavyweight, and they tended to use the phone for shorter interactions.

Our experience with desktop videoconferencing also revealed some important ways in which it is different from other forms of interaction. In desktop videoconferences, all participants were located in their offices where each person had access to his or her resources and distractions (e.g., phone calls, e-mail arrivals, visitors). Thus, it was not unusual for people to read e-mail or take phone calls during a conference. Furthermore, these interruptions were managed without causing confusion or offense because the aural and visual cues enabled remote collaborators to interpret what was happening when one person temporarily stopped participating. Thus, desktop videoconferencing was a medium for focused interaction (like a phone call or meeting), but also one that tolerated long periods of independent work.

One implication of this observation is that desktop videoconferencing is a distinct collaboration setting that has its own characteristics and limitations. As such, it is not intended to replace other forms of interaction (as some marketing promises might suggest). Our data showed that there were no statistically significant decreases in the amount of phone or face-to-face meeting activity when the full DVC prototype was available compared to the other two conditions (Tang & Isaacs, 1993). Desktop videoconferencing offers a communication choice that complements, rather than replaces, face-to-face, phone, e-mail, and other interactions.

In summary, the quantitative measures of DVC prototype use helped us detect that people stopped using the prototype once we removed the video. Interviews with the users confirmed that they did so in fact because of the lack of video. Qualitative analyses of the videotaped activity revealed ways in which video helped them accomplish and enrich their interactions, which helped explain why they found the video-mediated interactions so satisfying. The studies also revealed some design implications that led to our next project.

MONTAGE

Goals

Our experiences with the DVC prototype prompted us to take a broader perspective on how audio–video connections could be used to support remote collaboration. We realized that it is important to support the process of finding an opportune time to interact. To understand this problem better, we interviewed a range of people in the United States (including those who spent a portion of their work time physically separated from their work group) to explore how people want to be aware of and accessible to their colleagues. These interviews confirmed the need to help people find good times to make contact. People commented that they wanted help finding people who were not in their office or the ability to "leave a note on their chair" to set up a future contact. When presented with the idea of using audio–video connections to see when people were available, interviewees expressed strong concerns about preserving their privacy.

Design

Guided by these interviews, our previous experiences with the DVC prototype, and lessons learned from other videoconferencing efforts (e.g., Dourish & Bly, 1992; Fish et al., 1993), we developed a prototype called Montage (Tang & Rua, 1994), which tries to provide a sense of proximity for distributed groups. It does so by providing an easy way to make audio–video connections between computer desktops and by integrating other communication applications.

Montage uses momentary, reciprocal glances among networked, media-equipped workstations to make it easy to peek into someone's office. It is modeled on the process of walking down a hallway to visit a colleague in her office. If you peek in and see that she is not available (e.g., not in the office, busy on the phone), you might pass by the door without stopping. If you find her in, you might pause at the doorway to indicate what you want to discuss before entering and settling in for a discussion. By basing Montage on the hallway model, we hoped to provide a familiar way of increasing the accessibility of colleagues without disrupting their privacy.

In Montage, a user typically selects the name of a person they wish to glance from a menu (Fig. 9.3). Within a few seconds, a sound notifies the recipient of the onset of a glance and video windows fade in on both users' screens. The fade-in effect provides a graceful approach for the people involved in a glance. Either party can acknowledge the glance by pressing the audio button to open an audio channel. If neither party enables the audio channel, the glance fades away after 8 sec. Once either person presses the audio button, a two-way audio–video connection is established. The relatively small (128 × 120 pixels) video windows of the glance are intended to support short, lightweight interactions. If participants want to have an extended interaction, either one can initiate a full-featured desktop video-conference by pressing the Visit button. A visit offers enlarged video windows (256 × 240 pixels) and access to tools for sharing bitmap graphics (ShowMe Whiteboard, a product version of the shared drawing tool from the DVC prototype) and short text messages (Stickup notes). Glances and visits are ended by pressing a button that immediately dismisses the video window.

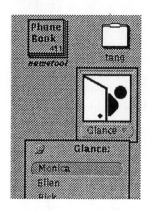

FIG. 9.3. John initiates a glance at Monica by selecting her name from the Montage menu.

If the glance shows that the person is not available, the buttons along the bottom of the glance window (see Fig. 9.4) provide quick access to browse her online calendar, send her a Stickup note, or send her an e-mail message. The online calendar and e-mail functionality are adaptations of existing tools widely used in our company. We developed Stickup, which enables users to type a text note that appears in a popup window on the recipient's screen (shown in Fig. 9.5). Stickups also include a Glance Back button that quickly starts a Montage glance back to the person who posted the Stickup, and a Reply button that opens a Stickup to post back. By integrating quick access to these other communication tools, we hoped that Montage would help coordinate opportune times to make future contact.

Because Montage allows audio–video connections with any other user, it is important to enable users to protect their privacy. Montage addresses this issue in part by building on existing social mechanisms for protecting privacy. Because all Montage glances are reciprocal, users can see if anyone is glancing them. Just as it is considered rude to stand outside someone's door and stare in, it is equally impolite to do so through Montage, which

FIG. 9.4. After John glances Monica, a small window appears on his screen providing a view into her office. At the same time, he sees a preview of his own image.

FIG. 9.5. A Stickup from Ellen. Note the Glance Back and Reply buttons that quickly initiate a glance or Stickup back to the person who posted the Stickup.

provides the aural and visual cues to make such eavesdropping obvious. This symmetry enables users to socially negotiate their privacy. In addition, Montage offers a "do not disturb" mode that blocks incoming glances.

Study

To learn how people would use Montage, we deployed the prototype in an existing working group (Tang, Isaacs, & Rua, 1994). We selected a group of 10 people distributed among three buildings on a campus site. The group was multidisciplinary (including marketers, engineers, a manager, and a project coordinator), and it included people who worked part time or telecommuted. As with our other studies, we chose a group that had not been involved in the design or implementation of Montage.

We studied the group's communication patterns for 4 weeks before we installed Montage, 12 weeks while they had Montage, and 4 weeks after we removed Montage. To determine how Montage affected their communication, we collected logs of their use of Montage, logs of their voice-mail system use, copies of all e-mail sent within the team, and logs of appointments scheduled in their online calendars. Unfortunately, we were unable to collect reliable information about their phone calls and face-to-face meetings. In each of the conditions, we videotaped samples of the group's work activity by leaving a video camera running in individual offices throughout a day. We administered surveys to the team during the study to gather their perceptions of their work activity and their reactions to Montage.

Lessons Learned

Even more than with the DVC prototype, the logs of Montage use demonstrated how frequently attempts to contact someone were unsuccessful. The Montage logs showed that on average, users attempted to glance others 2.9 times per day, but that 75% of glance attempts were not acknowledged (i.e., neither party enabled the audio). This high rate of unacknowledged glances underscores the importance of helping people find opportune times to make contact. Despite the likelihood that a glance would not immediately turn into an interaction, people continued to use Montage. This continued use suggested that glancing was sufficiently lightweight and even if it did not immediately initiate an interaction, it was valuable in arranging for one in the future.

The logs showed further evidence of the lightweight nature of interactions in Montage. Of the acknowledged glances, resulting interactions tended to be relatively short, with a median duration of 1 min 8 sec. This median compares to 8 min 55 sec in our previous DVC prototype, which suggests that Montage glances were used for shorter, more lightweight interactions. In the interviews, participants indicated that they tended to use Montage for small issues just as they arose. Without Montage, they either handled the issue themselves or waited to contact someone until a few such issues had accumulated.

However, the quantitative data demonstrated that the Montage features for coordinating future contact were not extensively used. There were 886 unacknowledged glance attempts, when the user might be expected to use the other communications applications integrated with Montage. However, the logs showed that people posted Stickups only 77 times, they browsed calendars only 20 times, and they sent e-mail only 16 times. These results surprised us, especially because the users' perceptions collected in the surveys told a different story. Eight of the 10 users said they especially liked Stickups and found them to be very useful. However, taking the usage data and user comments together, we concluded that even infrequent use of Stickups was enough to demonstrate their value to the users.

In the interviews, users were generally enthusiastic about Montage and the visual access provided by the video. Analyzing the videotapes identified specific ways in which the video was useful. The tapes provided more examples of the subtle benefits of using the video to convey nonverbal cues during an interaction, similar to what we saw with the DVC prototype. In addition, video was also used in Montage to interpret people's availability and willingness to interact. The information in the video window enabled the person being glanced at to identify who was requesting their attention and to convey whether they welcomed an interruption. Furthermore, when a glance revealed that someone was on the phone or occupied with a visitor, the participants often used nonverbal signals to set up future contact (e.g., a look and a hand gesture to indicate "I see you, I'll glance you back"). Other times, they used visual cues to interrupt the activity gracefully. Thus, in addition to the advantages of "talking heads" video, we also observed the benefits of "silent heads" video in leading up to an interaction.

Both quantitative and qualitative measures indicated that Montage provides a communication medium that is between face-to-face visits and the phone. Like the phone, it provides quick access to people who are located elsewhere, and allows both participants to remain in their own offices with access to their own resources. Like face-to-face interactions, the video channel in Montage allows rich interactions and facilitates more frequent, shorter interactions that addressed specific issues just as they arise.

FORUM

Goals

After focusing exclusively on small group coordination, we decided to explore the use of networked video and audio to provide a sense of community in a large organization. Presentation and training sessions are often used to communicate information to large groups of people. These sessions help large groups create common knowledge and shared experiences and they help reinforce the organization's culture.

As organizations become distributed, they have to work harder to create these shared experiences. We felt that it could be useful to enable people from different locations to attend presentations from their computer desktops. Presenters could reach more of their intended audience, and individuals could attend more presentations that interested them. This idea led to the development of Forum, a tool that enables distributed video-based presentations.

Before designing Forum, we observed face-to-face presentations and interviewed people who gave or attended many presentations. In doing so, we became especially aware of the interactive nature of presentations. Speakers rely heavily on feedback from the audience in the form of questions and nonverbal cues. Audiences also pick up information from each other by chatting among themselves and by seeing how others react to the speaker's comments. In designing Forum, we tried to find ways to build in tools that enabled interaction between the audience and speaker and among the audience. We also tried to provide a basic level of awareness so that participants would know who else was attending a talk.

Design

Forum is a distributed application that enables speakers to broadcast talks over a network and enables audience members to participate in the talks from their workstations. Speakers sit in front of a media-equipped workstation that lets them control the display of their slides, manage their interaction with the audience, and see a list of audience members. Audience members receive live audio and video of the speaker as well as the slides and slide annotations. Audience members can interact with the speaker in three ways: they can speak to the presenter, they can "vote" anonymously on an issue raised by the speaker, and they can send in written comments. Because they are in a multitasking environment, they can switch their attention between the Forum talk and other applications on their desktop or other activities in their office.

The audience's interface is shown in Fig. 9.6. The main window in the upper left shows video of the speaker, and the controls below it manage the audio parameters. The control panel to the right of the video provides three mechanisms to interact with the speaker: spoken questions, polls,

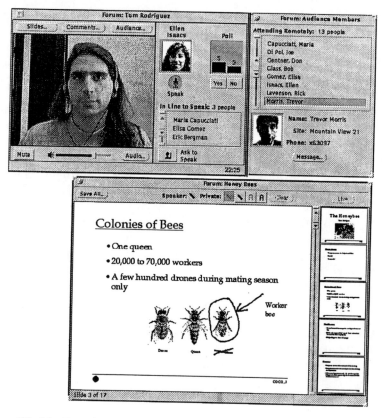

FIG. 9.6. Forum's audience interface. Audience members watch the video and interact with the speaker in the upper left window. Here, Ellen Isaacs is asking a question as three others wait in line to speak; the results of an earlier poll appear in the Poll meter. Audience members view the slides in the lower window, using the thumbnails to view slides independently of the speaker. The audience window shows a list of attendees and allows audience members to send each other text messages.

and written comments. An audience member who wants to speak gets in the queue by clicking on the button at the bottom of the window. When the speaker calls on her, she presses and holds down the Speak button. Everyone can hear her speak and they can see her picture with her name above it. Speakers use the poll meter in the upper right to ask the audience a question. To vote on a poll, an audience member clicks on the Yes or No option and the bar chart changes accordingly. To submit a written comment, the user clicks on the Comments button, types a comment into the popup window that appears, and sends it to the speaker.

Audience members can also find out who else is watching a presentation by clicking on the Audience button, which brings up the Audience window, shown to the right. Users can click on a name to see that person's icon, their location and phone number. They can send that person a short message by clicking on the Message button, which brings up a small window pre-addressed to that recipient. When they send the message, it pops up on the other person's screen in a small window with a Reply button. Finally, audience members see the speaker's current slide in the slides window, and they can click on a thumbnail to view a different slide at any time. Users can see the speaker's annotations and they can make their own private annotations.

Study

We studied the use of Forum using both informal and formal approaches. The informal testing went on throughout the process of developing Forum. On a weekly basis, we asked people around the company to give talks over Forum on a topic of their choice. The talks were attended by a small community of people who were willing to test Forum and, for any given talk, were interested in the topic. During each talk, we videotaped the speaker and at least one audience member. We sent out periodic questionnaires to the audience members, and we interviewed the speakers and some audience members. During that period, we made many refinements to the functionality and interface, many to enable smoother interactions. We also learned a great deal about both speakers' and audiences' experiences (Isaacs, Morris, & Rodriguez, 1994).

After a series of design iterations based on informal testing, we ran a more rigorous test to compare Forum presentations with those given in a local setting (Isaacs, Morris, Rodriguez, & Tang, 1995). In this study, seven talks were given once over Forum and once in a local setting. The talks ranged in topic and style (e.g., lecture, informal talk, discussion session). For each talk, we videotaped the speaker and an audience member, sent questionnaires to all audience members and the speaker, interviewed the speakers, and logged Forum user activity.

Lessons Learned

Much of what we learned about video stems from the fact that video is used asymmetrically in Forum. Although the audience members can see the speaker, the speaker cannot see the audience. We chose this design to minimize network bandwidth and because very few audience members had video equipment. In the future, these limitations will disappear, but our goal was to design something that could be used with current technology.

Our most striking finding was that audiences were extremely enthusiastic about Forum and in most cases preferred it to local talks, whereas speakers found it less rewarding to give a talk over Forum than in a face-to-face setting. Although other factors contributed to this difference, video played an important role. The questionnaire data and interviews indicated that speakers' biggest complaint was that they could not see the audience. They found it difficult to gauge the audience's level of interest, degree of understanding, and general attitude toward their material. One speaker said he liked trying out Forum because it was an interesting technology, but "insofar as a way to actually communicate the content, it was less fun, because of the inability to judge audience response and to get to know any members of the audience." Unless they worked hard to draw out the audience through the other interaction channels, speakers found it difficult to adjust and respond to the audience. Even the static image that appeared when an audience member asked a question was a welcome visual cue for speakers.

On the other hand, audiences could see the speakers and felt more connected to the speakers than vice versa. We can tell from analyzing videotapes that the video played an important role in helping audience members focus on the presentation. Still, few audience members explicitly mentioned the value of video in their questionnaires. Instead, when asked about the value of the visual information, most audience members mentioned that the slides were helpful and that they liked it when speakers showed videotapes or demos through the video channel. It appears that audiences, who had video of the speaker, took that information for granted, whereas speakers, who didn't have video of the audience, felt limited by its absence.

A second major finding was that more people attended Forum talks than local talks (for the same talk), by more than a 2 to 1 margin. An average of 141 people attended Forum talks, compared with 60 for local talks. As a result, Forum speakers received greater exposure than they would have otherwise. By interviewing speakers, we learned of many cases when speakers were approached long after their talk by people who recognized them from their Forum talk. We suspect that audiences felt as if they knew the speaker more than they might at a large presentation because each person had a close-up image of the speaker, who appeared to be talking directly to them.

The video channel was also used to transmit visual information other than the speaker's head and shoulders. A number of speakers played videotapes during Forum talks, which appeared in the same video region of the interface, temporarily replacing the speaker's image. The speaker could be heard while the video was playing. In addition, two speakers showed demos during their talks, pointing the camera at an object and manipulating it as they described how it worked. In these cases, the video channel was used to provide visual information about objects, rather than to support face-to-face interaction (Nardi et al., chapter 23, this volume).

These observations indicate that video plays an important role in establishing relationships among the participants and in demonstrating objects. However, we once again found that video is most effective when combined with other interaction tools. Clearly, the speaker's audio was the most important channel for the audience; it was not uncommon for people to listen to a talk while doing other work, focusing on the video when they wanted to pay closer attention. We know from the videotapes and speakers' interviews that the audio questions from the audience also provided the richest source of information about the audience. The importance of audio is highlighted by one of the audience's frustrations, which was their inability to express laughter or applause. The "press to talk" audio model was required to avoid audio echo problems, but it prevented audiences from giving ongoing audio feedback to the speaker. Some Forum audience members even sent in written comments to speakers at the end of their talks explicitly praising the talk. Because they could not applaud, they had to find another way to show appreciation.

One of the more surprising findings was how effectively the poll provided a sense of the audience. The poll is a very simple device that gives anonymous, yes–no information about the audience, but it was because of this simplicity that it became so useful. Speakers could ask frequent questions to get a feel for the audience's attitude and the audience could easily and anonymously convey their opinion. The poll served to keep the audience involved and the speaker connected to the audience. The effectiveness of the poll was a good reminder that interactivity can take many forms; the key is to provide the right tool for the right situation. In some cases, video provides the right information; in others a simple yes–no or text-based interaction tool fills the need.

THE ROLE OF VIDEO

Based on our work with these prototypes, we have come to appreciate the variety of ways in which video supports and enhances collaboration. There is no one right use of video. Each is appropriate for different tasks and settings, and in many cases video serves multiple purposes.

Enhancing the Users' Experience.   Perhaps our most obvious finding is that people like to see each other when they interact (Gale, 1990; Rudman et al., chapter 10, this volume). Regardless of any cognitive benefit video may provide, people like having it, whether they are in one-on-one interactions or watching lectures. We saw from the DVC study that people stopped using the prototype when the video was removed. Later we saw that people contacted each other for impromptu interactions over Montage more often than they did when they had to use the phone. In Forum, the video is an important reason why audiences had such an enthusiastic response to the technology.

Interpreting Visual Information in Interactions.   Video helps people interpret the many subtle visual cues that accompany interactions (Isaacs & Tang, 1994; Rudman et al., chapter 10, this volume). In one-on-one interactions, people use video to help time their contributions and interpret each others' attitudes. We saw cases when people used gaze awareness to indicate that they disagreed with a speaker. A smile along with a sarcastic remark helped defuse a comment. Gestures were used to enhance descriptions. In addition, video opened up room for more casual and less focused conversations. If someone paused to consider an issue, the other person understood that they were not simply being unresponsive. If a visitor dropped by or a person became distracted, the other person could easily understand what was happening. As a result, we, like others, saw cases of longer "office share" connections with intermittent focused interactions (Bly et al., 1993; Fish et al., 1993; Mantei et al., 1991).

In multiparty interactions, video also helps people manage not just when to speak but who will speak next. It also helps a speaker get a sense of the groups' reaction and to adjust as they speak. The lack of this video feedback in the one-to-many situation of Forum clearly disrupted speakers. They had few cues of the audience's understanding of, agreement with, or appreciation for their presentation, and so could not adjust their remarks accordingly. They ended up less satisfied with the experience relative to a face-to-face presentation.

Enabling Distributed Conversations That Would Not Happen Otherwise.   Because video enables the interpretation of subtle visual feedback, it opens the possibility of having conversations about sensitive or private issues that people are reluctant to conduct over the telephone. Although people prefer face-to-face settings for such delicate discussions, we found that people were willing to hold them over video but not over the phone. During one conversation, two people turned off the video camera that was observing their activity for our study purposes because they thought the topic was too sensitive for us to record, but apparently it was not too sensitive to discuss over a video link. When people work across distant locations, they rarely have the opportunity to have face-to-face conversations, so the video enables them to talk about issues they simply would ignore if only the phone were available. This is a subtle issue that affects groups that work together over long periods of time; conflict is bound to emerge and it must to be handled well to keep the group functioning productively. This effect has not been explicitly or extensively studied, so it remains an open question how far we can generalize from our findings.

Awareness. Video plays a critical role in providing awareness. From the DVC prototype, we learned that interactions are greatly facilitated if people know when others are around and whether they are available to talk. Video is perfectly suited to providing these cues. The video glance mechanism of Montage enabled people to interpret effortlessly whether someone was available to interact or whether they should try again later. Through video it is easy to tell if a person is on the phone, busy with a visitor, engrossed in some work, or not there. If someone is glanced when they are busy, they can look toward the video and recognize the glance, perhaps using nonverbal cues to indicate that they will get back to the person later. Of course, awareness usually trades off against privacy, so it is important to enable users to control others' access to them.

Our experience with Forum expanded our understanding of the role of awareness. Among large groups, awareness involves knowing not only who is around and their level of activity, but the size of the group and their level of responsiveness. An awareness of others present helps participants in large groups frame their contributions, and it sets up later interactions. An awareness of the size of the audience shapes participants' style of interaction, and knowledge of participants' level of responsiveness influences everyone's interpretations of the event. The role of video in enabling awareness has been noted for some time (see Isaacs et al., chapter 22, this volume).

Providing Identity and Recognition. Forum also demonstrated the importance of video for establishing the identity of a person, especially when the participants have never seen each other. When people first meet, they feel they know each other better if they have previously seen each other than if they have only heard each other. In the case of Forum, where speakers' images were broadcast to people distributed across many locations, the video provided valuable recognition to the speaker. Others see that person later and identify them, and perhaps approach them for an interaction. This role of video has not been discussed much in the video-conferencing literature, but we note that television has demonstrated convincingly the power of video to enable widespread recognition.

Creating a Focus. We were reminded by Forum of the simple point that video helps provide a point of focus. We noted that people often did other lightweight work while attending Forum talks, but when they wanted to pay closer attention, they watched the video, even though the "talking head" image provided relatively little dynamic information. In other cases, speakers used the video to show an object, which also gave the audience a focus and a shared understanding of the visual material. Nardi et al. (chapter 23, this volume) further discussed this use of "video as data."

DESIGN OF VIDEO

During the course of our work, we also have learned some design guidelines for using video in applications for face-to-face interaction, which we describe here. We qualify these comments with a reminder that we have worked with low-quality digital video (4–10 frames per second, low resolution), which may reduce the visibility of subtle social cues. Previous work indicates that very-high-quality video only marginally improves the quality of work (Olson et al., 1995), but that it does affect the mechanics of conversation and users' satisfaction with the experience (O'Conaill, Whittaker, & Wilbur, 1993).

Audio Latency Matters More Than Audio–Video Synchronization for Real-Time Interaction. In our DVC prestudy, we first learned the importance of minimizing audio latency when supporting live interaction, a finding that has been confirmed by others (Kurita, Iai, & Kitawaki, 1993; O'Conaill et al., 1993). When the time is longer than about 400 msec between when one person says something and the other person hears it, conversations become far less interactive. We found this effect even with constant delay from a switched system. Because it is difficult to time a response, people can no longer rapidly exchange utterances. Because humor heavily depends on timing, it starts to disappear. Because conflict management depends on quick responses to feedback, people back away from controversial issues. As a result, conversations with delayed audio are not only frustrating for participants, but they consist of extended monologues about straightforward topics with little humor (Krauss & Bricker, 1967; O'Conaill et al., 1993). If a design trade-off must be made, it is best to sacrifice audio–video synchrony to enable low-latency audio. Although it is also disturbing to see someone's mouth moving after hearing their utterance, people seem to be able to adjust to this much more effectively than they do to audio delays. Of course, when video and audio are used in noninteractive contexts, audio and video should be synchronized.

Video Is Often More Effective When Combined With Other Means for Interaction. Although video can be used alone in some cases, it is usually more effective when combined with other media. Audio is the obvious complement to video, but other types of media are often useful. When people interact, they often want to show each other things and write things down so they can be saved for later use. It is useful to enable them to share graphics, text, and applications. In Forum, we provided a "poll mechanism" to enable the relatively common technique of surveying the audience. Even if video of the audience had been provided, it would have been too unruly to manage this process. The lesson is that one should consider providing mechanisms to support visual behavior that cannot be accomplished comfortably through video.

Very Short Connection Times Are Critical for Supporting Lightweight Interactions. To effectively support lightweight interaction, audio and video connections among computers must be established very quickly. When using the phone, people often expect to make contact within three rings (about 10 sec). Our experience with the DVC prototype indicated that longer delays caused users to resort to the phone for short interactions. Even with Montage, it took an average of 11 sec for a glance to appear after it was initiated. This delay sometimes detracted from the goal of supporting lightweight interactions. Although responsive performance is always an issue with applications, it is especially important with desktop conferencing. If connections take longer (or even feel like they take longer) than a few seconds, users will use another mechanism or use videoconferencing only for more formal, extended interactions.

Provide a Sense of Approach When Establishing Video Connections. When video is used to connect people, designers should let people prepare for the pending connection by providing some warning. In the physical world we can often hear people approach, which smoothes the transition from the previous activity to the interaction. The designers of Cruiser found that people were disturbed when large video images of others' faces suddenly appeared on their monitor, even though they were aware that this could happen (Fish et al., 1993), whereas the RAVE system found audio cues to be helpful (Gaver et al., 1992). Based on these observations, we designed Montage glances to fade in rather than pop up and to be preceded by an audio cue. This approach felt more comfortable and natural to users.

Provide Ways for People to Protect Their Privacy. When people are told about applications that allow them to contact people over video, many react by expressing concern about their privacy. Although most users do not often take advantage of privacy controls, we have found that they will not even experiment with the system without the possibility of blocking access. Therefore, it is very important for the adoption of the technology to provide reasonable privacy controls. It would be a mistake to try to convince someone that they don't need access control because most people don't use it. They "use" it to feel comfortable that the system will let them control their privacy.

THE ROLE OF METHODOLOGY

Our understanding of our prototypes is shaped by the type of use studies we conducted and the measures we took. As we have shown, we believe it is important to use a combination of approaches and measures when collecting and analyzing data. Each method provides useful information, but when different ones are combined, a richer picture emerges of the effect of technology on people.

In particular, we prefer to combine both quantitative and qualitative measures. Quantitative results, such as usage statistics or frequency counts of specific behaviors, can identify reliable patterns in the data, which can be used to confirm or deny theories about user behavior. But quantitative information often provides only broad descriptions of phenomena. To understand how and why the behavior takes shape, we use qualitative measures, such as descriptions of specific events detected in the videotapes or comments from user interviews. It is also important to distinguish objective and subjective data. For example, it is helpful to use videotapes to count the occurrences of a certain behavior (an objective measure), but asking users why they chose that behavior (a subjective measure) helps fill out our understanding.

During the Forum study, we used findings from different sources to motivate investigations with other types of data. For example, we used the videotapes and the logs to count the number of questions asked in local and Forum presentations (a quantitative, objective measure of interactivity). However, we noticed from the tapes that the local talks "felt" more interactive (a qualitative analysis), and the questionnaires indicated that local audiences thought the questions were handled better (a quantitative measure of a subjective reaction). We returned to the videotapes and noticed that questioners in local talks seemed to ask more follow-up questions, which created a dialogue between the speaker and the audience member. From this qualitative analysis, we then counted the number of follow-up questions in Forum and local talks (quantitative measure) and found that indeed they did occur significantly more often in local talks. Finally, the interviews confirmed that this type of dialog contributed to the speakers' satisfaction with the experience. By combining measures, we not only know that local talks had more speaker–audience interactions, but we know the form they took and their effect on the participants.

In some cases, we noticed a conflict between the objective and subjective findings. In the Montage study, early interviews indicated that people considered protecting their privacy to be critical, which led us to build in a "do not disturb" mechanism to block video access. Once Montage was deployed, the logs showed that most people rarely used the privacy control. Interviews confirmed that they felt comfortable with the privacy offered. By combining these subjective and objective data, we determined that user acceptance depends in part on making privacy controls available, even though in practice most people do not actively use them. The behavioral measure would lead us to conclude that access control is not a necessary feature because it is rarely used, but the subjective reactions help us understand its importance to users.

In general, we have found that objective performance or usage data do not fully reveal the effect of a technology on users. We do not always know what aspects to measure to predict users' reactions (e.g., we may measure efficiency when users are more concerned with the quality of social interaction), and some aspects are difficult to measure (e.g., whether people feel comfortable using video to discuss sensitive matters). Because we do not understand when and why objective and subjective measures are not well correlated, we should explore both aspects of technology to fully understand its implications for use.

CONCLUSION

We have reported on use studies of a variety of prototypes that use video to support collaborative work. Our studies not only confirmed that users like video, but also uncovered concrete information about the value of video in supporting interaction. In many ways, our work builds on the emerging body of work that conflicts with the earlier literature that did not find any demonstrable value of video. Studies by Ochsman and Chapanis (1974) and Gale (1990) found no significant differences in comparisons of collaborative activity with and without video. There are two fundamental reasons why our studies found evidence for the value of video where earlier studies did not.

First, our studies involved prototypes whose design was shaped by an understanding of the needs of remote collaborators. Our question has not been "Is video useful?" but rather "How can video be usefully integrated into people's work practice?" As is often the case, it is not raw technology that is useful, but rather its design into artifacts that fit into users' work practice. By doing studies of users' work activity with existing technology, we come to understand people's needs well enough to integrate video with other technology to develop useful designs.

Second, our use studies combined methodologies and observed the prototypes in the context of real work activity. By combining quantitative measures of user behavior (computer logs, behavior frequency counts from videotape data, questionnaires) with qualitative analyses (descriptions of videotaped activity, interviews, essay questions in surveys) we could appreciate a variety of perspectives on people's use of the technology. Also, studying people using technology in the context of their real work over time can reveal patterns of use that may be missed in laboratory studies, which often must use relatively contrived short-term tasks, sometimes with groups that would not otherwise work together. Those studies enable researchers to isolate specific causes of behaviors, whereas field studies reveal realistic responses among representative groups of users doing naturalistic tasks.

We are encouraged that so much innovative research is being conducted, both in the lab and in the field, in the spirit of understanding users' goals and needs. Taken together, this research will help us design video-based technology that not only supports people's tasks but expands their ability to work with a wider range of people who may be located around the globe.

NOTE

1. We use the term *use studies* rather than the more common term *user studies* because we study the *use* of the technology in context, rather than the *users* of the technology.

REFERENCES

Bly, S. A., Harrison, S. R., & Irwin, S. (1993). Media spaces: Bringing people together in a video, audio, and computing environment. *Communications of the ACM, 36*(1), 28–47.

Brun-Cottan, F., & Wall, P. (1995). Using video to re-present the user. *Communications of the ACM, 38*(5), 61–71.

Dourish, P., & Bly, S. (1992). Portholes: Supporting awareness in a distributed work group. *Proceedings of the Conference on Human Factors in Computing Systems* (pp. 541–546). New York: ACM Press.

Fish, R. S., Kraut, R. E., Root, R. W., & Rice, R. E. (1993). Video as a technology for informal communication. *Communications of the ACM, 36*(1), 48–61.

Gale, S. (1990). Human aspects of interactive multimedia communication. *Interacting With Computers, 2*(2), 175–189.

Gaver, W., Moran, T., MacLean, A., Lövstrand, L., Dourish, P., Carter, K., & Buxton, W. (1992). Realizing a video environment: EuroParc's RAVE system. *Proceedings of the Conference on Human Factors in Computing Systems* (pp. 27–35). New York: ACM Press.

Isaacs, E. A., Morris, T., & Rodriguez, T. K. (1994). A forum for supporting interactive presentations to distributed audiences. *Proceedings of the Conference on Computer-Supported Cooperative Work* (pp. 405–416). New York: ACM Press.

Isaacs, E. A., Morris, T., Rodriguez, T. K., & Tang, J. T. (1995). A comparison of face-to-face and distributed presentations, *Proceedings of the Conference on Human Factors in Computing Systems,* (pp. 354–361). New York: ACM Press.

Isaacs, E. A., & Tang, J. C. (1994). What video can and cannot do for collaboration: A case study. *Multimedia Systems, 2,* 63–73.

Ishii, H., & Kobayashi, M. (1992). ClearBoard: A seamless medium for shared drawing and conversation with eye contact. *Proceedings of the Conference on Human Factors in Computing Systems* (pp. 525–532). New York: ACM Press.

Krauss R. M., & Bricker, P. D. (1967). Effects of transmission delay and access delay on the efficiency of verbal communication. *Journal of the Acoustic Society of America, 41,* 286–292.

Kurita, T., Iai, S., and Kitawaki, N. (1993). Assessing the effects of transmission delay: Interaction of speech and video. In *Proceedings of the 14th International Symposium: Human, Factors in Telecommunications* (pp. 111–121). Darmstadt, Germany: R. V. Decker.

Mantei, M. M., Baecker, R. M., Sellen, A. J., Buxton, W. A. S., Milligan, T., & Wellman, B. (1991). Experiences in the use of a media space. *Proceedings of the Conference on Human Factors in Computing Systems* (pp. 203–208). New York: ACM Press.

Ochsman, R. B., & Chapanis, A. (1974). The effects of 10 communication modes on the behavior of teams during co-operative problem-solving. *International Journal of Man–Machine Studies, 6,* 579–619.

O'Conaill, B., Whittaker, S., & Wilbur, S. (1993). Conversations over video conferences: An evaluation of the spoken aspects of video-mediated communication. *Human–Computer Interaction, 8,* 389–428.

Olson, J. S., Olson, G. M., & Meader, D. K. (1995). What mix of video and audio is useful for small groups doing remote real-time design work? *Proceedings of the Conference Human Factors in Computing Systems* (pp. 362–368). New York: ACM Press.

Sellen, A. (1992). Speech patterns in video-mediated conversations. *Proceedings of the Conference Human Factors in Computing Systems* (pp. 49–59). New York: ACM Press.

Tang, J. C., & Isaacs, E. (1993). Why do users like video? Studies of multimedia supported collaboration. *CSCW: An International Journal, 1*(3), 163–196.

Tang, J. C., Isaacs, E. A., & Rua, M. (1994). Supporting distributed groups with a montage of lightweight interactions. *Proceedings of the Conference on Computer-Supported Cooperative Work* (pp. 23–34). New York: ACM Press.

Tang, J. C., & Rua, M. (1994). Montage: Providing teleproximity for distributed groups. *Proceedings of the Conference Human Factors in Computing Systems* (pp. 37–43). New York: ACM Press.

Chapter 10

Channel Overload as a Driver for Adoption of Desktop Video for Distributed Group Work

Carrie Rudman
Richard Hertz
US West Advanced Technologies

Catherine Marshall
Collaborative Technologies

Elizabeth Dykstra-Erickson
Apple Computer, Inc.

In this chapter we build a theory of what may influence groups to invest in desktop video to support their work, given the relatively high costs of networks, software, and computers. The theory is motivated by a synthesis of two studies. In the first, groups of graduate students volunteered to use desktop conferencing to complete multiple, highly complex class assignments (Dykstra-Erickson et al., 1995, Rudman, Dykstra-Erickson, Hertz, Schmidt, & Marshall, 1996). In the second, we identified preexisting needs of distributed organizations for long distance visual information exchange (Rudman, Hertz, & Roberts, 1996). These two studies allowed us to see how people learn to communicate visually with long-term exposure to videoconferencing and how real-world pressures may drive the need to take advantage of such newly acquired skills to overcome the restricted channel capacity of audio and data communication.

INTRODUCTION

If we could accurately anticipate the future role of video for supporting collaborative work, the communications industry could more effectively justify the cost of developing the prerequisite network infrastructure. The future value of video may be underestimated because it has been evaluated

199

using traditional research techniques. We argue that short-term laboratory evaluations with artificial tasks cannot reveal the role that visual feedback plays in reacting to real-world social and logistical pressures and that simply observing audio conference calls cannot fully reveal problems that could be addressed by video. Conference calls that appear successful on the surface hide serious problems. People limit their goals for such meetings to fit the constraints of the communication media. These limitations ultimately force teams to travel to face-to-face meetings and expand the time required to complete their work. To predict the value of video, we believe we need to combine knowledge of organizational goals (e.g., quality and timeliness of work products), economic factors (e.g., access to distributed markets), logistical constraints faced by the teams, and the human dynamics critical to team collaboration. This combined knowledge provides the context for understanding why travel, reduced access to expertise, and time delays are costly, and how they drive the use of video for information exchange.

Based on data from our real-time observations of long-term collaboration and analysis of distributed organizations, we propose that eight factors contribute to the need for video:

1. The number of participants in a meeting.
2. The level of familiarity of the participants.
3. The distribution of knowledge between contributors to the team.
4. Task complexity.
5. The time pressure associated with the team's work.
6. The level of negotiation required to complete the task.
7. Power dynamics.
8. The extent to which visual information is shared.

We describe how each factor contributes to overloading the capacity of audio and data sharing channels in conference calls and how video works to compensate for that overload. We provide supporting evidence from students' long-term usage and from our analysis of the needs of real-world distributed groups. Finally, we speculate about how the eight factors interact with each other to influence a group's potential need for the video channel. We begin with overviews of the two studies and their results.

GRADUATE STUDENT TEAMS

Students in two 10-week business courses agreed to carry out all their team meetings using desktop conferencing. The students worked on case studies from real businesses or on marketing projects from other MBA courses.

The desktop conferencing system was installed in four offices in a building at the University of Oregon Graduate School of Business (Dykstra-Erickson et al., 1995; Rudman, Dykstra-Erickson, Hertz, Schmidt, & Marshall, 1995). The workstations provided four-way, full-duplex audio, video views of all the participants, file sharing, and a shared workspace (Timbuktu™). The bandwidth of the audio and video could be set high (15 kHz audio, NTSC video at 30 frames per second) or low (3 kHz audio, 64 kbps video at 15 frames per second). Both the video and audio low-bandwidth transmission were delayed by 500 msec to mimic current low-bandwidth systems. The offices had telephones and fax machines. Observation cameras recorded face, screen, and full-room views.

Course 1

Eleven students enrolled in a Business Strategies course created three teams to solve four complex business cases. They worked in the lab for one session per week and had to produce case recommendations during the meetings themselves. All teams used (a) audio conferencing and fax machines for their first assignment, (b) low-bandwidth audio and video conferencing with file transfer for their second assignment, and (c) high-bandwidth audio and video with application sharing for their third. The increasingly complex configurations were provided progressively to avoid overloading users with new capabilities. In the last project, different teams received one of the three configurations.

Course 2

Fifteen students in a separate Marketing Communications course created four teams that worked on three open-ended marketing projects. Each team built a marketing strategy for a local business using data collected from the outside world. They created one report for each 3-week project. The teams could use the conferencing system as often as they liked but could not meet face-to-face. They also could use e-mail and the equivalent of "overnight" mail. For their first project, they used full-duplex audio, file sharing, and the shared workspace, but no video. For their second and third projects, NTSC video was added.

Qualitative analysis of the videotaped meetings identified classes of communication transmitted through the audio, video, and data-sharing channels. We also documented the problems the students encountered when attempting to complete the assignments with the varying levels of communication support. Multiple questionnaires and interviews carried out after most of the individual sessions explored the seriousness of these problems and the perceived value of the video and data-sharing channels for supporting each class of communication. The students in the Marketing Communications course also wrote term papers in which they explicitly evaluated the value of video.

Problems with Audio Conference Calls

The analysis of the tapes from the Business Strategies course revealed that there were dramatic problems trying to use audio conferencing to solve the business cases, even though there was no delay of the audio. These problems demonstrated that the channel capacity of audio and fax was not sufficient to complete these complex tasks in real time. The 3- or 4-person teams needed to share complex data and then negotiate strategies for analyzing and solving the cases using only voice and fax. They needed to confirm each others' level of understanding of the data they faxed and determine their level of agreement on strategies without seeing each other's faces. Only one person could give feedback at a time because they could not see each others' nonverbal reactions. Without visual feedback from the other team members, they had difficulty knowing when they were paying attention—let alone whether they agreed with each others' suggestions. They also could not tell whether they were understood by the silent members of the team, and they sometimes had to interrupt each other awkwardly. When new data, concepts, variables, contingencies, justifications, and conclusions were introduced, other participants often provided no feedback about their relevance or level of importance. Key ideas that were needed to solve the case were often lost.

For all the cases, students needed to identify subtasks (e.g., locate information, calculate numbers, develop documentation) and plan ways to integrate the information during the meetings. But in the audio calls, they could not see each other to determine how willing others were to take on tasks. During the work, they could not see what others were doing (e.g., when they were out of the room, looking at paper, looking at the screen, typing). They sometimes did not know who was talking to whom. They delayed asking others about their status for fear of interrupting their work. When they did ask, they sometimes created ill-timed interruptions and when they got no immediate response they sometimes started yelling. They had problems knowing when others needed help because they could not see each other's level of frustration as we could through our observation cameras. Nor could they see each other's level of discomfort about bad assumptions, about intermediate calculations, or about errors in logic and overall conclusions. It was difficult to anticipate good times to break into discussions (Jefferson, 1973; Sacks, Scheclos, & Jefferson, 1974) because individuals could not presignal their need to talk with facial expressions and gestures and they could not get nonverbal feedback from the speaker.

Both our observations of the sessions and the students' comments in the following interviews showed that, in general, the students had problems evaluating each other's level of attention, concentration, and frustration, determining how angry or happy people were, determining how easy or difficult a task was for them, and deciding when was an appropriate time to speak. They couldn't read each other's moods when they were silent, and the need for division of labor discouraged interruptions. Acknowledgment, thanks, critiques, feedback on acceptable social behavior, and jokes were infrequent because they needed to use the auditory mode for task-oriented communication. Conclusions generally were shared verbally, and team members' widely varying levels of confidence in those conclusions were not visible.

The Moment-to-Moment Role of Video

Video later allowed the students in both courses to watch each other's faces, body language, and gestures. They also held up reports and graphs and enacted visual jokes (e.g., unfocusing the camera). In both courses, gestures were used to help regulate the flow of conversations (e.g., hands up, wiggle finger, cup hands around mouth). Other gestures conveyed important messages without interrupting the ongoing conversation of others (e.g., pretending to point a gun to say they didn't agree, tilting hand side to side), whereas others allowed all members of the team to respond simultaneously to a question posed to the group (e.g., thumbs up, OK, head shake). Students mimicked each other's gestures to acknowledge understanding (cf. the concept of "local language," Dykstra & Carasik, 1989; Dykstra-Erickson et al., 1995) Heath and Luff (1991), in contrast, found gestures to be ineffective for videoconferencing—presumably due to equipment differences and shorter length of exposure.

After the students in the Business Strategies course were exposed to all three configurations with the first three case studies, they rated the usefulness of audio, video, and data sharing for 14 classes of information exchange that we had abstracted from the videotapes. They used a scale from -1 (interferes) to $+2$ (highly valuable). Overall, high-bandwidth audio was rated 1.5 and low-bandwidth audio, 0.8. The delayed audio resulted in frequent audio collisions (e.g., multiple people responding to a delayed question or the speaker restating a question just as an answer comes back). Kurita et al. (1993) reported that an audio delay of 380 msec would be more tolerable than 500 msec even if the video delay remains at 500 msec. However, fast turn-taking would likely require a delay of 60 msec or less to avoid audio collisions. File transfer and the shared work space were rated 1.1 and 1.0, respectively. High-bandwidth video was rated 0.8 overall but low-bandwidth video received a -0.3 rating. The video ratings are shown in Fig. 10.1 for each of the types of information exchange that we had identified.

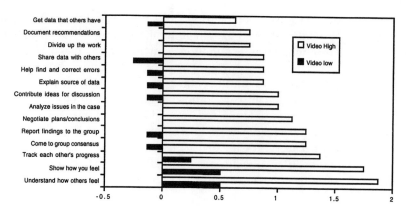

FIG. 10.1. Value of high- and low-bandwidth video for conveying information.

The high-quality video was particularly valued for understanding how others feel, and showing how you feel (above 1.75). It was rated as useful for tracking progress, coming to consensus, negotiating, reporting findings, contributing ideas, and analyzing issues (all 1 or above). The low-bandwidth video received much lower ratings, due to reduced resolution and the ½-sec delay. It was rated as actually interfering with sharing data and contributing ideas. This is in part because the students resorted to using regular phone lines to communicate with each other with no audio delay. The video with a 500-msec delay was therefore not synchronized with the immediate audio they heard over the phones. Data reported by Wilson, Smith, and Wakeman (1993) suggest that negative ratings are likely even if there is no synchronization problem. They presented subjects with degraded spoken words that could be recognized 50% of the time and measured the impact of adding progressively better video channels on increasing the recognition of the words. Their 64-kb video (similar to the low bandwidth used in our study) actually lowered recognition rates marginally. This was presumably due to the fact that the poor-quality video was distracting. The 128-kb video raised recognition by only 6%, whereas the 384-kb video raised recognition by almost 16% (slightly higher than the rate for NTSC video).

We later asked students in this course to rate the value of the high-bandwidth video for conveying specific types of visual information that we had observed during the sessions. Their ratings are shown in Fig. 10.2. We see in later discussion that a number of these types of information are particularly important to real-world distributed businesses.

In interviews with groups from the Marketing Communications course, the students tended to report gleaning information about transient mental states, like level of understanding, from the video more than more stable

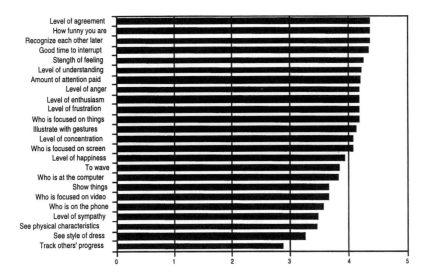

FIG. 10.2. Value of high-bandwidth video for visual information exchange (0 = *no value* and 5 = *very high value*).

characteristics of the individuals, like physical appearance—although these students already knew each other fairly well before taking the course and would not necessarily have had to rely on the video for this information.

REAL-WORLD ORGANIZATIONS

For this second study, we worked with 20 real-world distributed organizations to determine practical and economic factors that would drive the need for desktop conferencing in general and video in particular (Rudman, Hertz, & Roberts, 1995). Our methods were to a large extent anthropological. We attempted to identify a range of cases that had relevant characteristics (distributed groups dependent on highly complex collaboration). We then explored the goals and communication patterns of these organizations with open-ended interviews at their places of work. In addition, we observed face-to-face meetings of 11 of the groups, noting instances of classes of information exchange and documenting illustrative scenarios.

After the interviews, 14 of the groups tried out a desktop conferencing system either to run one of their standard meetings or to more generally evaluate ways in which the technology could support their work. The system was set up in the business schools at Oregon State University (OSU), University of Oregon, and Portland State University (PSU). Two Silicon Graphics Indy™ workstations at each site provided the InPerson™ conferencing software (version 1.0). This provided simultaneous video views of all conference participants, full-duplex audio (16 kHz sampling rate), and a shared whiteboard which allowed participants to capture and annotate application windows or video frames. A computer-aided design program and a World Wide Web browser were available as needed, and Xtelescreen™ supported sharing of applications. An emulation package supported Microsoft Windows™, Word™, Excel™, and PowerPoint™. Audio was captured with room-sensitive microphones and heard through headphones to avoid feedback. Video images were captured with gooseneck cameras.

We worked with groups from high-tech companies including computer sales managers, software developers, a factory automation company, and a high-tech asphalt testing company. We also worked with a variety of designers including architects and graphic designers. We worked with administrators like university deans, the managers of a national laboratory, and the staff of a venture capital firm. We also worked with groups that were responsible for managing and evaluating distributed systems, including evaluators of US West's repair methods and managers of bookstore inventory and point-of-sale systems. Finally, we worked with educators, including computer science faculty and faculty from a community college providing programs for small businesses.

Macro Factors: Trade-offs Between Travel, Access to Collaborators, and Quality of Communication

This study provided a "larger picture" of groups' overall motivation. All the groups constantly traded off the costs of travel with the benefits these contacts made for exchanging quality information that allowed them to reach their goals more effectively. We are able to draw inferences based on this macro view provided by these groups as well as on the micro view that we had obtained by observing the students. The distributed groups' preexisting communication problems, which we summarize next, clearly suggested needs for data sharing tools. But we also uncovered needs for video, and the participants' value ratings for video concurred.

Nature of Team Distribution

The real-world teams collaborated between Eugene, Corvallis, and Portland—Oregon towns that are spaced along Interstate 5 about 2 hr drive from one another. They also worked with groups distributed across the Pacific Northwest and the rest of country. A variety of pressures forced them to work at a distance. Some groups like the Bureau of Mines distributed responsibilities between locations, whereas others like the asphalt testing company had distributed customers and suppliers. Educators tried to reach students who were widely distributed. Members of professional associations like the Pacific Advanced Communications Consortium (PACC) shared common interests independent of location. All of the groups had challenges locating people and scheduling time to meet with them. For many of the groups, collaboration bridged multiple cities and institutions, making meetings especially difficult to schedule. Communication problems were multiplied by the fact that people belonged to multiple groups. For example, the Apple Computer sales manager for the universities in Oregon coordinated with three distinct groups in each of the three universities. In general, representatives of relevant organizations were not always available to meet, and experts sometimes could not contribute in a timely manner. This caused delays in completing group objectives.

Costs of Travel

The people in these 20 organizations traveled up and down Interstate 5 frequently to collaborate within their own organizations and traveled to other states on a regular basis. The costs of travel included airfare and hotels, lost work time, and fatigue—and these costs were sometimes prohibitive. Costs increased, of course, with the number of participants and with the dispersion of those participants. Advanced Control Technologies sometimes rejected clients on the basis of travel costs. They also could not afford multiple trips to equipment vendors or subcontractors who were distributed in multiple cities, and this resulted in costly surprises about design requirements for factory automation. All teams found it difficult to include key people in meetings and sometimes had to travel to track them down after meetings.

Problems with Audio Conference Calls

All of the groups could articulate their frustrations with audio conference calls. As with the student teams, the distributed group members reported that they couldn't see when others were paying attention or see nonverbal feedback. Again, key problems were regulating the flow of conversation and communicating attitudes. Conference calls were particularly ineffective for reviewing graphic information. The architects needed to assure that people could view and approve changes of building designs. They resorted to driving between sites only to find that the person they needed to talk to was not available. Leaving the design drawings there and discussing them afterward by phone caused problems because of difficulty coordinating visual reference points and explaining possible fixes verbally.

Need for Visual Contact During Meetings

People needed to recognize faces and learn about each other's work styles. For example, the PACC invited experts in computer science and journalism that did not know each other to evaluate opportunities for distance education. They claimed personal styles were garnered by face-to-face contact, providing social leverage for renewing contacts in the future.

In addition, the management at the Bureau of Mines indicated that visual contact was important for building organizational trust between people who know each other. Directives from management in Washington sometimes required downsizing or redistribution of areas of responsibilities among the nine labs across the country. Interpreting these mandates and getting information about their effect on the local personnel was very challenging using only telephone lines. They missed having the visual contact that leads to trust and translates to confidence in decisions.

In a face-to-face meeting to plan the construction of the OSU Alumni Center building, we saw how visual feedback regulated the flow of the conversation in larger, task-oriented groups. Presenters looked at the other 18 people that were present for feedback on a question and others raised their hands to break in. Silent gestures were used (e.g., nodding to support a proposal or interpretation, one hand representing budget and the other building options). Expressions (e.g., smiles) of participants provided a test of the "pulse" of how the meeting was going. Approximately fourteen 3 ft × 3 ft design drawings were tacked on the walls, and others were shown on an overhead projector. Presenters constantly (and audience members occasionally) pointed to parts of the drawings and shifted focus of attention using such visual cues.

We had hints that visual feedback on level of understanding was also important any time new data were shared. For example, the OSU bookstore system administrator needed to resolve problems with point-of-sale terminals and called the database company on the phone for help. He indicated that feedback on level of understanding was very important in these dialogues and was not clearly available over the phone. During their initial trial of our conferencing system, these same OSU and the PSU administrators shared a view of the database in a window and discussed differences in each other's menu customization and some of the more advanced configurations. With this system, they could observe each other's level of enthusiasm and understanding of various parts of the conversation with the video of their faces.

Needs to Share Prerecorded Video

Prerecorded video was used fairly frequently by a variety of the teams. During the face-to-face Alumni Center meeting, they played a video documentary about a different Alumni Center as an example. The presenter talked over the video to interpret it for the audience. Another group of architects used video clips to show progress on a site. The asphalt testing company used video to document problems with broken equipment. And the US West field analysts used video to justify the replacement of lead cable. In that case, they first taped damaged wires, illustrated covarying factors (weather, squirrel damage), and later recorded the time and equipment needed to repair the wires. During their initial test of our conferencing system, one of the US West analysts played the video tape of the damaged telephone wires for his partner in a different city using the alternate video input jack and his own camcorder. Both people commented as they played the tape. One of them copied a frame of the video on to the whiteboard. Both then annotated it, pointing out the nature of the repair and the nest of the squirrels that had done the damage. The analysts felt that showing this to management from a distance would have made their business case easier to defend. They suggested that transmitting tapes of damage could help repair teams more effectively plan their work. The video frames were captured and viewed with larger frame size at NTSC resolution, overcoming problems with the transmitted video.

The importance of visual views of working equipment was also discussed. Bureau of Mines staff had to fly between sites to use scarce equipment like scanning electron microscopes. Sometimes these trips were ineffective because the researchers discovered that they didn't have the materials they needed after the first test runs were completed. These interactions always involved multiple experts with multiple types of expertise and remote video views of the equipment would allow any contributor to direct equipment changes.

Unmet Needs of Subgroups

During face-to-face meetings, subgroups often contributed to only a part of a discussion and wasted time listening to the rest. Further, subgroups could not work together on subtasks during meetings because this disrupted others. The Advanced Control Technologies software people left a meeting so they could work to meet their deadlines even though important topics were discussed by the remaining staff that included managers and hardware experts. The conferencing system allowed the participants to freeze their video image. Several participants used this feature while they performed other tasks but still participated in the meeting. One participant froze the video for the first half of a meeting while he prepared to lead the second half. With this system, participants also could mute the outgoing audio. The PACC group insisted that the mute be used so side conversations between people in one room would not disrupt the group. It also was possible to start a separate video conversation during a larger meeting by putting the other meeting on hold. This feature was used repeatedly by our US West research team when we needed to contact a variety of people with specialized expertise distributed between the universities (e.g., network managers) during our own team meetings.

Limitations of Asynchronous Communication

For these groups, documentation tended to be developed by individuals and shared using paper mail and electronic mail. Meetings were usually used only to review changes to the material after it was developed. But there was ample evidence that this type of asynchronous communication was causing problems that might be addressed by desktop conferencing. For example, the US West reengineering committee jointly developed documentation on a new strategy for providing telephone services. Missing expertise sometimes required complete revisions to fill in missing data. Errors (e.g., omission of a job category in a staffing plan) also could lead to a loss of credibility with other departments.

Once, two separate data analyses couldn't be integrated because people did not use the same sampling assumptions. This group did not have the benefit of verbal and nonverbal feedback from other remote team experts during the development of the documentation itself. In contrast, during their initial trial of our conferencing system, the US West analysts worked together to revise PowerPoint slides using data pulled from spreadsheets. They indicated that reading each other's nonverbal reactions about satisfaction with the content, level of agreement, and so on assured they were working with the same assumptions and made their meetings more efficient, helping them complete their work during the meetings themselves.

Value Ratings

After the teams completed their first "test drives" they filled out a questionnaire in which they rated the value of video, whiteboards, and application sharing to support various needs (0 = *no value*, 1 = *low value*, 2 = *moderate value*, and 3 = *high value*). Figure 10.3 shows that even with minimal exposure, the highest ratings for supporting some of these functions were for the video.

FACTORS CONTRIBUTING TO THE NEED FOR VIDEO

We analyzed the combined results of both studies to identify factors contributing to the need for video as well as the interdependencies between them. We first describe each factor separately and then provide our theory

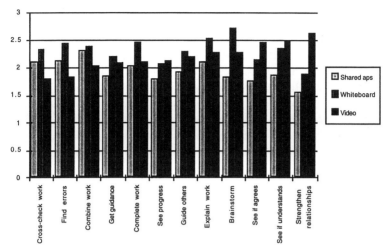

FIG. 10.3. Value ratings for communication categories.

of their interactions. Finally, we illustrate how these factors could be used to identify groups with high needs for video support. In general, we propose that the need for video will be highest (and that groups will be more likely to invest in the added network and computer power required) when their moment-to-moment communication demands exceed the available channel capacity of the other less expensive communication channels (e.g., audio and data sharing) and where time constraints, distribution of contributors, and budgets reduce the motivation to travel. We propose that these factors combine to influence overload of the previously available communications channels during specific units of time. Although the audio, data, and video channels are qualitatively different in the types of information they can carry, we suggest there is considerable functional overlap. Consequently, video can be used to relieve pressure for information exchange in the other channels.

The Influence of Team Size

One of the key factors that we propose leads to overload of the audio and data communication channels is team size. In related studies (Marshall & Novick, 1995; Marshall, 1996), we observed that people in two-party meetings can share their level of understanding, agreement, and concern about tasks verbally with backchannel utterances (e.g., "uh huh"), acknowledgments (e.g., "yeah right"), repairs (e.g., restatement to repair misunderstanding or lack of understanding), intonation cues, and so on. We have also observed that turn-taking seems to require minimal coordination in two-party meetings. In contrast, the three- and four-member student teams we observed using the video used much more complex mechanisms for providing feedback and turn-taking. We saw that the students learned to use the video channel to transmit and monitor facial expression, body language, and gestures (e.g., hands up) to indicate the need to talk, to invite feedback from specific individuals, and to provide silent feedback showing level of understanding, thereby also influencing who needed to talk next. The video channel thus can be used to manage the flow of conversations between multiple contributors in circumstances where the other channels are needed for detailed data exchange.

Increasing the number of participants can increase the amount of content that needs to be communicated. Additional team members add different perspectives on the problem at hand, or have responsibility for completing a subset of the work. All of the real-world groups we interviewed involved more than two participants, with some meetings ranging up to 19 members. Such teams need to ensure that the opinions of each are understood by the group and influence the outcome of the group's work. As more team members are added, coordination also increases. The work of each person is often dependent on the work of the other contributors. In order to ensure that interdependencies are addressed, group members need to know what each of the others is working on, whether they are paying attention when interdependencies are discussed, and whether they agree. In larger groups, multiple parallel conversations can go on at once. Sequential questioning in conference calls is tedious and the video provides an additional channel for this information, allowing the audio and data channels to be used for data transfer.

The Level of Familiarity of the Participants

Another factor that we propose influences channel overload is the level of familiarity of the participants. In face-to-face meetings, information about what people look like and their attitudes can be gleaned by observing their faces. When a team first comes together, the video channel may be used simply to glean information about facial characteristics for later face recognition. The study of real-world teams showed that they notice things like faces, hair color, age, and style of dress that allow them to recognize each other when they meet in other contexts, and also to make judgments that influence their discussions (e.g., estimate someone's age). They felt telephone contacts were frustrating as initial contacts because there was no way to "put faces to names."

However, we also saw that people learned to interpret person-specific visual cues. Characteristic gestures, body movements, and small changes in facial expression started to have meaning ("I don't agree") that could be communicated via video, leaving open the audio channels for other types of data transmission. In work preliminary to the studies already described, we informally observed a business class in which students were asked to form their own teams. The students who knew each other and had worked together previously quickly grouped into teams, leaving the others in the class the challenge of forming teams with less well-known peers. In their initial face-to-face meetings, the teams who were familiar with one another seemed to have an advantage. Their communication seemed more compact and less comprehensible to us. Facial expressions, directed gazes, and gesture were used constantly. They seemed to be able to divide up the work more quickly, possibly due to their use of feedback from the visual channel.

Distribution of Knowledge/Responsibility Between Contributors

When information is unevenly distributed between people with interdependent responsibilities, it often needs to be communicated, and those passing on the information need to verify whether it has been heard and understood. Facial expressions, body language, and gesture were found to be important indicators of level of attention and level of understanding for the students. As the disparity of knowledge increases, the need for feedback required also increases. Also, progress during meetings will be best evaluated by those with the deepest knowledge of the specific subject being discussed or responsibility for the outcome of the meeting. Facial expressions of such experts/managers can have an important controlling influence on what is said, who talks next, and what actions are agreed on. We propose that this also frees up channel capacity in the audio and data channels for complex data exchange.

Many of the distributed business groups had uneven distribution of knowledge. The OSU bookstore system administrator's responsibilities included troubleshooting software errors that the clerks did not understand. The balance of distribution of knowledge was reversed when the same system administrator needed to get help from the database company personnel who walked him through fixes over the phone. This administrator foresaw uses of desktop conferencing both to support his troubleshooting efforts with software vendors and to support communication within the bookstore. The analyst specifically wanted to be able to communicate remotely with the sales clerks to provide on-the-fly training on how to interpret the database user interface, and to provide remote troubleshooting support. He indicated that the video views would have provided information on level of understanding and frustration of the store clerks and would have provided an opportunity to convey information, support, and humor. And although shared data would allow the vendors to see which files were loaded, they felt that the video would allow the vendor to directly see the level of understanding of the analyst.

Not only did individuals have different types of expertise and responsibilities, but so did subgroups. In the study of students, it was not infrequent for two subgroups to carry on two distinct conversations using shared communication channels. These intertwined discussions tended to time share the audio channel with few actual audio collisions. We now hypothesize that this type of pressure increased the value of, and was substantially dependent on, the video channel (e.g., the ability to use gesture, and to interpret other subgroups members' facial expressions). We suspect that the experimental Hydra system (see Buxton, Sellen, & Sheasby, chapter 18, this volume) helps users disentangle several conversations even better by providing spatially separated video views and spatially localized audio.

Task Complexity

If we loosely define task complexity as the number of variables being considered simultaneously in solving a problem, as well as the extent of interdependency among those variables, then it seems likely that as task complexity goes up, so does the overall amount of information that needs to be communicated during distributed meetings. As the number of variables goes up, the importance of reading nonverbal reactions to that data increases because of the priority of using the data and audio channels for data communication. We must be cautious here, however. To the extent to which team members already share knowledge of the variables and interdependencies of those variables, such information does not need to be shared within a meeting.

The influence of complexity was not at first obvious in the face-to-face meetings of the real-world organizations. Although all of the teams were dealing with highly complex problems (e.g., designing a global positioning system for utility truck dispatch, designing campus buildings, analyzing inventory database customization options, selecting candidates for job positions), the meetings always seemed to be manageable within the time allowed, taking advantage of substantial amounts of shared knowledge. But the interviews revealed that the overall need for information exchange always exceeded the channel capacity of the meetings. The complexity of topics covered in the meetings was carefully adjusted to fit practical constraints. For example, when highly complex topics were addressed, team members were careful to limit the number of people involved. When status meetings were held to coordinate multiple subteam contributions, only the topics that were relevant to all team members were discussed. And even the topics in these meetings tended to be limited to changes: new data from outside the team that changed the overall direction of the work, or problems that had arisen during the work that required the team to change the methods they would use or their timelines. Often topics were not discussed in detail in the meetings but rather relegated to action items for individuals to attend to, or to agenda items for smaller meetings with a subset of participants.

Although these adjustments ensure that standard meetings are useful, they certainly increase the overall length of a project and reduce the perceived usefulness of the meetings for affecting actual deliverables. The students in the Business Strategies course did not have the option to make many of these adjustments. This allowed us to predict the role that video could play in supporting complexity where such adjustments have costs in real-world settings including travel to face-to-face meetings, excluding contributions of distributed collaborators, and extending time lines. As we have seen, the students were presented with highly complex tasks (e.g., setting prices for products) and they were required to address these problems in very limited time frames.

The increased bandwidth created by the data-sharing capabilities certainly helped them cope with this complexity. Yet all the students in the Business Strategies course had no doubt that the video was providing them information about their colleagues' mental states, which was helping them coordinate complexity. A questionnaire revealed that knowing colleagues' level of understanding was generally important for all types of coordination. Knowing level of attention being paid was particularly important for establishing division of labor and creating a high-quality result. Knowing level of agreement was, not surprisingly, particularly important for coming to agreement, and knowing level of enthusiasm was particularly important for tracking progress.

Highly complex tasks also can be supported by blocking transmission of information that may not be relevant to the discussion at the time to ensure a better signal to noise ratio during the meeting but also allowing parallel progress. We saw this during the trials of our desktop conferencing system, when team members purposefully shut down the video channel to avoid distracting others. Although this decreased the total amount of visual information transmitted, it increased the signal-to-noise ratio for the other participants. Thus the participants adjusted the amount of information transmitted dynamically without having to reduce the complexity of their own contribution.

Level of Negotiation Required

We also propose that high levels of negotiation can contribute to the overload of the audio and data channels. If team members disagree on actions that need to be taken, they need methods for influencing each other beyond the audio channel that must be used for information exchange. This pressure encourages use of the video channel. (See also Short, Williams, & Christie, 1976.) The previous section illustrates that negotiation is a fact of life for complex collaboration where trade-offs must be resolved on a regular basis. Students' methods included increasing "social presence" by using facial expressions to show the level of seriousness of a proposal. They also sometimes brought the lenses close to their faces when they wanted to break into a heated conversation or to show a high level of engagement.

Alternatively, they moved away from the camera apparently to indicate lack of commitment to the negotiation process. The student teams became conscious of monitoring and consciously using facial expressions to show level of agreement, level of frustration, and level of enthusiasm to influence decisions. They also used the video channel to negotiate cursor control, a very important method for influencing the outcome of the work. They developed gestures to show who was not using the cursor (i.e., hands up, palms forward) and used additional video feedback to pass control (e.g., hand waves, directed stares). Many of the distributed organizations focused on the importance of reading their clients' faces in negotiations and influencing their teammates through "strength of character." In summary, high levels of disagreement (including strength of disagreement and number of issues) and high needs for negotiation to resolve differences add a need for an additional level of communication that seems to be well supported by video.

Power Dynamics

In a related way, the power dynamics of a group can create pressure to exchange information, and video may play a particularly crucial role, especially when there are more than two participants. Mechanisms for gaining power and control include assessing the level of dissonance among members, determining who agrees with whom, and "taking control" by asserting one's self. The value of video for supporting such evolving social dynamics was described in the Marketing Communications students' final term papers. They felt that because of the video, each member had the opportunity to:

- " 'Take charge' of an individual session or phase of the project"
- "Visually monitor signs of increasing group dissonance through body language"
- "Reduce the group separation factor that could occur without visual stimulation"
- "Reduce the group-splitting effect of distance"

Others noted that the video:

- "Makes you feel more a part of the group, even when you are not actively speaking up"

- "Allows expressions that are 'written all over your face' to be picked up and understood"

Again, students purposefully influenced social dynamics by adjusting the camera. They moved in and out of camera range, used the camera to show their own emotions (facial gestures, zooming themselves out or in), and used the camera to serve as a proxy (wiggle the camera to connote dizziness, nod the camera to show agreement, cover the camera to request others to stop something distracting). Students used gestures to vie for control (e.g., raising hands, cupping hands around mouth and mouthing words without speaking, and zooming face into camera to gain attention of others). All of these activities had an influence on the changing power dynamics (e.g., who grabbed the focus of attention and thereby influenced the strategies of the group). The students indicated they were able to gauge the appropriateness of their own reactions to socially charged comments by viewing their own faces and comparing their reactions to their teammates'.

Although the power dynamics of the real-world organizations were not always visible to us, it was clear they drove the progress of these meetings. Individuals on the teams could clearly indicate who played what roles and who was in charge. Different people had different priorities and needed to influence the other team members to ensure that their agendas were addressed and that time lines were met. We saw many instances of individuals moving the focus of conversation to new topics on what appeared to be "strength of character," "strength of their message," or "position of authority." This appeared to be a complex process that interacted with the social hierarchy within the group and elicited nonverbal reactions from multiple participants simultaneously. We have seen that negotiating influence is particularly difficult during conference calls, and this can be confounded by lack of ability to share data. For example, the Dynamix software person drew a picture on a whiteboard for his peers in Portland and received numerous affirmative head nods creating pressure to develop consensus, but neither the picture nor the head nods were visible to the remote designer.

Time Pressure Associated with the Work

Time pressure is fundamental to our theory of the value of video because it forces information exchange to occur within time constraints, and therefore increases load on the audio and data-sharing channels. In the Business Strategies course, students were required to produce each assignment within a single session of fixed length. They needed to transfer substantial amounts of information quickly and needed to react fast to proposed plans and strategies. Video allowed silent confirmation that this information was heard and understood, and also allowed fast feedback when the problem-solving strategies were going awry. Time limits do not inevitably lead to increased channel overload, however. In a related study (Marshall, 1996), we imposed time limits for standardized tasks, but participants responded to this by adjusting the complexity of the discussion to comfortably fit the allotted time. Students in the Business Strategies course could not use this strategy without jeopardizing the quality of their reports.

Asynchronous communication was used to good effect when it was available to reduce time pressure during meetings. For example, the students in the Marketing Communications course not only sent each other e-mail to negotiate strategies but they also used "overnight mail" to share annual reports and marketing brochures. But these alternative channels were not available in the time frames allocated in the Business Strategies course.

In the study of preexisting organizations, we couldn't compare specific meetings where the team members were more or less time pressured. However, in the interviews, time pressure was a recurring theme and we extrapolate that communication systems that allow teams to complete work within shorter time frames would be valued. Although asynchronous communication (e.g., e-mail) helps to relieve pressure to communicate information during meetings, this does not provide the minute-to-minute feedback we have identified that can control the direction of a collaboration and the outcome of a negotiation. Meetings are often called when a sufficient number of these issues have accumulated to require multiple people to be in the same room at the same time in order to progress. But in reality these issues do not come up only at neatly scheduled meetings. A system that allows spontaneous contacts at the time a critical decision is first identified could be predicted to speed the overall time frame of distributed projects. All of the preexisting organizations were working against demanding schedules. The Alumni Center Steering Committee, for example, spent a substantial amount of time in their meeting reviewing Gantt charts to ensure that interlocking activities would conform to the overall schedule of the project. One of the universal complaints of these teams was resenting the time it took to travel to meet with the other team members face-to-face, and this presumably delayed critical decision making. For all of the businesses we worked with, time translated into money, and whenever travel was avoided, both time and money were saved. The more quickly these groups could complete projects, the more revenue they could generate.

Visual Information Sharing

Accurate verbal descriptions of visual information tend to be lengthy (e.g., descriptions of damage to telephone wires and its causes). So without video, the need to share highly visual information is likely to overload the audio channel because of this costly translation. Such pressure is relieved by video and, in fact, some information can only be adequately conveyed this way (see also review by Whittaker & O'Conaill, chapter 2, this volume). Some types of information (e.g., changes to packaging designs) were very difficult to share without a visual communication mode and resulted in increasing information exchange in the audio channel. This was illustrated in an earlier study by Marshall and Novick (1995) in which two-party teams worked on a geometric puzzle with and without video. When video was available, they used it to show the puzzle pieces, and this took precedence over use of the camera for anything else. When no video was available, participants were forced to give lengthy descriptions, which proved to be inadequate despite their complexity.

Some visual information can be shared by transferring still images, whereas other information is more effectively shared with motion video. If sharing this type of information is central to the progress of work, the visual channel is more likely to be valued. Video also affords the opportunity to share live or prerecorded views of objects and scenes. We have seen that videotapes were used on an ad hoc basis in face-to-face meetings, but for distant collaboration, mailing tapes to remote collaborators does not allow the sender to get feedback from the audience during the showing of the video, and there is no way to provide comments over the video to tune the message to the audience needs.

Interaction Between Factors

The eight factors just listed are not predicted to work independently in many cases. For example, the number of participants will sometimes be a function of the level of complexity of the task or time constraints (e.g., to allow division of labor and input from multiple types of experts in a pre-specified time frame). But this would not always be the case. Complexity would not necessarily drive the number of students that would sign up for a course, and neither complexity nor the number of students would drive the length of time allocated to the course. The impact of time pressure clearly trades off against the complexity of the problem being solved. If time frames are lax, then team members may not feel the same pressure to use video to deal with complexity. This includes relegating problem solving to individuals and communicating via electronic mail. However, we did find in the Marketing Communications course that, even with groups setting their own pace for work, they all preferred using video.

Not only do the factors sometimes interact with each other, but they ultimately influence which communication modes take precedence. We saw that when both high-quality video and data sharing were available, the types of communication occurring in the audio mode tended to shift. For example, the audio channel was sometimes silent as data communication shifted to silently reviewing files or videotapes. Thus, willingness to pay for these channels may at first be driven by overload of the other channels, but the relative strengths of these channels for specific types of information may actually give them momentary precedence over audio, once they have been purchased and integrated into work.

Although we would not expect each of the factors we have listed above to work independently in all cases, they are offered as classifications that allow us to identify work groups that are likely to benefit from video, at least after sufficient exposure to its benefits. Video feedback may be most valuable for teams larger than two. Highly familiar teams may value interpreting their colleagues' expressions. And groups who need to become familiar with each other quickly (e.g., establishing trust between salespeople and customers) may particularly value video. Distributed groups under time pressure are also likely candidates. Evidence that particular groups score high on even one of the factors may be justification for exploring their needs on the others, in order to determine whether they would be appropriate to include in a future evaluation of the match between their needs and video technology.

CONCLUSIONS

The combined data from these two sets of studies has allowed us to see how macro pressures on communication—including costs of travel, dispersion of contributors, and time pressures—may be addressed by the moment-to-moment support provided by video. This conclusion is based on extrapolation from a range of observations of detailed coordination of groups within meetings to their needs for meeting broader organizational objectives. Although distributed meetings would benefit from the data-sharing and high-quality audio alone, these capabilities would not support the same level of coordination of multiple, widely distributed contributors that would be provided by the addition of video. We conclude that audio and data alone could not as easily allow participants to

- See what others look like
- Observe and assimilate each others' facial reactions to data content.
- Smoothly coordinate turn taking
- Influence each others' activities to meet their objectives

Future research is needed to determine under exactly which circumstances data and audio sharing alone would allow groups to avoid expensive travel or allow groups to extend their geographic range. We suggest that groups that rank high on the eight factors we have described are likely to need visual feedback for a significant proportion of their meetings, and may be able to use video to reduce travel and increase the dispersion of activities to take advantage of resources in a wider geographical area.

Taken together, these data help to explain discrepancies in past research on the value of video. Several studies have shown limited or no advantages of audio/video collaboration over audio collaboration alone (Gale, 1989; Ochsman & Chapanis, 1974; Olson & Olson, 1995). Many of these studies have measured the time it takes to complete specific tasks and the quality of work created in meetings with and without video. In general, relatively simple tasks that had minimal personal consequence for the participants were carried out for relatively short time periods. Studies where there is low pressure to exchange information may show that the capacity of the audio channel is sufficient—where there are only two participants, where there is little vested interest in the outcome of the task, and where the task complexity can be dealt with or without division of labor. These circumstances are likely to show much lower ratings of the value of video. The value of video may be more salient in contexts where social variables hold sway (e.g., where there is a strong "pecking order"). Although the impact of video on time to complete task may not be obvious because of the wide array of methods for adjusting meeting content or communicating asynchronously, overall project length may be affected.

Also, studies where team members do not have control over their own image size either through movement of the camera or resizing of the images on the screen are less likely to reveal the importance of using video for effecting their own ends. Guidelines for designers are implied by this theory, including allowing

- Visual scanning of large groups (e.g., Sheasby, 1995)
- Flexible adjustment of the camera angle
- Flexible aiming of the camera to alternative subject matter
- Close juxtaposition of video to the work content of the meetings

In general, studies where users have only limited exposure are likely to show much weaker effects then when they have enough experience with video to learn to take advantage of it. (See Dykstra-Erickson et al., 1995, for a more complete treatment of adaptation.)

We further propose that with experience, participants come to understand in detail the effectiveness of the communication channels that are available to them during distributed meetings, and that this determines the type of work they attempt to accomplish. With even a small amount of exposure to video desktop conferencing, users will increase their expectations. We predict that as the cost for videoconferencing goes down and users gain more experience, the drive to use video will increase, as will the geographic dispersion of communication that is tolerated.

ACKNOWLEDGMENTS

We thank our colleagues in all of these projects including Terry Roberts, Jill Schmidt, and Arent Kartik Mithal. We also thank Ellen Isaacs, Steve Whittaker, Abi Sellen, Doug Corey, and Pat Somers for very helpful reviews of earlier drafts of this chapter. The study of student teams was supported in part by National Science Foundation grant HRD-9252943 to Catherine Marshall.

Timbuktu is a trademark of Farallon. Indy and InPerson are trademarks of Silicon Graphics. SoftWindows is a trademark of Insignia. Windows, Word, Excel, and PowerPoint are trademarks of Microsoft. Xtelescreen is a trademark of VisualTek.

REFERENCES

Dykstra, E. A., & Carasik, R. P. (1991). Structure and support in cooperative environments: The Amsterdam Conversation Environment. *International Journal of Man–Machine Studies, Special Edition on Groupware and CSCW, 34,* 419–434.

Dykstra-Erickson, E. A., Rudman, C., Marshall, C., Hertz, R., Mithal, K., Schmidt, J., & Marshall, C. (1995, March). Supporting adaptation to multimedia desktop conferencing. *Proceedings of the 15th International Symposium on Human Factors in Telecommunications* (pp. 31–38). Melbourne, Australia.

Gale, S. (1989, September). Adding audio and video to an office environment. *Proceedings of the First European Conference on Computer Supported Cooperative Work EC-CSCW '89* (pp. 121–130). London.

Heath, C., & Luff, P. (1991). Disembodied conduct: Communication through video in a multimedia office environment. *Proceedings, Human Factors in Computing Systems, Reaching Through Technology: CHI '91* (pp. 99–103). New Orleans, LA.

Jefferson, G. (1973). A case of precision timing in ordinary conversation: Overlapped tag-positioned address terms in closing sequences. *Semiotics, 9,* 47–96.

Kurita, T., Iai, S., & Kitawaki, N. (1993). Assessing the effects of transmission delay: Interaction of speech and video. In *Proceedings of the 14th International Symposium: Human Factors in Telecommunications* (pp. 111–121). Heidelberg: R.V. Decker.

Marshall, C. R. (1996). *An experimental study of multimedia conferencing* (Document TR-96-003). Collaborative Technologies, Monterey, CA.

Marshall, C. R., & Novick, S. (1995). Conversational effectiveness in multimedia communications. *Information, Technology and People, 8*(1), 54–79.

Ochsman, R. B., & Chapanis, A. (1974). The effects of 10 communication modes on the behavior of teams during co-operative problem solving. *International Journal of Man–Machine Studies, 6,* 576–619.

Olson J. S., & Olson, G. M. (1995, May). What mix of video and audio is useful for small groups doing remote real-time design work? *Proceedings of CHI '95* (pp. 362–368). Denver, CO.

Rudman, C., Dykstra-Erickson, E., Hertz, R., Schmidt, J., & Marshall, C. (1996). *Identifying barriers to team communication addressed by multimedia desktop conferencing.* US West internal technical report, Boulder, CO.

Rudman, C., Hertz, R., & Roberts, T. (1996). *Contextually-driven needs for multimedia desktop conferencing.* US West internal technical report, Boulder, CO.

Sacks, H., Scheclos, E., & Jefferson, G. (1974). A simplest systematics for the organization of turn-taking for conversation. *Language 50*, 696–735.

Sheasby, M. (1995). *The Brady Bunch, or privacy and peripheral awareness in video teleconferencing.* Unpublished master's thesis, Dept. of Computer Science, University of Toronto.

Short, J., Williams, E., & Christie, B. (1976). *The social psychology of telecommunications.* London: Wiley.

Wilson, F., Smith, W., & Wakeman, I. (1993, May). Quality of service parameters for commercial application of videotelephony. *Proceedings, 14th International Symposium: Human Factors in Telecommunications* (pp. 139–148), Darmstadt, Germany.

Chapter 11

Video in Support
of Organizational Talk

Abigail Sellen
Richard Harper
Rank Xerox Research Centre

We report on a study of the use of video in an organization outside of a research laboratory, and in doing so, discover two sets of issues that have significant implications for the use of video in real work contexts. The first set of issues concerns the ways in which video provides support for organizational talk—in particular, problem-solving talk during geographically distributed meetings. The second concerns the issue of organizational ownership of video technology and the ways in which this impacts the choice of which system to use for what kind of meeting. We argue that such findings, which cannot be revealed through controlled laboratory experimentation, complement our understanding of how video can support distributed work.

INTRODUCTION

Convincing arguments can be made for studying video-mediated communication (VMC) in day-to-day organizational use rather than within the confines of controlled laboratory experimentation. The use of video technology by real working groups doing real work can be examined over weeks and months. This raises a whole class of issues that are impossible to capture by observing experimental subjects carrying out contrived tasks over short periods of time. These include the interaction of video with established group dynamics and hierarchies, and long-term adaptation to the technology (Dourish, Adler, Bellotti, & Henderson, 1996; Dykstra-Erickson et al., 1995; Isaacs & Tang, chapter 9, this volume; Rudman et al., chapter 10, this volume).

However, one charge that can be leveled against many of the studies that look at the use of video systems in real organizational contexts is that they confine themselves to studying use within their own research communities. Our own research laboratory is no exception. Over the years, it has produced a great number of publications on the use of its own RAVE media space and attendant technologies (e.g., Bellotti & Sellen, 1993; Dourish & Bellotti, 1992; Dourish & Bly, 1992; Dourish, 1993; Dourish et al., 1996; Gaver et al., 1992; Gaver, Sellen, Heath, & Luff, 1993; Heath & Luff, 1991, 1992[1]; Lövstrand, 1991), but only two on the use of video in real-world settings outside the research community (Harper & Carter, 1994; Pagani & Mackay, 1993). We have been, in effect, "looking at ourselves." Doing so, unfortunately, raises a host of methodological and analytic questions.

First of all, and as noted elsewhere (Harper, 1992), research environments are, organizationally speaking, quite unlike most other places of work. In particular there is a disproportionately large number of professional staff with all the rights, autonomy, and aloofness from organizational constraint that goes with that status. Second, these professional groups are often riven by factionalism and mutual antipathy, which creates communities within communities, each supporting different technologies (Harper, 1996). And third, there appears to be a systematic unwillingness to recognize and report on how these and other social structural factors impact on the use of technology. Instead, studies of technological use in research labs describe workplaces that appear extraordinarily benign and devoid of social structure—hardly like workplaces at all, but more like easy-going playgrounds (e.g., Adler & Henderson, 1994; Dourish et al., 1996; Fish, Kraut, & Chalfonte, 1990). The result is that studies that purport to be of "real" people doing "real" jobs in research laboratories tell us very little about the actual circumstances those people find themselves in or of the actual organizational role the technology plays.

There may be a number of reasons for this, relating perhaps to a desire to hide the political context of research, a lack of expertise in the analysis of the social, or simply an inability to see the woods for the trees. The result, however, is that there are only a few substantive and analytically powerful studies on the use of video in organizational contexts (exceptions include Isaacs & Tang, 1994, and Tang, Isaacs, & Rua, 1994[2]). The extensive body of experimental literature effectively stands alone and in want of complementary empirical studies of "people at work" with video.

It was to remedy this perceived absence that we set about to research the use of a video link between two sites for the distributed design and manufacture of a photocopier we call "Jaspers" by the Xerox Corporation.

It is this research that we report on here. We first describe the project in some detail, and outline our methodological approach in analyzing the use of the video link. We then discuss the more general impact of the technology before focusing on two features of the use of the link by the Jaspers team.

The first feature we discuss is the way in which the link supported both the nature and distribution of the work manifest in what we call *organizational talk*. The second feature of interest relates to the fact that in real work settings, users have a range of technologies supporting their work. Choices between different types of technology, in this case, VMC systems, were sometimes based on considerations external to the technology itself. In particular, we discuss the way in which the organizational framework surrounding two types of video systems supported different kinds of meetings, which we may describe as problem-solving versus decision-making meetings.

BACKGROUND

The Jaspers project primarily involved two sites: one in Welwyn Garden City, England (just north of London), and one in Henrietta, in upper New York State (near Rochester). Jaspers was planned as a fast-track project with the aim of designing and developing a new photocopier in less than the time Xerox products typically take. For this reason, ongoing exchange of information and discussion between Welwyn and Henrietta was even more crucial to the process of distributed work than might normally be the case.

In the year prior to implementation of the video link in mid May 1994, the Jaspers team relied mainly on telephone, fax, and e-mail for communicating with Henrietta. Technical meetings for discussing hardware, software, or the user interface were accomplished mainly by telephone conferencing. Documents were shared by faxing them beforehand, or by having access to electronic documents that were printed out prior to meetings. Regular but infrequent meetings for management updates and status reports used a system called *XTV*. XTV is a fixed-link, leased-line videoconferencing system supporting multipoint conferencing. This used ISDN 2 lines offering 128 kbps of bandwidth (although under certain circumstances this could be increased). Welwyn has a dedicated room for XTV, shared by the whole site, which encompasses large screens, document cameras, and remote control facilities. In addition, frequent travel between the two sites was also taking place.

The project ordered a PictureTel codec unit 4000 and a large monitor and camera. The codec model was operated using a tethered control box containing the microphone and had standard features such as a video inset on the main monitor to show the outgoing video signal. The codec[3] itself was fairly large and heavy compared to some of the newer models now available, and so required quite a large trolley in order to make it mobile. The codec, like the XTV system, used ISDN 2 lines, but on a dial-up on-demand basis. With XTV, the lines were paid for whether they were used or not.

METHOD

The study came out of an 18-month ethnographic examination of work practice in the design center, the purpose of which was to determine the role of current and future technologies in work, video included. More specifically, one fieldworker (R. Harper) followed the hypothetical process that any photocopier design would take within the organization, and interviewed staff from apprentice up to senior management level. Key tasks within the design process were also observed in detail. These included early "precommitment" design processes, prototype machine building, testing, fault analysis, warehouse management and administration processes, and soft and hard tooled assembly and manufacture. These interviews and observations provided a background to specific and actual design instances, such as Jaspers. Once a focus on Jaspers had been agreed, a second field worker (A. Sellen) began work. The focus on Jaspers occurred during the last 6 months of the research period.

More specifically, interest with Jaspers commenced in May 1994, 2 weeks after the Jaspers team had acquired the video codec equipment and had set it up at both sites. At this point, management meetings that used to take place via XTV were already beginning to take place over the link, and they had become regular Friday events. In addition, the codec was being used for software and hardware development meetings, and by the user interface design team.

In general, only members of the Jaspers team used the equipment, although from time to time one or two people outside the project were also allowed to use the system. Scheduling use of the system involved booking one of the two meeting rooms with digital lines, and also booking the equipment. (Digital lines were also available in the software laboratory, but this did not require booking.) Both bookings were done through paper diaries in the charge of a single administrative assistant.

Throughout the 6-month period of observation of the Jaspers project, we supplemented our already extensive ethnographic knowledge with a variety of different methods to evaluate the use of the system and its impact on the project. In particular, we undertook the following:

1. In situ observation. For several of the meetings, one of us was present, helping in the setup of the system and taking notes during the course of the meetings. Most of our in situ observation of use of the link took place in the regular Friday management meetings.
2. Analysis of videotapes. Eleven meetings (both Friday meetings and others) were videotaped for subsequent analysis (some when we were present and some when we were not).
3. Interviews. Members of the Jaspers team were interviewed throughout the course of the project's development and after varying degrees of experience using the system. (Many of these individual had previously been interviewed during the early stages of the ethnography.)

Evaluation of use of the system through these different methods was interleaved with attempts to introduce modifications to the technical setup driven by observation of difficulties or problems the users were encountering. We were thus particularly interested in the results of these modifications in an attempt to do some iterative design. Such modifications ranged from rearranging tables and chairs and improving the lighting, to providing additional equipment to add to the basic setup already in place. For example, we provided an additional camera on an angle poise so that members of the Jaspers team could show and share documents and artifacts. We also provided a separate monitor to view the outgoing image, as the meeting participants had problems in viewing the video insert on the main monitor that was intended for this purpose. One side effect of providing additional equipment was that it then became more difficult to transport if a meeting was taking place in another room. We then experimented with different forms of trolleys to attempt to make the system more mobile.

For the purposes of this chapter the details of these modifications are unimportant. The benefits of video showed themselves in reference to the particular organizational purposes at hand, two of which are the focus of our discussion.

FINDINGS

Figure 11.1 shows the number of hours the system was booked during the 6-month period of the study. This is not an entirely accurate measure of its actual use as some impromptu meetings would not necessarily have been booked, and others that were booked may in fact have been canceled. However, it does give a general indication of the number of hours per week the system was in use. Figure 11.1 shows that there was a general trend of increasing use, despite large fluctuations.

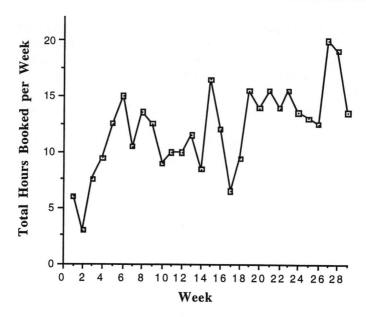

FIG. 11.1. Use of the system over 6 months as indicated by the number of
hours the system was booked per week.

More telling testimony as to the system's impact came from interviews with
members of the Jaspers team after 6 months of use of the system. The video
link had clearly and significantly changed the way they were working with
the remote site. After having the codec equipment for 6 months:

1. The video link was used in preference to telephone conferencing
for conversations among more than two people. In fact telephone conferencing had virtually ceased.

2. The XTV system was used much less frequently, and only for "formal"
meetings.

3. The travel budget for the Welwyn end of the project was underspent
by nearly 30%. Use of the video link was cited as a significant factor in
this. Members of the team said that most problem solving in terms of
software debugging, hardware diagnosis, and system integration was now
done over the link. For example, collaborative software debugging was
carried out on one occasion using the digital lines in the software lab and
simultaneously logging into the software system, which could be used to
remotely control the Jaspers prototype. The codec was then used to show
the responses of the prototype machine to various software. The ability to
work remotely in this way meant that the team almost never had to send
someone out to Henrietta.

4. In the opinion of many of the team members, the video link was at least partly responsible for greater productivity and improved communication within the project. Users believed that the video link was instrumental in facilitating collaborative processes within the Jaspers development cycle. One example used to illustrate this had to do with what are called *electromagnetic emissions* tests. These require the simultaneous testing of identically configured yet geographically distributed machines. The codec was cited as a significant benefit in enabling the engineers at the two sites to configure the systems identically.

Thus the video link not only fundamentally changed the way in which the team worked together, but also it was viewed by the team members as facilitating the work practices of the team.

Points 1 to 4, and Fig. 11.1, only skim over matters of interest, however. We wanted to understand *why* the video link was used in preference to telephone conference calling, for example. We wanted to understand what sort of processes visual information was supporting and enabling, and how it was being used for various meetings and distributed tasks. To obtain a deeper understanding of such issues, we turned to an analysis of the videotapes, the notes from our in situ observation, and the results of our interviews with the team members.

VIDEO AND ORGANIZATIONAL TALK

The first set of issues that arose from our analyses had to do with how video supported what we call the *sociality* of work. We had assumed, on the basis of our previous studies, that work practice is social in two senses: one, in that decision making, design, and indeed many of the processes that constitute engineering and technical work, are essentially social; and two, that these are underscored by the sociability of individuals in the workplace—a sociability that builds such things as effective teamwork and morale. Certainly, that this is so was attested to by users of the Welwyn–Henrietta link themselves: Several commented that meetings using a video connection seemed more lively and comfortable than a telephone conference. Somehow the use of video link gave participants a greater sense of participation.

The "somehow" is of course the rub of the matter. For the actual nature of sociality is quite difficult to specify. Indeed, a number of users made precisely this comment: It was hard to "put your finger on what's better about it." Gradually, however, our analysis led us to discover that the video link provided a set of benefits supporting the organization of Jasper meetings—benefits that could not be provided by audio alone.

Reference to Objects

One can begin to unpack these benefits by considering what might seem an obvious fact: that video supports visually oriented work. In practice, we found this assumption was borne out with the Jaspers team, but only on a handful of occasions.

For example, the video link was used when there was a problem integrating the various components of the safety shutter system for the Jaspers prototype. By using the document camera that we had provided, engineers in Welwyn and Henrietta were able to look at paper traces of data as they were coming in, and jointly diagnose the problem. In another case, the video link was used by a user interface design team at Welwyn who wanted to discuss the design of another new photocopier (not Jaspers) with Henrietta. Their purpose was to ensure consistency of the new product with other related products. They could do so by showing their product to designers in Henrietta, and using the document camera to "walk through" the design of the new machine. As it happened, one of the issues that emerged was the choice of color in the casing, and this, it was believed, was not accurately conveyed on the video. The group agreed to send Henrietta high-quality photographs subsequent to the video meeting.

The issue of the quality of the video image in cases where the distributed group was viewing documents and artifacts was an interesting one. Although the document camera offered important flexibility and mobility, its mobility made it unsatisfactory in many respects: It was difficult to focus and zoom, and needed to be clamped in position to prevent a fuzzy image from being transmitted. However, despite the poor-quality image, in the cases we observed, the groups at both sites were still able to "talk around" the documents and artifacts using the image as a basis for discussion. In other words, it seemed that the real benefit of showing work-related documents and objects was to provide a common frame of reference and a focus for discussion, rather than for the transmission of detailed information to the other site. Even a poor-quality video connection provided sufficient grounding for the discussion, and supported the need to show things to one another.

This is important. We discovered through our analysis that even in situations where the work was fundamentally visually oriented, the link was not used to provide visual information in what one might describe as obvious ways. Rather, visual information provided a general background, a demonstrable set of concerns for talk about those "seeable objects."

In short, though the showing of objects was intrinsic to the activities, the main business at hand was talk—talk *about* those objects. By talk we do not mean idle chit-chat, but discussion and exchange, requests for clarification, debate about specifying problems, attempts to agree on solutions, and so on. Being able to show things enabled and facilitated this talk. Pointing to an object allowed the participants to get to the point rapidly, supporting what Garfinkel (1967) has noted as the remarkable parsimony of talk. People used such things as visual references (provided in this case by video), their knowledge of the purposes at hand (i.e., the problems on the agenda), and their understanding of the discussion to avoid having to say everything and to fill in the missing parts in their understanding of what was said.

The bulk of meetings between Henrietta and Welwyn did not involve the showing of any objects at all. These meetings really did only involve talk. But for similar kinds of reasons, video provided visual information that helped support the effectiveness of this talk, and it did so in a number of ways.

Judging the Reactions of Others

Perhaps the most obvious benefit, and certainly one that users mentioned themselves, was that the video connection enabled participants to more effectively judge the reactions of their colleagues. Reactions occurred on a variety of levels. One level was being able to see whether their coparticipants were paying attention. In meetings that often fragmented (as we discuss later), and where a variety of concerns were brought to the table, it was not unusual for individuals or even groups to disattend from the main business at hand. Being able to see when people were ready to give attention, and conversely, when they were not, enabled individual members of the Jaspers team to know when they could move on to a new topic, or to know when they should hold off from doing so. It also indicated when the concentration of individuals "on the other side" was flagging, perhaps because they had not been directly involved in some preceding discussions.

For example, transcripts from the videos show that there were numerous instances of long pauses at the end of sequences of talk relating to some topic. These pauses continued until one or more parties who were "visibly" disattending, say, talking between themselves or flicking through some plans, were brought back to the main stream of talk either through invitation or by their own declaration. Although the word "invitation" implies a certain degree of politeness and ritual, in many instances these invitations took a fairly robust form (e.g., "Frank, are you going to listen now?"; "Come on now. Deal with this will you"). Transcripts also showed that ongoing discussion would sometimes be interrupted by one of the speakers drawing attention to the fact that one of the parties was "obviously not listening." Thus, being able to see if coparticipants were giving attention enabled more effective management of meeting activities.

At a more subtle level, being able to see coparticipants enabled individuals to better gauge such things as how serious an issue was perceived to be. Reactions to the mention of some problem gave participants an indication of whether there were other issues related to that problem that they did not know about but clearly ought to know about. Sometimes the less than interested reaction of their colleagues across the Atlantic resulted in the individuals who brought a problem to a meeting recognizing that it was effectively their own, and should not involve the team as a whole. What the video connection provided the Jaspers team with was access to a broad range of responses, verbal and otherwise. These responses were cues enabling the team and its members to effectively determine such things as the relative significance of some issue, the distribution of the "ownership" of that issue, and, related to that, the relevant parties in any problem solution.

Showing Presence

In addition to nonverbal responses, the video connection also meant that individuals could have a presence in a Jaspers meeting without having to say anything.[4] Sometimes it was important that someone be *seen to hear* of a problem or an issue, even if they had no comment to add to the related discussion. If their presence could be seen, their participation and acquiescence in any decision could be assumed. In this sense, video enabled individuals to participate in Jaspers decision-making and problem-solving activities without necessarily talking.

Presence was particularly important in these meetings because there was considerable fluctuation in the membership of the group over the course of any single meeting. People would come and go frequently, either because they had no interest in the discussion at that time, or because they had other commitments, or because they had been asked to join the meeting for a particular reason that had been previously unanticipated when the meeting was scheduled. We noticed that in particular, the arrival of new people would often significantly alter the course of the discussion. Sometimes it allowed decisions to be made that previously could not be made. Sometimes it reminded other members of the group of items that needed to be discussed but that hadn't been scheduled. Similarly, people leaving the meeting would often be noted and would shift the course of the discussion.

The point is that, in our observation of Jaspers meetings, having visual presence was clearly an important feature of team work: It enabled individuals to know and to some degree to understand the work of others. It enabled individuals to deepen their understanding of the division of labor they were part of. And, importantly, it enabled individuals to become participants in discussions as and when they needed to. The video connection clearly supported these aspects of organizational talk. This leads to the next benefit of the video link: the support of fractionated discussions.

Supporting Fractionated Talk

In our observations of Jaspers video meetings, it was quite common for some members of the group to break off from the main discussion to confer among themselves. Our observation of the Welwyn–Henrietta link showed that it was often the case that discussions would take place only at one site, while the other site would carry on a parallel discussion or would watch and listen in a peripheral way.

To illustrate, in one meeting, discussion was undertaken for several minutes about the issue of when a redesigned part was going to be introduced into the United Kingdom production line. This redesign was being undertaken because testing in Welwyn Garden City had shown that a previous design was not robust enough. When this was explained, the team in Henrietta broke off to have a discussion among themselves for just under 7 min. They used this time to determine what would be a good point for them to introduce the changed part into their own production line. One concern was that it would take them longer to effect the redesign, and so the "point of entry" into the production line in the United States would have to be different from the United Kingdom. Matters of relevance for this were solely their responsibility, so it was quite proper that the Welwyn Garden City end had nothing to contribute. Once the Henrietta team had made the assessment, they moved on to the next issue. In another instance, various topics were discussed (again by Henrietta) that resulted in a break that lasted 20 min. Far from being counterproductive, these local discussions served to address particular issues as they arose, for which it was only appropriate that the problem be solved locally. In other words, this fractionation of talk simply reflected the proper ownership of problems by the two sites.

It is important to recognize that such splitting up of talk is natural in many face-to-face meetings. People will, as a matter of course, turn away from the group at large to discuss with one another matters that are of no interest to the rest of the group. The issue we are highlighting here is that having visual access to what others are doing is important in allowing this to happen. As several users commented, without visual access (as in telephone conferencing), it is much more difficult to know what other discussions might be going on. Therefore breaking off from telephone conferences to have such prolonged discussions at the local sites would be both rude and inappropriate. With video, knowing that the remote site could see the group's activities meant that problem solving taking place at one geographical site could occur during the course of a meeting instead of being deferred until later. Group members knew that they could be seen to be conferring among themselves, and that the remote site would know how to take account of this hiatus in the interaction across sites. Thus another benefit of the video channel was that it supported the on-going, fractionated discussion that naturally arose in problem-solving talk.

Summary

In summary, video supported important aspects of what we have called organizational talk, in several ways:

1. Visual information about objects provided a framework of reference for discussion and for problem solving.
2. Video provided information about the reactions and relative involvement of individuals in distributed meetings. This provided a basis for assessing the participation of individuals in decision making, and emphasized issues such as the ownership of problems.
3. Video enabled group members to show presence, thereby allowing them to participate in group discussion and decision making without necessarily talking. Presence also had implications for accountability and the allocation of working responsibilities.
4. Visual information enabled the distributed team to flexibly separate into subgroups for smaller group discussions, and to reform as necessary as the meetings progressed.

Taken together, video helped support what we would call the "real-world" organization of problem definition and solution talk in distributed teams.

VIDEO AND ORGANIZATIONAL OWNERSHIP

The second set of issues we wish to discuss relates to the organizational framework surrounding two types of video systems used by the Jaspers team—namely, the video codec link, and the XTV system, which the Jaspers team still continued to use, albeit infrequently. We argue that differences in the organizational ownership of these two systems provided benefits for different kinds of meetings, which we might describe as *problem-solving* versus *decision-making* meetings.

As mentioned earlier, XTV continued to be used from time to time in preference to the codec system, but only for formal management meetings. In interviews of the Jaspers team, some of the reasons given for this had to do with the technical differences in the two systems. For example, the video codec link was, at that time, not configured for multipoint meetings, whereas XTV could be used when a third party needed to be brought in. XTV also offered better sound and image quality.

However, on further probing, these technical differences did not emerge as crucial to why XTV was appropriate for formal management meetings. Our analysis led us to discover other important differences between the video codec and the XTV facility. These relate to what we might call their different "organizational ownership." These differences derive primarily from the fact that the video codec system was locally owned by the Jaspers team, whereas the XTV system was shared by the whole site at Welwyn.

On Demand Versus Prescheduled Meetings

One consequence of the fact that the video link technology was locally owned was that meetings with Henrietta could be and indeed were often called at very short notice. Although there was a booking procedure, open slots were usually available throughout the course of the day, and, if needed, time was found or negotiated. Thus, for the Jaspers team, the codec equipment offered something close to a dial-up on-demand system. It was these demands that drove the use of the system, rather than, say, a prebooked session of the system demanding a meeting. Team members said that the ability to contact the remote site as and when needed was particularly useful during periods where there were urgent technical problems to be solved. One person pointed out that the codec was used almost constantly during critical periods of the Jaspers project when system integration, troubleshooting, and debugging were needed. The flexibility of scheduling meetings on the video codec meant that distributed collaborative teamwork could be undertaken as and when needed. In this sense the video link supported one of the important features of sociality that ensures the effectiveness of work practice: organizational flexibility and adaptability. In our observation, the use of the video link was demand driven in ways that reflected the natural ebb and flow of collaborative work.

Although XTV could support some of this flexibility, the simple fact that it was a shared facility meant that it required booking sometimes weeks in advance. As a result, the XTV system could rarely be used in response to the unexpected demands of a project. However, this lack of flexibility provided XTV with a different set of advantages. For example, one side effect of booking in advance was that it encouraged people to commit to attending a meeting. In organizations where staff find themselves involved in many meetings (as they do in Xerox!), the only way of guaranteeing their participation is to stake a claim on their time well beforehand. This is especially important if one wants senior staff to attend. This is one reason why XTV was more appropriate for formal management meetings than for ad hoc problem-solving meetings.

Adherence to Agenda

Another element of temporal flexibility concerned the fact that it was organizational practice to book XTV meetings for a specific length of time. Because the XTV facility was shared by the entire Welwyn site, it was understood that XTV meetings must finish when that time was up. Often this meant that issues had to be taken "offline" so as to get more important elements of an agenda dealt with before the meeting's end.

In contrast, the video link meetings we observed varied enormously in length. As one user put it, "they take as long as they need to take." Even the so-called management meetings, which ostensibly had strict agendas, tended to deviate away from the agenda in order to deal with specific problems or issues as they arose. In other words, video link meetings were characterized by the fact that a large degree of business was "completed" within them. When problem-solving discussion took a long time, it did not result in those discussions being terminated and continued later "offline," as has to be the case with XTV. Rather, the video link was used to get things solved within the course of the meeting (and within limits, of course). These solutions often involved the fractionated discussions mentioned earlier, and, much less frequently, the conveying of visual information about artifacts and documents.

However, the fixed length of time for XTV meetings could also be used to advantage. In addition to being more formal because of its prearranged times, the fixed duration of an XTV meeting was useful in ensuring that group members adhered to an agenda. Not only was the time limit useful in this respect, but it was also useful in forcing decisions to be made. Indeed, certain decision-making activities within Jaspers were undertaken on XTV precisely to ensure that decisions were made quickly. If there was a strict time limit on when a decision could be made, this forced the participants in the decision process to agree and come to a choice. Clearly, one aspect of this is that agendas for XTV meetings had to be carefully planned so that they contained the kinds of decision issues that could be reasonably decided in the time available.

Geographical Ownership

There was one final, crucially important feature of the video codec that gave it an advantage over XTV as regards supporting problem-solving activities. We have already mentioned that the Jaspers team had organizational ownership of the codec, but this was further reinforced by a geographical ownership. The codec equipment was located within the physical environment of the Jaspers workgroup. This enabled access to persons, equipment, and documentation as and when needed. Given the problem solution focus of many of Jaspers video link meetings, this access was crucial to the process. The meetings we observed, for example, showed a constantly changing group of people. As discussed previously, some members of the group would leave when the topic was no longer relevant to them, and others were brought in when their input was needed. There were also many occasions in which some document or printout from a software debugging session was needed to address a problem. These items could be fetched quickly and used as the focus for the discussion. In other words, one characteristic of the video link meetings was that they were dynamically changing in terms of people and artifacts; these changes reflected the natural order of problem solving.

The XTV site, by contrast, was deliberately located in a more "public" place, where all workgroups could get access. This resulted in some distance between the XTV room and the location of the offices of the Jaspers team—indeed, it was a separate building elsewhere on the site. This meant that participants could not easily bring in other team members or equipment and documentation if they were not anticipated prior to the meeting, especially given the time constraints of XTV meetings. Thus geographical location was one other factor that served to enforce the prearranged, preplanned, and more formal nature of XTV meetings.

Summary

Table 11.1 shows a summary of the different benefits of the video codec versus XTV facilities. From this analysis it is clear that the two facilities served very different purposes for the Jaspers team, and thus broadened the options available to them for communicating with the remote site. In this case, the different benefits of the two systems could only be understood by looking at the organizational practices surrounding the systems, and by looking at the larger context of which the systems were a part.

CONCLUSION

This chapter has been concerned primarily with two sets of findings: first relating to the use of video in the support of organizational, and particularly problem-solving, talk, and second, in relation to the importance of understanding the ways in which video systems are used within a broader organizational context.

TABLE 11.1
Benefits of Video Codec and XTV Technology

Video Codec	*XTV*
Supports ad hoc meetings	Supports formal meetings
Flexible meeting length	Fixed meeting length
Flexible agenda	Adherence to agenda
Facilitates problem solving	Facilitates speedy decision making
Access to people as needed	Secures prior commitment to attend
Access to documents and artifacts as needed	Preplanned and preread documentation

As regards the first set of findings, we had taken it for granted that video would be used to share visual information about objects. What we found instead is that although being able to see objects was clearly useful at times, mainly the video system was used to support conversation. Visual information provided a framework for reference in the course of talk, and was not an end in itself.

Furthermore, and moving away from issues to do with showing objects, we found that organizational talk had specific characteristics. These showed themselves in such things as the dynamics of group structures within meetings, and conversational turn-taking within those meetings. One characteristic of these real-world meetings was that individuals and groups spent considerable time defining and solving problems. This kind of talk fragments in ways that reflect the distribution of responsibilities and knowhow within the group. Because this distribution cannot necessarily be known before a problem is defined, often certain individuals come to a meeting, including a video meeting, only to discover that, after the problem is defined, much of the content of the discussion may be none of their concern. Thus in these meetings not every one participates all the time, and some individuals may "slip out of view" for quite long periods of time.

Nonetheless, even when individuals slip out of view in terms of taking turns at talking, it is important that they be seen to remain at the meeting. For eventually the talk, the concerns of the meeting, will come to coincide with their own. However, their silence in these circumstances should not be viewed as a failure of communication, deriving perhaps from the video communications system they are using. It is simply the demonstrable outcome of their waiting for business relevant to them to come up. Meanwhile, the fact that they are there, and the fact that others can see that they are there, is important for their later participation, and for enabling talk to fractionate again later in different ways. It also provides a basis for developing a shared understanding of the state of the project.

Video supports this kind of organizational talk in various ways. It enables individuals to show presence, which is important when questions to do with the significance and relevance of some problem are being assessed; it enables participants in a meeting to assess the reactions of others, leading to better allocation of task and job responsibilities; and finally, it allows the mutual monitoring of fragmented groups, enabling those groups, or subsections of them, to coalesce as the meeting progresses through its agenda.

We do not believe that these features of real-world working life would have been discovered unless we had chosen to look at the real world. As regards experimental studies of, say, turn-taking, the failure of someone to say anything for periods of up to 20 min would be viewed as a catastrophic failure either of the system itself or of experimental design—not as a proper course of action reflecting the natural unfolding of distributed problem solving. This casts experimental research on turn-taking, including our own (e.g., Sellen, 1992, 1995), in a very different light.

Our studies have also led us to rethink our understanding of the criteria individuals (or groups) use to determine the selection between similar technologies. Our previous research had led us to focus on what may be described as the local relationship between video technology and its users, not the organizational structures they were part of, such as the policies, procedures, and ownership aspects surrounding the use of a video system.

In the real-world setting described here, we found that users have a range of alternative technologies and that sometimes they will select one or another based on factors that are to various degrees extraneous to the technology itself. For example, we discovered that users in our study selected the XTV system as opposed to the video codec system because doing so enabled them to leverage decisions more quickly. In effect, users were taking advantage of the fact that XTV meetings were subject to constraints that the video link technology was not. These "organizational affordances" were recognized and exploited by members of the Jaspers team.

The criteria used in choosing between technologies are, like the issues surrounding organizational talk, difficult to replicate in laboratory experiments. Partly this is a matter of practical difficulties such as time constraints. But partly it is theoretical: The particular mix of organizational, procedural, interactional, and technical concerns that influence the use and choice of one kind of technological system over another cannot be replicated in experiments because the *sine qua non* of experiment is to separate out elements of a *Gestalt*, not preserve them.

In studies of "real people" doing "real things" within research laboratories, certainly some of the issues we have discussed here could be examined within our workplaces. There is certainly much more to say about organizational talk, and the instrumental use of different types of video systems in research laboratories would doubtless shed more light on the issues. However, in order to do so, we believe such studies need to take into account the social structural context of laboratory life, and need to consider how working activities within these places are bound by organizational constraints, time limits, immediate and overarching processes, moral accountabilities, and more.

Having raised these objections to experimental laboratory studies, and studies of real work in research laboratories, it must be made clear that we are not arguing that VMC research should only be conducted outside of these places. That would be a spurious and somewhat sanctimonious argument, especially given our own research history in this area. Our case is that studies of the world outside our front doors are needed to supplement the bulk of research, which has been, and in all likelihood will continue to be, undertaken within research laboratories. We hope we have shown that studying the world outside can provide new insights and new perspectives on the ways in which video can support collaborative, distributed work.

ACKNOWLEDGMENTS

We are grateful to Mike Molloy of RXRC Cambridge, who was the technical expert involved in this study, and on whose help and advice we relied throughout the project. As in our previous projects with RXTC in Welwyn Garden City, we have found Welwyn personnel to be extraordinarily helpful, patient, and sanguine. We wish to thank especially Garry Blackmore, Jim Keeping, Peter Walshe, and the members of the Jaspers team. For comments on the chapter itself, we thank Paul Dourish, Christian Heath, Ellen Isaacs, and Paul Luff.

NOTES

1. It should be noted that Heath and Luff (1992) do not confine themselves to research within the laboratory but also report on the use of video over the same XTV system we report on in this chapter.
2. Such studies do not need to be confined to video, of course. See, for instance, O'Conaill, Geelhoed, and Tofgt (1994).
3. We use the term *video codec* or *video link* to refer to the PictureTel technology used by Jaspers. Members of the team itself referred to this technology as their *media space*. We also contrast what we call "video codecs" with XTV even though, technically, XTV also makes use of codec technology. However, the XTV system is located within different organizational processes than the video codec system, which we discuss.
4. The importance of presence is also an issue that arises in experimental work. For example, in a comparison of different video systems, those systems that maintained the continuous presence of all group members were preferred to those that selectively focused on group members depending on who was talking (Sellen, 1995). Reasons given by the subjects were similar to those cited earlier, such as the ability to judge the reactions of people who were not talking, and the importance of being aware of who was present.

REFERENCES

Adler, A., & Henderson, A. (1994). A room of our own: Experience from a direct office-share. *Proceedings, ACM Conference on Human Factors in Computer Systems* (pp. 138–144). New York: ACM Press.

Bellotti, V. M. E., & Sellen, A. J. (1993). Design for privacy in ubiquitous computing environments. *Proceedings of the European Conference on Computer-Supported Cooperative Work* (pp. 61–92). Amsterdam: Kluwer.

Dourish, P. (1993). Culture and control in a media space. *Proceedings of the Third European Conference on Computer-Supported Cooperative Work* (pp. 125–137). Amsterdam: Kluwer.

Dourish, P., Adler, A., Bellotti, V., & Henderson, A. (1996). Your place or mine? Learning from long-term use of video communication. *Computer-Supported Cooperative Work, An International Journal, 5*(1), 33–62.

Dourish, P., & Bellotti, V. (1992, November). Awareness and coordination in shared work spaces. *Proceedings of CSCW'92* (pp. 107–114). Toronto.

Dourish, P., & Bly, S. (1992). Portholes: Supporting awareness in a distributed work group. *Proceedings of ACM Conference on Human Factors in Computer Systems* (pp. 541–547). New York: ACM Press.

Dykstra-Erickson, E., Rudman, C., Marshall, C., Hertz, R., Mithal, K., & Schmidt, J. (1995, March). Supporting adaptation of multimedia desktop conferencing. *Proceedings of the 15th International Symposium on Human Factors of Telecommunications* (pp. 31–38). Melbourne, Australia.

Fish, R., Kraut, R., & Chalfonte, B. (1990, October). The video window system for informal communication. *Proceedings, ACM Conference on Computer-Supported Cooperative Work.* Los Angeles, CA.

Garfinkel, H. (1967). *Studies in ethnomethodology.* New York: Prentice Hall.

Gaver, W. W., Moran, T., MacLean, A., Lövstrand, L., Dourish, P., Carter, K. A., & Buxton, W. (1992). Realizing a video environment: EuroPARC's RAVE system. *Proceedings of ACM Conference on Human Factors in Computing Systems* (pp. 27–35). New York: ACM Press.

Gaver, W. W., Sellen, A., Heath, C. C., & Luff, P. (1993, April). One is not enough: Multiple views in a media space. *Proceedings of INTERCHI '93* (pp. 335–341). Amsterdam.

Harper, R. H. R. (1992). Looking at ourselves: An examination of the social organisation of two research laboratories. *Proceedings of CSCW '92* (pp. 330–337). New York: ACM Press.

Harper, R. H. R. (1996). Why people do and don't wear Active Badges: A case study. *Computer Supported Cooperative Work, CSCW, 4*, 297–318.

Harper, R. H. R., & Carter, K. (1994). Keeping people apart: A research note. *Computer Supported Cooperative Work, 2*, 199–207.

Heath, C. C., & Luff, P. (1991). Disembodied conduct: Communication through video in a multi-media office environment. *Proceedings of ACM Conference on Human Factors in Computing Systems* (pp. 99–103). New York: ACM Press.

Heath, C. C., & Luff, P. (1992). Media space and communicative asymmetries: Preliminary observations of video mediated interaction. *Human–Computer Interaction, 7*, 315–346.

Isaacs, E. A., & Tang, J. T. (1994). What video can and cannot do for collaboration: A case study. *Multimedia Systems, 2*, 63–73.

Lövstrand, L. (1991). Being selectively aware with the Khronika system. *Proceedings of ECSW'91* (pp. 265–277). Amsterdam: Kluwer.

O'Conaill, B., Geelhoed, E., & Tofgt, P. (1994). Deskslate: A shared workspace for telephone partners. *Companion Proceedings of CHI'95, Human Factors in Computer Systems* (pp. 303–304). New York, ACM Press.

Pagani, D. S., & Mackay, W. (1993). Bringing media spaces into the real world. *Proceedings of the European Conference on Computer-Supported Cooperative Work* (pp. 341–356). Amsterdam: Kluwer.

Sellen, A. (1992). Speech patterns in video-mediated conversations. *Proceedings of CHI '92* (pp. 49–59). New York: ACM Press.

Sellen, A. (1995). Remote conversations: The effects of mediating talk with technology. *Human–Computer Interaction, 10*(4), 401–444.

Tang, J. C., Isaacs, E., & Rua, M. (1994). Supporting distributed groups with a Montage of lightweight interactions. *Proceedings of the ACM Conference on Computer-Supported Cooperative Work,* (pp. 23–34). New York: ACM Press.

Chapter 12

Rant and RAVE: Experimental and Experiential Accounts of a Media Space

Victoria Bellotti
Apple Computer, Inc.

Paul Dourish
Rank Xerox Research Centre (EuroPARC)

Much has been written in this and other publications about the many ways in which VMC falls short of face-to-face communication. This perspective on VMC use emphasises its failure to support the rich detail of interaction and resources available in face-to-face situations. In this chapter, we take a different view. Rather than focusing on the comparison of experimental experiences with VMC, we show how a media space system designed to support everyday interactions via audio–video (AV) devices, as part of a lived experiment, can be seen not just as a substitution for copresence, but as providing new resources for communication and collaboration. We describe the design of this system and how it supports a wider range of social possibilities than just telephony-style connections. We outline a series of short-term experimental studies assessing the utility of this system. Further, we use experience of living day-to-day with long-term AV connections to highlight important benefits that only become apparent over time. In particular, short-term and experimental studies miss the benefits that emerge through observing evolving cultural adaptations to such technology over the longer term and those that become apparent through thinking of such systems as an additional space for everyday interaction alongside face-to-face communication.

INTRODUCTION

Since 1988, Rank Xerox's research laboratory in Cambridge has used a "media space"—a network of audio, video, and computing technologies— both as a focus of research and as an infrastructure to support daily activity.

Users of the system include technical and nontechnical researchers as well as technical support and administrative staff working in a variety of computational environments. Although most of this chapter serves primarily as a description of the Cambridge laboratory's media space technology, of its design and philosophy, and of research undertaken to evaluate its impact on interpersonal interactions, a key element of our presentation is the distinction between media spaces and more traditional notions of desktop videoconferencing (DVC) applications that are becoming common in the software marketplace today. Some important distinguishing features of media spaces include enablement of a range of degrees of interpersonal engagement, the diversity of applications that they support, their availability for use, and the overhead involved in being "connected."

Orientation

Media spaces are not based around a "telephony" model of communication involving only explicit "call-style" connections. Instead, cameras and monitors and systems that sense electronic events are left "on" continuously, providing accessibility to public and sometimes personal spaces. Similarly, media spaces are not necessarily directed toward support for explicit person-to-person focused interactions. From a social perspective, a media space can be viewed as providing a wider set of services based around people's different reasons for wanting to be in contact with one another. Not all interactions between people have an explicit group of participants or explicit onset and termination, nor are they necessarily focused on some common goal or even clearly task oriented (Goffman, 1963). Different media space services, such as one-way glances or views onto public spaces, afford many different ways of being "in touch" so that users can extend their awareness of others, their presence, and the scope of their actions beyond localized encounters in physical space.

A media space is also unlike a telephony-style service from a technical standpoint. It may be made up of a variety of systems and components that play very different roles such as providing audiovideo services, sensing electronic events, coordinating services and events with feedback, enabling sharing of objects like drawings or a group calendar, and so on. None of these roles is necessarily related to every other role; in Rank Xerox's Cambridge laboratory the media space is comprised of a constellation of more or less interdependent parts. Integration between these components is as much a matter of use as of construction; such technology can be appropriated by its users for an unlimited variety of collaborative and social activities (see Harrison et al., chapter 13, this volume). Consequently, we regard media spaces as *infrastructures* rather than as *applications*.

In this chapter we seek to underline some important issues that have been overlooked in the research literature but that are key to the appreciation of the significance of media space design, setting it apart from other, perhaps more familiar forms of VMC. We start by outlining the background and history of the design of one particular media space at Rank Xerox's EuroPARC laboratory in Cambridge.[1] We then summarize some of the main findings of studies and analyses that have looked at the effects, benefits, and problems from its use. We also assess the utility of these studies themselves as indicators of how well media spaces support communication, collaboration, and mutual awareness.

To contrast with these formal investigations, we relate some of our own understandings based on the experience of living inside and using a media space for several years. We then conclude with a discussion of the two most important issues that have emerged as key to our understanding of media spaces. These are:

1. Evolution. Studies that involve contrived experimental or short-term working setups cannot tell us about the likely significance of the observed behaviors over the longer term. They also ignore the fact that media spaces are not immutable and that one of their main strengths is in their flexibility and reconfigurability. It is only over time, working and living with unfamiliar technologies, that users begin to appropriate and adapt them to fit their practices and preferences. Phenomena that at first seem awkward or important may recede, perhaps to be replaced by others that at first do not show up. Studies that focus directly on particular, collaborating users cannot capture the ways in which the technology impacts and involves others who may not seem to be explicitly collaborating, or the evolution of the surrounding society at large. Furthermore, focusing on particular tasks or locations means that the range of possible behaviors in relation to media space technology is not observable. It is not possible to determine what people prefer to use particular aspects of the technology for, nor what their wider experience of it is across a variety of situations and contexts.

2. Debunking the Video-as-Copresence Hypothesis. Evaluative studies of media spaces, including those conducted at EuroPARC, have often focused only upon the substitution of VMC for face-to-face, copresent collaboration. The premise that VMC simulates face-to-face communication is what we call the *Copresence Hypothesis.* Although it is clear, as other chapters attest, that there is much to learn from observing the effects and shortcomings of VMC in comparison to physical copresence, we feel that this is too narrow a construal of both the nature of the technology, and of its potential value. Media spaces do not replace real-world encounters; they extend the range of possible encounters, both in form and opportunity. Consequently, we highlight a diversity of important phenomena that arise outside the traditional analytic perspectives on media spaces. These phenomena tend to emerge over time, underlining the importance of analytic perspectives that accommodate the effects of evolution. They also rely on a broader view of the technology, which goes beyond its role as a substitute for face-to-face encounters, incorporating issues such as its role in everyday practices and its societal impact.

Throughout this chapter we seek to guide the reader toward a deeper appreciation of media spaces as more than glorified videotelephone exchanges. Our arguments, in particular those relating to the two issues just described, are intended to broaden the scope of discussion about how such systems might play a valuable part in widening the range of ways in which people might work and play together in the future. First, however, we begin by looking back at how such a system came to be developed.

HISTORY AND PERSPECTIVES

Building on the pioneering Media Space work at Xerox PARC (Bly, Harrison, & Irwin, 1993; Stults, 1989), the use of audiovideo (AV) technologies to support collaborative work became a major research theme early in EuroPARC's history. Like the PARC work, our research focused on the impact and usage of multimedia systems, rather than the development of the technology per se. A prototype media space called IIIF (the Integrated, Interactive, Intermedia Facility), was constructed in 1988–1989 using baseband transmission, off-the-shelf components, and custom-built switching software. In essence this meant placing a camera, monitor, microphone, and speakers, or media space node, in every office in the lab and connecting these with AV switching devices. A simple network control protocol supported interface development and exploration on various hardware platforms. By mid-1989, the hardware infrastructure was complete and a number of prototype interfaces were in place. For more details, see Buxton and Moran (1990).

The RAVE project—for Ravenscroft[2] Audio-Video Environment—was inaugurated in late 1989. At the outset, RAVE served three explicit purposes.

First, it was to become an umbrella under which a range of technologies then under development would be collected. As well as the ongoing development of the audiovideo system itself, this included the design and study of a number of related collaboration support systems. Second, it was a showcase of our technologies and research perspectives. With a focus on integration, RAVE pulled together a number of strands of ongoing work and demonstrated aspects of collaborative working in an integrated computational and multimedia environment. Third, it was very much a lived experiment. The technologies we were developing would be in day-to-day use, supporting ongoing work and activity. This, in turn, reflected an orientation toward studies of in situ usage, and the impact of introducing novel technologies into work settings. As such, the technology was to be available throughout the lab, to anyone who wanted it; indeed, subsequent developments were strongly shaped by the fact that the technology was in everyday use by lab members other than the developers.

The RAVE infrastructure continued as a research project at EuroPARC until late 1993. Gaver et al. (1992) provided a succinct summary of this project and some of the main design concerns. Although it is still in use in a number of projects organized around multimedia communication, RAVE itself is no longer an explicit program of research activity.

RAVE as an Environment

The key to a critical perspective behind RAVE is captured by the final letter of the acronym—"E" for Environment. Three aspects of the "environmental" view are particularly important when looking at the history and development of RAVE.

1. *Ubiquity.* As an environment within which laboratory members lived, widespread deployment was crucial. RAVE was available to all research and administrative staff, not just media space researchers. In addition, RAVE facilities were integrated into public spaces in the building. Although individuals would vary in the nature and extent of their use of it, the pervasiveness of the technology was crucial, and accessibility from all points of the lab and all the major desktop software environments in use was very important.

2. *Flexible organization.* A key property of our media space was the ability to flexibly organize and reorganize the configuration of tools and connections, so that users could integrate the facilities it offered into their everyday activities. The focus, then, was on providing tools and technologies that fostered this kind of adoption. Services ranged from short-term video-only "glances," to long-term "office-share" connections that could last for hours, days, weeks, or even years. The flexible organization—the ability, at any point, to turn off the connection, reconfigure it, look somewhere else or "be" somewhere else—was an essential motivation shaping the development of the technology.

3. *Range of tools.* RAVE is an infrastructure incorporating many tools, rather than itself being a single tool. It encompasses not only the interfaces by which people make and break connections, and tailor their accessibility, but also collaborative workspace tools, tools for integrating and sharing awareness information, calendar information, and so forth. With the inclusion of a framework for sharing UNIX applications, any UNIX application becomes part of RAVE. This is another element of the "flexible organization" aspect of RAVE's design, but it also encompasses a flexibility

in how work is conducted and what facilities will be deployed to a particular end, rather than flexibility in how they might be deployed.

TECHNOLOGIES

We have indicated that the media space comprises a wide range of component technologies that can be deployed flexibly in support of working activity. Starting with the central elements of AV connection switching, this section describes the most important technologies that form the basis of specific experimental studies and longer term experiences.

RAVE Core

The core RAVE technologies are those that control media space connections and allow users to tailor their accessibility. Before mid-1990, the primary mechanisms that supported media space connectivity were constructed using Xerox Buttons (MacLean, Carter, Moran, & Lövstrand, 1990) and an RPC interface to the iiif[3] switch management software (Milligan, 1989).[4] The iiif service provided a connection abstraction over the raw hardware. In particular, it provided naming facilities, grouping devices together into media space nodes referred to with meaningful names rather than cable numbers (often the name was that of the node's owner or the room it was in); a *connection* service, which abstracted away from the details of switch configuration, transparently handling the routing required to make connections specified in terms of their endpoints; and a *query* service, allowing clients to examine the status of nodes, devices and connections.

Xerox Buttons were on-screen button-like objects encapsulating simple behaviors; they had been designed as part of an earlier project investigating tailorability and were in use throughout the lab at the time. As well as providing an easy path for gradually more complex tailoring behavior, they could also be directly stored in formatted text documents (including e-mail messages) and grouped into libraries. Their simplicity, extensibility, and familiarity made them a natural vehicle for prototyping media space services. Users created new buttons for services like "glancing" at each other, "sweeping" through the building, watching common areas and VCRs, and so forth; these spread quickly through the building, perhaps being modified by other users along the way.

By late 1989, a core set of services was in common use, and we began to encapsulate them as an official "reference set" of RAVE buttons. At the same time, based on interviews and consultation with most lab members, the RAVE team began the design of an integrated privacy and access control mechanism. The result was the Godard system (Dourish, 1991), which manages access control in a media space, providing protection, feedback, and control facilities. Godard is based on two concepts:

1. Abstract *services*, which define connection modalities. Services are the means by which users address the system, and encapsulate system functions. Services are loosely based on real-world behaviors, rather than on technological descriptions of system action. Godard distinguishes between two services if they describe different behaviors in which users might engage, even when the technology to support the two services is identical. For example, the "videophone" and "office-share" services are both dyadic, reciprocal audio and video connections, but because they support different sorts of behaviors, they are different services.

2. An *agent*, which semiautonomously fields service requests on behalf of a user. The agent responds to service requests from other media space participants, according to preferences expressed by the user. By setting service property preferences, the user can tailor both their accessibility within the media space and the appearance of the service to them (changing, for instance, their level of feedback for particular services).

Godard itself does not define the services and their tailorable service properties, but provides a framework within which services can be defined and created. Our initial set of services were *glance*—a one-way, short-duration, video-only connection; *vphone*—a two-way, arbitrary-duration, video and audio connection; *office-share*—a two-way, arbitrary-duration, video and audio connection; *watch*—a one-way, arbitrary-duration, video and audio connection (for VCRs); and *background*—a one-way, arbitrary-duration, video-only connection (for public areas, window camera, etc.).

Early on, we discovered that a primary concern of our users was feedback on system action, rather than protection from intrusion. So, although an access control scheme allowed users to selectively define people from whom they would accept connections of each type, they placed much more emphasis on the range of ways in which they could be informed who was making a connection, and when. The primary form of feedback for all services was nonspeech audio cues (Gaver, 1991), whereas textual messages also provided a browsable history of recent RAVE activity.

The RAVE team developed both the Godard access and control mechanism and interfaces for user interaction. Buttons were used to make and break connections; control panels were used to set service properties and control accessibility. A "buttonizing" facility on the control panels allowed panel state to be "captured" within a dynamically created button; pressing that button would restore the state of the panel at the time it was buttonized. In this way, users could essentially create "macros" for various common states, such as general accessibility, more restricted access when they didn't want to be disturbed, suitable response messages when they were out at lunch or away from the office, and so forth.[5]

As well as this software architecture, hardware developments were also under way to ensure that users could control information that could be captured by the media space (Bellotti & Sellen, 1993). Footpedals, which switched off audio out of an office, enabled those who wished to maintain video communication but temporarily (or permanently) turn off audio to do so.[6] These also provided a simple way to reduce distracting noise in office shares between the semipublic open areas where administrators worked and where people would frequently stand around talking.

In "the commons," a public room in EuroPARC, people were concerned about not knowing when they were on camera. Visitors, moreover, were sometimes unpleasantly surprised to find out that they could have been "watched" by unseen viewers from a camera that they had not noticed. Two steps were taken to alert people to its presence and to its role as an eye for remote viewers. A large "feedback monitor" was placed close to it so that people quickly saw themselves "on TV" as they entered the room. They could also use this to see when they were safely out of shot. Also a mannequin, "The Toby," was used to draw people's eyes to what appeared to be a person facing them. Initially Toby had a small camera in his eye socket, but later on it was thought to be clearer to newcomers what was going on if he was placed standing behind the camera on a tripod. Toby's sweatshirt read, "I may be a Dummy, but I'm watching you."

Some people also adopted the use of a feedback monitor in their offices, using either a dedicated monitor or a picture-in-picture facility on their normal RAVE monitor.

Awareness Services: Polyscope, Vrooms, and Portholes

One early usage observation was that, when "idle," most video monitors were tuned to watch the commons, which houses mail trays, kitchen facilities, and lounge space, and where most large meetings are held. Users frequently commented that this was very useful for seeing when people arrived and collected their mail in the morning, gathered informally or for meetings, and so forth. Observing that this used the media space to support the same sorts of *passive awareness* of ongoing activities in our surroundings as does physical space, Alan Borning and Mike Travers developed *Polyscope*, an "awareness service." Gathering sets of images from around the media space, Polyscope presented users with short looped animations of activity at different RAVE nodes. These images or animations would be updated every few minutes, providing a regular snapshots of activity in the lab. A related system, Vrooms, employed a stronger spatial metaphor, and used the relative positioning of snapshots to control other access mechanisms, such as full-quality video connections (Borning & Travers, 1991).

Based on the success of Polyscope and Vrooms, we subsequently developed and deployed *Portholes* (Dourish & Bly, 1992). Portholes was aimed at providing awareness support for distributed work groups—in this case, the distributed group of media space researchers at EuroPARC and Xerox PARC in Palo Alto, California. Using still images rather than animations (mainly because of network bandwidth restrictions), Portholes provided Polyscope-like functionality that crossed the Atlantic and linked EuroPARC and PARC's media spaces into a single awareness space. Although the initial motivation had been to support the same sorts of awareness as had proved useful with Polyscope, experiences with Portholes over the first year or so moved us toward a view of fostering more of a sense of community in this distributed group, through increased familiarity and casual interaction. (This is discussed in more detail later, as is the entire issue of connection versus awareness.)

Sharing Work

The audiovideo tools within the RAVE environment provided users with a range of ways to become aware of ongoing activities and engage in more focused interactions. However, because focused interactions in physical space are supported with a range of artifacts (such as whiteboards and notebooks), it was important that RAVE also provide some tools for collaboration over artifacts. A number of tools were designed and deployed. As with the other RAVE technologies, they served multiple purposes, acting not only as tools for our own activities, but also as experimental prototypes for investigating issues in the user interface or data sharing architecture of collaborative tools. In general, these tools were small and lightweight, with an emphasis on interface simplicity and casual use rather than on structured interaction.

Khronika (Lövstrand, 1991) provided a shared online calendar system to which all lab members could contribute and offered the opportunity to specify daemons that could initiate some electronic event (such as an e-mail message or a nonspeech audio cue from the media space) in response to calendar or electronic events. *Shdr* provided a simple shared whiteboard with rudimentary textual annotations and continual telepointers. Designed to operate over the low-bandwidth connection that linked PARC and Euro-PARC, it used a replicated design and an adaptive algorithm for maintaining continual telepointing, the value of which had been pointed to in PARC's experiments with Commune (Minneman & Bly, 1992). *Shcl* was an even simpler tool that linked UNIX terminal sessions and the applications that ran over them, through a network multiplexer. This allowed simple work-sharing and, perhaps most usefully, facilitated remote or collaborative system support and debugging.

It is important to emphasize that these tools were never designed as fully functional shared applications supporting complex or large-scale work. Indeed, the other sharing facilities that we incorporated into our environment, such as Shared-X (Garfinkel, Gust, Lemon, & Lowder, 1989), were almost never used in preference to the lighter, simpler tools. Similarly, these tools were not designed for stand-alone operation; rather, they were created and used as an explicit part of a larger environment.

STUDIES: WATCHING OURSELVES WATCHING EACH OTHER

In this section we overview a collection of studies conducted with the RAVE infrastructure in order to give a flavor of the understandings that arose from examining behaviors around or reactions to the media space. We then step back and consider our own, more informal experiences gained over extended use of the "office-share" feature of our media spaces.

Because RAVE afforded a kind of copresence for remote collaborators, several studies were undertaken to assess the media space as a substitute for face-to-face interaction. In particular, some experimental, observational studies were conducted looking at task-oriented, interpersonal interactions (Gaver, Sellen, Heath, & Luff, 1993; Gaver, Smets, & Overbeeke, 1995; Heath, Luff, & Sellen, 1995; J. Olson, G. Olson, Storrøsten, & Carter, 1992; Smith, O'Shea, O'Malley, Scanlon, & Taylor, 1989). There was also a study on the effects of use of media space technology in people's usual offices (Heath & Luff, 1991, 1992).

Each study used intensive observational techniques to focus on details of a subset of behaviors and particular technology configurations, rather than the utility of a media space in general. However, we also consider another survey and interview-based study of the video-based awareness server, Portholes (Dourish & Bly, 1992), which is less detailed but gives a wider coverage of the perceived impact of such technology on people's practices and sensibilities over a longer period of time. We then relate our own day-to-day experiences of the utility of a media space as intensive users of the technology for well over 3 years.

Close analytic observations, surveys, and experiences, such as our own, each foster different kinds of appraisals of the pros and cons of technology in how it supports or disrupts social interaction. For this reason, it is not surprising that the various studies and our experiences sometimes support conclusions that seem to be at odds with one another. This suggests to us that the results of working within any traditional methodological framework should be considered with some caution when determining the worth of a technology that is clearly capable of interceding in people's relationships to their environment and to each other at so many different levels of analysis. In this section we therefore draw the reader's attention to differences in the various studies and accounts, which are at least partly responsible for conflicting views on the utility of media space technology.

Experimental Use of Video in Collaborative Problem Solving

One of the first media space studies at EuroPARC compared audiovideo (AV) mediated communication with face-to-face using a shared simulation environment to solve an everyday physics problem (Smith et al., 1989). Eye contact was simulated using arrangements of camera, monitor, and half-silvered mirror known as *video tunnels*. Five pairs of subjects used the video tunnel; three worked face-to-face; and two used audio only. Although the quality of the problem solving was not assessed, the main observation was that, with audio-only, there was less stepping back from problem details (meta-level discussion; typically associated in the research literature with enhanced problem solving). In the AV and face-to-face conditions, subjects increased eye contact in such discussions. A similar difference between audio-only and AV was also observed in the study of Commune by Minneman and Bly (1992) referred to earlier.

The next of the studies that we report (J. Olson et al., 1992) examined how different communications setups and the use of a synchronous shared editing tool, ShrEdit (McGuffin & Olson, 1992), changed how design meetings ran. Designers worked in groups of three on an artificial design problem using ShrEdit while situated in different offices, connected by continuous, two-way AV or audio-only links. In the AV condition, each participant had AV nodes on each side of the workstation to provide a virtual presence for the other two group members. Audio was supported by a single microphone and speaker arrangement for each participant.

The Olsons found that adding video did not produce a discernible difference in the quality of the design of the groups. This finding correlates strongly with that of many other researchers who have explored the use of AV to support remote focused collaboration (e.g., Chapanis, 1975; Egido, 1990). On the other hand, it conflicts with the tentative findings of Smith et al. (1989), who suggested that video seemed to improve users' problem-solving discussions.

Further experiments conducted by J. Olson, G. Olson, and Meader (1995) suggested that there was only a slight improvement in performance of groups in face-to-face over those using AV. However, face-to-face was significantly better than using audio-only. Even so, although audio-only subjects complained about communication problems, the quality of their work did not suffer very greatly.

We revisited the Olsons' experimental video data to analyze how audio–visual communication was used in maintaining the groups' awareness of each other's actions and coordinating group activity as a whole (Dourish & Bellotti, 1992). Continuous AV connections permitted chatting and comments to be made in a lightweight fashion. In particular, the spontaneity and general availability of verbal communication to the group at large made it easy for each member to call on others' attention. Each participant could explain the character of their work as they were doing it and engage in rapid exchanges without switching from what they were doing or necessarily disrupting others' activities. In this way, the open channel of audio communication enabled participants to overcome many problems imposed by the limitations of ShrEdit for supporting awareness of collaborators' activities.

In terms of assessing the value of AV-mediated communication, the data of Smith et al. and the Olsons show that it can support closely coordinated work by remote collaborators with a shared workspace. Continuously open audio channels offer an efficient means to attract attention and debate ongoing activity, because speakers are not required to type their conversations and can continue to work while communicating; however, from this research it is not clear what, if anything much, is added by video.

Experimental Use of Multiple Camera Views

The third laboratory study we report explored the use of multiple camera views to support focused remote collaboration. Six pairs of subjects in separate rooms drew each other's offices and designed the layout of furniture in a dollhouse (Gaver et al., 1993). One participant in the "design office" had direct access to the dollhouse and furniture, whereas the other in the "remote office" had only video-mediated views of these artifacts. Each subject had four camera views of the remote office: one face-to-face, one in-context view of each participant in relation to that person's workspace, and one desk view to permit the sharing of documentation. The design office also had a dollhouse view, and the remote office a bird's-eye view showing most of the room. Subjects were able to switch freely between these views during the experiment, which were shown on a single monitor on their desk.

Face-to-face views were used significantly less than other views by subjects and hardly at all in the design task. Typically subjects remained with one view for long periods interspersed with bursts of frequent switching. They had problems with the view selection control, which was hard to learn. The disjointedness of the different views was also found to be disorienting.

They also had extreme difficulty communicating references to their own and their partner's workspaces. Subjects often pointed at their own screen, which the remote partner could not see, or made abortive attempts to switch their own view for the partner's benefit, and there were several awkward verbal transactions when subjects tried to direct each other's attention to some object in their own or the remote office.

Face-to-face views often seemed to be used to assess the mood of the other while working or during episodes of negotiation, whereas the other views were selected as and when required for the best view onto the current task activity. The main conclusion drawn from this study was that the standard face-to-face view typical of most media spaces was not particularly useful for focused collaborative work involving shared artifacts.

We note that this experiment was contrived to emphasize the importance of artifacts in a non-face-to-face view. For this reason alone, one would expect a bias away from a preference for face-to-face interaction given the limited time available for the accomplishment of a specific task. On the other hand, this research clearly establishes the importance, for remote collaborators, of views that permit shared access to shared physical workspaces, concurring with the conclusions of previous studies by Harrison, Minneman, and Irwin (1992) and Ishii and Miyake (1991). Harrison et al., on the other hand, described how, in a realistic setting used to support real design work between two remote sites over an extended period of several weeks, face-to-face views were very common and were alternated or combined with (rather than rejected in favor of) views of desktops and artifacts.

This finding of Harrison et al. was later reinforced in a further study in which Heath et al. (1995) looked at the use of multiple cameras with multiple monitors so that subjects did not have to switch views but had them simultaneously available. They used three cameras and three monitors showing the shared document or model, a face-to-face view, and an in-context view. Subjects still focused on the desktop view, but the face-to-face view was looked at much more frequently than in the earlier study where explicit view switching on a single monitor was necessary.

A further experimental study by Gaver et al. (1995) used a single moving remote camera controlled by tracking head movements with a local camera using image processing software. The remote camera was mounted on two heavily modified electronically controlled flat-bed plotters, allowing it to move around a focal viewpoint. With this setup, viewers could visually explore the scene on their video monitor by moving their head from side to side, gaining more information about partially occluded objects and depth information from parallax effects.

Although the prototype technology was somewhat crude and unreliable, six pairs of subjects did similar drawing and design tasks to those in the multiple cameras experiments with largely positive results. The moving camera gave remote viewers better views than a fixed camera and, more interestingly, gave local collaborators better awareness of their remote partner's current view. Although the continuous nature of the changes of viewpoint was far less disruptive to the viewer than having to switch between multiple cameras as in the previous study, some subjects complained that sometimes they would prefer to be able to move around without having their view also move.

To sum up so far, it seems that for certain kinds of experimental task, video does not appear to confer any major benefits, whereas for others, involving the sharing of work objects remotely, it seems to be crucial. The earlier studies suggest that face-to-face views rather than video per se are not demonstrably of value. However, what the later studies show is that, when it is easier to do so, subjects take more opportunities to assess the expression and orientation of their partner or shift their viewpoint. What this research suggests above all is that conclusions about the value of media space technology based on such studies should always be regarded in the light of the fact that experimental modifications of the task and technological setup change the behavior of users. In other words, it is dangerous to make generalizations about the value or problems of VMC from a particular experimental study to VMC as a whole because the particulars of the experimental setup are highly influential over observed behaviors.

Video and Interaction in the Workplace

The next study takes a critical look at the ways in which AV-mediated communication falls short of the face-to-face situation in nonexperimental work settings. Heath and Luff (1991, 1992) conducted a detailed study of conversation and interpersonal transactions over media space nodes, drawing on ethnomethodological and conversation analytic frameworks. At the time of this study, AV nodes were being installed in offices in EuroPARC, and the researchers recorded more than a hundred hours of video tape and analyzed in detail the way in which people used the new system as they went about their daily work.

There are several important differences between this study and the previous ones, the first being that the technology was situated in the day-to-day workplaces of subjects doing real work, rather than an experimental task over which performance might be measured. Second, the study captured an important property of the media space in that it is on all the time and therefore supports opportunistic collaboration and communication that would not be possible using the telephony model of connectivity. Third, and crucially, the audio, unlike the video channel, was not continuously open in the situations observed, introducing overheads to participants in establishing conversation. Finally, the placement of the AV node was constrained by desk space and cable length, rather than by requirements for interaction; unlike the experimental AV setups, devices in offices were not necessarily placed such that participants' video equipment (and hence, their remote colleague) was within their field of view.

Subjects were seen to make regular use of the continuous video access they had to one another; however, a consequence of the technological arrangements was that problematic situations arose—for example, with one participant resorting to ever more extreme gesticulations to attract the attention of the other (and still failing to do so). Participants also exhibited behaviors that suggested to the researchers that the role of posture and gesture for illustrating and directing conversation and for awareness of where the other is directing their attention was noticeably disrupted through the video medium. The limited field of view of participants into each other's office space, and the discontinuity of the two spaces, meant that much gestural or postural information was attenuated, particularly with the remote participant's presence being restricted to a small flat display on the desktop.

Although observing that AV mediated interactions are clearly problem-atic in some circumstances, Heath and Luff also observed that some of the differences between it and copresent situations may be positive ones. For example, the apparent ease with which one can disengage from a remote colleague and their potentially disruptive office environment, by closing audio and turning away, was seen as a useful way of avoiding possible distraction at certain times.

As with the observations and findings from the experimental studies, the somewhat arbitrary particulars of the technological setups seem highly significant as explanatory phenomena (in this case, placement of monitors and who controls, or whether one can control, when audio is on or off during a connection). Furthermore, the technology was still unfamiliar and was imposed on the subjects in a predetermined configuration that they had to make the best of. We return later to some experiences of longer term AV connectivity in which more artful, creative use of the technology's limitations and capabilities could be made by participants who had developed a greater familiarity with AV connectivity as part of everyday interaction.

Portholes: A Video-Based Awareness Server

The preceding studies share a focus on explicit communication and collabo-ration in VMC, often contrasting their results with face-to-face situations. They do not expose some of the other properties of media space technology which derive from the notion that if the technology is continuously switched on, different kinds of video services are possible. The Portholes system described earlier provides an alternative kind of service demonstrating how video can also be useful for less explicit communication based on passive awareness of remote events.

Shortly after its introduction, a survey study was conducted to determine how well the system was doing in serving its intended purpose for its user population at EuroPARC and PARC. "Shortly" here means about 8 to 10 months, so most users had considerably more experience with the technology than in any of the previous studies. Eleven of the 22 subscribers noted their use of Portholes over a period of 3 days and completed a questionnaire about their reactions to and use of the system. Although this study did not get at details of interactions with Portholes or among its users, it revealed information about how beneficial the system was proving to be in general. A good deal of anecdotal, long-term information was also obtained from informal conversations with users about day-to-day or habitual use.

Portholes was originally intended to let users monitor when remote colleagues (perhaps across the Atlantic) were in and available for a phone call (or a visit, if within walking distance) or busy and not to be disturbed, and to provide a sense of distributed activity, both "at-a-glance" and slowly over time. Once the system was installed, however, it became clear that its primary value was in fostering a "sense of community" among users, enabling them to be aware of lab visits, meetings, absences, comings and goings, and so on at both EuroPARC in England and PARC in California. This was particularly noticeable for images of colleagues transmitted between the labs, because there was no other means by which people 6,000 miles apart could gain any awareness of each other's daily activities.

The notion of ongoing, passive awareness that had been our initial focus was an important route toward the sense of community Portholes supports. It is also a good example of how video can be used in ways that go beyond the telephony-based model used to support relatively short, focused work sessions. Since the time of the study, and long after Portholes ceased to be a subject of research, continued use has been made of the system (which requires almost no overhead to run) by people at both labs. This suggests that, although it supports few specific tasks explicitly, and presumably would be hard to justify in terms of increased productivity or demonstrably improved working relationships, its users seem to regard it as a worthwhile service.

Long-Term Office-Share

The final part of this section also deals with accounts of media space technology that go beyond focused collaboration and telephony-style connections. We relate our own experiences as long-term users, which parallels that of two other researchers at PARC[7]: We are all self confessed "addicts" of media spaces (see Dourish, Adler, Bellotti, & Henderson, (1996) for a more detailed account of our symptoms). Our experiences cover a period of 3 years of continuous "office sharing" between one pair of colleagues at EuroPARC and 1½ years between two colleagues at PARC lasting until the autumn of 1994, when one of each pair left Xerox.

Our accounts are, to be sure, informally derived but resonate with the reports of office neighbors and colleagues who have also office shared with someone and whose experiences we polled in a questionnaire survey undertaken at EuroPARC and PARC in 1991. We have found no other published accounts (let alone studies) of such long-term connections and the transformations in how individuals and communities use and experience them.[8]

Like our PARC colleagues, we began our office-share to support explicit collaboration (in particular, coauthoring a conference paper), but quickly found that there were many implicit benefits from having a "hole in space," arising primarily out of its long-term continual availability rather than the specifics of interaction. Crucially, we discovered that these benefits accrued not only to ourselves as the owners of the office-shares, but also to other colleagues in physical and organizational proximity. In what follows, we illustrate some of the emerging practices and associated benefits, organizing our illustrations in relation to four different perspectives that we have found useful in accounting for our views.

Four Perspectives. First, the *individual* perspective highlights the relationship between the individual and the technology in their office, and the software governing that technology. This draws on our experience of learning how to use the media space effectively, including our choices of physical placement and setup of camera, microphone, monitor and speakers. We found camera positions that gave optimal views not only of ourselves in our usual working position, but also of our offices and out of our doors into the public areas beyond. We kept the audio and video channels open all the time and placed the cameras on monitors well within our field of view even when we were facing our workstation. Over time we learned roughly what the field of view of the camera was (although one of us also used a feedback monitor, which was especially helpful for visitors). We also learned to tailor our pointing and gesturing to relate to the perspective of the other's space when appropriate (e.g., when remotely pointing to "the car park" or "up the street").

Second, the *interactional* perspective highlights the nature of interpersonal interactions mediated by technology. We developed sensitivity to each other's gaze direction (or "gaze awareness;" see Ishii & Kobayashi, 1992, or Tang & Isaacs, 1993), so that we were able to discern when the other was concentrating on the workstation or looking at the AV monitor (our own image). We adapted to the limitations of our microphones and speakers to reduce the number of occasions when confusion arose for our remote colleagues over whether we were speaking to them or to someone colocated in our own office. We used the continuous availability of open communication channels to engage in lightweight exchanges, such as asking quick questions about spelling, research citations, and so on.

Third, there is the *communal* perspective, which is typically outside the scope of investigations into VMC, but which we found critical to the patterns of interaction which emerged around our connections. This refers to the wider view of AV connections within an organizational and social context. We and other sharers noticed how our colleagues at EuroPARC and PARC who shared the same (or nearby) physical space with us began to make use of our office-shares. Colleagues might enter an office to talk not to its occupant but to the virtual occupant, or even to colleagues whose offices adjoined the remote office. We have returned to our offices to find another person in each of them talking over "our" office-share. We have even had reports of visitors assuming someone was in an office when they were hearing only the remote office noises or assuming that a meeting was going on, when what they were hearing was the local occupant talking with the remote one.

Sounds coming from activity in neighboring spaces also come from and are propagated back into the general community around an office-share, so aerobics workout tapes from down the remote hall or videotapes being analyzed in the remote neighbor's office were frequent contributions to an occasionally distracting awareness of remote activity. This projection of sound into surrounding areas could also be capitalized on. Speaking close to the microphone worked as a PA system for all of the offices near the remote office so that it was possible to summon anyone in that area. This was particularly useful for gathering people together when it was "pub time."

A further aspect of the communal perspective on this long-term connection arose out of our own use of it, as participants. When we first established the connection, the views from our cameras showed the remote participant a typical "head and shoulders" shot, reflecting a traditional preoccupation with "face-to-face" video conversations. Soon, however, we found that we wanted to change these views to encompass not only more of the local environment (offices, desk, and so forth) but, most importantly, the view out of each of our doors, beyond our offices and into the space beyond. This semipermanent connection was not simply linking us to each other; rather, it was linking our spaces, and hence linking the groups that inhabited those spaces; the ability to see and participate in their activities became especially valuable.

Finally there is the *societal* perspective on technology use, which reveals an area where our experiences differ from those of our PARC colleagues. In EuroPARC, a small lab with around 30 people, everyone became familiar with our office share. Visitors exhibited reactions such as awkwardness in front of our cameras or suspicion about the possibility of being spied or eavesdropped on. These reactions began to seem naive after we came to see the media space as a benign part of everyday life. We forgot our own initial, negative reactions to the system once we understood how it worked and learned how to make good use of it. In PARC, with more than 300 employees in the building, many people were unaware of the media space technology being used by our colleagues. These people behaved much like the visitors to EuroPARC because they also did not know and were dubious about the purpose of the technology. In both labs, however, our office shares became public affirmations of our working and social relationships with our colleagues.

We have come to see that behaviors are altered not only by the details of interactions with technology but also, often indirectly, by its very existence within a society. In this we strongly concur with the observations of other writers such as Gergen (1991), Meyrowitz (1985), and McLuhan (1964). Simply the presence of technology (or of specific uses of technology) as an everyday part of life leads, in itself, to a number of interesting transformations in behavior. In much the same way as we do not have to be watching television, or even own a television set, in order to be affected by the role of television in our culture, the presence of the media space as a whole introduced transformations that affected all the members of the laboratory, whether or not they made active use of the system. The existence of our office-share and those of others, alongside things like the widespread use of the Portholes awareness service, gradually became unremarkable aspects of the context within which the practices, social interactions, shared understandings, and expectations of all were grounded. Furthermore, particular uses (or misuses, or nonuses) of the technology in turn attained significance against this background of organizational relationships and practices. This wider reading, then, constitutes another perspective on the role of VMC in social settings, looking at the impact of video connectivity on the social, rather than the interpersonal.

WIDER ISSUES IN LONG-TERM MEDIA SPACE USAGE

To conclude this chapter, we wish to underline two themes that have been present throughout. These themes have informed our appraisals of the technology and of the observational and experiential accounts that we have presented and point to profound analytic and methodological implications for VMC research. The first relates to issues surrounding the gradual *evolution* of the technology and the practices of its users. The second relates to the analytic perspectives taken to assess the *utility* of the technology and is most profoundly linked to what we feel is the inappropriateness of the "copresence hypothesis."

Evolution

Throughout the preceding sections we have emphasized the media space as an environment in which people live and work, selecting from it as appropriate and organizing it around their activities. One of the key issues that is often overlooked in experimental and some observational studies is that users as individuals are highly adaptive to their environment and so are the cultures, norms, and practices that those individuals share. In addition, technology tends to be adapted, not just by designers but also by its users (e.g., Mackay, 1991). Furthermore a process of coadaptation both at the individual and at the societal level is continually at work on the people and the technology they use and may have profound effects on the appropriateness of particular metrics for evaluation.

Our analysis of the impact, importance, and use of media spaces is based strongly on these aspects of our experience. As a result, we present conclusions and open issues of a very different sort from those that we might base on a laboratory study. Along with our colleagues from PARC, we have been investigating the wider issues that arise out of long-term use of media space technology: issues of evolution and coadaptation of technology and of practices, both within individual use and more widely in the social groups to which media space users belong. We can see a variety of ways in which adaptations of technology and its use highlight the need to be circumspect in drawing conclusions from experimental and short term studies either of a class of technology as a whole, or of the effects it has on society. Four different kinds of evolution serve to illustrate this point:

Evolution of Individual Behavior. We have noted, as have others (e.g., Dykstra-Erickson et al., 1994; Tang & Rua, 1994), that people's behavior with new VMC technology changes over time. For example, Dykstra-Erickson et al. pointed out that observation over a significant stretch of time is essential, not only to allow users to become acquainted with new technology but also to see how new adaptations in behavior develop as users begin to learn how to make the best use of it. They noted how users developed new gestural conventions, *local visual languages*, which had no face-to-face parallel, and which both helped to overcome the ways in which VMC attenuates gestural information and made use of the properties of the technology itself (e.g., wobbling or covering the camera) to convey information. This parallels our own experience at EuroPARC where the behavior of those familiar with the media space gradually changed so that they learned, for example, to stand within the view of a camera when talking to a remote colleague, or to check with a remote colleague about who might be around to overhear a private conversation.

Evolution of Culture. Typical studies of media space technologies—including many in this volume—focus on conversation across AV connections, and on transformations in the behaviors of direct participants in the mediated conversation. One of the most striking features of our experience, though, was the gradual transformation that long-term usage and extended connections introduced not only in the behavior of primary users of the technology but also in the wider groups surrounding the media space participants: our colleagues, workgroups, and so on. This caused us to broaden our focus, beyond the individual and interpersonal aspects of media space use, to encompass communal and societal impacts also (Dourish et al., in press).

At EuroPARC, attitudes and acceptable practices gradually evolved as RAVE became part of everyday life. Although some were initially anxious about being "spied on," this concern tended to dissolve once they learned that there were no spying facilities available to (other) privileged users, and that everyone—from the managers to the receptionists—had the same services available to them. Eventually some of the most fearful became loyal users. As the technology was appropriated by the participants, new practices emerged and became standard (such as hanging a sign announcing the weekly seminar in front of the common room camera or using other people's continuous office shares as a shortcut to someone in another part of the building). Similarly, Cool et al. (1992) identified a phenomenon they call *autonomous system drift* with new, culturally accepted practices evolving around the installed technology, exploiting its positive features to good effect, but also substantially altering its effective performance for the culture as a whole.

Evolution of Personal Configurations. When the media space nodes were installed in people's offices they were alien devices, the properties and limits of which were unknown. Users gradually began to develop a sense of ownership and started modifying their node to suit their preferences or to improve others' views into their space (as mentioned earlier). Some users obtained larger monitors; others acquired or threw away footpedals that could shut off audio in and out of their office. Other users, given footpedals initially, took to using large "bulldog clips" to hold the pedal in the "on" position permanently. People usually moved their camera and monitor, with some preferring to have them right next to their workstation monitor and others placing them further away. Some preferred to point their camera away from themselves, or at their keyboards. Xerox Buttons, during the period when they were available, were readily exploited by many people to configure their interface and create specialized access to particular nodes or services.

Evolution of Technology. The media space (like many other similar research prototypes) continued to evolve in situ over a period of 5 years, with refinements and new services (such as Godard and Portholes) being added as time went by. All of these additions increased the utility and popularity of the media space and were generally responses to observed reactions and discussions with lab members. In particular, the need to address people's concerns about privacy was a strong motivating force for the evolution of technological control over access built in to the interface so that unwanted connections could be prevented. However, the provision of *feedback,* informing users of RAVE activity, became far more important than the provision of technical access control *per se.* Bellotti and Sellen (1993) discuss a number of measures taken over time to improve people's sense of confidence in the technology.

It is worth highlighting the relationship between technological and social "functionality," and the mutually influential adoption of technology into a set of established cultural norms. We would expect this to play out differently in different settings. Dourish (1993) provided a brief analysis of the different roles and forms of access control in four laboratory media spaces, showing the ways in which the detailed technological arrangements are carried out differently and to different purposes. This makes the observational analysis of styles of interaction and access control problematic, because they reflect organizational needs and expectations that are highly setting specific.

Each of these different kinds of evolution tended to interact with the others and affected how useful and acceptable the media space at EuroPARC was thought to be by its users. It is quite conceivable that detailed studies after the initial introduction and at the end of each year at least for the first 3 years would have supported different conclusions about how effective this infrastructure was. Although we do not have such systematic data, we can confirm that practices, attitudes, and technology configurations changed radically over the years.

Utility: Beyond Copresence and Telephony

Certain phenomena tend not to be visible in experimental evaluations and short-term analyses, particularly those focusing on interpersonal interactions, and yet within these phenomena lie potential problems that may present far greater barriers (or challenges, depending on how one looks at it) for uptake of the technology than how wide a field of view is available of a remote office, or whether eye contact is possible. This makes it important, when designing and studying systems such as a media space, to be conscious of the kind of analytic stance we are taking. Our presumptions about appropriate comparisons, or the uses to which we put the technology we are evaluating and the kinds of studies we should conduct, can strongly affect how we present our arguments about its utility and the phenomena we focus upon. This last section of our chapter deals with some important points surrounding this area of concern.

The Copresence Hypothesis.   Our perspective on media spaces centers on a reconsideration of what we term the *Copresence Hypothesis*—the premise that "media spaces attempt to simulate physical copresence." This has motivated many VMC research papers, and indeed was a motivation in our own beginnings in media space research. The hypothesis leads almost inevitably to the use of the "real world" as an evaluative baseline for AV communication technologies, as well as a focus on conversation and communication as a copresent phenomenon.

However, our experiences are that the most interesting effects resulting from the long-term, everyday use of a media space are those that highlight the way in which media space technology is appropriated and used as part of the real world supporting real people in real working relationships engaging in real conversation and work. Rather than attempting to simulate or recapture elements of everyday interaction in the purely physical environment, our concern is with the interplay between that context and the intriguing extensions offered by the facilities and functionality of media space technology. Our interpretation of *media space as the resulting "environment"*—a set of facilities that can be adapted and flexibly deployed in support of collaborative activity—arises out of this perspective.

Beyond Telephony.   One of the most notable features of a media space is that it is more than an infrastructure for point-to-point, telephone-style connections to support focused collaboration. Therefore, the focus of many different analyses of media spaces on that element is to presuppose, once again, a potential value that resides only in its ability to act in place of face-to-face, focused encounters. We have described the use of the Portholes awareness server and indefinite AV connections that go beyond telephony both in a technical sense and especially in the practices which emerge around them. So, although AV telephony may be useful, there are other kinds of real-time services that AV can provide that also deserve attention.

Beyond Short-Term Studies.   Some key points have been made in this chapter about the use of media space technology that have not, so far, been acknowledged in the many of the studies undertaken. The reasons for this, which have been hinted at earlier, include the fact that formal studies are necessarily short due to the expense and effort of intensive observation or data collection; they are often conducted immediately or very soon after introduction of the technology of interest, when the incentives are naturally highest to publish results[9]; they tend to trade depth of analysis against breadth of scope, once again due to the limits imposed by time and expense; and, due to paradigmatic tendencies, they often focus on objectification and analytic structure underplaying the importance of the development of intuitive insights by users and long-term experiential accounts.

The first and most important point we wish to make contrasts strongly with other accounts of media space technology.[10] It is that short-term observational studies, no matter how intensive and painstaking, fail to distinguish between abiding and serious problems and ephemeral problems or experimental peculiarities (such as the awkward view selection control in Gaver et al., 1993) that, although real enough and often providing valuable design insights, may recede in perceived importance as technological details, user expectations, and skills change over time. For example, some early difficulties (such as loss of eye contact) that we experienced with long-term AV connections became unproblematic as as we adapted the medium to our behaviors, and our behaviors to the medium. Even so, other difficulties persisted, such as the difficulty of judging how loud one is in a remote office; a whisper close to the microphone could be heard well outside a remote office. Also, after over a year of use, one of us failed to remember that if one's partner has covered the camera in their office, one's own camera is still on (our colleagues at PARC report similar experiences of this sort). Such difficulties, as revealed by our extended experiences, are not likely to be picked up in studies such as the ones reported earlier, yet they may be at least as important as the problems that are.

Second, a sense of *ownership* of or *responsibility* for the technology is critical to its uptake and use. The sense of ownership, which develops over time, is also a necessary precursor to the kinds of innovations and personal reconfigurations that enable users to get the best out of what has evolved to be a highly flexible technology. This element is clearly absent in experimental setups or in studies conducted immediately after introduction of the technology.[11]

Third, collaborative technology requires a *fostering culture* and *explicit organizational support* (i.e., investment of people and their time) in order to ensure that it is maintained and that newcomers to the culture within which it exists are carefully introduced to it and helped through any teething problems. Whatever the potential group benefits, users tend to be self-directed in their efforts to make technology work. If they see no personal benefits they will not waste precious time making it easier for others to see them or share what they do. Thus, cameras and microphones that don't work and calendars that are not up to date are all seen as someone else's problem. Rejected connections may be personally frustrating, but if they appear to be due to someone else's setup, they will not be reported.

Finally, problems observed in studies, such as the inability to attract a remote colleague's attention (Heath & Luff, 1991, 1992), are not necessarily inherent in media space technology as a whole. They may sometimes be a by-product of a particular setup (in that case having no control over remote audio) and are tractable to improvement by redesign. Indeed, the two studies by Gaver et al. (1993) and Heath et al. (1995) illustrate how changes in VMC configurations can substantively affect how users behave in interactions.

Experiences such as those arising from our office-shares, then, lead us to underline two major points. First, we argue that changes in the details of behavior are not necessarily problems. They may be better viewed as successful or unsuccessful adaptations to the affordances of new circumstances. We make a distinction between *behaviors* such as the use of eye contact, which are intrinsically linked to the peculiar affordances and limitations of the communication medium, and *achievements* such as the management of conversational flow, which are extrinsic to them. It is on the achievements resulting from successful adaptations (and, of course, the failures to achieve) that we must focus our analytic attention and design modifications. Second, the problems and benefits experienced by individual users when they first encounter a technology in a controlled study are only a fragment of a wider context that may render comparisons such as VMC with face-to-face inappropriate (when, say, the participants could otherwise not meet) and that may call for a longer term and broader view of emerging adaptations and societal changes around the technology as a whole, which in turn is adapted by its users as well as its designers.

CONCLUSION

This chapter has reported on a long-term "lived experiment"—one in which the technology was intimately entwined with everyday action for a wide range of participants, and that reflects the insights of a wide range of investigators and analytic perspectives. The detailed investigations of VMC based on techniques such as conversation analysis are clearly critical to the development of future technologies supporting communication and collaboration, but we feel it is important that these be balanced by broader investigations in which the issues at stake are those of the deployment of technologies, their integration into working situations, and the organization of working activities around them.

ACKNOWLEDGMENTS

We thank the following people for their part over the last 6 years, in sharing and shaping the ideas in this chapter: Annette Adler, Sara Bly, Alan Borning, Bill Buxton, Kathy Carter, Ian Daniel, Bill Gaver, Richard Harper, Steve Harrison, Christian Heath, Austin Henderson, Susan Irwin-Anderson, Lennart Lövstrand, Paul Luff, Wendy Mackay, Allan MacLean, Chao-Ying Ma, Tom Milligan, Hugh Messenger, Scott Minneman, Mike Molloy, Tom Moran, Toby Morrill, Gary and Judy Olson, Daniele Pagani, Abi Sellen, Mike Travers, and Alex Zbyslaw.

NOTES

1. The EuroPARC laboratory was named after Xerox's Palo Alto Research Center (PARC) in California. Since the work reported in this paper was conducted, EuroPARC has become the Cambridge Laboratory of the Rank Xerox Research Centre. We refer to the lab as EuroPARC, partly out of historical accuracy and partly out of nostalgia.
2. EuroPARC is located in Ravenscroft House.
3. The iiif software was originally written at EuroPARC. Subsequently, the software was provided to the University of Toronto, where the original iiif developers were engaged in the design of the CAVECAT media space. The Toronto work was subsequently based on a considerably more sophisticated version of iiif than the basic service which runs at EuroPARC.
4. A UNIX command-line interface was also provided, and a variant of it is still in common use; however, it has primarily been used for administrative and debugging purposes, rather than as a general user service.
5. To our regret, this highly useful feature was lost when we moved from the Xerox Lisp environment to UNIX and the X Window System, and hence no longer had access to Lisp's Buttons.
6. Interestingly, footpedals clamped in the "on" position with bulldog clips became a common sight.
7. The analysis presented here was developed in collaboration with Annette Adler and Austin Henderson.
8. Cool, Fish, Kraut, and Lowery (1992) only briefly alluded to office sharing at Bellcore during the development of their media space, although details of their connections differ, and the timescales were considerably shorter.
9. We are reminded of Mackay's (1991) observation that most software tailoring activity occurs when the software is installed, when the users have the least knowledge of its behavior and capabilities.
10. See, in particular, Heath and Luff (1991) for their ethnographic and interaction analysis based account of media space use, and Gaver (1992) for an ecological psychological account of use.
11. For a striking example of this effect, compare the experiences of Fish, Kraut, and Chalfonte (1990) with those reported by M. Olson and Bly (1991), of linked common areas with very different sorts of video technology—on the one hand, a complex, very precisely configured experimental wide-screen video window, and on the other, simple cameras and monitors that anyone could pick up and move around.

REFERENCES

Bellotti, V., & Sellen, A. (1993, September). Design for privacy in ubiquitous computing environments. *Proceedings, Third European Conference on Computer-Supported Cooperative Work ECSCW'93*. Milan, Italy.

Bly, S., Harrison, S., & Irwin, S. (1993). Media spaces: Bringing people together in a video, audio and computing environment. *Communications of the ACM, 36*(1), 28–47.

Borning, A., & Travers, M. (1991, April). Two approaches to casual interaction over computer and video networks. *Proceedings, ACM Conf. Human Factors in Computer Systems CHI'91*. New Orleans, LA.

Buxton, W., & Moran, T. (1990). EuroPARC's Integrated Interactive Intermedia Facility (IIIF): Early experiences. *IFIP Conference on Multi-User Interfaces and Applications*. Herakleion, Crete.

Chapanis, A. (1975). Interactive human communication. *Scientific American, 232*(3), 36–42.

Cool, C., Fish, R., Kraut, R., & Lowery, C. (1992, November). Iterative design of video communication systems. *Proceedings, ACM Conf. Computer-Supported Cooperative Work CSCW'92*. Toronto.

Dourish, P. (1991). *Godard: A flexible architecture for A/V services in a media space* (EuroPARC Tech. Rep. No. EPC-91-134). Cambridge: Rank Xerox EuroPARC.

Dourish, P. (1993, September). Culture and control in a media space. *Proceedings, Third European Conference on Computer-Supported Cooperative Work ECSCW'93*. Milan, Italy.

Dourish, P., Adler, A., Bellotti, V., & Henderson, A. (1996). Your place or mine? Learning from long-term use of video communication. *Computer-Supported Cooperative Work, An International Journal, 5*(1), 36–62

Dourish, P., & Bellotti, V. (1992, November). Awareness and coordination in shared workspaces. *Proc. ACM Conference on Computer-Supported Cooperative Work CSCW'92*. Toronto, Canada.

Dourish, P., & Bly, S. (1992, May). Portholes: Supporting awareness in distributed work groups. *Proc. ACM Conference on Human Factors in Computer Systems CHI'92*. Monterey, CA.

Dykstra-Erickson, E., Rudman, C., Hertz, R., Mithal, K., Schmidt, J., & Marshall, C. (1995). Supporting adaptation to multimedia desktop conferencing. *Proceedings, 15th International Symposium on Human Factors in Telecommunications*. Melbourne, Australia.

Egido, C. (1990). Teleconferencing as a technology to support cooperative work: Its possibilities and limitations. In J. Galegher, R. Kraut, & C. Edigo (Eds.), *Intellectual teamwork: Social and technical foundations of cooperative work* (pp. 351–373). Hillsdale, NJ: Lawrence Erlbaum Associates.

Fish, R., Kraut, R., & Chalfonte, B. (1990, October). The VideoWindow system in informal communication. *Proceedings, ACM Conference on Computer-Supported Cooperative Work CSCW'90*. Los Angeles.

Garfinkel, D., Gust, P., Lemon, M., & Lowder, S. (1989). *The SharedX multi-user interface user's guide, Version 2.0* (Software Technology Lab Rep. No. STL-TM-89-07). Palo Alto, CA: Hewlett-Packard Laboratories.

Gaver, W. (1991, September). Sound support for collaboration. *Proceedings, European Conference on Computer-Supported Cooperative Work ECSCW'91*. Amsterdam.

Gaver, W. (1992, November). The affordances of media spaces for collaboration. *Proceedings, ACM Conference on Computer-Supported Cooperative Work CSCW'92*. Toronto.

Gaver, W., Moran, T., MacLean, A., Lövstrand, L., Dourish, P., Carter, K., & Buxton, W. (1992, May). Realizing a video environment: EuroPARC's RAVE system. *Proceedings, ACM Conference on Human Factors in Computing Systems CHI'92*. Monterey, CA.

Gaver, W., Sellen, A., Heath, C., & Luff, P. (1993, April). One is not enough: Multiple views in a media space. *Proceedings, Conference on Human Factors in Computer Systems InterCHI'93*. Amsterdam.

Gaver, W., Smets, G., & Overbeeke, K. (1995, May). A Virtual window on media space. *Proceedings, ACM Conference on Human Factors in Computing Systems CHI'95*. Denver, CO.

Gergen, K. (1991). *The saturated self: Dilemmas of identity in contemporary life*. BasicBooks, Harper Collins.

Goffman, E. (1963). *Behavior in public places*. New York: Free Press.

Harrison, S., Minneman, S., & Irwin, S. (1992). *Graspable implications: A study of 3-D objects in remote collaboration*. Unpublished report, available on request from the authors at Xerox PARC, 3333 Coyote Hill Rd., Palo Alto, CA.

Heath, C., & Luff, P. (1991, April). Disembodied conduct: Communication through video in a multi-media environment. *Proceedings, ACM Conference on. Human Factors in Computing Systems CHI'91.* New Orleans, LA.

Heath, C., & Luff, P. (1992). Media space and communicative asymmetries: Preliminary observations of video-mediated interaction. *Human–Computer Interaction, 7*(3), 315–346.

Heath, C., Luff, P., & Sellen, A. (1995). Reconsidering the virtual workplace: Flexible support for collaborative activity. *Proceedings, Fourth European Conference on Computer-Supported Cooperative Work ECSCW'95.* Stockholm.

Ishii, H., & Kobayashi, M. (1992, May). ClearBoard: A seamless medium for shared drawing and conversation with eye contact. *Proceedings, ACM Conference on Human Factors in Computing Systems CHI'92.* Monterey, CA.

Ishii, H., & Miyake, N. (1991). Toward an open shared workspace: Computer and video fusion approach of TeamWorkStation. *Communications of the ACM, 34*(12), 36–50.

Lövstrand, L. (1991, September). Being selectively aware with the Khronika system. *Proceedings, European Conference on Computer-Supported Cooperative Work ECSCW'91.* Amsterdam.

Mackay, W. (1991, April). Triggers and barriers to customizing software. *Proceedings, ACM Conference on Human Factors in Computer Systems CHI'91.* New Orleans, LA.

MacLean, A., Carter, K., Moran, T., & Lövstrand, L. (1990, April). User-tailorable systems: Pressing the issues with buttons. *Proceedings ACM Conference on Human Factors in Computing Systems CHI '90.* Seattle, WA.

McGuffin, L., & Olson, G. (1992). *ShrEdit: A shared electronic workspace* (CSMIL Tech. Rep.) Ann Arbor, MI: Cognitive Science and Machine Intelligence Laboratory, University of Michigan.

McLuhan, M. (1964). *Understanding media: The extensions of man.* London: Routledge & Kegan Paul.

Meyrowitz, J. (1985). *No sense of place: The impact of electronic media on social behavior.* London: Oxford University Press.

Milligan, T. (1989). *The iiif design report* (version 3, working paper). Toronto: Computer Science Research Institute, University of Toronto.

Minneman, S., & Bly, S. (1992, May). Managing a trois: A study of a multi-user drawing tool in distributed design work. *Proceedings, ACM Conference on Human Factors in Computing Systems CHI'92.* Monterey, CA.

Olson, J., Olson, G., Storrøsten, M., and Carter, M. (1992, November). How a group-editor changes the character of a design meeting as well as its outcome. *Proceedings, ACM Conference on Computer-Supported Cooperative Work CSCW'92,* Toronto.

Olson, J., Olson, G., & Meader, D. (1995, May). What mix of audio and video is useful for small groups doing remote real-time design work? *Proceedings, ACM Conference on Human Factors in Computing Systems CHI'95.* Denver, CO.

Olson, M., & Bly, S. (1991). The Portland experience: A report on a distributed research group. *International Journal of Man–Machine Studies, 34,* 211–228.

Smith, R., O'Shea, T., O'Malley, C., Scanlon, E., & Taylor, J. (1989, September). Preliminary experiments with a distributed, multi-media, problem solving environment. *Proceedings, European Conference on Computer-Supported Cooperative Work ECSCW'89.* London.

Stults, R. (1989). *The experimental use of video to support design activity* (Tech. Rep. SSL-89-19). Palo Alto, CA: Xerox PARC.

Tang, J., & Isaacs, E. (1993). Why do users like video? Studies of multimedia-supported collaboration. *Computer-Supported Cooperative Work, An International Journal, 1*(3), 163–196.

Tang, J., & Rua, M. (1994, April). Montage: Providing teleproximity for distributed groups. *Proceedings, ACM Conference on Human Factors in Computing Systems CHI'94.* Boston, MA.

Chapter 13

The Media Space

Steve Harrison
Xerox PARC

Sara Bly
Consultant

Susan Anderson
Xerox Corporation

Scott Minneman
Xerox PARC

This chapter uses 10 years of experience with the PARC Media Space to show how groups can use video-mediated communication (VMC) to keep connected as though they were in a large, open-plan office. Turning this space into useful places for people and work requires that it fit the group's ways of being and working. Illustrated by a scenario of a typical day in the PARC Media Space, the chapter outlines how physical space and electronic connection combine to form media space, how media space is appropriated for use by different people for different activities, and how, through this appropriation, it becomes a fluid and flexible number of places. This leads to a discussion of the characteristics that enable a spatial approach to electronic connection, which results in some radical design guidelines for interfaces and privacy control that are at odds with the systems developed for video telephony, desktop videoconferencing, distance learning, or corporate telecommunications systems.

INTRODUCTION

This chapter uses 10 years of experience with the PARC Media Space (Bly, Harrison, & Irwin, 1993; Irwin, 1991; Stults, 1989) to show how groups can use VMC to keep connected as though they were in a large, open-plan office. Others in this book report on how pairs of people can employ the technology—certainly one aspect of a media space—but we discuss how close working groups (typically ranging from 3 to 30 members) use it as though it were part of their office space. Although the initial PARC Media Space was geographically distributed, we have accumulated several additional years of experience with a single-site installation. The bulk of the findings we discuss have their roots in a highly distributed setting; however, many of the phenomena and system design considerations are useful for groups in which colleagues are only a few feet apart.

The media space is a mix of audio, video, and computation that extends the world of desks, chairs, walls, and ceilings. This space formed by video connection is always "there," always on, always "present"—so present as to become part of the background of everyday work, just like the furniture. Turning this space into useful *places* for people and work requires that it fit the group's ways of being and working. It must provide the kind of accessibility that supports the subtle social phenomena enabling the work of a group to proceed. This requirement results in some radical design guidelines for interfaces and privacy control. The resulting designs are, in some ways, at odds with the systems and infrastructures developed for video telephony, desktop videoconferencing, distance learning, or corporate telecommunications systems.

Getting a handle on the particulars that distinguish a media space from a teleconference is useful. More important, however, is to understand the particular gestalt of a media space—why the whole is greater than the sum of its parts. Although the best way to understand media spaces is to participate in a group that relies on one to carry out its work, this chapter endeavors to give readers the perspective that would result from working in one. Thus, we begin by describing the PARC Media Space through the experiences of people working in it. This leads to a discussion of the characteristics that enable a spatial approach to electronic connection. Finally, we discuss the social and technical entailments of this approach.

A TYPICAL DAY IN THE PARC MEDIA SPACE

In this section we interweave an illustrative story (in italics) with a description of the two-site version of the PARC Media Space. Events depicted in the typical day are an amalgam of incidents observed in course of use of the PARC Media Space. Names have been changed and characters combined.

Imagine you are interviewing for a job with a 25+ person R&D group near your Oregon home. Most of their project work has to do with object-oriented technologies focused on support for remote collaboration. In fact, two thirds of the group is in another city about 700 miles away. These folks are not only building technologies, they are putting themselves in a situation where they have to understand the needs of people doing remote work and where they have to use the technologies they are developing.

The first research media space was created at the Xerox Palo Alto Research Center (PARC) in the mid-1980s. From 1985 to 1988, the System Concepts Lab (SCL) was geographically split between Palo Alto, California, and Portland, Oregon, with the intent of maintaining a single, coherent working group. Group members capitalized on the split to make their research issues on collaboration real and vital, and the fruits of their research were used to conduct their day-to-day work. SCL conducted its research in an office environment typical of so-called "knowledge workers," focusing on the rich social underpinnings of joint work as much as on the problems of sharing specific work content. One of the main technological enablers was the creation of a video, audio, and computing environment that spanned the two locations. This suite of technologies came to be called a media space.

You show up at 8:30 in the morning for your interview, and the site manager is there to greet you. Ron begins to show you around. The group is located in a new building. The facilities are nice enough—window offices primarily situated around a spacious and open common area with rooms interspersed for meetings and lab work.

The initial PARC Media Space grew out of the experiences and ways of working of the group. SCL was a close group of about two dozen people who collaborated on projects and management alike. Although there was a hierarchical management structure, lab members regularly attended staff meetings, and most decisions were made by consensus. In addition, weekly lab meetings ensured that there was frequent exchange not only of research progress but also of social activity. The social orientation was an acknowledged part of SCL's agenda and way of working.

Each researcher was encouraged to make two trips a year to the other site; reporting relations evolved so that some people reported to managers at the other location; and almost all projects came to have cross-site memberships. Although SCL was organized in groups that nominally carried responsibility for separate projects, project membership was fluid across these organizational boundaries.

Along the way Ron stops by one of the offices and introduces you to Katherine. From the look of things, you gather that she's in uncharacteristically early, working on a paper. Your attention is drawn to the television monitor and camera perched on the low filing cabinet next to her desk. Appearing on the monitor is a view into another office, now vacant, and a smaller inset image of a common area, similar to but different from the one behind you. That small image, you learn, is referred to as a PiP (picture in a picture).

As you move on, Ron strolls back to the common area and the couches arrayed in a U-shape around a big-screen rear-projection TV. There is not much to see on the TV except the other, slightly darker commons with its sofa and microphone. "That's Palo Alto . . . no one's there yet," Ron explains. You see that the overhead lights are still off and there is no life in any of the visible offices. Ron notes that it's pretty early for many folks to be in at either site; work times are flexible.

Initially, the two sites were linked by routers and twin 9.6-kbps links between their computer networks for shared file system access and electronic mail, as well as by telephone (speakerphones were used in group meetings). The system connection grew to include video compression equipment, two 56-kbps data lines, audio teleconferencing gear, a standard phone line, crossbar video/audio switches, numerous consumer-quality video cameras and monitors, and software controls. A camera and monitor were provided for each researcher's office and for the various conference rooms. In the two common areas, the monitor was a large screen display and a half-duplex speakerphone was added. Figure 13.1 diagrams this arrangement; Figure 13.2 shows a typical office.

Dedicated phone lines transmitting one audio and one video link were left open continuously. Walking through the commons provided an opportunity to see, hear, and speak with anyone in either common area. This electronic visibility mimicked the visibility of the physical environment: Many offices had windows facing onto the common area so that activity in the common area could be seen by people in their offices and vice

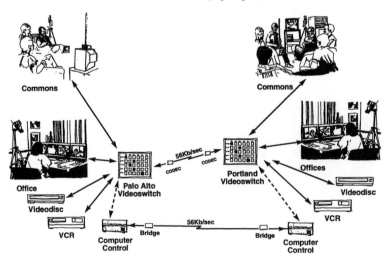

FIG. 13.1. The PARC Media Space linking offices, open areas, and audio–video services in Palo Alto and Portland.

FIG. 13.2. A typical office.

versa. Although it had been intended as a cross-site meeting tool, the primary use of the link was for frequent spontaneous discussions between researchers at the two sites. This electronically extended the casual inter-actions that were already part of the routine in the common areas.

Meanwhile in Oregon, Katherine has come in early to get a jump on some revisions that she wants to work into their paper before Doug takes another stab at the draft. They'd been working in parallel on the Friday before, Doug in his office and she in hers, linked with both video and audio connections (although Katherine also keeps the Palo Alto commons in view with her PiP). Deep in thought, she barely notices the conversation going on outside her office, and she relishes the remaining moments of relative quiet before the others arrive.

As Ron is talking, you look around. Strewn about the space are lots of flexible, reconfigurable furniture and equipment (e.g., video cameras on rolling tripods, com-puters on mobile desks, video monitors of various sizes). You are facing the big TV; offices around three sides of the space are visible through their glass walls. Between you and the screen is a low table with a prominent microphone, a couple of UNIX and SmallTalk manuals, and a brightly colored child's xylophone. Just to the right of the TV is a video camera on a tripod pointed in your general direction. On top of the big TV is a much smaller one (a 13-inch color monitor) that displays what the camera is shooting. There are bookshelves and mailboxes nearby; there's also another work area with a big whiteboard.

Down the hall and out of sight, Doug wanders into his Portland office, switching on the lights and saying hello to Katherine. She's prominently visible in one quadrant of his media space monitor (the two common areas and Roger's office occupy the others). "Hey Kath, your clothes are different; you must've gotten home sometime this weekend?" He's not sure whether the reply was a grunt or a nod, but he gets the hint and goes about getting settled in and reading his e-mail.

Through an analog crossbar switch that linked cameras, monitors, and microphones in each office, the computer gave switched access to persons in each office (Stults, 1986). The switch was critical in providing highly modifiable connections; participants could flexibly configure the electronic space to align with their current activity. Signals from distant places could be displayed on any monitor; views of multiple locations could be assembled for private or public consumption with the various PiP hardware; audio need not be coming from the same places as were visible on a particular screen. The modification of electronic space had a physical aspect as well, because the placement and number of audio and video pickups and displays in each office were also frequently changed (shown in Fig. 13.3). Lab members could move fluidly from using the public video/audio connection in the commons to a more private use of media space in their individual offices. The media space could exist or not exist in a variety of places.

You and Ron are deep in conversation about shared databases when, out of the corner of your eye, you see movement in the previously empty commons on the TV. Two people walk in, glance your way and stop, looking out at you and Ron. Ron waves and laughingly says, "Hey, you're way early for the interview talk, but you might want to join us anyway; we're talking about shared databases as a basis for collaboration." After introductions are made, you reiterate a bit and all four of you continue the database conversation.

   Katherine, paragraph completed, gets around to more completely answering Doug, "Yeah, my weekend wasn't all that bad. I decided it'd be better to go hiking and come in early today than to try to work straight through. Give me a couple more minutes here, OK? I wanna wrap this section up before the candidate talk." "Sure, I think I saw Dan's backpack; I've gotta grab some coffee and talk to him about a hack we've been cooking up."

FIG. 13.3. An office equipped with multiple monitors and cameras; note the over-the-shoulder camera capturing work surface and user orientation.

The PARC Media Space linked a dozen offices in Palo Alto, connections to various devices (such as video recorders and videodisk players), locations in other laboratories, eight offices in Portland, several shared areas in both Portland and Palo Alto, and the cross-site connection. Computer servers were implemented to control the media space's crossbar switches and other devices; computer workstations could communicate with the servers to control the topology of the audio/video network. Audio and video were entirely separable in both in the hardware and in the software. Because the split lab was planned as an experiment in which the demands of the setting would drive the technological explorations, anyone wanting an office node was provided with one.

Still in the commons as your conversation with Ron continues (the other two having apologetically wandered off to get settled before your talk), you notice more people, one or two at a time, walking by with briefcases or backpacks in hand and heading for their offices. Some you see over the link; some you see walking by the sofa on which you are sitting. Whether they are right next to you or on the TV, each person glances at you and nods or smiles.

Then something really peculiar happens: a person (whom later you'll be introduced to as Doug) comes out of the kitchen carrying a cup of coffee and heads into a nearby empty office displaying the nameplate "Dan Tenfu." You hear a rather loud, "Dan, are you there?" Doug then stands for a minute gazing at a small TV, tuts, and quickly turns to leave. Walking out the door, he asks Ron, "Have you seen Dan come in yet? That looks like his pack next to the pillar down there." Glancing toward the big TV, Ron says, "Not yet."

A bit later, you walk around to meet others in the group. Passing by Doug's closed office door, you see him through the glass panel working away and seemingly talking aloud to himself.

As it nears the time for your technical talk, you return to the commons. In addition to setting up the overhead projector, Ron wheels the camera around so that the group in Palo Alto can see both you and the screen. Seeing yourself on the small TV you ask, "Can that be turned off?" "Sure, but it will help you know if Palo Alto can see you." "Oh."

At the appointed hour, Ron makes the requisite introduction and you launch into a description of your work. Still in his office, Doug notices the first overhead on his monitor and realizes that the time has come to attend this talk. He also remembers that Roger had expressed some interest in the presentation and that he has been known to rush to his office and completely ignore talks he'd meant to attend. Because Roger is not in yet, Doug switches the current source of Roger's audio and video from Doug's office camera to one in the commons area before heading off himself.

Even though you're nervous, the talk in the commons is rather intimate: There are only four people sprawled around the corner of the room and about six people in Palo Alto visible on the TV. As you talk, someone in Palo Alto interrupts with a request to zoom the camera and not to fidget with the slide so they can read it. Later, someone in Portland interrupts to point out that there is a question in Palo Alto. "As you know, we use SmallTalk here—how would you do that in SmallTalk?" You move to the whiteboard to sketch out a solution and Katherine, who is sitting near the camera, reaches over and repositions it to show what you are writing.

When the talk ends, you and Ron keep working over different ways to implement your system in SmallTalk. Another researcher walks by and joins the conversation, quickly adding a few insightful observations. You're introduced to Roger, who sheepishly admits that he watched your presentation from his nearby office while reading e-mail. He figured he'd seen the bulk of your work at last month's OOPSLA, but this porting issue looked intriguing enough to get him out of his office. When the conversation draws to an end, Ron says he'd like to make a videotape record of the idea. "We do this pretty routinely. We have a closet full of tapes of meetings, presentations, project notes, even some office parties." After Ron starts a recorder in a back room, he prompts you so that you quickly explain the idea, pointing out salient aspects on the whiteboard diagram.

You and Ron next move into his office for lunch and a private meeting with Carl, the lab manager from Palo Alto. Ron steps over to his computer and switches the video to a two-way direct connection to Carl's office. He also quickly dials Carl on his office speakerphone; this conversation will not be available in the general media space. Carl has his back to the camera but you can see his workstation over his shoulder. From the freewheel atop his monitor and the cycling calendar, you figure Carl to be an avid cyclist. You see yourself appear on a video monitor in his office, delayed by a couple of seconds from Ron's actual camera switch. "Nice talk," Carl says, picking up his phone and turning toward the camera, which he proceeds to wheel to somewhere that you suspect is near the TV monitor you'd seen adjacent to his workstation.

After chatting for a few minutes, Carl repositions the camera to point to his whiteboard and outlines the larger organization. Sketching, gesturing to parts of the diagram, and occasionally adjusting the camera, he and Ron take turns answering questions you have. When Ron points to the image of the org chart on the screen, he also says he is pointing at the screen, presumably so Carl knows what he is doing. When Carl dashes off to another meeting, Ron restores the connection to the commons view.

As you get up to leave Ron's office, you hear a xylophone playing up and down. Then a voice comes over the speakerphone in the commons: "Is Jason around?" There is a reply from a Portland office: "Sandy, I think he's just gotten here, wait a sec." Then a few moments later, "Jason, Sandy wants you," is called out from the same office. Jason comes running up to the commons camera saying, "Oh, Sandy, hello . . . I just got in." As you're heading down to Katherine's office, you hear Jason and Sandy launch into a fervent discussion of an upcoming conference talk and what they plan to do there.

Katherine still has Doug on her screen (he seems to be working away on his computer), but turns to talk with you. Instead of immediately talking with her, you stare at the monitor. Now you realize that you hadn't seen Doug talking to himself, but that he'd probably been talking with Katherine. What a relief! In fact he now says, "That was a great idea that you all were working on." Then, noting the confused look on your face, "I saw your chat with Roger and Ron out in the commons." "But aren't you looking at Katherine?" "Well, yes. I can see both Kath and the commons. I just switched my audio to the commons for your talk." Doug briefly switches Kath-

erine's monitor to show the 4-PiP display that he is watching. It's like everyone must have an open door on everyone else; you shake your head, wondering if you could really get used to this.

Katherine flips off her microphone, and as you talk, you see two people who stop to talk with Doug; the volume is low, but you can definitely notice the conversation. Although the activity in Doug's office is sometimes distracting, Katherine keeps focused on your work and your interests. She even finds a few unexpected intersections with her own work. When you head off to your next appointment, Katherine flips her microphone back on and pointedly asks Doug if he's gotten lots done on the paper.

Strolling back through the commons to the next interview, you glimpse the image on the big TV cycling through a couple of offices in Palo Alto and notice that the occupants are in. You also catch sight of Carl walking through the open area.

At the end of the day, you hear people walking out and saying goodnight to people as they pass by. Someone calls out your name and says "Goodnight" and you respond to the voice from the commons with a "Nice to meet you—hope to see you again soon." By now you've stopped paying attention to whether the person left through the door in Portland or the one in Palo Alto.

It is important to reiterate that the Palo Alto–Portland Media Space was constantly in use, functioning like an extension of physical space. It was not something that was turned "off" or "on" during the day but something that was continuously available. The media space supported a sense of playfulness, the casual acceptance of each other's presence, and for people in Palo Alto, a closer sense of familiarity with those in Portland than with many in the same building.

The motivating problem for the media space was to recreate the sense of embeddedness in a working group separated geographically. We tried a variety of devices (both social and technical) and we used those in a variety of ways, some anticipated and some unanticipated. We iterated frequently and quickly, always keeping the participants in control of the technology and of their work activity, and always allowing the technology and the work activity to evolve together. The PARC Media Space began not with a single technological goal, but with a diverse group of people exploring new ways of working and of working together.

MAKING A PLACE IN MEDIA SPACE

The experiences of a day in the PARC Media Space illustrate how audio and full-motion video together can extend the physical world to include people and events taking place elsewhere. The physical and technological attributes of a media space create a space that is as real as, but different from, the everyday office environment. This space is appropriated for use by different people for different activities, and through this appropriation it becomes a fluid and flexible number of places. In functional terms, spaces are resources and places are uses crafted of spaces, but this does not do justice to the experiential qualities that give this distinction its power.

A media space is simultaneously a surrogate for three things that are usually seamless in the physical world: people, events, and places. When the media space system is demonstrated to visitors, one is just as likely to point at the screen and say, "That's Carl," or "There's a meeting," or "That's the conference room." Not only are all of these equally sensible descriptions, they are also accurate reflections of ways of relating to the display. Users see images of people as individuals, things happening, and the people participating in interactions occurring over time as namable events, and a workplace of familiar objects—tables, chairs, and walls—juxtaposed in (often strange) relation to one another.

Space is the opportunity; place is the understood reality. Our use of space, our activities within a space, our naming a space can make it a place. One way that public spaces become places is by being appropriated by a person or group for some particular use. Users project their own uses and their own meanings onto a location, transforming it from space to something richer. Urban design critic Jill Stoner, describing a street in Montisi, Italy, sees it evolve from cabinetmaker's shop to meeting hall to auto body shop to laundry to porch over the course of a day (Stoner, 1990). In the transformation, each group of people that occupy the street makes this space its own. The street is not just neutral, but a space where physical relationships, spatial form, traditions, and values interact to support the range of activities and become appropriate for each.

In our earlier discussions of experiencing a media space, the focus was on the people and their activities. A space and place perspective provides a powerful formulation of issues and analysis beyond looking only at technology as a link between people. To understand how a media space is enabled by the spatial qualities of the electronic environment, we need to explain what we mean by *space* (further distinguishing it from *place*) and how telecommunications systems can be spatial.

What Is a (Media) Space?

The room you are probably in now is a space; so is the table or desk where you are sitting at in that room; and so is a footbridge over a stream. *Space is the differentiated environment in which we act and are acted on.* Thus, it is more than a Cartesian ideal of multiple contiguous dimensions; it is the world with boundaries (like walls and oceans) and properties (like gravity and color). In what ways can video-mediated connection be "spatial"?

First off, the space of media space is a kind of space unto itself. It is like the notion of "theatrical space"—when a play is performed, the conventions of theater take over: time and place are dictated (or, at least, strongly suggested) by the play. Media space, too, is a construction that brings disparate places and times together in a physical space. Miles and time zones are swallowed up by coax and electrons; the melting pot of phosphors becomes a site for new rituals.

Robert Stults, one of the initiators of the PARC Media Space, describes how audio and video can provide a new kind of space:

> McLuhan's observations and vision [of nonlinear electronic space] gave form to the experiences of my childhood. One day in 1953, in the second grade, our mothers rounded us up, and in a station wagon, drove us to New York, where we were shepherded through hallways, around corners, over cables, under bright lights, looking up at the puppeteers in dark glasses, and then, ". . . What time is it? . . . It's Howdy Doody time!"
>
> Fifteen years later, reading McLuhan, I saw that in my family's den watching Howdy Doody, I had been personally present in the peanut gallery, in a space created by the networks and the technology of television. Because I was young, because I hadn't yet learned to read, because I had once been in the peanut gallery in person, my experience was so involved that even now, despite my intellectual knowledge that I was only watching a show, I remember that I was there, in the peanut gallery, participating. In this way, Howdy Doody is a precursor to the media space. (Stults, 1986, p. 4)

As the virtual worlds of audio and video intersect and combine with the physical worlds, spatial concepts of the physical world become part of the new hybrid experience. Media spaces deliver the messenger *and the environment of the messenger* along with the message. From the outset, Carl isn't just the disembodied voice of the Palo Alto manager; he's a thinning blond with a pleasant manner and a penchant for bicycles. These enriched notions accrue into substantially improved relations.

The power of the spatial within these hybrids is not limited to our experiences reported here. For instance, it is evidenced by the pervasive emergence in the body of media space research of shared offices (Adler & Henderson, 1994; Bellotti & Dourish, chapter 12, this volume), even in cases where that capability was not intentionally supported (Fish, Kraut, Root, & Rice, 1993). These electronically shared offices often persist for days or months at a time, becoming a resource not only for those who initiate the connection, but also for others who find it a convenient way to reach their distant colleagues.

In addition, spatial phenomena are often used as explicit metaphors for interfaces and system architectures. For example, a number of interface schemes for VMC systems use a door metaphor to represent access control (Mantei et al., 1991). Extending the utility of spatial metaphors from the user interfaces to entire system paradigms, social virtual realities (or MUDs) use a room metaphor for collaboration activity (Curtis, Dixon, Frederick, & Nichols, 1995). However, spatial ideas are often misunderstood by technology innovators, in part because our names for places are often confused with names of people. Thus, we often think that *Brian's house* or *Brian's phone* designates the same thing that *Brian's eyes* does. *Brian's house* may gloss *the place where Brian lives,* whereas *Brian's eyes* refers to part of Brian. This lack of distinction between person and image becomes problematic when we make the simplifying assumption that they are the same and build systems accordingly. Seeing someone's office on a video monitor is not the same as walking into that person's office through an open door; we can't expect the same behaviors and activities as a result.

But what does "space" provide as a framework for understanding? Why does it matter? Like the water that the unaware fish swims through, the space of human activity matters. Human experience is tied to it and organized by it; human relations are established in it; it shapes the activity; it shapes the communication carried out within it; and it therefore shapes the very thoughts of the people within it. It is exactly this opportunity for experience, for establishing relationships, for shaping activity and communication that underlies a media space.

What Is a Place?

What does it take to make a space into a place? Places are often socially constructed. A particular tree in a forest may be a significant place to someone who visits it regularly; the same tree may be nothing more than background to a city dweller walking in the woods. Places impart identity and aid with orientation. To be someplace in particular is meaningful: A corner office is both a location and a suggestion of some status for the occupant. Patterns of space that are memorable are "places." Memorable qualities can be scenographic (Yosemite Valley), personally meaningful (my chair), or the result of social convention (the entry to a house).

One way to think of place is the way that architects and historians do:

> But architecture is more than protective shells. In seeking to bring about place for ritual action, it must set out to define the boundless, that is, to limit space without necessarily enclosing it in all three dimensions. It does this in two specific ways: through circumscription and accent. In the first, it arrests and patterns the flow of ground. This we might call architecture as boundary. The second way involves the setting up of free structures that focus an otherwise undifferentiated stretch of open space. (Kostof, 1985, p. 21)

Additionally, place derives from a tension between connectedness and distinction. Place-making is as often the result of subtle actions—the arrangement of personal items on a desk, for example—as it is of large ones like constructing buildings. Take the example of the space of a table. The table top defines the physical limits of access: It blocks the path of people walking; it has a surface on which it is convenient to place things; and it defines some additional space for chairs and people seated around it. A table becomes a place through the differentiation of the space that results from its use. For example, a conversation across the table makes it a place. The free-standing object "table" disappears into the "place" of the conversation. As we saw with Katherine and Doug, the cameras and monitors disappeared into the place of their paper-writing project.

Within the confines of telecommunications systems, the idea of place provides identity, orientation, and a mode of control. Within a media space, actual media places are created, sometimes existing just within the electronic world, sometimes as hybrids of the surrounding physical environment and the electronic realm. Just as space provides the underlying opportunity for a media space, place-making provides the realities of a media space.

The Consequences of Place in Media Space

Thinking back to the examples of a typical day, the anecdotes illustrate the ways in which the media space is, in fact, a shared space. First, electronic places existed as adjuncts to the physical places that gave them name. Second, the patterns of the surrounding physical environment were continuous across the electronic link in both directions and were present in the virtual acoustic and virtual visual spaces as well. The extended rooms were not "out of place" with the office environments they were in. And they were distinct in two ways: They were still the specific spaces, and they were hybrids of physical and virtual spaces.

The activity of using a media space is not a primary activity itself, but one enabling other activities; unlike *phone* or *teleconference, media space* has not become a verb. Media spaces evolve through use as part of everyday activity rather than through a priori hardware and software design. Key to this is human mediation and appropriation.

Varieties of Uses. Remembering again the scenario of a typical day in the PARC Media Space, there are various uses for the connection: maintaining an awareness of others and their activities, chance encounters, locating colleagues, videotelephones, group discussions, recording and replaying video records, envisionment, presentations, and social activities. Media spaces are open-ended, malleable, and accessible in ways that can be appropriated for these varied uses. When some new activity arises, people can appropriate the system for that too.

"Appropriability" is a particular feature of the connections made in the PARC Media Space, which can be at one minute a public hallway, then a conference room, a project room, the outside world, a lobby, and a private office. It was not designed as the multipurpose solution to be these things or to afford some functions that accommodate these activities; it was appropriated to become these places. The system design reinforces this fluid appropriation: the system is always on, cameras and monitors can be freely repositioned and refocused, the state of everyone's connections is visible to all, and anyone can switch another's connection to show something (Bly et al., 1993; Harrison & Minneman, 1992; Irwin, 1991; Stults, 1989). One of the most common appropriations was of public common areas and the electronic link between them for casual conversations; one of these is illustrated in Figs. 13.4, 13.5, and 13.6.

Most people immediately think of head-and-shoulder shots when they think of VMC. Just as a visual encounter in physical settings is rarely just face-to-face, a media space is marked by the ability to see or be shown things from various vantage points: over-the-shoulder, out-the-window, down-the-

FIG. 13.4. Interaction in public area, 1: A discussion in Portland is noticed by someone (visible in the inset) strolling through the open space in Palo Alto.

FIG. 13.5. Interaction in public area, 2: Person in Palo Alto sits down to observe conversation and is noticed by one person in Portland.

hall, work-surface, head-mounted, swivel-chair-cam, in-the-audience, and yes, head-and-shoulders. There can be multiple images coming from the same or disparate locations, multiplexed together or displayed on separate monitors. There is no requirement that there be spatial isomorphism. Although at times confusing, visual and auditory discontinuity is a powerful part of the spatial repertoire. However, the confusion usually arises when attempting to *explain* a media space configuration or when trying to *orient* to a foreign one, not from *being* in a topologically complex configuration.

As an example, one media space project implemented a video work surface as though both participants were sitting in the same seat, but augmented it with a separate head-and-shoulders camera and monitor pair. Although your collaborator's hand appeared to be coming from a phantom sitting in your chair, the image of your collaborator's head and shoulders was sitting opposite you; if the collaborator reached forward, the head came toward you and the hand appeared to move out from your belly. Users never expressed any difficulty with this arrangement and in careful studies of its use, it was found that the two channels reinforced one another (Tang & Minneman, 1990)—see Fig. 13.7.

FIG. 13.6. Interaction in public area, 3: Cross-site orientation of conversation initiates new conversational place that includes both open areas and the technology that links them.

The Social Construction of Place.   Much more so than many other spaces (e.g., a private office), media spaces are jointly constructed. Joint construction means that there is interlocking activity; no single person or group decides on the arrangement or use of cameras, monitors, and connections. As we just saw, in the commons areas both the cameras and microphones were typically on, but the camera was regularly moved (or not) as the focus of attention changed and the participants in the area shifted position. Conversation is also jointly produced, with ongoing tests of understanding, signals of agreement, continuations of phrases and sentences from one speaker to another. Media space relies on this natural human tendency toward joint production.

Users of the system rely on human mediation to control access, to explain system state, to orient each other, and to adjust camera position to current activities. The computer interfaces that controlled switching includes no access or connection restrictions, so users establish their availability across the medium by directly controlling the technology, making requests of their remote colleagues, or switching others' displays. There is

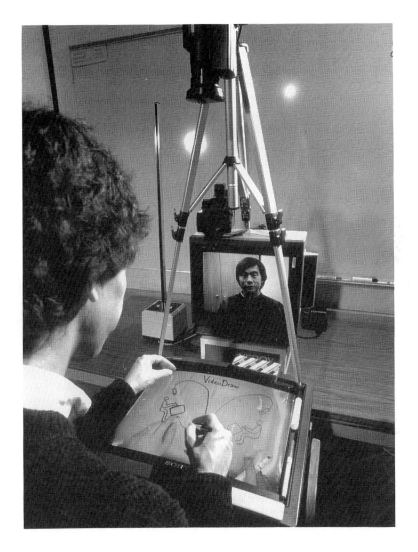

FIG. 13.7. Shared drawing. The work surface maintains the same orientation for all users, as though sitting in the same seat. It is augmented with a separate head-and-shoulders camera and monitor pair. Collaborator's hands appear to be coming from a phantom sitting in your chair; if the collaborator reached forward, the head came toward you and the hand appeared to move out from your belly. Users never expressed any difficulty with this arrangement, and in careful studies of its use, it was found that the two channels reinforced one another.

not automatic notification when someone was watching (although such a facility is available), so the observed person is not responsible for responding in "polite" ways. Similarly, observers take responsibility for changing their display if they're bothered by the image or audio. Individuals, not the technological system, evolve and maintain their own boundaries of personal and private space in much the same way that they negotiate activity within projects. In fact, explaining who is off camera is part-and-parcel of explaining an idea in a project discussion.

Furthermore, people jointly construct bridges between their activities. People are natural-born intermediaries—it's a social thing we all do. Humans can provide directions about improving connection, reflective commentary about the content, directions about focus, and management of conversational participation. This joint construction was evident in a number of the places in the PARC Media Space scenario. Here are just a few: Katherine repositioned the camera during the presentation, Ron told Carl where he was pointing since the camera remained on the visitor, and people verbally relayed the message, "Jason, Sandy wants you."

Places result from this joint construction. Returning to the comparison with theatrical space, the event is where the space becomes a place. In the example where PARC researchers strike up a conversation in the two common areas, a place is formed from the cameras, monitors, people, and furniture. People orient to the cameras and monitors so as to be included and including of others. They mutually allow the place of conversation to happen.

Human mediation is bound up in the sense of connectedness of a media space in two ways: First, human mediation smoothes the rough edges of the technology and makes it appear more seamless; second, it is a measure of how well it fits with the pattern of space that human mediation is continuous between copresent and transmitted settings.

This fit with the existing pattern of physical space is illustrated by the example of Doug going to Dan's Portland-connected-to-Palo-Alto office to find Dan. In this case, Dan kept an open audio (and, whenever possible, video) line between his office and the one he was visiting in Palo Alto. People would frequently walk into his office and ask, "Dan, are you there?" before they could see his image on a video monitor or themselves be seen by the camera. In other words, they acted as though he were available in the same space, or as if the place, Dan's office, were a combination of the two locations and the technology that connected them.

There can also be shared hybrid space at a smaller scale than whole rooms linked together. In another media space study, two engineers worked remotely from one another using a media space set up between PARC and an existing office a few miles away (Harrison & Minneman, 1992). Each engineer referred to the space on the table between himself and the monitor as the place where he worked. Working together to design a mechanism, they would show parts to one another. They simultaneously reviewed the parts, guiding each other through the salient details and directing repositioning of the others' cameras. They would sit in relation to one another as they would in physical space, but they were not able to use this new arrangement as they would a real table. Although it wasn't a table in physical space, it was more than a window into a space.

The linked tables provided a place to meet "across" that resulted in different experiences for the engineers. Gestures and objects in each engineer's space never crossed into the other, only their images. They showed up in different relation because the placement of cameras and monitors is a compromise between the separate physicality of the apparatus and the convenience and preferences of each designer. Although the physical relationship of people was similar, the space was different for each person and at times invisible to the other. Nonetheless, each engineer working through video apparatus had a place that was well defined, clearly owned and named—the engineer himself on one side and monitor on the other.

There was an ambiguous relation between the image on the monitor, the objects under discussion, and the continuity of the electronically created office. It was two places at once, one that created a single environment by linking two separate physical environments and one that contained the image of the other. This is illustrated in the sequence of Fig. 13.8 to 13.14.

Presentation and Presence. Users of media space not only construct the places out of media space, they also construct their presence to others using the technology. People are on camera a lot in a media space; as a result, conventions arise for being visible. This is often reflected in forms of human mediation—when it is acceptable to move a camera or to ask to have a camera moved. It has been our experience that people become comfortable with this joint responsibility for presentation. Furthermore, people become comfortable with displaying a particular point of view.

Interaction Sequence

FIG. 13.8. Interaction in office, 1: Engineer, taking a phone call outside of media space. Note that the chair in the monitor is vacant.

FIG. 13.9. Interaction in office, 2: Arriving at a remote office, another engineer sees and hears the engineer (sitting across the table, to the right of this photo) talking on the phone. He waits for him to complete his call.

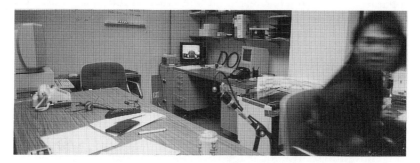

FIG. 13.10. Interaction in office, 3: Seeing the visitor in the small monitor on his desk, the engineer turns toward the large monitor and less directly toward the camera and speakerphone.

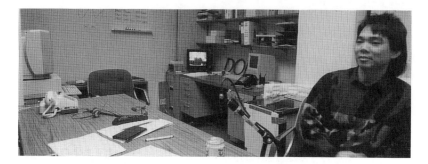

FIG. 13.11. Interaction in office, 4: The conversation begins.

FIG. 13.12. Interaction in office, 5: As the conversation proceeds, the visitor substitutes the handset for the speakerphone so as not to intrude on the other occupants of the remote office. The designer carries out the discussion with the visitor as though in his office. Note the outgoing image shown on the small monitor is framed to show mostly the designer's head and shoulders and very little of the work surfaces. Although the physical relationship of people to the equipment and furniture is similar, the space is different for each person and at times invisible to the other.

FIG. 13.13. Interaction in office, 6: Showing the visitor some of his sketches, the designer positions a sheet of paper under the small camera and he looks for visual signals of recognition and acknowledgment from his visitor. The session will soon conclude with the visitor saying good-bye and standing up, and the designer turning his back to the camera, returning to the work on his desk.

It is not so much that a media space offers an alternative to face-to-face interactions but that it offers an alternative to not being together. In this way it communicates the presence of others—not just random others, but close members of a group. Although facial expressions, gestures, side conversations, and intonation are important aspects of working dialogue, the ability to see and be seen, to speak to one another or to pass by are the more frequent activities of the media space environment. Such activities are the basis of the community life.

Presence works because the audio and video represent living, breathing people who are familiar to one another. These people have a shared

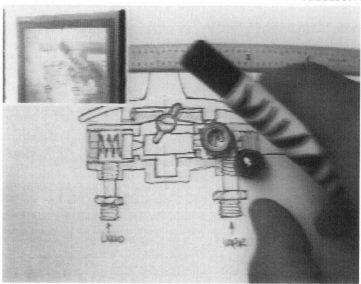

FIG. 13.14. Using the desktop camera, one engineer shows drawings and parts to the other. The space is now more asymmetric and discontinuous: The desktop (horizontal, close-in, malleable, and manipulable) becomes the screen image of the other (vertical, more distant from the user, larger scale, and unmanipulable), and the remote end shows the monitor as means for pointing, gesturing, and animating over it.

engagement with issues that matter on an ongoing basis. These people have the deep reciprocity of people who share a space together. It is here that being present outweighs, in fact dissolves, privacy.

The Social Construction of Privacy. The PARC Media Space derived in large part from architectural studios where everyone sits in the same room together; utility and companionship took precedence over a desire for complete and continuous privacy. At any time anybody could be with anybody or everybody else. The system locking mechanisms were rarely employed to create secured communications—people trusted one another enough. People would turn off their microphones to create acoustic privacy and they would signal that they were very busy by pointing their cameras at closed doors or out the window. Even in those cases, they were still present because the action was visible to all; such actions signaled their desire not to be interrupted.

Privacy has been a major concern of critics of media space and designers of related projects (Bellotti & Sellen, 1993; Dourish, 1993). However, in general, the debate has not been conducted with a rich view of the meaning of privacy. Technologies (such as walls, doors, or permission lists) are not the only way to create privacy, nor are such measures enough by themselves. Social convention gives meaning to the act of visual separation. A place-centric view emphasizes important distinctions: Privacy is not the same as private events nor is it a direct consequence of private places, and in contrast, being seen or even heard is not absolutely and inevitably public.

There are many dimensions to the notion of "privacy"—convenience, turf, control of embarrassment, and control of information. Privacy is relative, not a set of psychological primitives. For example, the discussion with the two managers, Ron and Carl, was conducted with the video being generally available for any lab member to look in on, although the audio was transmitted more privately using speakerphones. The public resource of the video link had been appropriated for this private conversation; it would have been possible for lab members to have observed the conversation—and even made some sense of it—but this was observably a private conversation.

Public Space, Civic Life. Just as "privacy" tends to be oversimplified, so does "public." Experiments in the public and semipublic use of media spaces (Borning & Travers, 1991; Root, 1988) have tended to focus on the *creation* of casual encounter, defining public as that which is explicitly available. There are, however, many kinds of public spaces. *Public* does not mean the absence of *privacy*, like privacy, it is another social construct that is expressed and experienced largely through spatial phenomena. In this way there are shadings and interrelations between the two: there are various kinds of semipublic places (e.g., parties) where it is okay to join into a private discussion. In our example, we see how Roger looks in on activity in the commons from his office without announcing his presence. He does this because he understands the limits of acceptable behavior within the group. In the later conversation, Roger acknowledges his apparent absence to the visitor who is not part of the community and could not be fully aware of nor could have agreed to the norms of that community.

Public space that reinforces (and depends on) the workings of a community can be described by analogy with civic places—the town square or street corner where the political life of the city has traditionally been carried out. The value of public space is that it is a platform for public activity and, most importantly, public discourse. Public places are made by and a requisite ingredient of communities (Mumford, 1938; Jacobs, 1961; Whyte, 1988; Entrikin, 1990). Meaningful chance encounter occurs in real public space as part of this fabric. The issue for understanding the notion of "public" in electronic media is not how to recreate a counterpart of the kinds of things found in a street (or in a hallway, for that matter), but for the public facility to be public—and for those to be constructed of places with shared, stable meaning and activities. The discourse that sustains a community carries with it the facility to talk about itself; it is these qualities of public space that make them "appropriable."

WHAT MAKES A MEDIA SPACE?

As we indicated in our discussion of the importance of space, a media space is constructed in special circumstances. To make video connection into useful places for people to work requires that it fits the group's ways of being and working; that is, it provides the kind of accessibility that supports the subtle social phenomena enabling the work of a group to proceed. Remembering back to the discussion of space and the joint construction of place, the properties of media space make demands on groups employing them and have consequences for the design of media space systems. Consideration must be given to the role of people in the operation of the system; the separation of social relations and system constraints; the availability of the system for appropriation; trust; privacy; and the availability of group members.

These characteristics, which have evolved with and been crucial to our long-term use of media spaces, are also present in other media spaces and even other electronic environments that may not be considered media spaces by their designers and users.

Human Mediation

In order for media spaces to be flexible and appropriable, they should both support and rely on human mediation wherever possible. This applies first to the control interface. Just as we are all pretty good at assessing situations and negotiating with whom we want to talk in physical space, a media space can use social negotiation to handle connection management. This design choice does not represent implementation laziness, but rather the realization that anything less will become unduly restrictive to a closely knit working community.

Furthermore, the system must be malleable along the lines of the collaborative activity in which the members of the community are engaged. This ranges from chance encounter in situations that make sense (versus systems which create artificial encounters) to being able to talk about, look at, point to, and show others the artifacts of work. The users must be comfortable with adjusting the communications system as part of their daily work.

Social Relations and System Structure

To maximize reliance on human mediation and allow for changing circumstances, do not build a model of social relations into the system. Instead, provide a framework to create places that work in the context of the activity. Models of social relations will inevitably become wrong and constraining. As we tried to illustrate by comparison with a city street, the notion of a proscribed place for chance encounter seems odd and contrived.

Consequently, *control* means different things depending on the kinds of accessibility present in a group. A media space for two people has almost no user interface; for 10–20 people, everyone can have a little window that leads to a bigger screen. It is hard to imagine an interface for a 1,000-person media space, as it is very difficult to imagine 1,000 people having close working relations with one another. This is not to say that a *network* of media spaces could not serve 1,000 people or more. However, it is a major design challenge to create a system that allows for subgroups with widely differing needs and norms to form and re-form and to socially negotiate access control among the subgroups.

Appropriation

The technology must create spaces that provide for places that align with the activity of the users and that are available for appropriation to that activity. Equipment must be flexible: movable, added to or taken from the network, available in a range of sizes and configurations. For example, cameras and microphones may be used over a shoulder or on the desktop or in a meeting room. Some situations might need many cameras and microphones, and another only a few. There is no predetermined set of media space equipment for all groups or all activities within a group. One size does not fit all.

The activity will necessarily change over the course of a day or a project or the life of an organization. Thus the primary requirement is that the technology be always on, always there, and maximally flexible. This is in stark contrast to systems that work like telephones or that have a notion of disconnecting.

Trust, Privacy, and Availability of Group Members

Clearly, media spaces are not for everyone; they are not for every kind of collaborative endeavor. First and foremost, there must be trusting working relations within the group; there needs to be trust among the project members and trust should be integral to the continuance of the project. A media space will succeed to the degree that it matches the trust and the expectations for trust that group has about itself.

Media spaces are particularly good sustainers of relations. We often found that people who first worked with others solely through our various media spaces often would spend time getting "reacquainted" when meeting face-to-face for the first time. If a group has poor relations already, the concern over exposure that might accrue from a media space will tend to make those relations much worse.

Privacy has a multitude of interpretations, uses, and possible implementations. Addressing privacy issues among members of a group solely with technological safeguards can compromise flexibility and place-making. This is not to deny that people sometimes need to work undisturbed or that some conversations should not be interrupted or overheard. Those needs, though, should be communicated among people, not blindly enforced.

CONCLUSIONS

We have seen how, within the confines of telecommunications systems, the idea of place provides identity, orientation, activity venue, and a mode of control—and how, in the realm of the users' experience, it affords an extension of space with many of the attendant properties of the physical world. The major technological implication of the people, events, and places framework is that there is no one way to view the technology of communication. Emphasizing any one view undermines the others; encoding one as a metaphor or analogy will dislocate the other interpretations. Although people and events are useful, places are where work gets done. It is not enough to create a representation of the phenomena of placeness; systems must provide the opportunity for multiple parallel experiences.

Although the media space primarily delivers sights and sounds from one location to another, this approach suggests new questions about the equipment doing the delivery. Are cameras and monitors just objects in a room? If they are objects, are they also spaces? Is the monitor with a moving image on it another person, and if it is, why is that person sitting on a desk jumbled up with lots of mail and documents? Is the monitor a window, and if it is, why is it on a desk instead of in the wall? And, of course, the approach raises many research possibilities about the relation of people and places to the range of events that need to be supported.

Finally a note of caution: Like the street, a media space is many "places" at once, not because the technology is designed to be these things, but because the users live it that way. In that sense, these are not communications systems but rather systems for the maintenance and manipulation of social worlds. This raises a very troubling question about our ability as researchers to perform the requisite decontextualization central to most forms of technological systems analysis. Where do the properties that we ascribe to the technology really come from? Just as the residents' experiences are not tied just to the street in Montisi but to the wider world of the town and their individual lives, our media space is tied to our lives and our experiences.

ACKNOWLEDGMENTS

We acknowledge the immense support that our reviewers, Victoria Bellotti, Bill Gaver, and John Tang, gave us in shaping this chapter. Without their input this would have been a great jumble of anecdotes, deeply felt opinions, and smatterings of reason. We would also like to thank our many colleagues over the years who have built and lived the PARC Media Space, and the Xerox Corporation for funding this project.

REFERENCES

Adler, A., & Henderson, A. (1994). A room of our own: Experiences from a direct office-share. *Proceedings of the ACM Conference on Human Factors in Computing Systems CHI'94* (pp. 138–144). Reading, MA: Addison-Wesley.

Bellotti, V. M. E., & Sellen, A. J. (1993, September). Design for privacy in ubiquitous computing environments. *Proceedings of the European Conference on Computer Supported Cooperative Work (ECSCW)*. Milan, Italy.

Bly, S., Harrison, S., & Irwin, S. (1993). Media Spaces: Bringing people together in a video, audio, and computing environment. *Communications of the Association of Computing Machinery, 36*(1), January. (pp. 28–47).

Borning, A., & Travers, M. (1991). Two approaches to casual interaction over computer and video networks. *Proceedings of the CHI'91 Conference on Human Factors in Computing Systems* (pp. 13–19). Reading, MA: Addison-Wesley.

Curtis, P., Dixon, M., Frederick, R., & Nichols, D. (1995). The Jupiter audio/video architecture: Secure multimedia in network places. *Proceedings of the Third ACM International Multimedia Conference and Exhibition* (pp. 79–90). Reading, MA: Addison-Wesley.

Dourish, P. (1993, September). Culture and control in a media space. *Proceedings of the European Conference on Computer Supported Cooperative Work (ECSCW)*. Milan, Italy.

Entrikin, J. (1990). *The Betweeness of Place: Towards a Geography of Modernity*. Baltimore, MD: Johns Hopkins University Press.

Fish, R., Kraut, R., Root, R., & Rice, R. (1993). Video as a technology for informal communication. *Communications of the Association of Computing Machinery, 36*(1), January. (pp. 48–61).

Harrison, S., & Minneman, S. (1992). The Media Space: A research project into the use of video as a design medium. *Proceedings of the Fourth National Symposium on Concurrent Engineering* (pp. 91–106). Rockford, IL: Society for Computer-Aided Engineering.

Irwin, S. (1991). *Technology, talk, and the social world: A study of video-mediated interaction*. PhD dissertation, Michigan State University.

Jacobs, J. (1961). *The death and life of great American cities*. New York: Vintage Books/Alfred A. Knopf.

Kostof, S. (1985). *A history of architecture: Settings and rituals* (p. 21). New York: Oxford University Press.

Mantei, M., Baecker, R., Sellen, A., Buxton, W., Milligan, T., Wellman, B. (1991). Experiences in the use of a media space. *Proceedings of the CHI'91 Conference on Human Factors in Computing Systems* (pp. 203–208). Reading, MA: Addison-Wesley.

Mumford, L. (1938). *The culture of cities*. New York: Harcourt Brace.

Root, R. (1988). Design of a multimedia vehicle for social browsing. *Proceedings of the Conference on Computer Support for Cooperative Work* (pp. 25–38). Reading, MA: Addison-Wesley.

Stoner, J. (1991). The House of Montisi. *Places, 7*(2), 19–22.

Stults, R. (1986). *The media space* (p. 4). Palo Alto, CA: Xerox Corporation.

Stults, R. (1989). *Experimental uses of video to support design activities* (Rep. No. SSL-89-19). Palo Alto, CA: Xerox Corporation.

Tang, J., & Minneman, S. (1990). VideoDraw: A video interface for collaborative drawing." *Proceedings of the Conference on Computer Human Interaction (CHI)'90* (pp. 313–319). Reading, MA: Addison-Wesley.

Whyte, W. (1988). *The city, Rediscovering the center.* New York: Doubleday.

Chapter 14

Sharing Faces, Places, and Spaces: The Ontario Telepresence Project Field Studies

Gale Moore
Ontario Telepresence Project

The Ontario Telepresence Project (OTP) was a 3-year cross-disciplinary project that focused on understanding how the work activities of groups, especially groups separated by distance, could be supported by organizationally grounded media space design. In addition to designing and developing a prototype media space to support our own distributed workgroup, we deployed the prototype into workplaces outside the laboratory. The objective was to work with users in real-world organizations to refine the initial design through an iterative process and to study the impact of this video-mediated communication (VMC) system on work practices and organizational activities. In this chapter I discuss the findings from a number of field studies and note specifically some of the challenges encountered in grounding the research in the real world. The findings demonstrate the ways in which a variety of contexts—including the work practices of individuals and groups and broader organizational factors such as culture—condition use and adoption. A number of the findings have direct implications for designing video-mediated communication systems.

I arrive at my Toronto office, unlock the door, and hear a cheery greeting. There's Gerald, in Ottawa, on the television monitor on my desk (I've left my "electronic door" open), who wants me to attend a meeting in Waterloo later in the day. I comment on the fact that he's wearing a suit and he tells me about a businessman he's off to see. I notice in Postcards[1] that he's out of the office most of the day, but arrives in time for our Waterloo meeting. A few clicks of my mouse and the three of us are together. The meeting over, I prepare to leave for the day. It was cloudy earlier so I glance out of my video window—it's raining. I grab my umbrella as I head out.

301

INTRODUCTION

The Ontario Telepresence Project (OTP)[2] was a 3-year cross-disciplinary project that focused on understanding how the work activities of groups, especially groups separated by distance, could be supported by organizationally grounded media space design.[3] In addition to designing and developing a prototype media space to support our own distributed workgroup, our goal was to move the prototype into workplaces outside the laboratory. The objective was to work with users in real-world organizations to refine the initial design through an iterative process and to study the impact of this VMC system on work practices and organizational activities. In addition, the move from the laboratory drew us into questions about deployment, and we used this as an opportunity to develop a model for deploying technology that takes the multiple contexts of the user and the organization seriously. This move from the laboratory to the workplace distinguished OTP from other media space research.

The chapter starts with some background on the project and moves on to a discussion of several field studies in which we either deployed Telepresence Media Space (TMS)[4] in the field, studied commercial videoconferencing systems in use in organizations, or both. The move from the lab to the field was complex, and throughout this chapter I highlight the challenges we faced in adopting this approach. Finally, having lived in a media space for over 2 years, we knew what to do when we were offered an ATM (asynchronous transfer mode) service for several months. The chapter concludes with the ATM studies.

Our experiences and results show the extent to which social factors shape the use or nonuse of technology in organizations. We paid careful attention to the work practices of individuals and groups, and worked closely with the users in a number of cases. We also attended to the broader organizational context in an attempt to understand how such things as organizational culture and policies condition interaction. Situating interactions within the organizational context extends the analysis. Computer-mediated communication systems that support cooperative work have people in at least two places, and we found in the case of VMC that there was a need to support the negotiation of multiple user contexts to improve effective use of the system. Finally, we found evidence to support our contention that the way in which technology is introduced and innovation managed in an organization is bound up with adoption outcomes.

BACKGROUND

The Ontario Telepresence Project (OTP) built on the work of the CAVECAT (Computer Audio Video Enhanced Collaboration And Telepresence) Project, one of the early experiments in the design and use of media space. The

CAVECAT system consisted of four nodes (each equipped with a personal computer, camera, TV monitor, speaker, and microphone, and connected by an audiovideo digitally switched network) located in offices and labs. OTP took advantage of the research findings of CAVECAT, particularly in the areas of cognitive psychology and human–computer interaction (Mantei, Baecker, Sellen, Wellman, & Buxton, 1991; Sellen, 1992, 1995). A social network analysis of CAVECAT users was also carried out (Haythornthwaite, Wellman, & Mantei, 1995). The psychological experiments on VMC begun in CAVECAT continued in OTP, but as they were independent of the field studies and have been previously published they are not discussed in this chapter.[5]

By intent, the OTP research team was cross-disciplinary—including sociologists, psychologists, engineers, and computer scientists—and cross-institutional—primarily the University of Toronto and Carleton University in Ottawa.[6] The project directly employed 14 people, but over its 3-year history involved over 30 people in its various activities. A core of the Toronto group had worked together during the CAVECAT Project, but the Ottawa members had neither worked with each other nor with members of the Toronto team previously. The experience of working in a media space that spanned hundreds of kilometers would be new to everyone. The immediate challenge was to install a second media space in Ottawa and to provide codecs at each end to permit interconnectivity between the sites. With this basic infrastructure in place the team could begin to work together, and to think about how the services and applications might be improved and extended.

Although the emphasis in OTP was on moving from the laboratory to the workplace, we continued to develop and evaluate new applications internally. Much was gained by giving the first versions of new applications to team members familiar with the system and tolerant both of continuous change and of software that was not sufficiently robust for the field sites. Furthermore, not all the social scientists—whose work practices and concerns differed from the technical staff—had previous experience with a media space, so there was a set of "naive" users in-house to inform the design. We were trying not only to support our work practices, but to design an environment that was flexible enough to let us and other real-world users "discover" new ways of working together. Living in a media space ourselves was an important part of the plan.

The research program was organized around three interlocking themes; social science and field studies, applications and user interface, and engineering. Each thematic group had members from both Toronto and Ottawa, and as travel between the sites was limited, the team quickly learned where some of the problems in VMC lay! We appreciate the irony in the fact that this process of team building was counter to our belief that video is best suited to supporting, not creating, teams, but we viewed it as a stronger test of our ability to deliver "telepresence"—a sense of shared presence or shared space among geographically distributed team members (Buxton, 1992).

A DESCRIPTION OF THE TMS ENVIRONMENT

What did the OTP media space "look" like, and how did it differ from desktop and conference room videoconferencing systems? The vignette with which I began this chapter is one attempt to capture the flavor of the OTP media space. One way in which media spaces can be distinguished from desktop and conference room videoconferencing systems lies in their central concern with "space" and the goal of creating an *environment* to support communication and collaboration, as opposed to designing a new tool or appliance. For example, the OTP media space—eventually called Telepresence Media Space (TMS)—provided us with the opportunity to meet and work with one or more colleagues in Ottawa and/or Toronto from a variety of locations (offices, conference rooms, and labs) and to attend meetings in any of these locations from our desks or offices. The conference room had a small monitor strategically placed at the back of the room so that it was possible to attend meetings from an office, and signal a desire for less than full participation. If at some point the person at the back of the room wished to participate more fully in the meeting, that person could "move" to the larger monitor and take a place at the table. In this way, through the use of video surrogates, virtual colleagues could move about the space and manage their social interactions in ways that respected well-understood social protocols. Buxton (chapter 17, this volume) illustrates a number of ways in which activities were supported (a concept Buxton calls *ubiquitous media*) and discusses why it is inappropriate to channel all communication through a single multipurpose device such as a workstation.

We did not conduct *formal* research on our own adoption process or use, but it was out of the experience of living in a media space that our ideas evolved. The insights we gained in everyday practice sensitized us to issues that might emerge in the field.

We learned that some activities were well supported by video—the weekly seminar series between the two sites was quite successful—whereas others were not. The Halloween party was dismal. The general activity and noise at both ends made it virtually impossible to hear anyone at the other end—never mind attend to their conversation or even to their costumes! The "live" window view that was the default view of TMS at each location was highly valued, particularly by those in windowless offices. From Toronto we could check on the weather conditions in Ottawa or note that a colleague's car was in the parking lot. For those in the same location, the window was a source of shared experiences—we all saw the fire engines arrive on campus, we all saw the window washer and the hooded man sandblasting the window sill where the camera was located. This became part of office lore.

We also found that distance, bandwidth, and speed of making a connection all made a difference in terms of use.[7] Contrary to the findings of Tang and Isaacs (1995) that collaborators as close as a few tens of feet did not use the system, there was frequent use of the system locally when colleagues were physically colocated in the same corridor. One possibility is that the reasons for use change as the distance changes. For example, even when colleagues were next door, it was useful to check if they were free, had visitors, or looked engrossed in a problem, before contacting them or stopping by. Somewhat later, when a new interface and improvements in the software meant that the overhead involved in making a local connection decreased—the choice of TMS versus the telephone or e-mail became a "real" choice—and use further increased. There still appeared to be little use of the system for informal communication between Ottawa and Toronto—due to issues of both bandwidth and speed of connection. However, when the ATM connection was in place between the two cities, both the speed at which connections could be made and the quality of the video improved dramatically. For several members of the team, myself included, the intercity use increased dramatically, only in part because we were developing the ATM studies. We began to "drop in" on each other frequently, and "hang out" in each other's offices for extended periods.

When the project ended there were approximately 50 nodes in a variety of offices, conference rooms, and labs, distributed over four physical locations in three cities.

WORKING IN "REAL-WORLD" SETTINGS

A major goal of the OTP, as noted in the introduction, was to work with users in "real-world" settings to refine the media space prototype. As we were to discover, there are a number of unique challenges and practicalities encountered when moving beyond the lab and the research team, in particular to sites outside the organization. Before discussing the field studies I want to highlight two issues with which we had to contend throughout—access, and ethics and privacy—and briefly describe our experiences.

Access

The difficult and time-consuming task of gaining access to an organization for any type of field study is well known. However, interest in the Ontario

Telepresence Project was high and we began negotiations for access with representatives from a number of organizations, but our success in securing sites was limited.[8] The usual difficulties were compounded by the fact that the financial investment for the prospective client was high (in the range of $100,000–$250,000), and that our small team could not deliver the level of technical support offered by commercial vendors of traditional videoconferencing systems. Necessity led us to develop a parallel strategy, namely, to look for opportunities to study the use of commercial videoconferencing systems—both conference room and desktop systems—already in organizations or being introduced. Access under these conditions was far easier to negotiate and we could leverage these studies to support the design of TMS. We had already identified two typical models of technological innovation: the Field of Dreams Model—"if you build it they will come" and the Velcro Model—"toss in the technology and see where it sticks" (Moore, 1994, p. 15). By working with organizations with real-world problems and experiences, much could be learned. We broadened our goals to include the development of a methodology to introduce TMS in the field (Moore, 1993). Methodologies, after all, are technologies too. The way in which TMS would be introduced into an organization we felt would condition subsequent stages and had implications both for adoption and use and ultimately for design itself.[9]

Ethics and Privacy

A committee to discuss privacy had been formed in CAVECAT days, and a paper by Clement (1994) outlined the issues and design solutions of four multimedia communication research teams.[10]

The version of the media space first used by OTP brought with it:

- A "hard wired" concept of reciprocity—that is, "if I see you, you can see me" was enforced by software control
- Parity of electronic and physical visitors
- A door metaphor (also "hard wired") to allow people not only to signal their degree of availability but also to enforce it

Over the course of the project we had considerable experience in talking about, and demonstrating video-based technologies to both technical and nontechnical people who had no previous experience with VMC. In spite of the diversity of the group, the almost universal response to the question of whether they would like video in their own workplace was, "But what if I was picking my nose?" Privacy, or the potential for observation, was clearly on the agenda, and we adopted this cliche to stimulate a discussion of privacy with any group who had not raised it themselves.

In the series of preinstallation meetings for the primary field site, Indigo,[11] we gathered data on staff concerns around privacy, in particular in the context of video in the workplace. Our primary goal was to assure the users that as individuals they controlled their communication space. In demonstrations to the staff of the first version of TMS that they would receive, we stressed the physical as well as the software controls available. For example, users were shown the mirror function—to see the view they were sending—and how to move the camera to send a different view. They were told that they could cover the lens and were shown how to disconnect the camera. We went as far as saying they could pull the main power cord with the assurance that this would not "take down" other users or other applications they might be running.

The 6-month lead time between the proposal to carry out the study in Indigo and the actual deployment of TMS proved important, as the way in which the issues were articulated changed over time. It was in the context of an ongoing relationship that the "deeper" concerns about the video began to emerge. For example, one staff member believed that the system was "on" at all times—regardless of whether it was in use—and that a master tape of everything that occurred in the office could be produced. In part this may have been because the media space in OTP (which the group had visited) was using camcorders and not small monitor cameras at the time.[12] Allaying these concerns may not actually encourage use, as use will depend on a number of factors, for example, how well the system supports work practices. But our experience suggests that the privacy issue will emerge when video in the workplace is being considered and that failure to address it is likely to be a source of stress that could negatively impact adoption. Finally, we consulted each user individually as to the placement of the hardware on their desks. This provided another opportunity to discuss TMS and to further reduce concerns.

In the end, we were fortunate to gain access to a number of sites, several of which are discussed later. We deployed TMS in two organizations: Provitel and Indigo.[13] Much of the interface design for the TMS prototype was done in connection with Indigo, and the design process to produce an interface for Indigo's version of the TMS was both facilitated and constrained by the need to consider the broader context.[14] The deployment of TMS in the Provitel site was primarily a demonstration project as it consisted of only two nodes. However, as the users also had access to a commerical desktop videoconferencing system that had been deployed more widely in their organization, this was an unique opportunity. In the ResCorp study we were invited into the organization to study a commercial conference room videoconferencing system that had been installed 1 year earlier. In this case they were interested in "growing the use." Finally, we carried out in two universities a series of studies that explored a number of innovative ways to use the high bandwidth provided by an ATM connection.

One final note before discussing the studies themselves: As I noted earlier, the research team was cross-disciplinary and cross-institutional in composition, and interacted with a large number of external organizations over the course of the project. The HCI literature has, in the past, paid attention to cross-disciplinary relationships when design teams have a human factors component (e.g., Mantei & Teorey, 1989; Newell & Card, 1985), and more recently, the CSCW literature has addressed the question of the relationship of ethnography to design (e.g., Hughes, King, Rodden, & Andersen, 1994; Hughes, Randall, & Shapiro, 1992; Shapiro, 1994). We were self-reflective as to how the composition of the team affected our own design practice. Harrison, Mantei, Beirne, and Narine (1994) reported on how the dynamics of interface design were affected by the addition of sociologists to the design team.[15] The cross-institutional linkages across government, universities, and industry central to the project added additional complexity as the representatives of each group often held different background assumptions about design goals and timetables. Taking the time to understand and unpack these assumptions *before* they are violated is recommended. Although this foundational work may be resisted, it is central to developing a program that satisfies the needs of all the participants. As globalization, restructuring, and strategic alliances across organizations become facts of organizational life in the 1990s, the need for groupware will increase, as will the need for a better understanding of the management of cross-disciplinary and cross-institutional teams.

THE FIELD STUDIES

The Provitel Study: A Comparison of a Commercial Desktop Videoconferencing System and TMS

Background. In May 1993 a prototype of TMS was installed in the offices of two representatives of Provitel, a telecommunications organization working with the technical staff at OTP. At the same time, VISIT[16] systems were being deployed at Provitel. This provided a unique opportunity to evaluate the two systems—one a commercial product and the other a prototype media space (Moore & Schuyler, 1994). The participants agreed to keep a record of their use and experiences with both systems. When the systems had been in place for several months in-depth interviews were conducted with the participants.

This was an exploratory study. It was constrained by the small user communities—a limited number of VISIT systems had been installed in

Provitel at the time, and only the two participants had access to TMS. However, given the virtually nonexistent data on real-world use of video systems, we gained a number of early insights into the factors that affect the use of these technologies.

As installed, the significant differences between the systems were in the location, quality, and size of the video image and in the additional services provided. The TMS image appeared on a separate 14-inch monitor, was a high-quality analog signal, and supported eye contact and gaze awareness; the VISIT image was digital and scalable and located on the workstation. VISIT was integrated with the telephone system, which permitted sophisticated call support and messaging, and supported file-sharing and file-transfer activities. TMS provided a "live" window view from the roof of the office high-rise as the default on the monitor.

Findings. There appears to be a definite threshold for video quality and size if the video is actually to be used. Participants felt that the video really added value in the case of TMS and in conference-room systems that both representatives had experienced, but that the small size and grainy quality of the VISIT image meant that it was seldom used as people frequently "disappeared." It was very easy for participants in a meeting to move out of camera range. However, although the image was not particularly useful for foreground communication it was a resource they appreciated when it was reconceptualized as providing background awareness, as it helped "keep track" of people in a multiparty meeting (see Buxton, Sellen, & Sheasby, chapter 18, this volume, for a discussion of the related "Brady Bunch" concept).

The location of the image was also important. Screen real estate is limited, and frustration was experienced with VISIT as colleagues got "lost" or mixed up with documents when a screen-sharing application was simultaneously in use. The separation of the person space and the task space was felt to be an important aspect of TMS, and provided support for our contention that video surrogates, although adding more hardware, help preserve social relations and support communication. Interestingly, it was the window—the default view on TMS—that attracted the attention of nonparticipants in the office and provided an opportunity to initiate informal discussions on the role of videoconferencing in the workplace.

The integration of telephony and video communication in VISIT was rated highly in reducing the overhead of managing messages. It also provided useful features such as automatic redial and a personal memo pad linked to the subscriber directory. Both participants pointed out that their work group had a voice-oriented culture—they received and responded to dozens of voice-mail messages a day, and that e-mail, while used, was not reliable in terms of receiving a fast response. In addition, a written record of communication was neither required or desired. Their work required them to be out of the office frequently, and remote access to their messages was essential—something neither TMS nor VISIT provided.

Indigo: A Study of TMS (Telepresence Media Space)

Background. The research discussed in this section took place in our primary field site, which we named Indigo. Indigo is a small, publicly funded administrative organization whose primary work is to foster relationships between university research communities and industry. Headquarters is on a university campus in a large metropolitan area and includes the majority of the staff (seven or eight at any time). The satellite office (from two to three)—including the vice-president—is on a university campus approximately 100 km away. We began negotiations with Indigo in November 1992, the first version of TMS was installed in March 1993, and we left the site in December 1994—a total of 27 months.

The organization has had frequent changes at the presidential level in its 6-year history. These frequent changes had left Indigo without a clearly defined mission or organizational structure—staff worked independently, and regular meetings were not held. A new president arrived in late 1992. His top priorities were to generate a mission statement, to define the "business" they were in, and to highlight Indigo's role as a "catalyst for innovation and entrepreneurship." Some work activities were restructured in an attempt to increase collaboration between the sites. The introduction of TMS was seen by the president as one way to support this objective, as well as to gain recognition for Indigo as a leading organization committed to technological innovation.

We had several objectives: to manage the field site (responding to organizational requirements while representing users); to develop and test our methodology for the introduction of new technology; to develop methods for social science research and to carry out the research; to develop a robust version of TMS with the users in a specific organizational context; and to develop training sessions, coordinate a user group, and support the technology. What follows is, in part, a story about the ways in which the real world shaped the process of design.

The process of negotiating a *formal* contract took time, but it was required by the president, who had come from a business environment where contracts are routine. The president had agreed to provide the necessary financial support on the condition that the staff agreed to have video technology in their workplace. Fortunately, the staff agreed—we had no hidden agenda, and as OTP espoused a philosophy of user-centered design we wanted these early adopters as partners. We did, however, question how realistic it was for staff to refuse, especially in a small organization. This was an ethical issue that was not resolved.

The design conundrum was just where, when, and how to break into the feedback loop in the user–technology development feedback cycle. We had been "contracted" to deliver a system and time was short. Our solution was to provide a version of TMS that was robust, minimal, and reflected what we were learning in the prestudies of the organization.[17] At the same time we attempted to keep it as flexible as possible so that the users could have "real" input into the subsequent iterations of the design.

Frequent meetings were held with Indigo staff prior to the deployment of the first version of TMS in April 1993. The day the system was formally "launched," OTP staff were at both sites for a training session that ended with a connection between the sites and a "video coffee party." We prepared a 12-page user guide[18] and established a user group that included all members of the organization. The user group was designed to be informal, and regular meetings were not scheduled due to the already busy timetables of the Indigo staff. As various OTP team members were in the organization almost daily gathering data or providing support, we kept in close contact with the site. Four versions of TMS were introduced in the organization over the course of the field study, and the user group met six times.

Design and Methods. The study employed an interrupted time series design. This approach can be viewed as a series of data collection periods—prior to the installation of the system, immediately after the installation, and several months later when the use of the system had stabilized.

We carried out a series of workplace-based studies using a variety of methods and developed a number of instruments. Traditionally there has been a deep divide in social science research between those using qualitative versus those using quantitative methods. In the case of Indigo we were committed to gathering as much in-depth information as possible, yet saw some advantage to developing objective measures that could be interpreted in the context of the qualitative results. We felt this would also help communicate the research to our industrial sponsors.

Observation and in-depth interviews were the primary ways in which we gathered qualitative data. This consisted of "hanging out" in the organization for several weeks as well as shadowing each employee for a period of a week to observe their work practices. Each period of observation was followed by an in-depth interview.[19]

We also developed and administered a number of surveys. The Technology Inventory was designed to determine not only what was available in the organization, but where it was located and if it was used.[20] The Nature of Work survey inquired into staff perceptions of the way in which time was spent, such as percentage of meetings prescheduled versus spontaneous and the broader environmental context in which their work took place (e.g., interorganizational contacts and activities). This was to gather background information not easily collected in interviews. After TMS had been in place for approximately a year and a half we administered the Diffusion of Innovation survey, which was designed to supplement the second round of observational and social network data being gathered at the same time.[21]

A social network questionnaire was distributed prior to the installation of TMS and repeated when the system had been in place for 20 months. The intent here was to identify existing patterns of communication and media choice and subsequently to assess how the use of TMS affected interaction and/or offered new opportunities for collaboration.

Finally, we explored using a stripped-down version of the system log kept by the developers as part of maintenance activities as input to a statistical analysis package. This was a way to gather objective data on the use of the system, which could be compared with the more subjective reports.[22]

Some Findings. Indigo provided a unique opportunity to gain insights into the design, deployment, and use of a media space by primarily non-technical staff in a real-world organization. Two members of Indigo used the system frequently, but the overall use remained low throughout the study. Several factors, independent of TMS, contributed to this. The president's original goal of restructuring of work activities to encourage cross-site collaboration (which in theory TMS could then support) was hampered by the fact that the staff at the remote site was early on reduced to two people. At headquarters, four of the seven staff members could physically see each other and the others were only a few feet away. The president and vice-president did, however, use the system regularly, and both agreed that TMS had been essential for a series of difficult budget negotiations that would otherwise have required the vice-president to travel to headquarters for face-to-face meetings.

It is interesting to note that both staff members in the remote location perceived that TMS had affected their autonomy and that they had lost a degree of control over their personal communication space. The remote site was now but "a mouse click away," and the president or other Indigo staff could simply drop by at any time. In addition, work was more likely to be allocated to them because they were "visible." Before TMS the Indigo staff at the remote site had been able to "manage" their interactions with headquarters—for example, by using an answering machine—but with TMS they were more closely tied into the day-to-day activities of the organization.[23] In contrast, a director who joined Indigo late in the study and was located in a third city 600 km away commented that he hoped to get a TMS node as soon as possible. His concern, being new, was that he might inadvertently be overlooked if he could not participate by video! The evaluation of TMS by the users was conditioned by their expectations about how the organization worked, their role in Indigo, and the point in the innovation process at which they joined the organization.

The following example illustrates how a small change can have an impact on use. The "live" window that provided an outside view at each end was kept "on" virtually all the time by the majority of the staff at headquarters—a practice that continues today. At the remote site, however, where the staff each had a real window, the TMS window was seldom used until the view was changed to show the front lobby. This view now provided the staff with useful information, as they shared quarters with another organization. Now they could see who was coming and be alerted to the arrival of visitors.

The TMS installation gave Indigo high visibility and status in its external environment where technological innovation was highly valued. An unanticipated consequence of this was that one of the primary uses of the system was for demonstrations of the system itself. The symbolic meanings that emerged around TMS furthered the president's organizational mission to be an information technology leader. One of the staff summarized it this way: "It's new, it's modern, it's where it's at." During the period of the study, Indigo developed and promoted a conference-room videoconferencing service based on this part of the media space environment.

Two findings relate to methodology and innovations in data collection: the "dynamic" notebook and the systems log. One of the challenges in doing real-world research is gathering self-reported data from subjects who are busy and engaged in their regular activities—they forget to report, they don't have time, and so on. In Indigo we provided the users with a "dynamic" notebook in the form of a "comment" button on the TMS interface. The TMS interface used by OTP had a "bug" button that activated a messaging service that sent reports directly to the system developers, thereby reducing the overhead of making a report. By relabeling the "bug" button a "comment" button, we hoped both to encourage the reporting of experiences as well as to get more spontaneous responses. Although our file of comments is not large (in part explained by the low overall use of the system), this method of collecting qualitative data deserves to be explored further.

We also attempted to analyze the Indigo systems log—a log of all the transactions on TMS which was kept as part of troubleshooting and maintenance activities.[24] This is potentially a rich source of data for use in conjunction with more qualitative reports. The idea, simple in conception, proved difficult to execute. In the case of Indigo, we could not navigate the variety of ways in which the codes had changed as features and functionality were added. Log data are a potentially valuable source for social analysis,[25] but the ways in which they are to be used needs to be specified in detail at the outset and closely monitored to assure continuity throughout the study period.

ResCorp: A Study of a Commercial Conference Room Videoconferencing System

Background. In 1992, ResCorp, a research division of a large multinational corporation, invested heavily in a conference-room videoconferencing facility, but 1 year later it was still seldom used. The senior management at ResCorp continued to feel that videoconferencing offered important opportunities for the corporation and were interested in finding out both why the system was not being used, and how use might be encouraged. In late 1993 OTP began a study to explore the issue of underutilization and used the opportunity to test the methodology for introduction of new technologies being developed at the project. Full details of this study can be found in Moore (1994).

A series of meetings was held with the ResCorp manager concerned about the problem, and a site visit to ResCorp grounded for the researchers the reality of the corporate installation and their experiences. The time spent in developing the relationship at this stage to negotiate a shared understanding of the rights and responsibilities of both parties laid the foundation for cooperation throughout the study. We collected a variety of documents—both formal and informal—to get some insight into how the company was organized and how their work was coordinated. Our aim was to identify a workgroup that might benefit from the use of videoconferencing. An unexpected document, a list of recent patents, provided us with a way to identify individuals who had worked together but were not colocated.

The next step was to set up a meeting with the members of the organization who had been involved in establishing the videoconferencing conference room, early users, and the potential users identified from the patent analysis. The group identified from the patent analysis appeared to be the most appropriate, and they agreed to participate in a study. The remainder of the attendees constituted themselves as a Core Group to manage relations between ResCorp and OTP and to receive reports on the research.

The study involved observation of a series of biweekly videoconferences of a technical working group whose members were in two research centers of the corporation. The centers were separated by an international boundary and located approximately 300 km apart. The observation period was for 4 months, followed by interviews with participants at each site.

Findings. In spite of a variety of technical problems (which had contributed to the history of underutilization), the participants expressed satisfaction with the use of videoconferencing for their meetings. The most significant finding was that the interaction of two organizational contexts created a unique communication space. We had already seen how the interaction space could be affected by the way in which hardware had been deployed—for example, a large monitor versus small—but this revealed how social factors such as organizational culture, policies, and practices at each end were also "shaping" the shared space. In this case, the fact that one end of the communication was from a site that took a highly regimented and bureaucratic approach to the provision of videoconferencing services (DevCorp), whereas the other was laissez-faire (ResCorp) affected the video meetings in significant ways. For example, a senior scientist at ResCorp had to come to the conference room—a considerable distance from his lab and office—a half hour before the meeting start time in order to receive the video call from DevCorp. This annoyed him, but the participants at DevCorp insisted that this was how it always worked. Yet the DevCorp participants were never there for the setup! It was not until the researcher visited the DevCorp site that the dramatic differences in the organizational practices around videoconferencing were revealed. DevCorp had staff dedicated to scheduling, setting up, and taking down videoconferences and a book of procedures—one of which was a mandatory conference setup 30 minutes in advance of any meeting. The scientist at ResCorp reported reduced frustration with complying once he understood that there was a rational explanation.

This story illustrates the need to pay more attention to the fact that communication media have *at least two ends*. A videoconference between any two sites creates a unique interaction space that is not controlled by either end—in fact, the space emerges in the interaction. The users of videoconferencing systems need to be aware of this aspect of "meeting by video" and negotiate the meeting space at the outset with each group of remote participants. In the case of ResCorp the lack of shared understandings about the video meeting had an impact on reported satisfaction, a factor we suggest will impact subsequent use.

The ATM Studies

In October 1994 the Ontario Telepresence Project had the opportunity to incorporate an ATM network[26] into the existing TMS.[27] The ATM service offered television-quality image regardless of the location of the connected sites, stereo sound, high-speed connections, no visible delay, and multiple audiovideo channels. The 2 years of living in a media space helped us see beyond the obvious technical advantages. We designed a series of studies to explore innovative ways in which the technology could be used. A set of working papers is currently in preparation that includes the following studies.

The Telepresence Tunnel. The Telepresence Tunnel was a live audio video link between a corridor at Carleton University and a corridor at the University of Toronto. The goal was to see how people in two widely separated buildings, with some common background—primarily engineering and computer science students and faculty—would socialize using an open audio and video channel if given the opportunity. The sample was self-selecting as the Tunnel was in operation 24 hours a day and questionnaires were simply left at the location. Additional observations were gathered by OTP staff who stopped by the Tunnel regularly to talk to the users. Overall, the response was highly positive. The Tunnel was used for serendipitous encounters and over time for prearranged meetings. Almost 70% of the respondents reported they would use a home video system or go to a specific facility to use this type of service for long distance calls. Almost 60% suggested they would use such a facility for local calls.

TeleLearning. Three remote teaching studies were conducted. Although our primary interest was in workplace-based studies we had all experienced a variety of distance education classrooms and we were particularly interested in what advantage, if any, would be gained from the use of two audiovideo channels instead of the single channel normally available. The key question was whether different ways of using the second channel, such as provision of various close-ups or panoramic views, would affect the student's evaluation of "presence," comfort and ease of interacting. The Conference Room at Carleton University was the location for all the Ottawa participants, but in Toronto, where the lectures originated, the venue was changed for each lecture—a large conference room, a midsize demo suite, and an office. With each class, the lecturers' options for viewing the audience were also changed. Poll-type evaluations were completed by the Ottawa participants at the end of each lecture. Evaluations of the sessions showed that the projection of one channel on a standard monitor and the second on a large wall screen at the lecturer's end made a difference in terms of the attendees' perceptions of "presence" and in their perceptions of the ease with which they could interact with the lecturer. This suggests that the availability of both background and foreground awareness for the lecturer had a consequence for the remote participants. Once again, this was support for the importance of taking both ends into account when evaluating communication systems. This will be increasingly important as interorganizational VMC increases.

The Virtual Office. Two members of the OTP engineering group (one in Toronto, one in Ottawa) who were working on a joint project, used the media space over the ATM network to link their offices for approximately 4 weeks. Overall, both reported extreme satisfaction with the experience. Although they had worked together intensely for over 2 years (daily exchange of e-mail, weekly meetings of the engineering group by videoconference, and face-to-face at annual meetings) they had not developed a social relationship. With the virtual office they discovered a similar taste in music and talked about their personal lives—they even brought their wives in to meet over video! Both felt that their productivity had increased, and although they enjoyed the social relationship they had developed during this period, they felt that it would be impossible to maintain when the available media were e-mail, telephone, and traditional videoconferencing. And indeed, when the ATM connection was gone they resented the amount of time they had to spend on e-mail. They also missed the spontaneity that the ATM had made possible, and similar to others who used TMS over ATM extensively, they experienced what might best be described as "video withdrawal." Bandwidth clearly makes a difference. And, as restrictions on the availability of bandwidth disappear in the future, the potential for discovering new ways of working across time and space is enormous. The flexibility and tailorability of media spaces suggest they are a good place to look for novel applications of VMC.

CONCLUSION

A great deal was accomplished in a period of less than 3 years. We designed, built, deployed, and studied the use of a prototype media space, TMS, in a variety of environments. Along the way we encountered a number of challenges that related directly to our goal of grounding our research in the real world. Gaining access to external organizations, especially when a prototype system was involved, was one challenge, and the issues around privacy and ethics were another.

A number of our findings have direct implications for designing video-mediated systems. The most important is that a variety of *contexts*—including the work practices of individuals and groups and broader organizational factors such as culture, structure, deployment strategy, and so on—condition use and adoption. Situating interactions within the organization context extends the analysis. There is a definite need to attend to the fact that VMC systems have at least two ends. A video meeting creates a unique interaction space that is not controlled by any single participant; in fact, the space emerges in the interaction. This is relevant for communication within a single organization, particularly if there are multiple subcultures and especially for interorganizational communication. When technology supports existing work practices or enables new and valued practices it is more likely to be adopted. Designs should be sufficiently open and flexible to continue to accommodate "discovery" as the system is used. The unanticipated uses and meanings are a rich source of insight for future services and applications.

More concretely, we found that there is a threshold for video quality and size, and that the location of the "person" image makes a difference. We found that the speed of making a connection and the bandwidth available also affect use. Services such as the "live" window were highly valued as they were perceived to add value. But once again, these factors must be understood within the broader contexts just described.

Do media spaces work? Our experiences in OTP suggest that they offer a unique potential to enrich communication and facilitate collaboration—if they are designed and deployed with sensitivity to work practices and organizational culture. Although the project ended more than a year ago, a number of us continue to work together—even though we live in different cities—and the insights we gained are being carried into new environments. Media space withdrawal might be seen as a lingering symptom of the project's success.

ACKNOWLEDGMENTS

This chapter reflects countless discussions and debates among all members of OTP, in particular those whose work is represented here. Special thanks to Laura Garton and Dick Dillon for their comments on earlier drafts. Funding from the Ontario Government and our industrial partners is gratefully acknowledged. Finally, special thanks to the organizations who granted us access and to the users who gave generously of their valuable time. They are the real pioneers.

NOTES

1. A background awareness service based on a concept originating in the work on Polyscope by Borning and Travers (1991) and further developed by Dourish and Bly (1992).
2. The project's major sponsor was the Province of Ontario and it was administered through two Centres of Excellence—the Information Technology Research Centre (ITRC) and the Telecommunication Research Institute of Ontario (TRIO). OTP ended December 31, 1994.
3. We understand media space as an *environment* in which audio, video, and computer technologies are integrated in novel ways to both support ongoing communication and to provide an opportunity to discover new ways of interacting.
4. The system originated at Rank Xerox's EuroPARC laboratory in 1988 (Buxton & Moran, 1990). It was given to the CAVECAT Project at the University of Toronto in early 1990 where development continued. The resources were transferred to the OTP in 1992. By 1993 the system had fundamentally changed and was named TMS: Telepresence Media Space. The TMS system was transferred to Xerox PARC in 1993 where it was implemented as Kasmir and to Xerox's Webster Research Center (Rochester, NY) in 1994.
5. For accounts of the psychology experiments, the reader is referred to Harrison, Chignell, and Baecker (1992a, 1992b) for work on group communication processes and Harrison, Ishii, and Chignell (1994) for a study on the effect of spatial discontinuities and distortions in VMC collaboration on the ability of participants to carry out a task.
6. Over the life of the project a number of staff from industry, research institutes, and universities in Canada, Europe, and Japan participated in the project.

7. Local connections were analog, which provided both high-quality video and audio; connections between cities involved the use of a codec and a digital signal where the quality, although good, was inferior to the analog and had approximately a half second transmission delay, which gave what one researcher described as the "Max Headroom" effect.

8. The cost to OTP in terms of the time spent preparing proposals for the potential clients was high. In several cases we even carried out preliminary studies in the organization.

9. From the perspective of pure research this approach could be seen as "interference." Our goal was to create a positive climate for adoption by working with the users and involving them in the process. Thus we were not neutral observers. However, there are many factors in any organization over which outsiders have no control. This is part of the design challenge.

10. OTP, Xerox PARC, Rank Xerox EuroPARC, and Bellcore.

11. All research involving human subjects carried out by the University of Toronto is subject to review and approval by the Human Subjects Experimentation Committee and written consent must be obtained from all participants. This is standard practice for social scientists and was noted by some of the technical staff (who had not previously thought of their work as involving human subjects) as an additional set of responsibilities inherent in the design of technology.

12. We were to pay particular attention to these concerns at the time of the deployment, and when we wished to use video for data collection we had participants sign a video consent form to reinforce the distinction between the use of TMS—video for communication with no permanent record—and the use of video as data for analysis.

13. These are code names.

14. The original interface to the CAVECAT system (the precursor of TMS) was never intended for use outside a research community of sophisticated users. The challenge was to design an interface that was easy to use and powerful, although at the same time remaining sufficiently flexible that it could be tailored to accommodate users in a variety of contexts. Gathering information to guide design for CSCW applications requires, in addition to understanding the psychology of the users and their tasks, a consideration of the interaction of individuals and groups and the cultural and sociological underpinnings of these interactions. Cooperation and coordination with the sociologists working in the organization at the same time gave the interface team access to additional data, but also constrained traditional HCI design practices. See Harrison, Mantei, Beirne, and Narine (1994) for details.

15. For example, with tight time schedules the need of the HCI designers to involve users in the design process came into conflict with the sociologists' efforts to gather baseline information on the organization and work practices prior to detailed discussions about TMS with the future users. On the one hand, access to the client was restricted; on the other hand, the HCI team was able to use a portion of the rich work practices data collected by the sociologists. When both groups required similar types of information, instruments were designed collaboratively. In the process, both groups developed a better understanding of each other's requirements.

16. VISIT is a registered trademark of Northern Telecom and at the time of the study was one of the first commercial desktop videoconferencing systems on the market.

17. The time required to get results from traditional social science research is in conflict with the timelines of systems developers and researchers. This problem is now being addressed in the CSCW community (e.g., Hughes, Randall, & Shapiro, 1992; Hughes, King, Rodden, & Andersen, 1994). This problem crosses both disciplinary boundaries and pure/applied research boundaries within disciplines.

18. The guide was intentionally short as our goal had been to design an interface that accommodated the skills of this group of experienced Macintosh users. In addition, we

wanted to encourage the staff to take "ownership" of the guide, modifying it to reflect *their* work and organizational practices.

19. Prior to starting the data collection we had collected and reviewed the formal publications of the organization.

20. We were interested in both the visible (e.g., fax, copier, etc.) and the invisible technology (e.g., software). We sought to discover discrepancies between what staff maintained on their personal machines and what we observed them to be using. The management of technical resources was the primary interest here.

21. This was based on Rogers' (1983) work on diffusion of innovation.

22. All participants in Indigo were informed that this log was being kept and that it was for research use only.

23. There was always the option of closing the software door to prevent glances, but the users were aware that this was not value neutral. TMS provided opportunities that didn't exist without the media space, but the responses to these opportunities, on both sides, are not without consequence.

24. There are ethical issues involved in archiving this type of data for future analysis.

25. It is interesting to note that the head of engineering became interested in the problem and developed some new software to visually display the data (Karam, 1994).

26. The ATM network provided three logical connections between the OTP sites in Ottawa and Toronto over a dedicated 45-Mbps DS-3 line: two full-duplex analog audiovideo circuits and an Ethernet link.

27. For technical details see Karam (1995).

REFERENCES

Borning, A., & Travers, M. (1991, April–May). Two approaches to casual interaction over computer and video networks. *Proceedings of CHI '91* (pp. 13–19). New Orleans, LA.

Buxton, W. (1992). Telepresence: Integrating shared task and person spaces. *Proceedings of Graphics Interface '92* (pp. 123–129). Vancouver, B.C.

Buxton, W., & Moran, T. (1990). EuroPARC's integrated interactive intermedia facility (IIIF): Early experiences. In S. Gibbs & A. Verrijn (Eds.), *Multi-user interfaces and applications* (pp. 11–34). Amsterdam: Elsevier.

Clement, A. (1994). Considering privacy in the development of multi-media communications. *Computer Supported Cooperative Work, 2,* 67–88.

Dourish, P., & Bly, S. (1992, May). Portholes: supporting awareness in a distributed work group. *Proceedings of CHI '92* (pp. 541–547). Monterey, CA.

Harrison, B., Chignell, M., & Baecker, R. (1992a, October). Do perceptions match reality? A comparison of objective and subjective measures in video mediated communication. *Proceedings of the 25th Conference of the Human Factors Association of Canada* (pp. 35–41). Hamilton, Ont.

Harrison, B., Chignell, M., & Baecker, R. (1992b, October). Out of site, still in mind? A case study of video mediated communication. *Proceedings of the Human Factors Society, 36th Annual Meeting* (pp. 242–247). Atlanta, GA.

Harrison, B., Ishii, H., & Chignell, M. (1994). *An empirical study on orientation of shared workspaces and interpersonal spaces in video-mediated collaboration* (OTP Tech. Rep. 94-2). Toronto: Ontario Telepresence Project.

Harrison, B., Mantei, M., Beirne, G., & Narine, T. (1994, April). Communicating about communicating: Cross-disciplinary design of a media space interface. *Proceedings of CHI '94* (pp. 124–130). Boston.

Haythornthwaite, C., Wellman, B., & Mantei, M. (1995). Work relationships and media use: A social network analysis. *Group Decision and Negotiation, 4*(3), 193–211.

Hughes, J., King, V., Rodden, T., & Andersen, H. (1994, October). Moving out from the control room: Ethnography in system design. *Proceedings of CSCW '94* (pp. 429–439). Chapel Hill, NC.

Hughes, J., Randall, D., & Shapiro, D. (1992, October–November). Faltering from ethnography to design. *Proceedings of CSCW'92* (pp. 115–122). Toronto.

Karam, G. (1994). Visualization using timelines. *Proceedings of the 1994 International Symposium on Software Testing and Analysis* (pp. 125–137). New York: ACM.

Karam, G. (1995). *Telepresence—Current and future technologies for collaboration* (SCE-95-01). Ottawa: Carleton University, Department of Systems and Computer Engineering.

Mantei, M., Baecker, R., Sellen, A. J., Wellman, B., & Buxton, W. (1991, April–May). Experiences in the use of a media space. *Proceedings of SIGCHI '91* (pp. 203–208). New Orleans, LA.

Mantei, M., & Teorey, T. J. (1989). Incorporating behavioral techniques into the system development life cycle. *MISQ, 13*(3), 257–276.

Moore, G. (1994). *A tale of two cities: A study of conference room videoconferencing* (OTP Tech. Rep. 94-04). Toronto: Ontario Telepresence Project.

Moore, G., & Schuyler, K. (1994). *Videoconferencing 1990s style: Sharing faces, places and spaces* (OTP Tech. Rep. 94-03). Toronto: Ontario Telepresence Project.

Moore, G. (1993). Methodology for the introduction of new technology in the workplace. In *Technology/Methodology Inventory* (OTP Tech. Rep. 93-06). Toronto: Ontario Telepresence Project.

Newell, A., & Card, S. (1985). The prospects for psychological science in human-computer interaction. *Human–Computer Interaction, 1*(3), 209–242.

Rogers, E. (1983). *Diffusion of innovations* (3rd ed.). New York: Free Press.

Sellen, A. J. (1992, May). Speech patterns in video-mediated conversations. *Proceedings of CHI '92* (pp. 49–59). Monterey, CA.

Sellen, A. J. (1995). Remote conversations: The effect of mediating talk with technology. *Human–Computer Interaction, 10*(4), 401–444.

Shapiro, D. (1994, October). The limits of ethnography: Combining social sciences for CSCW. *Proceedings of CSCW '94* (pp. 417–428). Chapel, NC.

Tang, J. C., & Isaacs, E. A. (1995). Studies of multimedia-supported collaboration. In S. J. Emmott (Ed.), *Information superhighways: Multimedia users and futures* (pp. 123–160). London: Academic Press.

Chapter 15

Reconfiguring Media Space: Supporting Collaborative Work[1]

Christian Heath
Paul Luff
University of Nottingham

Abigail Sellen
Rank Xerox Research Centre

Despite the substantial corpus of research concerned with the design and development of media space, the virtual workplace has failed to achieve its early promise. In this chapter, we suggest that a number of problems that have arisen with the design and deployment of media space derive from an impoverished concept of collaborative work. Drawing from our own studies of video connectivity, coupled with analyses of work and interaction in real-world settings, we consider ways in which we might reconfigure media space in order to provide more satisfactory support for collaboration in organizational environments.

INTRODUCTION

Advances in telecommunications will undoubtedly have a profound impact on organizational life and collaborative work over the next decade. Their ability to enhance and transform distributed activities, as well as enriching how people work when with each other, has been well documented, and we wait with some impatience to witness the extraordinary contribution of such technologies to our ordinary lives. Despite the optimism that greets successive innovations in telecommunications, it is not at all clear whether current developments provide satisfactory support for even the most simple or apparently straightforward collaborative activities. Indeed, the debates that have arisen concerning the actual contribution of experimental systems when deployed in organizations such as research laboratories reveal perhaps not only the potential shortcomings of the technology, but also our lack of understanding of the ways in which it might contribute to interpersonal communication and collaborative work. Even the very basic question as to the advantage of audiovisual communication over telephony remains subject to debate and curiosity. In fact, we have been reliably informed that in a large-scale study of the use of videotelephones by domestic users in a city in southwestern France, many subscribers preferred to look at themselves while on the phone rather than the person with whom they were talking.

As yet, therefore, we have relatively little understanding of the characteristics of video-mediated communication (VMC) or the contribution that audiovisual technologies including telecommunications might provide for collaborative work. In this brief chapter we wish to discuss the contribution and design of "media spaces": computer-controlled networks of audio and video equipment intended to support collaboration among physically distributed colleagues. In particular, by exploring the actual use of media space technology and comparing the support it provides to the resources that people ordinarily rely on when working together in more conventional environments, we wish to consider the requirements for developing more satisfactory technological environments for collaborative work. These requirements form the basis for a number of experiments in which we develop and evaluate prototype support for working together at a distance.

VIDEO-MEDIATED CONDUCT

EuroPARC's Media Space: Background and Setting

In common with several other system research laboratories, Rank Xerox has in place an audiovisual infrastructure in its laboratory in Cambridge, formerly known as EuroPARC. This infrastructure allows scientists and administrative staff to establish visual and audible contact with each other, or to view public areas such as the commons area and the conference room. EuroPARC's offices straddle three floors, and in part the technology was introduced to facilitate informal contact and sociability among organizational personnel. The system basically consists of a camera, 14-in monitor, speaker, and microphone in each office, with larger monitors in the public areas. The monitor, with camera typically placed on top, is positioned to one side, roughly at a 120 degree angle to the workstation (Fig. 15.1). A flat, multidirectional Pressure Zone Microphone (PZM) is normally positioned on the desk by the workstation, operated by a footpedal.

A   B

FIG. 15.1. Two offices using the audiovisual infrastructure at EuroPARC.
(A) The camera and monitor are to the left of the workstation and the
microphone is multidirectional, consisting of a small, flat metal plate on
the wall, operated by a foot switch. (B) More detail of the common
relationship between camera and monitor positions.

Over the past 3 years the infrastructure has become increasingly sophisticated, and we have experimented with various alternative configurations
that might enhance contact and cooperation among EuroPARC personnel.
A number of these developments have been designed to provide "users"
with more delicate ways of scanning the local environment or establishing
connectivity; (see, e.g., Borning & Travers, 1991; Gaver et al., 1992). Despite
these technological developments, the most prevalent use of the system
within EuroPARC is to maintain an open video connection between two
physical domains, typically two offices. These "office-shares" are often preserved over long periods of time (weeks and sometimes months). They
provide two individuals based at different parts of building with continual
video access to each other. Audio connections are normally switched off
until one of the participants wishes to speak with the other.

Methodological Considerations

As part of the introduction and development of the EuroPARC media space,
we undertook audiovisual recording of connections between individual
offices. To diminish the potential influence of recording on the way people
used the system, and to enable us to gain an overall picture of how frequently
and for what purposes individuals used connections, we undertook "blanket"
recording of a particular connection for up to 2 or 3 weeks. This data corpus
was augmented by more conventional field observation of both connections
and discussions in the laboratory concerning the system. We also collected
audiovisual recordings of experimental systems and of the use of related
technologies in environments other than EuroPARC, for example, the
Xerox Television (XTV) link between Britain and the United States.

Although our analytic orientation to the audiovisual materials and field
observations was relatively catholic, it drew in part from recent developments

in the social sciences, in particular ethnomethodology and conversation analysis. Our central concern was with the accomplishment of ordinary activities in and through media space technology and in particular the ways in which the participants themselves produced and recognized visual as well as vocal actions within the developing course of their interaction. Thus, nonverbal behavior is not treated in isolation from the talk with which it occurs or the context in which it arises. Conduct in interaction, whether visual, vocal, or a combination of both, is addressed with regard to the actions it performs in situ within the local configuration of activity. The meaning or, better, the sense of a particular actions is embedded in the context at hand, accomplished in and through a social organization that provides for the production and intelligibility of activities in interaction.

In examining VMC, we had a particular interest in the ways in which participants were able to organize each other's involvement in the course of various activities and to coordinate their vocal and visual actions. We were also driven by an interest in various substantive concerns, such as how individuals established mutual engagement; the extent to which they were able to remain (peripherally) aware of each other's activities and immediate environments; and whether video connectivity provided a suitable medium for accomplishing object-focused (such as screen- or paper-based) collaborative tasks. Analysis developed on a case-by-case basis, in which we began by transcribing particular fragments of data, identifying potential phenomena such as sequences of actions, and assembling collections of candidate instances. Comparing and contrasting the organization of specific activities across numerous instances found in data of both VMC and more conventional face-to-face interaction, provided ways in which we could begin to delineate a body of observations and findings (cf. Heath & Luff, 1991, 1992b).

Observations

Given the various, sometimes contradictory arguments concerning the significance of video to communication between physically distributed individuals, it is perhaps worth beginning by summarizing the conclusions from our analysis concerning the contribution of real-time visual access to informal sociability and collaborative work. There are three such contributions worth mentioning.

The first is that, unlike a telephone or audio connection, at EuroPARC video provides the opportunity for individuals to assess visually the availability of a colleague before initiating contact. More precisely, the video channel allows an individual not only to discern whether a colleague is actually in his or her office, but also to assess more delicately the state of his or her current activity and whether it might be opportune to initiate contact. The infrastructure supports the possibility of momentarily glancing at a colleague before deciding whether it is opportune to establish engagement. In this way, video makes an important contribution not only to the awareness of others within a physically distributed work environment, but also to one's ability to respect the territorial rights and current work commitments of one's colleagues.

Second, once individuals have established contact with each other, video provides participants with the ability to coordinate talk with a range of other activities in which they might be simultaneously engaged. This aspect of video's contribution is particularly important to computer-supported cooperative work (CSCW), where individuals are frequently undertaking screen-based activities while speaking with colleagues. Mutual visual access provides individuals with the ability to discern, to some extent, the ongoing organization and demands of a colleague's activities, and thereby coordinate their interaction with the practical tasks at hand. Moreover, mutual visual access provides individuals with the ability to point at and refer to objects within the shared local milieu. Such facilities have become increasingly important in recent years as designers have begun to develop shared real-time interfaces (cf. Bly, 1988; Olson, Olson, Mack, & Wellner, 1990). Recent experiments (Olson & Olson, 1991; Smith, O'Shea, O'Malley, & Taylor, 1989) have demonstrated the importance of providing video for participants to coordinate simultaneous screen-based activities.

Third, the video channel provides participants in multiparty conversations with the ability to recognize who is speaking and to "track" the thread of the conversation. This is of particular importance where videoconferencing facilities support multiparty interactions and where each connection involves more than single participant. In our analysis of multiparty audiovisual connections at both EuroPARC and the Xerox videoconferencing facility at Welwyn Garden City, we noted that video plays an important part in the allocation and coordination of speaker turns. The advantage of video in helping to identify and discriminate among speakers is also supported by experimental studies of multiparty videoconferencing systems (Sellen, 1995).

Despite these contributions, our observations of VMC suggest that this kind of technological medium provides a communicative environment that markedly differs from physical copresence. We next sketch some of the more significant differences between human conduct performed through technological media, and actions and activities undertaken in face-to-face settings.

The Insignificance of a Look. In recent years a growing body of research has noted the ways in which looking at another person not only serves to provide certain information, but is itself a social action that engenders a response from the person who is being looked at (cf. Kendon, 1990;

Goodwin, 1981; Heath, 1986). For example, all of us have been aware of being looked at by another in in a public setting such as restaurant or a train, and felt the discomfort that another's gaze can cause. We are perhaps less aware of the ways in which we attempt to distract the other and avoid their gaze, by becoming "preoccupied" with a book we are reading or shielding our eyes with a gesture. On the other hand, a look may serve to encourage another to return the gaze, and, having established a mutual orientation, allow the participants to move progressively into conversation or more generally focused interaction. Indeed, in research we conducted some years ago concerned with the medical consultation, we found the doctor would often initiate the business at hand in direct response to the patient turning toward him. In those particular cases, in the passing moment between the preliminaries of the consultation and discussing the patient's reason for visiting the doctor, a momentary look was enough to engender the doctor's initiating utterance. More generally, it has been found, throughout a range of ordinary settings, that turning and looking at another serves to elicit a response and most frequently a return of gaze from the person who is being looked at. Turning toward another, like other forms of bodily conduct such as talk, can be sequentially or interactionally implicative, generating a position (in immediate juxtaposition) where a particular action(s) is relevant, and if absent is "noticeably" or "accountably" absent (cf. Schegloff, 1972).

One of the interesting aspects of the ways in which gaze can serve to engender action is that the person who is looked at, and responds, is not necessarily looking at the other. Whether in conversation or simply walking down the street, individuals are able to monitor peripherally the local environment and, in particular, others within the local milieu, and respond where necessary or appropriate. Indeed, our ability to remain sensitive to and monitor people's behavior outside the direct line of our regard seems a critical element of the ways in which we produce and coordinate our actions with each other, whether they are produced through visual conduct or talk.

When we began to look at VMC, there seemed to be some curious differences in the ways in which the participants looked at each other and responded to each other's looks. In particular, we began to notice that although people would turn toward each other in the way they might in a copresent setting, their looks would often pass unnoticed by the person at whom they were looking. Moreover, it was not that the other was simply ignoring the look, because we knew from our research on face-to-face interaction that in "declining" another's gaze the recipient would frequently produce various actions to enable him or her to avoid the gaze of the other. Rather, in the cases at hand, one person would simply not notice that the other was looking at him, even where the other person upgraded, or exaggerated the look. The social and interactional significance of the look appears to be undermined by the technology; the look loses its sequential relevance.

For example, in the fragment illustrated in Fig. 15.2 drawn from a recording of a video connection between a scientist and a member of the administration at EuroPARC, we find Maggie, the scientist, attempting to initiate contact with Jean. To do this, Maggie turns toward Jean and then waves. For more than 10 sec she stares at Jean but receives no response. Finally, Maggie looks away to her phone and dials Jean's number, summoning Jean to the telephone. Only when Jean replies to Maggie's greeting do the parties establish visual contact.

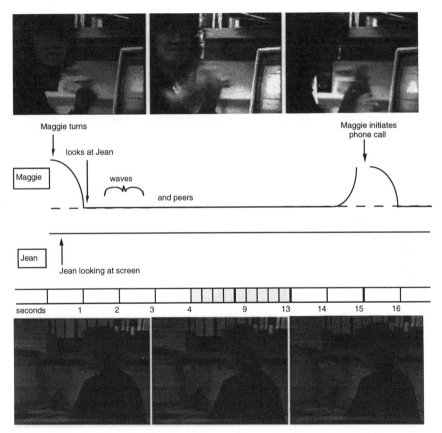

FIG. 15.2. A fragment of activity between a scientist, Maggie (top), and a member of administrative staff, Jean (bottom). For presentation purposes, the gaze direction of each of the participants is indicated by a line. Gaze toward another is shown by the line moving toward a central dashed line, and gaze away by their line moving away. In this fragment, Jean's gaze remains fixed on the screen, whereas Maggie first looks toward Jean and then, several seconds later, turns away.

In this example, therefore, the user presupposes the effectiveness of visual conduct through the media, assuming that a glance and then, more dramatically, a series of gestures will "naturally" engender a response from the potential coparticipant. However, the glances and their accompanying gestures, the power of the look to ordinarily attract the attention of another, appear to be weakened when performed through video rather than face-to-face. In neither this nor the many other instances we have examined is there evidence to suggest that the potential coparticipant is deliberately disattending the attempts to attract their attention. Rather, the looks and gestures of their colleagues simply pass unnoticed as if their appearance on a screen rather than in actual copresence diminishes their performative and interactional impact. It is as if the sequential significance of such actions is weakened by the medium. In consequence, the relatively delicate ways in which individuals subtly move from disengagement to engagement in face-to-face environments, especially when they are in a "state of incipient talk," appear to be rendered problematic in video-mediated copresence.

In consequence, at least during the initial introduction of the media space into EuroPARC, we found that users frequently had to resort to more formal or explicit ways of initiating mutual engagement. Unlike copresence where participants can delicately and progressively move, step by step, into a state of focused interaction, users would summon the other with a noise, as when calling someone on the telephone.

The Articulation of Talk and Recipient Insensitivity. Looking at another not only serves to initiate interaction, but plays an important part in the production and coordination of talk within an encounter. We have already mentioned how a look may encourage another to talk; gaze serves to display that the participant is not simply available but is also prepared to listen or "receive." During the course of talk speakers themselves are sensitive to the gaze of the person to whom they are talking and draw various inferences from the direction of the other's gaze concerning involvement in the activity at hand. Indeed, it has been found that speakers have various devices for encouraging a coparticipant to turn toward the speaker. These devices include speech perturbations such as pauses, the elongation of sounds, and various forms of self-editing and repair. They also include body movements such as gestures (cf. Goodwin, 1981; Heath, 1986). A critical element of the use and success of these various devices turns on the speaker's ability to encourage the recipient to reorient by looking at the coparticipant. The speaker's gaze in many cases works with these various devices to establish a reorientation from the coparticipant and thereby establish heightened involvement in the activity at hand.

The gaze of the speaker and the person to whom he or she is speaking therefore is consequential to the production of talk. For example, the speaker may delay the onset of an utterance until the speaker has secured the gaze of the recipient. Or, the speaker will stall the production of an utterance, withholding the gist of the talk, until he or she establishes a reorientation from the recipient. Or, in some cases, speakers will abandon the projected course of an utterance, and even a sequence of utterances such as a narrative, in the light of the failure to establish an appropriate orientation from the person to whom they are speaking. The production and articulation of talk in face-to-face interaction are embedded in, and interrelated with, the visual conduct of the participants; both talk and body movement inform the accomplishment of action and activity in interaction.

In consequence, the ineffectiveness of a look in video-mediated copresence can be consequential for the production of talk and more generally the interaction between the participants.

In the following example, we find the relative ineffectiveness of looking generating difficulties for the emergence of a conversation between two scientists at EuroPARC who are discussing a networking problem. We join the action as Ian initiates contact with Robert by enquiring what he should tell Marty, a colleague in the United States, to do:

```
 1  I:   What I shall I tell Mar::ty↑ to do(hh).
 2       (1.2)
 3  R:   Er:°m::
 4       (1.2)
 5  R:   Let's see:: well first >first off I'd (.2) what I did
 6       las: t night which seemed to (work) was send it tw::ice
 7       under different names:: <an then she did (a di::ff:).
 8       (1.6)
 9  R:   en then she: could clean up the er::: (.8) line
10       noi:se.
11       (. . . .)
12       (2.3)
13  R:   °thhh
14       (.3)
15  I:   O:k ay
16  R:   (Such a hak)
```

At the outset notice that Robert delays his reply to Ian's question first by pausing, then by producing "Er:°m::" (line 3), and then once again by pausing (line 4). Even when he does begin to reply, the actual answer is not immediately forthcoming; indeed, the gist of the reply appears pushed away from the beginning of the speaker's turn, by virtue of the preface "Let's see::"

and various forms of speech perturbation, including a sound stretch ("see::"), a .2-sec pause (line 5), and consecutive restarts "well first > first off I'd (.2) what." The speaker's actions and in particular his apparent difficulty in beginning his reply may be systematically related to the conduct of the (potential) recipient, and in particular to Robert's inability to secure his coparticipant's gaze. The more detailed picture in Fig. 15.3 may be helpful.

Withholding the reply fails to engender any reorientation from Ian, and following "Er:°m::", Robert begins progressively to shift his gaze toward Ian, as if attempting to encourage a reorientation while avoiding actually staring at his potential recipient. Both the withholding of the reply and the subtle shifts in Robert's orientation fail to encourage any display of recipiency from the coparticipant. Robert begins the preface "Let's see::" and looks directly toward his colleague. The alignment of gaze toward the coparticipant, the preface, the sound stretch, the pause, and the restarts are all devices that are regularly used to secure recipient alignment at the beginning of a turn. The pause appears to engender a response from Ian, and following his realignment of gaze from the screen to his colleague, the speaker begins the gist of his reply.

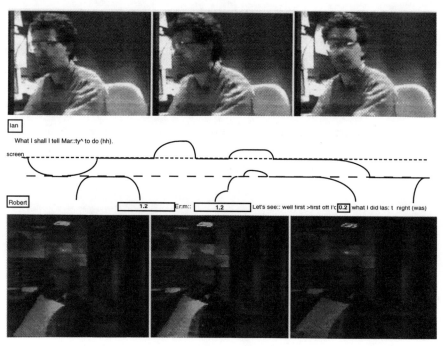

FIG. 15.3. A fragment of interaction between Ian (top) and Robert (bottom) over a video-mediated "office-share" connection. Ian's talk and Robert's talk are presented above and below the gaze line, respectively. Intervals between utterances are in tenths of a second.

It is apparent, therefore, that in this example the respondent has various difficulties in securing the relevant form of coparticipation from the potential recipient, ironically the party who initiated the interaction in the first place. The potential recipient displays little orientation to the speaker's successive attempts to secure his gaze. The difficulties faced by the speaker in attempting to secure a realignment from the recipient may derive from the relative ineffectiveness of his visual conduct and, in particular, the apparent inability of the coparticipant to notice the successive shifts in orientation undertaken by the speaker. Unlike face-to-face, the relative scale and presentation of a speaker's more delicate shifts in orientation and gaze in a media space appear to pass unnoticed and thereby undermine the interactional significance of conventional devices to establish mutual orientation.

In passing, a further point should be mentioned. To provide individuals with the ability to vary their position while speaking with colleagues through the media space, we deliberately used multidirectional microphones to provide audio connections. These multidirectional microphones are designed to conceal relative changes in the direction of a sound within a circumscribed domain. In consequence, they mask changes in the sound level of the voice as a speaker changes his or her orientation. These changes may allow another to discern whether his colleague is changing his physical orientation, for example, when the other is turning toward him. Thus, the relative ineffectiveness of a speaker's shift of gaze to engender response during the course of utterance may derive not only from the accessibility of their visual conduct, but also from the absence of changes in tone and loudness of the voice.

The Impact of Gesture.   Other forms of bodily conduct movements, ranging from relatively gross shifts in postural orientation through to minor head nods and the like also accomplish, often in combination with talk, social actions and activities. They are "locally" or contextually significant, serving to engender or provide opportunities for particular actions from a coparticipant. We have already mentioned, for example, how gestures can be used to elicit the gaze of the person to whom one is speaking, and how the utterance itself may be delayed until the gesture's accomplished its particular work. In some cases we find gestures accomplishing two or three actions simultaneously, with the sequential relevance of the movement engendering particular actions from the coparticipant at different points within the emergent of the activity. The significance of the participants' bodily conduct is accomplished within the developing course of the interaction and achieves its particular sequential significance then and there within the local configuration of action.

In video-mediated interaction, speakers use gestures as they might in face-to-face interaction. For example, in Fig. 15.4 we find a lengthy de-

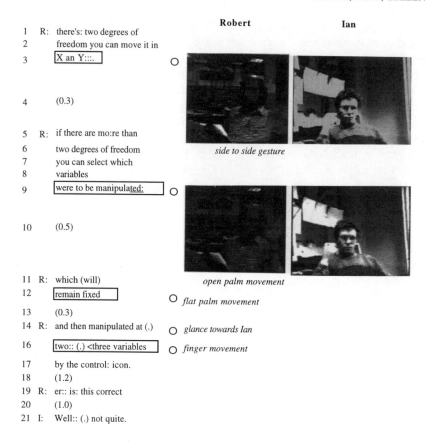

```
                                        Robert              Ian
1   R:  there's: two degrees of
2       freedom you can move it in
3       | X an Y:::. |                O

4       (0.3)

5   R:  if there are mo:re than
6       two degrees of freedom
7       you can select which
8       variables
9       | were to be manipulated: |   O

10      (0.5)

11  R:  which (will)
12      | remain fixed |              O  flat palm movement
13      (0.3)
14  R:  and then manipulated at (.)   O  glance towards Ian
16      | two:: (.) <three variables |  O  finger movement
17      by the control: icon.
18      (1.2)
19  R:  er:: is: this correct
20      (1.0)
21  I:  Well:: (.) not quite.
```

FIG. 15.4. A transcript of a conversation over an office-share connection between Ian and Robert.

scription of an interface in which the speaker appears to encourage his recipient to participate. The description itself is accompanied by a series of iconic or illustrative gestures through which Robert shows the operation of an icon in the interface. These include a side-to-side gesture occurring over "X an Y:::." (line 2) followed by an open palm movement from side to side with "were to be manipula<u>ted</u>:" (line 6). Robert moves his palm down and flat as he utters "remain fixed" (line 8) and moves his second and third fingers down as he says "two:: <three variables" (line 8). These gestures illustrate the ways in which the variables might be manipulated. Robert has the gaze of the recipient during much of this extract but only turns toward his coparticipant during the final part of the description.

On the one hand, the speaker's gestures appear to be designed to provide a visual portrayal of the objects and actions mentioned in the talk (see, e.g., Birdwhistell, 1970; Bull, 1983; Ekman & Friessen, 1969; Schegloff,

1984). There is little evidence, however, either in this fragment or in numerous other instances of iconic gestures in video-mediated interaction, that the illustrative component successfully provides the coparticipant with relevant or sequentially significant information. On the other hand, the gestures also appear to be designed to encourage Ian to participate more actively in the description. They fail, however, to transform the way in which he is participating in the talk; indeed, he provides little indication, despite various opportunities and encouragements to display that he is actually following the emergent description. Consequently, the speaker, who has been unable to encourage the recipient to indicate whether he agrees, disagrees, or fails to follow the description, is then faced with having to explicitly elicit confirmation and clarification.

The relative inability of the speaker's visual conduct to effect some response from the recipient during the production of turns at talk is found elsewhere, among different users within the data corpus. Even relatively basic sequences that recur within face-to-face interaction, for example, when a speaker uses a movement to elicit the gaze of a recipient and coordinates the production of an utterance with the receipt of gaze, tend to be absent from the materials at hand. Speakers continue to gesture and produce a range of bodily behavior during the delivery of talk in video-mediated communication. Yet visual conduct largely fails to achieve its performative impact or sequential significance.

Asymmetries in Video-Mediated Conduct

The foregoing analyses suggest that social interaction within a media space reveals asymmetries that, as far as we are aware, are found neither within face-to-face interaction nor in other technologically mediated forms of communication such as telephone calls. Indeed, even in the light of the growing corpus of literature concerned with asymmetries within various forms of institutional language use and interaction such as that in the medical consultation or in the courtroom, the distribution of communicative resources is particularly peculiar in video-mediated presence. For example, in institutional environments we find the incumbents of preestablished roles, such as doctor and patient, having differential access and influence to activity types throughout the course of an event. By contrast, in the materials at hand, the asymmetries parallel the categories of speaker and hearer and are in constant flux as the conversation and different forms of participation emerge. The asymmetries undermine the very possibility of accomplishing certain actions and activities.

Despite providing participants with the opportunity of monitoring the visual conduct of the other, and gearing the production of an activity to the behavior of the potential recipient, media space and videoconferencing systems can undermine the interactional significance of nonvocal action and activity. On the one hand, the speaker, or more generally the interactant, has visual access to the coparticipant. The speaker is able to monitor how the coparticipant behaves while speaking to him or her and remains sensitive to the recipient's behavior, state of involvement, and so on. But on the other hand, the resources on which a speaker ordinarily relies to shape the ways in which a coparticipant listens and attends to the talk appear to be interfered with by the technology. In video-mediated interaction, the speaker has visual access to the other but may be communicatively impotent.

Incongruent Environments of Action

Asymmetries in video-mediated conduct appear to arise in the light of two interrelated issues:

First, "recipients" have limited and distorted access to the visual conduct of the other. The other's conduct is available on a monitor that not only distorts the shape of a movement, transforming its temporal and spatial organization, but also presents the image of the other in toto. It destroys the relative weighting of different aspects of an individual's conduct. Moreover the presentation of the other on a conventional monitor undermines the possibility of peripherally monitoring the different aspects of the coparticipant's conduct.

Second, an individual's limited and distorted access to the other and the other's immediate environment undermines the individual's ability to design and redesign movements such as gestures in order to secure their performative impact. These problems become more severe when one recognizes that in contrast to physical copresence, a person undertaking an action, such as speaking, cannot change his or her own bodily orientation in order to adjust the perception of the recipient and the local environment. The speaker is unable to see how his or her actions appear to the other, and in consequence has relatively few resources to enable him or her to modify conduct in order to achieve a performative impact. It is not surprising, therefore, that in reviewing the data corpus, one finds numerous instances of upgraded and exaggerated gestures and body movements as speakers attempt to achieve some impact on the way that others are participating in the activity, literally, at hand.

Our observations of EuroPARC's relatively sophisticated media space, as well as more conventional videoconferencing systems, have shown that such systems provide users with incongruent environments in which to communicate and collaborate. Despite this incongruity, individuals presuppose the effectiveness of their conduct and assume that their frame of reference is "parallel" with the frame of reference of their coparticipant.

This presupposition of a common frame of reference and a reciprocity of perspectives is, as Schutz (1962) and others have pointed out, a foundation of socially organized conduct.

> Now it is a basic axiom of any interpretation of the common world and its objects that these various co-existing systems of coordinates can be transformed one into the other; I take it for granted, and I assume my fellow-man does the same, that I and my fellow-man would have typically the same experiences of the common world if we changed places, thus transforming my Here into his, and his—now to me a There—into mine. (Schutz, 1962, pp. 315–316)

In video-mediated presence, camera and monitor inevitably transform the environments of conduct, so that the bodily activity that one participant produces is rather different from the object received by the coparticipant. The presupposition that one environment is commensurate with the other undermines the production and receipt of visual conduct and suggests why gesture and other forms of bodily activity may be ineffectual when mediated through video rather than undertaken within a face-to-face, copresent environment.

COLLABORATIVE WORK IN ORGANIZATIONAL SETTINGS

The difficulties that people have when using media spaces, and perhaps the general lack of enthusiasm for the technology, becomes clearer when one considers how collaborative work is organized in more conventional environments. Alongside our research of media space use, we have undertaken a series of naturalistic studies of work, interaction, and technology in a range of organizational settings. These settings include line control rooms in the London Underground (Heath & Luff, 1992a, in press), primary health care (Greatbatch, Luff, Heath, & Campion, 1993), architectural practices (Luff & Heath, 1993), and news agencies (Heath & Nicholls, in press).

Although the settings encompass a broad range of tasks and technologies, the studies reveal that collaborative work in more conventional environments appears to reveal generic features that are relevant to how individuals organize their own activities and coordinate their own contributions, in real time, with others. So for example, if we take the London Underground control rooms we find that personnel have developed a body of informal and tacit practices for distributing information to each other and coordinating simultaneous, multiple activities. These practices allow personnel to distribute information to colleagues and to monitor each other's activities, while apparently engaged in a single, individual task. In this way, personnel coordinate their actions with each other and sustain a mutually compatible sense of the "business at hand" while managing their own specific responsibilities within a complex division of labor. The studies reveal the ways in which copresent collaborative work relies on a complex body of interactional practices through which personnel "peripherally monitor" and participate in each others actions and activities. Indeed, in such settings, it becomes increasingly difficult to demarcate the "individual" from the "collaborative" as personnel mutually sustain multiple activities that ebb and flow within various forms of coparticipation and production.

More generally the studies reveal various aspects of collaborative work that are of relevance both to the design and deployment of media space and to understanding the current limitations of such technologies. Of particular relevance are the findings that:

- Both focused and unfocused collaboration are largely accomplished not through direct face-to-face interaction, but through alignment toward the focal area of the activity, such as a document, where individuals coordinate their actions with others through "peripheral monitoring" of the others involvement in the activity "at hand." For example, much collaboration is undertaken side by side where the individuals are continuously sustaining a shared focus on an aspect of a screen- or paper-based document, such as a section of an architectural drawing.
- Collaborative work relies on individuals subtly and continuously adjusting their access to each others' activities to enable them to establish and sustain differential forms of coparticipation in the tasks "at hand."
- Collaborative work involves the ongoing and seamless transition between individual and collaborative tasks, where personnel are simultaneously participating in multiple, interrelated activities.
- Individuals' ability to contribute to the activities of others and fulfill their own responsibilities relies on peripheral awareness and monitoring; in this way information can be gleaned from the concurrent activities of others within the "local milieu," and actions and activities can be implicitly coordinated with the emergent tasks of others.
- Much of the interaction through which individuals produce, interpret, and coordinate actions and activities within copresent working environments is accomplished using various objects and artefacts, including paper- and screen-based documents, telephones, and the like. The participants activities are mediated and rendered visible through these objects and artifacts.

These observations stand in marked contrast to the support that media space provides for collaborative work. It becomes increasingly apparent, when you examine work and collaboration in more conventional environments, that the inflexible and restrictive views characteristic of even the most sophisticated media spaces provide impoverished settings in which to work together. This is not to suggest that media space research should simply attempt to "replace" copresent working environments; such ambitions are way beyond our current thinking and capabilities. Rather, we can learn a great deal concerning the requirements for the virtual office by considering how people work together and collaborate in more conventional settings. A more rigorous understanding of more conventional collaborative work can not only provide resources with which to recognize how, in building technologies, we are (inadvertently) changing the ways in which people work together, but also with ways that demarcate what needs to be supported and what can be left to one side (at least for time being). Such understanding might also help us deploy these advanced technologies.

DEVELOPING THE WORKSPACE

On the basis of the research we have described, we can begin to discern the limitations of a media space, at least as it is currently conceived. In part, these problems emerge as a result of assumptions that appear to inform the design of media spaces and related technologies such as videotelephones and videoconferencing systems. One such overriding assumption appears to be that a face-to-face, head and shoulders view is the most important for interpersonal communication and collaboration.

Yet, as we have discussed, face-to-face interaction is only one among a variety of cooperative activities that take place. Indeed, in many settings, face-to-face interaction constitutes a relatively small part of working together, and is one of a diverse configuration of spatial and bodily arrangements through which personnel participate in each others' activities and accomplish the "business at hand." In working together, individuals are continually and seamlessly shaping their participation and involvement in each other's activities as the demands of the task(s) and the interaction emerge. Individuals not only coordinate their actions with each other through various artifacts such as documents (whether on paper or screen) but continually adjust their access to each other and the tasks in which they are engaged. Perhaps the most important element of this interactional work is the ways in which individuals monitor each other's involvement in, or alignment to, an object or artifact. It is not simply a case of seeing what another is seeing, but rather seeing the other in relation to what he or she is looking at and doing. We need to consider ways of expanding access to the remote participant's activities, taking into account the flexible ways in which people accomplish collaborative tasks.

To explore some of these issues and in particular to consider the consequences of various ways of providing users with increased access to the remote space, we decided to undertake a series of experiments. The ultimate aim of the experiments was to inform the design of a system in which people could flexibly vary their access to their coparticipants and their coparticipant's activity and working environment. To do this, in collaboration with our colleague William Gaver, we began by constructing two simple systems offering variable, expanded access. The purpose of experimenting with these systems was to explore some of the interactional consequences of providing users with variable accessibility: to find out what the possible advantages and disadvantages of different design solutions might be.

The Multiple Target Video (MTV) Studies

One of the obvious ways of expanding access into another's domain is simply to increase the number of views a participant has of the remote environment. Thus, it should be possible to enhance the capabilities of media spaces by adding cameras and positioning these so that an individual has more than just a single face-to-face view of his or her coparticipants. Several commercial multimedia systems provide such possibilities, often by having an additional "document camera" pointed down onto the desk. However, the research we have outlined has suggested that having two views may still be limiting, being too restrictive and not providing a sense of colleagues' orientation to particular activities.

We therefore began by designing a system which offered more visual access: the Multiple Target Video (MTV) system. In the first of these experiments (MTV I), we offered different perspectives via four cameras: a conventional face-to-face view; a "desktop" camera to focus on the details of any activities on the work surface; a wider "in-context" view providing an image of the coparticipant in relation to their work; and a "bird's-eye" view giving access to the periphery of a colleague's environment. The difficulty for the design of such a system was how to display these different views to an individual.

In the first experiment, participants were given a single monitor to view the coparticipant, and could change their view on the remote site by turning a knob. Thus, each participant could select for display on the monitor only one view at a time, doing so by sometimes momentarily passing through other views. To provide further information, each participant was also given a "feedback monitor" showing which view the coparticipant had currently selected (see Fig. 15.5).

In this experiment, the participants were given two tasks in collaboration with another colleague: The first was to draw a plan of the coparticipant's

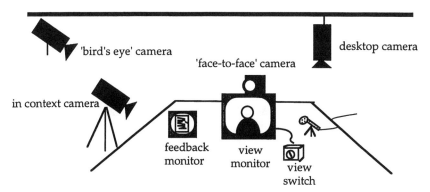

FIG. 15.5. Schematic diagram of the configuration of the MTV I system using multiple cameras and a single monitor for each participant.

office, and the second was to carry out a simple design task. In the design task, one of the participants, in the "design office," had a 3-D model of a room, complete with miniature furniture. The two participants' task was to agree on a layout for the room, subject to certain design constraints. The other person, in the "remote office," had to draw the final design. So that the individual in the remote office could see the model, one camera was used to focus on this model. This meant that the two participants did not have an identical range of views; only the individual in the "design office" had access to the bird's-eye view.

The experiment revealed some interesting results with regard to the use of the four different views.[2] For example, the face-to-face view was rarely used in the accomplishment of either task. Instead, participants mainly switched between the in-context, model, desk, and bird's-eye views. Given the nature of the design task it is perhaps not surprising that the participants in the "remote office" focused on the view showing most details of the model.[3] It appears that the in-context and bird's-eye cameras afforded similar possibilities for the subjects in the design office, allowing them to assess their colleague's orientation and to make sense of particular aspects of visual conduct, for example, gestures pointing to objects. Finally, some participants appeared to make use of the switch to track their colleagues as they moved around the room. It also seemed that the intermediate views that appeared while the user switched between settings provided opportunities to monitor aspects of a colleague's conduct and see, momentarily, other features in their domain.

However, the participants in the experiment did have difficulties with the system. As might be expected given the previous analysis, the MTV I system did not appear to alleviate the asymmetries revealed by our prior study of video-mediated communication. Participants still had difficulties when establishing and reestablishing engagement, with perturbations in

talk accompanying the beginning of turns, and with designing their gestures in the course of the interaction.

Moreover, the possibility of having different views of each other's domain appeared to exacerbate problems associated with these asymmetries.
Because each person could select from multiple views, participants appeared to be even more uncertain about what view the other had chosen
at any point in time. This fact, combined with the possibility that the
other's perspective could be transformed at any moment, further undermined the presumption of a reciprocity of perspectives. It is perhaps not
surprising that participants appeared to have difficulties both in achieving
a common orientation to focused tasks and in managing the disengagement from collaborative activities. Participants often had to make apparent,
through talk, their orientation to objects in the local environment and to
the technology. For example, they had to reformulate directions given by
their colleague, comment on their own movements and orientations, and
explicitly attempt to establish what the other could see. It seems that
variable access to the other and their respective domain can make it more
difficult for participants to preserve a sense of the (shifting) perspective
of the other and to thereby coordinate their actions and activities with the
contributions of their colleagues.

Interestingly, ascertaining the other's perspective did not seem to be
alleviated by the presence of the feedback monitor, through which it was
possible to find out what the other person was viewing. Instead, participants
appeared to make use of this to refer to objects in their own domain, pointing
to objects on the screen (such as their own documents) rather than pointing
to those same objects in their local environment. Of course, this strategy was
prone to difficulties, as pointing to the image on the feedback monitor was
difficult, if not impossible, for the remote person to see.

In addition to interfering with the establishment of a common frame
of reference within which to work, the need to switch between views also
appeared to be problematic because it precluded the ability to make a
smooth and natural transition amongst views. Having to think about and
negotiate the switch usually meant a break in the ongoing stream of activity.
This may have presented enough of a distraction to discourage full use of
the various views.

In maintaining the effort to provide variable accessibility to another's
domain, one possible solution to these difficulties was to remove the need
for sequential access via a switch. In a second study, we used a system (MTV
II) where each participant had multiple monitors each connected to a
different camera in the colleague's office (Fig. 15.6). In order to provide a
symmetrical range of views for both participants, each person had three
monitors showing an in-context view, a desktop view, and a face-to-face view.
The desktop view could be used either for viewing the model or a document.

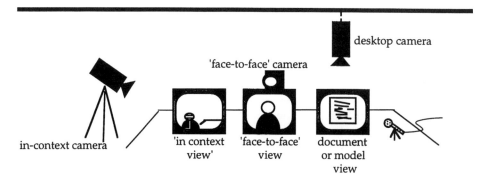

FIG. 15.6. Schematic diagram of the configuration of the MTV system using multiple cameras and multiple monitors for each participant.

The wide angle previously provided by the bird's-eye view was, in effect, provided by a wide-angle, in-context view. The three monitors were arranged in both rooms in a similar fashion with the face-to-face view in the middle. This meant that a orientation toward the face-to-face view would also appear to a coparticipant as a reorientation away from their in-context or desktop view, and vice versa. As both participants had access to all views simultaneously, there was no need for a feedback monitor. The tasks in this study were the same as those used in the first study.

Analysis of this second experiment showed that participants used all the views. Further, their pattern of looking at the different monitors showed that they "switched" views much more frequently than in MTV I. It may be that removing the necessity of having to switch views manually allows participants to use the available views more fully. Taking advantage of a different view was less cumbersome and did not require a break in the activity at hand.

Although they used all three views, participants oriented mainly to the desktop monitor when engaged in focused collaborative work, either to view documents or the model. However, the face-to-face view was found to be used much more frequently than in MTV I. During the course of the interaction participants would often glance briefly at each other between more prolonged sequences of looking at the model or document. Thus, although the face-to-face view was not looked at for long periods of time, it appeared to be pivotal as subjects tended to return to it frequently. Often, coparticipants utilized the view in order briefly to glance at their colleague. At other times, and especially after periods of prolonged silence, the face-to-face view was utilized with the in-context view to assess the other person's involvement in the activity.

Despite the advantages of having multiple views simultaneously available, the MTV II system still presented problems for the participants. Separate, fixed cameras still failed to offer complete access to the remote space. In addition, there still appeared to be difficulty in ascertaining the other person's perspective as evidenced by conversations in which participants attempted to make their orientation to the other explicit. The lack of access to a shared space for working, such as the inability to point to a shared document or artifact, also presented a problem. These findings point out the issues that such simple experimental configurations fail to address, and clearly need to be considered in the design of future technologies.

Although the MTV experiments must be regarded as only preliminary attempts to build a more flexible environment for collaborative work, they are important in that they represent a break from the assumption that collaboration and communication is mainly face-to-face. This is an assumption that we believe has led to the impoverishment of much media space research. Multiple views of another's environment do appear to provide facilities for undertaking more complex and wide-ranging collaborative work. However, the MTV studies have shown that design solutions that introduce variable access do this at the risk of imposing their own set of problems, as well as accentuating problems arising from the discontinuities and incongruencies that tend to be present in media space. It is important, however, to recognize these underlying problems, and to take them into account when envisaging how we might reconfigure media space. A more thorough understanding of the complex skills and competencies used by individuals in undertaking collaborative work not only can serve as a benchmark with which to evaluate our crude attempts to develop technologies, but also can provide an important resource in envisaging more innovative systems.

SUMMARY

In the light of research concerned with interaction and collaboration in both a media space and more conventional working environments, it is not surprising that recent developments in video-mediated communication have not met with the success that we might have envisaged. Although we will undoubtedly find markets for the videotelephone and for videoconferencing facilities, as well as more sophisticated forms of connectivity, we may have to go some way before we develop a technology that can support more complex forms of collaboration both within and across organizational environments. The limitations of current audiovisual infrastructures do not simply derive from the asymmetries that they inadvertently introduce into interpersonal communication. Indeed, as we have suggested elsewhere (Heath & Luff, 1992b), a certain insensitivity to another with whom one is intermittently working may have certain advantages in fulfilling one's own individual responsibilities. Rather, audiovisual connectivity, including the development of more sophisticated media spaces, has been primarily concerned with providing physically distributed personnel with face-to-face views of each other, whereas collaborative work recurrently involves variable and contingent access, not simply to each other's physical domain and artifacts but to the emergent activities in which the participants are engaged. Many forms of audiovisual connectivity, from basic videophones to advanced media spaces, have attempted to support interpersonal communication rather than collaboration and in consequence, perhaps, built relatively impoverished resources for working environments.

In attempting to address some of the issues concerning the requirements for and development of a media space, we inevitably confront some of the underlying "difficulties" that give rise to the peculiar forms of interpersonal conduct we find in communication mediated through audiovisual technologies. The relative insignificance of a look, the impotence of gestural activity, and their consequences for the articulation of talk derive not only from the distorted presentation of the coparticipants to each other, but also from the incongruent interactional environments provided by a media space. As Dourish, Adler, Bellotti, and Henderson (1996) recently argued, some of the difficulties that derive from this incongruence may be dealt with by an informal culture emerging among frequent users to manage the problems that arise in the operation of the system. This is undoubtedly the case. And yet, the interactional asymmetries that arise by virtue of the incongruent environments provided within a media space remain, and become increasingly severe, as we attempt to develop more sophisticated technologies to support collaborative work. Indeed, as the MTV experiments demonstrate, the more we try to develop a technological infrastructure to support variable access to each other's activities and the environments this necessitates, the more we can generate difficulties for users. Rather than rely upon the emergence of ad hoc informal culture to manage these problems, we need to explore systematically ways in which we can provide personnel with the resources with which to collaborate and participate, where necessary, in each other's activities, while unobtrusively preserving the individual's sensitivity to his own and his colleague's environment. If we can begin to address these issues and build a technology that can support task-based interaction and collaboration, then we might well be surprised with the impact of media spaces and telecommunications on work and organizational life.

ACKNOWLEDGMENTS

Part of the work reported in this chapter was supported by the EC RACE Programme (R2094) under the auspices of a research project entitled MITS

(Metaphors for Telecommunication Services). The MTV experiments were carried out in collaboration with William Gaver of the Rank Xerox Research Centre Cambridge EuroPARC (now at the Royal College of Art). We are also grateful to Wendy Mackay for assisting with the design of the MTV experiments. We would also like to thank Mike Molloy, Paul Dourish, and others at Rank Xerox Research Centre, Cambridge (EuroPARC), as well as Michel de Fornel, for their support and ideas during our studies of media space.

NOTES

1. This chapter also appeared in the book by S. Emmott (Ed.; 1995), *Information superhighways: Multimedia users and futures* (pp. 161–187). London: Academic Press, as the chapter "From video-mediated communication to technologies for collaboration: Reconfiguring media space." Reprinted by permission of Academic Press Ltd.
2. See Gaver, Sellen, Heath, and Luff (1993) for more details of the method and results of these experiments.
3. Although one "remote" subject mainly opted for the in-context view that provided access to the coparticipant in relation to the model.

REFERENCES

Birdwhistell, R. L. (1970). *Kinesics and context: Essays on body motion communication.* London: Allen Lane.
Bly, S. A. (1988, September). A use of drawing surfaces in different collaborative settings. *CSCW '88*, (pp. 250–256). Portland, OR.
Borning, A., & Travers, M. (1991). Two approaches to casual interaction over computer and video networks. In G. M. Olson, J. S. Olson, & S. P. Robertson (Eds.), *Proceedings of the ACM Conference on Human Factors in Computing Systems, (CHI '91)* (pp. 13–19). New Orleans, LA: ACM Press.
Bull, P. (1983). *Body movement and interpersonal communication.* Chichester: John Wiley and Sons.
Dourish, P., Adler, A., Bellotti, V., & Henderson, A. (1996). Your place or mine? Learning from long-term use of video communication. *Computer-Supported Cooperative Work, An International Journal, 5*(1), 33–62.
Ekman, P., & Friessen, W. V. (1969). The repertoires of nonverbal behavior: Categories, origins, usage and coding. *Semiotica, 1,* 49–98.
Gaver, W. W., Moran, T., Maclean, A., Lovstrand, L., Dourish, P., Carter, K. A., & Buxton, W. (1992). Realizing a video environment: EuroPARC's RAVE system. In G. Bennett, G. Lynch, & P. Bauersfeld (Eds.), *Proceedings of the ACM Conference on Human Factors in Computing Systems, (CHI 92),* (pp. 27–35). Monterey, CA: ACM Press.
Gaver, W. W., Sellen, A., Heath, C. C., & Luff, P. (1993). One is not enough: Multiple views in a media space. *Proceedings of the ACM Conference on Human Factors in Computing Systems, (INTERCHI '93)* (pp. 335–341). Amsterdam: ACM.
Goodwin, C. (1981). *Conversational organisation: Interaction between a speaker and hearer.* London: Academic Press.

Greatbatch, D., Luff, P., Heath, C. C., & Campion, P. (1993). Interpersonal communication and human–computer Interaction: An examination of the use of computers in medical consultations. *Interacting With Computers, 5*(2), 193–216.

Heath, C. C. (1986). *Body movement and speech in medical interaction.* Cambridge: Cambridge University Press.

Heath, C. C., & Luff, P. (1991). Disembodied conduct: Communication through video in a multi-media office environment. In G. M. Olson, J. S. Olson, & S. P. Robertson (Eds.), *Proceedings of the ACM Conference on Human Factors in Computing Systems (CHI '91)* (pp. 99–103). New Orleans, LA: ACM Press.

Heath, C. C., & Luff, P. (1992a). Collaboration and control: Crisis management and multimedia technology in London Underground Line control rooms. *CSCW Journal, 1*(1–2), 69–94.

Heath, C. C., & Luff, P. (1992b). Media space and communicative asymmetries: Preliminary observations of video mediated interaction. *Human-Computer Interaction, 7,* 315–346.

Heath, C. C., & Luff, P. (in press). Converging activities: Line control and passenger information on London Underground. In Y. Engestrom & D. Middleton (Eds.), *Cognition and communication at work: Distributed cognition in the workplace.* Cambridge: Cambridge University Press.

Heath, C. C., & Nicholls, G. M. (in press). Animating texts: Selective readings of news stories. In L. B. Resnick & R. Saljo (Eds.), *Discourse, tools and reasoning: Situated cognition & technologically supported environments.*

Kendon, A. (1990). *Conducting interaction: Studies in the behavior of social interaction.* Cambridge: Cambridge University Press.

Luff, P., & Heath, C. C. (1993). System use and social organisation: Observations on human computer interaction in an architectural practice. In G. Button (Ed.), *Technology in working order* (pp. 184–210). London: Routledge.

Olson, G. M., & Olson, J. S. (1991). User-centered design of collaboration technology. *Journal of Organisational Computing, 1*(1), 61–83.

Olson, J. S., Olson, G. M., Mack, L. A., & Wellner, P. (1990). Concurrent editing: The group interface. In D. Diaper, D. Gilmore, G. Cockton, & B. Shackel (Ed.), *Interact '90—Third IFIP Conference on Human–Computer Interaction* (pp. 835–840). Cambridge: North Holland.

Schegloff, E. A. (1972). Notes on a conversational practice: Formulating place. In D. Sudnow (Eds.), *Studies in social interaction* (pp. 75–119). New York: Free Press.

Schegloff, E. A. (1984). On some gestures' relation to talk. In J. M. Atkinson & J. C. Heritage (Eds.), *Structures of social action: Studies in conversation analysis* (pp. 266–296). Cambridge: Cambridge University Press.

Schutz, A. (1962). *Collected papers I: The problem of social reality.* The Hague: Martinus Nijhoff.

Sellen, A. (1995). Remote conversations: The effects of mediating talk with technology. *Human–Computer Interaction, 4,* 401–444.

Smith, R. B., O' Shea, T., O' Malley, C., & Taylor, J. S. (1989, September). Preliminary experiments with a distributed, multi-media problem solving environment. *First European Conference on Computer Supported Cooperative Work* (pp. 19–35). London.

DESIGN

Chapter 16

Models and Metaphors for Video-Mediated Communication

Sylvia Wilbur
Queen Mary & Westfield College, University of London

This chapter provides an introduction to Part III on design of video-mediated communication. Various approaches have been taken to this area, each based on a particular view of how video can serve the social and task-related needs of distributed workgroups. Examples of different models of video-based communication are media space, virtual meeting room, shared workstation, multiparty conferencing, and "dense-mode" (large-scale) conferencing. This chapter aims to identify common threads among these models and show how each reflects a different perspective on a common abstraction: shared virtual space. A virtual space provides a context for real-time collaboration over audio, video, and data channels. The properties of contextualized communication vary for different interaction scenarios and the characteristics of virtual spaces for generic types of video communication are discussed.

INTRODUCTION

Part III of this volume focuses on the design of systems for video-mediated collaboration. This area of research, now well established after a decade of experimental work, has produced a variety of different approaches to the use of visual communication in collaborative technology. Each approach presents a "model of communication" that incorporates both a context for collaboration and an implied style of user interaction. Examples are media space, virtual meeting room, shared workstation, and multiparty conferencing. Systems based on these abstractions are described within the following section and elsewhere in this volume. By way of introduction to Part III, this chapter aims to identify common threads among these models and show how each reflects a different perspective on the design of collaborative contexts.

Despite their different approaches, experimental systems based on video-mediated communication (VMC) share a common view of the medium as a general-purpose, ubiquitous tool in the workplace of the future. Advances in digital video transmission and improvements in workstation architectures will ultimately make this vision realizable. Buxton, in chapter 17 on augmented reality, envisages a range of video devices in every office, each designed to serve a specific communication purpose. For the present, however, experimental work with multiparty video is still largely based on analog technology. Separate video networks and computer-controlled switching devices together offer more or less unlimited connectivity and bandwidth, without affecting the performance of the local data network. For remote collaboration, high-quality, full-size color images on desktop monitors provide a sense of copresence, and images can be multiplexed for group discussions. Collaborative systems for real-time interaction typically offer users a range of desktop applications integrating video, audio, and data communications.

Experimental systems for informal, intraorganizational communication include Xerox PARC's media space (Bly, Harrison, & Irwin, 1993), Rank Xerox Cambridge EuroPARC's RAVE (Gaver et al., 1992), Bellcore's Cruiser (Fish, Kraut, Root, & Rice, 1993), and the Ontario Telepresence Project (Buxton, 1992). An experimental analog system on a smaller scale was built at Queen Mary & Westfield College, University of London (Wilbur & Ing, 1993). More recently, SunSoft's Montage, a prototype system based on digital video, has aimed to provide a sense of teleproximity for distributed groups (Tang, Isaacs, & Rua, 1994). For wide-area conferencing, AT&T's Rapport system (Ensor, Ahuja, Connaghan, Pack, & Seligman, 1992) provides a range of services for users in the context of virtual meeting rooms, and other multisite conferencing systems include MAJIC (Okada, Maeda, Ichikawaa, & Matsushita, 1994), Bellcore's Rendezvous (Hill, Brinck, Patterson, Rohall, & Wilner, 1994), and Touring Machine (Arango et al., 1994). The United Kingdom-based MICE project has experimented with multisite videoconferencing over the Internet (Bilting, Sasse, Schulz, & Turletti, 1994).

The unifying thread among all these systems is the integration of real-time video and audio connections in a computer-supported context for remote collaboration. By context is meant not only the setting in which remote meetings are held, but also one where opportunities for opening unplanned collaborations can occur. The general aim has been to emulate the characteristic richness of face-to-face encounters through support for naturalistic ways of making contact, engaging in conversation, and performing collaborative tasks. In face-to-face conversations, the design of the physical environment in which meetings take place is important for contextualizing the communication. Meeting places are typically designed for specific types of communication, for example, board rooms, lecture theaters, and reception areas. When distributed meetings take place over video, appropriate contextualization of users' interactions in a *virtual space* is then required. Mediated by real-time media, and existing in parallel with the physical space in which each user resides, this virtual space becomes the context for users' interactions. As in real space, the effectiveness of remote collaboration is enhanced if participants feel close to those they are communicating with and are aware of where their attention is directed. Creating an environment where participants experience *awareness* and *teleproximity* is therefore an essential aspect of the design of virtual space (Tang et al., 1994; Gaver, 1992).

But is the contribution of real-time media simply to provide channels of communication? In earlier studies of video-based interaction, media appeared to have a quality of *social presence* (Short, Williams, & Christie, 1976) during remote conversations. Short's research on the impact of telecommunication media on collaboration suggested that nonverbal communication has effects on the outcomes of mediated interactions by determining feelings of social presence. Viewed from this perspective, media do not just afford remote collaboration, they are components of the virtual context itself. In this case, mediated environments can never be facsimiles of real space, and the social presence of the media will influence the interactions that occur.

The concept of a virtual space (VS) where people meet for real-time interaction is central to the various models of VMC discussed in the following chapters. Each model provides a particular perspective on remote interaction that must be understood in order to use the system effectively. As an introduction to the section on VMC design, we attempt to reconcile these different perspectives within a single, generalized view of a VS. We show how each model of video communication reflects a particular social or task-focused view of collaboration. Whether the design of a VS emphasizes its role as a "person space" or a "task space" (Buxton, 1992) is an important distinction among media spaces, virtual meeting rooms, shared workspace, and conferencing systems.

SPATIAL CONTEXTS FOR COLLABORATION

Designers of VMC systems have generally aimed to imitate the affordances of face-to-face communication. What different kinds of communication need to be considered? A generic scheme for classifying communication was defined by Applbaum (1973) in which "levels" of human interaction were described. These levels were:

- Nonverbal
- Dyadic
- Small-group
- Intercultural
- Public speaking

For each level, a physical context is required that reflects the characteristics of that type of communication. A public speech, for example, normally requires a large, open space with a platform for the speaker, whereas dyadic conversations can start almost anywhere. Attributes that distinguish these categories of communication include group size, mode of interaction, and degree of formality. In general, these attributes are closely linked. During a public address or lecture, for example, communication is mainly one way, and attendees do not expect to be able to interact freely with others in the room during the talk. The design of lecture theaters, therefore, reflects these expectations. In contrast, a coffee area where small groups tend to congregate is designed to enable people to mingle freely and engage with whom they please.

Dyadic or small-group communication tends to be informal, by which we mean it is often unplanned, transient, and social in nature. Open, uncluttered areas with good access, such as hallways, corridors, and coffee areas, enable people to "sight" others and start informal conversations. The physical proximity of small-group interactions lets people establish eye contact, observe bodily posture, and give visual responses (smiles, nods, etc.) to the person they are listening to.

That informal communication plays a significant role in organizational communication is becoming increasingly clear from recent studies (Whittaker, Frohlich, & Daly-Jones, 1993; Fish et al., 1993; Kraut, Egido, & Galegher, 1988). The following categories of informal interaction were proposed by Kraut:

- Intended—when one person seeks out another for a specific purpose
- Opportunistic—when one person by chance sights someone he or she wishes to speak to
- Spontaneous—two or more people meet and begin an unplanned conversation

These categories differ mainly in terms of their "openings." Shared areas around a coffee machine or in corridors provide a context for spontaneous and opportunistic conversations to start. The spatial design of these areas—for example, room for people to stop and chat—is important for promoting this type of communication. In contrast, intended collaborations often originate in private offices, when one person "drops by" the office of another for a brief, ad hoc consultation. Both private and shared areas can therefore provide the setting for the opening of informal communications, whereas more preplanned activities take place in designated meeting rooms.

Areas designed for preplanned meetings typically contain objects such as whiteboards, projectors, and VCRs to aid the discussions. Participants in a meeting may bring additional artifacts to the meeting place, for example, documents, designs, and transparencies. During the collaboration, these may be utilized for generating ideas, sharing information, or collaborative design. In some cases, some participants may be allowed only to view shared information, whereas others can modify its contents. Membership of the group, and hence entry to the meeting place, may be controlled if discussions are confidential.

In summary, the design and furnishings of a physical meeting place reflect the type of communication it is intended for. Important aspects of the design of meeting rooms include physical dimensions, accessibility, affordances for visual and verbal interaction, and the objects in the room. Such rooms, however, are used mainly for preplanned collaborations; informal, unplanned collaborations occur in wider settings, such as corridors, hallways, or in the context of private offices. Providing opportunities for the "openings" of informal communication in these settings is an important aspect of a generalized virtual space.

VIRTUAL CONTEXTS FOR COLLABORATION

Figure 16.1 depicts the components of a generalized VS intended to provide opportunities for openings of conversations as well as for engaging in collaboration. Spatial contexts for openings (private, public, and group meeting places) are shown around the meeting context itself. During the opening stages of collaboration, "sightings" may be made, the availability of others is checked out, and people move to establish copresence. Successful openings lead to collaborations, when the task-related and social aspects of the interactions rely on the quality of both visual and auditory channels, and on the availability of shared objects. The figure is intended to show how the different aspects of collaboration—the shared "person space" and "task space," first proposed by Buxton (1992)—are integrated in a virtual space for collaboration. Mané, in chapter 19 on group space,

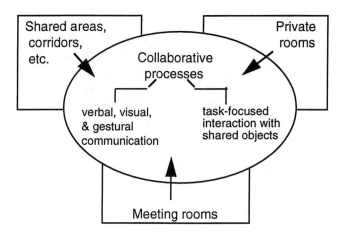

FIG. 16.1. Contextualized collaboration.

extends these ideas further and suggests that the roles of participants affect their requirements for communication channels.

When a multimedia environment becomes the context for remote collaboration, the characteristics of the VS created should, like physical space, reflect the type of social and/or task-related interaction it is intended for. For informal communication, opportunistic conversations should be supported by helping users be aware of who is around to talk to over video channels. A model of informal communication, where awareness of others is a key concept, is the basis for design of a *media space*. In contrast, a more task-focused environment will emphasize support for interaction with the tools and information required for that activity. The user interface to a VS implementation reflects its social or task-related goals, and here metaphors from the real world can be usefully employed to suggest the kind of context intended. The Cruiser system, for example, presents the user with a virtual corridor for social browsing (Fish et al., 1993), whereas Rapport provides a representation of a virtual meeting room for more task-focused activities (Seligmann, Mercuri, & Edmark, 1995).

Currently, implementations of virtual spaces do not attempt to address every social and task-related aspect of contextualized collaboration. Constraints on design of current systems include both the cost and the technical capabilities of current hardware, plus the demands placed on the underlying network infrastructure by multiple video channels. In addition, further research is required into the impact of various design options on specific tasks and social functioning of workgroups. For these reasons, designers have tended to concentrate on specific aspects of real-time collaboration. The various models of communication presented in this volume, then, can be regarded as different, but complementary, views on a virtual space, or alternatively, as different levels on which collaboration operates.

Media Spaces

The media space concept originated in work at Xerox PARC in the mid 1980s (Bly et al., 1993), although its roots can be traced back to earlier work with videophone and videoconferencing technologies. The researchers at PARC defined a media space as "an electronic setting in which groups of people can work together, even when they are not resident in the same place or present at the same time." The design of a media space emphasizes the social nature of work, and the importance of informal communications. Gaver (1992) described media spaces as indicating "an analogy to everyday space . . . media spaces support 'virtual copresence' and act as tailorable office-spaces." Media spaces aim to support informal communication among participants by promoting awareness of who is around to talk to, and by providing interfaces for contact and engagement with others. For intended communication, a video glance application enables the initiator to take a brief look into the office of someone they wish to consult (Tang et al., 1994; Wilbur & Ing, 1996). The glance must be reciprocal—that is, anyone who is glanced at over a brief video connection has the right to know who initiated the operation.

Earlier media spaces were often discontinuous, reducing the opportunity, for example, to move seamlessly from glancing at someone to starting a conversation. More recently, this issue has been addressed in systems such as SunSoft's Montage and QMW's MEET system. Facilities for hovering in the background of a conversation or leaving a message are also provided, enabling users to use their natural styles of interaction in the workplace.

At the user interface, the virtual space may be represented, for example, by a corridor (Cruiser), a hallway (Montage), or a set of doors (Telepresence). Each provides a useful metaphor for browsing the virtual space for people to communicate with. Because a media space is essentially a social place, issues such as privacy controls are important to address. The Ontario Telepresence project, for example, uses door icons to indicate several degrees of privacy (Harrison, Mantei, Beirne, & Narine, 1994). If the graphical representation of a door indicates it is open, no permission is needed to glance inside. If the door is closed, permission must be obtained, via an auditory "knock," before entering. Montage has similar levels of accessibility.

As this discussion shows, in media spaces the role of video is not just an accompaniment to voice communication. A glance application is just a two-way video connection for a few seconds where auditory channels would be an intrusion. In Portholes, single video frames were used in a representation of a kind of picture gallery showing the recent status of people in remote offices (Dourish & Bly, 1992). As these examples show, video is already a medium with a range of different applications.

Virtual Meeting Rooms

Virtual meeting rooms (VMR), described by Ensor in chapter 20, are a model adopted by AT & T Bell Laboratories as the basis for the design of Rapport and other systems for long-distance interpersonal communication. As the name suggests, the components of the model are based on the basic properties of a physical meeting room, and the constraints and affordances these properties imply. Although opportunistic communication can occur when two people enter a shared VMR at the same time, this type of virtual space focuses mainly on task-related aspects of collaboration. Computer-based tools and shared information are important objects associated with a VMR, and can be protected from unauthorized access. A "meeting" in the VMR context need not involve interpersonal interactions—a meeting takes place "whenever any person or computer program accesses information within a room."

An important property of a VMR is its persistence. It represents a place that exists for as long as it is needed, where people can meet or deposit shared information and tools. Members of the room are represented by graphics that convert to video feeds when the user enters the room. Because the group that owns a VMR may consist of any number of people, who may be long distances apart, "talking heads" video is used. Graphical simulations can be used to provide additional visual feedback concerning where people are focusing their attention and to provide backchannel responses such as smiles and nods (Seligmann et al., 1995).

The perspective of VMRs, then, is on the task space of collaboration. Video denotes presence, but does not attempt to provide the full range of visual cues available in face-to-face. Instead, assurance cues (about connectivity, level of attention, gaze, etc.) are provided by other means.

The DIVA virtual environment (Sohlenkamp & Chwelos, 1994) is also based on a model of a persistent meeting room. The prototype DIVA supports a simple abstraction that models in a virtual space the basic elements of the physical world: people, rooms, desks, and documents. Users are able to have synchronous and asynchronous communication, and a glance in the virtual office window provides awareness of the activities of other members of a collaborative workgroup.

Multiparty Videoconferencing

In multiparty videoconferencing, participants from multiple sites hold a meeting over video and audio communication channels. Conventional approaches to videoconferencing have concentrated on the technical aspects of setting up connections, transmission of real-time data, and session management. Less attention has been paid to the dynamics of participants' visual and verbal interactions. In face-to-face meetings, participants can get a sense of both the group as a whole and of individuals' contributions; the ability to establish eye contact, have "side" conversations, and be aware of where others are looking are all aspects of group interaction that are usually missing in videoconferencing.

Chapter 18 by Buxton, Sellen, and Sheasby describes experimental work on user interfaces and display technologies aiming to overcome these limitations. Rapid prototyping techniques have been used to evaluate a variety of new design approaches in systems such as Hydra, LiveWire, and the Brady Bunch. The main perspective of this area of work, then, is enhancement of the "person" or social aspects of virtual space. Issues such as the way meetings are set up, task outcomes, access controls, and the persistence of collaborations are not addressed.

Another prototype system that attempts to imitate even more closely the characteristics of interaction in physical space is the prototype MAJIC system (Multi-Attendant Joint Interface for Collaboration). MAJIC aims to provide a feeling of the correct "social distance" (proxemics) that users need in a meeting where decisions are to be taken, by supporting multiple eye contact among participants and life-size images projected on a 4 ft × 8 ft curved screen constructed from thin transparent film (Okada et al., 1994). Each video camera is set up behind the screen at the center of the user's face, allowing users to make eye contact and providing life-size images. The project has concentrated on the technical issues of simulating physical closeness without addressing the social aspects of how people establish connections.

Chapter 19 by Mané, on group space, emphasizes the asymmetric value of "talking heads" video. Most research into the value of video communication in remote multiparty collaboration has focused on the visual needs of listeners. However, anecdotal evidence suggests that the lack of visual cues may, in fact, have more impact on the speaker, by depriving him or her of feedback on reactions to the message. Voice-activated video switching does not address these issues.

Shared Workstation

NTT's TeamWorkStation provides a shared workspace for two users working on a shared design. While essentially focused on the specific task of design, the system integrates video images of the users with the shared drawing surface, using overlaying techniques and specialized technology for the drawing space. The metaphor here is "talking through and drawing on a large glass board." Because video images are overlaid on the drawing surface, each user can see the image of his or her partner while drawing. Being aware of the direction and expression of the other's gaze, a designer can gauge the other's reaction to a drawing action, and adapt behavior accordingly. In this way, the social aspects of collaboration are successfully integrated with the task.

VIRTUAL CONTEXTS FOR LARGE-SCALE COMMUNICATION

Applbaum's levels of communication provided a starting place for our discussion of contextualized communication. So far, we have described virtual spaces for nonverbal (i.e., glances, gaze), dyadic, and small-group levels of communication. There remain the intercultural and public-speaking levels of communication. These needs are met by videoconferencing on the Internet, over the multicast virtual network known as the Mbone.

Mbone conferencing is sometimes called CB for short—the video version of Citizens' Band radio, or the "Tune in, turn on, and audio drop-out" model described by Jon Crowcroft in chapter 24 on Internet conferencing in this volume. Current Internet services are able to support only limited interaction during real-time conferencing. Indeed, most events conform to a noninteractive, receiver-join approach that is the only practical model for large-scale participation. Although some private conferences for smaller groups do take place, the broadcasting of major events and conferences attracts the most attention. These include events of international interest, like the NASA Space Shuttle launch, public addresses by public figures, poetry recitals and concerts, and academic conferences.

Although basically a connection-based approach, Mbone conferencing has aspects of a virtual space. At the user interface, a "rendezvous" metaphor lets users set up private, ad hoc conversations by selecting a name from the list of participants. Receivers can get a feeling of "being there" when the remote camera transmits pictures of the conference setting when no speaker sessions are scheduled.

BEYOND THE CONSTRAINTS OF PHYSICAL SPACE

We began this chapter by observing that designers of VMC systems have aimed to emulate the affordances of face-to-face collaboration. Each model of communication we have discussed has addressed specific aspects of a virtual context for collaboration that incorporates the fundamental components of physical environments.

The affordances of a virtual space need not, however, be limited by the constraints of real environments. In Rapport, for example, users can participate in more than one collaboration at a time, and any number of participants can be accommodated in a virtual meeting room. In the Brady Bunch system, a participant is able to start a "side conversation" with any member of the group, unlike face-to-face meetings where asides are only possible with those in close physical proximity. And with TeamWorkStation, two coworkers can maintain eye contact while simultaneously drawing. These examples illustrate how a VS can imitate the characteristics of real space and at the same time provide opportunities for an even richer set of visual and verbal exchanges.

It seems likely that the various models and metaphors for video-mediated collaboration we have discussed will eventually merge into a single, powerful model for remote communication. The signs of this are already there, as systems that were previously labeled plain old "videoconferencing" begin to absorb the concepts of awareness and teleproximity that have emanated from media space systems.

DESIGN TOPICS COVERED IN THE REMAINDER OF THIS SECTION

In chapter 17, Buxton discusses "Living in Augmented Reality." This chapter describes the experience of living with ubiquitous video and media space systems over a period of 7 years, providing insights that may have important implications for the future of video in the workplace. A rather different perspective on design of video systems is given in chapter 18, "Interfaces for Multiparty Videoconferences," by Buxton, Sellen, and Sheasby. This chapter focuses on the problems of supporting with video the complex dynamic interactions that characterize multiparty meetings. The theme of group interaction is continued in chapter 19, in which Mane explores the value of video in multiparty discussions, its asymmetric properties, and its contribution to grounding in multiparty conversations. He describes an implementation of group space based on multiple control units (MCUs), with voice-activated switching. This "meeting room" representation provides a link with chapter 20 by Ensor on virtual meeting rooms. Ensor elaborates the VMR concept and describes various implementations, emphasizing the importance of information-sharing and persistence in collaborative environments. The final chapter in this section is by Ishii, Kobayashi, Arita, and Yagi: Design concepts for video are illustrated by reference to TeamWorkStation, a shared workspace with overlaid video, and to ClearBoard. The latter system seamlessly integrates a shared workspace and interpersonal space for remote design collaboration between two people.

REFERENCES

Applbaum, R. L. (1973). *Fundamental concepts in human communication.* New York: Harper and Row.

Arango, M., Bahler, L., Bates, P., Cochinwala, L., Cohrs, D., Rish, R., Gopal, G., Griffeth, N., Herman, G., Hickey, T., Lee, K. C., Leland, W., Lowery, V., Mak, V., Patterson, J., Ruston,

L., Segal, M., Sekar, M. P., Vecchi, M., Weinrib, A., & Wuu, S.-Y. (1994). The TOURING MACHINE system. *Communications of the ACM, 36*(1), 68–77.

Bilting, U., Sasse, A., Schulz, C.-D., Turletti, T. (1994, June). Remote seminars through multimedia conferencing: Experiences from the MICE project. *Proceedings of INET '94.* Prague.

Bly, S. A., Harrison, S. R., & Irwin S. (1993). Media spaces: Bringing people together in a video, audio, and computing environment. *Communications of the ACM, 36*(1), 28–43.

Buxton, W. (1992, May). Telepresence: Integrating shared task and person spaces. *Proceedings of Graphics Interface '92* (pp. 123–129), Vancouver, BC.

Dourish, P., & Bly, S. (1992, May). Portholes: Supporting awareness in a distributed work group. *Proceedings of CHI'92* (pp. 541–547). Monterey, CA.

Ensor, J. R., Ahuja, S. R., Connaghan, S. R., Pack, R. B., & Seligmann, D. D. (1992, May). The Rapport multimedia communication system. *Proceedings of ACM SIGCHI '92* (pp. 581–582). Monterey, CA.

Fish, R. S., Kraut, R. E., Root, R. W., & Rice, R. E. (1993). Video as a technology for informal communication. *Communications of the ACM, 36*(1), 48–61.

Gaver, W. W. (1992, November). The affordances of media spaces for collaboration. *Proceedings of CSCW 92* (pp. 17–24). Toronto.

Gaver, W., Moran, T., MacLean, A., Lövstrand, L., Dourish, P., Carter, K., & Buxton, W. (1992, May). Realizing a video environment: Europarc's RAVE system. *Proceedings of CHI'92* (pp. 27–35). Monterey. CA.

Harrison, B., Mantei, M., Beirne, G., & Narine, T. (1994, April). Communicating about communicating: Cross-disciplinary design of a media space interface. *Proceedings of CHI '94* (pp. 124–131). Boston.

Hill, R. D., Brinck, T., Patterson, J. F., Rohall, S. I., & Wilner, W. T. (1994). The Rendezvous language and architecture. *Communications of the ACM, 36*(1), 62–67.

Kraut, R., Egido, C., & Galegher, J. (1988). Patterns of contact and communication in scientific research collaboration. *Proceedings of CSCW 88* (pp. 1–13). Portland, OR.

Okada, K.-I., Maeda, Y., Ichikawaa, Y., & Matsushita, Y. (1994, October). Multiparty videoconferencing at virtual social distance: MAGIC Design. *Proceedings of CSCW '94* (pp. 385–395). Chapel Hill, NC.

Seligmann, D. D., Mercuri, R. T., & Edmark, J. T. (1995, May). Providing assurances in a multimedia environment. *Proceedings of Human Factors in Computing Systems ACM SIGCHI '95* (pp. 250–256). Denver, CO.

Short, J., Williams, E., & Christie, B. (1976). *The social psychology of telecommunications.* London: Wiley & Sons.

Sohlenkamp, M., & Chwelos, G. (1994, October). Integrating communication, cooperation, and awareness: The DIVA virtual office environment. *Proceedings of CSCW '94* (pp. 331–345). Chapel Hill, NC.

Tang, J., Isaacs, E. A., & Rua, M. (1994, October). Supporting distributed groups with a Montage of lightweight interactions. *Proceedings of CSCW '94* (pp. 23–35). Chapel Hill, NC.

Whittaker, S., Frohlich, D., & Daly-Jones O. (1994, April). *Proceedings of CHI '94* (pp. 2–10). Boston.

Wilbur, S., & Ing, S. (1993, March). Interaction management in office-based multimedia collaboration. *Proceedings of Telepresence 93, 3rd European Congress.* Lille, France.

Wilbur, S., & Ing, S. (1996). Real-time video for informal workgroup communication. *Computer Networks and ISDN Systems, 28,* 491–497.

Chapter 17

Living in Augmented Reality: Ubiquitous Media and Reactive Environments

William A. S. Buxton
Computer Systems Research Institute, University of Toronto
and
Alias | Wavefront Inc.

One thread of this chapter presents a particular approach to the design of media. It is based on the notion that media spaces can be thought of as the video counterpart of ubiquitous computing. The combination of the two is what we call Ubiquitous Media. *We go on to discuss the synergies that result from approaching these two technologies from a unified perspective.*

The second thread is of a practice and experience nature. We discuss ubiquitous media from the perspective of having actually "lived the life." By basing our arguments on experience gained as part of the Ontario Telepresence Project, we attempt to anchor our views on practical experience rather than abstract speculation.

INTRODUCTION

In 1991, Mark Weiser, of Xerox PARC, published an article that outlined a vision of the next generation of computation (Weiser, 1991). He referred to this model as *ubiquitous computing,* or *UbiComp.* UbiComp was based on the notion that it is inappropriate to channel all of one's computational activities through a single computer or workstation. Rather, Weiser argued that access to computational services should be delivered through a number of different devices, each of whose design and location was tailored to support a particular task or set of tasks. It is on this notion of delivering computational services throughout our work, play, and living spaces that the ubiquity in the name is based.

In addition to ubiquity, UbiComp assumes that the delivery of computation should be *transparent*. There is a seeming paradox that arises between the principle of ubiquity and that of transparency. The resolution of this paradox, through the use of examples, constitutes a significant part of this chapter.

Around the same time that Weiser and his colleagues were developing the ideas that were to emerge as UbiComp (Fig. 17.1), others down the hall at Xerox PARC were developing video-based extensions to physical architecture, so-called *media spaces* (Stults, 1986; Bly, Harrison, & Irwin, 1993). These were systems through which people in remote offices, buildings, and even cities could work together as if they were in the same architectural space. Although they are prototypes, these systems enabled one to work side by side at one's desk with someone in a remote location (Fig. 17.2). You could call out of your door and ask "Has anyone seen Sara?" without thinking about whether the answer would come from Portland, Oregon, or Palo Alto, California. Nor did it matter at which of these two centers either you or Sara was at. The technology supported a sense of shared presence and communal social space that was independent of geographical location. The result can perhaps best be described as a *social prosthesis* that afforded support of the links that hold together a social network—links that are typically only maintainable in same-place activities.

Weiser's paper gave no hint of the activities of the media space group, and vice versa. However, I increasingly began to see the two projects as two sides of the same coin. Consequently, in my work with the Ontario Telepresence Project (at the University of Toronto, partially supported by

FIG. 17.1.   Xerox PARC tab. (Photo: Xerox PARC.)

FIG. 17.2. Shared open office via Media Space (Photo: Xerox PARC).

Xerox PARC), I began to consciously apply the tenets of UbiComp to the media space technology. Thus, just as UbiComp deems it inappropriate to channel all of your computational activity through a single workstation, so in *ubiquitous video* (*UbiVid*) we deemed it inappropriate to channel all of our communications through a single "video station" (viz., camera, video monitor, microphone, loudspeaker). And as in UbiComp, the location, scale, and form of the technology were determined by its intended function. And although ubiquitous, our focus was to render access to the services of these communications technologies transparent.

UbiComp and UbiVid—let us call them collectively *ubiquitous media*—represent an approach to design that is in contrast to today's multimedia computers, in which functionality is inherently bundled into a single device, located at a single location, and operated by a single individual. Ubiquitous media, on the other hand, is an architectural concept in that it is concerned with preserving, or building on, conventional location–function–distance relationships.

Ubiquitous media can also be understood in relation to artificial reality. Rather than turning inward into an artificial world, ubiquitous media encourage us to look outward. It expands our perception and interaction in the physical world. (For example, in the attempt to find Sara, consider the augmentation of the social space to include the physical space of both Palo Alto and Portland. The augmentation was socially transparent. There was no "user interface" other than that used in conventional architecture: One just called blindly out the door.) In contrast to "virtual" or "artificial" reality, we consider our use of ubiquitous media as *augmented reality* (Wellner, Mackay, & Gold, 1993).

In this chapter, we discuss our experience living in such an environment over the past 7 years. From this experience emerge insights that we believe have important implications to the future deployment of media—insights that we feel are doubly important in this period of technology convergence, especially because they are derived from actual experience, rather than theoretical speculation.

UBICOMP: A BRIEF OVERVIEW

As described by Weiser, UbiComp can be characterized by two main attributes:

- *Ubiquity:* Interactions are not channeled through a single workstation. Access to computation is "everywhere." For example, in one's office there would be tens of computers, displays, and so on. These would range from watch-sized Tabs, through notebook-sized Pads, to whiteboard-sized Boards (Fig. 17.3). All would be networked. Wireless networks would be widely available to support mobile and remote access.

FIG. 17.3. Xerox Liveboard and PARCpads (Photo: Xerox PARC).

- *Transparency:* This technology is nonintrusive and is as invisible and as integrated into the general ecology of the home or workplace as, for example, a desk, chair, or book.

These two attributes present an apparent paradox: How can something be everywhere yet be invisible? Resolving this paradox leads us to the essence of the underlying idea. It is not that one cannot see (hear or touch) the technology, but rather that its presence does not intrude into the environment of the workplace (either in terms of physical space or the activities being performed). Like the conventional technology of the workplace (e.g., architecture and furniture), its use is clear, and its physical instantiation is tailored specifically for the space and the function for which it is intended. Central to UbiComp is a break from the "Henry Ford" model of computation, which can be paraphrased as: "You can have it in any form you want as long as it has a mouse, keyboard, and display." Fitting the square peg of the breadth of real needs and applications into the round hole of conventional designs, such as the GUI, has no place in the UbiComp model.

Technology Warms Up

We can most easily place Weiser's model of computation in historical perspective by the use of an analogy with heating systems. In earliest times, architecture (at least in cold climates) was dominated by the need to contain heat. Special structures were built to contain an open fire without burning down. Likewise, in the early days, special structures were built to house computation. These were known as *computer centers.*

As architecture progressed, buildings were constructed where fires were contained in fireplaces, thereby permitting heat in more than one room. Nevertheless, only special rooms had fire because having a fireplace required adjacency to a chimney. Similarly, the analogous generation of computation was available in rooms outside of computer centers; however, these required access to special electrical cabling and air conditioning. Therefore, computation was still restricted to special "computer rooms."

The next generation of heating system is characterized by Franklin stoves and, later, radiators. Now we could have heat in every room. This required the "plumbing" to distribute the system, however. The intrusion of this "plumbing" into the living space was viewed as a small price to pay for distributed access to heat. Again, there is an analogous generation of computational technology (the generation in which we are now living). In it, we have access to computation in any room, as long as we are connected to the "plumbing" infrastructure. And like the heating system, this implies both an intrusion into the space and an "anchor" that limits mobility.

This leads us to the newest generation of heating system: climate control. Here, all aspects of the interior climate (heat, air conditioning, humidity, etc.) are controllable on a room-by-room basis. What actually provides this is invisible and is likely unknown (heat pump, gas, oil, electricity?). All that we have in the space is a control that lets us tailor the climate to our individual preference. This is the heating equivalent of UbiComp: The service is ubiquitous, yet the delivery is invisible. UbiComp is the computational analogy to this mature phase of heating systems: In both, the technology is seamlessly integrated into the architecture of the workplace.

Within the UbiComp model, there is no computer on my desk because my desktop *is* my computer. As today, there is a large whiteboard on my wall, but with UbiComp, it is active, and can be linked to yours, which may be 3,000 km away. What I see is way less technology. What I get is way less intrusion (noise, heat, etc.) and way more functionality and convenience. And with my Pads and Tabs, and the wireless networks that they employ, I also get far more mobility without becoming a computational "orphan."

MEDIA SPACES AND UBIQUITOUS VIDEO

UbiVid is the video complement to UbiComp in that it shares the twin properties of ubiquity and transparency. In "desktop videoconferencing," as it is generally practiced, what we typically see is a user at a desk talking to someone on a monitor that has a video camera placed on top. This was illustrated in Fig. 17.2. Generally, the video interactions are confined to this single camera–monitor pair.

In UbiVid, we break out of this, just as UbiComp breaks out of focusing all computer-mediated activity on a single desktop computer. Instead, the assumption is that there is a range of video cameras and monitors in the workspace, and that all are available. By having video input and output available in different sizes and locations, we enable the most important concept underlying UbiVid: *exploiting the relationship between (social) function and architectural space.*

One example of this approach can be seen in the *Hydra* units for multiparty videoconferencing, discussed in chapter 18 by Buxton, Sellen, and Sheasby. In what follows, we explore the significance of this relationship in more detail. We start by articulating some of the underlying design principles, and then proceed to work through a number of other examples.

Design Principle 1: Preserve function/location relations for both tele and local activities.

Design Principle 2: Treat electronic and physical "presences" or visitors the same.

Design Principle 3: Use the same social protocols for electronic and physical social interactions.

Example: My Office

Let us work through an example to illustrate how these principles apply in a specific context, namely my office. A floor plan of my office is given in Fig. 17.4. There is a desk where I work and a coffee table, around which I have small informal meetings. There are five chairs, one of which is normally behind my desk. The others are around the coffee table. There are three distinct locations where remote visitors can appear. If we are working closely one-on-one, they appear on my desk. (This is shown as location A in Fig. 17.4.) Here, they appear right beside my computer screen (which might contain information that we are both viewing simultaneously). This type of meeting is illustrated in Fig. 17.5.

If someone wants to glance into my office to see if I am available, they can do so from the door (location B in Fig. 17.4), whether they come physically or electronically. A camera mounted above the door gives them approximately the same view that they would have if they were glancing through my physical door. This is illustrated in Fig. 17.6. I can see who is "at the door" on a small monitor mounted by the camera, and—as in the physical world—I can hear their approach by means of an auditory icon, or *earcon*.

Likewise, when I am engaged in a meeting in my office, if someone comes by the door to see if I'm available, this same arrangement provides me with the same options regardless of whether the person comes electronically or physically. I can ignore them if I don't want to be interrupted, and due to their position and distance, they don't intrude on my meeting. If I want, I can glance up and discretely determine who is there. If it is someone that I don't want to speak to at the moment, I can then glance down and continue

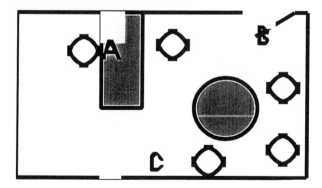

FIG. 17.4. My office showing key locations: (A) desk, (B) door, and (C) meeting table.

FIG. 17.5. Remote face-to-face collaboration at the desktop.

my meeting. The person at the door is aware that I know of their presence, and by my action, they know that I can't see them at the moment. On the other hand, if it is someone who could contribute to the meeting, I invite them in. Finally, if it is someone that I know needs urgent attention, I will suspend the meeting and deal with the issue (hopefully briefly).

Although some may claim that this additional technology is superfluous or an added "luxury," we believe that it may well make the difference between success and failure of a system. We can illustrate this with an example. In

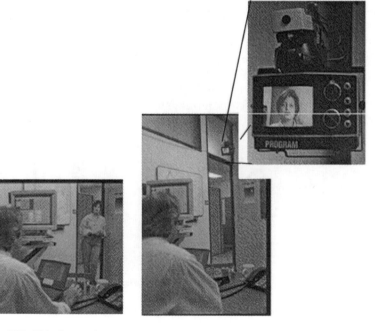

FIG. 17.6. Interactions at my office door: (a) physically and (b) electronically.

1993–1994, Hiroshi Ishii visited us from NTT for a year. When he first came, this "door cam" was not deployed. After he had been with the project for a while, he explained to me that when he first came he was reluctant to use the system to contact me because he felt that it was rude to just "arrive" on my desktop. His reasons were partially due to not knowing me that well at the time, and partially out of "respect" for my position as director of the project. To him, the distance and means of approach afforded by the "door cam" was an important affordance to his making effective use of the system. Our claim is that such social sensitivities are not rare.

In addition to working at my desk and interactions at the door, there is a third location-sensitive function that takes place in my office: informal meetings. These normally take place around the round coffee table, and may involve up to five or six people. Frequently these include a participant from a remote site. In order to enable him or her to do so from an appropriate location, a special "seat" is reserved for the remote participant at the table. This is located in position C in Fig. 17.4, and is shown in Fig. 17.7.

By having the remote participant appear in a distinct and appropriate location, participants physically in my office are able to direct their gaze at the remote participant just as if that person were physically present. Likewise, the remote participant has a sense of gaze awareness, that is, who is looking at whom, and when. The reason is that the remote participant has a physical presence in the room—a presence afforded by the location of the video *surrogate* through which the remote participant communicates.

In our discussion, we have mainly dealt with social function and distance in relation to fixed locations. These are issues, however, which normally

FIG. 17.7. An informal meeting with remote participation.

have a strong dynamic component. People move. In so doing, functions change. In this regard, our system is still lacking. One can move from location to location within the room, but the transitions are awkward. This is an area that needs improvement. But before one can work on movement, one has to have places to move to. This has been our main focus to date.

As we have lived in this environment in this form for almost 3 years, perhaps the most striking thing is a seeming paradox. By adding this extra equipment into the room, there actually appears to be less technology and far less intrusion of the technology in the social interactions that it mediates. Our argument is that this is due to the technology being in the appropriate locations for the tasks undertaken in the room. In a single desktop solution, for example, one would be twisting the camera and monitor from the desk to the coffee table when switching between desktop and group meetings. Also, due to the multiple cameras and monitors, we avoid the contention for resources that would otherwise result. For example, I can be in a desktop conference on one monitor, monitor a video that I am copying on another, and still not prevent someone from appearing at my electronic door.

As we have pointed out in the preceding examples, through increased ubiquity we have achieved increased transparency. This last point is achieved, however, only through the appropriate distribution of the technology—distribution whose foundations are the social conventions and mores of architectural location–distance–function relationships.

Example: Back-to-Front Videoconferencing

Another example of using spatially distributed video is the implementation of "back-to-front" videoconferencing at the University of Toronto. In conventional videoconferencing rooms, the camera and monitors are placed at the front of the room. This location works well if the remote participant is the presenter; however, if the remote party is intended to be part of the audience, then the location is inappropriate. In this case, the remote party should be located with the rest of the audience. If both social functions are to be supported, then so should both locations. Figure 17.8 illustrates how we enable remote participants to "take their place at the table" with the other members of the audience.

The scenario shown in the figure illustrates the notion of transparency. Due to the maintenance of audio and video reciprocity, coupled with maintaining "personal space," the presenter uses the same social mechanisms in interacting with both local and remote attendees. Stated another way, even if the presenter has no experience with videoconferencing or technology, there is no new "user interface" to learn. If someone raises a hand, it is clear the person wants to ask a question. If someone looks confused, a point can be clarified. Rather than requiring the learning of new

FIG. 17.8. A back-to-front videoconference: The remote attendee sits at the table.

skills, the design makes use of existing skills acquired from a lifetime of living in the everyday world.

> *Concept:* Video surrogate: Don't think of the camera as a camera. Think of it as a surrogate eye. Likewise, don't think of the speaker as a speaker. Think of it as a surrogate mouth. Integrated into a single unit, a vehicle for supporting design Principles 1 and 2 is provided.

> *Premise:* Physical distance and location of your video surrogate with respect to me carries the same social weight, function, and baggage as if you were physically in your surrogate's location. Furthermore, the assumption is that this is true regardless of your actual physical distance from me.

> *Qualification:* This equivalence is dependent on appropriate design. It sets standards and criteria for design and evaluation.

UBIQUITOUS MEDIA: UBICOMP + UBIVID

Up to this point, we have discussed computation separately from the media spaces. Clearly, however, these two classes of technology coexist. They complement each other in a number of ways. First, there is a dependence relationship: It is only through the computational resources that the control and operation of media spaces can be deployed.

Second, there is a cumulative relationship. In collaborative work, the media space technology provides the shared space of the people, and the computers the shared space of electronic documents. Both types of shared space are required to establish a proper sense of shared presence, or *telepresence*. When used together, a sense of awareness of the social periphery is afforded—a sense that would otherwise only be possible in a shared corridor or open concept office.

In the remainder of this section, we give examples that illustrate each of these cases.

Making Contact

It is misleading to think about computation as separate from collaboration via media spaces. The notions of UbiComp and UbiVid go hand-in-hand. This is most easily seen in the example of how the computer is used to mediate interactions within a media space. Figure 17.9 shows the user's view of the main application used to mediate connections among people and resources. (The cross-disciplinary process which led to this design is documented in Harrison, Mantei, Beirne, & Narine, 1994.) The left panel in the figure is what users normally see. It is primarily a scrolling list of names of the people and resources to which I can connect. Operationally,

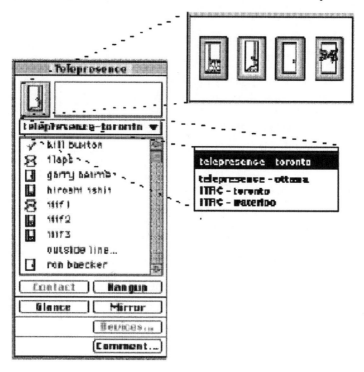

FIG. 17.9. The telepresence client: making connection and specifying accessibility.

one selects the desired name, then selects the "Contact" button, shown in the lower portion of the panel.

Notice that beside each name in the list is an icon of a door. The door icon can be in one of four states. Each indicates a different degree of accessibility for that name. If it is *open*, you are welcome to "pop in." If it is *ajar*, you can glance in and determine availability, but you must "knock" if you want to enter. If it is *closed*, you must knock and wait for a response before entering, and glancing is not possible. Finally, if the door is *boarded shut*, you can only leave a message.

I can set my door state by clicking on the door icon in the top left corner of the panel. This causes the menu shown on the upper right to pop up, from which I select one of the four icons. The icon beside my name is then accordingly updated for all users. Hence, a means is provided to control accessibility which is based upon everyday social protocols.

The application enables me to contact people at various sites, not just those who are local. In the example, residents at the Toronto Telepresence site are displayed in the name list. However, selecting the site name displayed above the name list causes a menu listing all sites to pop up. This is illustrated in the lower right panel. Selecting a site from this menu causes its residents' names to appear in the name list.

Shared Presence of Person and Task

In an earlier publication (Buxton, 1992), we argued for the need to support a sense of shared presence of both task and person. The main argument was that being able to move seamlessly from one to the other was important in undertaking a number of common interactions. This point was argued by others, especially Ishii, Kobayashi, and Grudin (1992).

Figure 18.7 in chapter 18 on multiparty conferencing by Buxton, Sellen, and Sheasby is one example of our efforts to support the seamless and natural redirection of gaze, and gaze awareness through the affordances of our design.

The next two examples illustrate how we can support this seamlessness, but in a manner appropriate to different application needs, by integrating UbiComp and UbiVid technologies with industrial design.

Example: The Active Desk

Figure 17.10 illustrates a collaborative design application. The design appears on what we call the *Active Desk* (developed jointly by the Ontario Telepresence Project and the Arnott Design Group of Toronto). This is a large electronic drafting table. It employs a 100 × 66 cm rear projection display. One interacts with the system with a stylus (4000 × 4000 points resolution) or a keyboard. In the illustration, a Hydra unit is mounted on each of the two upper corners of the desk (only one visible in the figure),

FIG. 17.10. The Active Desk, equipped with a Hydra unit.

thereby supporting three-way collaboration. The design being worked on is visible to all parties, and all parties can interact with it, such as pointing, making annotations, or adding to it.

Little technology is actually visible, and the form of the system is specifically tailored to the task: graphic design. Industrial design has rendered the technology transparent to the task. In essence, there is no desktop computer and no desktop metaphor. The desktop is the computer.

Design Principle 4: The box into which we are designing our solutions is the room in which you work/play/learn, not a box that sits on your desk.

Example: Sitting Across the Desk

This final example, illustrated in Fig. 17.11, is the UbiVid equivalent to sitting across the desk from someone. Here, through rear projection, the remote participant appears life-size. What we are trying to capture in this example are two people working together on a joint project, such as a drawing or budget. Although not the case in the example, the shared documents would appear on the desktop, using a technology similar to the Active Desk seen in the previous figure.

First, notice that having one's counterpart displayed this way is not like seeing the person on a regular video monitor. Because of the scale of the image, the borders of the screen are out of our main cone of vision. Hence, the space occupied by the remote person is defined by the periphery of his or her silhouette, not by the bezel of a monitor. Second, from being life-size, there is a balance in the weight or power exercised by each participant. Third, the gaze of the remote participant can traverse into our own physical space. When the remote party looks down on his or her desk, our sense of *gaze awareness* gives us the sense that the person is looking right onto our own desktop, and with his or her gaze, the person can direct us to look at the same location. This power of gaze awareness is so strong that people have even argued that the eyes actually emitted "eye rays" that could be sensed (Russ, 1925). It is this same power of gaze that we have tried to expoit in order to achieve an ever more powerful sense of *telepresence*.

FIG. 17.11. Face-to-face, life-size, across the desk.

POSTCARDS AND AWARENESS
OF THE SOCIAL PERIPHERY

Portholes was a system jointly developed by Xerox PARC and Rank Xerox EuroPARC (Dourish & Bly, 1992). Its purpose was to provide a sense of peripheral awareness and social proximity among a group of geographically distributed coworkers. The approach to doing so was to present a tiled view of video snapshots of all members of the distributed workgroup, with the images updated about once a minute.

With the cooperation of the original developers, we further developed the system. In our case, these snapshots are updated every 5 min. Unique to the Ontario Telepresence Project implementation is the superimposition of the door icons on the snapshots. A typical display of our version of Portholes is shown in Fig. 18.5 in the chapter on multiparty conferencing by Buxton, Sellen, and Sheasby.

The snapshot and door state icon provides information as to the presence or activities of group members, as well as their degree of accessibility. Furthermore, the snapshots provide a user interface to certain functions concerning individuals. For example, after selecting the snapshot of me on your screen, you can then click on the "Info" button on the top of the frame to get my phone number, name, address, and e-mail address. Or, double clicking on my image or selecting the "Contact" button asserts a high-band-width connection to me (thereby providing an alternative means to make a connection to that illustrated in Fig. 17.9).

Portholes takes advantage of the fact that each office has a video camera associated with it. It goes beyond the stereotyped notion of desktop video as simply a videophone. Rather, it supports a very important sense of awareness of the social periphery—an awareness that normally is only available in shared-office or shared-corridor situations. It introduces a very different notion of video on demand and delivers its potential with a transparent user interface.

Finally, discussions about Portholes always touch upon the issue of privacy. We are frequently asked, "How can you live in an environment where people can look in on you like that?" There are a couple of responses to this. First, Portholes is not an "open" application. It embodies a sense of reciprocity within a distinct social group. People cannot just randomly join a Portholes group. Members know who has access to the images. Second, even within the group, one can obtain a degree of privacy, because the distribution of your image can be controlled by your door state. Finally, remember that the images have no motion and no audio. What is provided is less than what would be available to someone looking through the window of your office door. This is especially true if the snapshot is taken from the "door camera," such as illustrated in Fig. 17.6.

ACTIVE SENSING AND THE REACTIVE ENVIRONMENT

In the examples thus far, the use of computational and video technologies has been complementary. However, the net effect has been cumulative. Our argument is that the benefits go well beyond this. In this section we show a synergy that occurs when these two classes of technologies are used together. The result can be far more than the sum of the parts. We illustrate this in examples of what we call *proximal sensing, reactive environments,* and *context-sensitive interaction* (Buxton, 1995).

Video, Portholes, and "Call Parking"

We can leverage the video and computational technologies of ubiquitous media by recognizing that the same cameras that I use for videoconferencing can give my computer "eyes." Furthermore, the same microphone through which I speak to my colleagues can also provide my computer with an "ear."

> Design Principle 5: Every device used for human–human interaction (cameras, microphones, etc.) is a legitimate candidate for human–computer interaction (and often simultaneously).

By mounting a video camera above the Active Desk and feeding the video signal into an image-processing system, one can use the techniques pioneered by Krueger (1983, 1991) to track the position of the hands over the desk. This is illustrated in Fig. 17.12, which shows a prototype system developed by Yuyan Liu in our lab. In the example, the system tracks the position and orientation of the left hand as well as the angle between the thumb and forefinger. The resulting signal enables the user to "grasp" computer-generated objects displayed on the desk's surface.

Such use of video is relatively nonintrusive. One need not wear any special gloves or sensors. The system sees and understands hand gesture much in the same way that people do: by watching the hands or body. Furthermore, the Digital Desk of Wellner (1991) has shown how the position objects, as well as the hands, and their relationship to the diplayed data can be used as the basis for interaction.

Another simple, yet effective, use of video to support interaction can be demonstrated by an extension of the Portholes application. A prototype written by Luca Giachino, a visiting scientist from CEFRIEL in Milan, Italy, demonstrated this. The underlying observation is that two Portholes images in a row constitute a motion detector. In comparing two frames, if more than 40% of the pixels change, there has been motion. Hence, one can have a rather reliable indication whether there is someone there. By keeping 1 bit of state for each frame, one can determine—within 5 min of resolution—if someone is still there, still away, come in or gone out.

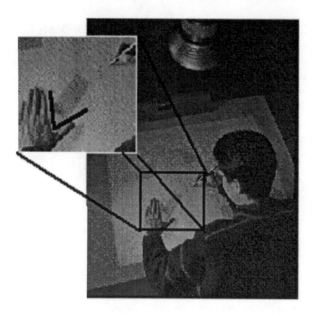

FIG. 17.12. Using video to enable the computer to react to hand position and gesture.

With this observation and the resultant code, the mechanism for a new type of "call parking" is provided. If I want to call you, I could look up at Portholes to see if you are there. If so, I could double click on your image to assert a connection. Otherwise, I could instruct the system that I want to talk to you. In the background, while I get on with other work, it could monitor the state of your office and alert me when you appear to be in and (by virtue of your door state) when you are available. The benefit of such a utility increases dramatically when it is a conference call that one wants to set up.

Doors Revisited: The "Door Mouse"

The cameras and microphones found in the office are not the only sensory devices that can be taken advantage of in the domain of ubiquitous media. Other alternatives include the full repertoire of motion and proximity sensors used in home automation and security. Let us revisit an earlier example, the specification of door state, as a case in point.

Specifying door state using the mechanism illustrated in Fig. 17.9 preserves the protocols of the physical world by metaphor; however, it fails to comply fully with the design principle of using the same mechanism in both the electronic and the physical domain. The reason is that although the protocols are parallel, they are not *one*. One still has to maintain two systems: the physical door and the logical one, as represented in the computer application.

Using the physical door to control both means that accessibility for both electronic and physical visitors are handled by the same mechanism. Hence (naturally subject to the ability to override defaults), closing my physical door is sensed by the computer and prevents people from entering physically or electronically (by phone or by video). One action and one protocol controls all.

Such a system was implemented in a number of rooms in our lab by a student, Andrea Leganchuk. Her simple but elegant solution is illustrated in Fig. 17.13.

> *Observation:* A door is just as legitimate an input device to a computer as is a mouse or a keyboard.

Proximal Sensing and Context

What characterizes the previous examples is the increased ability of the computer to sense more than just the commands that are typed into it. Our experience suggests that computation is moving toward a future where our systems will respond to more and richer input.

One hint of this today is *remote sensing,* the gathering of data about the earth and environment by sensors in satellites. What we are describing is similar, except the sensors are much closer, hence the term *proximal sensing.* In this case, it is the ecology and context of the workspace which is being sensed.

> When you walk up to your computer, does the screen saver stop and do the working windows reveal themselves? Does it even know if your are there? How hard would it be to change this? Is it not ironic that, in this regard, a motion-sensing light switch is "smarter" than any of the switches in the computer, AI notwithstanding?

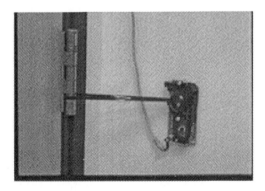

FIG. 17.13. The "door mouse."

We see this transition as essential to being able to deliver the expanded range of functionality being promised as a result of technological convergence. Our perspective is that if considerable complexity is not off-loaded to the system, much (if not most) of the promised functionality will lie beyond the complexity barrier, or the user's *threshold of frustration.* Our final example briefly introduces some of our ongoing work based on this premise.

Reactive Environment

The way in which proximal sensing and context-sensitive interaction can help reduce complexity while supporting new services is illustrated in our final example, an augmented meeting room. Much is promised in the way of meeting support by new technologies. Videoconferencing, electronic whiteboards, audio- and video-based meeting capture, and annotation and electronic presentations that support video and computer graphics are just some examples. The components for nearly all of these services are now commercially available. And yet, our ability to deliver them in a way that augments a meeting, rather than intruding on it, is limited, to say the least. Delivering them to a techno-novice in a walk-up-and-use conference room is virtually unthinkable.

The reason is the amount of overhead associated with changing the state of the room to accommodate the changing demands and dynamics of a typical meeting. Take a simple example. Suppose that you are in a videoconference and someone asks, "Record the meeting." This turns out to be nontrivial, even if all of the requisite gear is available. For the meeting to be recorded, the audio from both sites must be mixed and fed to the VCR. Furthermore, the video from each site must be combined into a single frame using a special piece of equipment, and the resulting signal also fed to the VCR. Somehow, all of this has to happen. And recognize that the configuration described is very different than if just a local meeting were to be recorded, a video played back locally, or a video played back so that both a remote and local site could see it.

In each of these cases, let us assume that the user knows how to perform the primary task: to load the tape and hit "record" or "play." That is not the problem. The complexity comes from the secondary task of reconfiguring the environment. However, if one takes advantage of proximal sensing, the system knows that you put a tape in, which key you hit ("play" or "record"), and whether you are in a videoconference or not, and if so, with how many people. Hence, all of the contextual knowledge is available for the system to respond in the appropriate way, simply as a response to your undertaking the simpler primary task: loading the tape and hitting the desired button.

Over the past year, we have been instrumenting our conference room (the one seen in Fig. 17.8) to react in such a way. Furthermore, we have been doing so for a broad range of conference-room applications, in order to gain a better understanding of the underlying issues (Cooperstock, Tanikoshi, Beirne, Narine, & Buxton, 1995).

SUMMARY AND CONCLUSIONS

We have hit the complexity barrier. Using conventional design techniques, we cannot significantly expand the functionality of systems without passing users' thresholds of frustration. Rather than adding complexity, technology should be reducing it, and enhancing our ability to function in the emerging world of the future.

The approach to design embodied in ubiquitous media represents a break from previous practice. It represents a shift to design that builds on users' existing skills, rather than demanding the learning of new ones. It is a mature approach to design that breaks out of the "solution-in-a-box" superappliance mentality that dominates current practice. Like good architecture and interior design, it is comfortable, nonintrusive, and functional.

To reap the benefits that this approach offers will require a rethinking of how we define, teach, and practice our science. Following the path outlined here, the focus of our ongoing research is to apply our skills in technology and social science to both refine our understanding of design, and establish its validity in those terms that are the most important: human ones.

ACKNOWLEDGMENTS

Virtually all of the work described in these examples was designed and implemented by the members of the Ontario Telepresence Project, of which I had the pleasure to be Scientific Director. The excellence of the work comes partially from the excellence of the team itself, and partially from strong support and collaboration with colleagues at Xerox PARC and Rank Xerox EuroPARC. To all of those who have helped make these such stimulating environments, I am very grateful.

The research discussed in this chapter has been supported by the Ontario Government Centres of Excellence, Xerox PARC, Hewlett-Packard, Bell Canada, the Arnott Design Group, Object Technology International, Sun Microsystems, NTT, Bell Northern Research, Hitachi Ltd., Adcom Electronics, IBM Canada, and the Natural Sciences and Engineering Research Council of Canada. This support is gratefully acknowledged.

REFERENCES

Bly, S., Harrison, S., & Irwin, S. (1993). Media spaces: Bringing people together in a video, audio and computing environment. *Communications of the ACM, 36*(1), 28–47.
Buxton, W. (1992). Telepresence: Integrating shared task and person spaces. *Proceedings of Graphics Interface '92* (pp. 123–129). May 11–15, Vancouver, British Columbia.

Buxton, W. (1995). Integrating the periphery and context: A new model of telematics *Proceedings of Graphics Interface '95* (pp. 239–246). May 17–19, Québec, Québec.

Cooperstock, J., Tanikoshi, K., Beirne, G., Narine, T., & Buxton, W. (1995). Evolution of a reactive environment. *Proceedings of CHI '95* (pp. 170–177). May 7–11, Denver, CO.

Dourish, P., & Bly, S. (1992). Portholes: Supporting awareness in a distributed work group. *Proceedings of CHI '92* (pp. 541–547). May 3-7, Monterey, CA.

Harrison, B., Mantei, M., Beirne, G., & Narine, T. (1994, April). Communicating about communicating: Cross-disciplinary design of a Media Space interface. *Proceedings of CHI '94* (pp. 124–130), Boston, MA.

Ishii, H., Kobayashi, M., & Grudin, J. (1992, November). Integration of inter-personal space and shared workspace: Clearboard design and experiments. *Proceedings of CSCW '92* (pp. 33–42), Toronto, Ontario.

Krueger, Myron, W. (1983). *Artificial reality.* Reading, MA: Addison-Wesley.

Krueger, Myron, W. (1991). *Artificial reality II.* Reading, MA: Addison-Wesley.

Russ, C. (1925). An instrument which is set in motion by vision. *Discovery, Series 1, 6,* 123–126.

Stults, R. (1986). *Media space* (Systems Concepts Lab Tech. Rep.) Palo Alto, CA: Xerox PARC.

Weiser, M. (1991). The computer for the 21st century. *Scientific American, 265*(3), 94–104.

Wellner, P. (1991, November). The DigitalDesk Calculator: Tactile manipulation on a desktop display. *Proceedings of the Fourth Annual Symposium on User Interface Software and Technology (UIST '91)* (pp. 27–33), Hilton Head, SC.

Wellner, P., Mackay, W., & Gold, R. (Eds.).(1993). Computer-augmented environments: Back to the real world [Special issue]. *Communications of the ACM, 36*(7).

Chapter 18

Interfaces for Multiparty Videoconferences

William A. S. Buxton
Computer Systems Research Institute, University of Toronto
and
Alias | Wavefront Inc.

Abigail J. Sellen
Rank Xerox Research Centre (EuroPARC)

Michael C. Sheasby
SOFTIMAGE/Microsoft, Montreal

We describe how conventional approaches to multiparty videoconferences are limited in their support of participants' ability to establish eye contact with other participants; be aware of who is visually attending to them; selectively listen to different, parallel conversations; make side comments to other participants and hold parallel conversations; perceive the group as a whole; share documents and artifacts; and see coparticipants in relation to work-related objects. We present some design alternatives to these conventional videoconferencing approaches, describe the prototypes we have developed, and discuss their experimental evaluation.

INTRODUCTION

Designing to support multiparty videoconferences—conferences that involve more than two sites or more than two people—presents challenges beyond the design of simple point-to-point video systems. In a conventional videoconferencing setup, everyone is seen on one or two monitors, cameras are fixed, and what control is available comes typically through a cumbersome interface. Even in the two-party situation, such technology presents a variety of problems including lack of eye contact, limited fields of view, asymmetrical control of cameras, and difficulty in knowing how one's voice is perceived by one's coparticipant. Contrast this with meetings where all participants are in the same room—each person is his or her own "display" (i.e., their body), has full control over his or her own "camera" and "speaker" (i.e., their eyes and voice), and is fluent with the user interface to this "technology."

This chapter focuses on the particular problems of supporting multiparty meetings with video. In some respects, multiparty meetings exacerbate the problems inherent in two-party video meetings. In other respects, they present problems specific to the multiparty case. By experimentally evaluating conventional approaches to multiparty videoconferencing, we are able to explicate many of these problems. We then suggest design alternatives in the form of prototype systems that are themselves subjected to empirical evaluation. The primary intent of this chapter is to communicate the rationale behind our different design ideas, what we have learned from implementing and evaluating them, and the direction that we are heading in the future.

THE PIP APPROACH

The most common method of supporting multiparty video conferences involving several sites is to use a picture-in-picture (PIP) approach.[1] Using this technique, a single video screen is tiled into a number of sub-screens, each containing the output of one video source. Figure 18.1 shows a schematic of a four-way PIP, where the picture from each camera appears in a different quadrant of the screen. Figure 18.2 shows a user involved in a four-way conference using such a PIP device. This technique has the advantage that all parties can see each other. It is also technologically straightforward and reasonably economical, and therefore commonly used in commercial systems.

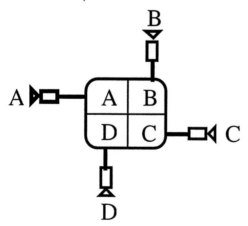

FIG. 18.1. The output of multiple cameras A, B, C, and D (each at different sites) shown tiled, in separate quadrants of the screen. Typically, the images are combined at a central location using the PIP device. The output is then broadcast to each participant.

FIG. 18.2. A four-way videoconference using a PIP device. All participants see the same split screen, which includes an image of themselves.

One obvious problem with this approach is that it breaks down as the number of remote sites increases, due to the decreasing size of the tiled images. But closer consideration reveals a number of other problems in supporting multiparty videoconferences this way.

First, participants using this approach are limited in their ability to establish eye contact with other participants, and to be aware of who, if anyone, is visually attending to them. Because there is a single camera and monitor, participants cannot tell who is looking at them as opposed to the other participants. Neither can they establish eye contact with any one of the participants to the exclusion of the others (mutual gaze). Further, because all participants occupy the same general area in the visual field (i.e. a single monitor), there is no need to turn the head to speak or listen to different participants. One can assume that supporting head-turning and gaze is an important consideration, as they have been shown to serve a number of communicative functions as well as helping to manage turn-taking and floor control (Argyle, Ingham, Alkena, & McCallin, 1973; Exline, 1971).

Participants using this approach are also limited in their ability to listen to simultaneous conversations. One significant factor contributing to this problem is the way the audio is configured. Typically, the audio from all participants comes from a single speaker. In contrast, when people physically occupy the same room, separate speech streams emanate from different points in space. It is this in part that makes it possible to selectively attend to ongoing parallel conversations (the "cocktail-party effect," Cherry, 1953; Egan, Carterette, & Thwing, 1954). This is made difficult when these spatial cues are eliminated.

These problems taken together represent serious design deficiencies that motivated us to try a different approach, which would offer support for selective gaze and head-turning, and for selective listening.

HYDRA

We call our first alternative design *Hydra*. The basis for the Hydra system is to preserve the notion of personal space in an attempt to preserve the everyday skills of conversational acts afforded by such space.

The underlying concept behind Hydra is to replace each of the remote meeting participants with a video surrogate (Sellen, Buxton, & Arnott, 1992).[2] In simulating a four-way round-table meeting, the place that would otherwise be occupied by a remote participant is held by a camera, monitor and speaker, as shown in Fig. 18.3.

Using this technique, each participant is presented with a unique view of each remote participant, and that view and its accompanying voice

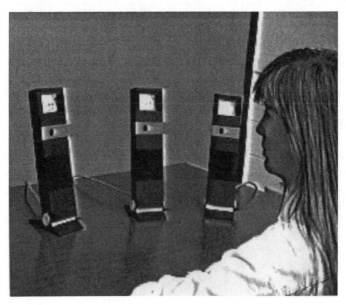

FIG. 18.3. A four-way videoconference using Hydra. Each Hydra unit contains a video monitor, camera, and loudspeaker. A single microphone conveys audio to the remote participants.

emanate from a distinct location in space. The net effect is that conversational acts such as gaze and head-turning are preserved because each participant occupies a distinct place on the desktop.

The fact that each participant is represented by a separate camera–monitor pair means that gazing toward someone is effectively conveyed. In other words, when person A turns to look at person B, B is able to see A turn to look toward B's camera. The spatial separation between camera and monitor is small enough to maintain the illusion of mutual gaze or eye contact. Looking away and gazing at someone else is also conveyed, and the direction of head turning indicates who is being looked at.[3] Furthermore, because the voices come from distinct locations, one is able to selectively attend to different speakers who may be speaking simultaneously.

We carried out a series of empirical studies to more closely examine and quantify the behavioral differences between Hydra and the PIP system (Sellen, 1992, 1995). These studies focussed primarily on objective measures of speech such as turn length, amount of simultaneous speech, and floor control parameters.

We hypothesized that the lack of support for selective gaze and head-turning and for selective listening in the PIP system would affect conversational interaction and make certain conversational acts difficult in comparison to the Hydra system. For example, we predicted that turn-taking might be adversely affected with the PIP system, and that holding parallel conversations and making side comments to others in a group would be difficult.

Although there was no significant difference between the PIP and Hydra approach with respect to some measures of turn-taking behavior, Hydra did, as expected, support parallel and side conversations. No such conversations were observed in the PIP approach. In addition, the majority of subjects expressed a preference for Hydra in their subjective evaluations, citing the ability to selectively attend both visually and auditorially as the major reason for preferring it over the PIP system. Some subjects commented that Hydra has much more of an interactive "feel" about it than the PIP approach to multiparty meetings. Thus the results are in line with the original intentions motivating the design of Hydra.

We are exploring ways to further exploit the properties of the preserved personal space. For example, by adding a proximity sensor to each Hydra unit, one will be able to establish a private audio link to another participant by leaning toward that person's unit. The gesture is the same as in everyday conversation, and conventional social mores are preserved, because the others can see not only that one person is making a side comment, but to whom. Once this mechanism is in place, and with the benefits of dedicated speakers for each participant, we hope to support parallel conversations, side comments, and breaking into conversational subgroups even more effectively. All of these important aspects of conversations and meetings are poorly supported by existing technology.

Since this system was developed, Ichikawa, Okada, and colleagues (Ichikawa, Okado, Jeong, Tanaka, & Matsushita, 1995; Okada, Maeda, Ichikawa, & Matsushita, 1994) have developed a multiparty system that contains some of the same properties of Hydra. The MAJIC system projects life-size images on a semitransparent surface allowing cameras to be placed behind the screen. Speakers are also placed behind the screen image of each participant. Thus the MAJIC system also provides support for selective gaze and head-turning. The much larger images may be a much better approach for many multiparty situations. However, because it uses projection and large screens, one drawback of the system is that it does not sit unobtrusively on a desktop, but is an altogether more imposing type of configuration, with less flexibility to be moved around and combined with other systems, as described in the last section of this chapter.

LIVEWIRE: VOICE-ACTIVATED SWITCHING

Although Hydra appears promising for small meetings of up to about four participants, like the PIP system, the approach does not scale up very well to larger groups. Furthermore, despite design ideas that we have developed to minimize the effect, Hydra is equipment intensive.

As a result, we have been looking at alternative design approaches. One that we have implemented is often used in broadcasting and in some videoconferencing systems. The approach, our implementation of which is called *LiveWire* (see Sheasby, 1995), involves changing who is visible on the monitor over time, depending on who is speaking. This is illustrated in Fig. 18.4. A number of simple assumptions formed the basis of this approach:

- All nonspeakers see the current speaker "full screen."
- The speaker sees the previous speaker.
- Only one person "owns" the screen at any one time.

The advantage of this approach is that it scales up well to large groups. It is also an interactive system responding to the dynamics of the conversation. However, it also has some serious drawbacks, which were revealed in our empirical studies (Sellen, 1995):

1. Subjects commented that they quickly lost a sense of the larger group—people who were not speaking had virtually no presence in this system.
2. Speakers complained that they got no feedback or confirmation from the system that they were being seen by the others, because any speaker continues to see the previous speaker. Subjects remarked that this was a serious problem.
3. The fact that LiveWire allows people only to monitor the speaker and not other people's reactions to what is being said was perceived

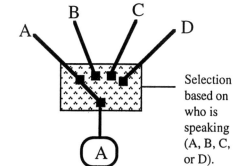

FIG. 18.4. Voice-activated switching. LiveWire is an implementation of a voice-activated switching system. The voice of the speaker causes the speaker's image to be seen full frame on all other screens.

Selection based on who is speaking (A, B, C, or D).

to be unnaturally restrictive. Subjects disliked the fact that they had no control or choice over whom to monitor.

4. The ability to have side conversations, or to make side glances and other nonverbal communicative acts, was not supported as it was in Hydra. This was largely due to the fact that subjects had difficulty, especially at first, assessing who was looking at whom.

5. The automatic switching was often distracting and inappropriate, especially when people in the group coughed or laughed, causing the screen to quickly switch from one person to the next.

These design flaws represent considerable problems for systems like LiveWire that depend on voice-switched full screen images. Not only have we found that this sort of "tunnel vision" is inappropriate in a multiparty situation, but the lack of control over this selective view is also problematic. When LiveWire was compared with the PIP system and an audio-only system (Sellen, 1995), the majority of the subjects said they liked the PIP system best, preferring the LiveWire system only slightly more often than having no video at all.

Although obviously not an ideal solution to supporting multiparty conferences, one advantage of developing LiveWire was to allow us to assess a system similar to what is commercially available, and to use it to compare our alternative designs to current practice. In addition, evaluating the shortcomings of such systems can serve as a basis for further design innovations, as described in the next section.

THE BRADY BUNCH: LIVEWIRE MEETS PORTHOLES

Taking some of the shortcomings of LiveWire into account, we designed a successor that builds on the voice-switching approach. A prototype of this system, which we have named the *Brady Bunch*,[4] was implemented and evaluated (Sheasby, 1995).

Building on the LiveWire technology, the Brady Bunch was partially inspired by two systems developed at Rank Xerox EuroPARC and Xerox PARC: *Portholes* (Dourish & Bly, 1992), and its predecessor, *Polyscope* (Borning & Travers, 1991). In brief, Portholes (illustrated in Fig. 18.5) is a system that repeatedly takes and distributes snapshots of the work group to the work group. The images are shot using one or more frame-grabbers, which have access to the group members' video cameras (without disrupting other uses of the cameras, such as conferencing). The individual snapshots are subsampled and distributed over the local (or wide) area network servicing the group, and combined with the shots of others in the group. The net effect is that each group member receives relatively recent still pictures of the office or workspace of each group member, which are

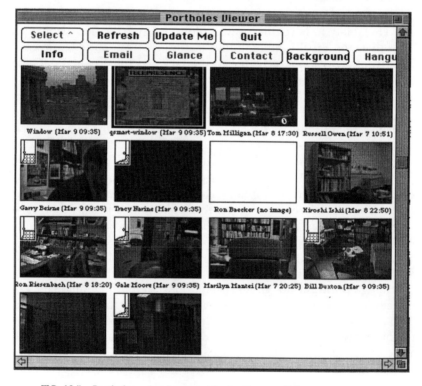

FIG. 18.5. Portholes as implemented by the Toronto Telepresence Project. Every 5 min, a snapshot of each member of the workgroup is distributed to all other members. In the Telepresence implementation, this is accompanied by an icon of that member's door icon, which indicates that person's degree of accessibility. The resulting tiled image of one's work group affords a strong sense of who is available when. It also can serve as a mechanism for making contact, finding phone numbers, and avoiding intruding on meetings.

displayed on their workstation. Portholes also has embedded functionality that permits users to access one another over the accompanying audiovideo (AV) network. Hence, it has a control as well as an awareness function.

The Brady Bunch design combines the Portholes/Polyscope approach with LiveWire. A live voice-switched image is supported by a set of slow-scan video images. The static images are snapshots of the other meeting participants, grabbed using a technique similar to Portholes. Although the initial design placed the slow-scan images in a ring around a larger live image directly on the workstation monitor, the first implementation of the Brady Bunch (Sheasby, 1995) placed the live image on a separate monitor, leaving the slow-scan images on the user's workstation desktop.[5]

The Brady Bunch was designed to be used in focused group interaction, where all group members play an active role in a discussion. In normal operation, the current speaker is displayed in the large LiveWire image, whereas the other meeting participants are displayed in the slow-scan images. The slow-scan images provide a sense of the context of the larger group and give group members who are not talking some presence in the meeting. This addressed the first problem that we found with LiveWire.

The second problem of lack of feedback was addressed by the addition of an "on camera" indicator to the LiveWire system. This consisted of superimposing a red dot on the live image displayed in the current speaker's video monitor to confirm to the person that he or she was being viewed by the others.

The third and fourth problems—the ability to glance at others and to have side conversations with them—were addressed by the addition of two features. The first feature allows a user to "glance" at another user (view someone other than the speaker in the main window) by clicking on that person's slow-scan image. That person is then displayed as full-motion video on the live monitor, replacing the speaker. This allows participants to override the voice-activated switching system to monitor nonspeaking members of the meeting. The second feature allows two users to have "side conversations" by allowing them to drop out of the group meeting to communicate privately with each other. In this mode, pairs of users can communicate via a private and secure audiovideo link. This method of connecting is similar to that for glancing at another user but involves acceptance by the remote user.

In face-to-face meetings, there are many inherent visual cues that convey the fact that one is being glanced at. In order to provide this kind of information in the Brady Bunch system, we used the slow-scan images to present status cues. For example, if one was being glanced at, the name of the person glancing would alternate with the word "glancing" in the slow-scan window representing that person. Requests for side conversations were handled similarly.

The Brady Bunch was tested using the board game Diplomacy. In this game of strategic negotiation, players attempt to dominate a stylized map of the world by invading one another's territory (see Fig. 18.6). The rules are set up so that a player is unlikely to win alone; the players are intended to form alliances with one another to win specific battles. The point of the game is that players must negotiate with skill and persuasiveness, because treaties can be ignored and cheating one's allies is common behavior.

The game was chosen because it depends heavily on the accurate assessment of the sincerity of a distant user. In this respect the game reflects actual negotiation, a common and important business practice. Thus, although difficult to measure, a player's success at the game is directly related to the translation of their face-to-face communication skills to the teleconferencing medium.

In the experiment, subjects made heavy use of the glance and side conversation features in the Brady Bunch system, although the difference between them appeared hazy to some subjects. During these side conver-

FIG. 18.6. The Brady Bunch approach used with the game Diplomacy. A full-motion voice-switched video image of the current speaker on a separate monitor is supported by slow-scan images of all meeting participants in separate windows on the workstation display.

sations, users could be seen to spend a great deal of time visually monitoring each other as if trying to assess the truth of what the other was saying. Thus, the ability to monitor someone other than the speaker and to break into conversational subgroups was shown to be important, at least in this kind of game situation.

The experimental evaluation also revealed that users wanted the system to enable them to engage in side conversations of more than two people. They also wanted the system to provide them with information about when side conversations or glances were occurring between participants other than themselves.

In a subsequent version of the Brady Bunch, we intend to explore better ways of providing feedback. One potential solution is to highlight the borders of the slow-scan windows of users to tell each participant who is viewing them. For example, if I am talking, under normal circumstances, all participants' borders will be highlighted to indicate that everyone is viewing me. If I then lose the floor, the windows revert to their normal state. If I am not talking, I may still be glanced at by others, which would be indicated by those people's windows being highlighted. Notice that this solution removes the need for the red "on camera" dot in the live monitor.

What is missing in this approach, however, is the provision of feedback to users to tell them that *other* people are glancing at or are having side conversations with each other. Private conversations between distant users could be indicated with another form of highlighting, but other solutions need to be explored, such as altering the layout of the windows to indicate connections between distant users.

This method of providing information about who is attending to whom is intended to compensate for the lack of head-turning and gaze cues people use in everyday conversation, and that we have sought to provide in Hydra. We hope to experiment to see whether this kind of compensation is effective.

In addition, like most existing practice, this approach does not have the spatial audio cues that formed the basis of Hydra. We may be able to effectively spatially distribute the individual voices using techniques such as those described by Ludwig, Pincever, and Cohen (1990) and Cohen and Ludwig (1991).

INTEGRATION OF SHARED PERSON
AND TASK SPACES

Up to this point, our discussion has focused exclusively on the shared "person space" of the participants involved in a multiparty conference. The discussion is not complete, however, without considering the shared space of the documents, applications, or other artifacts that are part of the reason for meeting. This we call the shared *task space*. What we have elsewhere (Buxton, 1992) is that these two notions of shared space must be seamlessly integrated in order to achieve a true sense of *telepresence*. This is as important in the multiparty case as it is in the dyadic meetings. However, the multiparty case presents additional design and engineering complications. In this section, we outline two examples of how we have approached this problem.

The Electronic Whiteboard Case

In this case, illustrated in Fig. 18.7, we combine the Hydra technique with a large data display, reminiscent of the Xerox Liveboard (Elrod et al., 1992). In this configuration, the Hydra units function much as before. The major addition is that the sense of gaze awareness afforded by Hydra now extends to the shared document displayed on the large screen, as well as among the participants. For example, if the other participants are looking at the current speaker, and that speaker looks up at the large screen, the other participants will be aware of this, and follow the speaker's gaze. Thus, this configuration not only provides access to shared documents but also gives some sense of one's coparticipants' orientation to those shared documents.

FIG. 18.7.   Shared task and person space. A multiparty meeting concerning a technical drawing is illustrated. The technical drawing is displayed on the large screen behind the Hydra units (which are used for the shared presence of the participants). Each participant can see and mark up the technical drawing. The configuration supports gaze awareness toward people and document.

It is worth briefly contrasting this configuration with the ClearBoard system of Ishii and his colleagues (Ishii, Kobayashi, & Grudin, 1993; chapter 21, this volume). Briefly, ClearBoard superimposes the image of the remote person on the work surface. In the dyadic case, this affords excellent and seamless fine-grain gaze awareness. However, although elegant, the technique breaks down in the multiparty case. Hence, we need to pursue other design alternatives.

Finally, note that in at least one way, this electronic configuration improves on the analogous "same-place" configuration. Assuming that the configuration is replicated for all participants, each participant has the electronic whiteboard right in front of them. In contrast, in the same-place, round-table situation, some participants would have to turn partially or completely around in order to see the physical whiteboard.

The Active Desk Case

In another case, we have configured the Hydra units around an electronic desktop, which we call the *Active Desk*.[6] With the Active Desk, the user's desktop is an active surface, which is in fact a 100×66 cm rear projection computer display. There is no desktop computer, nor is there any desktop metaphor—the desktop *is* the computer. Electronic documents, shared or otherwise, appear on its surface, and one interacts with them with a stylus, keyboard, or some other input device.

Key to this configuration is the fact that the Hydra units can be placed around the periphery of the desk, thereby affording a seamless way of integrating conversation and collaborative interaction with a document. Overall, the approach has been to model the social and interaction skills seen in the everyday world: that is, people standing around a drafting table, discussing the document, and changing their gaze from document to person by simply raising, lowering, or turning their heads. Again, this approach tries to provide some support for conveying people's orientation to shared, work-related documents.

Worth noting is how the previous two examples can be combined. Imagine that the person shown in Fig. 18.7 is also working on an Active Desk. Furthermore, let us assume that information on an individual's desk is their private space, and information on the electronic whiteboard is public. From the resulting relationship between space and function, the power of gaze awareness is extended. Now, for example, I can tell if you are looking at me, at the public space, or your private notes. Our assumption (one which we are exploring more formally) is that these additional cues—being based on everyday skills—facilitate the quality of the interaction and the naturalness of the ensuing dialogue.

CONCLUSIONS

The support of multiparty meetings with remote participants presents a challenging interface design problem. There are a number of behavioral aspects of meetings that need careful consideration in order to build these interfaces effectively. Throughout the course of evaluating and designing multiparty systems, we have enumerated a number of everyday conversational and communicative acts that are poorly supported by existing technologies. Our evaluation of conventional approaches to multiparty video-conferences (namely, the picture-in-a-picture or the voice-switching approach) has shown that they are limited in their support of participants' ability to:

- Establish eye contact with other participants
- Be aware of who, if anyone, is visually attending to them
- Selectively listen to different, parallel conversations
- Make side comments to other participants
- Hold parallel conversations
- Perceive the group as a whole, in order to sense the "mood" of the group, for example
- Share documents and artifacts, and see coparticipants in relation to those objects

Some of the more unconventional approaches we have described provide much better support for these aspects of multiparty meetings, and as much as possible we have tried to evaluate and assess the extent to which they do so. We have also tried to document the particular design problems that still exist, and suggest how the designs might be improved. So far, we have found that the process of evaluation acts to inspire new design possibilities as much as it reveals design flaws.

The design space for multiparty video systems is rich and the issues are important. Our view is that in any such investigation, field trials and experiments with real subjects are critical. The dilemma is that to test, one needs a working system without making too much of an investment in a working system that has not been tested. Clearly, this is a case for iterative design and rapid prototyping, as we hope we have demonstrated in this chapter.

ACKNOWLEDGMENTS

We acknowledge the contribution of the Arnott Design Group of Toronto for the design and fabrication of the Hydra models. We also thank Sara Bly, Paul Dourish, Bill Gaver, and Hiroshi Ishii for their helpful comments on earlier drafts of this chapter. The work described was supported by the Ontario Information Technology Research Centre (ITRC), the Natural Sciences and Engineering Research Council of Canada (NSERC), Xerox Palo Alto Research Center (PARC), Rank Xerox Research Centre, Cambridge, the Arnott Design Group, Toronto, Object Technology International, Ottawa, Digital Equipment Corp., Maynard, Massachusetts, and IBM Canada's Laboratory Centre for Advanced Studies, Toronto. This support is gratefully acknowledged.

NOTES

1. The term *picture-in-a-picture* can also refer to the technique of embedding one small video picture into a larger full-screen background picture. We use the term here to refer to a 2 by 2 video tiling approach.
2. After designing and implementing this system, we became aware of earlier work that used the same approach (Fields, 1983). So, the basic approach is not original, just uncommon. But like conventional videoconferencing, just because it has been done before does not mean that there is not significant room for improvement.
3. Note that it is important to preserve the geometry of the virtual round table with Hydra. That is, if I appear across the table from you, you must similarly do so from me. Likewise, the person to my left must be to your right, and so on. This is solved by assuming that whoever calls the meeting configures the seating of the table. Software can then ensure that the "seating" is consistent for all participants.
4. Named because of its similarity in appearance to the opening credits of the TV series of that name.
5. One benefit of this was that it made it simple to determine a user's focus of interest for the purposes of evaluation (i.e., whether the user was looking at the current speaker on the live monitor, the rest of the group on the workstation monitor, or elsewhere).
6. The Active Desk was developed jointly by the Ontario Telepresence Project, and the Arnott Design Group of Toronto.

REFERENCES

Argyle, M., Ingham, R., Alkena, F., & McCallin, M. (1973). The different functions of gaze. *Semiotica, 7*, 10–32.

Borning, A., & Travers, M. (1991). Two approaches to casual interaction over computer and video networks. *Proceedings of CHI '91, ACM Conference on Human Factors in Computing Systems* (pp. 13–19). New York: ACM.

Buxton, W. (1992). Telepresence: Integrating shared task and person spaces. *Proceedings of Graphics Interface '92* (pp. 123–129).

Cherry, E. C. (1953). Some experiments on the recognition of speech with one and two ears. *Journal of the Acoustical Society of America, 22*, 61–62.

Cohen, M., & Ludwig, L. (1991). Multidimensional audio window management. *International Journal of Man–Machine Studies, 34*(3), 319–336.

Dourish, P., & Bly, S. (1992, May). Portholes: Supporting awareness in a distributed work group. *Proceedings of CHI '92* (pp. 541–547), New York: ACM.

Egan, J. P., Carterette, E. C., & Thwing, E. J. (1954). Some factors affecting multichannel listening, *Journal of the Acoustical Society of America, 26,* 774–782.

Elrod, S., Bruce, R., Gold, R., Goldberg, D., Halasz, F., Janssen, W., Lee, D., McCall, K., Pedersen, E., Pier, K., Tang, J., & Welch, B. (1992, May). Liveboard: A large interactive display supporting group meetings, presentations and remote collaboration. *Proceedings of CHI'92* (pp. 599–607), New York: ACM.

Exline, R. V. (1971). Visual interaction: The glances of power and preference. In J. K. Cole (Ed.), *Nebraska Symposium on Motivation* (Vol. 19, pp. 163–206). Lincoln: University of Nebraska Press.

Fields, C. I. (1983). *Virtual space teleconference system.* United States Patent 4,400,724, August 23.

Ichikawa, Y., Okada, K., Jeong, G., Tanaka, S., & Matsushita, Y. (1995). MAJIC videoconferencing system: Experiments, evaluation, and improvement. In H. Marmolin, Y. Sunblad, & K. Schmidt (Eds.), *Proceedings of the Fourth European Conference on Computer-Supported Cooperative Work (ECSCW '95)* (pp. 279–292). Dordrecht: Kluwer.

Ishii, H., Kobayashi, M., & Grudin, J. (1993). Integration of interpersonal space and shared workspace: ClearBoard design and experiments. *ACM Transactions on Information Systems (TOIS), 11*(4), 349–375.

Ludwig, L., Pincever, N., & Cohen, M. (1990). Extending the notion of a window system to audio. *IEEE Computer, 23*(8), 66–72.

Okada, K., Maeda, F., Ichikawa, Y., & Matsushita, Y. (1994). Multiparty videoconferencing at virtual social distance: MAJIC design. In R. Furuta & C. Neuwirth (Eds.), *Proceedings of CSCW '94* (pp. 385–394). New York: ACM Press.

Sheasby, M. C. (1995). *Brady Bunch and the LiveWire engine: Peripheral awareness in video teleconferencing.* MSc thesis, Department of Computer Science, University of Toronto.

Sellen, A. (1992, May). Speech patterns in video mediated conversations. *Proceedings of CHI '92* (pp. 49–59). Monterey, CA.

Sellen, A. (1995). Remote conversations: The effects of mediating talk with technology. *Human–Computer Interaction, 10*(4), 401–444.

Sellen, A., Buxton, W., & Arnott, J. (1992, May). Using spatial cues to improve desktop video conferencing. 8 minute videotape. *Proceedings of CHI '92.* Monterey, CA.

Chapter 19

Group Space: The Role of Video in Multipoint Videoconferencing and Its Implications for Design

Amir Mané
AT & T Bell Laboratories

Video-mediated communication can afford participants a much-needed sense of the group space—that is, a sense of being together and interacting with a group of people. To achieve the desired experience of telepresence the visual channel should display information concerning who is participating, what their level of engagement is, the current speaker, and who is making short verbal contributions. Furthermore, it would allow the listeners, without "taking the floor," to provide the speaker with visual backchannel responses that are so needed to achieve grounding and effective communication. The implications for design include the need in multiparticipant conversation to continuously present not only the current speaker, but also the other participants in the conversation.

INTRODUCTION

For over half a century, the field of videotelephony has drawn the attention of scientists and entrepreneurs. For the most part, the focus was on a point-to-point conversation between two individuals (e.g., Williams, 1977; Rutter, 1987). However, the proliferation of videoconference rooms and "rollabout" videoconferencing systems indicates that video-mediated communication (VMC) is often used in a group activity. Indeed, some have observed that even when the system is designed for two participants, it often draws multiple participants at each point (Mantei et al., 1991). The

401

recognition that much of the work accomplished in today's economy is done in groups is the basis for the emergence of the field of computer-supported cooperative work (Olson et al., 1993). This leads us to focus on implications of VMC research for the design of multipoint desktop video-conferencing, and specifically for the integration of the image of participants into the display of such systems.

The attraction of multimedia collaboration lies in the belief that people who are physically remote can work together in a fashion that is close to that of a face-to-face meeting. The goal has been defined as *telepresence*— "the use of technology to establish a sense of shared *presence* or shared *space* among geographically separated members of a group" (Buxton, 1992, p. 123). Buxton suggested that telepresence consists of two kinds of spaces: person space and *task* space. Sharing a person space creates the sense of being physically together with the other person; it relies on our ability to observe signs like voice, facial expressions, eye gaze, and body language. Sharing a task space is the sense of being copresent in the task domain. This implies, for example, being able to share a text document, point to elements in it, modify it, and expect the other parties to see your actions and their results.

GROUP SPACE

The main thesis of this chapter is that in order to achieve a sense of telepresence in a conversation that involves more than two parties, there is a third space that has to be shared—the *group space*. Sharing a group space is the sense of being together and interacting with a group of people. Of interest to our discussion is the use of the term *group space* by researchers who attempt to bridge the gap between environmental and social psychology. Contrasted with personal space, which is central to the field of environmental psychology, group space is viewed as "a collectively inhabited and socioculturally controlled physical setting" (Minami & Tanaka, 1995, p. 43). These studies attempt to capture the way that people view a physical space as belonging to the group, and argue that changes to the group space would bring about conflicts among groups and renegotiation of its use. In contrast, the term *group space* in this discussion is focusing on the fact that there are multiple individual that are taking part in the meeting, not on the (virtual) space that they occupy. The sense of a group space is best described as the accumulation of four levels of cues about the participants. First comes the simple knowledge and awareness of the presence of other parties in the virtual meeting. This includes the *connectivity assurance* cues (Seligmann & Edmark, 1994) that provide information about the multiple connections that support the meeting. How many people are there? Who they are? This may sound trivial, but contrast it to the many audio conference calls in which participants may not even know who is on the line.

The second level of cues concerns how participants are differentiated according to their contribution to the discussion. Participants need to be aware of the identify of the current speaker, who is asking questions, and how participants are reacting to what the speaker is saying. In an environment where events may not necessarily be clearly associated with the person who triggered them, these *focal assurances* (Seligmann & Edmark, 1994) provide information about the involvement of each participant. In a situation where the participants are not familiar with each other, it is especially hard to develop a sense of where people stand on issues when the contributions are not tied to a specific participant.

Third, and probably most important to our discussion, is the ability to have a sense of the audience response to the content of the discussion throughout the meeting. How do listeners feel about the topic, and what is their level of engagement with the conversation? How committed are they to the group activity? The way in which listeners respond to various suggestions is also important.

The final level of cues is concerned with sensing the relationship among individuals in the group. This introduces the notion of group structure. It is important to recognize that a multiperson interaction is more than the sum of interactions among any two individuals. Rather it is the interaction of a group. Whether one focuses on the relatively stable structure of the group or on the dynamics by which such a structure changes, it is clear that the behavior of the group can be abstracted with the group, rather than the individual in the focus. Group performance, cohesion, relative power of individuals, the emergence of coalitions and of leadership—all these can be described and studied as the characteristics of group structure and behavior (Collins & Raven, 1969).

Indeed, the social psychological study of group structure acknowledges the importance of the communication pattern. Recognized as sometimes a cause, sometimes an effect, and often as both, the pattern of communication has been studied extensively as an independent variable (Collins & Raven, 1969). The goal was to assess how the imposed pattern of communication may determine aspects of the group process (Bavelas, 1950). Varying the pattern of communication and through it manipulating independent variables such as position centrality was found to influence morale and leadership nomination (Leavitt, 1951). Although the typical studies involved a small group of people sharing a physical space, and separated by partitions, one can see how the pattern of communication that is dictated by the virtual physical space would affect group structure and performance.

The person space focuses on an individual, and presumably provides us with all the signals and signs that are needed for effective communication with another individual, whereas the group space provides us with cues about the group as a whole and about its dynamics. To understand the role and the value of the visual channel in representation of group space, one needs to review what in general is the role of video in person to person communication.

THE ROLE OF VISION IN CONVERSATION

Before discussing the role of the visual channel in remote communication, it is useful to have an understanding of the role of visual cues in face-to-face conversation. Communication relies heavily on *signals* and *signs*. Signals are actions intended to convey a message to the recipients. Signs are actions that, although not consciously intended to do so by the sender, are interpreted by the recipient as part of the communication. Signals consist of a code, an encoder, and a decoder. The code is the message itself, for example, the word "Hello" or a culturally anchored body gesture. The encoder is the person who makes something public via that code, and the decoder is the person who responds systematically to that code (Wiener, Devoe, Rubinow, & Geller, 1972). Most of the signals that humans use are linguistic. Visual signals are used either as illustrations to complement the words or to substitute for the words altogether (Argyle, 1969). In addition to the signals, which are intentional, people also send and interpret signs, acts such as blushing or yawning that are not intended to communicate to others, but do so (Clark, 1985). Some of the signs may be conveyed through voice and speech qualities, but many of them are conveyed visually. Of course, the boundaries of between signs and signals are fuzzy, and the way that one dresses, grooms, and accessorizes is both a sign and a signal.

Nonverbal cues have a specific role in conversation, providing *expression*, *regulation*, and *monitoring* functions (Kendon, 1967). Expression refers to the emotional realm, and addresses issues such as arousal, fear, embarrassment, shame, sorrow, aggression, and so forth. Facial expressions, eye gaze, blushing, yawning, hand gestures, and body posture are interpreted as an indication of the person's emotional state. Although we may not always be able to identify these cues, we are fairly apt at perceiving and interpreting indications of emotion. The regulation function refers to turn-taking and "floor control" in the conversation. Eye gaze, eye movement, and head nods all facilitate the smooth transition between speaker and listener, and serve as a social mechanism to facilitate the conversation. The monitoring function refers to the use that the speaker is making of the listeners' responses in interpreting the impact of the message. Here the role of the nonverbal cue is to serve as an indication of the cognition of the listener— indicating understanding, agreement, or confusion.

The study of socially shared cognition has sharpened our understanding of both the monitoring and the regulation functions. In constructing their messages, people use the feedback that they get from the listener to adapt the content of the message (Kraut, Lewis, & Swezey, 1982). Grounding is the process by which participants in communication establish the mutual understanding needed both to convey information and to recognize that the message has been understood (Clark & Brennan, 1993). It impacts both the content of the message and the flow of the conversation. A key aspect of grounding is the role of backchannel responses—feedback that the listener provides to the speaker, without "taking the floor," as to the level of understanding or agreement that was achieved. Some the back-channel responses are verbal, for example, "yes," or "uh-hum." However, often the backchannel responses will be visual—a nod of the head, a shake of disapproval, raised eyebrows, or a puzzled expression.

EVALUATING THE VISUAL CHANNEL IN REMOTE COMMUNICATION

The study of communication and social psychology is congruent with the very intuitive appeal of adding video to audio for remote communication—it conforms, after all, to our experience in everyday life. However, the value of video was profoundly questioned by the demise of the Picture-Phone during the 1960s. Arguably, the main reason for its failure in penetrating the market was the fact that people did not find real value in the video connection (Noll, 1992). In the following years, a wave of research focused on the psychology of the telephone and the possible merit of the visual channel. Numerous studies compared communication in a face-to-face meeting, an audio connection, and an audio plus video connection (typically closed-circuit TV), as well as other variants. With few exception, the studies focused on the interaction between two individuals (Short, Williams, & Christie, 1976; Williams, 1977; Rutter, 1987). These studies focused on the display of the faces of participants in a conversation. It is only recently that attention has been drawn to video as data (Nardi et al., 1993), even when the data are the talking heads themselves (e.g., Kamata & Hirama, 1995).

For a variety of tasks that require transmission of information or joint problem solving the audio channel was quite adequate. In fact, from this earlier work there was no evidence of any advantage for adding a video channel or for performing the task in a face-to-face meeting (e.g., Ochsman & Chapanis, 1974). When the task involved persuasion, in negotiation, in conflict resolution, or in attitude change, the media of communication did make a difference. For example, in several studies a cooperative solution of the prisoner's dilemma was achieved when vision was available (Rutter, 1987). Another example: When speaking out of conviction, people were more persuasive using the visual channel; when arguing against their true beliefs, they were more persuasive in the absence of video (Short, 1974). Overall, the observation was made that discussion over voice only tends to be more task oriented, less person oriented (Short et al., 1976).

The overall adequacy of the audio channel led Williams (1977) to conclude that although visual cues are employed in a face-to-face conversation, either they are redundant, or else people can compensate rather well for their absence. When differences between audio and audio plus video were detected, the explanation focused mostly on the emotional aspects of the situation. Short et al. (1976) argued that the degree of salience of the other party—how visible and prominent they are—is a key construct, and the "social presence" is the quality of the communication media that determines this salience. The degree of social presence afforded by a device will determine its use. When audio only is available, people tend to perceive the other party in a more abstract manner, less as a full human being. When video is available, the social presence is higher and people are more likely to conform to the norms of behavior that were established in face-to-face communication. This model seems to gain further support from observation of the phenomenon of "flaming" in e-mail—use of abusive and aggressive language that is so common when the communication channel affords a very low level of social presence. Arguably, flaming takes place "because a person composing an electronic message lacks tangible reminder of his or her audience" (Sproull & Kiesler, 1991, p. 49). Similarly, the "cuelessness model" (Rutter, 1987) argues that in the absence of social cues, people experience a psychological distance, which in turn influences the outcome and the style of interaction.

THE ASYMMETRIC VALUE OF TALKING HEADS VIDEO

An alternative explanation emerges when one looks at the role of backchannel responses in communication. Because the speaker formulates the message according to the listener (Kraut et al., 1982), it is the availability of these feedback messages that may make the difference in those cases where persuasion is needed. A speaker may be clueless about the audience reaction to his or her message and thus be less effective in communicating it. The term *cuelessness* that Rutter used to describe the psychological distance created by the lack of social cues can be applied to the cognitive impediment that is created by the absence of cognitive clues. The speaker is deprived of the feedback that is normally used in the production of the message.

An event shared by many in the research community may serve to illustrate the problem. A keynote speaker in the CSCW '94 program, known for his charismatic and inspiring style of delivery, gave a presentation via a VMC system. His image, delivered through a desktop videoconferencing system, was projected onto a large screen. The fact that his image was small and of low quality did not seem to bother the audience. The problem appeared to have been that, in the lack of immediate audience, his talk was flat and tentative. It seemed, both from the content of his conversation and from his overall demeanor, that he did not have a sense of his audience. This experience is in an interesting contrast to another talk, given at the same conference. This time the speaker, a CSCW researcher, was giving a presentation to an audience of thousands in another location via a telecast. In attendance was a small local audience. The presentation went smoothly, and at its conclusion the speaker commented spontaneously that she was very appreciative of having the local audience, and that in fact she did not have any sense of her larger intended audience. The way she experienced it, she gave her talk to the people in the room.

These anecdotes illustrate an interesting implication of the "cognitive cluelessness" that the absence of video creates. The function of video can be described as "asymmetric": The video image of the listener is far more important to the speaker than is the image of the speaker to the listener. For those of us who are not hearing-impaired, rarely does the "talking head" provide much information beyond the auditory content of the speech. However, for the speaker, the "listening head(s)" may carry information that is essential for the speaker in order to formulate his or her contribution.

Most of the studies of VMC have been exploratory in nature (e.g., Abel, 1990; Mantei et al., 1991). Some succeeded in pointing to the fact that when afforded a video channel, people liked it, and indeed seem to use some nonverbal cues in a fashion that is similar to the way that they are used in a face-to-face communication (Isaacs & Tang, 1993). Others have provided insights about parameters in the use of video (e.g., Prussog, Mühlbach, & Böcker, 1993). But for the most part, when discussing the role of "talking head" video, they failed to show that the outcome of the task has been significantly different from a similar situation with audio only as the medium of communication. The body of research focuses on the value of the "talking head" to the listener. An alternative direction for research might be to look at the value of the "listening head" to the speaker.

THE ROLE OF VIDEO IN REPRESENTING
GROUP SPACE

For very practical reasons, most of the research on the role of audio and video in communication has focused on the conversation between two participants. Study of videoconferencing does provide us with some insights about conversation between multiple participants at two points and about multiple participant in multiple points(e.g., O'Conaill, Whittaker, & Wilbur, 1993; Sellen, 1992). However, there is relatively little discussion of the group dynamics—that is, about the impact that the physical arrangement has on variables such as leadership, cohesion, power, attraction, and satisfaction from belonging to the group.

One exception is a study of coalition formation, in which four participants were divided into two groups that were either separated by a table in a face to face meeting, or else were communicating with the other pair through an audio-only or audio and video connection (Williams, 1975). The investigation seems to indicate clearly that with audio as the only channel of communication, people formed a less favorable opinion of the people on the other side and were more likely to oppose their suggestions. Both audio-only and audiovideo subjects were more likely to second a proposal made by a person who was physically with them than the proposal of the person who was remote. This research gives credence to the observations about different dynamics of interaction among the people who are physically copresent, versus those who are copresent through the VMC system. It appears to be easy to slide to an "us versus them" approach where "us" is the group that is present physically and "they" are at the other end of the connection (Mantei et al., 1991).

User experience in VMC is highly influenced by the constraints of current technology (Angiolillo, Blanchard, Israelski, & Mané, chapter 3, this volume). Indeed most systems that are available commercially are operating within tight price–performance trade-offs and provide a picture whose quality falls far short of the expectations that we develop as viewers of broadcast TV. Even with ISDN bandwidth, the picture does not provide an adequate rendering of fine facial expressions. In fact, even with analog video, when the image was split to four quadrants (which is still bigger and clearer than most digital systems) viewers felt that fine points of the interaction were not visible and that the saliency of the visual information was reduced. The limitation of framing the "talking head" rules out the possibility of incorporating much of the body language. At the existing level of technology one can argue that the video technology is falling short in presenting the user with the "person space" that was hoped for.

However, the technology does provide some level of visual backchannel response. In fact, one recent study shows how users of a "quadrature" video system developed a "visual language" that consisted of exaggerated gesture to express position and to assist in the regulation of the conversation and the collaboration (Dykstra-Erickson et al., 1995). Gestures such as thumbs ups, thumbs down, as an indication of approval, or holding up one finger to indicate "wait, I'm ready to talk," illustrate how visual backchannel responses are used to provide content and to coordinate turn-taking. The fact that users have to resort to these exaggerated gestures suggests that more subtle signs, those that we use in a face-to-face conversation, may be lost in VMC systems that use today's technology. Much is lost when implicit signs have to be turned into explicit signals. Much of what is known as "social grace" hinges on our ability to convey a message with subtlety, and to allow the other party to respond or not to respond without explicitly ignoring or explicitly responding to our message. It is feasible that with a more advanced VMC system these subtleties may be preserved, but at least today's technology can offer a first approximation.

Paradoxically, the video may be rather adequate in establishing an acceptable level of group space. The crude and small representation of multiple participants may be adequate to address three of the four levels of group space representation mentioned earlier in this chapter. Assuming that it is feasible to do so, one can incorporate into a single display the multiple images or a composite single image of all the participants, and thus present clearly who is and who is not part of the group at any given time. With that in place, users have a continuous and clear visual representation of the identity of the various contributors that are being heard on the auditory channel. Indeed, they can have a clear indication of the level of engagement of the various participants and notice "secondary" activities (reading mail) or events (private conversation) that the participant may be engaged in. Furthermore, listeners have ample opportunity to provide explicit messages that convey their reaction to the group activity. Granted, what in a face-to-face meeting may be a subtle gesture has to be presented as an explicit body gesture, but the existence of the visual backchannel response affords the user a level of interaction that does not exist in an audio-only condition.

The fourth level of group space, one that focuses on the social interaction among the group participants, is, for the most part, outside the reach of current technology. Exploratory systems are able to preserve an indication of who is looking at whom in a multipoint connection, and allow the user to look at any participant at any time (Okada, Maeda, Ichikawaa, & Matsushita, 1994). But they can do so realistically only at a great cost, within very demanding constraints, and they fail to scale easily for groups larger than three. It is hard to see how a solution that will probably require a true-to-life size and high-quality display of each participant and a system configuration that conveys eye contact and captures the spatial relationship among the participants can become commercially viable in the near future.

GROUP SPACE AND ITS IMPLEMENTATION

Practical implementation of the representation of group space is highly dependent on the technology in use. Multiple control units (MCU) are used for bridging multiple participants, summing up the audio signal from the various points, and composing a single video channel. One common algorithm used by the MCU for selection of the video signal is known as voice-activated switching. In this technique everyone gets to see the speaker, who in turn gets to see the image of the previous speaker. This imposes quite a challenge for representing group space. One way of meeting this challenge is provided by a user interface that incorporates still images of all the participants in a "meeting-room" representation (Benimoff et al., 1995). The image of the speaker is presented, based on the switching done in the MCU, in one window; events in the life of the group, such as participants joining in or dropping out, are represented through still images of the participants in the meeting-room window (see Fig. 19.1).

The quadrature display, which integrates the images of up to four participants into a single video stream and sends this stream to the participants, is moving a step closer to representation of listeners as well as speaker and recreation of a group space, but does so at the expense of dedicating only a quarter of the available image size to any given participant. It is interesting

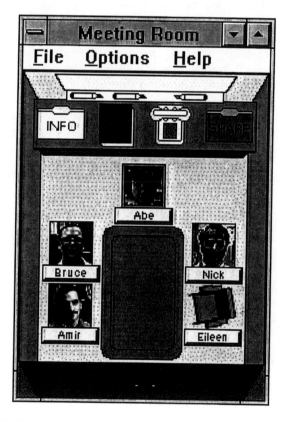

FIG. 19.1. A desktop display with a meeting-room representation.

to note that when such a system was used, as in the case of CAVECAT (Computer Audio Video Enhanced Collaboration And Telepresence), subjects found it annoying when the placement of individuals in the four quadrants changed in the course of a single meeting (Mantei et al., 1991). The use of the quadrature system in CAVECAT also provides some affordances about the reduced sense of social presence that is associated with the reduction of any individual participant to a quarter of its full size. Since CAVECAT did not use compressed video, one can only speculate about the effectiveness of a composed quadrature picture presented in the CIF format; actual testing and comparison to other modes of presentation would be of great value.

Although the quadrature solution is limited to four participants (five if self-view is sacrificed), a more general solution for n participants was proposed by the developers of Rapport (Ensor et al., 1991), who integrated into a single display a stamp-size representation of each participant and a larger display of the individual who is the current speaker. By so doing, they balanced the benefit of a larger image of the current speaker with a minimal representation of all the other participants, integrating the person space with the group space.

This idea was carried further by the development of sophisticated ATM-based multipoint video bridging architecture that makes it possible for each participant to display an arbitrary number of full motion (30 fps) video streams varying in size from full size to $1/4$, $1/16$, and $1/64$ of the screen (Gaglianello & Cash, 1995). Thus, a user could designate the entire screen as the window for the current speaker, hold a quarter-sized corner for a particular participant whose reaction the user is interested in monitoring, and populate the other participants in stamp-size representations. Clearly, such a technology would bring not only a better representation of group space, but also a better sense of sharing a person space.

In selecting the optimal presentation, one has to make a choice between the size of the visual image of any particular participant and the incorporation of images of multiple participants, possibly all of them. Users seem to prefer the continuity that the "split screen" affords. At the same time there are clear indications that the size of the image is an important factor in determining the sense of "telepresence" (Prussog et al., 1994). In fact, some observed that the size of the video image seems to be influencing the participant's effectiveness in conversation and that switching between a split-screen view and a full-screen view caused the viewers to switch from a conversation among those who were physically present at the room to a conversation with those that were connected through the VMC system (Mantei et al., 1991). If, as multipoint systems make their way into the marketplace, it turns out that users prefer the group view over the "speaker" view, this would indicate that sharing a group space may be more valued than sharing the person space.

CONCLUSION

To understand the role of the visual channel in a multipoint VMC system one has to look at the group, rather than the individual, as a subject of inquiry. The main argument of this chapter is that in addition to person space and task space there is a group space—the sense of copresence with the other participants in the virtual meeting. The sense of group space is created to the degree that participants are aware of who is participating, what others are doing, responses to the content of the discussion, and get a sense of the group mood as a whole.

The role of the visual channel in human communication was studied mostly from the perspective of the listener, and the question was, what is the benefit that the listener could have from having access to the image of the speaker in addition to being able to hear their voice? A different approach would be to focus on the benefit that the speaker has from viewing the image of the listener. If the value of the visual channel in VMC is "asymmetric" and its major contribution is to present backchannel information about the listeners, then multipoint videoconferencing may be the environment where this technology can prove its worth. Although current technology may not meet our expectations with regard to the delivery of facial expressions and minute gestures, it may be sufficient to present important information about the group space—who is present, who is active, and how they react to the content of and events in the meeting. The video channel should be able to create a sense of a group space, and in doing so, it may give VMC systems an advantage over multipoint audio connection.

REFERENCES

Abel, M. J. (1990). Experiences in an exploratory distributed organization. In J. Galegher, R. E. Kraut, & C. Egido, C. (Eds.), *Intellectual teamwork: Social and technological foundations of cooperative work* (pp. 489–510). Hillsdale, NJ: Lawrence Erlbaum Associates.

Argyle, M. (1969). *Social interaction.* London: Methuen.

Bavelas, A. (1950). Communication patterns in task-oriented groups. *Journal of the Acoustical Society of America, 22,* 725–730.

Benimoff, N. I., Altom, M. W., Farber, J. M., Kirby, D. J., Mané, A. M., Montero, R. C., Pastore, R. L., Roberts, L. A., Sauer, R. F., Todd, S., & Whitten, W. B. (1995, March). A user interface design for desktop multimedia collaboration. *Proceedings of HFT'95; 15th International Symposium on Human Factors in Telecommunications* (pp. 23–30). Melbourne, Australia.

Buxton, W. A. S. (1992). Telepresence: Integrating shared task and person spaces. *Proceedings of Graphic Interface '92* (pp. 23–129). San Mateo, CA: Morgan Kaufmann.

Clark, H. H. (1985). Language use and language users. In G. Lindzey & E. Aronson (Eds.), *Handbook of social psychology* (pp. 179–231). New York: Random House.

Clark H. H., & Brennan, S. E. (1993). Grounding in communication. In L. B. Resnick, J. M. Levine, & S. D. Teasley (Eds.), *Perspectives on socially shared cognition* (pp. 127–149). Washington, DC: American Psychological Association.

Collins, B. E., & Raven, B. H. (1969). Group structure: Attraction, coalitions, communication, and power. In G. Lindzey & E. Aronson (Eds.), *Handbook of social psychology* (pp. 102–204). Reading, MA: Addison-Wesley.

Dykstra-Erickson, E., Rudman, C., Marshall, C., Hertz, R., Mithal, K., & Schmidt, J. (1995, March). Supporting adaptation to multimedia desktop conferencing. *Proceedings of HFT'95; 15th International Symposium on Human Factors in Telecommunications* (pp. 31–38). Melbourne, Australia.

Ensor, J. R., Ahuja, S. R., Connaghan, R., Horn, D., Pack, M., & Seligmann, D. D. (1991). Control issues in multimedia conferencing. *Proceedings of TRICOMM '91* (pp. 33–143). Chapel Hill, NC: IEEE.

Gaglianello, R. D., & Cash, G. L. (1995). Montage: Continuous presence teleconferencing utilizing compressed domain video bridging. *Proceedings of ICC'95* (pp. 573–581). Seattle, WA: IEEE.

Isaacs, E. A., & Tang, J. C. (1993) What video can and can't do for collaboration: A case study. *Proceedings of ACM Multimedia 93* (pp. 199–206). New York: ACM Press.

Kamata, K., & Hirama, A. (1995, March). The use of 64 Kbit/s videophones for hearing impaired people. *Proceedings of HFT'95; the 15th International Symposium on Human Factors in Telecommunications* (pp. 321–328). Melbourne, Australia.

Kendon, A. (1967). Some functions of gaze direction in social interaction. *Acta Psychologica, 32*, 1–25.

Kraut, R. E., Lewis, S. H., & Swezey, L. W. (1982). Listener responsiveness and the coordination of conversation. *Journal of Personality and Social Psychology, 34*, 718–731.

Leavitt, H. H. (1951). Some effects of certain communication patterns on group performance. *Journal of Abnormal Social Psychology. 46*, 38–50.

Mantei, M. M., Baecker, R. M., Sellen, A., Buxton, W. A. S., Milligan, T., & Wellmand, B. (1991). Experiences in the use of a media space. *Proceedings of CHI '91* (pp. 203–208). New York: ACM Press.

Minami, H., & Tanaka, K. (1995). Social and environmental psychology transaction between physical space and group dynamic processes. *Environment and Behavior, 27*(1), 43–55.

Nardi, B. P., Schwartz, H., Kuchinski, A., Leichner, R., Whittaker, S., & Sclabossi, R. (1993). Turning away from talking heads: The use of video-as-data in. *Proceedings of CHI '93* (pp. 327–334). New York: ACM Press.

Noll, A. M. (1992). Anatomy of failure: Picture phone revisited. *Telecommunication Policy, 18*, 307–316.

Ochsman, R., & Chapanis, A. (1974). The effects of 10 communication modes on the behavior of teams during co-operative problem-solving. *International Journal of Man–Machine Studies, 6*, 579–619.

O'Conaill, B., Whittaker, S., & Wilbur, S. (1993). Conversations over video conferences: An evaluation of the spoken aspects of video mediated communication. *Human–Computer Interaction, 8*, 389–428.

Okada, K. I., Maeda, F., Ichikawaa, Y., & Matsushita, Y. (1994). Multiparty videoconferencing at virtual social distance: MAJIC design. *Proceedings of CSCW '94* (pp. 385–393). New York: ACM Press.

Olson, J. S., Card, S. K., Landauer, T. K., Olson, G. M., Malone, T., & Leggett, J. (1993). Computer supported co-operative work: Research issues for the 90s. *Behavior & Information Technology, 12*(2), 115–129.

Prussog, A., Mühlbach, L., & Böcker, M. (1993, May). Telepresence in stereoscopic videoconferencing. *Proceedings of the 14th International Symposium HF in Telecommunication* (pp. 201–211). Darmstadt, Germany.

Prussog, A., Mühlbach, L., & Böcker, M. (1994, October). Telepresence in video communications. *Proceedings of the Human Factors and Ergonomic Society* (pp. 180–184). Nashville, TN.

Rutter, D. R. (1987). *Communicating by telephone.* Oxford: Pergamon.

Seligmann, D. D., & Edmark, J. T. (1994, May). User interface mechanisms for assurances during multimedia multiparty communication. *1st International Workshop on Networked Reality in Telecommunication* (Section 6–2). Tokyo.

Sellen, A. A. (1992). Speech patterns in video-mediated conversations. *Proceedings of CHI '92* (pp. 49–59). New York: ACM Press.

Short, J. A. (1974). Effects of medium of communication on experimental negotiation. *Human Relations, 27,* 225–234.

Short, J., Williams, E., & Christie, B. (1976). *The social psychology of telecommunications.* London: Wiley.

Sproull, L., & Kiesler, S. (1991). *Connections: New ways of working in the networked organization.* Cambridge, MA: MIT Press.

Wiener, M., Devoe, S., Rubinow, S., & Geller, J. (1972). Nonverbal behavior and nonverbal communication. *Psychological Review, 79,* 185–214.

Williams, E. (1975). Coalition formation over telecommunications media. *European Journal of Social Psychology, 5,* 503–507.

Williams, E. (1977). Experimental comparisons of face to face and mediated communication. *Psychological Bulletin, 84,* 963–976.

Chapter 20

Virtual Meeting Rooms

J. Robert Ensor
Bell Laboratories

The virtual meeting room is a computer-based collaborative environment in which people may access and exchange shared information. This chapter discusses the origins of the communication model on which this collaborative framework is based. It then describes three systems—Rapport, VPE, and Archways—that use virtual meeting rooms to provide communication services. Rapport is a multimedia, multiparty desktop conferencing system that allows its users to exchange information in both synchronous and asynchronous long-distance interactions. VPE is a software system that helps people use Rapport-managed virtual meeting rooms to create, store, and retrieve meeting histories, as well as conduct conferences. Archways is a knowledge-based system that automatically generates three-dimensional visualizations of communication activities, illustrating Rapport-managed virtual meeting rooms and the real-world environments of meeting participants.

INTRODUCTION

Most people spend part of each day in a room. This common experience makes the room one of the most universally familiar objects in our world. Such a well-known object makes an attractive metaphor for guiding the construction and use of computer-based systems. For example, Austin Henderson and Stuart Card (1986) created a window manager whose user interface was based on a room metaphor. Similarly, Sudhir Ahuja and I

415

developed an extensive and detailed abstraction of rooms in which meetings occur. We used this model to define a class of distributed, computer-based collaborative environments, which we term *virtual meeting rooms,* and the model guided the development of several systems that create communication frameworks conforming to its constraints. We included in the virtual meeting room model those elements of physical rooms that we feel are needed to provide computer-based analogs for the physical space in which face-to-face meetings occur. In other words, the model suggests ways to build and use systems through which long-distance interpersonal communications can be as convenient and effective as face-to-face meetings.

We originated the virtual room concept in the autumn of 1986 during our initial studies of computer-supported cooperative work (CSCW). The virtual meeting room model is based on generalizations of earlier computer-based systems that supported real-time conferencing among remote parties (e.g., Sarin & Greif, 1985, Lantz, 1986). The model was influenced by the Colab project (Stefik, Bobrow, Lenning, & Tatar, 1986) of Xerox PARC, which was a seminal study in CSCW. Colab was based on the hypothesis that people could communicate more effectively if they had access to their office computers' data and programs during face-to-face meetings. The Colab studies were conducted in a specially equipped room where people could access private and shared data from computers during meetings. The virtual meeting room is based on a complementary notion. Rather than have people go to a meeting room with computer access, an electronic "meeting room" is distributed among participants' computers. The virtual meeting room model describes environments for multimedia conferences in which collaborators can converse over long distances while remaining in their homes or offices and, therefore, maintaining access not only to their computers but also to other local stores of information—books, magazines, newspapers, and so forth.

Figure 20.1 illustrates the major components of the virtual meeting room model. These components are abstractions of fundamental properties of a physical room—its location, its doors, its walls, the means of transmitting information inside it, and the objects within it. The model components form the basis for its descriptions of computer-based communication environments and the interpersonal activities that are supported by them. The model of a virtual meeting room includes the room's name, its access methods, its admission policies, its boundary or scope, its transmission media, and descriptions of objects associated with ("within") the room. A *meeting* is any period during which a person or computer program is sending or receiving information within the scope of the room. A meeting description includes its name, the name of the room in which it is taking place, and descriptions of meeting participants (also termed room occupants), who are the persons and computer programs accessing information within the room.

FIG. 20.1. Virtual meeting room: model components.

Each virtual meeting room has a name, which permits that particular collaborative environment to be referenced by other programs (e.g., calendar managers). It also allows the room to act as a designated rendezvous site for interactions (meetings). Figure 20.1 illustrates a virtual meeting room named The Sierra Room. The operations defined for a virtual meeting room create means of accessing the collaborative environment (providing a metaphorical "door" for each room). Security or other restrictions may be associated with the controls for entering or leaving a room. These restrictions are represented in Fig. 20.1 as the analog of the receptionist's desk or guard's station that is often associated with a physical meeting room. The virtual meeting room operations also limit the distribution of a room's description and the shared information available within it. These restrictions are represented in the figure by the room's walls.

In a physical meeting room, people hear and see each other. They can also see and/or hear other objects displayed there. To provide similar communication opportunities in its distributed computer-based environment, a virtual meeting room must distribute shared information to room occupants. Because this information is generally represented in multiple media, a virtual meeting room is inherently a multimedia communication framework. Room occupants may be represented by textual and graphical descriptions and by real-time audio and video data "streams" originating from their microphones and cameras. These streams produce live audiovideo images of the occupants (called *talking heads*). In addition to creating occupant representations, the virtual meeting room provides operations by which occupants may introduce other shared data into the room's scope. An occupant may use audio and video streams as well as program outputs to create this shared multimedia information. For example, one might use video to show friends the cover and liner notes of a new CD and use stereo-quality audio to share a favorite song from the same disk. In the spirit of Colab, the virtual meeting room model places special emphasis on the role of computer-based tools and data in group work. When a computer program is associated with a virtual meeting room, it is metaphorically "brought into" the room, and its output is made available to room occupants. (The displays produced by these programs are represented as video wall monitors in Fig. 20.1.) Of course, not everyone who gathers in a physical room has the same ability to see and hear the information available there. Similarly, a virtual meeting room permits occupants to access its environment through different devices, offering them different input and output capabilities. For example, one person might access the virtual meeting room through a telephone, and another might access it through a multimedia computer.

The persistence of physical rooms helps people interact. By remaining in a fixed location, a room offers people a place for rendezvous. Because a room exists independent of meetings held within it, it may be used as a location for meeting preparation. For example, a slide projector may be placed in a room in preparation for a lecture. Similarly, a room can be used for a sequence of meetings and can hold results produced during these meetings. For example, a room in an advertising agency can be designated as the location of all meetings with a particular client, holding advertisement layouts produced during these design sessions. To offer similar benefits in a computer-based collaboration environment, virtual meeting rooms are able to persist beyond meetings held within them. Shared information may be placed in the virtual meeting room before a group of collaborators meets there. For example, a graphical editor may be associated with the room in preparation for a review of a group progress report. Furthermore, a series of meetings can be held within a virtual meeting room, and information may be stored within the room between these interactions. For example, an advertising agency can conduct all online meetings with a particular client in a designated virtual meeting room, which can store the advertisement layouts produced during these design sessions. The persistent electronic environment prescribed by the model supports not only real-time interactions among people, but also interpersonal communications in which people exchange messages asynchronously. That is, the virtual meeting room provides a means of exchanging multimedia messages, in which messages may be not only static e-mail notes, but also active programs. For example, a CAD tool, with its associated design data, can be left as a message in a virtual meeting room. This property of virtual meeting rooms makes them especially supportive environments for long-term collaborations.

According to the virtual meeting room model, whenever any person or computer program accesses information within a room, a meeting is taking place in that room. Meetings are given names, providing the same reference utilities as virtual meeting room names. Because all meetings "take place within," that is, are associated with, rooms, each meeting description contains the name of its associated virtual meeting room. Finally, meeting representations contain descriptions of meeting participants. The participant descriptions include their identifiers and information about their input–output capabilities. These capabilities are determined not only by the devices through which participants access the room, but also by permissions associated with shared information. For example, a participant may have both input and output capabilities for one shared computer program, but have only output capablities for another program. Meeting participants can enter and leave a virtual meeting room at their convenience; thus, the participant description also indicates whether that participant is currently a room occupant.

To make the virtual meeting room model applicable to a broad range of collaborative activities, we did not make most meeting procedures part of the abstraction. In other words, a virtual meeting room does not contain operations for specialized meeting activities. Hence, it can model a wide range of communications. For example, scheduled formal meetings and lectures in classrooms are based on rendezvous in named meeting spaces. The virtual meeting room abstraction can also model spontaneous chance encounters at a water cooler or espresso machine. In these cases, a person is in a virtual meeting room, and another person happens to enter there also. Each person is informed of the other's presence, and their talking heads and other shared information are exchanged. In fact, traditional meetings are not required for access to virtual meeting rooms. For example, a meeting with only one participant is allowed.

To support this wide range of interpersonal communications, the virtual meeting room cannot impose the limitations on communications and control found in most multimedia conferencing systems. For example, the virtual meeting room must not require that meetings be scheduled or that meetings have a chairperson, even though these restrictions would help implement billing and other activities typically associated with telecommunication services. The virtual meeting room is not tied to a particular multiuser program. The virtual meeting room concept is based on information sharing, and it permits specialized meeting tools, such as Cognoter or Argnoter (Foster & Stefik, 1986), to be brought into the meeting space to support particular activities. Thus, meetings in which participants use their existing day-to-day tools in meetings are encouraged.

RAPPORT MULTIMEDIA CONFERENCING SYSTEM

We designed and implemented the Rapport multimedia conferencing system (Ahuja, Ensor, & Horn, 1988) according to the virtual meeting room model. Rapport creates instances of virtual meeting rooms so that its users may collaborate over long distances from their homes and offices. Its call management mechanisms help users meet through scheduled and extemporaneous meetings. It coordinates communication network services to distribute audio, video, and computer program data to conference members. Meeting participants may access Rapport virtual meeting rooms through differing sets of input and output devices. For example, conferees with only telephone access to a virtual meeting room may participate in the exchange of audio-based information, whereas conferees with video cameras and monitors may send and receive video streams.

Computer programs based on the UNIX operating system and the X Window System (Scheifler & Gettys, 1986) may be associated with Rapport meetings. Such programs are termed *application programs* and are said to be "within the room." Rapport filters the input to, and the output from, application programs to create identical displays on the computer screens of meeting participants.

Figure 20.2 illustrates the relationships among the Rapport system components during a typical two-party call. In this example, David and Kate are collaborating over long distances to write a book. They produce audio-

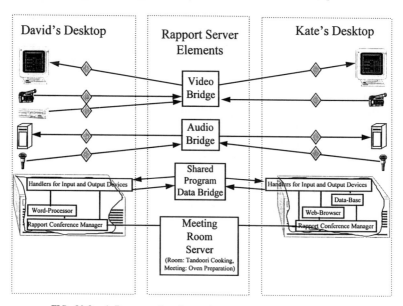

FIG. 20.2. A Rapport virtual meeting room: system components.

video talking heads with their cameras and microphones and display them with their monitors and speakers. David is also providing video-based information from his videotape player. Computer-based displays are being produced on both computer screens by program Word-Processor, executing on David's computer, and by the programs the Data-Base and Web-Browser, executing on Kate's computer. David and Kate can both provide input to the three programs.

Rapport's meeting room server creates and maintains room and meeting descriptions. Its data structures define a virtual meeting room, here labeled Tandoori Cooking, for the Oven Preparation meeting. Rapport media-specific subsystems—its audio bridge, video bridge, and shared program bridge—receive input from each camera, microphone, and computer program. They then combine or multicast the video, voice, and computer program output streams to create a bridged multimedia stream for each participant (Ahuja, Ensor, & Lucco, 1990). Desktop input and output devices may interface directly to the bridges through network connections. Alternatively, devices may connect to interfaces within David's and Kate's computers, which, in turn, have network connections to the bridges. These possibilities are represented in the figure by the diamonds that intersect each path between a desktop input/output device and a bridge. The bridged streams are composed according to each participant's use of the media. Conferees control their contribution of information to the communication system and also control their receipt of the bridged output. Rapport's control structure is represented in the figure by bidirectional communication paths between each Rapport conference manager and its local handlers and application programs and between each conference manager and the meeting room server. Additional control paths among the servers form a tree rooted at the meeting room server, but this structure is not illustrated in the figure.

Rapport must perform two primary tasks to implement virtual meeting rooms:

1. It must receive audio-, video-, and computer-based information from each meeting participant and use these data to create an integrated multimedia representation for each participant.
2. It must provide operations that allow users to manage the conduct of meetings and control the transmission and display of information during meetings.

Managing Communications

Rapport is a distributed program that manages information movement among meeting participants (Ensor et al., 1991). It is responsible for interfacing its users' input and output devices (that capture and display meeting data) to the appropriate underlying communication network (or collection of networks). It then makes use of the transmission services of this network to transmit data among participants. Finally, it makes use of media-specific bridging devices to integrate data.

The input and output devices of conference participants must be connected to exchange data. Rapport obtains the necessary communication links from one or more underlying transmission networks. The number and characteristics of these links depend on the media through which each participant communicates. Rapport provides controls for connection management by extending its underlying communication network(s) to coordinate communications over multiple links. This link management remains active during a conference. Participants may add or drop other conferees and use more or fewer media for information exchange as the conference progresses. This management occurs whether transmission is over one network or several. For example, in the Tandoori Cooking, Oven Preparation meeting of David and Kate, communications could take place over distinct networks, such as a baseband cable network for the distribution of video, a telephone network for exchange of voice, and a local-area network for the exchange of conference protocol messages and program data. On the other hand, they could also take place over an integrated multimedia network, such as ISDN. In either case, Rapport provides the same communication controls for its users.

To support multiparty conferences, bridges combine data from meeting participants and distribute the integrated data back to them. Bridges can also integrate separate media streams into a multimedia representation of a virtual meeting room. The bridges may be implemented in a variety of ways, ranging from software modules executing on participant computers to specialized hardware located in a centralized location. The different versions of Rapport have used various combinations of bridges to integrate conference data. The bridging requirements of a set of data streams depend not only on the media involved, but also on the use of the media in the meeting. For example, audio produced when a participant speaks is usually combined with other sounds in the room, but speakers are not presented with their own signals. On the other hand, audio generated when scanning shared scientific data would typically not be combined with any other signal and would be presented equally to all meeting participants. In general then, a medium-specific bridge must perform multiple bridging functions for data in its medium.

User Interfaces

As we have tested different aspects of multimedia interpersonal communication over long distances, we have given Rapport many user interfaces (Ensor, Ahuja, & Seligmann, 1993). Because we support participation in Rapport conferences from a variety of devices, these interfaces have presented a corresponding range of control operations. For example, participants with telephone-only access to a Rapport conference are not offered application program controls. Rapport interfaces have also used a variety of control surfaces, including telephone key pads, computer touch screens, and pen-based computers. Even within a fixed set of input and output devices and control surfaces, Rapport interfaces have varied. For example, the interfaces shown in Figs. 20.3 and 20.4 are both based on computer screen displays with mouse and keyboard control surfaces, but they represent common control operations with distinct look-and-feels. All Rapport user interfaces present two sets of operations. One set of commands supports meeting conduct; the other set supports media controls within meetings.

The controls for meeting conduct are based on management of rooms and meeting membership. Rapport user interfaces include operations that create and destroy meeting rooms. When rooms are created they are given names, providing access by other programs to the room's representation and also supporting meeting participant rendezvous. Conference membership can change at any time during a meeting. People can join ongoing meetings and people can step out of meetings (either permanently ending their participation in the meeting, or temporarily leaving the meeting to return later). When people enter or leave a meeting, Rapport activates or deactivates their representations (e.g., talking heads) to indicate their status. Meeting membership controls—add and drop member—require that meeting participants have names. Rapport provides a name directory service with personalized caches of names available to each user. The entries in these directories may include multiple communication ports for multiple data streams. A final set of meeting control operations is based on virtual meeting room communication. Sets of meeting participants can have subconferences or "sidebar conversations" with each other. Participants can be "paged," that is, receive signals, from outside a virtual meeting room. Within the meeting, participants can use Rapport-provided telepointers (Stefik et al., 1986) and attention-requesting signals, so-called *raised hands*.

Two fundamental metaphors have been used in developing the look and feel for the Rapport meeting controls listed above. The first approach to representing meeting controls, illustrated in Fig. 20.3, is based on the telephone call metaphor. In fact, a conventional telephone, as well as a computer screen-based graphic representation of the device, can be used to conduct meetings in this version of Rapport. Traditional use of telephone controls causes Rapport to create conventional telephone calls within the virtual meeting room framework. To support conventional telephony commands in a multimedia collaborative framework, this version of Rapport can supply default parameters to several meeting management operations. For example, when a call is initiated via a telephone, the names of rooms and meetings are generated by default (as caller identifier plus a sequence

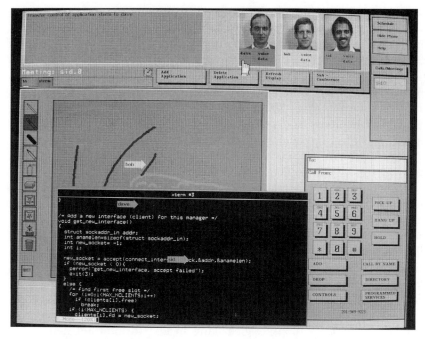

FIG. 20.3. A Rapport conference: phone-based meeting controls.

number). Similarly, a meeting and associated room are created and de-
stroyed together when the telephone goes off and on hook. Other controls,
invoked as additional telephone button-press sequences, permit conventional calls to be expanded to multimedia, multiparty collaboration environments. For example, parties can be added to the default two-party call by
using the mouse to "press" the "add" button on the telephone graphic of
Fig. 20.3 or by pressing programmed buttons on a telephone.

The second approach to representing meeting controls is based on the
meeting-room metaphor itself. This interface allows users to manipulate
room and meeting representations directly, as illustrated in Fig. 20.4. Because the control representations map directly onto the underlying system
framework, default actions in this version of the system are available simply
for the speed and convenience of specifying user requests. For example,
David can specify that the meetings he creates should allow audio and
video data exchange, whereas Kate can ask the system to start her meetings
with only audio data exchange as the default. In this interface, graphical
representations of rooms are labeled by their names. Additional media
and parties are added to meetings by putting their representations into a
room. Like the conferencing system of Michaelitz (1990), these Rapport
versions let users move among meetings by moving along a meeting hallway.

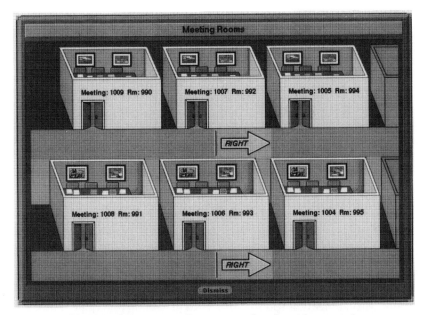

FIG. 20.4. A Rapport conference: room-based meeting controls.

Although the telephone-based look and feel is based on a more common call control metaphor and allows people to use Rapport without any training, the room-based interface requires only insignificant training.

In addition to the controls for overall conduct of meetings, Rapport user interfaces provide controls for transmission and display of information exchanged within meetings. These media-specific controls are common to the two versions of Rapport already described. The system's media controls are medium specific, not participant specific. That is, Rapport media controls provide means to add and delete media-specific subsystems to a meeting. These subsystems, which are all associated with bridges, make room and meeting descriptions, as well as the shared data associated with meetings, available to conferees. For example, audio and video bridges distribute talking head displays, as well as shared audiovideo presentations, to meeting participants. These subsystems are also responsible for providing more precise controls for distribution of information among meeting participants. For example, David and Kate can change a voice-only meeting into a data-only meeting by using Rapport commands to delete voice from, and add program sharing data to, the meeting. Once the program sharing data subsystem has been added to their meeting, it provides them with commands to specify distribution restrictions for program data. They might then request that David be allowed to provide input to shared programs and receive program output, whereas Kate be allowed only to receive output.

The subsystems also provide each Rapport user with individual controls for information displays. For example, David could place a talking head display of Kate in the middle of his screen, whereas Kate could iconify talking head displays on her screen. Individual display layouts are especially important in multimedia systems because input and output devices for audio and video tend to be limiting resources. People have trouble attending to more than one audio or video stream at a time, and people want to make their own decisions about how to focus their attention during meetings. For example, the common approach of "voice-activated" switching by video bridges, which automatically selects the speaker's talking head for display, has not been well received in our experiments. We have found greatest enthusiasm among users for "continuous presence" video, where multiple streams are continuously available to the meeting members. Each participant is provided controls for size and placement of the images selected for display (Gaglianello & Cash, 1995).

Persistence

Because virtual meeting rooms are persistent, long-term collaborations are especially well supported by the Rapport multimedia conferencing system. Continuity of a group's activities may be enhanced by conducting meetings in virtual meeting rooms. A virtual meeting room can relate one meeting to another by providing a common rendezvous site and by storing meeting results. For example, Charles, Max, and Jessie are long-term collaborators on the design of a windsurfing sail. They have used Rapport to create a long-lived room, Slalom 4.5, for their common project. This room is used as their meeting place and as a repository for their common project information. During a typical meeting, they use a collection of services to support their conversations, namely audio and video bridging services, and program sharing services. To help with their design tasks, the designers also make use of some specialized CAD tools—an aerodynamic simulator, a panel layout tool, and a material inventory control program. A subsequent meeting can continue the design in the same environment. Furthermore, the room, with its persistent information storage, can be accessed by one person for individual work with the common data. Hence this collaborative environment allows group members to leave each other elaborate messages in rooms and to move seamlessly between private and group activities.

The persistence of virtual meeting rooms also helps support mobile users. Rooms provide a rendezvous mechanism for accessing services and conducting communication sessions. Therefore, a user can move physical locations, change hardware configurations, and still access a given room. Connections are simply dropped when not needed and (re)established to hold meetings within a room. Users can access a room from any point as long as they can communicate with a Rapport meeting room server. For example, Kate can create a virtual meeting room by issuing requests from her office computer. She can begin to execute a program within the room. She may then leave the virtual room (although it continues to exist) and her physical office and drive to her house. During the drive, she may reenter the room through her car telephone, talking with other parties in the meeting and accessing information within the room through audio interfaces. At her house, she can use a different device, such as a set-top box, to reestablish contact with the Rapport server and reenter the virtual room where the still-executing program is located.

Project Status

Since the spring of 1987, Rapport has been a focus of work within the Multimedia Communication Research Department of AT & T Bell Laboratories. It has helped us, members of this department, study networking requirements for multimedia multiparty communications. We have used Rapport to create multimedia networks by coordinating information exchange over separate transmission fabrics. For example, Rapport has coordinated transport of data over Internet and the public switched telephone network during long-distance multimedia conferences. Rapport has also managed conferences over integrated digital networks, such as ISDN and ATM. Working with other members of AT & T, we have used Rapport to measure people's reactions to various means of controlling multimedia, multiparty communications. By incorporating different sets of media services as its subsystems, Rapport has helped us measure people's reactions to a variety of multimedia conferencing capabilities. For example, the role of video in multimedia conferencing has been studied. Experience shows that people usually position their cameras so that talking heads are actually talking "heads and upper torsos," providing some indication of body language during conversations. It also shows that when video bandwidth is low and lip synch is lost, people usually prefer fewer, higher qualtiy images for participant representations. Currently, members of our department are using Rapport as the basis for their multimedia communication research projects. Two of these are introduced next.

A SYSTEM FOR VISUALIZING PERSISTENT ENVIRONMENTS

VPE, or Visualizing Persistent Environments (Ginsberg & Ahuja, 1995), is a software system that helps people use Rapport-managed virtual meeting rooms to store and retrieve information as well as to conduct meetings. It also helps people locate and access rooms containing particular data. VPE provides its own interface through which users request actions involving rooms and meetings. However, it interacts with Rapport to act on these requests. More precisely, the Rapport meeting room server manages room and meeting representations according to requests that it receives from the VPE server, and it sends events to the VPE server describing the status of those rooms and meetings.

Generalizing the hallway of Rapport's room-based user interface, the VPE interface allows users to create multiple room groupings (see Fig. 20.5). VPE is designed to help people conduct meetings by automatically recording meeting activities, thus creating meeting histories. VPE records both participant interactions and their manipulations of multimedia information during conferences. In general, each server associated with a meeting provides information for the meeting minutes. For example, if voice, video, and data servers have been associated with a meeting, they all provide information to the VPE server, where it is recorded. The VPE server then correlates the information from these servers, thus allowing these data to be cross-indexed. For example, a user can retrieve records in which a participant is both speaking and using a whiteboard program. Information that the Rapport meeting room server contributes to the VPE server is

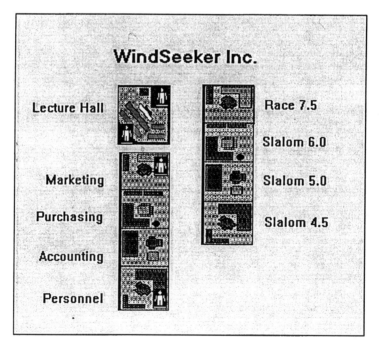

FIG. 20.5. VPE display: a set of rooms.

called *metainformation* because it is *about* the room and the meeting, rather than part of the service-specific information used during the meeting. VPE provides an effective way to represent the histories of distributed multimedia collaborations because it records and displays the generic meta-information associated with multimedia content in a way that allows users to focus on and access the associated content of interest. For example, one can find the video record of a specified meeting participant associated with the departure of another participant.

Figure 20.5 is a VPE display of three sets of virtual meeting rooms associated with a hypothetical manufacturer of windsurfing sails—Wind-Seeker, Inc. The rooms are grouped by three organizational functions. The room called Lecture Hall is a designated site for company-wide exchanges of information. The rooms labeled Marketing, Purchasing, Accounting, and Personnel are electronic environments associated with corporate management and financial functions. The rooms labeled Race 7.5, Slalom 6.0, Slalom 5.0, and Slalom 4.5 are environments for product development projects. Each of these rooms is long-lived. Lecture Hall, Marketing, Purchasing, Accounting, and Personnel might live as long as the company; Race 7.5, Slalom 6.0, Slalom 5.0, and Slalom 4.5 are expected to live as long as their corresponding product developments.

Figure 20.6 shows two VPE displays describing the activities associated with one meeting. The top display represents the "episodes" recorded in the meeting. Each episode description contains a time interval, a list of associated people, a list of associated programs, and an iconic visual representation. This figure contains the displays of five episodes. The second and third episodes are contemporaneous and indicate that Weimer was

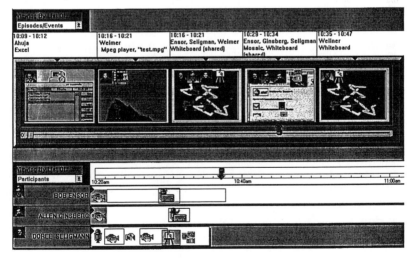

FIG. 20.6. VPE display: meeting information.

playing an MPEG movie clip, while he, Ensor, and Seligmann were using a shared whiteboard program. Episode four is shown in more detail in the bottom display of Fig. 20.6. Each row of the lower display lists the actions of a meeting participant associated with the event. This description shows when each participant uses video, voice, or computer programs to contribute information to the meeting. For example, the row describing Doree Seligmann's actions indicate that she was talking when the event began. It shows that she contributed video-based information in two periods, interrupted by her introducing a document into the room. She also worked with a whiteboard program and an unidentified graphical display program later in the episode.

VPE is currently in early stages of development. It is being integrated with a version of Rapport that contains media-specific subsystems for broadband transmission of digital audio and video. These data streams will support enhancements to VPE records by permitting the capture and storage of more meeting content as well as associated metainformation. However, increasing the quantitative and qualitative bandwidth of the VPE representation space raises issues and problems in generating clear and accurate visual representations of greater quantities of information. These issues are the subject of current research in the VPE project.

ARCHWAYS THREE-DIMENSIONAL VISUALIZATION SYSTEM

Archways (Seligmann, Mercuri, & Edmark, 1995) is a knowledge-based system that automatically generates three-dimensional visualizations of communications activities. The visualizations represent both Rapport-managed virtual meeting rooms and the real-world environments of meeting participants. Archways knowledge bases include descriptions of fundamental visual and aural relationships within simple spaces, design techniques for human–computer program interfaces, and ways to use services supplied by X Window System servers. The user interfaces generated by Archways are based on the following model of long-distance communication. When a person interacts with a remote entity, the person remains in his or her physical location but is, simultaneously, in a virtual environment defined by the long-distance interaction. For example, when people are talking via telephone, each of them is in a real-world location as well as the virtual place that hosts the conversation. These dual environments are not associated only with telecommunication among people; they also arise when a person or program accesses a remote service. For example, when a VCR player transmits a video stream to a remote viewer, it is in some physical place and in the virtual place it shares with the people and/or programs receiving its output. When an Archways user is communicating with one or more remote parties, Archways generates a representation of the real-world location of each communicating party and a representation of the virtual meeting room hosting their interaction. Furthermore, Archways generates customized views of each of these places for each party.

Figure 20.7 is an Archways visualization of a virtual room and the real-world locations in which the meeting participants are situated. The virtual room is represented as a cubic soap-bubble hovering over representations of the communicating parties' physical locations. The real-world locations are positioned within a stylized representation of their actual geographical relationships. In this case, the rooms are located within the same part of a building, so only that region of the world is illustrated. Representations of more separated locations are not yet generated. "Cables" connecting devices in real-world locations with objects in the virtual room are used to represent the flow of information into and out of the virtual room.

Figure 20.8 is an Archways visualization of a virtual room. In the situation illustrated, four people—Cati, Doree, John, and Sid—are browsing (i.e.,

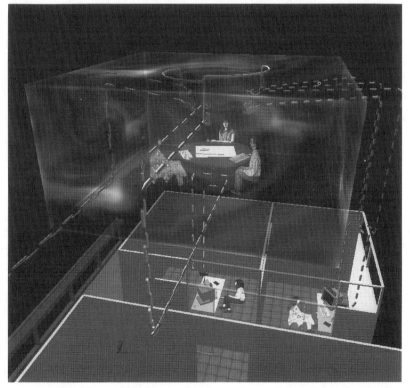

FIG. 20.7. An Archways visualization: a virtual meeting room and real-world locations.

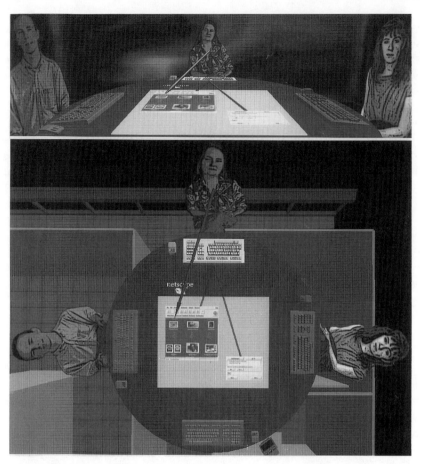

FIG. 20.8. An Archways visualization: inside a virtual meeting room.

surfing) the Internet together by sharing a Netscape browser during a
multimedia communication session. Archways creates a unique representation of this interaction for each "surfer"; the one in the figure has been
created for Sid. Because the views are from his perspective, he is not shown.
At the moment illustrated, all four people are looking at Cati's home page,
which features her stamp collection. Archways received notifications from
the Rapport meeting room server when the room was created, when the
media servers were associated with the room, and when various people
joined the meeting. As each notification was received, Archways generated
and placed object representations in the room display. The people are
represented by color-coded, texture-mapped images. The round table indicates that the room is hosting a conference. Archways received notifications from the X Window server when the browser was first associated with

the room and continued to receive updates on the browser's use, which enabled it to generate live copies of the program's windows and place these displays in the virtual room representation. Additional visual cues provide information about each meeting participant. For example, Archways generated the cables connecting Doree's keyboard to the two browser windows, indicating that she currently has input control of them. She is also using a telepointer, which is indicated by the cable connecting her to her point of attention—a stamp shown in the shared browser.

Archways, currently under development, is expanding in several ways. Both its knowledge bases and object descriptions are being enlarged to create more detailed visualizations. For example, descriptions of people have been enhanced so that meeting participants can be viewed from any angle. Also, people's representations are becoming animated. Participants sitting around a conference table in a virtual room now move in their seats to acknowledge the entry of a new person into the meeting. Archways descriptions of information flows are also being enhanced. For example, the cables that connect a virtual room to real-world locations can now be examined for detailed descriptions of the data they are transmitting.

CONCLUSIONS

A familiar part of daily experience, rooms have proven to be a useful metaphor for building and using communication programs. They have been especially useful in guiding the construction and description of environments for multimedia communication, where conventional telephony and Internet data exchange provide only partial foundations. Room metaphors suggest how people can join and leave conversations. They also indicate how people can add and drop participants and use more or fewer media during these conversations. Thus, room metaphors are becoming more common in communication systems, as telephone- and Internet-based systems extend to multimedia multiparty interactions.

However, not all room-based systems are created equal. Through our experiences with Rapport, VPE, and Archways, we have discovered that some aspects of the virtual meeting room model are especially important for building flexible, easy-to-use communication systems. Two parts of the model are of paramount importance—information distribution and information storage. The virtual meeting room model specifies that participants inside the room have access to all media-specific services associated with the room. Each media service defines mechanisms by which individual participants control the information they send to, or receive from, the room's shared environment. Because a room is persistent, it can serve as a long-term storage of shared information. Rooms may also be accessed by people who are moving about, perhaps from one device to another.

Long-term collaborations, in which groups of people conduct series of related meetings, are especially well supported by persistent rooms.

REFERENCES

Ahuja, S. R., Ensor, J., & Horn, D. (1988, March). The Rapport multimedia conferencing system. *Proceedings, Conference on Office Information Systems* (pp. 1–8). Palo Alto, CA.

Ahuja, S. R., Ensor, J. R., & Lucco, S. E. (1990, April). A comparison of application sharing mechanisms in real-time desktop conferencing systems. *Proceedings, Conference on Office Information Systems* (pp. 238–248). Cambridge, MA.

Ensor, J. R., Ahuja, S. R., Connaghan, R., Horn, D., Pack, M., & Seligmann, D. D. (1991, April). Control issues in multimedia conferencing. *Proceedings, TriComm* (pp. 133–143). Chapel Hill, NC.

Ensor, J. R., Ahuja, S. R., & Seligmann, D. D. (1993, May). User interfaces for multimedia multiparty communications. *Proceedings, IEEE International Conference on Communications ICC '93* (pp. 1165–1171). Geneva.

Foster, G., & Stefik, M. (1986, December). Cognoter, theory and practice of a Colab-orative tool. *Proceedings, Conference on Computer-Supported Cooperative Work* (pp. 7–15). Austin, TX.

Gaglianello, R. D., & Cash, G. L. (1995, June). Montage: Continuous presence teleconferencing utilizing compressed domain video bridging. *Proceedings, ICC '95* (pp. 573–581). Seattle, WA.

Ginsberg, A. B., & Ahuja, S. R. (1995, November). Automating envisionment of virtual meeting room histories. *Proceedings, ACM Multimedia '95* (pp. 65–75). San Francisco, CA.

Henderson, D. A., & Card, S. K. (1986, July). *Rooms: The use of multiple virtual workspaces to reduce contention in a Windows-based graphical user interface* (ISL Tech. Rep.). Palo Alto, CA: Xerox PARC.

Lantz, K. (1986, December). An experiment in integrated multimedia conferencing. *Proceedings, Conference on Computer-Supported Cooperative Work* (pp. 267–275). Austin, TX.

Michaelitz, G. (1990, November). *A new metaphor for multimedia desktop conferencing systems.* Presentation at 1990 International Seminar on Digital Communications, Bordeaux.

Sarin, S., & Greif, I. (1985). Computer-based real-time conferences. *IEEE Computer, 18,* 33–45.

Scheifler, R. W., & Gettys, J. (1986). The X Window system. *ACM Transactions on Graphics, 5*(2), 79–109.

Seligmann, D. D., Mercuri, R. T., & Edmark, J. T. (1995, May). Providing assurances in a multimedia environment. *Proceedings, Human Factors in Computing Systems ACM SIGCHI '95* (pp. 250–256). Denver, CO.

Stefik, M., Bobrow, D., Lanning, S., & Tatar, D. (1986, December). WYSIWIS revisited: Early experiences with multi-user interfaces. *Proceedings, Conference on Computer-Supported Cooperative Work* (pp. 276–290). Austin, TX.

Chapter 21

Iterative Design of Seamless Collaboration Media[1]

Hiroshi Ishii
MIT Media Laboratory

Minoru Kobayashi
Kazuho Arita
Takashi Yagi
Nippon Telegraph and Telephone Corporation

This chapter illustrates the concrete design examples of video-mediated communication systems: TeamWorkStation and ClearBoard. These systems were designed to support focused real-time collaboration by distributed group members. While most of the current video telephony has been designed to see "talking heads," our goal is to go beyond this model and demonstrate new usage of video-mediated communication technologies.

INTRODUCTION

Groupware is a label for computer-based systems explicitly designed to support groups of people working together. It is growing rapidly as a new application category in the computer industry (Baeker, 1993; Coleman, 1993; Ellis, Gibbs, & Rein, 1991; Galegher, Kraut, & Egido, 1990; Greenberg, 1991; Greif, 1988).

Most of the current groupware such as workflow systems and collaborative authoring tools are devoted to computational support and are designed under the constraint of limited communication bandwidth. However, the deployment of broadband digital networks opens a new future for multimedia collaboration environments that integrate realtime audio and video communication links with computer-based shared workspaces (Brittan, 1992; Lyles, 1993).

We have been exploring the future of collaboration media that make good use of real-time video through the iterative design of various group-

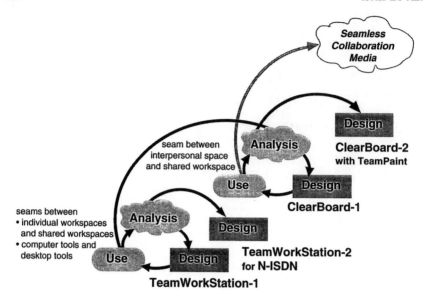

FIG. 21.1.   Progression of our collaboration media design.

ware systems.[2] Progression of our collaboration media design is illustrated in Fig. 21.1.

Our research started in 1988 and was motivated by the study on shared drawing space (Tang & Minneman, 1991) in the media space[3] environment (Bly, Harrison, & Irwin, 1993). Whereas most of the current videotelephony was designed to see "talking heads," our goal is to go beyond this model and demonstrate new usage of video-mediated communication technologies. Video is a powerful medium not for only seeing talking heads but also for creating shared workspaces and shared visual context for remote collaboration.

This chapter introduces the progression of iterative media design from TeamWorkStation to ClearBoard. These systems were designed to support focused realtime collaboration by distributed group members. The key concept behind our iterative design is *seamlessness*. Seamless design pursues the following two goals:

1. Seamlessness (continuity) with existing work practices:
People develop their own work practices after using a wide variety of tools and interacting with a large number of people. We believe the continuity with existing work practices and everyday skills is essential. Groupware that asks users to abandon their acquired skills and to learn a new protocol is likely to encounter strong resistance (Grudin, 1988).

2. Seamlessness (smooth transition) between functional spaces:
Collaboration requires us to shift among a variety of functional spaces or modes. Seamless design undertakes to decrease the cognitive load of users

as they move dynamically across different spaces. For example, TeamWork-Station was designed to enable smooth transition between individual workspaces and shared workspaces by allowing users to keep using both familiar desktop tools and computer tools. ClearBoard realizes seamless integration of interpersonal space and shared workspace allowing people to use various nonverbal cues such as a partner's gaze direction for smooth focus switching between these two spaces.

TEAMWORKSTATION-1 AND SEAMLESS SHARED WORKSPACES

People do a lot of their work without computers, or using different tools on different computer systems, and develop their own work practices for these situations. Even in a heavily computerized individual workplace, users often work both with computers and on the physical desktop. Neither one can replace the other. For example, printed materials such as books and magazines are still an indispensable source of information. Therefore, when designing real-time shared workspaces, depending on the task and the media of the information to be shared (paper or computer file), coworkers should be able to choose either computers or desktops and to switch between them freely. One person's choice should be independent of the other members' choices. Group members should be able to use a variety of heterogeneous tools (computer-based and manual tools) in the shared workspace simultaneously. To realize such a seamless shared workspace, we designed TeamWorkStation-1 (TWS-1; Ishii, 1990; Ishii & Miyake, 1991). The key design idea of TWS-1 is a "translucent overlay" of individual workspace images. TWS-1 combines two or more translucent live-video images of computer screens or physical desktop surfaces using a video synthesis technique. Translucent overlay allows users to combine individual workspaces and to point to and draw on the overlaid images simultaneously. We chose video as the basic medium of TWS because it is the most powerful for fusing presentations of a variety of traditionally incompatible visual media such as papers and computer documents.

System Architecture of TWS-1

Figure 21.2 shows an overview of the first prototype, TWS-1. Two charge-coupled device (CCD) video cameras are provided at each workstation: one for capturing live face images of the group member and the other for capturing the desktop surface images and hand gestures. TWS-1 provides two screens. The individual screen (private workspace) is on the left and the shared screen is on the right. These two screens are contiguous

CCD camera to capture face image

CCD camera to capture desktop image

individual screen

shared screen

FIG. 21.2. Overview of TeamWorkStation-1 prototype.

in video memory, and this multiscreen architecture allows users to move any application program window between the individual and shared screens by merely mouse dragging. Therefore, it is easy to bring one's own data and tools from each personal computer into the shared workspace to use in remote collaboration. Hardcopy information can also be shared easily by placing it under the CCD camera (i.e., on the physical desktop). Fig. 21.3 shows an image of a shared screen where two users are discussing the system configuration by annotating and pointing to electronic diagrams in a drawing editor by hand.

The first prototype TWS-1 was implemented on Macintosh computers to provide small work groups (2–4 members) with a shared workspace. The system architecture of TWS-1 is illustrated in Fig. 21.4 (Ishii & Miyake, 1991). The video network is controlled by a video server that is based on a computer-controllable video switcher and video effecter. The video server gathers, processes and distributes the shared computer screen images, desktop images, and face images. Overlay of video images is done by the video server. The results of overlaying are redistributed to the shared screens via the video network.

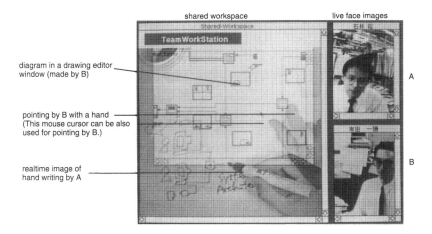

FIG. 21.3. A shared screen of TeamWorkStation-1.

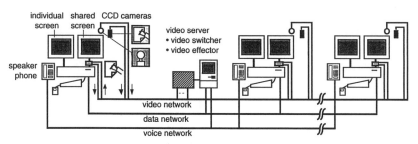

FIG. 21.4. System architecture of TeamWorkStation-1 prototype.

Experience of TWS-1

Through experimental use of TWS-1, we found that users liked the feature which allowed them to keep using their favorite individual tools, especially papers and pen, while collaborating in a desktop shared workspace. That is, there was no need to master the new sophisticated groupware. The drawback of this overlay approach is that the results of collaboration cannot be shared directly. Because individual workspaces are overlaid as video images, the marks and the marked documents occupy different "layers" in the shared screens. They are actually stored separately in different places in different media (in computer files or on paper). We mainly used a video printer or video tape recorder to record the results and the collaboration process.

Shared workspace is taken by many computer scientists to mean *data sharing*. However, we think it is not required that all the outcomes of the work-in-progress to be directly "manipulable" by all the participants. We seldom felt the necessity to edit the others' diagrams directly. If a diagram was to be changed, usually the originator would change it according to the comments made by the other. One reason appears to stem from the respect paid to the ownership of the outcomes. This seems to be a very natural feeling, even in a close collaborative session. The overlay solution provides us with a comfortable work environment, because the overlaid layers keep the person's own layer of work intact.

Because TWS-1 was designed for laboratory experiments to verify the concept of seamless shared workspaces, we did not pay much attention to the number of cables or the communication bandwidth. As a result, the system configuration became complex and difficult to maintain. This complexity prevented us from conducting the field tests using publicly available digital networks, and motivated us to start designing a completely new system, TeamWorkStation-2 (TWS-2).

TeamWorkStation-2 for N-ISDN

TeamWorkStation-2 (TWS-2) was designed to provide a shared workspace over narrowband ISDN[4] (N-ISDN) Basic Rate Interface (2B+D) and the Primary Rate Interface (H1/D) using the CCITT H.261 standard of moving picture transmission (Ishii, Arita, & Yagi, 1993). We chose N-ISDN, especially Basic Rate Interface, as the target network because of its widespread availability in Japan.

We devised a new multiuser interface called ClearFace for TWS-2. ClearFace superimposes translucent, movable, and resizable face windows over a workspace image to enable more effective use of the normally limited screen space. We found users had little difficulty in selectively viewing either the facial image or the workspace image.

System Architecture of TWS-2

We radically simplified the system architecture. Fig. 21.5 shows the system architecture of TWS-2. We targeted dyadic communication to make the centralized video server unnecessary and to eliminate complexities that would arise from multipoint connection. The two TWS-2 terminals are connected by one ISDN link. Each terminal is composed of three major components: a TWS-2 Box, a video CODEC, and a PC-9801™ personal computer. All video processing functions (e.g., translucent overlay, picture-in-picture) are supported at each terminal. All the hardware for video processing, camera control units, audio amplifiers, and power units were encapsulated into a single TWS-2 Box.

The PC-9801™ computer is mainly used to control the video processing hardware in the TWS-2 Box and the video CODEC. If direct sharing of information stored in the computer is required, we can use screen sharing

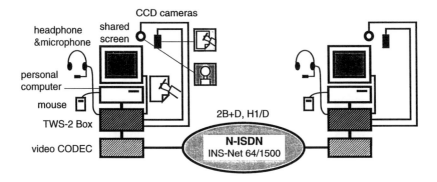

FIG. 21.5. System architecture of TeamWorkStation-2 prototype.

software while overlaying desktop video images with the shared computer screen.

Figure 21.6 shows the appearance of a TWS-2 terminal in use. A headphone with a small microphone is provided for voice communication. Like TWS-1, TWS-2 provides two CCD cameras, one to capture the user's face image and another to capture the physical desktop image. The TWS-2 Box also provides an external video input port that can be used to show recorded video clips by connecting a video player.

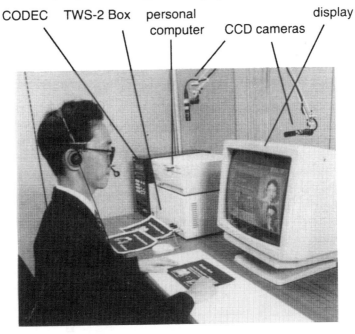

FIG. 21.6. Appearance of TWS-2 terminal.

TWS-2 provides only one screen instead of the two screens (individual and shared screens) of TWS-1. The experimental use of the previous system, TWS-1, led us to observe that most work was done in the desktop-overlay mode in which only the video images of physical desktop surfaces are overlaid. We decided to make desktop overlay the basic service of TWS-2, and to make computer screen overlay an option. This decision led to the one screen architecture of TWS-2.

Figures 21.7 and 21.8 show typical screen images of TWS-2 in use. In Fig. 21.7, users A and B are discussing the system architecture using hand drawing and gestures. In Fig. 21.8, teacher A is teaching calligraphy to student B using red ink to correct B's strokes made in black. This calligraphy example demonstrates the important TWS feature that all of the collaborators share not only the results of drawing, but also the dynamic process of drawing and gesturing.

Experimental Use of TWS-2

We have tested TWS-2 since 1992 by connecting our offices in Tokyo, Yokosuka, and Osaka by INS-Net 64.[5] We conducted several controlled laboratory experiments as well as the tests of real work outside of laboratories (Ishii, Arita, et al., 1993). Before we started the TWS-2 experiments, many people felt dubious about the ability of INS-Net 64 to support real-time activities because of their previous experience with the jerky displays of videophones. However, the subjects generally commented that they could interact smoothly with their partner and that they were absorbed in the task. Although the subjects noticed some delay and jerkiness in the remote desk- top video image, these did not hinder subjects from concen-

FIG. 21.7. Design session via TWS-2.

teacher A

A's hand   B's hand   student B

FIG. 21.8.   Calligraphy lesson via TWS-2.

trating on their work. However, all the subjects noted that they could not clearly see their partner's desktop image. This confirmed that the CIF (Common Intermediate Format; 352 pixels/line × 288 lines/picture) standard is definitely insufficient to see small characters or fine drawings in the remote documents.[6]

Beyond Videophone

Videophones and videoconferencing are the most typical video applications that use N-ISDN, and they represent the effort at imitating "being there" which has long been the goal of telecommunication technologies (Hollan, & Stornetta, 1992). Real-time video is used only to see the remote partners' facial expressions, postures and gestures in these applications.

In contrast to these "talking head" applications, TWS-2 demonstrates a new direction for the usage of real-time video: the creation of a virtual shared workspace. The main focus of TWS-2 is not the imitation of face-to-face communication but rather is the sharing of overlaid desktop images for collaboration.

The experiments to date confirm that TWS-2 has one large advantage over ordinary videophones as the pre-eminent N-ISDN service. The advantage is due to the bandwidth limitation and human perception. People are especially perceptive of changes in facial expressions. If facial expression is the main means of communication, even slight asynchrony between the voice and the movement of eyes and lips is immediately noticed, making smooth conversation difficult. Because facial expression is always changing and the face and body are always moving, delay in transmitting the partner's image increases perceived discontinuities and hence increases the negative impression of users.

The main difference between the desktop and face images is that the desktop images are relatively static. Images of papers and the marks drawn on the papers do not change quickly. Only the hands move on the desktop when users gesture or draw. Thus the total amount of motion is far less than that experienced with videophone displays. This more static nature of the desktop surface increases the effective video frame rate. Although quick hand motions looks jerky, TWS-2 users can be more productive than their videophone counterparts because they can visually share objects and work on them.

SEAMLESS INTEGRATION OF INTERPERSONAL SPACE AND SHARED WORKSPACE

One major focus of groupware development has been the creation of virtual "shared workspaces" in distributed computer environments. Shared workspace activities include sharing information, pointing to specific items, marking, annotating, and editing. These activities can be supported by computer-based groupware, including shared screen systems, shared window systems, and multiuser editors (Ellis et al., 1991).

In face-to-face meetings, we speak, make eye contact, and observe each other's facial expressions and gestures. These verbal and nonverbal channels are important in building confidence and establishing trust (Buxton, 1992). The focus of telecommunication technologies such as the videophone and videoconferencing has been the creation of "interpersonal spaces" that maintain a sense of "telepresence" or "being there" (Hollan & Stornetta, 1992) through the visibility of gestures and facial expressions of distributed group members.

Both shared workspace and interpersonal space are essential for remote, real-time collaboration. Many desktop multimedia conferencing systems, such as TeamWorkStation, Personal Multimedia-Multipoint Teleconference System (PMTC; Tanigawa, Arikawa, Masaki, & Shimamura, 1991), and MERMAID (Watabe, Sakata, Maeno, Fukuoka, & Ohmori, 1990) support both spaces, but they have a major limitation: an arbitrary seam exists between the shared workspace and the face images. We realized that this problem is not just the superficial physical discontinuity of spatially separated windows. Absent are the nonverbal cues that would enable a smooth shift in attention between the shared workspace and the partner's face image. Current groupware and videoconferencing technologies do not support these cues.

Lack of eye contact is another problem of TWS (see Figs. 21.3 & 21.8; Fig. 21.9). Camera positioning prevents one person from knowing the

Interpersonal Space   **Shared Workspace**

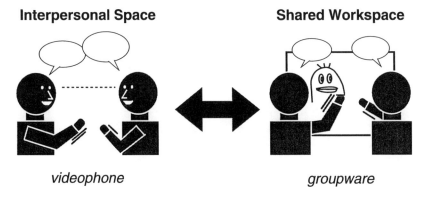

videophone   *groupware*

FIG. 21.9. Seamless integration of interpersonal space and shared workspace.

direction of the other's gaze; it could be directed toward the face image, toward objects in the shared workspace window, or elsewhere. A shift in focus is not apparent until accompanied by a visible gesture or an audible remark. Awareness of gaze direction and mutual eye contact are impossible.

ClearBoard is designed to overcome these limitations by seamlessly integrating interpersonal space and shared workspace (Fig. 21.9). A design goal of ClearBoard is to allow a pair of users to shift easily between interpersonal space and shared workspace using familiar everyday cues such as the partner's gestures, head movements, eye contact, and gaze direction.

ClearBoard Metaphor

The key metaphor of ClearBoard design is "talking through and drawing on a big transparent glass board." Fig. 21.10 shows "ClearBoard-0," which is the simple mockup of this ClearBoard concept for colocated pairs of users. ClearBoard-0 consists of a glass board positioned between the partners on which they draw or post objects. ClearBoard requires less eye and head movement to switch focus between the drawing surface and the partner's face than is needed in either the whiteboard or the desktop environment. However, a real glass board has the problem that written text appears reversed to one's partner; we were able to solve this problem by mirror-reversing video images in ClearBoard-1 and 2, as described in the following sections.

DESIGN OF CLEARBOARD-1

Figure 21.11 shows ClearBoard-1; our first prototype to support remote collaboration (Ishii & Kobayashi, 1992). Two users are discussing a route by drawing a map directly on the screen surface. Both users can share a

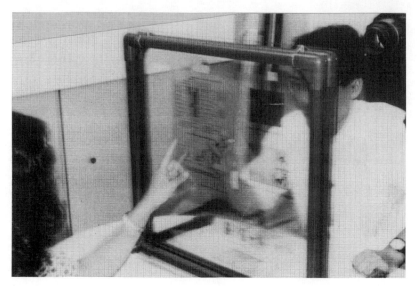

FIG. 21.10. A simple mockup of ClearBoard metaphor: ClearBoard-0.

common map orientation. The partner can read all the text and graphics in their correct orientation.

In order to implement the remote version of ClearBoard, we devised the system architecture called "drafter-mirror" architecture illustrated in Fig. 21.12. Each terminal is equipped with a tilted screen, a video projector, and a video camera. Users can write and draw directly on the surface of the screen using color paint markers. The video camera located above the screen captures the drawings and the user's image as reflected by the half-mirror as a continuous video image. This image is sent to the other terminal through a video network and projected onto the partner's screen from the rear so that both users can share a common orientation of the drawing space. The partner can draw directly over this transmitted video image.[7]

Experimental Use of ClearBoard-1

Since 1990, this prototype has been used in experimental sessions. We observed effortless focus switching between the task and the partner's face. Users could read their partner's facial expression, achieve eye contact, and utilize their awareness of the direction of their partner's gaze. Easy eye contact even during drawing-intensive activities increased the feeling of intimacy and co-presence. No subjects reported difficulty with the mirror-reversal of the partner. This may be because human faces are quite symmetric or because we are accustomed to seeing our own images reversed in mirrors. We found ClearBoard provides the capability we call *gaze aware-*

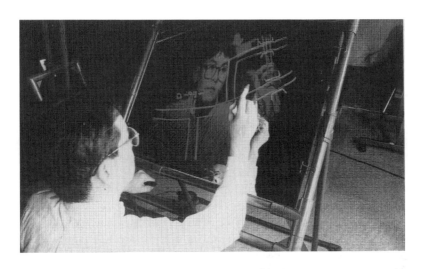

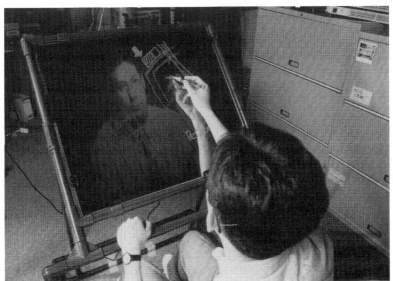

FIG. 21.11. ClearBoard-1 in use.

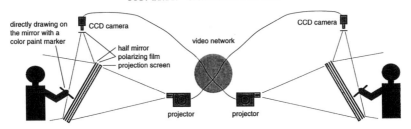

FIG. 21.12. System architecture of ClearBoard-1 prototype.

ness—the ability to monitor the direction of a partner's gaze and thus his or her focus of attention. A ClearBoard user can tell which screen objects the partner is gazing at during a conversation more easily and precisely than is possible in an ordinary meeting environment with a whiteboard.

To understand the implication of gaze awareness, we conducted a collaborative problem solving experiment on ClearBoard using the "river crossing problem" (Ishii, Kobayaghi, & Grudin, 1992/1993). This experiment confirmed that it is easy for the instructor to say which side of the river the student was gazing at. This information was quite useful in understanding the student's thinking process and in providing advice. The importance of eye contact in the design of face-to-face communication tools is often discussed. However, we believe the concept of gaze awareness is more generalized and is a more important notion. Eye contact can be seen as a special case of gaze awareness.

An interesting and less critical confusion manifested itself when users directly drew over their partner's image, playfully adding eye glasses or a mustache, for example. Clearly they had a "WYSIWIS" (what you see is what I see) expectation, not realizing that, although the drawing is shared, the facial images are not, with each person seeing only the other's image. Thus, the metaphor of the ClearBoard is not always entirely assimilated.

DESIGN OF CLEARBOARD-2

In using this ClearBoard-1 prototype, we found several problems. The projected video image of a drawing is not sufficiently clear. Lack of recording capabilities is an obstacle to re-using the work results. To overcome these problems in ClearBoard-1, we decided to design a new computer-based prototype, ClearBoard-2 (Ishii, Kobayashi, et al., 1992/1993). Instead of using color paint markers, ClearBoard-2 provides users with "Team-Paint," a multiuser computer-based paint editor and digitizer pen.

TeamPaint

TeamPaint is a groupware application for shared drawing. It runs on networked Macintosh™ computers, and it is based on a replicated architecture. TeamPaint offers several functions: recording of working results, easy manipulation of marks, and the use of data held in computer files. TeamPaint provides an intuitive interface based on the metaphor of drawing on a sketch pad with a color pencil as shown in Fig. 21.13.

Each user is provided with individual layers and can only modify his or her own layers by default. All members see the composite image of all the layers. Because each layer is isolated from the others, no access control is

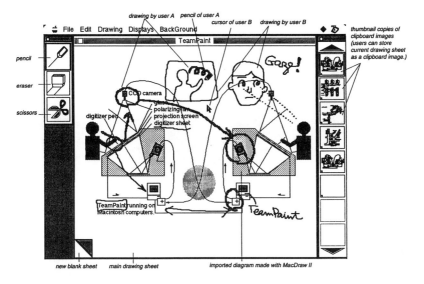

FIG. 21.13. A screen of TeamPaint.

necessary. TeamPaint has no floor control mechanisms but enables simultaneous gesturing and drawing by multiple users. Gestures, in the form of cursor movements, and through them the drawing process, are visually shared by all members.

ClearBoard-2 System and Its Use

Using TeamPaint, transparent digitizer sheets, and electronic pens, we implemented the computer-based prototype, ClearBoard-2. Figure 21.14 shows the ClearBoard-2 prototype in use, and Fig. 21.15 shows the system architecture of the prototype. The composite drawing image of TeamPaint is made to overlay the face images with a special video overlay board. The mixed RGB video image is projected onto the screen's rear surface. TeamPaint makes it easy to get a new blank sheet and the drawing marks are easier to see. The lower screen angle decreases arm fatigue but gives the impression that the partner is under the screen rather than behind it as in ClearBoard-1.

The use of RGB video and the chroma-keying overlay technique does increase image clarity. Furthermore, the capability of recording results and re-using the data produced in previous sessions or from any other application program promises to add tremendous value to an already practical tool. Through the use of ClearBoard-2, it was often observed that the user's gaze follows the partner's pen movements. We confirmed that "gaze awareness" is as well supported in ClearBoard-2 as it was in ClearBoard-1. One can easily tell which object on the TeamPaint screen the partner is looking at.

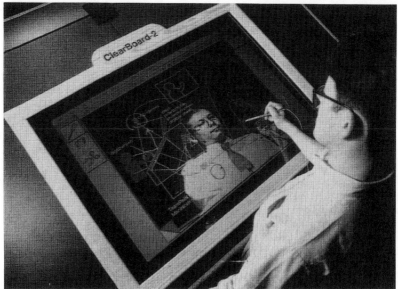

FIG. 21.14. ClearBoard-2 in use.

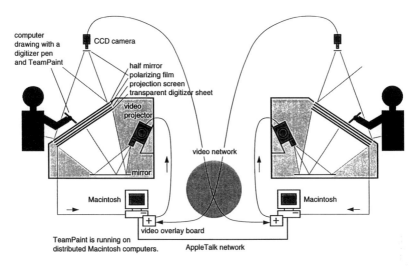

FIG. 21.15. System architecture of ClearBoard-2 prototype.

We see the evolution from ClearBoard-1 to ClearBoard-2 as being very important. Computer and video communication technologies have, until now, evolved independently. Although they have been loosely coupled using arbitrary multiwindow interfaces in many desktop multimedia conferencing systems, they have never been integrated seamlessly from the users' cognitive point of view. ClearBoard-2 succeeds in naturally integrating the user interfaces of computer-based groupware with that of video-conferencing. We expect that the seamless integration of computer and video communication technologies will be an integral part of the next generation of collaboration media.

Moreover, ClearBoard-2 can be seen as an instance of the paradigm shift from traditional HCI (human–computer interaction) to HHI (human–human interaction) mediated by computers. We are interacting not *with* computers, but *through* computers.

We believe the ClearBoard design is not only beyond the traditional desktop metaphor based on a multiwindow interface but also suggests a direction of "beyond being there" (Hollan & Stornetta, 1992). We expect ClearBoard to be useful both as a collaboration medium and as a vehicle to investigate the nature of dynamic human interaction.

SUMMARY AND FUTURE WORK

We have presented an evolution of our collaboration media design. Team-WorkStation (TWS) demonstrates a new usage of real-time video for collaboration, by providing distributed users with a seamless shared workspace.

Using a translucent video overlay technique, real-time information such as hand gestures and handwritten comments can be shared, as can information contained in printed materials and computer files. Users can continue to use their favorite application programs or desktop tools, so there is only a minor cognitive seam between individual workspaces and shared workspaces. TWS-2, a redesigned version which uses N-ISDN Basic Rate Interface, demonstrated the advantage of this application over ordinary videophones given the same bandwidth limitation.

In order to integrate the shared workspace and the interpersonal space seamlessly, we designed ClearBoard. ClearBoard-1 permits coworkers in two different locations to draw with color markers while maintaining direct eye contact and the use of natural gestures. Through experiments, we discovered that ClearBoard also supported the important feature of gaze awareness. In order to offer new functions, such as recording of working results, easy manipulation of marks, and the use of data held in computer files, we designed a computer-drawing version, ClearBoard-2. ClearBoard-2 supports shared drawing with TeamPaint and electronic pens.

Through the iterative design of these collaboration media, we believe it is most important to respect the skills that people use in everyday life (Buxton, 1990). Our design focuses on basic skills such as drawing, gesturing, talking, gaze reading, and using computers. We believe skill-based design will lead to cognitive seamlessness.

We are now very much interested in how the next generation of collaboration media may augment the process of collaborative creation by people such as artists, musicians, designers, and children. NTT's vision video, "Seamless Media Design" (NTT, 1993) illustrates our expectation of future collaboration media based on the ClearBoard concept.

Broadband Digital Network

Although, all these prototype systems except for TWS-2 were implemented using hybrid (analog video + digital data) networks, it is obvious that the hybrid networks have serious limitations in extending their scale.

We expect that the new international telecommunication standard broadband integrated services digital network (B-ISDN) and asynchronous transfer mode (ATM; Lyles, 1993) will provide a universal and scalable infrastructure for various collaborative applications including TeamWorkStation and ClearBoard. ATM is expected to be a common technology for both local area networks (LAN) and wide area networks (WAN). ATM also provides bandwidth-on-demand to meet the requirements of many applications.

Although N-ISDN provides users with fixed communication bandwidth, we expect that ATM technology will provide users with the flexibility to dynamically change the appropriate bandwidth and the balance between the frame rate and resolution of motion pictures on demand (based on the contents and the usage of video). For example, a TWS session using a detailed blue print for a new building may require more bandwidth for higher resolution of shared documents compared to a TWS meeting with shared sheets of blank paper for free hand drawing. Competitive negotiation tasks may require both higher frame rate and resolution to read one's colleagues' subtle facial expression rather than documents. ClearBoard requires much more communication bandwidth (higher resolution, higher frame rate, and less delay) than TWS because ClearBoard presents a life-size partner's image, and users want to read subtle and quick changes of a partner's gaze.

Because required bandwidth changes dynamically both within a single application depending on the contents and usage of video, and among various applications, rapid reassignment of bandwidth on demand will be a critical feature to support seamless transitions among various collaboration modes.

From Multimedia to Seamless Media

Multimedia is now becoming a big buzzword in the computer and communication industries. As a result, the number of cables behind a computer, the number of features users need to understand, and the number of incompatible data formats are increasing beyond the limits of human cognitive capability. A variety of media (such as text, video, audio, graphics) and services (on demand video, video conferencing, electronic newspaper) are becoming available through a single powerful computer on the desktop and a broadband communication network called the *information superhighway*. However, each medium and service are still separated from each other and they are not seamlessly integrated from a user's cognitive point of view.

The communication channels of human beings are inherently multimodal and seamless. It does not make much sense to decompose the representation of information into primitive data types such as text, video, audio, and graphics, and stress the "multi-ness" of the media. For example, we are speaking, gesturing, and drawing simultaneously in a design meeting. We have great skills to express ideas and understand each other in everyday contexts using all these media as a whole. We believe the multi-ness of media is not the main issue, but how to integrate them into a seamless media hiding the various low level representations, discontinuities among primitive media, and complexity of underlying technologies is the core issue in designing new applications. *Multimedia* sounds like a premature label that represents a stage of media evolution from the monomedia to the seamless media.

Toward Ubiquitous Media and Augmented Reality

We hope that ClearBoard will change our concept of a wall from being a passive partition to being a dynamic collaboration medium that integrates distributed real and virtual spaces. We are now exploring a vision of new architectural spaces where all the surfaces including walls, ceilings, windows, doors and desktops become active surfaces through which people can interact with other spaces, both real and virtual. In these spaces, both computers and video must be inherently ubiquitous media (Weiser, 1991). Many challenges exist to achieve a seamless extension of spaces and their interconnections. Nevertheless, our design will be based on the natural skills and social protocols people are using in everyday life to manipulate and interact with information, artifacts and each other.

ACKNOWLEDGMENTS

We would like to thank Masaaki Ohkubo at NTT for the contribution to building the TWS-1 prototype. We appreciate the contribution of Professor Naomi Miyake at Chukyo University and Professor Jonathan Grudin at University of California, Irvine, to the observational and experimental phase of this research. We thank George Fitzmaurice and Beverly Harrison at the University of Toronto for their careful comments on our early version of this chapter. Finally, the stimulating discussions with Professor William Buxton at the University of Toronto on the principles of skill-based design and the ubiquitous media were greatly appreciated.

NOTES

1. This chapter is based on the article "Interactive Design of Seamless Collaboration Media," originally published in *Communications of the ACM* [Special Issue on Internet Technology], *37*(8), 83–97. Copyright 1997, Association for Computing Machinery, Inc., reprinted by permission.
2. A videotape that introduces the entire history of this collaboration media design is available in the ACM SIGGRAPH video review, Issue 87 (Ishii, Arita, & Kobayashi, 1992).
3. *Media space*, originated by Xerox PARC (Bly, et al., 1993), is the environment that integrates video, audio, and computer technologies, allowing individual and groups to work together despite being distributed geographically and temporally. Recent developments include Cruiser (Bellcore; Fish, Kraut, Root, & Rice, 1993), RAVE (Rank Xerox EuroPARC; Gaver, 1992), and CAVECAT/Telepresence (University of Toronto; Mantei, et al., 1991).
4. In April 1988, NTT started an ISDN Basic Rate Interface service (called INS-Net 64) in Japan using the existing metallic cables providing two 64kbps B channels and one 16kbps D channel. In June 1989, ISDN Primary Rate Interface service (called INS-Net 1500) was started using optical fiber cables. INS-Net 1500 provides 1.5 Mbps channel at the maximum. Since the introduction of these ISDN services, the number of subscriber lines has grown steadily, and there were more than 200,000 INS-Net 64 subscriber lines in Japan at the beginning of 1994.

5. The latest version of TWS-2 is available via Ethernet as well as N-ISDN.
6. If both members need to see fine details, we expect facsimile to be the technological partner that offsets the weakness of TWS-2 in sharing detailed documents.
7. This shared video drawing technique, which allows remote partners to draw directly over the video image of their coworkers' drawing surface, was originally demonstrated in Video-Draw (Tang & Minneman, 1991).

REFERENCES

Baecker, R. (Ed.). (1993). *Readings in Groupware and Computer-Supported Cooperative Work*. San Mateo, CA: Morgan Kaufmann.

Bly, S. A., Harrison, S. R., & Irwin, S. (1993). Media spaces: Video, audio, and computing. *Communications of the ACM, 36*(1), 28–47.

Brittan, D. (1992). Being there: The promise of multimedia communications. *MIT Technology Review, May/June*, 42–50.

Buxton, W. (1990). Smoke and mirrors. *Byte*, July, 205–210.

Buxton, W. (1992). Telepresence: Integrating shared task and person spaces. *Proceedings of Graphics Interface '92* (pp. 123–129). San Mateo, CA: Morgan Kaufmann.

Coleman, D. (Ed.). (1993). *Proceedings of Groupware '93*. San Mateo, CA: Morgan Kaufmann.

Ellis, C. A., Gibbs, S. J., & Rein, G. L. (1991). Groupware: Some issues and experiences. *Communications of the ACM, 34*(1), 38–58.

Fish, R. S., Kraut, R. E., Root, R. W., & Rice, R. E. (1993). Video as a technology for informal communication. *Communications of the ACM, 36*(1), 48–61.

Galegher, J., Kraut, R., & Egido, C. (1990). *Intellectual teamwork: Social and technological foundations of cooperative work*. Hillsdale, NJ: Lawrence Erlbaum Associates.

Gaver, W. (1992). The affordance of media spaces for collaboration. *Proceedings of CSCW '92* (pp. 17–24). New York: ACM.

Greenberg, S. (Ed.). (1991). *Computer-Supported Cooperative Work and Groupware*. London: Academic Press.

Greif, I. (Ed.). (1988). *Computer-Supported Cooperative Work: A Book of Readings*. San Mateo, CA: Morgan Kaufmann.

Grudin, J. (1988). Why CSCW Applications fail: Problems in the design and evaluation of organizational interfaces. *Proceedings of CSCW '88* (pp. 85–93). New York: ACM.

Hollan, J., & Stornetta, S. (1992). *Beyond being there. Proceedings of CHI '92* (pp. 119–125). New York: ACM.

Ishii, H. (1990). TeamWorkStation: Towards a seamless shared workspace. *Proceedings of CSCW '90* (pp. 13–26). New York: ACM.

Ishii, H., & Miyake, N. (1991). Toward an open shared workspace: Computer and video fusion approach of TeamWorkStation, *Communications of the ACM, December*, 37–50.

Ishii, H., & Kobayashi, M. (1992). ClearBoard: A seamless medium for shared drawing and conversation with eye-contact. *Proceedings of CHI '92* (pp. 525–532). New York: ACM.

Ishii, H., Arita, K., & Kobayashi, M. (1992). Toward seamless collaboration media: From TeamWorkStation to ClearBoard [video]. *SIGGRAPH Video Review*. CSCW '92 Technical Video Program, *87*(6), New York: ACM.

Ishii, H., Arita, K., & Yagi, T. (1993). Beyond videophones: TeamWorkStation-2 for narrowband ISDN. *Proceedings of ECSCW '93* (pp. 325–340). Dordrecht, Netherlands: Kluwer Academic.

Ishii, H., Kobayashi, M., & Grudin, J. (1993). Integration of interpersonal space and shared workspace: ClearBoard design and experiments. *ACM Transactions on Information Systems (TOIS), 11*(4), 349–375. (Original work published 1992)

Lyles, B. (1993). Media spaces and broadband ISDN, *Communications of the ACM, 36*(1), 46–47.

Mantei, M., Baecker, R., Sellen, A., Buxton, W., Milligan, T., and Wellman, B. (1991). Experiences in the use of a media space. *Proceedings of CHI '91* (pp. 203–208). New York: ACM.

NTT. (1993). *Seamless media design* [video]. *SIGGRAPH Video Review,* CSCW '94 Technical Video Program, Issue 106, Item 10, ACM, New York, 1994.

Tang, J. C., & Minneman, S. L. (1991). VideoDraw: A Video Interface for Collaborative Drawing. *ACM Transactions on Information Systems (TOIS), 9*(2), 170–184.

Tanigawa, H., Arikawa, T., Masaki, S., & Shimamura, K. (1991). Personal multimedia-multipoint teleconference system. *Proceedings of INFOCOM '91* (pp. 1127–1134). New York: IEEE Communications Society.

Watabe, K., Sakata, S., Maeno, K., Fukuoka, H., & Ohmori, T. (1990). Distributed multiparty desktop conferencing system: MERMAID. *Proceedings of CSCW '90* (pp. 27–38). New York: ACM.

Weiser, M. (1991). The computer for the twenty-first century. *Scientific American, September,* 94–104.

THE FUTURE

Informal Communication Reexamined: New Functions for Video in Supporting Opportunistic Encounters

Ellen A. Isaacs*
Sun Microsystems

Steve Whittaker
ATT Labs—Research

David Frohlich
Brid O'Conaill
Hewlett Packard Laboratories

Many systems have focused on using video to support formal distributed meetings among groups of people, but recent research indicates that most workplace interactions occur spontaneously for short periods of time, frequently between two people who discuss topics that build on prior discussions. In this chapter, we characterize these informal interactions, describe their value, enumerate the functions they accomplish, and consider ways we might design video-based systems to support informal interactions among different types of distributed groups. We discuss some existing applications that support various aspects of informal communication and consider ways to build on those ideas to build a system designed specifically for opportunistic and spontaneous encounters.

INTRODUCTION

How and when do office workers interact? Most CSCW research and commercial software for video-based interaction presupposes that people most often interact in formal meetings. According to this view, people have long interactions on preplanned topics, often with multiple people and frequently in a room designed for meetings. However, according to some preliminary but detailed data about the interaction patterns of people in real-life workplace settings, the vast majority of interactions look rather

---

*Currently at Electric Communities.

different. Workplace interactions are short, on the order of seconds rather than minutes or hours (Kraut, Fish, Root & Chalfonte, 1990; Whittaker, Frohlich, & Daly-Jones, 1994). They tend to be opportunistic in that they occur because one person happens to be near another at a time when one wants to ask for or provide information. They are often continuations of prior conversations. They usually involve only two people who discuss a single piece of information, and they often involve a reference to a document.

As this book has shown, when video is used to support planned meetings, its benefits are relatively subtle and subjective. Video helps people manage the mechanics of conversation and understand nuances in meaning, and participants find meetings more satisfying if they can see one another (Isaacs & Tang, 1994; Dykstra-Erickson, Rudman, Hertz, Mithal, Schmidt, & Marshall, 1995; Rudman, Hertz, Marshall, & Dykstra-Erickson, chapter 10, this volume). But the presence of video does not have dramatic, immediately apparent effects on the work at hand, unless that work is inherently visual (Ochsman & Chapanis, 1974; Argyle, Lalljee, & Cook, 1968; Short, Williams, & Christie, 1976). Although we certainly consider it important to enable richer interactions in preplanned meetings, in this chapter we focus on the possibility of using video to support the more common, but less noticed, unplanned interactions, and in particular the initiation of such conversations.

Our notion is that video may be a natural medium to support impromptu interactions because such interactions depend on each person knowing that the possibility of an interaction exists. Visual information is crucial for supporting the "sightings" that are a prelude to impromptu workplace conversations (Kendon & Ferber, 1973; Fish, Kraut, Root, & Rice, 1993; Kraut, Fish, Root, & Chalfonte, 1990). We believe that, in addition to supplementing the verbal channel in interactions once they occur, video could also help make those impromptu interactions possible. Only a few systems have been designed to support the informal interactions that occur among co-located people in the workplace (Root, 1988; Tang & Rua, 1994; Bly, Harrison, & Irwin, 1993; Gaver et al., 1992), and none are designed to enable purely chance encounters (although they sometimes happened in the existing systems). In this chapter, we explore the type of applications that could be designed to support informal and, in particular, spontaneous communication.

Current VMC Systems

Most of the commercial video-based communication applications have focused on prearranged, relatively formal and extended interactions. For example, PictureTel supports meetings between groups of people sitting in meeting rooms at two or more sites. The use of a dedicated conference room means that such meetings are often arranged days or weeks in advance (Mosier & Tammaro, 1995; Tang & Isaacs, 1993; Sellen & Harper, chapter 11, this volume). Desktop videoconferencing products such as ProShare and ShowMe allow for conversations between two or more people who are sitting at their desks, but the design of these systems tends to encourage extended interactions. The long start-up time and complex activities necessary to set up connections make people less inclined to invest the effort for brief, single-topic interactions (Tang & Rua, 1994; Whittaker, Frohlich, & Daly-Jones, 1994a).

Various research labs have built systems to enable quick connections between two or more people. Bellcore's Cruiser (Root, 1988), Toronto's CAVECAT (Mantei, Baecker, Sellen, Buxton, & Mulligan, 1991), SunSoft's Montage (Tang & Rua, 1994), DEC's Argo (Gajewska, Kistler, Manasse, & Redell, 1994), and the Media Spaces at Xerox PARC (Bly et al., 1993) and EuroPARC (Gaver et al., 1992) are examples of systems designed to be used from the computer desktop. However, like their commercial counterparts, all these applications except the Media Spaces and a feature of the Cruiser system (described later) are "connection-based" in the sense that a person explicitly decides to initiate an interaction. We argue that these unplanned but intentional interactions are but one style of impromptu interaction; there are other more opportunistic types of informal interactions that have not been fully explored. We claim that these other classes of interactions are frequent and crucial for accomplishing work. Despite their importance, informal interactions are especially hard to support in distributed groups. We therefore characterize design requirement and discuss technologies to support informal communication across distance.

The systems just mentioned have three features that allow for the possibility of supporting opportunistic interactions. One is *virtual shared offices,* where people keep a connection open between their offices indefinitely. Users of Xerox's Media Spaces were encouraged to do this, and users of Cruiser and Montage also created virtual shared offices on their own. In these cases, people can have extremely quick, spur-of-the-moment interactions because the link is "always open." However, interactions can occur only among those who are already connected. There are no facilities for overriding or interrupting existing links, so others cannot join existing interactions unless they are physically near one of the people sharing a link.

Another example is the Autocruiser feature in Cruiser, which automatically made connections with a random series of people, each of which timed out if no one enabled the connection. This feature was intended to encourage opportunistic communication, but when it was tested, users found it "highly objectionable." The authors explained that "[u]nlike the random encounters that occur multiple time a day when two people are co-located, the Autocruises did not allow people to conduct the subtle nonverbal negotiations that regulate the entree into conversation" (Fish et al., 1993, p. 52). This experience indicates that it is not enough to simply enable opportunistic communication; rather, the system must be designed to help people initiate these interactions naturally.

Finally, Portholes enabled awareness through a matrix of static images of other people's offices, and those images were updated every 5 min (Dourish & Bly, 1992). Upon seeing that someone was available, users within a site could create an audio–video connection. The Argo system also included a "hallway" of slowly updating video images (Gajewska, Manasse, & Redell, 1995).

These findings give us a glimpse of the possible design requirements for a system that enables impromptu communication, but they are just the beginning. In this chapter we explore in more detail the requirements for a such a system. We do this by describing the current data about informal interactions, presenting a new classification of the functions they fulfill, and then speculating about desirable properties of an application designed to support informal communication among distributed people. We hope this exploration will help illuminate the value of video in supporting informal communication and stimulate ideas about how to do so successfully.

A LOOK AT INFORMAL COMMUNICATION

Types of Informal Communication

We begin with a taxonomy of interpersonal communication proposed by Kraut, Fish, Root, and Chalfonte (1990). They proposed four types of interactions:

1. Scheduled: meetings that are planned in advance by both parties.
2. Intended: interactions that occur when one person seeks out another to discuss a specific topic, but where there is no prearranged plan to talk.
3. Opportunistic: interactions that occur when one person happens to see another and remembers wanting to discuss a particular topic with them.
4. Spontaneous: interactions that occur because two people happen to see each other and get into a conversation on a topic not prepared by either person.

As mentioned, the majority of commercial and research focus has been on supporting scheduled interactions. We propose to focus on the latter three, all of which we include in the term *informal*.[1] As we have indicated, a number of systems have been developed to support intended interactions, but few have focused on opportunistic and spontaneous interactions. We are particularly interested in these last two types of interactions (which we call *unintended*), in part because of the absence of systems to support them, and in part because our data suggest that a great many workplace interactions are of this type. Our data remain suggestive, however, because they do not systematically distinguish among the three types of informal interactions. The following is a brief summary of the existing evidence about the nature of informal communication in the workplace.

Characteristics of Informal Communication

The following are two illustrative examples of informal communication in the workplace. They are taken from an observational study in which two mobile professionals were "shadowed" for a week. The first subject, Richard, was a British surveyor (or assessor, in U.S. English) working for a small city-center consultancy. The second subject, Bina, was a public relations manager for a large research laboratory. We used a remote camcorder and radio microphone to record their interactions with colleagues, clients, and others, resulting in a corpus of 402 face-to-face and telephone conversations with 99 interactants, 377 of which were found to be informal. We refer to these data as the HP corpus. The research method and more detailed results are described in Frohlich (1995), O'Conaill and Frohlich (1995), and Whittaker, Frohlich, and Daly-Jones (1994). In the following extracts Richard initiates brief conversations with Frank, a colleague working in the same open-plan office.

Extract 1.[2] A short opportunistic interaction (ROffice47, 0min:8sec).

Richard is standing up reading a document behind his desk when his colleague Frank walks into view on his way to his own desk from another office.

1 R: Frank can you reath read this report for me?
2 F: Now?
3 R: Aye if you've got a minute
4 F: Yeah

This interaction is completed in 8 sec. Richard sees that Frank is moving around the office and hence is not currently engaged in work, so he opportunistically solicits Frank's help. The shared visual environment affords Richard this information about Frank's availability and allows Frank and Richard to look at, and then physically exchange, the document. The interaction is brief and has no formal openings or closings, such as greetings or farewells.

The following interaction shows an unplanned conversation between Richard and Frank that occurred immediately after Frank had finished a phone call to a client. It arose because Richard heard Frank's phone call and opportunistically monitored the outcome. It continues with Richard offering unprompted advice and assistance.

Extract 2. An opportunistic interaction leading to unprompted advice (ROffice 66, 28sec of 1min:36sec).

Frank is on the phone across the office from Richard. Frank puts down phone.

1	R:	Is he all right?
2	F:	Yeah
3	R:	Which one's he's got? there's a restaurant
4	F:	I said that I'll do this one initially and then further afield
5	R:	Which one's that?"
6	F:	That's: eighty two whiteladies road it's the offices
7	R:	Oh, yeah we act for the landlord on that one. I did a rent review against him on that
8	F:	Right ()
9	R:	His shop it might be worth checking out he's got a sub-tenant
10		downstairs who's got a clothes shop
11	F:	Yeah
12	R:	Might be worth trying to get in with them as well
13	F:	Yeah all right

Again the interaction begins without formal initiation. The interaction has a history, revealed by the implicit shared context between the participants. Without being told, Richard knows the identity of Frank's caller (line 1), and details of the case (line 3). The shared context results in a condensed and cryptic conversational style. Toward the end of the fragment Richard offers unprompted advice to Frank (line 12), which eventually results in an agreed action for Frank to report back (not shown). Thus an unplanned conversation led to a detailed task-oriented discussion.

These conversations, which are representative of the HP corpus, along with data from various other sources, suggest a characterization of work in which people are engaged in multiple intermittent and interleaved collaborative tasks. Workers frequently seek out and are sought out by their coworkers for brief interactions. These conversations often have a history of prior interactions, and workers are often concurrently engaged in multiple interaction threads. More specifically, the available data show that, despite some variation due to job type, interpersonal communication has the following properties:

- Frequent. Office workers spend between 25 and 70% of their time in face-to-face conversations with others, depending on job specification (Kraut, Fish, Root, & Chalfonte, 1990; Panko, 1992; Reder & Schwab, 1990; Sproull, 1984; Whittaker, Frohlich, & Daly-Jones, 1994).
- Brief. Conversations generally last only a few minutes, with lower estimates at 1.9 min (Whittaker, Frohlich, & Daly-Jones, 1994), and higher estimates under 15 min (Kraut, Fish, Root, & Chalfonte, 1990; Reder & Schwab, 1990).
- Unscheduled. About 88 to 93% of professionals' interactions are unscheduled (Kraut, Fish, Root, & Chalfonte, 1990; Whittaker, Frohlich, & Daly-Jones, 1994), with lower figures of around 60% for managers (Panko, 1992).
- Often dyadic. For professional workers, 84% of meetings are dyadic (Whittaker, Frohlich, & Daly-Jones, 1994), although this figure is lower for managers. Panko (1992) estimated that dyads account for 40 to 45% of all managers' interactions, whereas MacLeod, Scriven, and Wayne (1992) found that figure to range from 58 to 63%, depending on level of management.
- Frequently supported by shared objects such as paper documents or designs (Luff, Heath, & Greatbatch, 1992; Tang, 1991; Whittaker, Froh-lich, & Daly-Jones, 1994a).
- Intermittent. The purposes of interpersonal interactions are seldom achieved in one interchange, so that such conversations occur over intermittent episodes (Whittaker, Frohlich, & Daly-Jones, 1994), with participants on average interacting with each other 2.5 times per day (Kraut, Fish, Root, & Chalfonte, 1990).
- Lacking formal openings or closings. Whittaker, Frohlich, and Daly-Jones (1994) showed that only 11% of the conversations observed were prefaced by greetings and only 3% included a formal farewell.
- Dependent on physical proximity. Numerous studies have shown that the closer together offices of coworkers are located, the more likely they are to interact (Allen, 1977; Festinger, Schachter, & Back, 1950; Kraut, Egido, & Galegher, 1990; Kraut, Fish, Root, & Chalfonte, 1990).

In other words, based on the available data, upward of 80 to 90% of interpersonal interactions in the workplace are not preplanned meetings. They are therefore are not studied in the literature and not supported by the majority of video-based systems on the market. However, these data examine exclusively office settings (and only a few at that), which of course are not representative of the full range of work settings. But we speculate that workers in nonoffice settings may be even less likely to engage in formal, meeting-based interactions. In any case, given the ubiquity of office work, these numbers provide a compelling argument for further pursuing this aspect of communication.

The Value of Impromptu Communication

Informal communication is vital for achieving certain types of work-related tasks. Research on scientific collaboration has shown that physical distance is the strongest predictor of collaboration between researchers. Physical proximity promotes frequent, impromptu face-to-face communications, which are crucial for the planning and negotiation phases of projects (Finholt, Sproull, & Kiesler, 1990; Kraut, Egido, & Galegher, 1990). Work on software development also has demonstrated that the degree to which projects engage in interpersonal communication strongly predicts project success (Kraut & Streeter, 1995). Furthermore, other work has shown negative impacts on teamwork when opportunities for ad hoc communication are reduced, as in remote collaboration. Work becomes more difficult to coordinate and advance, despite the use of longer and more task-focused meetings in remote settings (Kraut, Egido, & Galegher, 1990). This finding is confirmed in other work on the isolation experienced by teleworkers trying to collaborate over long distances (e.g., Kraut, 1987; Olson, 1987). Sociological studies of organizational life stress the primary role of mundane office conversations in helping workers learn, understand, adapt, and apply formal procedures and processes (Boden, 1994; Suchman & Wynn, 1984).

Data from the organizational communication literature add evidence that interpersonal communication improves group performance and helps keep organizations healthy. Several such studies have looked at strong and weak ties within organizations, where strength is a function of frequency of contact, reciprocal favors or obligations, emotional intensity, and intimacy (Granovetter, 1973). A common finding is that although both high- and low-performing groups maintain both strong and weak ties, high-performing groups tend to have a higher proportion of weak ties than do low-performing groups (Nelson & Mathews, 1991). It is likely that the weak ties examined in these studies are based largely on informal communication, and in particular on opportunistic and spontaneous communication. Nelson and Mathews (1991) explained that weak ties to those outside a work group reduce a group's tendency to become insular and to negatively stereotype other groups. Weak ties also have been found to enhance "information flow and permeability of organization boundaries," and to "foster flexibility and effective decision making" (Nelson & Mathews, 1991, p. 371).

Groups with many weak ties were also more accepting of innovations (Nelson, 1989).

Despite research from a various disciplines showing the value of informal interactions, evidence indicates that people in the workplace do not recognize its value. Kraut and Streeter (1995) found that impromptu communication is underutilized compared with its value, whereas formal communication techniques are overused relative to their value. Our own preliminary evidence supports this result. In a series of interviews with a dozen employees in a Fortune 500 U.S. corporation, we found that although people reported gaining most of their work-related news and information from informal interactions, those same people said they used almost exclusively formal approaches to convey information to other parts of the company (Isaacs, Tang, & Morris, 1996). Most commonly, they reported their information to a high-level management group and asked that they pass the information down the hierarchy in their staff meetings. In many cases, they wrote a document to convey information and either gave it to managers to give to their employees, or made it available to employees directly (in e-mail, mailings to the home, or by publishing it on the company's internal World Wide Web pages). Some also gave formal presentations to supplement the document. When we asked information disseminators if they had considered spreading their information through word of mouth, they either had not thought of it or did not trust it. They were concerned that information passed informally would be distorted and misinterpreted and might not become available to all the intended recipients.

How Does Informal Communication Achieve Its Effects?

Although current research indicates the value of informal communications, much less is known about how they deliver this value. A number of promising suggestions have come from McGrath (1991), who suggested that workgroup communication can contribute to the social as well as the production function of the group. He noted that the social function includes both member support (e.g., making sure people feel their contributions are valued) and group maintenance functions (e.g., keeping people informed of others' activities and ensuring that the groups' contributions are coordinated to achieve a common goal). In the rest of this section we develop these insights further with reference to the informal interactions contained in the HP corpus.

Based on a content analysis of 377 informal face-to-face and telephone interactions in the HP corpus, we developed a simple classification of the functions of informal communication. We identified six functions: tracking people, taking or leaving messages, making meeting arrangements, delivering documents, giving or getting help, and reporting progress and news.

Tracking People

Tracking people involves identifying the current whereabouts, activities, and future plans of intended interactants. Often people track each other by making requests as part of a search for a colleague, as in Extract 3 when Maureen asks Bina about the whereabouts of a mutual colleague.

Extract 3. A tracking request made by Maureen to Bina about Ian (BOffice35, 9sec).

Maureen pops her head over the wall of Bina's cubicle.

1   M: Bina you don't know when Ian's due- oh here's Jane now- know when Ian's back?
2   B: Tomorrow I expect
3   M: Ahh
4   B: Oh yeah he's out today yeah

In other cases, people volunteer information about their future whereabouts by announcing to nearby colleagues a planned departure from their workspace. In one typical example from the corpus, Bina's colleague told her of some forthcoming days off to flag a problem with their joint work plans. The benefit of tracking interactions seems to be that they provide coworkers with a sense of each others' current and future availability for help, advice, and joint work.

Taking and Leaving Messages

Taking and leaving messages refers to contacting someone via a third party. This situation was particularly common on the phone, because "two thirds" of outgoing calls from Bina and Richard failed to reach their intended recipient. There were numerous interactions in which the caller asked the recipient to take a message or accepted an offer to leave a message. When the recipient was a colleague rather than a receptionist, the message often developed into an extensive explanation of the context. A similar pattern can be seen in the roaming encounters of Richard and Bina around their office sites. When they failed to find someone, they often left detailed messages with "covering" colleagues, as when Bina leaves a message for Catherine with Sue (Extract 4).

Extract 4. Bina requests that Sue take a detailed message for Catherine (BRoam12, 1min02sec).

1   B: Sue would you do me a favor (.5sec) when Catherine's free could you

2   ask her about the Pisa Science Centre and (.4sec) say that they're

3   updating this new booklet?

4 S: Mmh hm

5 B: Of the () ninety three and do we really want this under there or not

6 S: Right

7 B: Because I think all contacts will want it through here as opposed

8   to centered there (.9sec)

9 S: Right what (do you call this)

10 B: Its called HP- I'm go- I can leave this with you

11 S: OK

This interaction continued for 11 more turns as Bina and Sue clarified the message. Although these interactions may seem inefficient, they have the positive side effects of informing message takers of their colleagues' activities, affording practice in covering behavior, and providing message leavers with natural opportunities to make new contacts for future enquiries. Thus, these interactions support both social and production functions for the workgroup.

Making Meeting Arrangements

Making meeting arrangements refers to scheduling future interactions. A few interactions in the corpus were devoted entirely to this function, as when Jane invited Bina for lunch (Extract 5).

Extract 5. A meeting invitation or offer made by Jane to Bina (BOffice31, 0min:16sec).

1 J: Had any lunch?

2 B: Yea::h

3 J. Oh you have

4 B: Oh have you already bee- you going now

5 J: No no I was just going to pop into the buffet to just get a couple of leftovers

6 B: No: I I went 'cos I couldn't wait

As with taking and leaving messages, such offers and requests often result in discussions that inform people of the commitments and plans of their coworkers.

Document Delivery

Document delivery refers to handing off a document with actions attached to it. A simple example is shown in Extract 6, where Rose requests a signature on a signed letter.

Extract 6. Rose hands over a letter to Richard for signing (ROffice50, 0min:8sec).

1 Ro: () *Hands over document*
2 Ri: Ah right
3 Ro: Do you need to sign the cross rep () yeah you do
4 Ri: Ah right

More complex examples of document delivery in the corpus involve discussions of individual actions associated with different parts of a document. All such interactions provide opportunities for each party to query, check, and discuss the quality of actions associated with their documentation. The coordination aspect of this activity helps explain why people often carry out apparently simple office tasks interactively, rather than develop or adhere to asynchronous "workflow" procedures that appear at first glance more efficient.

Giving or Getting Help

Giving or getting help refers to joint problem solving for one person's benefit. This type of interaction most commonly consisted of a question–answer exchange. Often these questions were shouted from a distance and resulted in short, simple answers as in Extract 7. They are equivalent to turning aside to look something up in a reference book.

Extract 7. Rose requests help from Richard (RRoam21, 28sec).

1 Ro: Richard have you got any of the amendments?
       On phone behind pillar
2 Ri: () nine three four (1.0sec) seven four three (1.1sec) okay thanks bye.
       Puts phone down.
3   erh yeah erhm hang on I haven't I've got a few there's only these little bits here.
       Walks over to Rose
4 Ro: Well ([)
5 Ri: [I can feed you them page by page if you want

Spontaneous offers of help also arise in the course of work-related conversations such as that shown in Extract 2 where Richard asks Frank about the progress of a phone call and ends up giving advice about what to do next. Another example was when Rose reminded Richard of an approaching deadline for a document delivery by walking up to him on the phone, pointing to her watch and saying, "It's twenty-five past four" (ROffice41). These interactions furnish workers with not only willing, fast, and effective resources for problem solving, but also lightweight forms of supervision that provide natural checks on the timing and quality of their work. The fact that everyone acts as resources and supervisors for each other is yet another mechanism by which everyone becomes informed about and involved with each others' work.

Reporting Progress and News

Reporting progress and news refers to updating people with relevant information. Such reports were often offered spontaneously upon some event or encounter, such as when Bina meets Nigel in the coffee area and begins an account of a meeting (Extract 8).

Extract 8. Bina offers a news report on Adjay to Nigel (BRoam42, 26sec of 1min:42sec).

Noise of coffee machine being switched on.

1 B: I just spoke to Adjay and he suggested splitting out the bit about fault

2   tolerance into two bits Rod's bit and his bit so two sessions I'm () but they

3   want to talk separately so

4 N: Ah OK I hadn't realized he was going to talk about fault tolerance

5 B: Well he he was going to be involved in that and they've decided

6   they'd like to split it and I thought well- yes we'll do that then

7 N: Mmh

Often the initial statement has a dramatic tone and prefaces a longer "story," as in one instance when a colleague begins a conversation with, "Can you believe it, Bina?" Furthermore, the end of the report is usually an occasion for the recipient to provide a reaction or assessment of the news. In this case, Bina told her own story by way of sympathizing with her colleague's complaint.

Direct requests for updates were also common, as in Richard's "Is he all right?" to Frank after Frank's phone call in Extract 2. Note that these exchanges are not always between teammates working on the same projects. Reporting progress and news is a flexible way of maintaining and consolidating contact with ex-teammates and others with whom there has been contact in the past.

We can now see how informal interactions contribute to McGrath's (1991) three functions of groupwork: production, social (group maintenance), and social (member support). Many help-, news-, and document-related interactions contribute to the production function of a group by solving individual or shared problems as they arise, providing relevant pieces of information at just the right time, and controlling the quality of transactions and outputs. In addition, tracking, message, and meeting arrangement interactions are indirectly supportive in that they provide ways of sustaining and planning the other kind of contacts with absent or busy partners.

These last three kinds of interactions, however, are more central to the social functions of the group, that is, group maintenance and member support. They help group maintenance by providing ways for members to learn about each other's activities, and therefore to adapt their contributions to the group's output. Document-, help-, and news-related interactions also help maintain the group by monitoring and controlling individuals' work in ways that bring it into line with group objectives. They also help keep people mutually accountable for their commitments. We can easily imagine that the combined effect of these interactions is to make people feel part of the group.

Finally, through message-, help-, and news-related interactions individuals receive several forms of "member support." Message-taking constitutes practice in covering for others and hence trains people in new roles and responsibilities. Getting help provides emotional as well as task support. Reactions to progress reports are natural occasions on which to praise people for achievement, whereas news updates help maintain long-term relationships with people who may become closer colleagues in future group work.

Types of Groups Engaging in Informal Communication

So far we have assumed that the nature, function, and value of informal communication are the same for all types of workgroups. However, these characteristics may differ depending on the type of group. In this section we present one way of looking at different types of workgroups so that we can draw conclusions for technology support. We do not suggest this is the definitive classification of workgroups; the literature here is vast, encompassing group theory and organizational behavior. Rather, we present one possible workgroup taxonomy as a thought exercise that highlights some of the issues that arise from different groups' needs in supporting informal interactions.

We often think of workgroups in terms of our immediate colleagues. These are the people with whom we perform our primary work function. However, people also have many interactions with colleagues throughout and outside an organization. We suggest that there are three types of workgroups in addition to project groups: cross-functional, peer, and external.

Cross-functional groups are those that cross organizational boundaries, often to perform a short-term activity. For example, a short-term workgroup crossing the finance and production departments may form to clear an expense claim or place a purchase order. *Peer* workgroups are networks between people of the same profession or past colleagues. These groups provide professional guidance and support that may not be available within the project group. Finally we use the term *external* to describe the many relationships that exist with partners outside the organization. Clients, suppliers and contract staff would fall into this category.

All four group types have different needs and constraints that affect their patterns of communication. Based on a preliminary analysis of the HP corpus using these definitions, we consider how communication in these workgroups might differ. These are summarized in Table 22.1.

Project Workgroup. A preliminary analysis of the HP data indicates the majority of communication occurs within project groups. These groups tend to be formed for long durations, and communication can be expected to be varied and frequent (McGrath, 1991). Project groups engage in all the communication functions described previously. Organizations commonly locate members of a project close together, although more groups are being asked to work across distance. Project groups are formally recognized by their organizations, so management is likely to support investments in technology for their work. Additionally, the group is likely to have control over their equipment and they may be able to customize solutions for specific group needs.

Cross-Functional. Cross-functional groups provide support to other groups within an organization. Their communication requirements focus more heavily on document delivery and discussion, giving and getting help, and taking or leaving messages. Because their communication is document-centric, these groups have traditionally been supported by structured work-flow systems designed to pass documents from one part of the organization to another. From this analysis, we see an additional need to facilitate discussion and advice-giving during handovers (see also Harper & Sellen, 1995).

TABLE 22.1
Characteristic Differences by Group Type

Parameter	Project	Cross-Functional	Peer	External
Functions of communication	All	Document delivery, giving and receiving help, taking and leaving messages	Giving and receiving help, reporting progress and news	Tracking people, taking and leaving messages, making meeting arrangements
Duration of group	Long term	Varies	Long term	Varies
Intensity of communication	Daily	Varies	Daily to intermittent	Sporadic
Physical location	Traditionally colocated	On/off site	On/off site	Off site
Recognized by organization?	Yes	Yes	No	Yes
Equipment under control of group?	Yes	May cross departments	May cross departments	No

The long-term duration of such relationships and their recognition by organizations again make them likely candidates for technology support. However, the communication requirements may be sporadic so the technology may appear at times to be underutilized, which may make expensive systems difficult to justify. Cross-functional group members are likely to be spread out, perhaps within a building or even across sites. The ability to track members or leave detailed messages during active periods would be useful. Although the control of equipment is within a single organization there may be departmental differences. Standardization of technology would be desirable.

Peer. Communication within this group is supportive in nature, giving and receiving advice, and reporting news and progress. Our preliminary look at the HP corpus indicates that these conversations are sporadic but last longer, possibly because peers are less likely to be co-located. Peer communications are less task-focused than those of project groups and provide more of the social rewards of communication. When peers are co-located, initiation of such communication often requires low effort, as when Richard remarks loudly on a report, inviting Jerry to enter into a discussion with no formal greeting or opening sequence. Support for such low-effort initiation represents a challenge when parties are distributed. Because peer groups are not formally recognized by organizations, they may be unlikely to receive formal support. However, the field of scientific research may be an exception, because peer collaboration is considered especially valuable (Pickering & King, 1992). Equipment compatibility may be an issue if members are in different organizations.

External. Communication with external parties is usually relatively formal and frequently revolves around formal meetings. External groups are not co-located, so their communications are especially likely to include meeting arrangements, taking and leaving messages, and tracking, in addition to task-focused communication. Activities among external parties can range from simple process tasks to complex negotiations. Communication may also vary from daily conversations to sporadic interchanges. Some of these relationships, such as those with customers, can be among the most important for an organization and are therefore likely to attract investment. However, equipment will span different organizations so standardized solutions will be required.

DESIGN IMPLICATIONS

So far we have characterized the subtlety and complexity of informal interactions among people who are co-located. We also have documented the sheer frequency of informal communications and their crucial contribution to the social and production aspects of team functioning. And we have noted the important role of a shared physical environment on the initiation and maintenance of informal conversations. But fundamental changes are taking place that reduce the frequency of informal communications. Many organizations have been spreading their operations across geographic sites, and they are forming strategic alliances with other organizations in distant locations. In addition, more people are telecommuting from home and connecting into work while traveling on business trips. As a result, many people are expected to collaborate with others who are distributed across many locations, sometimes in different countries and time zones.

Given the importance and frequency of informal communication, how can we support it in these newly distributed groups? In particular, what role will video play in that efort? Providing technological support for informal interactions is a challenge because, unlike meetings, which happen at predetermined times among predictable groups of people in predefined locations, informal interactions have few defined variables. They occur with little notice for short periods of time, often between participants whose identities cannot be predicted in advance. The topics are unplanned, but they often build on previous conversations, so any document or supporting material may become relevant. We attempt to take on the challenge of providing support for informal interactions by dividing the problem into two issues. We first consider how we might help people enter informal interactions and then discuss features that might help support those interactions once they begin.

Entering Interactions

We have been making the distinction between intended interactions, those that occur when someone decides on the spur of the moment to contact another person, and opportunistic and spontaneous interactions, those that happen when people happen to be at the same place at the same time. We first discuss lessons learned from existing systems for intended interactions, and then we speculate on ways to support opportunistic and spontaneous interaction.

Intended Interactions—The Connection Problem. From studies of informal communication in the workplace and of existing prototypes that support intended communication, we know that the majority of people's attempts to reach others are initially unsuccessful (HP corpus; Fish et al., 1993). We mentioned that 67% of attempted phone calls in the HP corpus did not reach the intended recipient, and in the Montage study 75% of all attempts to reach someone were unsuccessful (Tang, Isaacs, & Rua, 1994).

Why is this? One problem with intended interactions is that the availability of the recipient is not guaranteed. One method of helping people find good times to interact is to use techniques such as "glancing" (Root, 1988; Tang & Rua, 1994) to offer people information about the availability of the recipient. By "looking into" the recipient's office they can see whether the person is present and available for conversation. Once availability has been established, it is critical to establish connections (such as audio, video, and data sharing) extremely quickly and easily. Studies of existing prototypes show that if a connection is not made within a few seconds, people tend to use the system for longer, more formal interactions (Tang & Isaacs, 1993; Fish et al., 1993).

On occasions when recipients are unavailable, it is useful to provide mechanisms to set up future contact, most notably the ability to leave a note in a prominent place. Montage, for example, allows people to leave an electronic "Stickup" note on the screen of someone they tried to contact. The recipient can use that note when they return to establish a video connection with the sender. This feature was well received by users (Tang, et al., 1994).

In addition, we have shown that people often go to another colleague if they do not find the person they seek. Perhaps a system for intended interactions could allow people to designate a "next relevant colleague" to whom people could "go" when appropriate. A more sophisticated but complex design would allow the user to specify different people for different topics. Another possibility is to provide a "contact method" for the recipient. In addition, we noted that people often announce to their colleagues upcoming events that will take them away from their work area, thus encouraging others to handle pending business with them. A distributed system might support a similar activity, perhaps by enabling a group video connection or a prominent place to leave a note to a group.

In the Montage system, people can post an image for those who glance to indicate they are not in the office (Tang & Rua, 1994). They can also write a message on the image to give more information. Data from an extended use study showed that 87% of the times users put up the "not available" sign, they wrote a note indicating their whereabouts and/or when they would return. They never specified another person to contact, however. This finding indicates that a forwarding feature might need to be built in to facilitate the behavior.

Finally, it might be useful to provide a message capability that goes beyond text or voice alone. Users may want to make better use of missed connection events by leaving richer multimedia messages incorporating a combination of voice, gestures, writing, and documents. Wang's Freestyle system allowed users to do this by freezing the image of a document on the screen, which users then annotated and spoke about in a recorded "voice over" message (Francik, Rudman, Cooper, & Levine, 1991). Frohlich and Daly-Jones (1995) tested a similar pen-and-voice messaging facility called Voicefax against standard PC fax and voice-mail messages. They found that people used significantly fewer Voicefax messages to perform the same task with higher perceived quality. It is not hard to imagine a video-based variation on these systems that allowed users to switch on a local document camera to record a video message for dispatch with its associated documentation.

In sum, features that would be useful to set up contact include:

- The ability to very quickly glance into colleagues' offices to check their availability
- Rapid connection once availability is established
- The ability to leave a message if an attempt to contact is unsuccessful
- A way to leave a notice indicating where you are and when you will be back
- Multiple-way audiovideo connections for group announcements (e.g., to "preannounce" when you will be unavailable)
- Forwarding, that is, a way to designate a "next relevant colleague"
- Multimedia messages

Opportunistic and Spontaneous Interactions. Because unintended communication is initiated by the copresence of the interactants, technologies to support remote opportunistic and spontaneous communications need to provide methods for interactants to become aware of and encounter one another serendipitously. As we saw from the HP corpus examples, people develop awareness in the physical world by seeing others in nearby locations as they go about their workplace activities. People often run into others in common areas, such as hallways, coffee areas, office supply areas, cafeterias, printer areas, parking lots, etc. When people move into a common area, they recognize that they enter a "public" space where they might be observed and approached for conversation. As a result, people use visual cues to signal to others the degree to which they are receptive to interactions.

In a distributed environment, people can use video to stay aware of others' availability. In the PARC Media Space, for example, a camera was placed in a commons area largely to help people stay aware of others' whereabouts (Bly et al., 1993). People can use such video to see when people come into camera range. They can see such things as body position, facial expression, eye contact, and other cues about a person's focus of attention. They can tell whether a person is already involved in an interaction, and if so, whether it might be appropriate to join. In other words, video allows people to use many of the same cues they use in a shared physical environment to understand who is where and whether they are willing to interact. We described many examples from the HP corpus when people used visual cues to time their opening comments. There were other cases when people used visual cues to indicate they would prefer not to initiate conversation. People also used visual cues on occasion to show that they were ready to end interactions.

Still, simply providing video access among remote collaborators is not sufficient for enabling smooth entry into interactions. People also need to know when they are likely to encounter others so that they can adjust their demeanor appropriately. The Autocruiser feature of Cruiser was not well received in part because people were given no warning of pending video connections and because they had no relevant shared context when a connection was made (Fish et al., 1992). The Montage system used approach sounds to signal a pending interaction and a slow video fade-in effect to soften the intrusiveness of the video connection (Tang & Rua, 1994). Perhaps such sounds and video effects could be used to signal the proximity of others. In addition, certain "places" in a shared electronic work environment could be created where people could "run into" others. These places might provide other attractions that draw people (e.g., daily news, schedule of events, progress schedule) so that unintended interactions might occur.

In our experience, users of video systems often ask for the ability to control visual access. One way to do so is to design all connections to be symmetric so that no one can watch or listen without being seen and heard themselves. In addition, explicit access controls can be provided.

These ideas suggest the following components for a system to support unintended interactions:

- Use video (and possibly audio) to allow people to see (and hear) who is available.
- Use video to convey whether a person is open to an interaction.
- Provide cues when people are in an online "place" where they might see and be seen by others.
- Provide contexts with useful information where people are likely to see others.
- Provide symmetric audio and video; if you can see or hear, then you are being seen and heard.
- Provide the ability to control visual access.

Supporting Conversations

Once people successfully initiate an interaction, they need support for it, whether it began as an intended or unintended interaction. Many informal conversations include references to online and paper documents, from scribbled notes to published papers (Whittaker, Frohlich, & Daly-Jones, 1994; Harper & Sellen, 1995). People should be able to bring such documents into a discussion at a moment's notice. They also should be able to see each other pointing and writing on documents. Because many conversations are continuations of previous discussions, it may be useful to help people keep track of their concurrent discussions so they can easily restore the shared context when a new "installment" occurs. This function is supported in a prototype (Whittaker, Swanson, Kucan, & Sidner, in press) that kept track of conversational threads and represented them on the user's desktop as "piles." The piles could be accessed rapidly and used to regenerate the context of an ongoing conversation.

A related concept is to enable people to store different aspects of their conversations, including documents, audio, video, and screen snapshots. By storing these conversation components, people could keep track of progress, keep others informed, and perhaps resolve later misunderstandings. One such system is Filochat, a conversational support tool that co-indexed user's pen strokes during note-taking to an audio recording of the meetings. Field study results showed that this system helped people regenerate the context of prior meetings from handwritten notes (Whittaker, Hyland, & Wiley, 1994). A system developed at Xerox PARC called WhereWereWe enables real-time video capture, indexing, and playback during conversations, which was used successfully to support and track design and planning sessions (Minneman et al., 1995).

Storing conversations might also help those who wish to convey a message to a large group but do not trust word of mouth. For example, creators of information could make their message easily available online (in text, audio, video, or otherwise), so that anyone passing on that information could easily share the first-hand version. The information might include a link to the information creator so that people could easily contact them (though video or otherwise) if they had questions. Perhaps mechanisms could be included to track those who had seen the message so that the information creator could contact groups who had not received the message.

Ideas discussed to support interactions that happen spontaneously include:

- Ability to share existing online and paper documents and material created on the fly
- A mechanism to help track and restore multiple, ongoing conversations with different people
- The ability to store and retrieve parts of conversations in a variety of media

Range of Needs for Different Groups

As we discussed, not all types of groups are alike, and those differences suggest different requirements for supporting informal communication. One obvious design implication is that people tolerate different levels of privacy violations from different types of people, especially when video is involved. Our studies of workgroup communication indicate that many people find it acceptable for other workgroup members to interrupt them, overhear their conversations, view many of their documents, handle issues for them in their absence, and so on. Support for workgroup interaction could take advantage of this openness to provide ongoing, lightweight access to each other's whereabouts, activities, and stored materials. However, this arrangement would be unacceptable for external groups, or possibly peer and cross-functional groups. For those groups, it would be useful to create contexts where access is open while limiting or blocking awareness in other contexts.

In general, it may make sense to build in a notion of groups, which people may define and control as an entity rather than specifying access on a per-person basis. Of course, group membership is often fluid, especially for ad hoc teams. A community of peers may not even see themselves as a group. There may be a need for official groups, where all the members acknowledge the boundaries of the group, as well as unofficial groups, where a person creates a group to characterize the level of access they will allow a set of people.

To support external groups, tools must interoperate across computer platforms. Even within the same company, different groups often work on different hardware using different software. A system designed to support their ability to notice each other and enter into unplanned conversations should run smoothly across a variety of platforms.

Possible ways discussed to handle different types of groups include:

- A notion of groups built into the system
- A lightweight mechanism to easily specify and change levels of access for groups
- Easy access to the technology to accommodate fluid changes in group membership
- Interoperability across platforms to enable collaboration across external groups

CONCLUSION

Our goal in this chapter was to call attention to the importance of informal communication—and in particular opportunistic and spontaneous interactions—for the healthy, productive functioning of groups, and to point out how video is a natural tool for supporting such behavior. We have discussed a range of activities that occur through informal communication among a range of types of groups, and we have considered a variety of implications for the design of systems to support that work. We do not expect that any one system could provide all the support we explore; we raise the ideas as possible considerations when designing a system. We also do not expect that all our suggestions will turn out to be useful. Because no such system directly addresses unintended interactions, we can only speculate based on our knowledge of such communication in the physical world and on design principles of other CSCW systems. We hope we have stimulated thought on the issue and encouraged researchers and practitioners to consider either building tools to support informal communication or designing into other systems mechanisms to support informal communication.

NOTES

1. Note that "informal" refers to the way in which the interaction is initiated, not necessarily the tone of the interaction; scheduled interactions may also be conducted in an informal manner. Although we believe the term *impromptu* better characterizes the nature of these interactions, we use the term *informal* because it has been used in the past (Kraut, Fish, Root, & Chalfonte, 1990).
2. The following conventions are used in the transcriptions:
   () indicates an untranscribable utterance
   (0.5sec) indicates a pause length
   - indicates cut off
   ? indicates rising intonation
   : indicates stretch of the preceding phoneme

REFERENCES

Allen, T. (1977). *Managing the flow of technology.* Cambridge, MA: MIT Press.

Argyle, M., Lalljee, M., & Cook, M. (1968). The effects of visibility on interaction in a dyad. *Human Relations, 21,* 3–17.

Bly, S., Harrison, S., & Irwin, S. (1993). Media Spaces: Bringing people together in a video, audio and computing environment. *Communications of the ACM, 36*(1), 28–45.

Boden, D. (1994). *The business of talk: Organisations in action.* Cambridge: Polity Press.

Dourish, P., & Bly, S. (1992). Portholes: Supporting awareness in a distributed work group. *Proceedings of the Conference on Computer Human Interaction* (pp. 541–547). New York: ACM Press.

Dykstra-Erickson, E., Rudman, C., Hertz, R., Mithal, K., Schmidt, J., & Marshall, C. (1995). Supporting adaptation to multimedia desktop conferencing. *Proceedings of the 15th International Symposium on Human Factors in Telecommunications* (pp. 31–38). Melbourne, Australia.

Festinger, L., Schachter, S., & Bach, K. (1950). *Social pressures in informal groups: A study of human factors in housing.* New York: Harper & Row.

Finholt, T., Sproull, L., & Kiesler, S. (1990). Communication and performance in ad-hoc task groups. In J. Galegher, R. Kraut, & C. Egido (Eds.), *Intellectual teamwork* (pp. 291–325). Hillsdale, NJ: Lawrence Erlbaum Associates.

Fish, R., Kraut, R., Root, R., & Rice, R. (1993). Video as a technology for informal communication. *Communications of the ACM, 36*(1), 48–61.

Francik, E., Rudman, S. E., Cooper, D., & Levine, S. (1991). Putting innovation to work: Adoption strategies for multimedia communication systems. *Communications of the ACM, 34*(12), 53–63.

Frohlich, D. (1995). Requirements for interpersonal information management. In P. J. Thomas (Ed.), *Personal information systems: Business applications* (pp. 133–153). Cheltenham: Stanley Thornes, in association with Unicom Seminars.

Frohlich, D. & Daly-Jones, O. (1995). Voicefax: A shared workspace for voicemail partners. In *Companion Proceedings of Conference on Computer Human Interaction* (pp. 308–309). New York: ACM Press.

Gajewska, H., Kistler, J. Manasse, M. S., & Redell, D. D. (1994). Argo: A system for distributed collaboration. *Proceedings of Multimedia* (pp. 433–440). New York: ACM Press.

Gajewska, H., Manasse, M. S., & Redell, D. D. (1995). Argohalls: Adding support for group awareness to the Argo telecollaboration system. *Proceedings of User Interface Software and Technology* (pp. 157–158). New York: ACM Press.

Gaver, W., Moran, T., MacLean, A., Lövstrand, L., Dourish, P., Carter, K., & Buxton, W. (1992). Realizing a video environment: EuroParc's RAVE system. *Proceedings of Conference on Computer Human Interaction* (pp. 27–35). New York: ACM Press.

Granovetter, M. (1973). The strength of weak ties. *American Journal of Sociology, 78,* 1360–1380.

Harper, R., & Sellen, A. (1995). Collaborative tools and the practicalities of professional work at the International Monetary Fund. *Proceedings of the Conference on Computer Human Interaction* (pp. 122–129). New York: ACM Press.

Isaacs, E. A., & Tang, J. C. (1994). What video can and cannot do for collaboration: A case study. *Multimedia Systems, 2,* 63–73.

Isaacs, E. A., Tang, J. C., & Morris, T. (1996). Piazza: A desktop environment supporting impromptu and planned interactions. *Proceedings of the Conference on Computer-Supported Cooperative Work* (pp. 315–324). New York: ACM Press.

Kendon, A., & Ferber, A. (1973). A description of some human greetings. In R. Michael & J. Crook (Eds.), *Comparative ecology and behavior of primates* (pp. 591–668). London: Academic Press.

Kraut, R. E. (1987). Predicting the use of technology: The case of telework. In R. E. Kraut (Ed.), *Technology and the transformation of white collar work* (pp. 113–134). Hillsdale, NJ: Lawrence Erlbaum Associates.

Kraut, R. E., Egido, C., & Galegher, J. (1990). Patterns of contact and communication in scientific research collaboration. In J. Galegher & R. Kraut (Eds.), *Intellectual teamwork: The social and technological bases of cooperative work* (pp. 149–171). Hillsdale, NJ: Lawrence Erlbaum Associates.

Kraut, R., Fish, R., Root, B., & Chalfonte, B. (1990). Informal communication in organizations: Form, function and technology. In S. Oskamp & S. Spacapan (Eds.), *People's reactions to technology in factories, offices and aerospace,* The Claremont Symposium on Applied Social Psychology (pp. 145–199). Newbury Park: Sage.

Kraut, R. E., & Streeter, L. A. (1995). Coordination in software development. *Communications of the ACM, 38*(3), 69–81.

Luff, P., Heath, C., & Greatbatch, D. (1992). Tasks-in-interaction. Paper and screen based documentation in collaborative activity. *Proceedings of Conference on Computer Supported Cooperative Work* (pp. 163–170). New York: ACM Press.

MacLeod, L., Scriven, J., & Wayne, F. S. (1992). Gender and management level differences in the oral communication patterns of bank managers. *Journal of Business Communication, 29*(4), 343–365.

Mantei, M. M., Baecker, R. M., Sellen, A. J., Buxton, W. A. S., & Mulligan, T. (1991). Experiences in the use of a Media Space. *Proceedings of the Conference on Computer-Human Interaction* (pp. 203–208). New York: ACM Press.

484ISAACSETAL.

McGrath, J. E. (1991). Time matters in groups. In J. Galegher & R. Kraut (Eds.), *Intellectual teamwork: The social and technological bases of cooperative work* (pp. 23–61). Hillsdale, NJ: Lawrence Erlbaum Associates.

Minneman, S. L., Harrison, S., Janssen, B., Kurtenback, G., Moran, T., Smith, I., & van Melle, B. (1995). A confederation of tools for capturing and accessing collaborative activity. *Proceedings of the Conference on Multimedia* (pp. 523–534). New York: ACM Press.

Mosier, J., & Tammaro, S. (1995). Video teleconference use among geographically dispersed work groups: A field investigation of usage patterns and user preferences. *Journal of Organizational Computing, 4*, 343–366.

Nelson, R., & Mathews, K. M. (1991). Network characteristics of high-performing organizations. *Journal of Business Communications, 28*(4), 367–386.

Nelson, R. (1989). The strength of strong ties: Social networks and intergroup conflict in organizations. *Academy of Management Journal, 32*(2), 377–401.

Ochsman, R. B., & Chapanis, A. (1974). The effects of 10 communication modes on the behavior of teams during co-operative problem-solving. *International Journal of Man–Machine Studies, 6*, 579–619.

O'Conaill, B., & Frohlich, D. (1995). Timespace in the workplace: Dealing with interruptions. *Companion Proceedings of Human Factors in Computing Systems* (pp. 262–263). New York: ACM Press.

Olson, M. (1987). Telework: Practical experience and future prospects. In R. E. Kraut (Ed.), *Technology and the transformation of white collar work* (pp. 135–154). Hillsdale, NJ: Lawrence Erlbaum Associates.

Panko, R. (1992). Managerial communication patterns. *Journal of Organisational Computing, 2*, 95–122.

Pickering, J. M., & King, J. L. (1992). Hardwiring weak ties: Individual and institutional issues in computer mediated communication. *Proceedings of the Conference on Computer-Supported Cooperative Work* (pp. 256–261). New York: ACM Press.

Reder, S., & Schwab, R. G. (1990). The temporal structure of cooperative activity. *Proceedings of the Conference on Computer-Supported Cooperative Work* (pp. 303–316). New York: ACM Press.

Root, R. W. (1988). Design of a multi-media vehicle for social browsing. *Proceedings of the Conference on Computer-Supported Cooperative Work* (pp. 25–38). New York: ACM Press.

Short, J., Williams, E., & Christie, B. (1976). *The social psychology of telecommunications.* London: Wiley & Sons.

Sproull, L. (1984). The nature of managerial attention, In L. Sproull & J. Larkey (Eds.), *Advances in Information Processing in Organizations* (pp. 9–27). JAI Press.

Suchman, L., & Wynn, E. (1984). Procedures and problems in the office. *Office: Technology and People, 2*, 133–154.

Tang, J. (1991). Findings from observational studies of collaborative work. *International Journal of Man–Machine Studies, 34*, 143–160.

Tang, J. C., & Isaacs, E. A. (1993). Why do users like video? Studies of multimedia-supported collaboration. *Computer Supported Cooperative Work: An International Journal, 1*(9), 163–196.

Tang, J. C., Isaacs, E. A., & Rua, M. (1994). Supporting distributed groups with a Montage of lightweight interactions. *Proceedings of the Conference on Computer-Supported Cooperative Work* (pp. 23–34). New York: ACM Press.

Tang, J. C., & Rua, M. (1994). Montage: Providing teleproximity for distributed groups. *Proceedings of the Conference on Computer Human Interaction* (pp. 37–43). New York: ACM Press.

Whittaker, S., Frohlich, D., & Daly-Jones, O. (1994). Informal workplace communication: What is it like and how might we support it? *Proceedings of the Conference on Computer Human Interaction* (pp. 131–137). New York: ACM Press.

Whittaker, S., Hyland, P., & Wiley, M. (1994). Filochat: Handwritten notes provide access to recorded conversation. *Proceedings of the Conference on Computer Human Interaction* (pp. 271–277). New York: ACM Press.

Whittaker, S., Swanson, J., Kucan, J., & Sidner, C. (in press). TeleNotes: Managing lightweight interaction in the desktop. *Transactions on Computer–Human Interaction.*

Chapter 23

Video-as-Data: Technical and Social Aspects of a Collaborative Multimedia Application[1]

Bonnie A. Nardi
Apple Computer, Inc.

Allan Kuchinsky
Hewlett Packard Laboratories

Steve Whittaker
AT & T Laboratories

Robert Leichner
Hewlett Packard Laboratories

Heinrich Schwarz
Massachusetts Institute of Technology

We studied the use of a collaborative multimedia system for coordinating team-work among members of a neurosurgical team. We analyze the use of video within the operating room and the use of broadcast audio and video to other locations in the hospital to enable remote neurophysiological monitoring. We describe how the multimedia system was used in a real-world work context, including its benefits and problems. We argue that video can be useful as more than just pictures of people talking to one another; video can be a rich tool to enable analysis and problem solving. We discuss privacy problems inherent in collaborative multimedia technology and describe how they played out in the hospital during the course of our study.

INTRODUCTION

The rich information throughput afforded by multimedia makes it a logical extension to the computer-supported collaborative work technologies that have been under development during the last decade (Baecker, 1993; Bly,

Harrison, & Irwin, 1993; Buxton, 1992; Ishii & Kobayashi, 1992; Kuzuoka, 1992; Mantei et al., 1991; Sellen, 1992). To date, collaborative multimedia systems have tended to focus on the use of audio and video to enable synchronous interpersonal communication between remote participants. Video is used to communicate visual aspects of interaction such as eye gaze, gesture, facial expression (Chapanis, Ochsman, Parrish, & Weeks, 1972, 1977; O'Conaill, Whittaker, & Wilbur, 1993; Sellen, 1992; Tang & Isaacs, 1993), or information about the presence or absence of a remote collaborator (Bly et al., 1993; Dourish & Bly, 1992; Fish, Kraut, & Chalfonte, 1990; Tang & Rua, 1994). Where such "talking heads" systems have been evaluated, the effects have been both subtle and task specific. Few benefits have been observed for collaborative problem-solving tasks (Chapanis, 1975; Chapanis et al., 1972, 1977; Fish, Kraut, Root, & Rice, 1992), although tasks such as negotiation that require access to the motivations of others do show outcome differences when video information is provided (Short, Williams, & Christie, 1976). Commercial multimedia systems using talking heads video for supporting interpersonal communication have not been greatly successful (Egido, 1990; Noll, 1976, 1992). One consistent result, however, is a subjective preference by users for video over audio–only interaction (Sellen, 1992; Tang & Isaacs, 1993). More research is needed in this area.

Although multimedia offers many new and enticing technical possibilities in areas such as electronic publishing, interactive learning, and video on demand, such applications have not been explored to the same extent as those for talking heads. The few systems that do tackle the new applications have tended to be research prototypes, so we lack detailed information about their potential utility in real work settings.

The study we report in this chapter attempts to redress the balance. We describe and analyze a multimedia system used to coordinate work among members of a neurosurgical team in a teaching hospital. Although the system we studied was experimental in the sense that it was still under development, it was actually being used in the hospital for everyday work, and we conducted our study by observing its use in the real work setting.

The chapter focuses on four key issues: (a) the importance of video-as-data in contrast to talking heads video; (b) the need to develop new tools to make video a richer medium; (c) the differing uses of information in audio versus video channels; and (d) privacy problems associated with collaborative multimedia technology. Video-as-data contrasts with the traditional "talking heads" approach. In applications such as videophone and videoconference, video is used to show the head and upper body of remote interactants. By contrast, we focus here on using the video image to display *shared dynamic work objects* that are critical to the task being carried out by a distributed team.[2] We investigate the importance of these shared objects in mediating collaboration in distributed teams.

THE MULTIMEDIA SYSTEM IN THE HOSPITAL

In the hospital where we conducted the study, live color video is used in the operating room to coordinate team activity during neurosurgery. Both live and recorded video are used for training in neurosurgery. During the critical parts of an operation, such as the removal of a tumor, the neurosurgeon looks through a stereoscopic microscope to view the brain or spine as he[3] works. A camera co-mounted with the optics of the microscope captures a video image of what the surgeon sees. The image is then displayed on a cable TV link. The entire neurosurgical team—anesthesiologist, neurophysiologist, neurotechnician, resident or fellow neurosurgeon(s), surgical technician, scrub nurse, circulating nurse, nurse-anesthetist, and sometimes an anesthesiology resident—can see what the surgeon sees. The video image is two-dimensional (2D) and is a somewhat smaller view of the surgical field than the surgeon's view. This technology has been in existence (although not universally available) for over 20 years, and is now an indispensable part of operating room activity in many hospitals.

The multimedia system in the hospital also has a new and very innovative facility for remote broadcast of video, audio, and quantitative data from the operating room instrumentation. The multimedia system includes MediaBox, an appliance for the control of media peripherals and analog signals (Sclabassi, Leichner, Kuchinsky, Krieger, & Prince, 1991). MediaBox provides control, configuration, and integration with the workstation and network environment for multiple media sources. Figure 23.1 shows a schematic view of the multimedia medical network in the hospital.

The multimedia facility was developed by neurophysiologists who are interested in establishing how much of their job can be done from locations away from the operating room. Remote performance of their tasks would allow them to service a greater patient population, spreading their scarce

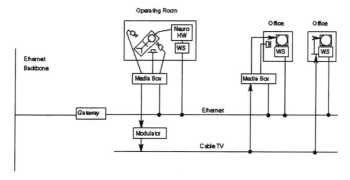

FIG. 23.1. The multimedia medical network. (Neuro HW = neurophysiological monitoring hardware, WS = computer workstation.)

expertise over a larger number of operations. Before describing how the neurophysiologists use the multimedia system for remote monitoring, we briefly sketch their role in the neurosurgery team.

Neurophysiologists monitor the patient's neurophysiological responses during an operation and feed information back to the neurosurgeon and anesthesiologist if they suspect a problem. Neurophysiological monitoring has been successful in reducing patient morbidity by constantly tracking central nervous system activity to see that it is maintained within acceptable parameters. During many neurosurgical operations there is a high risk of damage due to the anesthesia or surgery itself: for example, cutting, stretching, or compressing a nerve, or cutting off the blood supply to parts of the brain. Neurophysiological monitoring helps prevent such events. It has enabled neurosurgeons to perform more difficult and daring operations (especially going deeper into the brain) and is available only in some hospitals. It is used during operations in which the patient is at high risk.

But the neurophysiologist does not need to actually be in the operating room at all times in order to monitor effectively. His main source of information is the instrument data showing neurophysiological measures displayed as plotted line graphs on a computer screen. This information is routinely broadcast to remote network nodes, outside the operating room, enabling remote monitoring. The new multimedia system feeds the audio, video, and instrument data to nodes in a networked system allowing remote monitoring from other operating rooms, conference rooms, and offices (Sclabassi et al., 1991). The video and audio information supplement the neurophysiologist's view of the operation, supplying additional information for interpreting the instrument data (as we discuss later in detail). During routine parts of an operation, neurophysiologists can be in their offices answering patient calls, reading mail, editing papers, and tending to other duties while monitoring the operation as a background activity. In the future, the facilities for remote broadcast will also be used by remotely located neurosurgeons acting in an advisory role. Using the remote monitoring, neurophysiologists and neurosurgeons should be able to simultaneously monitor a larger number of operations, spreading scarce expertise over a greater area and making more efficient use of their time. Only a handful of nodes have operable video and audio capabilities at the present time, so our discussion of their use reports preliminary findings.

METHODOLOGY

To learn about the use of the multimedia system, we conducted an ethnographic study comprised of observations in the operating room; audiotaped, semistructured interviews; informal interaction (such as going to lunch with informants and casual conversation in hallways and offices); and "shadowing." The shadowing technique involved following around a single individual for several days to track and record activity in as much detail as possible. We used this technique with the neurophysiologists to study their use of the remote video and audio. We had originally hoped to quantify this information in terms of times-per-task, but because of the complexities of hospital life we would have needed at least 3 to 6 months of shadowing to iron out anomalies and make statistically valid statements. The shadowing was nevertheless very informative as we learned a great deal about the daily activities of neurophysiologists and had many opportunities for informal conversation. A total of 14 person-weeks of fieldwork was conducted. More than 500 pages of interview transcripts resulted from interviews with about 35 informants.

Our observations were conducted in the operating room during a series of brain and spine surgeries. In some cases we observed complete surgeries, and in others we spent a period of hours in the operating room (neurosurgeries can last from about 5 to 24 hours). Although it might seem odd that we were allowed in the operating room, the staff was accustomed to visitors because we were at a teaching hospital. We donned "scrubs" (soft, loose, cotton clothing) and masks, exactly the same as those worn by all operating-room personnel, and our presence was not conspicuous. We had opportunities to ask questions of all operating-room personnel during operations (except the attending neurosurgeon) as there are always times when a particular team member is not busy. The scrub nurse was only briefly accessible, but because circulating nurses are also trained and work as scrub nurses, we had good opportunities to talk to them in the operating room about both roles. The semistructured interviews were used to fill in gaps in our knowledge and to pose specific queries about many aspects of the use of the multimedia technology, especially the privacy concerns.

THE OPERATING ROOM: ROLES AND PROCEDURES

It is necessary to provide some background on work flow and work roles in the operating room during surgery to be able to make sense of the discussion in the following sections in which we analyze the use of the multimedia system in detail. Figure 23.2 is a photograph of the neurosurgical team at work. Figure 23.3 diagrams the work roles in the operating room.

Preparing the Patient

At the beginning of an operation the patient is tranquilized, anesthetized, and connected to a variety of monitors and drips. The attending anesthesiologist plans the general course of the anesthesia to be used for the operation and is usually present during the "prep" period. The attending anesthesiolo-

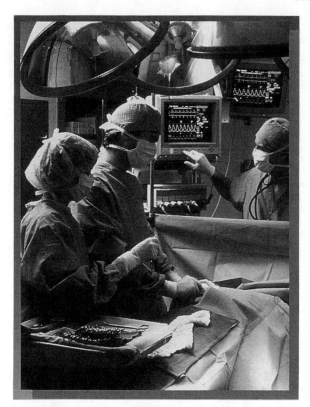

FIG. 23.2. The neurosurgical team at work. The neurotechnician is seated by the neurophysiological workstation display at the left of the photography. The scrub nurse is shown in the center, while the surgeon, on the right, works on the patient. The anesthesia team is situated behind the hanging drape at the right of the photograph. In the foreground is the surgical table, which contains instruments and supplies used by the surgeon.

gist works with the nurse-anesthetist and/or resident anesthesiologist to administer the anesthesia and insert the appropriate intravenous lines for blood and a catheter for urine. After the initial setup, the attending anesthesiologist generally leaves the operating room to attend to another operation or to take care of other tasks. The resident and/or nurse-anesthetist then monitors the patient's basic physiological functions: heart rate, blood gases, blood pressure, breathing, urine concentration, and so forth. The attending anesthesiologist returns to the operating room when necessary. He or she can be reached by phone via pager and makes "check-in" visits to see how things are going.

At this time, the nurses are busy setting up the operating room: arranging instruments on the sterile table that will be placed near the operating table, checking supplies, putting the patient's x-rays up on the wall.

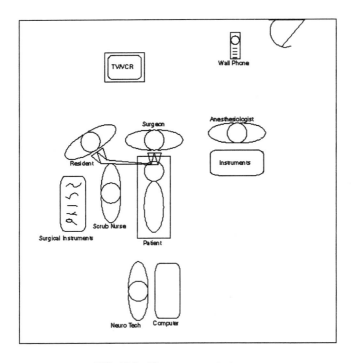

FIG. 23.3. The neurosurgical team.

The beginning of the operation is also the time when the patient, after being anesthetized, is connected to the electrodes that will be used to monitor muscle and nerve activity. The neurophysiologist and neurotechnician apply the electrodes that provide "evoked potential" data. Throughout the course of the operation the patient is given electrical stimulation (electrical potential for activity is actually evoked by stimulation) to make sure that muscles and nerves are responding appropriately and are not being damaged by the surgery. The neurophysiologist supervises the neurotechnician and all ongoing cases, and is ultimately responsible for the interpretation of the neurophysiological data. The neurotechnician does the more routine monitoring, sitting in front of the computer screen watching the plotted line graphs.

As mentioned, the neurophysiological data can also be viewed in other locations outside the operating room because the graphs can be displayed on remote nodes on the networked computer system. The system can display all of the neurophysiological data for any operating room to which the system is connected. Neurophysiologists, when on call, thus usually spend a part of the day in the various operating rooms and a part of the day in their offices, monitoring the evoked potentials via the computer displays. Neurophysiologists may monitor as many as six operations concurrently (they have a backup person assigned to help in case of overload). When not in the operating room, they communicate with the neurotechnician in the operating room via telephone, and they carry pagers. If during the course of the operation the neurotechnician suspects a problem, he or she reports it to the surgeon and may also telephone the neurophysiologist if this person is not in the operating room at the time. The neurophysiologist then returns to the operating room to evaluate the data and possibly communicate with other members of the surgical team such as the attending neurosurgeon or anesthesiologist.

"Opening" and "Closing" the Patient

After the prep, the patient is "opened"—that is, the incision made—by the resident or neurosurgical fellow. The resident or fellow then continues to cut and drill until he is down to the point in the brain or spine where the most delicate surgery is required: for example, the brain tissue that must be "picked through" to reach a tumor, aneurysm, or blood vessel compressing a nerve. At this point the attending neurosurgeon arrives in the operating room to take over. Often the procedures used by the neurosurgeon are "microprocedures," requiring the use of the microscope. The resident or fellow neurosurgeon watches the operation through a second (2D) lens on the microscope while the attending neurosurgeon views the surgical field through the main stereoscopic optics. When the microscope is being used, the video is on as well, so those in the operating room can watch a two-dimensional view of the surgery on the TV monitor. The audio portion of the system is on as soon as the microscope and VCR are turned on, often at the beginning of the operation, long before the microscope is needed.

Via the networked multimedia system, the neurophysiologist, if not in the operating room, can see the microscope video and hear a great deal of what is said and done in the operating room. The broadcast video image enables the remote neurophysiologist to see what the surgeon is currently doing. The broadcast audio also allows the neurophysiologist to hear what the surgeon is saying in the operating room as he calls for instruments, explains the procedure, and describes the patient's state to students and others in the operating room. The neurophysiologist also hears other ambient sounds of interest such as the equipment noise, which often provides (whether by design or not) auditory cues to the progress of the operation or the patient's state. For example, the sounds from the suction device tell everyone in the operating room how much blood is being suctioned; a lot of blood might indicate a problem. The audio broadcast to remote locations transmits such sounds and many others: The Doppler ultrasound emits the noise of the heart pumping, the noise of the drill reveals the kind of drill being used, and hammers, saws, and chisels have their characteristic sounds. Oscilloscopes used by the neurophysiologists and neurotechnicians have audio output that tracks responses produced by stimulation, responses that may go by so quickly they cannot be seen visually on the display but can be detected aurally.

The operation may be recorded on videotape, at the discretion of the attending neurosurgeon.

Throughout the surgery the scrub nurse hands the surgeon the instruments and supplies that he requests. The circulating nurse makes sure that the scrub nurse has all the necessary equipment; the circulating nurse is a bridge between the sterile operating area and nonsterile areas of the operating room. When the attending neurosurgeon has finished the procedure, the patient is "closed"—that is, the incision is repaired—by the resident or fellow. The patient is revived from the anesthesia in the operating room and asked to wiggle his toes and say something. He is then wheeled to recovery.

VIDEO-AS-DATA

To date, most research on video has focused on talking heads video in which the video images are of remote participants conferring, or checking on each other's presence in a particular location, or performing some task together (Baecker, 1993; Chapanis et al., 1972, 1977; Dourish & Bly, 1992; Egido, 1990; Fish et al., 1990, 1992; Mantei et al., 1991; O'Conaill et al., 1993; Sellen, 1992; Tang & Isaacs, 1993). In the operating room, video images of the workspace and work objects—that is, the data—are the focus of interest. We describe the central role of video-as-data in *coordinating team work* and *educating medical personnel* in the teaching hospital setting.

In the operating room, the live video is used to coordinate activity during the most critical part of the surgery, when the neurosurgeon is working deep in the brain or spine on very small structures that he sees only through the microscope. In a sense, even though operating room personnel are co-located, the video provides "remote" access; the surgical field is invisible, without the intervening video technology, to all but the surgeons. The video is used by the scrub nurse, anesthesiologist, nurse-anesthetist, circulating nurse, neurophysiologist, and neurotechnician, to see more precisely what the surgeon is doing.

The most important function of the live video in the operating room is to allow the scrub nurse to anticipate which instruments and supplies the surgeon will need. As one scrub nurse said, the video is "the only indication we have of what's going on in the [patient's] head." The TV monitor is on a movable cart, and its position changes depending on the orientation and position of the patient, which depends on the kind of operation being performed. The circulating nurse positions the monitor so that the scrub nurse has an unimpeded view, clearly revealing the importance of the video to the scrub nurse.

During the critical parts of the surgery, events move very quickly, and the surgeon must be able to work steadily and without interruption. He changes instruments as often as every few seconds, and he needs to work in tight coordination with the scrub nurse who is selecting an instrument from over one hundred instruments arrayed on the sterile table near the operating table. The scrub nurse may also need to hand the surgeon one of hundreds of types of supplies (sutures, sponges, Teflon pads, etc.) brought to her by the circulating nurse. The work of a neurosurgical operation is extremely detailed and fast-paced, and the better idea the scrub nurse has of the surgeon's needs, the more smoothly the operation proceeds. Even with the video, the surgeon calls out the instrument or supply he needs next, but the ability of the nurse to anticipate what the neurosurgeon will want is considered very important by operating room personnel. One neurosurgeon used a sports metaphor to explain how the video supports neurosurgeon–scrub nurse coordination:

> Neurosurgeon: . . . an operation is like team work, [for example], ice hockey—the center brings the puck around, and the forward goes to the appropriate position, and the puck is coming in and he hits it . . . Surgeon and scrub nurse . . . it's mutual team work . . . So a good scrub nurse looks at the video and knows what's coming next—instrument in and out, instrument giving and taking. It's all team work, [like] sports activity. . . . So if you don't have the video, there's no way to do so [coordinate activity quickly]. So [with the video] it's uniform, harmonious work.

As she watches the video, the scrub nurse is tracking the course of the operation and looking for unusual events to which she must respond with the correct instrument or supply. For example, she may know that the surgeon is approaching a time in the operation when a clip will be needed. Or she may see the surgeon nick some tissue, in which case a cautery device will likely be called for to repair the nick.

The scrub nurse's effective use of the video depends on her own knowledge and understanding of what she is seeing; the presence of the video image is not a guarantee that she will be able to anticipate the surgeon's needs and respond quickly. There is an interaction between her level of expertise and understanding and the presence of the video in the environment. As one neurosurgeon explained:

Neurosurgeon: Some scrub nurses are excellent when they look at the video, they know what's next and they are very good. But other scrub nurses are not at that level yet, so [I] have to tell her what I need and even if she's looking, [she] is not at level yet, so it is more time-consuming.

Because the scrub nurse is listening to the surgeon, selecting instruments and supplies and handing them to the surgeon, her use of the video involves very quick glances at the monitor to see what is happening. All the more reason she must instantly understand what she is seeing. In contrast to the scrub nurse's quick glances at the monitor, the others in the operating room who watch the video may watch it intently for long stretches of time. Their use of the video helps them keep track of the progress of the surgery, but generally they do not rely on the video for split-second reactions as does the scrub nurse. Anesthesiologists, nurse-anesthetists, circulating nurses, and neurotechnicians watch the video in part to remain attentive to the surgery, to maintain interest and concentration at times when they may have very little to do. For example:

Interviewer: What does [the video] tell you about what you have to do?

Anesthesiologist: In the neurosurgical procedure, the microscopic part actually is quite long and boring usually for us because once we get to that part of it . . . the patient usually is very stable. . . . It's nice to see where they are, how much longer are they going to be. Is he [the surgeon] still dissecting or is he [finishing] up? I don't have to ask the surgeon that.

Many anesthesiologists, nurse-anesthetists, circulating nurses, and neurotechnicians commented that watching the video was "interesting" and that it was much better than just sitting there with nothing to do. The video thus alleviates boredom and provides a focal point of attention that helps maintain shared awareness of the work being done by the surgeon.

This is critical because events can change very quickly during an operation. Suddenly what is seen on the video monitor can dictate that someone take action or that a new interpretation of an event applies. Operating-room personnel look for a variety of events such as the placement of a retractor or clip, where the surgeon is drilling, if there is bleeding, how close to a tumor the surgeon is. For example, a nurse-anesthetist explained:

Nurse-anesthetist: The anesthetic requirements [for] drilling through bone are different from the anesthetic requirements when they are working inside the head, where there are not pain fibers.

In this example, the actions of anesthesia personnel must be coordinated with those of the surgeon, and depend critically on what he is doing at a given moment in the surgical field. The video provides this information to anesthesia personnel.

Neurophysiologists and neurotechnicians interpret the graphs they watch on the computer display in concert with events shown on the video. One neurotechnician explained that they can "decipher the responses better" when they know what the surgeon is doing. For example, when a retractor is placed, a delayed response may result that should not necessarily be attributed to nerve damage, but may have been caused by the retractor itself. Interpreting the neurophysiological data is difficult because its meaning can be affected by signal noise, the type and amount of anesthesia used, surgical events, and random variation. The video provides an important source of information for making better inferences in a highly interpretive task. Again, the use of the video allows tasks to be coordinated appropriately by supplying neurophysiologists and neurotechnicians with critical information about the neurosurgeon's actions.

At a teaching hospital, education is of critical importance. Anesthesiology and neurosurgical residents and fellows, student nurses, and neurophysiologists- and neurotechnicians-in-training observe and/or take part in operations as a critical part of their education. While the neurosurgical resident or fellow uses the second 2D lens on the microscope to view the operation when the attending neurosurgeon is operating, others in the room watch the video. We observed students, residents, and fellows training at the hospital watching the video, and also visiting students, residents, and fellows from other hospitals. On several occasions they entered the operating room, parked themselves in front of the video monitor, and watched for the duration of the microprocedures (which may go on for several hours).

Because of the innovative and experimental character of the operations performed at the hospital, the operating room accommodates visiting neurosurgeons, anesthesiologists, and neurophysiologists from institutions around the world who come to learn about the new procedures. One of their main activities in the operating room is to watch the video.

Implications of Video-as-Data

The use of the video in the operating room is very different from the typical uses to which we imagine putting video. The neurosurgical team needs to view the *workspace*—that is, the data—on the video, rather than an image of a person talking. Video images of the workspace and work objects convey critical information about the work that enables tight coordination between members of the neurosurgical team and facilitates education. Team members, students, and visitors see lifelike images of the work objects and how they are changing and being manipulated. Video-as-data enhances task performance, rather than providing telepresence.

We were struck by the extent to which the use of video-as-data in the neurosurgical context serves a number of highly varied functions. The overall goal of the video is to provide a window into the unseeable world of the surgical field, but the uses to which the surgical information is put, and the way the information is gathered, vary greatly depending on the specific tasks associated with the differing roles on the neurosurgical team. As we have seen, the video image can coordinate fast-paced exchanges of instruments and supplies between neurosurgeon and scrub nurse; it can serve as a means of maintaining attention and focus over long stretches of time during which some team members are relatively inactive; it helps team members choose the correct action or interpretation depending on the event portrayed in the video; it educates a variety of medical personnel. The use of video-as-data in neurosurgery thus coordinates many activities all working toward a common goal.

Our study shows that the use of video in the neurosurgical context is quite different than standard notions of what it means to support collaborative work. Rather than facilitating direct interpersonal communication (as CSCW systems are often intended to do), in many crucial instances, the video in the operating room permits individuals to work *independently*, actually obviating or reducing the need for interpersonal communication. The video supplies enough information so that the need for interpersonal communication is reduced or eliminated, and individuals can figure out what they need to know based on the video itself, circumventing the need to talk to or gesture at someone. In the operating room, the provision of visual information at key moments provides a different channel of communication than that which would be provided through verbal, gestural, or written communication. Rather than facilitating collaboration through interpersonal interaction, the video itself informs operating-room personnel of the collaboration—in the sense of tasks that need to be performed to advance the work—that is needed. Collaboration and coordination are enabled as each member of the neurosurgery team interprets the visual information and proceeds to do his or her job based on an interpretation of that information. The video data, plus individual knowledge and understanding, combine to produce an interpretation that leads to the desired collaboration, with little or no interpersonal interaction.

There are parallels here to recent work on shared workspaces (Whittaker, Geelhoed, & Robinson, 1993). This work examined two-person telephone communication with and without the presence of a shared workspace, and two-person synchronous communication using shared drawing surfaces and documents for editing and design tasks (Whittaker et al., 1993). A key function of the workspaces in these investigations was that they served as a record of progress through the tasks, so that both participants could directly observe modifications and annotations to the document or design as changes were made. As with video-as-data in the operating room, this sometimes obviated the need for verbal interaction, because both participants could jointly see the changes made by the other. In addition, the other participant's actions such as turning a page in the shared document could be directly observed, without the need for verbal communication, so that people could always "see where they were" in the editing task. In contrast, for interaction using telephone only, participants were forced to make such actions explicit verbally.

Although the video image in the operating room sometimes obviates the need for interpersonal interaction, at other times the content of the video image becomes the basis for discussion and interaction, another aspect of its use as a shared workspace. For example, we observed a nurse-anesthetist in the operating room watching the video with a student nurse-anesthetist and describing to her the progress of the operation. Indeed, we ourselves profited from explanations in which the video was a key point of reference as operating room personnel educated us about many aspects of neurosurgery. Visitors, residents, fellows, and students also discussed what was being shown on the video monitor.

Video-as-data may change our sense of what it means to be "remote" or "co-located." In the operating room, even though people are co-located, the surgical field is remote, because it is invisible to anyone not looking directly through the microscope. The surgical field is accessible only through the video to most operating-room personnel. Thus it is not necessarily the location of people that is important in the video-as-data situation, but rather the location of the workspace. Aural information in the operating room, on the other hand, is not remote, so we have a situation in which the aural and visual have different values in terms of co-location. We can imagine other such situations; for example, the repair of a delicate piece of machinery with many small parts might be a situation in which a view of the workspace is remote, while aural information is not.

TOOLS FOR VIDEO

Our observations in the operating room persuaded us of the importance of video-as-data in contrast to an exclusive focus on "talking heads" video. Video-as-data has been used for many years in medical and industrial settings and has become indispensable in many applications. For example, in power plants, live video of remote locations is used to monitor plant operations (Tani, Yamaashi, Tanikoshi, Futakawa, & Tanifuji, 1992). Video is used in telerobotics and remote surveillance (Milgram, Drascic, & Grodski, 1990).

There are many exciting possibilities for extensions and enhancements to basic video capabilities. Milgram et al. (1990) developed a system that combines stereoscopic video and stereoscopic computer graphics so that users can point to, measure, and annotate objects within the video. Tani et al. (1992) proposed "object-oriented video" in which the real-world objects in the video become computer-based objects that can be manipulated so that users will be able to reference, overlay, highlight, and annotate them, as well as use the objects for control and information browsing. In Tani's prototype system for power plants, users can, for example, point to a burner on a boiler in the live video and bring up a document that explains how the ignition system of the boiler works. By pointing to a pipe on a live video they can view a graph that shows the amount of fuel running through the pipe. Users can get a more detailed video or related video of an object by pointing to the object, obviating the need to directly control remote cameras. Users can control remote devices through direct manipulation techniques such as clicking and dragging; for example, "pushing" a button on the video image engages a real button on the remote device (Tani et al., 1992).

Lieberman (1994) developed a system in which digitized video is used to allow domain experts to select and graphically annotate frames containing objects of interest in the operation of machinery, the assembly and disassembly of circuit boards, and so forth. Using programming by demonstration techniques, users describe the actions that represent transitions between frames. The video then runs to show the objects and procedures of interest. These techniques provide a way for experts to document operational and maintenance procedures for complex systems (Lieberman, 1994).

Work on interactive iconic annotation and visual parsing of video sequences is underway (Davis, 1993; Weitzman & Wittenburg, 1993), and such work is essential for making video-as-data an accessible and usable technology.

The application of iconic and object-oriented video would be especially useful for educational applications where students need to learn to analyze and not just passively view video images. If video-based educational software is to be more than just educational television, students need tools that will help them to actively engage the material they are working with. Once we see that video goes well beyond talking heads, we can begin to supply the kinds of tools that will take advantage of video-as-data, and that will make video into an interactive medium supporting analysis and problem solving.

For the medical application we studied, we found that recorded video is already used for classroom teaching and to review events in past operations. Integration of video with other computerized time-based data is the next critical step. Uniform storage, access, and presentation methods for data are needed. Means of visualizing complex relationships between data sets of varying types will support research and teaching. Medical personnel in our study underscored the need for future tools that will allow for the synchronization of video with other data sources, in particular the instrument data relevant to a particular specialty. Anesthesiologists, for example, want to see the video images synchronized with the physiological data they monitor such as blood pressure, blood gases, heart rate, pulse, and temperature. Such observations could be done during an operation, with video and instrument data they had just recorded. The synchronized data sets could also then be used for post hoc analysis, and for training purposes. Neurophysiologists want to see video synchronized with the many measures of nerve and muscle response that they monitor. Useful capabilities will include (a) "scrolling through" a video/instrument data set, and (b) finding a particular video event, or instrument event, or a particular time, so that users can then view all related contemporaneous data for the event or time.

Users would also like to be able to scroll through different data sets at different rates to capture latency in cause-and-effect relations between variables. For example, a neurophysiologist might want to scroll back through a videotape to find an event that took place a minute or two ago, such as the placement of a clip, which might just now be causing a reaction in the patient that would show up in the neurophysiological data seen in the plotted line graphs. Scrolling at different rates in different datasets might also be done in studying the recorded operation and related data, after the fact, to try to ascertain delayed effects of surgical events.

Again, it is easy to see how the provision of such analytical capabilities will have wide educational applicability in many domains. Students trying to understand complex relationships among many variables would have a vivid graphic image with which to visualize events. At the same time, the more abstract quantitative measures would be made more intelligible, giving students help with difficult concepts. Animation would be an interesting substitute for actual video in some applications where a video image is not available and a simulation is needed, such as a collapsing bridge. The idea of seeing the image as data to be analyzed against other variables is the same in both cases, and similar tools would be appropriate. It would also be possible to compare animated simulation information with actual video test data, that is, testing the data of the real object against the simulations run during the design phase. There are many exciting possibilities, then, for using video to analyze data and to support complex problem-solving activities. The integration of video-as-data with other data sources will be useful in many applications for analysis, training, legal, and archival purposes (Whittaker, Hyland, & Wiley, 1994). Users of such technology will want to be able to edit, browse, search, annotate, overlay, highlight, time-stamp, and display video data.

Of course, such manipulation of large amounts of relatively unstructured information presents a novel set of problems, particularly those related to indexing, search, and retrieval of video information. The user must be able to specify in a clear way what he or she is looking for. Unlike text systems and conventional database systems, where keywords to aid search may be generated automatically, keywords used today to describe the contents of video must be generated manually (but see Russell, 1994). This is labor-intensive and error-prone and may also introduce sources of bias as the description of content is subject to interpretation. For dynamically changing stores of video data, this task becomes particularly complex.

The alternative of content-based search and retrieval is promising, but remains an open research area. One needs to consider which features of the video information are represented, how these features are extracted, and how an index and search structure based on these features is computed. Often some level of user involvement is needed in the indexing; the effectiveness of the indexing mechanism, and the resulting level of ease with which a user can browse and navigate through the video information, may be thus dependent on the level of sophistication of the user.

One partial solution to the indexing problem for multimedia data is to analyze user activities during audio or video recording to automatically generate event-based retrieval cues. Research prototypes have been built to "co-index" audio or video with handwritten notes. Pen-based computer applications allow users to gesture at their original handwritten notes of a meeting, and have the system access video or audio recordings of exactly what was happening when that note was taken (Minneman & Harrison, 1993; Whittaker et al., 1994). Other techniques involve the construction of retrieval cues based on the intonational properties of the speech signal (Hindus & Schmandt, 1992; Arons, 1993).

Our findings about the importance of the ongoing use of video-as-data in a real work setting with demanding requirements (as opposed to brief experiments or testing within research labs) should encourage us to pursue our understanding of how video-as-data can be extended and used in other work settings. Within medicine, video is used in many kinds of surgery including orthopedic surgery, plastic surgery, and general surgery that employs microprocedures. Nonmedical applications of video-as-data could include monitoring and diagnostic tasks in complex mechanical or electrical systems such as a Space Station, power plants, or automated factories, and training for many aspects of using, designing, monitoring, and repairing such systems. Many companies, such as Xerox, use video to train people in the use of their equipment (Egido, 1990), and it is easy to imagine many training applications for video-as-data. Real estate agents might show properties remotely. Attorneys are making increasing use of video data in courtroom presentations. There are many potential applications for video-as-data.

AUDIO VERSUS VIDEO

We have described the function of the live video in the operating room. The broadcast video served the same purposes in the remote situation for the neurophysiologists. Now we would like to describe the use of the remote audio facility and compare video versus audio.

The audio channel provided additional information to the remotely located neurophysiologist trying to interpret the situation in the operating room. This information came from two sources: (a) what was being said in the operating room, and (b) the overall affective atmosphere in the operating room, as revealed by the audio. We look at each of these in turn.

There is often important conversation taking place in the operating room that is of direct utility to the neurophysiologist. As the neurosurgeon works, he often explains what he is doing or discusses his anticipated actions with the other neurosurgeon(s). Anesthesia personnel discuss the patient's physiological function. The neurophysiologist is better able to interpret the instrument data he is looking at by hearing the comments of the neurosurgeons which reveal the progress of and plans for the operation. The comments of the anesthesia team can also describe physiological information and help the neurophysiologist to anticipate what will happen next in the operation.

In many cases, the neurophysiologist actually has better access to what is being said when he is in a remote location than when he is in the operating room. Within the operating room, it is sometimes difficult to hear some of what is said because of the noise of equipment and conversations. In contrast, when listening to the audio in a remote location, one gets a clear transmission of what the neurosurgeons and the anesthesia personnel are saying, as they are positioned closest to the microscope (on which the microphone is mounted). One neurophysiologist explained:

> *Neurophysiologist:* In fact, the audio is better over the network than it is in the operating room because you can't hear what the surgeons are saying in the operating room. So if you don't know the case, you kind of guess what they're doing. With the audio, you know exactly what they are doing. Because they talk to each other about the steps they are going to take. So you can really anticipate what potentially might happen.

This is an example of "beyond being there" (Hollan & Stornetta, 1992), where at least one aspect of being remote is preferable to being colocated.

The audio also allows the remotely located neurophysiologist to hear what the neurotechnician is telling the surgeon and how the surgeon responds to that information. The neurophysiologist can see for himself what the neurotechnician sees on the graphs, but the response of the neurosurgeon is very important. The neurosurgeon may say that he's not doing anything that might be causing a problem, or that he doesn't understand the neurophysiological response, or that he will change an action he is taking. He may say nothing. These responses are of interest to the neurophysiologist.

The neurophysiologist may not agree with what he hears the neurotechnician tell the surgeon:

> *Neurophysiologist:* In that case, I heard the technician say something to the surgeon that I didn't agree with . . . [He] said there was a change in the response. There wasn't.

> *Interviewer:* . . . So what did you do, you called?

> *Neurophysiologist:* Called right away . . . Told the surgeon there was no change.

Here the audio information directly influenced the neurophysiologist's behavior: he telephoned the operating room to provide a different interpretation of the neurophysiological data than that given by the neurotechnician.

Other audio information provides an overall impression of the atmosphere in the operating room, information on how the operation is progressing. This information is of an emotive, affective type; the neurophysiologist infers a general sense of the conditions in the operating room. As one neurophysiologist said:

> *Neurophysiologist:* . . . What's the feeling in the room? The microphone is very close to the surgeon so I can really get a good feeling for whether he feels like the case is going well or not.

> *Interviewer:* When he is saying something.

> *Neurophysiologist:* Yeah, you can hear it from his voice. You can [also] hear how much activity there is in the room, whether the people are scrambling.

Here the neurophysiologist was listening for the emotional tone of the room as evinced in people's voices and the quality of their activity ("whether the people are scrambling"). Again, this information influenced his behavior, in this case his decision as to whether to go to the operating room from his office:

> *Neurophysiologist:* Well, if people are agitating, there's a lot going on. I probably would have a much lower threshold for going to the room because I'm alerted then that there's something going on in the room, and that's maybe an opportunity for me to make a significant contribution.

The neurophysiologists listened for situations such as a dead silence or nervousness in the surgeon's voice, which would indicate a problematic situation. On the other hand, what the neurophysiologist might hear was the radio playing and people telling jokes and having relaxed conversations. This would indicate that things were moving along nicely, according to plan.

Our preliminary findings suggest that the information from the remote audio concerning the course of the surgery, the surgeon's observed and anticipated actions, the content of key comments made by personnel such as the neurotechnician, and the overall atmosphere in the operating room allow the remotely located neurophysiologist to perform his job more efficiently and effectively. He can better plan and coordinate his visits to the operating room because he has richer information with which to decide when he needs to visit a particular operating room, or whether he wants to place a telephone call. If he does need to go to the operating room, he arrives with better information about the status of the operation. If the neurophysiologist is communicating with the neurotechnician via the telephone, the neurophysiologist has a better idea of what is happening in the operation because of the presence of the audio data.

One of the biggest differences we found between the remote audio and remote video was that the audio conveyed the emotive, affective side of the operation. This finding is in contrast to studies of videoconferencing such as those of Short et al. (1976) in which the visual images conveyed the more subtle emotional clues. In a sense this is not surprising since the video image of a brain or spine could hardly convey emotion, but it does show that we cannot assume a priori that any given communication channel will serve a particular purpose. During videoconferencing, participants read each other's facial expressions, gestures, and posture to gain additional clues to the information conveyed in the audio channel. People are making a conscious effort to use the expensive videoconferencing time to say what needs to be said, but there is more information that can be gleaned from an interpretation of faces and bodies. In the operating room we have almost a mirror image of this situation: The video channel conveys the "hard data" while the audio channel picks up on tension, humor, nervousness, and so forth, as conveyed in people's voices and activity patterns.

Taken together, we found that the audio and video in the broadcast facilities provided a much more complete picture of operating room activity than the neurophysiological data in the plotted line graphs alone: ·

Neurophysiologist: When you look at the computer data by itself [from a remote location], it seems to be one dimensional. When you add the rest of it [audio and video], you get a very rich picture of what's going on [in the operating room].

The use of remote multimedia facilities does not eliminate the need for neurophysiologists to be physically present in the operating room for at least part of the operation. Rather, it allows a reallocation of their time across operating rooms, offices, and conference rooms. The use of multimedia appears to give neurophysiologists more flexibility to move about the hospital on an as-needed basis, rather than to stay tied exclusively to a small number of operating rooms.

In the next section we continue our contrast of audio and video, but in the context of the privacy issues concerning the use of the multimedia system that arose during the period of our research.

PRIVACY IN COLLABORATIVE MULTIMEDIA SYSTEMS

Our assessment of the multimedia technology in the hospital is overall very positive, but there is a problematic side to it that cannot go unmentioned. Although many have pointed out the potential invasion of privacy inherent in the use of video (Mantei et al., 1991; Fish et al., 1992; see also Clement, 1994, on privacy in multimedia systems), in the hospital this became more than a possibility, as a situation of confusion and tension over the multimedia technology developed in which many misunderstandings and bad feelings arose. We describe the incidents related to the problem and suggest some potential remedies. We attempt to understand the nature of privacy concerns raised in the hospital, including concern over possible changes in the nature of communication within the operating room, fear of workplace video monitoring, and resentment over the way the multimedia technology was introduced.

Multimedia technology can facilitate collaboration in situations where people are not colocated, as we have described. This happens via a process in which information is taken out of its original context and presented in a different context. This very process reduces individual control over the kinds of information that people may consider private or personal. The context of information presentation and dissemination is suddenly radically altered; what was once an ephemeral event in a small, well-defined, visible space, with known participants, has now become a situation in which speech and action can be permanently recorded and/or broadcast live to remote, unseen, and possibly unknown viewers and/or listeners.

During the course of our research, we encountered a growing discussion about privacy in relation to the multimedia technology in the hospital. Early in the second phase of the data collection we attended a meeting that was convened to discuss the rising tensions over the multimedia technology. In attendance were anesthesiologists, nurses, neurophysiologists, and some members of our research team. Anesthesiologists and nurses aired grievances about the recording and live broadcast of audio to remote locations outside the operating room. The concerns expressed were varied, ranging from concern over malpractice suits to fear of "Big Brother" (a term we heard on several occasions) monitoring job performance. There was a great deal of confusion over which technologies were actually in use or about to be installed. It was felt by some that the design and installation of the remote audio facilities had taken place in bad faith, without considering the impact on those who did not benefit directly from the technology. As observers, we felt that some of the concerns were justified and some reflected political maneuvering and political cleavages from past hospital history.

As designers of technology we were concerned about the criticism of the technology articulated at the meeting and we scheduled a series of interviews with anesthesiologists, nurses, neurotechnicians, and neurophysiologists to discuss the issues in detail. An advantage of the ethnographic method is that unexpected but clearly important events can be followed up without feeling that a rigid study design is being violated. The privacy concerns inherent in collaborative multimedia technology are certainly not unique to the hospital setting and we were able to take the opportunity to find out exactly what concerned people in this environment. The most subtle and, to us, most worrisome concern expressed at the meeting, in remarks we heard in the operating room, and in the extensive interviews we conducted, was that the free and unfettered atmosphere in the operating room was being compromised by the remote audio broadcast. It was pointed out that both tension and boredom in the operating room are relieved by the relaxed talk and joking that often go on during an operation. During an operation the radio may be playing, the neurosurgeon may be making casual conversation, and informal side conversations are taking place. During one of our observations at a very routine part of an operation when everything was going exactly according to plan and the atmosphere was very relaxed, the resident asked, "Do you remember dead baby jokes?" It was not unusual for people to discuss topics such as movies they had recently seen, or to poke fun at some of the high-status doctors in the hospital not present in the room at the time. Such lightheartedness might seem quite inappropriate to those outside the immediate situation—such as a prosecuting attorney or the patient's relatives—but to the staff in the operating room it is a way to cope with an extremely demanding job and a rigid professional hierarchy. The banter and fun in the operating room provide social cohesion in a situation that is often stressful and that requires meticulous teamwork, as we have tried to document. A remote audio broadcast is surely a hindrance to establishing and maintaining an atmosphere in which people do not feel that they must censor themselves lest their comments be misunderstood or overheard by the wrong ears. By opening up the operating room to those beyond its four walls, the remote broadcast changes the nature of communication within the operating room in significant ways. We heard many statements of concern that the multimedia technology would suppress valuable communication in the operating room.

A related concern expressed by the anesthesiologists and nurses was that because students are in the operating room as part of their training, both they and their instructors might feel inhibited if unseen and possibly unknown listeners had access to their conversation. Students are already nervous enough when learning the difficult skills of neurosurgery, and comments such as an instructor remarking, "I can't believe you did that," might be open to significant misinterpretation on the part of those not present.

We tend to think of the visual part of video as being most revealing and hence potentially most intrusive, but in the hospital the broadcast audio was perceived to carry the most risk. One reason was that people felt that audio information could so easily be misinterpreted. Taking the information out of context was seen as being potentially damaging:

> *Anesthesiologist:* You can't distinguish between those two [a true problem and something that just sounds bad] on the audio. . . . It can sound terrible and not be, or the opposite. It can sound trivial and be horrible. And you get an incomplete picture without . . . an observer to fill in gaps. . . . What you have is something that could be misconstrued. People are concerned about many things—that real information can be misconstrued, that artifacts and abnormal information can get interpreted as truth, and that truth gets blown out of proportion. So it can be on all those kinds of levels.

There was much discussion of the legal implications of recording video within the operating room. These concerns are valid; recent court cases show that doctors and hospitals can and do lose cases because of interpretation (or misinterpretation) of the audio portion of video recordings. (The visuals on these videotapes of course show the operation itself, e.g., some portion of the patient's brain or spine, and attorneys do not attempt to interpret these images in court.) The hospital has been recording videotapes of operations for years, and the tapes go into a library maintained by the neurosurgery department. What drastically changes in the new situation with remote multimedia is that anyone at a remote node can record an operation (with the current low level of security in the analog CATV system) so it is no longer at the discretion of the attending neurosurgeon.

We found these concerns—communication style, student impact, and malpractice suits—to be well-motivated and reasonable in light of the kind of work performed in the operating room. Other concerns seemed to us to be more an expression of resentment over the way the remote audio and video facilities were installed, without consultation or buy-in from nurses and anesthesiologists. Although the neurophysiologists and neurosurgeons were in line to have the technology installed in their offices and conference areas so that they could remotely monitor several operations at once (neurosurgeons in an advisory role), the nurses and anesthesiologists were not. So they felt that not only did the technology not benefit them, it was to be used at their expense, and without their agreement. There were also issues concerning the manner in which the technology was introduced (see Grudin, 1988). Although those installing the system felt that they had informed the nurses and anesthesiologists, the nurses and anesthesiologists felt they had not. It is impossible to unravel the exact train of events now, but what is interesting is that some of the arguments advanced by the nurses and anesthesiologists against the multimedia technology seemed to stem from ill will aroused by their perception that they were being left out of the process.

We found that those in favor of versus those against the multimedia system (in its current configuration) were divided pretty neatly along professional lines. The nurses and anesthesiologists were against; the neurophysiologists and neurosurgeons were for. The neurotechnicians, who are closely allied with the neurophysiologists, expressed some mild annoyance over the broadcast facilities in private interviews, but on the whole supported the technology. Some spoke out in favor of it in informal exchanges with the study team.

The nurses, because of the nature of their jobs, do not stand to benefit from the remote broadcast facilities. They are at the lower end of the status hierarchy in the operating room, and thus they perhaps feel most threatened by the possibilities of the system. It was the nurses who worried about the multimedia system (or a future version) being used in a "Big Brother" capacity to monitor their job performance.

The anesthesiologists were an interesting case because they would like to have remote facilities for monitoring physiological responses, but they were not as far along in a separate development effort to create such a system, and they did not stand to gain directly from the current system. We noticed that they seemed to accept the utility of the technology, even though complaining about legal dangers and other issues, and they offered ideas for privacy safeguards (which we discuss in a moment).

Another argument that we heard against the use of the remote broadcast was that it would invade the patient's privacy. However, patients essentially sign away all of their rights to privacy in this setting, so this concern seemed somewhat manufactured. Individual doctors may go to great lengths to assure patient privacy, but legally, consent forms that patients sign remove rights. The recording of the video that has been going on for years in the operating room reduces patient privacy, yet patient privacy did not become an issue until the installation of the remote facilities.

We elaborate on the delicate political issues of these incidents not to dismiss the nurses' and anesthesiologists' complaints as politically motivated, but rather to suggest some possible remedies for future systems. We believe that the way the multimedia system was introduced in the hospital was less than optimal in two ways. First, it did not contain simple privacy safeguards such as an indicator showing when the video was being recorded. Second, and more important in our estimation, a serious, systematic, and thorough effort to inform staff of the benefits and features of the technology was not made. Many team members were genuinely puzzled about the utility of the remote audio broadcast. There was confusion about when the remote facilities were active, who might be listening at a remote node, when a recording would be made, whether both audio and video were recorded, and when new facilities would be installed and what they would be. Some of the nurses were not aware that their voices had been recorded on the videotape within the operating room as the tapes had been made over the years. The installation of the new multimedia system significantly raised awareness of, and concern over, not only the new system itself, but media capabilities that been in the hospital for some time.

In addition to the installed multimedia system, the neurosurgeons were considering the use of a wide-angle or "environmental" camera that would show the operating room itself and the staff as they worked. This bit of knowledge came out as gossip, not a formal statement to the staff. At the meeting on privacy issues it was stated that, "No one assumed an environmental camera would be a problem." The rationale for a wide-angle camera was given, vaguely, as "understanding the gestalt of the case." But an environmental camera is easily seen by almost any worker as a potential threat, and the idea of installing a camera with the ability to watch and record people as they work is clearly one that needs to be openly discussed. The offhand rationale invoking the "gestalt of the case" failed to explain the potential value of a wide-angle camera; rather, such a rationale suggested that staff input into decisions about the use of such cameras was not valued.

Of course, to a large extent we are looking at this problem with 20/20 hindsight and we see in retrospect that privacy concerns might be an issue with recorded and broadcast multimedia. But we present this case in detail because we believe we can learn from this experience for future projects. Thus we recommend that collaborative multimedia projects instigate some form of participatory design (Muller, 1993) in which those who are to be affected by the technology are systematically informed of, and contribute to, the design of relevant parts of the technology. Through a series of careful interventions with a skilled facilitator, those affected by a technology learn about and to some extent help to design the technology. Indeed, we saw this very process happen informally in the privacy meeting. Several suggestions for privacy safeguards were offered, such as a light showing when an operation is being recorded and an "on-air" light showing when the remote audio is being broadcast. It was suggested that the lights be placed not only in the operating room itself, but in the two hallways which have entrances into the operating room, so that people could mentally prepare themselves before entering the operating room. This is the kind of suggestion that can make a big difference to the success of a project, and that can only come from knowing the details of a particular situation, such as the layout of the operating room and the need to be prepared before beginning demanding work. This kind of site- and task-specific information is what participatory design techniques are good at discovering. In addition, through the process of negotiating the design of a system, people come to understand it more fully and feel less threatened by it. Participatory design allows concerns to be taken into account *before* they lead to the kind of tense situation we encountered in the hospital. An important lesson from our research is that for inherently social technologies such as collaborative multimedia systems, social and technical solutions must play together to utilize technology to its best advantage (see also Nardi, 1993).

There are other technical privacy safeguards that can be built into collaborative multimedia systems. In particular, it will be valuable for people to know which remote nodes are active at a particular time so that they will have some sense of who may be viewing or listening. This is an inexact solution, but certainly preferable to having no idea at all of who is part of the current context. A unidirectional microphone picking up only the surgeon's comments might also be appropriate. This solution does lose some data of interest to neurophysiologists, that is, picking up on the general atmosphere in the operating room and the sounds of the machinery, but it affords more privacy to the rest of the operating room staff. Such a trade-off might be appropriate in some situations. Alternatively, audio could be accessed via specific nodes for which access would be controlled by passwords or other security measures.

We noted that reactions to the multimedia system split out along professional lines. There was an important exception: One of the neurosurgeons expressed grave concerns about the technology. The neurosurgeon felt that its utility had not been justified while its legal ramifications were extremely serious. Like the anesthesiologists and nurses, he felt strongly that the technology had not been explained or introduced formally or appropriately. He expressed a sense of a loss of control because of the ability of those at remote nodes to record an operation without a neurosurgeon's authorization. He suggested the implementation of security measures such as passwords and locks on equipment at remote nodes. Although these solutions might seem obvious to computer experts, in the situation in which the system was being developed in the hospital it was not thought necessary to include such safeguards in the early phases of the project, even those as simple as "on-air" lights. Participatory design efforts might have channeled development energy into the security issues from the outset, showing good faith effort and allaying at least some concerns.

Because the audio portion of the multimedia system in the hospital was implicated much more than the video in notions of "public" and "private" during an operation, social solutions to privacy problems that allocate "public" and "private" times for audio broadcast and recording during an operation might be of use. (In another setting the video might be treated similarly.) In the hospital there seemed to be a fairly consistent view that certain phases of the operation—the critical phases—were appropriate for gathering and distributing audio information. Informal, personal conversation would not be taking place at these times and the spoken words of those in the operating room might be important for patient care. For example, a nurse-anesthetist observed,

> *Nurse-Anesthetist:* Anything that is directly related to the patient would be helpful. [Patient information is] more likely to be helpful to [the neurophysiologist] than us talking about, is it raining outside now? Or, what did they have for lunch today? Those kinds of things have very little to do with patient care whatsoever. What the surgeon is saying, what the neurophysiology technician is recording, seeing, and how he is communicating that to the surgeon, and how I am in between those two, and what dialogue takes place pertaining to a specific neurophysiological [event]—those things are pertinent and those things could be recorded without infringing upon anyone's rights.

These critical stages in the operation might well be viewed as *public* stages where all information was open to inspection and broadcast. Times before and after the critical stages in the operation, where personal conversation might take place, could be viewed as *private* times during which it would be appropriate to restrict distribution of audio information. It is possible that the agreement on conventions concerning public and private stages of the operation might be as effective as technologically based solutions to privacy concerns. Again, participatory design techniques exist that can help people to sort through such issues (Muller, 1993).

We must also face the fact that collaborative multimedia systems will in many cases reduce privacy and change the nature of communication. The possibility of being remotely monitored at all times while you are at your job is indeed a very serious one. It is unavoidable that we must accept the disadvantages as well as the advantages of the technology, if we choose to use it. People should understand that choices are being made; the use of any given technology is not inevitable. Through the application of participatory design techniques we hope that people can arrive at collective solutions with which the majority feels comfortable.

SUMMARY

We have described the use of video-as-data in a collaborative multimedia application. The promise of this approach is indicated by the application we studied in which the video image of a shared workspace served multiple but distinct functions in supporting complex teamwork. Many other activities, such as concurrent engineering and design that require distributed teams to coordinate, modify, and manipulate complex work objects, are likely candidates for the continued use of video-as-data. Future work should identify and refine these different applications of video-as-data.

Once we begin to view video as data, new analytic and display tools are required. We need techniques to directly manipulate video, in order to change the state of remote real-world objects (Tani et al., 1992). We also need techniques for annotating, indexing, and manipulating multiple streams of synchronized data. We can use these tools in educational settings to explain and depict relations between complex variables represented in different media streams and in research settings to analyze and discover underlying causal relations between variables.

Our study results suggest that we should broaden our view of audio beyond the simple transmission of verbal communications. In contrast to previous claims about the functions of audio versus video (Short et al., 1976), we found that remote audio was often used to judge the emotional state of the operating team, and video to supply hard data about the surgeon's actions and current state of the patient. We also found that provision of the video image often obviated the need for verbal interpersonal communication. Ambient audio proved of value in affording both local and remote team members access to gross aspects of patient functioning, such as heart rate, without having to read instruments directly. Thus, audio is a rich and varied communication medium whose potential goes far beyond simply carrying words.

Finally, care must be taken to preserve privacy in settings where audio, video, and data from real-work settings are broadcast to remote locations or recorded for future analysis. Study participants were concerned about the possibility of their work activity being broadcast to unseen and unknown observers. Fear of eavesdropping and/or unwished-for video recording may reduce the effectiveness of a collaborative multimedia system, impair interpersonal communication, and increase stress levels in the workplace. Steps should be taken to provide staff with feedback about precisely which data are being recorded or broadcast, when data are recorded or broadcast, and who is viewing or recording the data. The system should have appropriate security controlling who can view, listen to, or record data from remote nodes. Our experience indicated the potential value of the use of participatory design techniques for the development and installation of collaborative multimedia systems. The use of such techniques can serve to reduce participants' fears that they are being inappropriately observed and evaluated, and also to solicit their suggestions about how to better design such systems.

ACKNOWLEDGMENTS

Some of the material in this chapter was published previously in the *Proceedings of INTERCHI '93* (Nardi et al., 1993). We thank Erik Geelhoed and Bob Simon for their help with data collection. Steve Gale's previous work on the project was of great value. Robin Jeffries, Jim Miller, Vicki O'Day, Andreas Paepcke, and Dan Russell gave insightful comments on earlier drafts of the chapter. Bob Sclabassi facilitated our work greatly. At the hospital we thank the secretaries who helped us to track down and schedule interviews with peripatetic medical personnel. Our many informants in the hospital generously allowed us to follow them around, ask endless questions, and watch them for hours on end at their jobs. For their good cheer and thoughtful answers to our questions, we offer grateful thanks.

NOTES

1. This chapter is based on the article by B. Nardi, A. Kuchinsky, S. Whittaker, R. Leichner, and H. Schwarz (1995). Video-as-data: Technical and social aspects of a collaborative multimedia application. *Computer Supported Cooperative Work*. Reprinted by permission of Kluwer Academic Publishers.
2. The stance of recent media spaces applications is less clear about the role of video: Although media spaces work mainly emphasizes "talking heads" video, there is some discussion of using video to focus on objects or artifacts (Bly et al., 1993).
3. Our use of the pronoun *he* is for convenience's sake; any other construction would make it awkward to describe individual roles in the operating room. We alternate *he* and *she* as generics.

REFERENCES

Arons, B. (1993). Speechskimmer: Interactively skimming recorded speech. *Proceedings of ACM Symposium on User Interface Software and Technology* (pp. 187–196).
Baecker, R. (1993). *Readings in groupware and computer-supported cooperative work.* San Mateo, CA: Morgan Kaufmann.
Bly, S., Harrison, S., & Irwin, S. (1993). Media spaces: Bringing people together in a video, audio and computing environment. *Communications of the ACM, 36,* 28–45.
Buxton, W. (1992, May): Telepresence: Integrating shared task and shared person spaces. *Proceedings of Graphics Interface '92* (pp. 123–129). Vancouver, BC.

Chapanis, A., Ochsman, R. B., Parrish, R. B., & Weeks, G. D. (1972). Studies in interactive communication: I. The effects of four communication modes on the behavior of teams during cooperative problem-solving. *Human Factors, 14,* 487–509.

Chapanis, A. (1975). Interactive human communication. *Scientific American, 232,* 36–42.

Chapanis, A., Ochsman, R. B. , Parrish, R. B., & Weeks, G. D. (1977). Studies in interactive communication: II. The effects of four communication modes on the linguistic performance of teams during cooperative problem-solving. *Human Factors, 19,* 101–129.

Clement, A. (1994). Considering privacy in the development of multi-media communications. *Computer-Supported Cooperative Work, 2,* pp. 67–88.

Davis, M. (1993, August). Media streams. *IEEE Symposium on Visual Languages.* Bergen, Norway.

Dourish, P., & Bly, S. (1992, May): Portholes: Supporting awareness in a distributed work group. *Proceedings CHI'92* (pp. 541–547). Monterey, CA.

Egido, C. (1990). Teleconferencing as a technology to support cooperative work. In J. Galegher, R. Kraut, & C. Egido (Eds.), *Intellectual teamwork* (pp. 351–371). Hillsdale, NJ: Lawrence Erlbaum Associates.

Fish, R., Kraut, R., & Chalfonte, B. (1990). The videowindow system in informal communication. *Proceedings of the Conference on Computer Supported Cooperative Work* (pp. 1–12).

Fish, R., Kraut, R., Root, R., & Rice, R. (1992, May). Evaluating video as technology for informal communication. *Proceedings of CHI'92* (pp. 37–48). Monterey, CA.

Grudin, J. (1988). Why groupware applications fail. *Proceedings of the Conference on Computer Supported Cooperative Work* (pp. 85–93).

Hindus, D., & Schmandt, C. (1992). Ubiquitous audio: Capturing spontaneous collaboration. *Proceedings of the Conference on Computer Supported Cooperative Work* (pp. 210–217).

Hollan, J., & Stornetta, S. (1992, May). Beyond being there. *Proceedings of CHI'92* (pp. 119–125). Monterey, CA.

Ishii, H., & Kobayashi, M. (1992, May). ClearBoard: A seamless medium for shared drawing and conversation with eye contact. *Proceedings of CHI'92* (pp. 525–532). Monterey, CA.

Kuzuoka, H. (1992, May). Spatial workspace collaboration: A SharedView video support system for a remote collaboration capability. *Proceedings of CHI'92* (pp. 533–540). Monterey, CA.

Lieberman, H. (1994, August). A user interface for knowledge acquisition from video. *Proceedings AAAI.* Seattle, WA.

Mantei, M., Baecker, R., Sellen, A., Buxton, W., Milligan, T., & Wellman, B. (1991). Experiences in the use of a media space. *Proceedings of CHI'91* (pp. 203–215). New Orleans, LA.

Milgram, P., Drascic, D., & Grodski, J. (1990, August). A virtual stereoscopic pointer for a real three dimensional video world. *Proceedings of Interact'90* (pp. 695–700). Cambridge.

Minneman, S., & Harrison, S. (1993). Where were we: Making and using near-synchronous, prenarrative video. *Proceedings of the ACM Conference on Multimedia.*

Muller, M., ed. (1993). *CACM* [Special issue on participatory design], *36,* 4.

Nardi, B. (1993). *A small matter of programming: Perspectives on end user computing.* Cambridge, MA: MIT Press.

Nardi, B., Schwarz, H., Kuchinsky, A., Leichner, R., Whittaker, S., & Sclabassi, R. (1993, April). Turning away from talking heads: Video-as-data in neurosurgery. *Proceedings of InterCHI'93* (pp. 327–334). Amsterdam.

Noll, M. (1976). Teleconferencing communications activities. *IEEE Communications,* 8–4.

Noll, M. (1992). Anatomy of a failure: Picturephone revisited. *Telecommunications Policy,* 307–316.

O'Conaill, B., Whittaker, S., & Wilbur, S. (1993). Conversations over video-conferences: An evaluation of the spoken aspects of video-mediated interaction. *Human–Computer Interaction, 8,* 389–428.

Russell, D. (1994, August). Creating and using index links in multimedia documents: A simple knowledge-augmented approach. *Proceedings of AAAI-94, Workshop on Indexing Multimedia.* Seattle, WA.

Sclabassi, R., Leichner, R., Kuchinsky, A., Krieger, D., & Prince, F. (1991, January). The multi-media medical monitoring, diagnosis, and consultation project. *Proceedings of HICSS-24* (pp. 717–728). Kauai, HI.

Sellen, A. (1992, May). Speech patterns in video-mediated conversations. *Proceedings of CHI'92* (pp. 49–59). Monterey, CA.

Short, J., Williams, E., & Christie, B. (1976). *The social psychology of telecommunications.* London: John Wiley & Sons.

Tang, J., & Isaacs, E. (1993). Why do users like video: Studies of multimedia-supported collaboration. *Computer Supported Cooperative Work, 1,* 163–196.

Tang, J., & Rua, M. (1994, April). Montage: Providing teleproximity for distributed groups. *Proceedings of CHI'94* (pp. 37–43). Boston.

Tani, M., Yamaashi, K., Tanikoshi, K. Futakawa, M., & Tanifuji, S. (1992, May). Object-oriented video: Interaction with real-world objects through live video. *Proceedings of CHI'92* (pp. 593–598). Monterey, CA.

Weitzman, L., & Wittenburg, K. (1993, August). Relational grammars for interactive design. *IEEE Symposium on Visual Languages.* Bergen, Norway.

Whittaker, S., Geelhoed, E., & Robinson, E. (1993). Shared workspaces: How do they work and when are they useful. *International Journal of Man–Machine Studies, 39,* 813–842.

Whittaker, S. Hyland, P., & Wiley, M. (1994). Filochat: Handwritten notes provide access to recorded conversations. *Proceedings of the Conference on Computer Human Interaction* (pp. 271–277).

Chapter 24

Supporting Videoconferencing on the Internet

Jon Crowcroft
University College, London

This chapter is about the evolution of the Internet toward a system that can support videoconferencing and other applications that provide real-time interactivity. We describe the service contracts and techniques used to provide real-time delivery, and the routing needed to permit efficient multiparty communication, and look at some of the other pieces of the jigsaw that make these novel applications feasible and attractive.

INTRODUCTION

Internet-based videoconferencing has been in regular use since 1990. Ever since low-cost video capture hardware and audio input and output became common on desktop computers, people have tried using the same network they use for other communication to carry these continuous media (Casner & Deering, 1992; Huitema, 1992).

Initial use of audio and video (also known as "continuous" media) was constrained to multimedia mail through the Multipurpose Internet Mail Extensions (MIME) and other technology for enclosing more than plain text in e-mail, or information retrieved from a World Wide Web server. Because e-mail and Web pages are delivered "at leisure," there is not necessarily any need for high-capacity communication links unless a lot of users send a lot of MIME mail.

As it became apparent that long-haul parts of the Internet had the capacity to convey enough bits of audio and video per second to form

comprehensible sound and pictures, users started to use the net for interactive multimedia.

The current Internet (Clark, 1988; Leiner, Cole, Postel, & Mills, 1985)
was not designed for such traffic, and there have been a number of functional enhancements to the original architecture to make this both possible
and to make it attractive. This chapter is about these enhancements and
their deployment. It remains to be seen whether Internet-based videoconferencing takes off in a really big way, say as the use of WWW has. At the
moment, the jury is out (in fact, the jury is probably mainly sitting in
stockbrokers' offices using ISDN-based H.261 [CCITT, 1990] videoconferencing terminals).

A fictitious piece of the Internet is illustrated in Fig. 24.1, to show the
key components that provide the service, namely, links (whether local-area
networks or wide-area network lines), and routers interconnecting them.

In this chapter, first we look at the way the Internet provides communication and how that can be altered to meet users expectations for audio
and video traffic as well as ordinary data; then we look at the enhancements
that make it feasible for many people and programs to communicate from
one to many others simultaneously. After that, we look at the way that
computer-based multimedia traffic can adapt to varying network conditions, and how applications that have many simultaneous users can be
made adaptive. Then we consider the emerging model for how to ask the
network for guarantees about its performance. Following that, we look at
the aptly named "lightweight session" model for coordinating many-to-

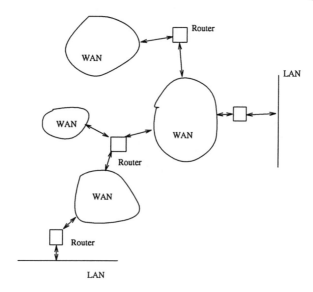

FIG. 24.1. A piece of the Internet.

many continuous media applications, and at how multiway applications can be controlled in the way that face-to-face meetings are controlled, or in other ways more flexibly. We wrap up with a look at the trade-off between timeliness and consensus in widespread multiway communications, and try to guess at where this is all heading in the longer term.

INTERNET SERVICE MODEL

The Internet was once intended to support multiple types of service (Cole, 1981), but this intent was lost in the mists of time as its most basic service model became hugely successful throughout the 1980s. This service model is the contract or, more accurately, the lack of contract that there is between the network and its users. A good analogy for a service model is that of a transport system: We do not expect the roads to take us to a destination. We expect them to allow us to drive there, and we expect a train or a plane to take us to a destination. These represent different levels of service guarantees. We can take the analogy further if we add that we have no expectation from the existence of roads about journey times, but we have an expectation from the existence of timetables for our train journey times (although the British reader could be forgiven for not taking this seriously!). Thus we can see that a service model refers both to the interface and to the performance that a system gives us. In this sense, it is more subtle and rich than most contracts.

In networks that are able to carry a range of different types of traffic from different applications, this contract is usually expressed in terms of a set of performance measures commonly known as *quality of service* parameters. (These might be more properly understood if they were called *quantity of service* parameters!) In its simplest form, one might express the applications in terms of whether each end was a human or a computer, and whether the medium was data, audio, or video.

For example, a file transfer is of data between two computers, whereas remote terminal access requires moving data between a computer and a human, an audioconference requires you to move audio between two (or more) humans, and so forth. The difference between human and computer reception lies in two places: the way human perception of sound and vision cannot be told to "wait"—there is a minimum rate for delivering continuous media (hence its name); and the way people interact—there is a maximum delay between utterance and comprehension above which natural "conversation" becomes impossible.

The Internet has no basic, widely implemented way of expressing these rate and delay parameters, qualitatively or quantitatively. This is because the very fundamental way that one accesses the network to convey anything from source to destination(s) is "without warning." Essentially, any computer connected to the Internet may attempt to communicate with any other computer(s) at any moment.

This is in direct contrast to traditional telecommunications networks used for example for telephony. The plain old telephone network requires users to do two things:

1. A receiver must put the phone on hook before . . .
2. A sender can call it.

This has the consequence that the telephone network gets a warning that a user wants to use it (and the opportunity to say "no"), and that once the network has said "yes," the receiver cannot be using up any more network resources (unless it has another line . . . but that is just like there being another receiver).

This means that the telephone network can be provisioned (*dimensioned* is another term used for this) easily for the expected number of calls at any time. Each call represents a fixed resource commitment. An unexpectedly high number of attempted calls (say on a popular holiday) can simply result in some calls being blocked (not getting through).

Another type of network beloved of telecommunications companies is what is called the *leased line.* This makes an even stronger commitment in terms of resource (and assumes an even stronger requirement for this guarantee) between the network and the user in that this is a service that is in place from when it is installed as opposed to when the call is placed. In other words, the opportunity to say "no" is not there after the lease has been signed.

The Internet model is commonly referred to as a "best effort" service. Each request to send is honored by the network as best it can. This works for communication of data between computers (usually), because the receiver can always wait for data that is late, and the sender can usually resend any data that is lost or distorted in transmission, however long it takes to discover this loss. This ability to cope with variable delivery rates and delays is often termed *elasticity.* If you picture the "communications pipe" between sender and recipient as a tube made of elastic carrying some liquid, then the delay and decrease in delivery rate is just like what happens if you stretch the tube.

The problems with using this type of technology to convey audio and video are twofold: that if the sender and/or receiver are humans, they cannot tolerate arbitrary delays; and if the rate at which video and audio arrive is to low, the signal becomes incomprehensible. Using the elastic pipe analogy, if a fire engine was trying to put out a fire with such a water pipe, whenever it got stretched too much, the water would arrive too little,

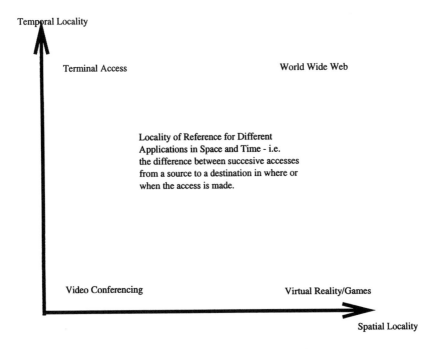

FIG. 24.2.   Temporal and spatial locality of reference.

too late. We illustrate the range of services in terms of the time or space between accesses to successive units of data in Fig. 24.2.

User Expectation and Service Models

The service model that a network provides has a profound effect on users' expectations. For example, users of the modern phone network expect that their phone call will very rarely be blocked (i.e., not get through), and furthermore that when they get through to the intended recipient, the call will practically never be dropped except by the receiver hanging up.

In contrast, the Internet users expect that they can always start an application, but that the quality of communication has no guarantee, and can vary between almost no throughput and very high delays, right through to perfect communication, with no apparent correlation between the behavior and their own actions.

This lack of expectation of quality has led to user acceptance of quite low quality audio and video communication, both in base level and in high variation of media quality and delay. This acceptance would seem quite surprising when compared with early experiments with video over phone-type networks, but is not so surprising given the users' previous experience of the highly variable performance of traditional Internet applications.

THE MBONE MODEL

The first major functional enhancement to the Internet that has made videoconferencing attractive has been the addition of *multicasting* (Macedonia & Brutzman, 1994). In a nutshell, multicasting is the ability of the network to efficiently deliver information to multiple recipients. The most useful analogy here is with TV and radio broadcasting. The electromagnetic spectrum ("ether") is divided into frequencies that are allocated by some authority to TV and Radio stations. These frequencies are then advertised in TV and radio listings magazines and so forth. Users then "tune in" to these frequencies by turning a dial on their set. If they have a smart set (or a TV and VCR with separate tuners) they can receive multiple stations.

The Mbone packet delivery model, illustrated in Fig. 24.3, is similar to broadcast, but superior. A multicast-capable host computer (or *host* for short) on the Internet that runs an application that receives multicast simply "joins" a set of receivers on the net, identified by a group address. As a side effect of the join, two things happen: The host reprograms its network interface to receive packets to the additional group address that is being used for this multicast. And the host informs all nearby routers of the fact that there is (at least) one recipient for packets to that multicast address.

Groups are distinguished by having separate multicast addresses (just as unique hosts are distinguished by having unique unicast addresses). Multicast address assignment is generally dynamic (although some addresses are set aside for well-known groups), and under the control of collections of the users. This is in contrast to frequency assignment in the electromagnetic spectrum, where the bandwidth (in the sense of number of different possible frequencies) is a scarce resource compared with the number of multicast internet addresses. In the radio and TV world, frequencies are assigned under global and national treaties and laws. In the Internet, there are some tools for multicast address management, which we will look at later. Again, it is instructive to compare the dynamic,

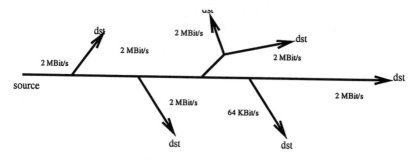

FIG. 24.3. Picture of Mbone.

soft/programmable nature of multicast groups with the more hardwired telephone networking models.

A host computer does not have to be in a multicast group to be able to send to it. Anyone, anywhere, at anytime (cue cocktail music) can send a packet to any group (in the time-honored Internet style!). Hosts can take part in multiple multicast sessions. It is up to the receiving applications to take care of whether they can deal with multiple receptions—for example, if you receive audio from multiple audio sessions, do you want to mix them and then play them out (to the confusion of the user) or let the applications allow the user to choose? Of course, if you are receiving audio from multiple sources sending to the same session, the user probably does want to hear them (although maybe not!). If you receive multiple video sessions, do you want to display the video in multiple windows, or let the user choose one or more sessions?

The routers in the Internet (the sorting offices or switching matrix glue that links everything together) that are capable of multicast use the location of groups or of senders to determine the delivery tree that is used to get packets from the source to the set of receivers. This tree is usually quite optimal in terms of the number of links that packets traverse. Packets are also not duplicated anywhere; they are only copied at appropriate points. We look at styles of delivery trees a bit more later. For now, imagine sending a memo to a group of people, but only having to print one copy at source. Then as the memo arrives at various sorting offices, if there are any local recipients, the sorting office puts the memo in the copier and delivers it to those recipients, saving on shipping a huge bag of copies from the original sender to all the sorting offices, but at some cost of copying along the way instead.

This model of packet delivery has had a profound effect on the way that application programmers have learned to construct multicasting programs. The tasks of figuring out who is in a conference, whether they are ready to receive or not, whether a user has the right to speak or not, and so forth are all moved to a completely separate level of the system because of this model. In other words, the Mbone multicast model is policy free in terms of call setup, floor control, membership control, activity and session information, and so on.

This is in direct contrast to existing models of conferencing. For example, in audiotelephony, the receivers must have their phones "on the hook." A particular caller must call them, one at a time, and add recipients to a conference call. Even if a phone bridge is used, the phone bridge needs to call each of the participants, and all of their calls typically go via the phone bridge. The way people have come to use Mbone conferences is in two styles:

1. The TV broadcast model is where a seminar or meeting is simply disseminated for anyone to see/hear.

2. The CB radio style is where users chat interactively and openly, coming in and out of a virtual meeting place as and when they like.

The addition of security/privacy features has also led to closed, more formally structured use, which we look at later. The popularity of this technology is indicated to some extent by the growth in the number of sites attached to the Mbone, as shown in Fig. 24.4.

It is instructive to think about alternative ways that group communication might be supported in a network. For example, we might put a list of addresses in a packet of information we wish to send to a list of recipients. This would work so long as the group was fixed and reasonably small, but would quickly become unmanageable for groups in the hundreds or thousands, which we already find in use in the Mbone. An alternative might be to employ a central distribution server where we send everything, and it "fans it out" to all the recipients. This would fly in the face of the entire Internet design philosophy, because it would be a central site, subject to failure and performance problems. Instead, the Mbone distributes both the group control and the data distribution tasks into the network.

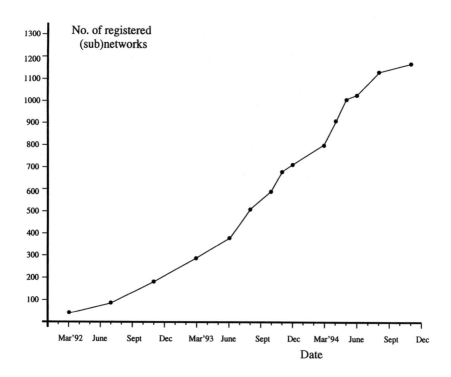

FIG. 24.4. Picture of Mbone growth.

Tree Topologies

The Mbone routing was initially based on the thesis work of Steve Deering (1989) and comprises two parts:

1. Tunnels. These are used to glue together Mbone sites that have multicast-capable routers but are separated by routers that do not support multicast, thus forming a virtual topology on top of the underlying Internet unicast routing. This has proved invaluable in this (and other) work in terms of deploying new versions of the routing.
2. Distance vector multicast reverse path (DVMRP) routing. This is the actual routing protocol, which is a natural extension to the age-old routing information protocol, using the paths that are calculated to get from a set of sources D to a particular destination, S for unicast, and as a way to get multicast from S to D.

DVMRP employs a scheme called pruning to eliminate branches from the network that do not contain members of a group whenever a source starts sending. As the Mbone has grown (in early 1995 it had 1500 sites, where a site might be a research laboratory or university campus, in 22 countries, internationally), there have been many groups that are small, and sparse. This has meant that the amount of routing control overhead from pruning traffic (and multicast traffic delivered unnecessarily to sites without members before they are pruned) has caused people to rethink the routing scheme. Several alternates have emerged:

- MOSPF (multicast extensions to the unicast routing scheme OSPF) allows aggregation of traffic and groups and also permits paths to be chosen based on different types of service.
- CBT (core-based trees) is based on a manager placing a "core" or center router appropriately in the network by calculating where the place is that all routing traffic would go through if we formed a minimal spanning tree from the center to all groups. This is a tricky calculation, and takes smart heuristics. It results in lower link usage than DVMRP, and doesn't need pruning, but it can increase the delays in paths between users, which may be critical for some kinds of multimedia interactions.
- PIM (protocol-independent multicast) is based on a mix of the ideas from CBT and DVMRP, and relies on the underlying unicast routing to calculate its paths. It is also capable therefore of exploiting underlying policies concerning routes, including potentially, type-of-service selection of paths.

The two extremes of multicast tree topology are illustrated in Fig. 24.5. At the time of writing, there is a great deal of research and development

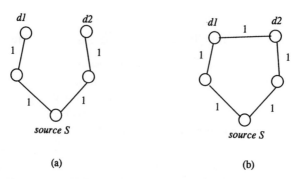

FIG. 24.5.   Center- and source-based trees.

in the area of multicast routing, and it remains to be seen what the main scheme will be. However, the power of the basic original Internet protocol (IP) multicast model is in no doubt.

ADAPTIVE PLAYOUT—COPING WITH VARIATION

As explained earlier, the Internet currently provides no guarantees. The throughput and delay along a path can vary quite drastically as other traffic comes and goes. When the network is overloaded, packets get lost leaving gaps in the information flow at a receiver. This is illustrated in Fig. 24.6. Two basic techniques have emerged to deal with these two problems:

1. Audio, video, and other interactive application receivers generally use an adaptive playout scheme.
2. Senders are generally adaptive to reported network conditions, falling back to lesser quality as the network becomes more highly loaded, and only, gingerly, increasing the quality and subsequent load as the network is perceived to have more spare capacity.

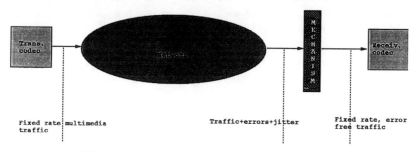

FIG. 24.6.   Adaptive playout, and adaptive transmitter.

The way these two techniques work is quite ingenious, but once seen, relatively simple (Jacobson, 1994). All sources that are generating information with time structure use a protocol called RTP, the real-time protocol, which places a media timestamp in each packet that is sent. All receivers use this timestamp for two purposes:

1. The interarrival time distribution is monitored. If the delay on the path varies, it will probably vary fairly smoothly, with some sort of reasonable probability distribution. By monitoring the mean difference between interarrival times, and adding this to a playout buffer that is used to delay sending thing between the receiving application and the output device (video window, audio, whiteboard, etc.), the receiver can be assured to a high degree of chance that it won't be starved of data ("run out of steam").

2. Receivers monitor gaps in the interarrival times (that correspond to missing data, as opposed just to, say, silence in an audio stream). Periodically, Mbone applications report the statistics about particular sources by multicasting a report to the same group. A sender/source can use this report to calculate whether the network appears congested or not. The scheme used to adjust the sending rate is basically that used in TCP (transmission control protocol), but must be implemented by degrading the quality of the input media for audio and video—many video compression schemes are easily altered to permit this. The total amount of traffic generated by these quality reports is constrained to be a constant percentage of any conference session (typically around 5%). The reason that this still works adequately to inform senders of network conditions is that as a conference grows, the number of samples of different parts of the net gets better and better, and hence the quality of information in fact improves, even though the quantity from any given receiver decreases. The receivers use the reception of other receivers reports to give an estimate of the number of receivers, and hence to reduce the frequency with which they send reports in a fully distributed way.

There are a number of tools that now exist, many in the public domain, that are in widespread use on the Mbone:

- From LBL: vic, vat, wb, sd is a full set of UNIX-based video, audio, whiteboard, and directory tools for Mbone conferencing.
- From Cornell: CuSeeMe/Reflectors is a set of MAC (and recently PC) based tools for unicast conferencing, but when combined with a reflector, which functions like an application level core-based tree Mbone router, they serve a similar function.
- From Xerox PARC, nv is a low-cost video tool, which works particularly well with slides.

- nevot is another UNIX audio tool from the University of Massachusetts.
- From the MICE project in Europe, IVS, Bat, Nt, and sdr are a set of UNIX-based alternates to the LBL tools.
- Imm is an image dissemination tool used to distribute weather maps received from satellites across the Mbone.
- Webcast is a tool for causing a number of World Wide Web client programs to synchronize which WWW pages they fetch at a time.

The audio and video tools are, as we have explained, loss tolerant, and can be made to adapt to variations in throughput (up to a point!) and delay. The whiteboard/shared editor type Mbone applications deserve a closer look.

Shared Applications in the Mbone

Shared applications that currently exist in the Mbone are what is termed *collaboration aware*, which is to say that they have been written specifically to be used by multiple simultaneous users, rather than simply being adapted through some kind of "wrapper," such as a shared windowing system with floor controller, to such use.

Wb and Nt represent a fairly radical departure from previous shared applications, in that they are engineered in the context of very large numbers of users (thousands) and over very long-haul networks, where there are very poor guarantees of full connectivity for the duration of a conference that is using the application, and where the capacity and delay from any given source to the group of users of the shared application may be varying by orders of magnitude.

To deal with this, the authors of both of these tools recognize up front that consistency of views for all users is a holy grail, and simply unachievable within finite resources. However, correctness of view should be possible up to some point.

The starting point for solving this is that an application-specific reliability is required, and that it is different for Wb and Nt.

Wb defines a set of operations that each user can carry out on the whiteboard, each of which is *idempotent*, or can be repeated without danger. The reliability in Wb is achieved through retransmission of missing operations. Again, to gain scaling to large numbers of participants, there is a very ingenious scheme to decide who requests a retransmission: Conventional schemes rely on recipients notifying senders of missing packets through negative acknowledgment packets or NACKs. However, a NACK/Retransmit style protocol would not scale, as typically, a loss that is incurred somewhere in the MBone might be perceived by entire cohorts of receivers when a subsequent operation arrives; an implosion of NACKs from all of them would then result. Wb uses multicast to its own benefit. All messages for all functions are always multicast. They also all contain timestamps, and all participants monitor their "closeness" to each other. When a recipient wishes to request a repair retransmission, they first "throw a dice" with a number of sides depending on how near they are to the source of the missing message, and wait for the time indicated by the dice. If they subsequently see a repair request from one of their cohorts, they suppress the timer that would otherwise have gone off and caused them to make the request. The Wb scheme is self-tuning, and works very well.

Nt is somewhat different, in that it is not a whiteboard, but a shared document editor ("network text"). Thus the operations by different users cannot be conveniently made idempotent. Nt attempts a stronger ordering than Wb, but uses similar schemes to achieve the repair. In the event of a partition of the network, followed by a healed network, Nt will offer the users a choice of which branch of the now disjoint edits to follow (or to revert to the prepartition version of the document).

INTEGRATED SERVICES MODEL

The Internet is not a static set of services and protocols, and there has been a great deal of effort since 1990 to add a broader range of services to the Internet model. The Integrated Services Working Group (Braden, Clark, & Shenker, 1994) of the IETF has now defined four classes of service that should match the vast majority of future applications (although the scheme is extensible, so that future applications which need new services are not excluded!).

The current four classes of service are:

1. Best effort. This is the "traditional" service model of the Internet, as described earlier, typically implemented through FIFO (first in, first out) queuing in routers.

2. Fair. This is an enhancement of the traditional model, where there are no extra requests from the users, but the routers attempt to partition up network resources in some fair share sense. This is typically implemented using a random drop approach to overload, possibly combined with some simple round-robin serving of different sources.

3. Predictive or controlled delay. This is where the delay distribution that a particular flow perceives is controlled. This requires the source (or a group where it is applied collectively to all sources sending to a group) to make some prestatement to the routers that a particular throughput is required. This may be rejected.

4. Guaranteed. This is where the delay perceived by a particular source or to a group is bounded within some absolute limit. This may entail both

an "admission test" as with group 3, and a more expensive forwarding queuing system.

These classes of traffic are roughly in line with those developed in the broadband integrated services digital networks (ISDN) standards communities (the ITU and ATM Forum), for ATM (asynchronous transfer mode) networks. They define the equivalent services in terms of the bandwidth rather than delay model, but the intent is similar. UBR, ABR, VBR, and CBR stand for *unspecified, available, variable,* and *constant bitrate* services, respectively. ATM is seen in some quarters to be the multiple service network of the future. It is clear that it is able to convey roughly the same services as are being devised for IP, which should lead to the possibility of layering one service on the other fairly easily.

The separation of these service classes is important, because the billing model of the network is related to the service model. For example, elastic services such as those we have traditionally used in the Internet do not require a usage charge for traffic that gets no guarantees. However, when an application needs or asks for guarantees, there is a requirement to present some feedback to prevent everyone idly asking for the maximum guarantee (so that the network can make an informed decision). This feedback can most easily be provided by billing, although some researchers assert that it is only necessary to actually incur a charge when the network would be unable to meet all the current requests, rather than whenever people make a request. This is analogous to billing people for road use during congested periods, and not at other times, and billing people with larger cards more so as to adjust the demand.

This aspect of the Internet is relevant to considerations of videoconferencing, because it may well be that large parts of the Internet will not permit such applications until either reservation or billing or both are in place as new technology.

RSVP

The protocol that has been devised to establish a reservation in the network for particular flow classes is called the Resource ReserVation Protocol, or RSVP (Zhang, Braden, Estrin, Herzog, & Jamin, 1994). It might be more accurate to describe it as a dual-function protocol that serves to install knowledge about classes of traffic in the network (a filter specification) as well as what particular type or quality of service that these flows will need (a flow specification). This separation is important, as the filter specification can be reused in a number of ways.

The simplest way that the filter specification is reusable is the fact that it can refer to a flow received by an application, rather than to one that is sent. This means that a sender can send video at a rate convenient to the sender, but receivers can select the subband rates that are most convenient to each of them. This receiver-based reservation is quite different from the telephony model of how to do things, and fits well with the multicast model of the Mbone—it is a bit like the way people can choose what size TV screen they have, independent of the TV transmitted signal (or choose whether the TV is color, or black and white, or has mono or stereo audio), The second way that the filter generalizes the idea of a reservation is that it can include a "wild card," so it can refer to groups of sources. For example, in an audio conference, there is no necessity to set aside resources for all the audio feeds at once, because humans are typically capable of organizing themselves in a conversation so that there is only one (or one and a bit!) person speaking at any one time. Hence, sources will ask for reservations that are only marginally more than a unicast audio reservation for a multiway audio conference on the Mbone.

Flow specifications are cast in terms of the class of service, combined with the quantitative parameters as needed. For example, a mean rate combined with a burstiness (also known as "leaky bucket" parameters by analogy with a water bucket with a given volume and size of leak) suffices to characterize many applications.

Future versions of the Internet protocol will incorporate tags (known as flow identifiers) to make the classification of packets by newer routers a more efficient task. Again, the flow identifier has been designed with possible future bearer networks such as ATM in mind. Thus it is 24 bits in size, just as the VCI/VPI field is in ATM used for roughly the same function.

LIGHTWEIGHT SESSIONS

The advent of the Mbone has led to the separation of the protocols used for conference media streams from the protocols used to set up and control various aspects of a conference, as mentioned earlier, such as membership, session information, media activity, floor control, and so on. But the usefulness of the IP multicast service has made itself felt in the control protocols too. A number of sites have used multicast as the way to disseminate control information within a conference. Again, as with the media streams, the advantages in terms of scalability are manifold.

Alongside the multicast group used to carry the media themselves, another associated multicast group can be used to disseminate this control information. The model is that of a computer bus, on which messages can be placed, and received by any device attached to the backplane. This "bus model" is used in two related ways:

1. The LBL tools (Jacobson, 1994) use this as a local bus, to distribute information between applications at a given site to coordinate the control activities that are common. For example, if a user runs a video, audio, and a whiteboard application, there is little point in each of these applications sending activity messages separately. They can be combined. Also, when a user is participating in multiple conferences, the coordination of ownership of devices such as exclusive use audio input and output can be carried out through messages on the local conference control bus.

2. UCL (University College London) researchers have carried this and the basic wide-area session message use of multicast to a general extreme, where the entire Mbone is used to coordinate all conference control messages using a conference control channel. This is illustrated in Fig. 24.7 as the multicast control bus.

The local bus can also be used to carry out receiver synchronization, If a machine is receiving different media streams with different delay variations that belong in the same session, then the adaptive playout buffer sizes can be exchanged by multicasting their status on the local Mbone (local to the receiver machine only), and used to add in a constant so that all streams are played out in synchronization, with no need for any complex end-to-end protocol to carry out complex delay-bound calculations, as are used in many other systems.

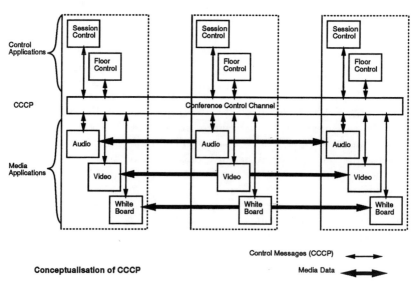

FIG. 24.7. Multicast control bus.

Mbone Session Directories

The growth in the Mbone has led to some navigation difficulties (just as there are in the World Wide Web, and in Usenet News Groups). This has led to the creation of a session directory service. This has several functions:

1. A user creating a conference needs to choose a multicast address that is not in use. The session directory system has two ways of doing this: First, it allocates addresses using a pseudo-random strategy based on how widespread the conference is going to be according to the user, and where the creator is; second, it multicasts the session information out, and if it detects a clash from an existing session announcement, it changes its allocation. This is currently the main mechanism for the management of allocation and listing of dynamic multicast addresses.

2. Users need to know what conferences there are on the Mbone, what multicast addresses they are using, and what media are in use on them. They can use the session directory messages to discover all of this. The latest versions of multicast include a facility for administrative scoping, which allows session creators to designate a logical region of interest outside of which traffic will not (necessarily) flow. This is mainly used to limit the network capacity used rather than as a privacy enhancement, because there is little guarantee that someone does not subvert the Internet multicast routing anyhow, so it cannot give a guarantee of protection against accidental or deliberate disclosure. It can, however, protect cooperating users and sites from being overrun by irrelevant video and audio traffic.

3. Furthermore, the session directory tools currently implemented will launch applications for the user.

CONFERENCE CONTROL

Conference control (Schooler, 1992) refers to the set of tasks concerned with managing the tools that mediate between users. This includes controlling access and membership, controlling starting and stopping media including coordinating this with any floor control mechanism, reporting activity by a user of a given media type, and so on.

Early conference control systems in the Internet were modeled around telephony and the T.120/T.GCC style of management, where each and every control action is specified for a unique participant, and each and every action is specified to each and every participant. Such systems were targeted at closed, secure, managed, and generally floor controlled (chaired) conferences. Often, the conference control architecture was dictated by the low-level network call control model, or even by the media distribution technology (as with MCU-based T.120-based videoconference systems).

The Mbone style of conferencing separates out this functionality, but in no way precludes using tight coupling of control actions, participants, and media. Indeed, the use of the local- and wide-area bus model to propagate control actions leads naturally to efficient scaling of all styles of conference. Yet again, we note the user expectation is of potential dynamics in membership, and quality of conferences. This is an advantage over hardwired groups and quality, because it is less constraining to designers of conferencing tools. They can always add constraints later. The use of multicast for conference control is shown in Fig. 24.8.

CONSENSUS AND THE MBONE

When we discussed the Mbone conference control and media delivery models, one of the claims made was that they scaled well for systems with large numbers of participants over very large networks, in the face of partial failures. Of course, this means that there are (at least temporary) inconsistencies that may be perceived by users. Luckily, humans (unlike bank

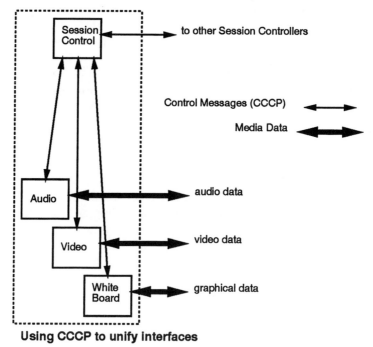

Using CCCP to unify interfaces

FIG. 24.8. Loose and tight conference control using CCCP.

managers) are quite capable of holding inconsistent views temporarily, and waiting for conflicts to resolve, so this is not necessarily a show stopper.

Unreliability and human tolerance work surpassingly well in the experience of many Mbone users. Ordering and human frailty may be a problem for some classes of user, though. For example, a distributed auction system would not be feasible using a scheme that did not constrain bids (and video/audio from bidders) in the correct order. In a large-scale system, it may be that this is only achievable at a very large cost. There has been quite a bit of research on reliable and on ordered reliable delivery multicast protocols, and the work at Cornell on Isis and Horus is particularly relevant. The most recent transport level work is that at Berkeley for NASA, and we look briefly at that next.

RMP

The reliable multicast protocol (RMP) is a multiservice protocol with the goal of supporting a range of services on top of the Internet Mbone delivery service. RMP supports various types of ordering, and organizes participants into virtual topologies to achieve levels of reliability. It remains to be seen whether a single protocol can carry out the very broad range of services that we have so far outlined.

Security

An often expressed concern about the Mbone "open channel" model of conferencing is that it is not secure. This is in fact simply not the case. Privacy and authentication are end-to-end functions, and whether media and media control are unicast or multicast is not relevant (Ballardie, 1995). There are only a couple of consequences of the fact that Mbone conferencing uses multicast:

1. Because this encourages multiway videoconferencing, there is a greater need for multiparty key distribution. Typically, this means that an asymmetric key system is needed such as PKC based on RSA or PGP.

2. Traffic analysis and denial of service, two threats to security that are often overlooked, are potentially easier with a multicast network. It transpires that the very techniques used to provide better resource guarantees (RSVP and integrated service IP routers) can prevent the denial of service attack. Traffic analysis may be a little harder to prevent in a multiprovider Internet. Generally, it may be that sites will use random traffic from other sources, and perhaps route their traffic so it appears to source from different entry points to the net (perhaps different RPs or cores in the multicast routing system), to avoid analysis. It remains to be seen if this is a serious threat.

WHERE NEXT?

There are two remaining problems to be solved in Internet videoconferencing research. One is concerned with the traffic service model and the other with the final scaling requirements for delivery of media and control messages.

One extreme view of future network evolution is that the capacity will simply be overprovisioned. Thus reservations will be unnecessary, and it will be adequate simply to state whether an application is elastic or needs a delay distribution with some bound (Mackie-Mason & Varian, 1993). In fact, an even more extreme view is that all applications are elastic in some sense, especially when audio and video applications are becoming more and more adaptive. In the future, processing power and intelligence might be sufficient that as bandwidth becomes scarce, very extreme forms of compression might be employed: For example, model based video entails sending coordinates of the features in a scene, and recreating and animating the scene accordingly at the receiver. Voice recognition (VR) techniques will make this easier. Similarly, speech recognition means that at worst, speech can be turned into phonemes, or even text, and sent at two orders of magnitude less bandwidth than a basic voice call.

Scaling conferences to millions, so that interactive Internet-based videoconferencing could replace bulletin boards, and perhaps be used for such large-scale social phenomena as participatory democracy (rather than representative democracy), is another vision held by some Internet proponents.

There is a more mundane school of thought that says that the telecommunications networks (ISDN- and ATM-based technology) are more suited to proper provision of services for voice and video. There is no particular evidence for this, because any valid comparison of installed base should include cost, and it is certainly the case that ISDN-based videoconferencing equipment is extraordinarily expensive (still), whereas the Internet technology is "cheap and cheerful." Just which way everyone jumps remains to be seen.

FURTHER READING

1. Service Model.

David D. Clark (1988, August.) The design philosophy of the DARPA Internet protocols. *SIGCOMM Symposium on Communications Architectures and Protocols* (pp. 106–114). Stanford, CA.

2. The Mbone.

Michael R. Macedonia and Donald P. Brutzman (1994). MBone provides audio and video across the Internet. *IEEE Computer*, April, 30–36.

3. The Internet Integrated Services Model.

R. Braden, D. Clark, and S. Shenker (1994). *Integrated services in the Internet architecture: An overview.* 1633, June 9. Los Angeles: ISI.

4. RSVP.

Lixia Zhang, Stephen Deering, Deborah Estrin, Scott Shenker, and Daniel Zappala (1993). RSVP: A new resource ReSerVation protocol. *IEEE Network, 7,* 8–18.

5. Lightweight Sessions.

Van Jacobson (1994, September). Tutorial. *ACM SIGCOMM Conference.* London. http://www.cs.ucl.ac.uk/mice/van.

Sally Floyd, Van Jacobson, Steve McCanne, Ching-Gung Liu, and Lixia Zhang (1995, September). A reliable multicast framework for light-weight sessions and application level framing. *ACM SIGCOMM 95.* Cambridge, MA.

6. Conference Control.

Eve M. Schooler (1993). Case study: Multimedia conference control in a packet-switched teleconferencing system. *Journal of Internetworking: Research and Experience, 4,* 99–120.

Handley, Wakeman, and Crowcroft (1995, September). The conference control channel protocol. *ACM SIGCOMM 95.* Cambridge, MA.

7. Consensus.

Scott Shenker, Abel Weinrib, and Eve Schooler (1994, November). Managing shared ephemeral state: Policy and mechanism. *Proceedings of the International Workshop on Multimedia Transport and Teleservices (COST237).* Vienna, Austria.

8. Reliable Multicast.

S. Armstrong, A. Freier, and K. Marzullo (1992). *RFC 1301, Multicast transport protocol.* February 19.

Paliwoda, K., and Crowcroft, J. (1988, August). A reliable multicast transport protocol. *ACM SIGCOMM.* Stanford, CA.

http://research.ivv.nasa.gov/projects/RMP/RMP.html.

Todd Montgomery <tmont@cerc.wvu.edu NASA/Berkeley, Concurrent Engineering Research Center.

9. Security.

T. Ballardie and J. Crowcroft (1994, October). *Multicast-specific security threats and counter-measures.* ISOC.

Proceedings, ISOC Symposium on Network and Distributed System Security (1995).

REFERENCES

Braden, R., Clark, D., & Shenker, S. (1994, September). *Integrated services in the Internet architecture: An overview* (RFC 1633). Network Information Centre, SRI International.

Casner, S., & Deering, S. (1992). First IETF Internet Audiocast. *Computer Communications Review, 22,* 3.

Clark, D. (1988, August). The design philosophy of the DARPA Internet protocols. *Proceedings, ACM SIGCOMM.* ACM. Stanford, CA.

Cole, E. (1981, August). PVP—A packet video protocol (USC-ISI Tech. Rep.). USC-ISI, Los Angeles.

CCITT. (1990). *Video codec for audiovisual services. Consultative Committee for International Telephone and Telegraph/H.261.* Geneva: Author.

Deering, S. (1989, January). *Host extensions for IP multicasting* (RFC 1112). Network Information Centre, SRI International.

Huitema, C. (1992, June). *Software codecs and work-station video conferences* (INET92). Internet Society, Kobe, Japan.

Jacobson, V. (1994, September). *Multimedia conferencing on the Internet.* ACM SIGCOMM Tutorial. London.

Leiner, B. M., Cole, R. H., Postel, J. B., & Mills, D. (1985, March). The DARPA Internet protocol suite. *Proceedings IEEE INFOCOM.*

Macedonia, M., & Brutzman, D. (1994). MBone provides audio and video across the Internet. *IEEE Computer, 27*(4), 30–37.

Mackie-Mason, J., & Varian, H. (1993). Some economics of the Internet. In *Networks, infrastructure and the new task of regulation.* Cambridge, MA: MIT Press.

Schooler, E. (1992, November). The impact of scaling on a multimedia connection architecture. *Proceedings of the Third International Workshop on Network and Operating System Support for Digital Audio and Video.* ACM, San Diego, CA.

Zhang, L., Braden, R., Estrin, D., Herzog, S., & Jamin, S. (1994, July). *Resource ReSerVation Protocol (RSVP)—Version 1 functional specification, Internet Draft.* IETF RSVP Working Group.

Chapter 25

Prospects for Videotelephony[1]

Robert E. Kraut
Carnegie Mellon University

Robert S. Fish
Bellcore

This chapter evaluates the likelihood that a videotelephony service could be commercially successful, in the face of the long history of failure that telecommunications and computer companies have had in offering videotelephony products. With recent improvements in algorithms for video compression, VLSI implementations that reduce the cost of video compression equipment to levels that small businesses and consumers can afford, industry's agreement on standards for video coder–decoder interoperability, and the availability of telecommunication transport services at data rates that support video transmission, the technological prerequisites for videotelephony will be largely met in the United States by the turn of the century or sooner. Although businesses might consider videotelephony because it supplements voice communication, with rich nonverbal images of the talking parties, this extra information is not the main value of video. Rather, the visual channel seems to have greater value for tasks with a major social component, and complex, ambiguous, or conflictive tasks. In addition, in business telephony can extend beyond interpersonal communication, including the use of video as data, to access multimedia services, and to sustain organizational awareness. In homes, video might be especially valuable to support routine social calls, with local calls most common, such as the daily chats of teenagers. As a result, videotelephony might be more valuable in a residential than in a business setting, because it is precisely these social functions for which the video channel seems best suited. However, concerns about privacy are likely to be more pronounced in residential settings than in business ones.

541

INTRODUCTION

The goal of this chapter is to help understand whether future videotelephony services can be commercially successful. Recently, Noll (1992) reviewed the history of AT&T's experience in offering several videotelephony services, all of which failed. He concluded from this history that people have no use for audiovideo interpersonal communication, and widespread use of videotelephones is unlikely ever to succeed. "[I]t seems very clear that AT&T's PicturePhone service failed not because of . . . any . . . technological factor, nor because of inadequate marketing efforts or price, but for the simple reason that most customers had no applications for it." Discussing the current generation of videotelephony, he observed that "there is nothing new in these recent attempts at reinventing PicturePhone for face-to-face video communication: they will only replicate the past with the same results: namely, market failure" (p. 315).

Our reading of the evidence, however, makes us skeptical of Noll's strong negative conclusions. We don't predict success for videotelephony, but its future is far more uncertain than Noll's analysis suggests. The growth of the videoconferencing market, recent successful field trials of videophone service in business settings, and experimental studies comparing visual communication to other forms all suggest conditions under which videotelephony is desirable. The first section of this chapter reviews the evidence about the value of videotelephony.

Our assessment is that the success of videotelephony will depend only moderately on whether customers have a compelling, instrumental application for it: The evidence suggests that many customers seem to enjoy the increased social sense that videotelephony provides, and that its value is as much esthetic as utilitarian. Rather, success will depend more on economic, quality of service, and social issues. Will terminal costs and usage charges be low enough to justify the modest benefit that people derive from the service? Will telecommunications companies, through their sales and advertising efforts, target the social uses for which video is best suited? Will the quality of the audio in video calls be high enough? Will videotelephony be integrated with the voice telephone network, so that subscribers have a critical mass of calling partners? And will residential customers and privacy advocates tolerate new communication norms, which may result from visual communication? The second section of this chapter examines some of the technological and service features that might shift the value of videotelephony service.

Throughout this chapter, we differentiate the use of videotelephony in business and residential settings for two reasons. First, the evidence about uses of visual communication and demand for it is much more complete for business settings than for residential ones. And second, there is reason to think that the typical uses, demand, and willingness to pay will be different in the two settings. We conclude that given appropriate price and privacy policy, it is within the residential market that videotelephony is most likely to succeed. Yet we acknowledge that conclusions about the residential environment are much more speculative than conclusions about the business one.

The Use of Video in Business Settings

Use. A substantial body of research over the past decade suggests that people can quickly adapt to videotelephony, that they enjoy using it, and that, depending on the quality of the particular implementation, they find it more natural than voice telephony and prefer audiovideo communication to audio-only communication when they have a choice. On the other hand, video by itself adds little to what people can do in a conventional phone conversation. People treat calls in which they can talk to and see each other very similarly to calls in which they can only talk to each other. Other chapters in this book presented the research on which these conclusions are based, so we only briefly sketch the evidence here.

Recent field experiments reviewed in Part II of this book have shown that when people have videophones on their desks and a sufficient population of others to call, they use the videophones frequently, on a daily basis, and virtually abandon their voice phone for those calls where the videophone is an alternative. Research on the Cruiser™ system from Bellcore is typical of the recent findings (Fish, Kraut, Root, & Rice, 1993, and unpublished follow-up evaluations). Over 100 employees of a research laboratory used a prototype desktop videophone system for many months. These users placed multiple calls per day to their most frequent communication partners. They used the videophone to call people who were within their own workgroups, who were physically close by, and with whom they communicated most over other media.

The popularity of video calls in diverse field experiments strongly suggests that organizational members routinely used videotelephony because of the intrinsic value they received from having a visual communication service. This conclusion contrasts with those from trials of AT & T's PicturePhone product in the mid-1970s, which suggested when people used those videophones, they did so for extrinsic reasons—because the videophone was answered sooner or was less likely to be busy than a conventional telephone (Noll & Woods, 1976). Most of the recent field experiments have involved professional employees from research and development companies and universities. Although one should be cautious about generalizing from their experiences, the experiences certainly contrast with the negative portrayal of use that Noll painted.

Value for Interpersonal Communications. If people in field trials use video-phones frequently, what value are they receiving from them? Research on this question started with Chapanis's studies of the early 1970s (e.g., Chapanis, Ochsman, Parrish, & Weeks, 1972; Williams, 1977) and have continued to the present day (e.g., Clark & Brennan, 1991). Much of the research and theorizing focuses on the way that video changes the amount and quality of information exchanged in a conversation.[2] Studies that have examined users' judgments about the tasks for which visual communication is valuable and experimental studies that have compared actual use across different media come to similar conclusions. For many tasks, videophones are equivalent to voice phones. Adding interactive voice to any communication medium has more profound influences on judgments and communication performance than adding a visual component (Williams, 1977).

The differences that do exist between voice and videotelephony depend on task and how the video is used. There are some tasks, for example, showing physical objects, for which videotelephony is obviously better suited than voice telephony. Indeed, both early marketing research by AT & T and more recent theorizing on the coordination of conversation (Clark & Brennan, 1991; Kraut, Miller, & Siegel, 1996; Whittaker& Geelhoed, 1993) suggest that video is more valuable when it shows the object of a conversation rather than the participants in it. Even the early AT & T videophones had an option to use the camera to show documents.

But most commercial videophones assume a "talking heads" model and focus their cameras on the conversational participants. Even under these conditions, the value of video depends on the task. Judgment studies show that both videotelephony and conventional audio-only telephony are evaluated as adequate for routine information exchange activities—checking on project status and exchanging information of various types. As the tasks became more socially sensitive (e.g., getting to know someone) or intellectually complex (e.g., explaining a difficult concept), videotelephony is often judged to be superior to the audio-only telephone (Fish et al, 1993; Zmud, Lind, & Young, 1990).

Experimental research, in which pairs and small groups engage in tasks using audio-only or audiovisual communication, leads to similar conclusions. Performance on information exchange and referential communications tasks is very similar whether pairs converse via audio-only or audiovisual communication systems (Chapanis et al., 1972; Krauss & Fussel, 1990; Short, Williams, & Christie, 1976). On the other hand, differences are more pronounced in tasks involving conflict or explicitly social motives. Compared to audio-only conversations, audiovideo conversations are more personalized, less argumentative, and broader in focus, and groups conversing over them tend to like each other more and are more likely to reach consensus easily. In negotiation or persuasion sessions, the negotiation is more gentle, and agreements tend to be influenced by the personalities of the bargainers rather than being dominated by the merits of the argument (Williams, 1977).

New Uses of Videotelephony. The experimental studies just reviewed asked how discrete conversations differ when they are conducted over audiovisual channels rather than over an audio-only channel. In contrast, recent field experiments, described in Part II of this book, in which communities of users have video networks available for months at a time, allow one to examine how new uses for videophones evolve. In these field trials important nonconversational uses of the systems emerge, even though dyadic audiovideo "calls" are the most common use. If the systems support storage, then video mail is popular (Hopper, 1994). If the system allows it, people use videotelephony as they would a television, although less frequently than they place point-to-point calls or exchange video mail messages (Fish et al., 1993; Hopper, 1994). People also use video for benign surveillance—to maintain awareness of what their colleagues are doing even when they are not immediately communicating with them. In addition, people use video to lower barriers to spontaneous communication, much as physical proximity allows people to bump into each other (Abel, 1990; Buxton & Moran, 1990; Dourish & Bly, 1992; Fish et al., 1993; Fish, Kraut, & Chalfonte, 1990; Kraut, Fish, Root, & Chalfonte, 1990; Mantei et al., 1991).

These novel uses—to view broadcasts, to maintain organizational awareness, to keep communication channels open, and to support spontaneous communication—are enabled by video. Although histories of the telephone identified early applications for entertainment and social awareness, these uses are rare in contemporary business settings (Fischer, 1992).

Summary. In business settings people like and place videotelephone calls frequently when they have videotelephony available, even though for conversational purposes they perceive it and use it more like voice telephony than like face-to-face communication. When cameras are focused on parties to a conversation, the visual information does little to improve conversation, at least if the main goal is the exchange of information. The visual channel is more useful when it focuses on the object of conversation. On the other hand, "talking heads" video seems valuable for complex, ambiguous, or conflictful intellectual tasks and for tasks in which the social component is key. It facilitates the conduct of conversations, especially multiperson conversations. Moreover, when organizations use videotelephony over long periods of time, they develop uses that supplement the basic interpersonal communication function, including the use of videophones to access information services, to maintain workplace awareness, and to promote unplanned contact.

The Use of Video in Residential Settings

The published literature documents virtually no experience with video communication in residential settings, and our discussion of this topic is speculative, based on inferences from studies of how households use voice telecommunications. This is a reasonable strategy, because even though the two technologies differ subtly, we have seen that at least initially video-telephony use will be patterned after voice telephony use.

Among residential subscribers, the modal telephone call is a pairwise conversation between friends or family who are located geographically close to each other and who call each other to have a convenient way to chat. This pattern has been stable since the early days of residential telephone service (Fischer, 1992). In a contemporary study, Dordick and LaRose (1992) had a national sample of households record who they talked to and why, for a sample of their telephone calls. About two thirds of residential calls are to family and friends (see Fig. 25.1). About a third of residential calls have chatting or the exchange of news as their primary motive (see Wurtzel & Turner, 1977, for similar conclusions based on a very different methodology). These data on calling patterns lend credence to proprietary market research in which the vast majority of potential residential subscribers reported "keeping in touch with family and friends" as a top application for a videotelephony service.

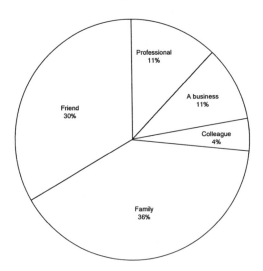

FIG. 25.1. Calling partners for residential telephone subscribers. From Dordick and LaRose (1992). Reprinted by permission.

Advertising for videophones often portrays distant family members using the video to keep in touch at emotionally charged occasions (e.g., grandparents sharing a child's birthday party). While distant communication may drive the purchase of videophones, it is unlikely to be the driving use of a videophone. People communicate most with those who are geographically close to them. This pattern is consistent across many studies and occurs across different communication media (e.g., Eveland & Bikson, 1987; Mayer, 1977). In the case of telephone calls, most studies show that between 40% and 50% of telephone calls are made within a 2-mile radius from a household (Fig. 25.2).

Moreover, calling patterns are quite concentrated, and become more concentrated the farther apart calling parties are from each other. Over half of the median household's telephone calls go to only 5 different numbers, and about half of their long distance calls go to a single number (Mayer, 1977).

Two of the best predictors of residential telephone use are the presence of an adult woman in the household and the presence of teenagers of either gender (Brandon, 1980). Both "need" and "opportunity" probably account for these demographic correlates of telephone use. Women, for example, as part of their sex-role obligations, often have the responsibility to maintain the household's social networks, and, because they are less likely than men to work outside of the household, they have more time to talk on the phone. Similarly, teenagers are at a life stage when they are developing their personal social networks and have substantial free time. Teenagers are also large consumers of other communication services, such as "chat lines," electronic mail, and electronic bulletin boards (Kraut, Scherlis, Mudkopodhyay, Manning, & Kiesler, 1996).

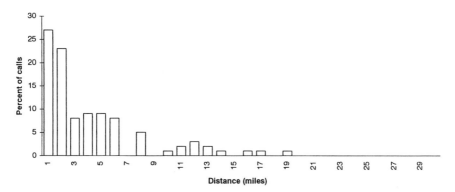

FIG. 25.2. Calling distances for residential telephone subscribers. From Mayer (1977). Reprinted by permission.

Residential telephone use is elastic, and is constrained by two resources: time and money. During weekdays, telephone use peaks during the late afternoon, when students come home from school, and during mid-evening, when people come home from work and have finished dinner chores. During these times, calls are both more frequent and longer (Brandon, 1980). These calling patterns are muted in households headed by a person over age 65, which are less likely to contain students and members of the paid workforce, and disappear entirely on the weekends, when time use is less constrained.

Price and income shift the extent to which customers buy communication and when they buy it. Across the United States, the price of toll calls differs by time of day, and the hour that discount rates go into effect has changed over the years. Customers typically place twice as many calls in the hour following the evening discount as in the hour before it goes into effect (Brandon, 1980). Household income is associated with the number of toll calls made per month, but not the number of flat-rate local calls.

Summary. Although we have virtually no hard evidence about the uses of residential videotelephony, there is little reason to think that initial uses of videotelephony will differ from traditional and long-standing patterns of use for audiotelephony. These data suggest that the dominant use of residential videotelephony would be for routine social calls, with local calls most common, and with women and teenagers the dominant users. Because demand for social communication is highly elastic, price and convenience may be especially important determinants of the success of residential videotelephony.

Market Prospects

Evidence about the market success of videotelephony is mixed. As Noll documented, early introductions of videotelephony and videoconferencing were failures. But now growth, at least in the business-oriented videoconferencing market, seems to be increasing (Institute for the Future, 1993). Although the total size of the videoconferencing market is minuscule compared to the market for audioconferencing systems (including speakerphones and lines with three-way calling), it does show substantial growth, especially for low-cost equipment.

One key enabler for this growth has been the substantially reduced costs for teleconferencing equipment and for long-distance telecommunication services. The second key enabler of the growth in the videoconferencing market is interoperability standards, which allowed units from different manufacturers to communicate with each other, albeit at a lower quality than through the proprietary algorithms used for communication between units from a single manufacturer. Other improvements in videoconferencing technology may have also supported the growth in the market. Echo cancelers and echo suppressers have substantially improved the audio quality in videoconferences over the years. Technology, known as multipoint control units, now exists for bridging multiple locations, meaning that multiple locations can be connected in a single videoconference. Additionally, the use of computers in conjunction with videoconferences has sometimes made these systems easier to control and has provided a channel for meeting participants to share data.

Relatively low-cost videophones (less than $1,000 per device) have only recently come on the market, and it is too early to forecast their success, especially because prices are still declining rapidly and some of the major manufacturers have models that do not interoperate. In 1992 AT&T introduced its latest incarnation of the videophone. It has a 3 by 3-inch LCD display and works over regular telephone lines using a 19.2-kbps modem, with a maximum of 10 frames per second. The device was initially introduced at $1,500 and then reduced to $1,000 per phone. It was sold both in AT & T phone center stores and consumer electronic outlets. British Telecom offered its own version of an analog videophone in 1992. Sales in both the United States and Great Britain have been disappointing. *Forbes Magazine* estimated that fewer than 30,000 videophones had been sold worldwide by mid 1994, with an unknown number of these being sold for residential use (Samuelson, 1994). High price, poor image quality (indicating that these units are below some threshold of acceptability), and lack of critical mass (in general, if you want to use these units you have to buy two and give one to the other person you wish to see) are factors that may be causing the poor sales of these personal videophones. Like stand-alone videophones, affordable videophone add-ons to personal computers are just coming on the market, rapidly dropping in price from over $7,000 in 1993 to under $1,000 in 1995 to under $150 for a rudimentary black and white system in 1997. As prices continue to fall, it is likely that this will be a cost-effective configuration for many white-collar workers who use computers routinely.

Surveys of the general public show moderate interest in videotelephony. For example, according to Dordick and LaRose's survey (1992), about a third of a random sample of the U.S. population expressed interest in a videophone—more than were interested in voice mail, but substantially fewer than were interested in burglary and fire alarms, energy monitoring, or caller-ID. Table 25.1 indicates the proportion who expressed positive interest (i.e., "interested" or "very interested") for each of several telecommunications services.

Several potential suppliers of videotelephony services have conducted proprietary market research attempting to predict demand for videotelephony. In a typical study, a sample of respondents is given some experience with videotelephony, either by viewing video tapes of simulated conversa-

TABLE 25.1
Percent of Americans Interested in New Telecommunication Services
(Dordick & LaRose, 1992)

New Technology	Percent Interested
Alarm service	62%
Caller-ID	50%
Energy monitoring	46%
Personal communication services/mobile phone	41%
Videophone	34%
Voice mail	28%
Information gateways	28%
ISDN	25%

tions or having an actual conversation on prototype equipment. Respondents are then asked about their likelihood of subscribing to such a service, under different assumptions about features the service would offer (e.g., variation in visual quality, screen size, calling features, user interfaces, or connection to the public telephone network), and their willingness to pay a lump sum for equipment and monthly fees for service. These subscription and willingness-to-pay estimates are then discounted for the overoptimism endemic to market research and projected to the population as a whole.

Under the most optimistic scenarios, the market research of which we are aware projects more than 1.5 to 3 million videotelephony subscribers in the United States by 2000, with business subscribers outnumbering residential subscribers approximately 2 to 1. One should be skeptical about the absolute sizes of these estimates, because of the history of poor prior prediction, because potential customers are not very good predictors of their purchase behavior when asked about services they have experienced only briefly, and because of the assumptions in the analysis about improvements in costs, visual quality, interconnectivity, and other factors influencing the desirability of a service.

Comparisons of predicted demand under several different scenarios, however, give insight into service features that might influence the ultimate success of a videotelephony offering. The market research suggests that the demand for videotelephony increases with increased visual quality, with the addition of supplementary calling features similar to those available for voice calls (e.g., three-way calling, call waiting, call hold, and call forwarding), and with greater integration with the voice telephone network. Of these three variations, connection to the voice network has the greatest impact on demand.

Summary. Although previous market introductions have failed, business videoconferencing is becoming more widespread, and potential residential consumers express moderate interest in videotelephony. However, the projected demand for videotelephony is based on very limited data. Market trials, especially those in which videotelephony is used in residential settings, are necessary to better understand demand and how videotelephony will actually be used.

BASIC AND DESIRABLE SERVICE FEATURES

Although Noll maintained that videotelephony failed because the concept is fundamentally flawed, it is plausible to assume that the details of the service will strongly influence how it is received. This section describes the basic attributes that are a prerequisite for a mass-market videotelephony service, and concludes that they will be in place by the end of the 1990s. It also describes supplemental service features that could add value to a videotelephony service in residential and business settings.

Basic Attributes

The minimum attributes for an acceptable videotelephony service are the following:

- Simultaneous, two-way video and audio telecommunications.
- Adequate service quality, including audio quality, video quality, and user interface quality at least comparable to the quality of service on the voice network (e.g., initiation of calls by dialing a single number, maintaining call progress tones and announcements, and maintaining acceptable call setup times).
- Interoperability of videophones from different manufacturers, operating at different bandwidths.
- Integration with voice telephony, so that users can call any phone or pick up on any phone, even though connections between a videophone and a voicephone would involve only voice.
- Acceptable prices for both equipment and telecommunications service.

If the appeal of videotelephony is indeed that it is a more natural technology for interpersonal communication than conventional telephony, then the following will shape the success of a videotelephony service: (a) a critical mass of communication partners; (b) service quality, including minimally acceptable video and audio quality and convenience; and (c) cost. In terms of service quality, although both video and audio quality are important, we believe that audio is the more important of the two.

Visual Quality

Interactive experiments, in which people actually converse over a video system, and judgment studies, in which they view one side of simulated conversations, both show that perceived service quality, subscription intention, and willingness to pay increase with increases in telecommunications bandwidth. These studies show little differences in visual quality requirements between potential residential and business subscribers and between residential and business content. They show that the current generation of video compression algorithms operating at 384 kilobits per second (kbps) is adequate for videotelephony and that the impact of extra bandwidth on perceived quality is greatest at the lowest bandwidth levels (i.e., adding 64 kbps to a 64-kbps call has more effect than adding it to a 256-kbps call).

Most of the evidence about low-bit-rate encoding comes from judgment studies, in which viewers observe a number of simulated conversations, as if they were on one end of a videotelephony call, and make judgments of visual quality after each scene. In a recent Bellcore experiment, Judd (1993) had subjects view several simulated conversations differing in group size, scene context and topic, and screen size. For example, one scene showed a wife and children showing off party costumes to a husband on a business trip, whereas another showed an insurance salesman explaining a policy to a customer. The main independent variable was the bandwidth setting on an H.261 compliant codec (video coder/decoder) manufactured by GPT. Compression is necessary for video calls to be placed through contemporary data networks, to reduce the resources they consume. In general, though, compressing an image degrades quality, as information is lost. With the H.261 algorithm, compression results in blockiness, blurring of movement, and delay.

Figure 25.3 shows the result from this experiment. It suggests that compressing a video call down to 64 kbps using a 1992 implementation of the H.261 algorithm led to a visual quality that viewers judged inadequate (almost 60% of them judged the image as poor). On the other hand, compression to 128 kbps may be marginally adequate for videotelephony (39% judged the images as poor).

Interactive experiments, in which participants actually converse over these bit rates, show that early H.261 implementations running at 384 kbps are acceptable for extended business meetings, and real videoconferencing frequently occurs at lower rates. According to vendors of variable-rate codecs, in business videoconference settings, about three quarters of customers set their codecs at 112–128 kbps. Even when a videoconferencing system is running at 112 kbps, video quality is often the least important problem users experience (e.g., Tang & Isaacs, 1992). The compromise between visual quality and hourly costs—about double the cost of a voice-only telephone call—make the 112–128 kbps level a useful one.

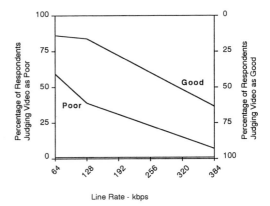

FIG. 25.3. Relationship between bandwidth and perceived visual quality of stimulus materials coded using an H.261 algorithm.

The visual quality that can be achieved at 128 kbps will undoubtedly improve over time, as algorithms improve and as hardware advances allow faster implementations. A recent proprietary report on videotelephony polled seven experts from research organizations and major codec manufacturers. The median judgment of these experts was that by 1997, codecs will be available to allow the visual quality that in 1993 required 256 or even 384 kbps to be achieved at 128 kbps. Moreover, if videophones are configured as small windows on the screen of a personal computer, as we expect them to be in business settings, the small image size will lead to increased perceived quality, compared to today's levels. If these predictions are true, by the end of the decade the video quality at 128 kbps will have improved enough so that it would not be an obstacle to the acceptance of videotelephony. This data rate of 128 kbps corresponds to ISDN basic rate access now being introduced in the United States and Europe.

Audio Quality

Most researchers find that audio quality is more important to the success of videotelephony than is visual quality. Without talk, there is no communication. But, unfortunately, the audio quality in videotelephony systems is almost invariably worse than the audio quality in audio-only systems. There are three critical technical factors that contribute to the lowered audio quality in videotelephony. These are (a) limited bandwidth for the audio signal, (b) acoustic feedback and echo resulting from hands-free operation, and (c) delay introduced by video processing. Of the three, degradation introduced by delay is the one most likely to undermine a commercially successful videotelephony service.

Bandwidth.   Currently, combining both an audio and a video signal on a limited-transmission channel leads to either degraded audio or degraded video quality. However, new audio compression algorithms are reducing the bandwidth needed to transmit speech while maintaining or improving quality. Using traditional pulse code modulation algorithms, telephony-quality (3.1 Hz bandwidth) speech requires 64 kbps to transmit. However, the International Telecommunications Union (ITU) standard G.722 only requires 48 kbps when providing an extended quality 7-kHz channel. The increased fidelity provided by the wider bandwidth results in improved speaker recognition in multiple-participant conferences because the distinguishing characteristics of different voices are better preserved. The recent ITU G.728 standard transmits telephony-quality speech (3.1 kHz) in only 16 kbps. These ITU algorithms have been widely endorsed by telecommunications companies.

Acoustic Feedback and Echo. One of the most attractive features of experimental video telephony systems is hands-free, full-duplex audio. Yet this feature often leads to acoustic feedback and echo. There are two solutions for eliminating the howl and echo. By using a handset or headset, one can acoustically isolate the speaker from the microphone. This is an unattractive solution, because it reduces the naturalness that videotelephony affords, and is impractical for multiparty conversations. Or one can use a variety of signal processing techniques—such as dynamic gain adjustment, echo suppression, or echo cancellation—to prevent acoustic feedback. Current techniques work adequately for conversations taking place in small offices and involving two to four sites. The digital signal processing technology to implement these solutions is currently expensive, but prices are dropping rapidly. Advanced forms of these solutions could be incorporated into low-end videophones by the turn of the century, if not sooner (e.g., Addeo & Shtirmer, 1993).

Delay. The availability of a visual signal can influence the perception of audio quality and the intelligibility of speech. For example, in understanding speech in face-to-face conversation, people typically use lip-reading to augment the acoustic signal. Similarly, under ideal conditions in videotelephony, one can improve the intelligibility of speech by adding a small (3-inch diagonal) LCD display of the speaker (Ostberg, Lindstrom, & Renhall, 1989).

However, in the typical commercial video telecommunications system, video degrades speech intelligibility rather than improving it. Audio delay is the primary culprit in this degradation. The video processing needed for digital compression and transmission introduces delay. Designers of codecs can accommodate this delay in the audio domain through one of two strategies. First, they can desynchronize the audio and video signals, sending the audio through immediately, while delaying the video. This technique gives users incorrect lip-reading cues from the visual signal, thus degrading intelligibility.

The other technique is to keep the audio synchronized with the video, but this introduces audio delay. Research on audiotelephony shows that round-trip delays of as little as 200 msec are noticed and disrupt conversations (Riez & Klemmer, 1963); round-trip delays introduced by codecs are typically two to four times as long. These delays cause participants in conversation to experience slow responses, excessive interruption, and failures to respond in conversation, which in turn result in less interactive conversation with fewer and longer speaking turns. Research on the dynamics of such disrupted conversations suggests they are less successful, in the sense that participants in them communicate information less well, feel the conversations are less natural, and terminate them sooner (Krauss & Bricker, 1966).

Trade-offs between audio delay and audiovideo synchronization are inherent to videotelephony, because video processing requires some delay to eliminate the temporal redundancy in the video signal. This is because removing temporal redundancy requires buffering successive video frames in order to find picture elements that remain unchanged from frame to frame. However, the delay can be reduced with greater bandwidth for video transmission, with faster video processing hardware, and with faster algorithms for video coding. All of these improvements are happening.

Availability of Network Services

In order for videotelephony to be practical, a network service must exist to transport audio, video, and signaling information among the subscribers' terminals. How this is done depends on how the signals are created, how far the signals must be transported, and what sort of processing is to be done along the way. Although the voice telephone network is close to ubiquitous in the United States, it is for the most part unsuitable for carrying video signals, because of limited bandwidth and large signal losses that occur with transmission distance. Hence, the availability of alternative and suitable network services is critical for the spread of videotelephony.

In businesses, local-area data networks (i.e., within a location or campus) have become the method of choice for networking computers. These same networks cannot carry video traffic, however, because video is an isochronous signal, requiring constant bit rate, whereas these networks are typically engineered for data traffic that occurs in bursts, and they can easily become overloaded. Wide-area networks for business have traditionally used dedicated private lines, which, if they have sufficient bandwidth, are suitable for video traffic. However, wide-band dedicated services are expensive, so wide-area videotelephony will probably rely on public network services for which users pay only when the services are used. An example of this is the integrated services digital network, or ISDN, which provides constant-bit-rate service access at 128 and 1,536 kbps. Hybrid networks, which combine local-area network technologies for local service and ISDN for wide-area service, are a way for businesses to cost-effectively combine available network services for both local- and wide-area videotelephony. In the future, new network services based on asynchronous transfer mode (ATM) fast cell-switching techniques may provide a single technology that can support high-bandwidth isochronous services on a local network as well as provide a transparent mechanism to interconnect with public wide-area services.

In residences, network access for video services depends on the delivery of two-way wide-bandwidth services to the home. Because homes have traditionally not subscribed to these services in the past, their availability is limited. The ISDN basic rate interface provides a 128-kbps service that can be used for video and audio over the copper telephone cabling currently used for voice telephony. This service is predicted to be widely available to residences within the next few years. Alternatively, for homes served by television cable systems, recent developments in these systems may permit two-way video services using digital services over an upgraded cable network.

Integration With the Voice Network

The value of any communication system grows with the number of people it connects (Allen, 1988). Research specifically about videotelephony shows that identical services can succeed or fail based simply on the numbers of subscribers connected (Kraut, Rice, Cool & Fish, 1994). Initially, very few businesses or households will have videophones. Although residential subscribers may buy a pair of videophones to support an important personal relationship (e.g., between older parents and their adult children), given the residential calling patterns reviewed previously, videophones will need to communicate with voice telephones to create the widespread connectivity that is important in the development of any new telecommunications service. Subscribers will need to be able to call and receive calls from conventional audio telephone (although, obviously without a video component). Most videoconference systems and videotelephony applications on personal computers do not have this feature.

Given the elasticity of telephone communication, to be successful, videotelephony service should be at least as convenient to use as the current voice network. A user should be able to place a call with a single call initiation (even if the terminals must place multiple calls in order to allocate sufficient bandwidth to achieve acceptable visual quality levels), with alerting and other tones to indicate call progress and outcome, and with comparable call setup times.

Inexpensive Terminals

Many industry analysts predict that videotelephony will not grow substantially until the price for a residential videophone is less than $500 and the incremental price of video equipment in the business environment is $1,000 or less (Insight Research Corporation, 1992). This in turn is likely to depend on the size of the market for these terminals, because manufacturers need a large market to recover their fixed costs to make a product.

Desirable Features

Whether the addition of video to conventional telephony adds enough value to be the basis of a successful service is unclear. The availability of supplemental features could make or break the emergence of videotelephony. Both the early trials of AT & T's PicturePhone system and more recent experiments with desktop video telephony in business settings show that two features—the ability to add shared work objects, like documents and spreadsheets, and the ability to add other people to calls in progress—will be important features of a business videotelephony service. In a residential setting, custom-calling features popular with audiotelephony and features to handle privacy concerns are likely to be crucial.

Shared Work Objects. In the original PicturePhone trials, people often used the system to show objects that they were discussing, rather than to look at each other, and this capability was added after human factors trials. Shared drawing spaces and other ways of sharing data are important in both commercial and experimental video systems (Fish et al., 1993; Kuzuoka, 1992; Tang & Isaacs, 1992). Because all members of the conversation must be able to view, point at, and, if appropriate, modify objects, fax only partially solves the problem of sharing text and graphics information. Using the video itself to show text is only occasionally appropriate because of video's low resolution but is useful for showing three-dimensional objects (Kraut et al., 1996).

Multiparty Conversations. In a business setting, multiparty conversations are essential (Panko, 1992). Experiences with both commercial and experimental video communication systems confirm the importance of multiperson conversations. For example, in the Sun Microsystems corporate network, multisite conversation was the third most desired new feature (after shared drawing tools and a larger screen) (Tang & Isaacs, 1992). Experience with one experimental system indicates that once multiparty conversations become available, users will need control over them (Fish et al., 1993). They will want to add or drop parties, control whom to view, and adjust the volume of each party to the conversation.

Custom Calling Features. In the short term, residential videotelephony is likely to require different supplementary features than is videotelephony in a business setting. The most popular call management features associated with conventional telephony—call waiting, call forwarding, speed calling, and three-way calling—are likely to be the features that customers will want for their videotelephony service as well (Link Resources, 1993).

Privacy. Privacy features are likely to be needed for videotelephony in ways they are not for conventional telephony, especially in residential settings. Videotelephony field experiments suggest that in business settings videotelephony is perceived as intrusive before it is used, but that privacy concerns diminish rapidly with use (Fish et al., 1993). Privacy concerns in residential settings are likely to be greater than in business settings, because video is perceived to be more revealing than audio and because the residence is a less public place (Katz, 1988, 1990, 1991). Personal Technology Research (1993), for example, found that almost a quarter of the residential customers they surveyed viewed a videophone at home as an invasion of privacy.

At a minimum, a videotelephony service must provide users control over whether video is being sent from their camera. Exactly how these privacy controls should work, however, will depend on the still-evolving norms around residential telecommunications privacy.

Interworking With Information Services. Video for interpersonal communication and video to view information and entertainment are converging, as the growth of videotelephony over the Internet and the experience with field trials of videotelephony demonstrate. Once subscribers have a video terminal in their house capable of switched point-to-point connections, it is likely they will use it to connect to entertainment and information sources, even though the video quality of this connection may be less than they could obtain from TV, a VCR, or a video-based information service. For example, interactive games in which players can see the people they are playing with and the game objects are attractive extensions to the stand-alone video games that are prominent in homes today. Similarly, once a substantial number of potential consumers have videophones available, information providers are likely to offer video information and entertainment services optimized for the limited technical capabilities of these terminals. Indeed, in anticipation of these services, the British equivalent of the FCC is proposing to preemptively ban adult-oriented video information services.

If video information services become an important use of videophones, then the videophone itself will probably change. In particular, it will need to be equipped with a richer input interface than the conventional telephone keypad. Keyboards, mice, or touch screens typical of screen phones or PCs may be appropriate.

SUMMARY

In summary, with the right service attributes, videotelephony—viewed as an enhanced version of conventional telephony—is likely to be used for the same interpersonal communication tasks as conventional telephony. In the residence, this means handling the socialization with family and friends for which the video medium is especially good. In the business environment, the dominant use is still likely to be pairwise communication, perhaps disproportionately targeted for applications like sales and negotiation, where the social component of communication is especially important. In the business environment, multiparty calls may be an important supplementary use. Smooth interworking with the current public voice-switched network is probably a prerequisite for market success, because it provides a mechanism to leverage off an installed customer base.

However, these conclusions are inferences from limited data. Market trials, especially those in which videotelephony is used in residential settings, are necessary to better understand how it will be used. Although videotelephony will initially be deployed for and applied to interpersonal communication, it will probably soon be used for video information and entertainment services, ranging from catalog shopping to adult-oriented services. Further analysis is necessary to understand the impact of videotelephony-based information services on the design and deployment of videotelephony.

ACKNOWLEDGMENTS

We would like to thank Bryant Mordecai and Jane Siegel for careful readings of this chapter, and Thomas Judd, C. T. Chen, and Martin Honig for access to unpublished data. The opinions expressed in this chapter are those of the authors and do not necessarily reflect the position of Bellcore or its owner companies.

NOTES

1. Reprinted with permission from R. Kraut & R. Fish (1995). Prospects for video telephony. *Telecommunications Policy, 19*(9). Elsevier Science Ltd., Oxford, England.
2. Note that making the assumption that video changes the quality of information exchanged has restricted the research questions that have been asked. Research on the esthetics of the communication experience or the nonutility determinants of the adoption of video communication are equally important topics of study, but have rarely been conducted.

REFERENCES

Abel, M. J. (1990). Experiences in an exploratory distributed organization. In J. Galegher & R. Kraut (Eds.), *Intellectual teamwork: Social and technological foundations of group work* (pp. 489–510). Hillsdale, NJ: Lawrence Erlbaum Associates.

Addeo, E. J., & Shtirmer, G. (1993). *Audio processing system for teleconferencing.* U.S. Patent 5,271,057.

Allen, D. (1988). New telecommunications services: Network externalities and critical mass. *Telecommunications Policy, 12,* 257–271.

Brandon, B. (1980). *The effects of the demography of individual households on their telephone usage.* Cambridge, MA: Ballinger.

Buxton, B., & Moran, T. (1990). EuroPARC's integrated interactive intermedia facility (IIIF): Early experiences. *Proceedings of the IFIP WG8.8 Conference on Multi-User Interfaces and Applications* (pp. 11–34). Heraklion, Crete.

Chapanis, A., Ochsman, R. B., Parrish, R. N., & Weeks, G. D. (1972). Studies in interactive communication: I. The effects of four communication modes on the behavior of teams during cooperative problem solving. *Human Factors, 14,* 487–509.

Clark, H. H., & Brennan, S. E. (1991). Grounding in communication. In L. B. Resnick, R. M. Levine, & S. D. Teasley, (Eds.), *Perspectives on socially shared cognition* (pp. 127–149). Washington, DC: American Psychological Association.

Dordick, H., & LaRose, R. (1992). *The telephone in daily life: A study of personal telephone use.* Unpublished manuscript, Temple University, Philadelphia.

Dourish, P., & Bly, S. (1992). Portholes: Supporting awareness in a distributed work group. *Proceedings of CHI'92* (pp. 541–547). New York: ACM.

Eveland, J., & Bikson, T. (1987). Evolving electronic communication networks: An empirical assessment. *Office: Technology and People, 3,* 103–128.

Fischer, C. S. (1992). *America calling.* Berkeley, CA: University of California Press.

Fish, R. S., Kraut, R. E., & Chalfonte, B. L. (1990). The VideoWindow system in informal communications. *Proceedings, ACM Conference on Computer Supported Cooperative Work* (pp. 1–12). New York: Association of Computing Machinery.

Fish, R. S., Kraut, R. E., Root, R., & Rice, R. E. (1993). Video as a technology for informal communication. *Communications of the ACM, 36,* 8–61.

Hopper, A. (1994). Communications at the desktop. *Computer Networks and ISDN Systems, 26,* 1253–1265.

Insight Research Corporation. (1992). *Multimedia computing and the network: Applications and telecommunications, 1992–1997.*

Institute for the Future. (1993). *Groupware and video market trends report* (Special Rep. No. SR-497). Menlo Park, CA: Author.

Judd, T. H. (1993). *Visual quality issues in low bit rate digital video applications* (Bellcore Rep. No. TM-ARH-022643). Morristown, NJ: Bellcore.

Katz, J. E. (1988). Telecommunications privacy policy in the U.S.A.: Socio-political responses to technological advances. *Telecommunications Policy, 12,* 353–368.

Katz, J. E. (1990). Caller-ID, privacy, and social processes. *Telecommunications Policy, 14,* 372–411.

Katz, J. E. (1991). Public concern over privacy: The phone is the focus. *Telecommunications Policy, 15,* 166–169.

Krauss, R. M., & Bricker, P. D. (1966). Effects of transmission delay and access delay on the efficiency of verbal communication. *Journal of the Acoustical Society, 41,* 286–292.

Krauss, R. M., & Fussell, S. R. (1990). Mutual knowledge and communicative effectiveness. In J. Galegher, R. Kraut, & C. Egido (Eds.), *Intellectual teamwork: Social and technological bases of cooperative work* (pp. 111–145). Hillsdale, NJ: Lawrence Erlbaum Associates.

Kraut, R. E., Fish, R. S., Root, R. W., & Chalfonte, B. (1990). Informal communication in organizations: Form, function, and technology. In S. Oskamp & S. Spacapan (Eds.), *Human reactions to technology: The Claremont Symposium on Applied Social Psychology* (pp. 145–199). Beverly Hills, CA: Sage.

Kraut, R. E., Miller, M. D., Siegel, J. (1996). Collaboration in performance of physical tasks: Effects on outcomes and communication. In *Proceedings of the ACM Conference on Computer Supported Collaborative Work '96* (pp. 57–66). New York: Association of Computing Machinery.

Kraut, R. E., Rice, R. E., Cool, C., & Fish, R. S. (1994). Life and death of a videophone: Structural and social influences on the use of a new communications medium. *Proceedings of the Conference on Computer Supported Cooperative Work* (pp. –). New York: Association of Computing Machinery.

Kraut, R. E., Scherlis, W., Mukhopadhyay, T., Manning, J., & Kiesler, S. (1996). HomeNet: A field trial of residential Internet services. *Communications of the ACM, 12,* 55–63.

Kuzuoka, H. (1992). Spatial workspace collaboration: A sharedview video system for remote collaboration capability. In *Human Factors in Computing Systems, CHI'92* (pp. 533–540). New York: ACM.

Link Resources. (1993). *Home media consumer survey.* New York: Link Resources Corporation.

Mantei, M., Baecker, R., Sellen, A., Buxton, W., Milligan, T., & Wellman, B. (1991). Experiences in the use of a media space. *Proceedings of CHI'91: Human Factors in Computing Systems* (pp. 203–208). New York: Association of Computing Machinery.

Mayer, M. (1977). The telephone and the uses of time. In I. de Sola Pool (Ed.), *The social impact of the telephone* (pp. 225–245). Cambridge, MA: MIT Press.

Noll, A. M. (1992). Anatomy of a failure: PicturePhone revisited. *Telecommunications Policy, 16,* 307–316.

Noll, A. M., & Woods, J. P. (1976). *PicturePhone® usage at Bethany-Garfield Hospital* (Tech. Mem. TM-76-1228-4). Murray Hill, NJ: Bell Laboratories.

Ostberg, O., Lindstrom, B., & Renhall, P. (1989). Contribution of display size to speech. *International Journal of Human–Computer Interaction, 1,* 149–159.

Panko, R. R. (1992). Managerial communication patterns. *Journal of Organizational Computing, 2*(1), 95–122.

Personal Technology Research. (1993, August). *Person video communications: Desktop conferencing and consumer videotelephony report.* New York: Author.

Riez, R. R., & Klemmer, E. T. (1963). Subjective evaluation of delay and echo suppressers in telephone communication. *Bell System Technical Journal, 4,* 2919–2942.

Samuelson, J. (1994, May 23). Voyeurs vs. exhibitionists. *Forbes, 153*(11), 210.

Short, J., Williams, E., & Christie, B. (1976). *The social psychology of telecommunications.* New York: Wiley.

Tang, J. C., & Isaacs, E. A. (1992). Why do users like video? Studies of multimedia-supported collaboration. *Computer Supported Cooperative Work, 1,* 163–196.

Whittaker, S., & Geelhoed, E.. (1993). Shared workspaces. How do they work and when are they useful? *International Journal of Man–Machines Studies, 39,* 813–842.

Williams, E. (1977). Experimental comparisons of face-to-face and mediated communication: A review. *Psychological Bulletin, 84,* 963–976.

Wurtzel, A. H., & Turner, C. (1977). Latent functions of the telephone: What missing the extension means. In I. de Sola Pool (Ed.), *The social impact of the telephone* (pp. 246–261). Cambridge, MA: MIT Press.

Zmud, R., Lind, M., & Young, F. (1990). An attribute space for organizational communication channels. *Information Systems Research, 1,* 440–457.

Afterword

If, as it is said to be not unlikely in the near future, the principle of sight is applied to the telephone as well as that of sound, earth will be in truth a paradise, and distance will lose its enchantment by being abolished altogether.

—Arthur Strand, 1898

The goal of true telepresence, through the mediation of visual and verbal channels of telecommunication, has still not been fully realized almost a century after Strand's prediction. The feeling of "being there," and of communicating with remote colleagues just as if they were copresent, turns out to be much harder to achieve than was realized in the early days of video communication. As the findings in this book show, even high-quality video currently fails to reproduce the same level of awareness and engagement with others as face-to-face meetings.

A lot has been learned, however. Designers of video-mediated communication systems are now benefitting from the earlier work of research laboratories such as Xerox PARC, Rank Xerox Cambridge EuroPARC, Bellcore, AT&T, and the University of Toronto. Together with technical advances, understanding of the social and task-related requirements of remote collaborators is now resulting in the development of integrated video, audio, and data environments in which groups of people can collaborate more effectively at a distance. An important aspect of this work is the recognition that video is useful for informal communication as well as more formal conferencing. Another is the realization that collaboration is much more than face-to-face talk, but also requires access to artifacts, to activities in relation to these artifacts, to remote environments, and to the activities of remote participants in those environments. Design work is now beginning to reflect these advances in thinking. As a consequence, designers are expanding beyond initial notions of video systems as video telephones, and are beginning to support richer forms of interaction.

We predict that video in the future will play many roles in workplace communication. As the medium becomes increasingly available at the office and in the home, people will evolve new ways of using it. Integrated in computer environments with novel user interfaces, this new form of visual communication will be adapted to meet the needs of a range of different scenarios. We believe the research reported in this book to be just the first phase of this new era for video communication. We must continue the work of understanding how people use visual channels in order to realize the full potential of this new medium.

Subject Index